THE GAZETTEER
OF ENGLAND

Volume 2   L – Z

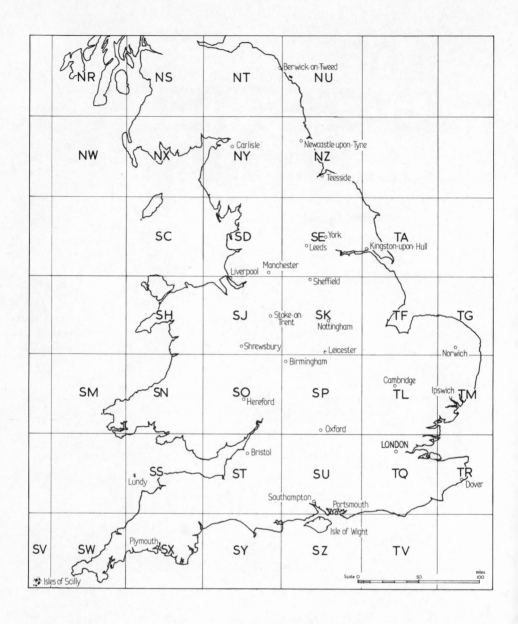

Plan showing incidence of the 100-kilometre squares of the Ordnance Survey National Grid

(Crown copyright reserved)

The GAZETTEER of England

England's Cities, Towns, Villages and Hamlets:
a comprehensive list with basic details on each

Volume 2 L-Z

OLIVER MASON

ROWMAN AND LITTLEFIELD

The grid references in this gazetteer are taken from the Ordnance Survey National Grid, Crown copyright reserved.

The map is extracted from the index to the quarter-inch series, with permission.

Population data, which is Crown copyright, is used with the permission of the Controller of HM Stationery Office.

ISBN 0–87471–139–8

Rowman and Littlefield
81 Adams Drive
Totowa: NJ 07512
Printed in Great Britain

CONTENTS

EXPLANATORY NOTES

GENERAL

The aim of this gazetteer is to provide a comprehensive list of English places, from the largest cities down to all but the smallest hamlets, with certain essential information about each. (Administrative areas whose names correspond to no one place on the ground are, however, not listed, eg Aireborough, Yorks; Lakes UD, Westm; Tower Hamlets, London; Hawerby cum Beesby, Lincs; St Thomas the Apostle Rural, Cornwall. Nor are localities which are within boroughs or urban districts and which have become submerged in the larger place).

The main districts in Greater London are listed.

INFORMATION GIVEN

1 **Location** The name of each place is followed by that of the county in which it is situated. Then follows the number(s) of the one-inch Ordnance Survey (O.S.) map(s) (seventh series) on which it appears; its four-figure map reference (O.S. National Grid System); and its distance and direction from another place, the distance being given to the nearest mile measured in a straight line.

Example 1

> SHELFORD Notts
> 112, 121, 122 SK 6642 6m E of Nottingham.

Shelford appears on the three overlapping sheets 112, 121 and 122.

Example 2

> TIXOVER Rutland
> 123/134 SK 9700 5m SW of Stamford.

Tixover appears partly on sheet 123 and partly on sheet 134.

2 **Administrative status and population** according to the latest available information. If the official administrative name of a place differs from the name under which it is listed, the official name is shown in brackets, eg

> SALISBURY Wilts
> 167 SU 1430 21m NW of Southampton.
> MB(New Sarum),35,271 .

The official administrative name of the municipal borough of Salisbury is New Sarum.

3 **In the case of a civil parish, the rural district in which it is situated** is given, eg

> PIXLEY Herefs
> 142, 143 SO 6638 3m W of Ledbury.
> CP, 214. Ldbry RD.

The civil parish of Pixley is in the rural district of Ledbury.

In the case of a locality, the administrative area in which it is situated is given.

Example 1

> COTON CLANFORD Staffs
> 119 SJ 8723 3m W of Stafford.
> Loc, Seighford CP.

Reference to Seighford will show that it is in the rural district of Stafford.

Example 2

> TREVISCOE Cornwall
> 185 SW 9455 5m WNW of St Austell.
> Loc, St Stephen-in-Brannel CP. St Astll RD.

The civil parish of St Stephen-in-Brannel is not itself listed as there is no actual place of that name; therefore the rural district (St Austell) is given under the locality.

Example 3

> KEAL COTES Lincs (L)
> 114 TF 3661 8m SE of Horncastle.
> Loc, Spilsby RD.

Keal Cotes is not wholly included in any one civil parish, but is within the rural district of Spilsby.

For all boroughs and urban districts (and for Greater London and the Isles of Scilly), the populations shown are those given in the Census 1971 Preliminary Report. The populations of civil parishes are compiled from the 1961 census, since the 1971 census figures for these areas were not available at the time of going to press; where no population is given, this denotes a boundary change since 1961.

'Localities' have no population figures, since they have no defined boundaries.

4 Post Offices. If there is a post office named after the place listed, this is denoted by the letter P.

If the letter P only is shown, then the postal address is simply the name of the place followed by its county (see *Example 1* below).

If the letter P is followed by the name of another place, then that place is the post town and is included in the postal address (see *Example 2* below).

If the letter P is followed by the name of another place in capital letters, then that place is the post town and does not require the name of the county to be included in the postal address (see *Example 3* below).

If the letter P is followed by the name of the place listed, in capital letters, then the place listed is itself the post town and does not require the name of the county to be included in the postal address (see *Example 4* below).

If the name of a different county appears after the letter P, then that name, and not the name of the county in which the place listed is situated, is included in the postal address (see *Example 5* below).

If the name of the post office is different from the name of the place listed, this is indicated as in *Example 6* below.

EXAMPLES

No.	Place	Indication	Postal address
1	Buckfastleigh, Devon	P.	Buckfastleigh, Devon
2	Yedingham, Yorks(E)	P Malton.	Yedingham, Malton, Yorkshire
3	Guiseley, Yorks(W)	P LEEDS.	Guiseley, Leeds
4	York, Yorks	P(YK).	York
5	Soulbury, Bucks	P Leighton Buzzard, Beds.	Soulbury, Leighton Buzzard, Beds.
6	East Barming, Kent	P(Bmng), Maidstone.	Barming, Maidstone, Kent

Postal addresses of places in Greater London are not given unless the address contains the name of a county other than London, eg Croydon, Surrey; Enfield, Middx.

5 **Places of worship and schools.** These are denoted respectively by the letters Ch followed by the letter(s) for the denomination(s) concerned, and by the letters Sch followed by the letter(s) for the type(s) of school. (See list of abbreviations.) Private schools are not listed.

Places of worship and schools are listed for all civil parishes and localities therein, but not for boroughs or urban districts, from considerations of space.

6 **Parliamentary constituencies.** After the 1970 general election, a number of boundary changes, recommended by the Boundary Commission, were approved by Parliament. The constituency of each place for the next general election after that held in 1970 is shown. If this is different from the 1970 constituency, then the latter is shown in brackets.

Example 1

> ALNWICK Nthmb
> 71 NU 1813 17m N of Morpeth.
> UD 7,113. P. Berwick-upon-Tweed CC.

Alnwick is to be in the county constituency of Berwick-upon-Tweed; it was in the same constituency in 1970.

Example 2

> WROXHAM Norfolk
> 126 TG 2917 7m NE of Norwich.
> CP, 1,101. St Faith's and Aylsham RD. P Nrwch.
> Ch e. Sch p. N Nflk CC (Central Nflk).

Wroxham is to be in the county constituency of North Norfolk, although for the 1970 general election it was in the county constituency of Central Norfolk.

Example 3

> GROOMBRIDGE Kent and Sussex(E)
> 171, 183 TQ 5337 4m WSW of Tunbridge Wells.
> Loc, Tonbridge RD, Uckfield RD. P TNBRDGE WLLS.
> Ch e, m. Sch pe. Royal Tunbridge Wells CC (Tonbridge),
> E Grinstead CC.

Groombridge is partly in Kent and partly in East Sussex. The part in Kent is to be in the county constituency of Royal Tunbridge Wells, although for the 1970 general election it was in that of Tonbridge; the part in East Sussex remains in the county constituency of East Grinstead.

If the parliamentary constituency of a locality is not given in its own entry, it may be found by reference to the larger place in which it is situated.

7 **In the case of county and municipal boroughs,** London boroughs, urban districts, and civil parishes, the names of the localities within them which have their own entries are shown; eg under East Woodhay, Hants, will be found:

> See also Ball Hill, Broad Laying, E End,
> N End, Woolton Hill.

These five localities, all within the civil parish of East Woodhay, have their own separate entries in the gazetteer.

8 Descriptive matter. Brief descriptive notes are given in some cases. Properties open to the public are marked with an asterisk (*). Those open seldom, sporadically, or only by written application, are not so marked. Properties followed by the letters (A.M.) are in the care of the Department of the Environment and are open to the public. The public is usually given free access at all times to open spaces owned by the National Trust (NT) and these are not marked with an asterisk.

ABBREVIATIONS

airpt	airport	j	junior (school)
A.M.	ancient monument	Jcbn	Jacobean
	(in care of Department	km	kilometres
	of the Environment)	LB	London borough
b	Baptist	Ld	Lord
b	born	Lit	Little
b	boys (school)	loc	locality
BC	borough constituency	Lr	Lower
bldng	building	m	Methodist
blt	built	m	mile(s)
br	bridge	MB	municipal borough
bthplce	birthplace	mdvl	medieval
c	century (eg: 20c)	mkt	market
c	*circa*	mnfg	manufacturing
c	Congregational	mnftre	manufacture
CB	county borough	mnr	manor
CC	county constituency	monmt	monument
CC	cricket club	MP	Member of Parliament
ch	church, place of worship	mt	mount, mountain
chpl	chapel	Nmn	Norman
cmmn	common	NT	National Trust
CP	civil parish	orig	original, originally
cstle	castle	O.S.	Ordnance Survey
Ct	Court	P	post office
d	died	p	primary (school)
Dec	Decorated	par	parish
distr	district	Perp	Perpendicular
e	Church of England	pk	park
eccl	ecclesiastical	plpt	pulpit
EE	Early English	pop.	population
Elizn	Elizabethan	prob	probably
esp	especially	R	River
est	estimated	r	Roman Catholic
f	Society of Friends		(place of worship)
FC	football club	RAF	Royal Air Force
ft	feet	RC	Roman Catholic
g	girls (school)	rd	road
GC	golf club	RD	rural district
gdn	garden	rems	remains
Ggn	Georgian	Revd	Reverend
GLC	Greater London Council	Rgncy	Regency
Govt	Government	rly	railway
grn	green	rsdntl	residential
grnds	grounds	s	secondary (school)
Gt	Great	sch	school
hmlt	hamlet	scrn	screen
HQ	headquarters	St	Saint
hse	house	st	street
hsptl	hospital	stn	station
hth	heath	Tdr	Tudor
i	infants (school)	tn	town
incl	including, inclusive	Trans	Transitional
indstrl	industrial	TV	television
intntl	international	twr	tower

u	undenominational	vllge	village
UD	urban district	w	with (in place names)
Upr	Upper	wd	wood
v	religious denomination	wks	works
	other than b, c, e, f, m, r	YWCA	Young Women's Christian
Vctrn	Victorian		Association

ABBREVIATIONS USED FOR COUNTIES
AND THE ISLE OF WIGHT

*Beds	Bedfordshire	Lincs(K)	Lincolnshire
*Berks	Berkshire		(parts of Kesteven)
*Bucks	Buckinghamshire	Lincs(L)	Lincolnshire
*Cambs	Cambridgeshire		(parts of Lindsey)
Ches	Cheshire	*Middx	Middlesex
*Co Durham	County Durham		(for postal purposes only)
Cumb	Cumberland	*Northants	Northamptonshire
Derbys	Derbyshire	*Notts	Nottinghamshire
*Glos	Gloucestershire	Nthmb	Northumberland
*Hants	Hampshire	*Oxon	Oxfordshire
Herefs	Herefordshire	Shrops	Shropshire
*Herts	Hertfordshire	Som	Somerset
Hunts	Huntingdon and	*Staffs	Staffordshire
	Peterborough	Warwicks	Warwickshire
	(administrative county)	Westm	Westmorland
Hunts	Huntingdonshire	*Wilts	Wiltshire
	(parliamentary constituency)	*Worcs	Worcestershire
IOW	Isle of Wight	Yorks(E)	Yorkshire (East Riding)
*Lancs	Lancashire	Yorks(N)	Yorkshire
*Leics	Leicestershire		(North Riding)
Lincs(H)	Lincolnshire	Yorks(W)	Yorkshire
	(parts of Holland)		(West Riding)

*In the case of these counties the abbreviations approved by the post office are as shown. The post office abbreviation for Shropshire is Salop; for Lincolnshire it is Lincs, irrespective of the administrative division of the county. Other counties should be spelt out in full in postal addresses, although the administrative divisions of Suffolk, Sussex and Yorkshire are omitted.

Gazetteer

L - Z

LACEBY Lincs (L)
105 TA 2106 4m WSW of Grimsby.
CP, 1,369. Grmsby RD. P Grmsby. Ch e, m.
Sch pe. Louth CC.

LACEY GREEN Bucks
159 SP 8200 2m SSE of Princes
Risborough. CP, 1,367. Wycombe RD.
Ch e, m. Sch pe. Aylesbury CC (Wcmbe).
See also Loosley Row, Speen.

LACH DENNIS Ches
110 SJ 7072 3m ESE of Northwich.
CP, 171. Nthwch RD. P Nthwch.
Nthwch CC.

LACKFORD Suffolk (W)
136 TL 7870 6m NW of Bury St Edmunds.
CP, 146. Thingoe RD. Ch e. Bury St Eds CC.
St Eds CC.

LACOCK Wilts
156, 157 ST 9168 3m S of Chippenham.
CP, 1,363. Calne and Chppnhm RD.
P Chppnhm. Ch e, c, m. Sch pe.
Chppnhm CC. See also Bowden Hill,
Notton. Show vllge (NT). L. Abbey (NT)*;
13c cloisters, Tdr and and later hse.

LADBROKE Warwicks
132 SP 4158 2m S of Southam. CP, 211.
Sthm RD. P Leamington Spa. Ch e. Sch pe.
Stratford-on-Avon CC (Strtfd).

LADDINGFORD Kent
171 TQ 6948 6m E of Tonbridge. Loc,
Yalding CP. P Maidstone. Ch v. Sch pe.

LADOCK Cornwall
185, 190 SW 8950 6m NE of Truro.
CP, 819. Truro RD. P Truro. Ch e, m2.
Sch pe. Truro CC. See also New Mills.

LAINDON Essex
161 TQ 6889 3m S of Billericay. Loc,
Basildon UD. P Bsldn.

LAKE Wilts
167 SU 1339 2m SW of Amesbury.
CP(Wilsford cum Lke), 162. Amesbury RD.
Salisbury CC. L. Hse, much restored 16c
hse; gdns* with fine topiary work.

LAKENHEATH Suffolk (W)
135 TL 7182 5m WSW of Brandon.
CP, 4,512. Mildenhall RD. P Brndn.

Ch e, b, m2, v. Sch p2. Bury
St Edmunds CC. On edge of Fens. Large
airfield.

LAKES END Norfolk
135 TL 5196 6m E of March. Loc,
Upwell CP. P Wisbech, Cambs. Ch m.

LAKE SIDE Lancs
88, 89 SD 3787 8m SSW of Windermere.
Loc, Colton CP. Pleasure boats ply N along
lake in holiday season.

LALEHAM Surrey
170 TQ 0568 2m SSE of Staines. Loc,
Stns UD. P Stnss, Middx. Thames-side vllge.
Burial place of Matthew Arnold.

LAMARSH Essex
149 TL 8935 4m SSE of Sudbury. CP, 126.
Halstead RD. Ch e, b. Saffron Walden CC.
Ch has round Nmn twr, rare in Essex.

LAMAS Norfolk
126 TG 2423 4m SE of Aylsham.
CP(Buxton w Lammas), 1,041. St Faith's
and Aylshm RD. P NORWICH, NOR 59Y.
Ch e. Sch p. N Nflk CC (Central Nflk).

LAMBERHURST Kent
171, 183 TQ 6736 6m ESE of Tunbridge
Wells. CP, 1,356. Tonbridge RD. P Tnbrdge
Wlls. Ch e, b, m. Sch pe. Royal Tnbrdge
Wlls CC (Tnbrdge). See also Hook Grn.
Formerly important iron-working centre.
1m SE, Scotney Cstle (NT)*: shrub gdns
leading to moated ruins. 1½m NE, Owl Hse,
with gdns* and lakes.

LAMBETH London
160, 170 TQ 3075 3m S of Charing Cross.
LB, 302,616. BCs: Lmbth Central,
Norwood, Streatham, Vauxhall (Brixton,
Clapham, Nwd, Strthm, Vxhll). See also
Brixton, Clphm, Kennington, Nwd,
Stockwell, Strthm, Tulse Hill, Vxhll.
Wedge-shaped borough S of Thames with
short river frontage incl Vxhll, Lmbth,
Westminster, Hungerford (rly), Waterloo
Brs; also incl Wtrloo Stn and Lmbth Palace,
residence of Archbishop of Canterbury.

LAMBLEY Notts
112 SK 6245 5m NE of Nottingham.
CP, 979. Basford RD. P NTTNGHM.
Ch e, m2. Sch p. Carlton CC. Fine Perp ch.

LAMBLEY Nthmb
76 NY 6758 4m SSW of Haltwhistle. Loc,
Coanwood CP. P Carlisle, Cumberland.
Ch e, m.

LAMBOURN Berks
158 SU 3278 7m N of Hungerford.
CP, 2,627. Hngrfd RD. P Newbury.
Ch e, m2, r. Sch pe. Nbry CC. See also
Eastbury, Upr Lmbn, Woodlands St Mary.
Famous for racehorse training.

LAMBOURNE END Essex
161 TQ 4794 5m SSE of Epping. Loc,
Lmbne CP. Eppng and Ongar RD. Ch v.
Sch p. Brentwood and Ongr CC (Chigwell).

LAMBS GREEN Sussex (W)
170, 182 TQ 2136 3m W of Crawley. Loc,
Rusper CP.

LAMERTON Devon
175, 187 SX 4476 3m NW of Tavistock.
CP, 591. Tvstck RD. P Tvstck. Ch m2.
Sch pe. W Dvn CC (Tvstck). See also
Rushford.

LAMESLEY Co Durham
78 NZ 2558 3m S of Gateshead. CP, 4,206.
Chester-le-Street RD. Ch m2.
Chstr-le-Strt CC. See also Galloping Grn,
Kibblesworth.

LAMORNA Cornwall
189 SW 4424 4m SSW of Penzance. Loc,
W Penwith RD. P Pnznce. St Ives CC. Tiny
harbour; haunt of artists.

LAMORRAN Cornwall
190 SW 8741 4m ESE of Truro across river.
Loc, St Michael Penkevil CP. Ch e.

LAMPLUGH Cumb
82 NY 0820 6m SSW of Cockermouth.
CP, 586. Ennerdale RD. P Workington.
Ch e. Sch pe. Whitehaven CC. See also
Kirkland.

LAMPORT Northants
133 SP 7574 7m WSW of Kettering.
CP, 191. Brixworth RD.
P NORTHAMPTON. Ch e. Sch pe.
Daventry CC (Kttrng).

LAMYATT Som
166 ST 6535 2m WNW of Bruton.

CP(Lamyat), 131. Shepton Mallet RD.
P Shptn Mllt. Ch e. Wells CC.

LANCASTER Lancs
89, 94 SD 4761 20m N of Preston.
MB, 49,525. P(LNCSTR). Lncstr CC. See
also Scotforth. On R Lune. Nmn cstle*; Ggn
Old Tn Hall*. University (at Bailrigg, qv).
Linoleum manufacture and general industry.
New central shopping area opened 1970.

LANCHESTER Co Durham
85 NZ 1647 7m WNW of Durham.
CP, 4,053. Lnchstr RD. P DRHM.
Ch e, m2, r. Sch i, je, pr, s2. NW Drhm CC.
Ch of architectural interest, Nmn to Perp.
To SW, Roman fort.

LANCING Sussex (W)
182 TQ 1305 3m NE of Worthing.
CP, 13,319. Wthng RD. P. Ch e2, m, r, v.
Sch p2, s. Shoreham CC (Arundel and
Shrhm). Up the hill to N, L. College, boys'
boarding sch; mid-19c chpl is notable
landmark.

LANDBEACH Cambs
135 TL 4765 4m NNE of Cambridge.
CP, 648. Chesterton RD. P CMBRDGE.
Ch e, b. Camb's CC.

LANDCROSS Devon
163 SS 4623 2m SSE of Bideford. CP, 71.
Bdfd RD. Ch e, m.. N Dvn CC (Torrington).

LANDEWEDNACK Cornwall
190 SW 7112 10m SSE of Helston. CP, 703.
Kerrier RD. Ch e. Sch p. St Ives CC. See also
Lizard. Most southerly parish in England.
Contains Lizard Point, Kynance Cove.

LANDFORD Wilts
179 SU 2519 9m SE of Salisbury. CP, 662.
Slsbry and Wilton RD. P Slsbry. Ch e, v.
Sch pe. Slsbry CC.

LANDKEY Devon
163 SS 5931 3m ESE of Barnstaple.
CP, 824. Bnstple RD. P Bnstple. Ch e, m.
Sch p. N Dvn CC. Consists of L. Newland
and L. Tn.

LAND OF NOD Hants
169 SU 8337 5m NW of Haslemere. Loc,
Headley CP.

LANDRAKE Cornwall
186 SX 3760 4m WNW of Saltash.
CP(Landrake with St Erney), 611.
St Germans RD. P Sltsh. Ch e, m. Sch pe.
Bodmin CC. See also Markwell.

LANDSCOVE Devon •
187, 188 SX 7766 2m E of Buckfastleigh.
Loc, Staverton CP. P Newton Abbot. Ch e.
Sch pe.

LANDULPH Cornwall
187 SX 4361 2m N of Saltash. CP, 388.
St Germans RD. Ch e, m. Sch p.
Bodmin CC. See also Cargreen.

LANDWADE Cambs
135 TL 6268 3m NNW of Newmarket. Loc,
Fordham CP.

LANDYWOOD Staffs
119 SJ 9906 3m S of Cannock. Loc, Gt
Wyrley CP. P Gt Wly, Walsall. Ch m. Sch p.

LANEAST Cornwall
186 SX 2284 6m W of Launceston. CP, 142.
Lnstn RD. Ch e, m. N Cnwll CC.

LANE BOTTOM Lancs
95 SD 8735 3m NE of Burnley. Loc,
Briercliffe CP. Bnly RD. Clitheroe CC.

LANE END Bucks
159 SU 8091 4m W of High Wycombe.
CP(Fingest and Lne End), 2,063.
Wcmbe RD. P Hgh Wcmbe. Ch e. Sch pe.
Wcmbe CC.

LANE END Cumb
88 SD 1093 2m SSE of Ravenglass. Loc,
Waberthwaite CP. Millom RD.
Whitehaven CC.

LANE ENDS Co Durham
85 NZ 1833 1m SSW of Willington. Loc,
Crook and Wllngtn UD.

LANEHAM Notts
104 SK 8076 9m S of Gainsborough.
CP, 275. E Retford RD. P Rtfd. Ch e, m.
Bassetlaw CC. See also Ch Lnhm. (Ch is to E
at Ch Lnhm).

LANESHAW BRIDGE Lancs
95 SD 9240 2m E of Colne. Loc, Clne MB.
P Clne.

LANGAR Notts
112, 122 SK 7234 10m ESE of Nottingham.
CP(Lngr cum Barnstone), 520.
Bingham RD. P NTTNGHM. Ch e. Sch pe.
Rushcliffe CC (Carlton).

LANGBAR Yorks (W)
96 SE 0951 3m NW of Ilkley. CP(Nesfield
w Lngbr), 175. Wharfedale RD. Rpn CC.

LANGCLIFFE Yorks (W)
90 SD 8265 1m N of Settle. CP, 420.
Sttle RD. P Sttle. Ch e, m. Sch p.
Skipton CC. Quarries and limeworks.

LANGDALE END Yorks (N)
93 SE 9391 7m WNW of Scarborough. Loc,
Wykeham CP. P Scbrgh. Ch m.

LANGDON BECK Co Durham
84 NY 8531 7m NW of Middleton in
Teesdale. Loc, Forest and Frith CP.

LANGDON HILLS Essex
161 TQ 6787 4m S of Billericay. Loc,
Basildon UD.

LANGENHOE Essex
149, 162 TM 0018 S of Colchester. CP, 202.
Lexden and Winstree RD. Sh p. Clchstr CC.
Adjoins Abberton, qv.

LANGFORD Beds
147 TL 1841 2m S of Biggleswade.
CP, 1,379. Bgglswde RD. P Bgglswde.
Ch e, m, s. Sch p. Mid-Beds CC.

LANGFORD Devon
176 ST 0203 8m SE of Tiverton. Loc,
Cullompton CP.

LANGFORD Essex
162 TL 8309 1m NW of Maldon. CP, 182.
Mldn RD. Ch e. Mldn CC. Ch: Nmn apse at
W end, only example in England and one of
few in Europe.

LANGFORD Notts
113 SK 8258 3m NNE of Newark. CP, 145.
Nwk RD. Ch e. Nwk CC.

LANGFORD Oxon
157 SP 2402 3m NE of Lechlade. CP, 349.
Witney RD. P Lchlde, Glos. Ch e, c, m.
Sch pe. Mid-Oxon CC (Banbury). Ch has
Saxon and Nmn work.

LANGFORD BUDVILLE Som
164 ST 1123 2m NW of Wellington.
CP, 343. Wllngtn RD. P Wllngtn. Ch e, r.
Sch pe. Taunton CC. See also Runnington.

LANGFORD END Beds
147 TL 1653 3m N of Sandy. Loc,
Tempsford CP.

LANGHAM Essex
149 TM 0233 6m NNE of Colchester.
CP, 869. Lexden and Winstree RD.
P Clchstr. Ch e, m. Sch p. Clchstr CC. See
also Blacksmith's Corner, Lnghm Wick.

LANGHAM Norfolk
125 TG 0041 5m WNW of Holt. CP, 215.
Walsingham RD. P Hlt. Ch e, m. Sch p.
NW Nflk CC (N Nflk).

LANGHAM Rutland
122 SK 8411 2m NW of Oakham. CP, 823.
Oakhm RD. P Oakhm. Ch e, b. Rtlnd and
Stamford CC.

LANGHAM Suffolk (W)
136 TL 9769 8m ENE of Bury
St Edmunds. CP, 77. Thedwastre RD.
Ch e. Bury St Eds CC.

LANGHAM WICK Essex
149 TM 0231 4m NNE of Colchester. Loc,
Lnghm CP.

LANGHO Lancs
95 SD 7034 4m NNE of Blackburn. Loc,
Billington CP. P Blckbn. Ch e, m, r. Sch pe.

LANGLEY Bucks
159, 160, 170 TQ 0079 2m E of Slough.
Loc, Slgh MB. P Slgh.

LANGLEY Ches
110 SJ 9471 2m SE of Macclesfield. Loc,
Sutton CP. Mcclsfld RD. P Mcclsfld. Ch m.
Sch p. Mcclsfld CC.

LANGLEY (Lower Green) Essex
148 TL 4334 6m SE of Royston. Loc,
Lngly CP. Saffron Walden RD. Ch m.
Sch pe. Sffrn Wldn CC.

LANGLEY (Upper Green) Essex
148 TL 4434 7m SE of Royston. Loc.
Lngly CP. Saffron Walden RD. P Sffrn
Wldn. Ch e, b. Sch pe. Sffrn Wldn CC.

LANGLEY Hants
180 SU 4401 2m SSW of Fawley. Loc,
Fwly CP. Ch e.

LANGLEY Herts
147 TL 2122 2m SW of Stevenage. CP, 181.
Hitchin RD. Htchn CC.

LANGLEY Kent
172 TQ 8052 3m SE of Maidstone. CP, 704.
Hollingbourn RD. P Mdstne. Ch e. Sch pe.
Mdstne CC. See also Lngly Hth.

LANGLEY Nthmb
77 NY 8261 2m SSW of Haydon Br. Loc,
Hdn CP. Hexham RD. Ch m. Hxhm CC. To
NE, L. Cstle*, restored 14c pele twr. Part
used as sch.

LANGLEY Warwicks
131 SP 1962 5m N of Stratford. CP, 143.
Strtfd-on-Avon RD. P Strtfd-upon-Avn.
Ch e. Strtfd-on-Avn CC (Strtfd).

LANGLEY BURRELL Wilts
157 ST 9375 1m NE of Chippenham.
CP(Lngly Brrll Without), 473. Calne and
Chppnhm RD. P Chppnhm. Ch e. Sch pe.
Chppnhm CC.

LANGLEY HEATH Kent
172 TQ 8151 4m SE of Maidstone. Loc,
Lngly CP. Ch m.

LANGLEY MARSH Som
164 ST 0729 7m NW of Wellington. Loc,
Wiveliscombe Without CP. Wllngtn RD.
Taunton CC.

LANGLEY PARK Co Durham
85 NZ 2144 3m ESE of Lancaster. Loc,
Esh CP. P DRHM. Ch e, b, m2, r, s. Sch s.

LANGLEY STREET Norfolk
126/137 TG 3601 8m NNW of Beccles. Loc,
Langley w Hardley CP. Loddon RD.
P(Lngly), NORWICH, NOR 18W. Ch e, m.
Sch p. S Nflk CC. L. Hall, mid-18c Palladian
style hse, now sch.

LANGOLD Notts
103 SK 5887 5m N of Worksop. Loc,
Hodsock CP. P Wksp. Ch e, v. Sch p, s.

LANGORE Cornwall
174, 186 SX 2986 2m NW of Launceston.
Loc, St Stephens by Lncstn Rural CP.
Lncstn RD. N Cnwll CC.

LANGPORT Som
177 ST 4126 7m WNW of Ilchester.
CP, 777. Lngpt RD. P. Ch e, r, v. Yeovil CC.
Stone-blt mkt tn, once a port on R Parrett.
15c hilltop ch. Mdvl guild chpl in archway
over rd. Withy beds, nursery gdns.

LANGRICK Lincs (L)
114 TF 2648 5m NW of Boston. Loc,
Langriville CP. P Bstn. Ch e, m.

LANGRIDGE Som
156 ST 7469 3m N of Bath. Loc,
Charlcombe CP. Ch e.

LANGRIGG Cumb
82 NY 1645 6m WSW of Wigton. Loc,
Bromfield CP. P Carlisle.

LANGRISH Hants
181 SU 7023 3m W of Petersfield. CP, 311.
Ptrsfld RD. P Ptrsfld. Ch e. Sch p.
Ptrsfld CC. See also Ramsdean.

LANGRIVILLE Lincs (L)
114 TF 2748 5m NW of Boston. CP, 336.
Spilsby RD. Ch m2. Horncastle CC. See also
Langrick.

LANGSETT Yorks (W)
102 SE 2100 3m SW of Penistone. CP, 221.
Pnstne RD. Pnstne CC.

LANGSTONE Hants
181 SU 7104 1m S of Havant. Loc, Hvnt
and Waterloo UD. On edge of large
land-locked harbour where 'mulberry'
harbours blt for Normandy landings in
World War II (1944). Yachting.

LANGTHORNE Yorks (N)
91 SE 2591 2m NNW of Bedale. CP, 48.
Bdle RD. Ch e, m. Thirsk and Malton CC.

LANGTHORPE Yorks (N)
91 SE 3867 just NW of Boroughbridge.
CP, 418. Thirsk RD. Thsk and Malton CC.

LANGTHWAITE Yorks (N)
90 NZ 0002 11m W of Richmond. Loc,
Arkengarthdale CP. Reeth RD. Ch e.
Rchmnd CC.

LANGTOFT Lincs (K)
123 TF 1212 5m SSE of Bourne. CP, 445.
S Kesteven RD. P PETERBOROUGH. Ch e.
Sch p. Rutland and Stamford CC.

LANGTOFT Yorks (E)
93 TA 0166 6m N of Driffield. CP, 460.
Drffld RD. P Drffld. Ch e, m. Sch p.
Howden CC.

LANGTON Co Durham
85 NZ 1619 8m WNW of Darlington.
CP, 60. Barnard Cstle RD. Bishop
Auckland CC.

LANGTON Lincs (L)
114 TF 2368 2m W of Horncastle. CP, 35.
Hncstle RD. Ch e. Hncstle CC.

LANGTON Lincs (L)
114 TF 3970 5m SW of Alford. CP(Lngtn
by Spilsby), 70. Splsby RD. Ch e.
Horncastle CC. See also Sutterby. Ggn ch
and *cottage orné*. Dr Johnson used to stay
at the hall, now ruined.

LANGTON Yorks (E)
92 SE 7967 3m S of Malton. CP, 116.
Norton RD. P Mltn. Ch e. Sch p.
Howden CC. Blt round long grn.

LANGTON BY WRAGBY Lincs (L)
104/105 TF 1577 8m SSE of Mkt Rasen.
CP, 130. Horncastle RD.
P(Lngtn), LINCOLN. Ch e. Hncstle CC.

LANGTON, GREAT Yorks (N)
91 SE 2996 5m WNW of Northallerton. See
Gt Lngtn.

LANGTON GREEN Kent
171 TQ 5439 3m W of Tunbridge Wells.
Loc, Speldhurst CP. P Tnbrdge Wlls. Ch e.
Sch p.

LANGTON HERRING Dorset
178 SY 6182 5m WNW of Weymouth.
CP, 149. Dorchester RD. P Wmth. Ch e, m.
W Dst CC.

LANGTON LONG BLANDFORD Dorset
178, 179 ST 8905 just E of Blandford.
CP, 271. Blndfd RD. Ch e. N Dst CC.

LANGTON MATRAVERS Dorset
179 SY 9978 2m W of Swanage. CP, 950.
Wareham and Purbeck RD. P Swnge.
Ch e, m2. Sch pe. S Dst CC.

LANGTREE Devon
163 SS 4515 4m SW of Torrington.
CP, 463. Trrngtn RD. P Trrngtn. Ch e, m2.
Sch p. W Dvn CC (Trrngtn). See also Stibb
Cross.

LANGWATHBY Cumb
83 NY 5733 4m ENE of Penrith. CP, 613.
Pnrth RD. P Pnrth. Ch e, m. Sch pe. Pnrth
and the Border CC. See also Edenhall.

LANGWORTH Lincs (L)
104 TF 0676 6m NE of Lincoln. Loc,
Barlings CP. Welton RD. P LNCLN.
Ch e, m2. Sch pe. Gainsborough CC.

LANIVET Cornwall
185, 186 SX 0364 3m SW of Bodmin.
CP, 1,019. Wadebridge and Padstow RD.
P Bdmn. Ch e, m. Sch p. Bdmn CC. See also
Nanstallon, Ruthernbridge.

LANLIVERY Cornwall
185, 186 SX 0859 2m WSW of Lostwithiel.
CP, 373. St Austell RD. P Bodmin. Ch e, m.
Sch p. Bdmn CC. See also Sweetshouse.
Hill-top vllge; Perp ch with high granite twr.

LANNER Cornwall
190 SW 7139 2m SE of Redruth. Loc,
Camborne-Rdrth UD. P Rdrth.

LANREATH Cornwall
186 SX 1856 5m ESE of Lostwithiel.
CP, 356. Liskeard RD. P Looe. Ch e, m.
Sch pe. Bodmin CC. Ch has wooden monmt
to Grylls family, once owners of the 17c
mnr hse.

LANSALLOS Cornwall
186 SX 1751 5m W of Looe. CP, 1,427.
Liskeard RD. Ch e. Bodmin CC. See also
Polperro, Trenewan.

LANSDOWN Som
156 ST 7268 3m NNW of Bath. Loc,
Charlcombe CP. Mostly suburb of Bath.
Two large schs and two twrs: 19c folly now
used as cemetery chpl, and L. Monmt
(A.M.), commemorating Battle of
L. in 1643.

LANTEGLOS HIGHWAY Cornwall
186 SX 1453 5m SSE of Lostwithiel. Loc,
Lntgls CP. Liskeard RD. Ch m. Bodmin CC.

LANTON Nthmb
64, 71 NT 9231 5m WNW of Wooler. Loc,
Ewart CP. Glendale RD.
Berwick-upon-Tweed CC.

LAPFORD Devon
175 SS 7308 8m NW of Crediton. CP, 612.
Crdtn RD. P Crdtn. Ch e, c, m, v. Sch p.
Tiverton CC (Torrington). See also Filleigh.
Ch outstanding, esp scrn.

LAPLEY Shrops
119 SJ 8712 7m SSW of Stafford. CP, 840.
Cannock RD. P STFFD. Ch e.
SW Staffs (Cnnck). See also Wheaton Aston.

LAPWORTH Warwicks
131 SP 1671 8m NW of Warwick. CP.
Wrwck RD. P Solihull. Ch e. Sch pe. Wrwck
and Leamington CC. See also Kingswood.
Oddly shaped ch; monmt by Eric Gill.

LARKFIELD Kent
171, 172 TQ 7058 4m WNW of Maidstone.
CP(E Malling and Lkfld), 5,142. Mllng RD.
P Mdstne. Ch m. Sch p. Tonbridge and
Mllng CC (Sevenoaks).

LARKHILL Wilts
167 SU 1244 3m NW of Amesbury. Loc,
Durrington CP. P Salisbury. Sch p. Large
Army camp.

LARLING Norfolk
136 TL 9889 6m SW of Attleborough. Loc,
Roudham CP. Wayland RD.
P NORWICH, NOR 18X. Ch e. S Nflk CC.

LARTINGTON Yorks (N)
84 NZ 0117 2m WNW of Barnard Cstle.
CP, 146. Startforth RD. P Bnd Cstle, Co
Durham. Co Durham. Ch m, r.
Richmond CC.

LASBOROUGH Glos
156 SO 8294 4m W of Tetbury.
CP(Westonbirt w Lsbrgh), 226. Ttbry RD.
Ch e. Stroud CC. L. Mnr*, early 17c; typical
Cotswold mnr hse; gdn.

LASHAM Hants
168, 169 SU 6742 6m SSE of Basingstoke.
CP, 198. Alton RD. P Altn. Ch e.
Petersfield CC. Gliding centre.

LASTINGHAM Yorks (N)
86, 92 SE 7290 6m NW of Pickering.
CP, 147. Kirkbymoorside RD. P YORK.
Ch e, m. Thirsk and Malton CC. Trans-Nmn
ch incorporates part of 11c abbey.

LATCHINGDON AND SNOREHAM Essex
162 TL 8900 5m SSE of Maldon.
CP(Ltchngdn), 843. Mldon RD.
P(Ltchngdn), Chelmsford. Ch e2, c. Sch pe.
Mldn CC.

LATCHLEY Cornwall
175, 187 SX 4073 4m NE of Callington.
Loc, Calstock CP. Ch m.

LATELY COMMON Lancs
101 SJ 6698 1m SE of Leigh. Loc, Lgh MB.

LATHBURY Bucks
146 SP 8745 just N of Newport Pagnell.
CP, 109. Npt Pgnll RD. Ch e.
Buckingham CC.

LATIMER Bucks
159, 160 TQ 0098 3m SE of Chesham.
CP, 1,225. Amersham RD. P Chshm. Ch e.
Chshm and Amrsham CC (Aylesbury). See
also Leyhill Commn.

LATTERIDGE Glos
155, 156 ST 6684 7m ESE of Severn Rd Br.
Loc, Iron Acton CP.

LATTIFORD Som
166 ST 6926 2m SW of Wincanton. Loc,
Holton CP.

LATTON Wilts
157 SU 0995 6m SE of Cirencester.
CP, 456. Cricklade and Wootton
Bassett RD. P Swindon. Ch e. Sch pe.
Chippenham CC.

LAUGHTERTON Lincs (L)
104 SK 8375 9m WNW of Lincoln. Loc,
Kettlethorpe CP. P LNCLN.

LAUGHTON Leics
132, 133 SP 6689 5m W of Mkt
Harborough. CP, 75. Mkt Hbrgh RD. Ch e.
Hbrgh CC.

LAUGHTON Lincs (L)
104 SK 8497 5m NNE of Gainsborough.
CP, 244. Gnsbrgh RD. P Gnsbrgh. Ch e, m2.
Sch pe. Gnsbrgh CC. Ch: monmts, brasses.
To N, large forestry area; To S, open
commns.

LAUGHTON Sussex (E)
183 TQ 5013 5m SSE of Uckfield. CP, 771.
Hailsham RD. P Lewes. Ch e, m. Sch p.
Lws CC (Eastbourne). See also Shortgate.

LAUGHTON EN LE MORTHEN Yorks (W)
103 SK 5188 6m ESE of Rotherham. Loc,
Thurcroft CP. P(Lghtn), SHEFFIELD.
Ch e, m. Sch p, pe. Outstanding ch twr and
spire.

LAUNCELLS Cornwall
174 SS 2405 2m E of Bude. CP, 390.
Stratton RD. Ch e. Sch p. N Cnwll CC. See
also Grimscott. St Swithin's holy well; ch,
unrestored, noted for bench-ends.

LAUNCESTON Cornwall
174, 186 SX 3384 20m NNW of Plymouth.
MB(Dunheved otherwise Lncstn), 4,725. P.
N Cnwll CC. See also St Stephens. Once the
county capital. Dunheved is the old Celtic
name. Rems of Norman cstle (A.M.) on site
of earlier one.

LAUNTON Oxon
145, 146 SP 6022 2m E of Bicester.
CP, 597. Ploughley RD. P Bcstr. Ch e, c.
Sch pe. Banbury CC (Henley).

LAVENDON Bucks
146 SP 9153 2m NE of Olney. CP, 582.
Newport Pagnell RD. P Olney. Ch e, bc.
Sch p. Buckingham CC. Ch has Nmn twr.
Faint rems of Nmn cstle to N.

LAVENHAM Suffolk (W)
149 TL 9149 6m NNE of Sudbury.
CP, 1,305. Cosford RD. P Sdbry.
Ch e, bc, m, s, v. Sch p. Sdbry and
Woodbridge CC. Small 'wool' tn. Many
timbered hses. Guildhall (NT)*, 16c,
restored. Famous Dec to Perp ch with
massive twr.

LAVERSDALE Cumb
76 NY 4762 4m WNW of Brampton. Loc,
Irthington CP. Sch pe.

LAVERSTOCK Wilts
167 SU 1530 1m E of Salisbury. CP, 1,873.
Slsbry and Wilton RD. P Slsbry. Ch e.
Sch pe. Slsbry CC.

LAVERSTOKE Hants
168 SU 4848 2m E of Whitchurch. CP, 470.
Kingsclere and Whtchch RD.
P(Freefolk), Whtchch. Ch e22 Sch p.
Basingstoke CC.

LAVERTON Glos
144 SP 0735 2m SW of Broadway. Loc,
Buckland CP. P Brdwy, Worcs. Sch pe.

LAVERTON Som
166 ST 7753 3m N of Frome. Loc,
Lullington CP. Ch e.

LAVERTON Yorks (W)
91 SE 2273 5m WNW of Ripon. CP, 269.
Rpn and Pateley Br RD. Ch m. Rpn CC. See
also Dallowgill.

LAWFORD Essex
149 TM 0831 1m W of Manningtree.
CP, 1,974. Tendring RD. P Mnnngtree. Ch e.
Sch pe. Harwich CC. L. Place is plastics
research centre.

LAWHITTON Cornwall
186 SX 3582 2m SE of Launceston.
CP(Lhttn Rural), 215. Lncstn RD. P Lncstn.
Ch e, m. N Cnwll CC.

LAWKLAND Yorks (W)
90 SD 7766 3m NW of Settle. CP, 191.
Sttle RD. Skipton CC. See also Eldroth.

LAWLEY Shrops
118, 119 SJ 6608 2m SSE of Wellington.
Loc, Dawley UD. P Telford. The Wrekin CC.

LAWNHEAD Staffs
119 SJ 8324 6m WNW of Stafford. Loc,
Ellenhall CP.

LAWSHALL Suffolk (W)
149 TL 8654 5m NW of Lavenham.
CP, 543. Melford RD. P Bury St Edmunds.
Ch e, r. Sch pe. Sudbury and
Woodbridge CC.

LAWTON Herefs
129 SO 4459 3m W of Leominster. Loc,
Kingsland CP.

LAXFIELD Suffolk (E)
137 TM 2972 6m N of Framlingham.
CP, 651. Hartismere RD. P Woodbridge.
Ch e, b. Sch pe. Eye CC. Ch has splendid
twr, vast roof span, seven-sacrament font.
Half-timbered former guildhall opposite ch.

LAXTON Northants
133/134 SP 9596 6m NNE of Corby.
CP, 127. Oundle and Thrapston RD. P Cby.
Ch e. Wellingborough CC (Peterborough).

LAXTON Notts
112 SK 7267 4m E of Ollerton. CP, 293.
Southwell RD. P Newark. Ch e, v. Nwk CC.

See also Moorhouse. Rems of
motte-and-bailey cstle.

LAXTON Yorks (E)
97, 98 SE 7925 3m ENE of Goole. CP, 311.
Howden RD. P Gle. Ch e. Hdn CC. See also
Saltmarshe.

LAYCOCK Yorks (W)
96 SE 0341 2m W of Keighley. Loc,
Kghly MB. P Kghly.

LAYER BRETON Essex
149, 162 TL 9418 3m ENE of Tiptree.
CP, 195. Lexden and Winstree RD.
P Colchester. Ch e, f. Clchstr CC.

LAYER DE LA HAYE Essex
149, 162 TL 9620 4m SW of Colchester.
CP, 898. Lexden and Winstree RD.
P Clchstr. Ch e, m. Sch pe. Clchstr CC. See
also Malting Grn.

LAYER MARNEY Essex
149, 162 TL 9217 2m ENE of Tiptree.
CP, 220. Lexden and Winstree RD. Ch e.
Colchester CC. L.M. Hall*, Tdr brick
gatehouse of eight storeys, much decorated.
Ch has monmts to Marney family, early 15c
onwards.

LAYHAM Suffolk (W)
149 TM 0340 1m S of Hadleigh. CP, 390.
Cosford RD. P Ipswich. Ch e. Sudbury and
Woodbridge CC. To W, Overbury Hall,
painted by Constable.

LAYLAND'S GREEN Berks
158 SU 3866 3m ESE of Hungerford. Loc,
Kintbury CP.

LAYSTER'S POLE Herefs
129 SO 5563 4m SW of Tenbury Wells. Loc,
Middleton on the Hill CP. Sch pe.

LAYTHAM Yorks (E)
97, 98 SE 7439 8m W of Mkt Weighton.
Loc, Foggathorpe CP.

LAZONBY Cumb
83 NY 5439 6m NNE of Penrith. CP, 649.
Penrith RD. P Pnrth. Ch e, m. Sch pe. Pnrth
and the Border CC.

LEA Derbys
111 SK 3257 3m SE of Matlock.
CP(Dethick Lea and Holloway), 1,077.
Belper RD. P Mtlck. Ch e, v. Sch p. Blpr CC.

LEA Herefs
142, 143 SO 6621 4m ESE of Ross-on-Wye.
CP, 273. Rss and Whitchurch RD.
P Rss-on-Wye. Ch e. Sch pe. Hereford CC.

LEA Lincs (L)
104 SK 8286 2m SSE of Gainsborough.
CP, 621. Gnsbrgh RD. P Gnsbrgh. Ch e, m.
Sch pe. Gnsbrgh CC.

LEA Shrops
118 SJ 4108 5m WSW of Shrewsbury. Loc,
Pontesbury CP.

LEA Wilts
157 ST 9586 2m ESE of Malmesbury.
CP(Lea and Cleverton), 559. Mlmsbry RD.
P Mlmsbry. Ch e, v. Sch pe.
Chippenham CC. See also Garsdon.

LEADENHAM Lincs (K)
113 SK 9552 8m NW of Sleaford. CP, 477.
N Kesteven RD. P LINCOLN. Ch e, m.
Sch pe. Grantham CC.

LEADEN RODING Essex
148, 161 TL 5913 6m SSW of Dunmow.
CP, 364. Dnmw RD. P Dnmw. Ch e. Sch p.
Saffron Walden CC. One of eight Rodings,
pronounced 'roothing'.

LEADGATE Co Durham
77, 78 NZ 1251 1m ENE of Consett. Loc,
Cnstt UD. P Cnstt.

LEADGATE Cumb
83 NY 7043 2m SSW of Alston. Loc, Alstn
w Garrigill CP.

LEAFIELD Oxon
145 SP 3115 4m NW of Witney. CP, 787.
Chipping Norton RD. P OXFORD. Ch e, b.
Sch pe. Banbury CC.

LEAKE Yorks (N)
91 SE 4390 4m ESE of Northallerton.
CP, 4. Nthlltn RD. Ch e. Richmond CC.

LEAKE COMMON SIDE Lincs (H)
114 TF 3952 7m NE of Boston. Loc, Old
Lke CP. P Bstn. Ch m. Sch p.

LEALHOLM Yorks (N)
86 NZ 7607 7m SSE of Loftus. Loc,
Glaisdale CP. P Whtby. Ch e, m, r. Sch p.

LEA MARSTON Warwicks
131 SP 2093 3m N of Coleshill. CP, 295.

Meriden RD. P Sutton Coldfield. Ch e.
Sch pe. Mrdn CC. See also Mstn. To S, Hams
Hall Power Stn.

LEAMINGTON Warwicks
132 SP 3165 9m S of Coventry. MB(Royal
Lmngtn Spa), 44,989. P. Warwick and
Lmngtn CC. Largely rsdntl tn which grew
up late 18c and 19c. Rgncy hses. Pump
rooms. The 'Royal' and 'Spa' conferred
in 1838.

LEAMINGTON HASTINGS Warwicks
132 SP 4467 4m NNE of Southam. CP, 361.
Rugby RD. P Rgby. Ch e, m. Sch pe.
Rgby CC. See also Broadwell, Kites
Hardwick. To N, Draycote Reservoir.

LEAMSIDE Co Durham
85 NZ 3146 4m NE of Durham. Loc,
W Rainton CP. Ch m2. Sch p.

LEASGILL Westm
89 SD 4984 6m S of Kendal. Loc,
Heversham CP.

LEASINGHAM Lincs (K)
113 TF 0548 2m NNW of Sleaford.
CP, 514. E Kesteven RD. P Slfd. Ch e, m, v.
Sch pe. Grantham CC.

LEASINGTHORNE Co Durham
85 NZ 2529 3m E of Bishop Auckland. Loc,
Bshp Aucklnd UD.

LEATHERHEAD Surrey
170 TQ 1656 12m ENE of Guildford.
UD, 40,112. P. Epsom and Ewell BC
(Epsm CC). See also Ashtead, Fetcham,
Gt Bookham, Lit Bkhm.

LEATHLEY Yorks (W)
96 SE 2347 2m ENE of Otley. CP, 214.
Wharfedale RD. P Otley. Ch e, m.
Ripon CC.

LEATON Shrops
118 SJ 4618 4m NNW of Shrewsbury. Loc,
Pimhill CP. Atcham RD. Ch e. Shrsbry CC.

LEA TOWN Lancs
94 SD 4731 4m WNW of Preston.
CP(Lea), 3,657. Prstn RD. P(Lea), Prstn.
Ch r. Sch p, pe, pr. S Fylde CC.

LEAVELAND Kent
172 TR 0054 5m S of Faversham. CP, 114.
Swale RD. Ch e. Fvrshm CC.

LEAVENING Yorks (E)
92, 97, 98 SE 7863 5m S of Malton.
CP, 225. Norton RD. P Mltn. Ch m. Sch p.
Howden CC.

LEAVES GREEN London
171 TQ 4161 2m N of Biggin Hill. Loc,
Bromley LB. P Keston, Kent.
Orpington BC (CC).

LEA YEAT Yorks (W)
90 SD 7687 7m ESE of Sedbergh. Loc,
Dent CP.

LEAZES Co Durham
78 NZ 1656 7m SW of Gateshead. Loc,
Stanley UD. P Burnopfield, NEWCASTLE
UPON TYNE.

LEBBERSTON Yorks (N)
93 TA 0782 3m WNW of Filey. CP, 128.
Scarborough RD. Scbrgh CC (Scbrgh and
Whitby).

LECHLADE Glos
157 SU 2199 10m NNE of Swindon.
CP, 1,134. Cirencester RD. P. Ch e, b, m, r.
Sch pe. Crncstr and Tewkesbury CC. Old br
spans R Thames. Perp ch.

LECK Lancs
89 SD 6476 2m SE of Kirkby Lonsdale.
CP, 192. Lunesdale RD. Ch e. Sch pe.
Lancaster CC. Fellside parish.

LECKFORD Hants
168 SU 3737 5m S of Andover. CP, 152.
Romsey and Stockbridge RD. P Stckbrdge.
Ch e, m. Winchester CC.

LECKHAMPSTEAD Berks
158 SU 4376 6m NNW of Newbury.
CP, 323. Nbry RD. P Nbry. Ch e, m.
Nbry CC.

LECKHAMPSTEAD Bucks
146 SP 7237 3m NE of Buckingham.
CP, 178. Bcknghm RD. Ch e. Bcknghm CC.

LECKHAMPTON Glos
143, 144 SO 9419 2m S of Cheltenham.
CP, 3,509. Chltnhm RD. P Chltnhm. Ch e.
Sch i, j. Cirencester and Tewkesbury CC.

LECONFIELD Yorks (E)
99 TA 0143 3m NNW of Beverley.
CP, 1,412. Bvrly RD. P Bvrly. Ch e, m.
Sch p. Haltemprice CC. See also Arram,
Scorborough.

LEDBURN Bucks
146 SP 9021 2m SSW of Leighton Buzzard.
Loc, Mentmore CP.

LEDBURY Herefs
143 SO 7137 7m SW of Malvern. CP, 3,630.
Ldbry RD. P. Ch e, b, m, r, v2. Sch i, j, s2.
Leominster CC. 17c mkt hall. Many
timbered hses. 14c ch has detached twr;
monmts.

LEDGEMOOR Herefs
142 SO 4150 8m SW of Leominster. Loc,
King's Pyon CP. Ch m.

LEDICOT Herefs
129 SO 4162 5m WNW of Leominster. Loc,
Shobdon CP.

LEDSHAM Ches
109 SJ 3674 3m WSW of Ellesmere Port.
CP, 144. Chester RD. P Little
Sutton, Wirral. Ch m. City of Chstr CC.

LEDSHAM Yorks (W)
97 SE 4529 3m NNE of Castleford.
CP, 125. Tadcaster RD. Ch e. Sch pe.
Barkston Ash CC. Ch partly Saxon.

LEDSTON Yorks (W)
97 SE 4328 2m N of Castleford. CP, 346.
Tadcaster RD. Barkston Ash CC.

LEDWELL Oxon
145 SP 4228 7m E of Chipping Norton.
Loc, Sandford St Martin CP.

LEE Devon
163 SS 4846 2m WSW of Ilfracombe. Loc,
Ilfrcmbe UD. P Ilfrcmbe. Old world vllge in
deep combe; small beach (½m) in rocky
cove.

LEE Hants
180 SU 3617 5m NW of Southampton. Loc,
Romsey Extra CP. Rmsy and
Stockbridge RD. Ch e. Eastleigh CC.

LEE Lancs
94 SD 5655 7m SE of Lancaster. Loc, Over
Wyresdale CP. Lncstr RD. Lncstr CC.

LEE Shrops
118 SJ 4032 2m S of Ellesmere. Loc,
Ellesmre Rural CP. N Shrops RD.
Oswestry CC. L. Old Hall, half-timbered
Elizn hse. To E, White Mere, one of several
in distr.

LEEBOTWOOD Shrops
129 SO 4798 3m NNE of Ch Stretton.
CP, 191. Atcham RD. P Ch Strttn. Ch e.
Shrewsbury CC. Below Lawley Hill. Some
half-timbered hses.

LEE BROCKHURST Shrops
118 SJ 5427 2m ESE of Wem. CP, 120.
N Shrops RD. Ch e. Sch pe. Oswestry CC.

LEECE Lancs
88 SD 2469 3m E of Barrow. Loc,
Aldingham CP. P Ulverston.

LEE CLUMP Bucks
159 SP 9004 3m WNW of Chesham. Loc,
The Lee CP. P(Lee Cmmn), Gt Missenden.
Sch pe.

LEEDS Kent
172 TQ 8253 4m ESE of Maidstone.
CP, 733. Hollingbourn RD. P Mdstne. Ch e.
Sch pe. Mdstne CC. Large cstle, mostly 19c
reconstruction, rising from lake, in pk laid
out by Capability Brown.

LEEDS Yorks (W)
96 SE 2933 36m NE of Manchester.
CB, 494,971. P(LDS). BCs: Lds E, NE, NW,
S, SE, W. See also Eccup, Headingley,
Kirkstall. Major indstrl city; clothing,
engineering, etc. Centre extensively rebuilt.
University. Triennial music festival. To E,
Temple Newsam Hse*, Tdr and Jcbn.

LEEDSTOWN Cornwall
189 SW 6034 5m SW of Camborne. Loc,
Crowan CP. P Hayle. Ch m. Sch p.

LEEK Staffs
110 SJ 9856 10m NE of Stoke-on-Trent.
UD, 19,368. P. Lk CC.

LEEK WOOTTON Warwicks
132 SP 2968 2m N of Warwick. CP, 671.
Wrwck RD. P WRWCK. Ch e. Sch pe.
Wrwck and Leamington CC.

LEE MILL ESTATE Devon
187, 188 SX 6055 2m W of Ivybridge. Loc,
Ermington CP. Plympton St Mary RD
(Tavistock). P(Lee Mll Br), Ivybrdge.
W Dvn CC.

LEEMING Yorks (N)
91 SE 2989 2m ENE of Bedale. CP(Exelby,
Lmng and Newton, 2,097. Bdle RD.
P Northallerton. Ch e, m. Sch p. Thirsk and
Malton CC.

LEEMING BAR Yorks (N)
91 SE 2890 2m NE of Bedale. Loc,
Aiskew CP. P Northallerton. Ch e. Sch pe.

LEE MOOR Devon
187 SX 5761 5m NW of Ivybridge. Loc,
Shaugh Prior CP. P Plymouth. Ch m. Sch p.
China clay wks.

LEE-ON-THE-SOLENT Hants
180 SU 5600 3m W of Gosport. Loc,
Gspt MB. P. Resort. Naval flying HQ.

LEES Derbys
120 SK 2637 6m W of Derby. CP(Dalbury
Ls), 158. Repton RD. P(Dlbry Ls), DBY.
Belper CC.

LEES Lancs
101 SD 9504 2m E of Oldham. UD, 4,367.
P Oldhm. Oldhm E. BC.

LEE, THE Bucks
159 SP 9004 4m WNW of Chesham.
CP, 651. Amersham RD. Ch e, v. Chshm and
Amrshm CC (Aylesbury).

LEGBOURNE Lincs (L)
105 TF 3684 3m SE of Louth. CP, 347.
Lth RD. P Lth. Ch e, m. Sch pe. Lth CC.

LEGSBY Lincs (L)
104 TF 1385 3m SE of Mkt Rasen. CP, 280.
Caistor RD. P Mkt Rsn. Ch e, m2. Sch p.
Gainsborough CC. See also E Torrington.

LEICESTER Leics
121, 122 SK 5804 89m NNW of London.
CB, 283,549. P(LCSTR). BCs: Lcstr E, S, W
(NE, NW, SE, SW). See also Humberstone.
Indstrl city specialising in hosiery, knitwear,
footwear. Cathedral. University. Many
Roman and mdvl rems.

LEIGH Dorset
178 ST 6108 5m SSW of Sherborne.
CP, 347. Shbne RD. P Shbne. Ch e, m.
Sch pe. W Dst CC.

LEIGH Glos
143 SO 8726 5m NNE of Gloucester.
CP, 279. Cheltenham RD. Ch e. Cirencester
and Tewkesbury CC. See also Coombe Hill.

LEIGH Kent
171 TQ 5446 3m W of Tonbridge.
CP, 1,582. Sevenoaks RD. P Tnbrdge.
Ch e, m. Sch p. Svnks CC. Pronounced 'lie'.
Mock-Tdr Vctrn vllge with grn. Hall Place
has large lake and gdns*.

LEIGH Lancs
101 SD 6500 6m SE of Wigan. MB, 46,117.
P. Lgh BC. See also Lately Cmmn. Coal;
textiles.

LEIGH Shrops
118 SJ 3303 7m ESE of Welshpool. Loc,
Worthen CP.

LEIGH Surrey
170 TQ 2246 3m SW of Reigate. CP, 956.
Dorking and Horley RD. P Rgte. Ch e, v.
Sch p. Dkng CC. Ch: brasses.

LEIGH Wilts
157 SU 0692 7m SSE of Cirencester.
CP, 336. Cricklade and Wootton
Bassett RD. P Swindon. Ch e, m. Sch pe.
Chippenham CC. To N, some rems of
former par ch, part of which was pulled
down in 1896 and rebuilt in vllge.

LEIGH Worcs
143 SO 7853 4m W of Worcester. CP, 979.
Martley RD. P WCSTR. Ch e, m. Sch p.
Kidderminster CC. See also Lgh Sinton.

LEIGH DELAMERE Wilts
156, 157 ST 8879 4m NNW of
Chippenham. Loc, Grittleton CP. Ch e.

LEIGH GREEN Kent
184 TQ 9032 1m ESE of Tenterden. Loc,
Tntdn MB. P Tntdn.

LEIGH ON SEA Essex
162 TQ 8386 W distr of Southend. Loc,
Sthnd-on-Sea CB. P. Sthnd W BC. Rsdntl
and holiday resort; cockle-fishing.

LEIGHS, GREAT Essex
148, 169, 162 TL 7217 4m SSW of
Braintree. See Gt Lghs.

LEIGH SINTON Worcs
143 SO 7750 3m N of Malvern. Loc,
Lgh CP. P Mlvn. Ch v. Sch pe.

LEIGHTERTON Glos
156 ST 8291 4m WSW of Tetbury.
CP(Boxwell w Lghtrtn), 179. Ttbry RD.
P Ttbry. Ch e, b. Sch p. Stroud CC.

LEIGHTON Shrops
118, 119 SJ 6105 4m NNW of Much
Wenlock. CP, 387. Atcham RD.
P Shrewsbury. Ch e. Shrsbry CC. See also
Eaton Constantine, Longwood.

LEIGHTON Som
166 ST 7043 5m WSW of Frome. Loc,
Wanstrow CP.

LEIGHTON BROMSWOLD Hunts
134 TL 1175 8m WNW of Huntingdon. Loc,
Lghtn CP. Hntngdn RD. Ch e, m. Sch pe.
Hunts CC.

LEIGHTON BUZZARD Beds
146 SP 9225 11m W of Luton.
UD(Lghtn-Linslade), 20,326. P. S Beds CC.
Mkt tn, whose ch, All Saints, is 'considered
the finest parish church in the county'.

LEIGH UPON MENDIP Som
166 ST 6947 5m W of Frome. CP, 406.
Frme RD. Ch e, m. Sch p. Wells CC. Ch:
twr.

LEIGHWOODS Som
155, 156, 165 ST 5572 2m W of Bristol.
Loc, Long Ashton CP. Ch e. See Abbots
Leigh.

LEINTHALL EARLS Herefs
129 SO 4467 6m SW of Ludlow. Loc,
Aymestrey CP. Ch e.

LEINTHALL STARKES Herefs
129 SO 4369 6m SW of Ludlow. CP, 73.
Leominster and Wigmore RD. Ch e, m.
Lmnstr CC.

LEINTWARDINE Herefs
129 SO 4074 7m W of Ludlow. CP, 747.
Leominster and Wigmore RD. P Craven
Arms, Salop. Ch e, c, m. Sch pe. Lmnstr CC.
See also Marlow.

LEIRE Leics
132 SP 5290 4m N of Lutterworth.
CP, 347. Lttrwth RD. P RUGBY. Ch e, m.
Blaby CC (Harborough).

LEISTON Suffolk (E)
137 TM 4462 4m E of Saxmundham.
UD(Lstn-cum-Sizewell), 4,864. P. Eye CC.
Engineering wks. 1m N, rems of 14c L.
Abbey (A.M.).

LELANT Cornwall
189 SW 5437 3m SE of St Ives. Loc,
St Ives MB. P St Ives.

LELANT DOWNS Cornwall
189 SW 5236 3m SSE of St Ives. Loc,
Ludgvan CP. P Hayle. Ch m.

LELLEY Yorks (E)
99 TA 2032 7m ENE of Hull. Loc,
Elstronwick CP. Ch m.

LEM HILL Worcs
130 SO 7274 4m W of Bewdley. Loc,
Rock CP.

LEMINGTON Nthmb
78 NZ 1864 4m W of Newcastle. Loc,
Newburn UD. P NCSTLE UPON TYNE 5.

LEMSFORD Herts
147, 160 TL 2112 1m WSW of Welwyn Gdn
City. Loc, Hatfield CP. Ch e. Sch pe.

LENCHWICK Worcs
144 SP 0347 2m N of Evesham. CP(Norton
and Lnchwck), 803. Eveshm RD. Sch pe.
S Worcs CC.

LENHAM Kent
172 TQ 8952 9m ESE of Maidstone.
CP, 2,487. Hollingbourn RD. P Mdstne.
Ch e, c. Sch p, s. Mdstne CC. See also Lnhm
Hth, Platt's Hth, Sandway.

LENHAM HEATH Kent
172, 184 TQ 9149 3m W of Charing. Loc,
Lnhm CP. P Maidstone. Ch m.

LENTON Lincs (K)
113, 123 TF 0230 8m NNW of Bourne.
CP(Lntn Keisby and Osgodby), 186.
W Kesteven RD. Ch e. Rutland and
Stamford CC.

LENT RISE Bucks
159 SU 9281 3m WNW of Slough. Loc,
Burnham CP. P Bnhm.

LENWADE Norfolk
125 TG 0918 8m ENE of E Dereham. Loc,
Gt Witchingham CP. St Faith's and
Aylsham RD. Sch pe. N Nflk CC (Central
Nflk).

LEOMINSTER Herefs
129 SO 4959 12m N of Hereford.
MB, 7,071. P. Lmnstr CC. See also Aulden,
Brierley, Cholstrey, Ivington, Ivngtn Grn.

LEONARD STANLEY Glos
156 SO 8003 3m WSW of Stroud.
CP, 1,131. Strd RD. P Stonehouse. Ch e, m.
Sch pe. Strd CC.

LEPE Hants
180 SZ 4598 3m S of Fawley. CP(Exbury

and Lpe), 273. New Forest RD.
Nw Frst CC.

LEPPINGTON Yorks (E)
92, 97, 98 SE 7661 7m SSW of Malton.
Loc, Scrayingham CP. Ch e, m.

LERRYN Cornwall
186 SX 1457 3m SE of Lostwithiel. Loc,
Liskeard RD. P Lstwthl. Ch m. Sch pe.
Bodmin CC.

LESBURY Nthmb
71 NU 2311 3m ESE of Alnwick. CP, 946.
Alnwck RD. P Alnwck. Ch e. Sch pe.
Berwick-upon-Tweed CC. See also Bilton,
Hawkhill. Neat 19c vllge on R Aln. Main
line rly viaduct.

LESNEWTH Cornwall
174 SX 1390 4m NNE of Camelford.
CP, 76. Cmlfd RD. Ch e. N Cnwll CC.

LESSINGHAM Norfolk
126 TG 3928 7m ESE of N Walsham.
CP, 220. Smallburgh RD.
P NORWICH, NOR 26Z. Ch e, m. Sch p.
N Nflk CC. See also Hempstead.

LESSONHALL Cumb
75 NY 2250 2m WNW of Wigton. Loc,
Waverton CP.

LETCHMORE HEATH Herts
160 TQ 1597 1m SW of Radlett. Loc,
Aldenham CP. P Watford. Grn and public
hse impart vllge character.

LETCHWORTH Herts
147 TL 2132 5m N of Stevenage.
UD, 30,884. . Hitchin CC. See also Norton,
Willian. England's first gdn city (1903).
Considerable indstrl development. Singular
scarcity of licensed premises.

LETCOMBE BASSETT Berks
158 SU 3785 3m SW of Wantage. CP, 157.
Wntge RD. P Wntge. Ch e. Abingdon CC.
Thatch; watercress beds.

LETCOMBE REGIS Berks
158 SU 3886 2m SW of Wantage. CP, 473.
Wntge RD. P Wntge. Ch e. Sch pe.
Abingdon CC.

LETHERINGHAM Suffolk (E)
137 TM 2757 3m SSW of Framlingham.
CP, 87. Deben RD. Ch e. Eye CC.

LETHERINGSETT Norfolk
125 TG 0638 1m W of Holt. CP(Lthrngstt
w Glandford), 274. Erpingham RD. P Hlt.
Ch e, m. N Nflk CC. Ch by Butterfield.

LETTON Herefs
129 SO 3770 6m E of Knighton.
CP(Walford, Lttn and Newton), 86.
Leominster and Wigmore RD. Lmnstr CC.

LETTON Herefs
142 SO 3346 7m ENE of Hay-on-Wye.
CP, 92. Weobley RD, P HEREFORD. Ch e.
Leominster CC.

LETTY GREEN Herts
147, 160 TL 2810 3m WSW of Hertford.
Loc, Hertingfordbury CP. P HTFD.

LETWELL Yorks (W)
103 SK 5687 5m NNW of Worksop. CP, 93.
Kiveton Pk RD. P Wksp, Notts. Ch e.
Rother Valley CC.

LEUSDON Devon
175, 187, 188 SX 7073 4m NW of
Ashburton. Loc, Widecombe in the
Moor CP. Ch e.

LEVEDALE Staffs
119 SJ 8916 4m SSW of Stafford. Loc,
Pennkridge CP

LEVEN Yorks (E)
99 TA 1045 6m NE of Beverley. CP, 683.
Bvrly RD. P Hull. Ch e, m. Sch pe.
Haltempriceee CC

LEVENS Westm
89 SD 4886 5m SSW of Kendal. CP, 903.
S Westm RD. P Kndl. Ch e, m. Sch pe.
Westm CC. See also Cotes. Levens Hall*,
Elizn hse; topiary gdns. Steam engine
museum.

LEVERINGTON Cambs
124 TF 4411 2m NW of Wisbech.
CP, 2,920. Wsbch RD. P Wsbch. Ch e, m.
Sch p. Isle of Ely CC. See also Gorefield.

LEVERTON Lincs (H)
114 TF 4047 5m ENE of Boston. CP, 637.
Bstn RD. P Bstn. Ch e. Sch pe. Holland
w Bstn CC. See also Lvtn Outgate.

LEVERTON OUTGATE Lincs (H)
114 TF 4248 7m ENE of Boston. Loc,
Lvtn CP. Ch m.

LEVINGTON Suffolk (E)
150 TM 2339 5m NW of Felixtowe.
CP, 212. Deben RD. P Ipswich. Ch e.
Sudbury and Woodbridge CC. Broke Hall,
18c–19c, beside Orwell estuary.

LEVISHAM Yorks (N)
86, 92 SE 8390 5m NNE of Pickering.
CP, 80. Pckrng RD. P Pckrng. Ch e2, m.
Scarborough CC (Scbrgh and Whitby).

LEW Oxon
158 SP 3206 3m SW of Witney. CP, 78.
Wtny RD. Mid-Oxon CC (Banbury).

LEWANNICK Cornwall
186 SX 2780 4m SW of Launceston.
CP, 350. Lncstn RD. P Lncstn. Ch e, m2.
Sch p. N Cnwll CC. See also Polyphant. Ch
contains a cresset stone — ancient stone
candlestick; cf Marhamchurch.

LEWDOWN Devon
175 SX 4486 7m E of Launceston. Loc,
Tavistock RD. P Okehampton. W Dvn CC
(Tvstck).

LEWES Sussex (E)
183 TQ 4110 8m ENE of Brighton.
MB, 14,015. P. Lws CC. See also S Malling.
County tn of E Sussex on R Ouse between
downs. Nmn cstle* and several old hses.
High St climbs steep hill.

LEWISHAM London
161, 171 TQ 3874 2m SSW of Greenwich.
LB, 264,800. BCs: Deptford, Lwshm E,
Lwshm W (Dptfd, Lwshm N, S, W). See also
Blackheath, Catford, Dptfd, Hither Grn,
Mottingham, New Cross, Nunhead,
Sydenham. S of Thames with very small
river frontage at Dptfd Power Stn. L. itself
is on Ravensbourne Brook.

LEWKNOR Oxon
159 SU 7197 5m S of Thame. CP, 483.
Bullingdon RD. P OXFORD. Ch e. Sch pe.
Henley CC. See also Postcombe, S Weston.
At foot of Chilterns.

LEWORTHY Devon
163 SS 6738 8m NE of Barnstaple. Loc,
Bratton Fleming CP.

LEWTRENCHARD Devon
175 SX 4586 8m E of Launceston. CP, 167.
Tavistock RD. Ch e. Sch pe. W Dvn CC
(Tvstck). Incumbency for 43 years of
S. Baring-Gould, Vctrn hagiologist and
hymn-writer.

LEY Cornwall
186 SX 1766 5m W of Liskeard. Loc, St Neot CP.

LEYBOURNE Kent
171 TQ 6858 5m WNW of Maidstone. CP, 2,103. Malling RD. Ch e. Sch pe. Tonbridge and Mllng CC (Sevenoaks).

LEYBURN Yorks (N)
91 SE 1190 8m SSW of Richmond. CP, 1,357. Lbn RD. P. Ch e, m2. Sch p, pr, s. Rchmnd CC. Small mkt tn with large square. To E, L. Shawl, limestone escarpment.

LEYCETT Staffs
110 SJ 7946 3m W of Newcastle-under Lyme. Loc, Ncstle-undr-Lme RD. Sch p. N-u-L BC.

LEYHILL COMMON Bucks
159, 160 SP 9802 2m E of Chesham. Loc, Latimer CP. Ch m. Sch p.

LEYLAND Lancs
94 SD 5422 5m S of Preston. UD, 23,391. P Prstn. Chorley CC. See also Midge Hall. Motor and rubber wks. New Tn designated in area.

LEYLAND GREEN Lancs
100 SD 5400 4m NE of St Helens. Loc, Ashton-in-Makerfield UD.

LEYSDOWN-ON-SEA Kent
172, 173 TR 0370 8m ESE of Sheerness. Loc, Queenborough-in-Sheppey MB. P Shrnss. Holiday place; Thames estuary N, marshlands S.

LEYTON London
161 TQ 3786 6m NE of Charing Cross. Loc, Waltham Forest LB. Ltn BC. Rsdntl distr E of R Lee.

LEYTONSTONE London
161 TQ 3987 7m NE of Charing Cross. Loc, Waltham Forest LB. Leyton BC.

LEZANT Cornwall
186 SX 3379 4m S of Launceston. CP, 495. Lncstn RD. Ch e, m. N Cnwll CC. See also Rezare, Trebullett, Treburley, Trekenner. 2m ENE, Greystone Br, seven-arched mdvl br carrying A384 rd over Tamar.

LICHFIELD Staffs
120 SK 1109 15m NNE of Birmingham. MB, 22,672. P. Lchfld and Tamworth CC. Cathedral; close has old hses, incl former Bishop's Palace, now a sch. Samuel Johnson's bthplce (1709) in mkt square now a museum.

LICKEY Worcs
130, 131 SO 9975 4m NE of Bromsgrove. Loc, Brmsgrve UD, Brmsgrve RD. P Rednal, BIRMINGHAM. Brmsgrve and Redditch CC (Brmsgrve). At W foot of wooded L. Hills. Well known rly gradient (L. Incline).

LICKEY END Worcs
130, 131 SO 9672 1m NE of Bromsgrove. Loc, Brmsgrve UD. P Brmsgrve.

LICKFOLD Sussex (W)
181 SU 9226 4m NE of Midhurst. Loc, Lodsworth CP. Several timber-framed 17c cottages; picturesque hmlt.

LIDDINGTON Rutland
133 SP 8797 2m SSE of Uppingham. Alternative spelling for Lyddington, qv.

LIDDINGTON Wilts
157 SU 2081 4m SE of Swindon. CP, 346. Highworth RD. P Swndn. Ch e, m. Devizes CC. On hill 1m S, L. Cstle, Iron Age fort.

LIDGATE Suffolk (W)
135 TL 7257 6m SE of Newmarket. CP, 227. Clare RD. P Nmkt. Ch e, c. Bury St Edmunds CC.

LIDLINGTON Beds
147 SP 9939 3m W of Ampthill. CP, 917. Ampthll RD. P BEDFORD. Ch e, m, v. Sch p. Mid-Beds CC.

LIDSTONE Oxon
145 SP 3524 3m SE of Chipping Norton. Loc, Enstone CP.

LIFTON Devon
174, 186 SX 3885 3m E of Launceston. CP, 841. Tavistock RD. P. Ch e. Sch p. W Dvn CC (Tvstck). See also Liftondown, Tinhay.

LIFTONDOWN Devon
174, 186 SX 3685 2m E of Launceston. Loc, Lifton CP. Ch m.

LIGHTCLIFFE Yorks (W)
96, 102 SE 1325 3m E of Halifax. Loc, Brighouse MB. P Hlfx.

LIGHTHORNE Warwicks
132 SP 3355 6m S of Leamington. CP, 1,359. Southam RD. P WARWICK. Ch e. Stratford-on-Avon CC (Strtfd).

LIGHTWATER Surrey
169 SU 9262 4m ENE of Camberley. Loc, Windlesham CP. P. Ch e, m. Sch p.

LILBOURNE Northants
132, 133 SP 5676 4m ENE of Rugby. CP, 227. Daventry RD. P Rgby, Warwickshire. Ch e, m. Dvntry CC (S Nthnts). To E, M1 motorway on embankment. To S, Rugby radio stn.

LILLESHALL Shrops
119 SJ 7315 3m SSW of Newport. CP, 8,857. Wellington RD. P Npt. Ch e, v. Sch p. The Wrekin CC. See also Donnington. Ch: Leveson monmt, 17c. Rems of 12c abbey to S. 19c L. Hall in Tdr style, now National Recreation Centre.

LILLEY Herts
147 TL 1226 4m NNE of Luton. CP, 489. Hitchin RD. P Ltn, Beds. Ch e, m. Sch pe. Htchn CC.

LILLINGSTONE DAYRELL Bucks
146 SP 7039 4m N of Buckingham. CP, 121. Bcknghm RD. P BCKNGHM. Ch e. Sch pe. Bcknghm CC.

LILLINGSTONE LOVELL Bucks
146 SP 7140 4m N of Buckingham. CP, 143. Bcknghm RD. P BCKNGHM. Ch e. Bcknghm CC.

LILLINGTON Dorset
178 ST 6212 3m SSW of Sherborne. CP, 95. Shbne RD. Ch e. W Dst CC.

LILSTOCK Som
164 ST 1744 6m E of Watchet. Loc, Stringston CP. Ch e.

LIMBER, GREAT Lincs (L)
104 TA 1308 5m NNE of Caistor. See Gt Lmbr.

LIMBRICK Lancs
95, 101 SD 6016 2m SE of Chorley. Loc, Hth Charnock CP. Chly RD. Chly CC.

LIMEHOUSE London
161 TQ 3681 4m E of Charing Cross. Loc, Twr Hmlts LB. Stepney and Poplar BC (Stpny). In dockland to N of Thames. Formerly Lndn's Chinese quarter.

LIMINGTON Som
166, 177 ST 5422 1m E of Ilchester. CP, 230. Yeovil R. P Yvl. Ch e. Yvl CC.

LIMPENHOE Norfolk
126 TG 3903 8m WSW of Yarmouth. Loc, Cantley CP. P NORWICH, NOR 71Z. Ch e, m.

LIMPLEY STOKE Wilts
166 ST 7860 3m SE of Bath. CP, 523. Bradford and Melksham RD. P Bth. Ch e, b. Westbury CC. Rd, rly, canal, and R Avon share valley here. To N, Dundas Aqueduct.

LIMPSFIELD Surrey
171 TQ 4053 8m W of Sevenoaks. CP, 3,296. Godstone RD. P Oxted. Ch e, c. Sch pe. E Srry CC (Reigate). See also Chart. Picturesque vllge preserving some rural character. Burial place of Delius.

LINBY Notts
112 SK 5351 6m S of Mansfield. CP, 275. Basford RD. P NOTTINGHAM. Ch e. Sch pe. Carlton CC (Ashfield). Mining vllge. To E, Cstle Mill, where James Watt set up his first steam engine for cotton-spinning, 1785.

LINCHMERE Sussex (W)
169, 181 SU 8630 2m SW of Haslemere. CP, 1,526. Midhurst RD. Ch e. Chichester CC (Horsham). See also Hammer. Hill vllge near Surrey border.

LINCOLN Lincs
113 SK 9771 120m N of London. CB, 74,207. P(LNCLN). Lncln BC. County capital and cathedral city on site of Roman *Lindum Colonia*. Many mdvl hses. Cstle blt by William I. Extensive indstrl development, mostly engineering.

LINCOMB Worcs
130 SO 8268 2m SSE of Stourport. Loc, Hartlebury CP.

LINDALE Lancs
89 SD 4180 2m NNE of Grange-over-Sands. Loc, Upr Allithwaite CP. N Lonsdale RD.

P Grnge-over-Snds. Ch e. Sch pe. Morecambe and Lnsdle CC. Monmt to John Wilkinson (son of Isaac W. — see Backbarrow), early ironmaster who cast parts for br at Ironbridge, Shrops (qv).

LINDAL IN FURNESS Lancs
88 SD 2575 3m SW of Ulverston. Loc, Dalton-in-Fnss UD. P Ulvstn.

LINDFIELD Sussex (E)
182 TQ 3425 1m NE of Haywards Hth. Loc, Cuckfield UD. P Hwds Hth. Suburban vllge with fine main st of timber-framed and Ggn brick hses.

LINDFORD Hants
169 SU 8036 6m WNW of Haslemere. Loc, Whitehill CP. P Bordon. Ch m.

LINDISFARNE Nthmb
64 NU 1242 5m NNE of Belford. See Holy Island.

LINDRIDGE Worcs
129, 130 SO 6769 5m E of Tenbury Wells. CP, 577. Tnbry RD. Ch e. Sch pe. Kidderminster CC. See also Eardiston, Frith Cmmn.

LINDSELL Essex
148 TL 6427 3m NNE of Dunmow. CP, 217. Dnmw RD. P Dnmw. Ch e, v. Saffron Walden CC.

LINDSEY Suffolk (W)
149 TL 9745 3m NW of Hadleigh. CP, 143. Cosford RD. Ch e. Sudbury and Woodbridge CC. St James' Chpl (A.M.), 13c.

LINFORD Essex
161, 171 TQ 6779 3m NE of Tilbury. Loc, Thurrock UD. P Stanford-le-Hope. Thrrck BC (CC).

LINFORD Hants
179 SU 1707 2m ENE of Ringwood. Loc, Ellingham CP.

LINFORD, GREAT Bucks
146 SP 8542 2m WSW of Newport Pagnell. See Gt Lnfd.

LINGDALE Yorks (N)
86 NZ 6716 3m S of Saltburn. Loc, Skelton and Brotton UD. P Sltbn-by-the-Sea.

LINGEN Herefs
129 SO 3667 4m NE of Presteigne. CP, 152. Leominster and Wigmore RD. P Bucknell, Salop. Ch e, m. Lmnstr CC. See also Birtley.

LINGFIELD Surrey
171 TQ 3843 3m N of E Grinstead. CP, 6,871. Godstone RD. P. Ch e, b, m, r, v. Sch p, s. E Srry CC (Reigate). See also Dormans Land, Felcourt. Ch: monmts. Lock-up and restored boundary mark (St Peter's Cross). To S, L. Pk Racecourse. 2m NE, Puttenden Mnr*, half-timbered Tdr hse.

LINGWOOD Norfolk
126 TG 3608 8m E of Norwich. Loc, Burlingham CP. Blofield and Flegg RD. P NRWCH, NOR 79Z. Ch e, m. Sch p. Yarmouth CC.

LINKENHOLT Hants
168 SU 3657 8m N of Andover. CP, 59. Andvr RD. P Andvr. Ch e. Winchester CC (Basingstoke).

LINKINHORNE Cornwall
186 SX 3173 4m NW of Callington. CP, 1,087. Liskeard RD. P Cllngtn. Ch e, m. Bodmin CC. See also Henwood, Minions, Rilla Mill, Upton Cross. Ch has very tall granite twr; St Melor's holy well nearby.

LINLEY Shrops
130 SO 6898 4m NNW of Bridgnorth. Loc, Barrow CP. Ch e. Ch stands in trees beside drive of hall.

LINLEY GREEN Herefs
143 SO 6953 3m ESE of Bromyard. Loc, Linton CP. Brmyd RD. Leominster CC.

LINSLADE Beds
146 SP 9125 just W of Leighton Buzzard. UD(Lghtn-Lnslde), 20,326. P Lghtn Bzzd. S Beds CC (Buckingham). Transferred from Bucks 1965.

LINSTEAD MAGNA Suffolk (E)
137 TM 3176 4m WSW of Halesworth. CP, 56. Blyth RD. Eye CC.

LINSTEAD PARVA Suffolk (E)
137 TM 3377 3m W of Halesworth. CP, 91. Blyth RD. Ch e. Eye CC.

LINSTOCK Cumb
76 NY 4258 2m NE of Carlisle. Loc,
Stanwix Rural CP. Border RD. Penrith and
the Bdr CC.

LINTHWAITE Yorks (W)
102 SE 1014 3m WSW of Huddersfield.
Loc, Colne Valley UD. P Hddsfld. Clne
Vlly CC.

LINTON Cambs
148 TL 5646 5m NNE of Saffron Walden.
CP, 1,982. S Cambs RD. P CAMBRIDGE.
Ch e, s, v. Sch je, s. Cambs CC.
Half-timbered 'guildhall' near ch. Vllge
college.

LINTON Derbys
120 SK 2716 5m SSE of Burton-on-Trent.
CP, 1,958. Repton RD. P Btn-on-Trnt,
Staffs. Ch e, m2. Sch p. Belper CC.

LINTON Herefs
142, 143 SO 6525 4m E of Ross-on-Wye.
CP, 454. Rss and Whitchurch RD.
P Rss-on-Wye. Ch e. Sch pe. Hereford CC.
See also Gorsley Cmmn, Lnton Hill.

LINTON Kent
172 TQ 7550 3m S of Maidstone.
CP, 1,686. Mdstne RD. P Mdstne. Ch e.
Sch s. Mdstne CC.

LINTON Yorks (W)
90 SD 9962 7m N of Skipton. CP, 285.
Skptn RD. P Skptn. Ch e. Skptn CC. Blt
round grn beside R Wharfe and a beck.
Clapper and packhorse brs. Grand 18c
almshouse, Fountains Hsptl, with chpl
possibly by Vanburgh.

LINTON Yorks (W)
96 SE 3946 1m SW of Wetherby. Loc,
Collingham CP.

LINTON COLLIERY Nthmb
78 NZ 2691 5m NE of Morpeth. Loc,
Ellington CP. P Mpth. Ch m. Sch p.

LINTON HILL Herefs
142, 143 SO 6624 4m E of Ross-on-Wye.
Loc, Lntn CP.

LINTON-ON-OUSE Yorks (N)
91, 97 SE 4960 9m NW of York. CP, 1,346.
Easingwold RD. P YK. Sch p. Thirsk and
Malton CC.

LINWOOD Hants
179 SU 1809 4m NE of Ringwood. Loc,
Ellingham CP. P Rngwd.

LINWOOD Lincs (L)
104 TF 1086 2m S of Mkt Rasen. CP, 152.
Caistor RD. Ch e, m. Gainsborough CC. Ch:
15c brasses.

LIPHOOK Hants
169, 181 SU 8331 4m W of Haslemere. Loc,
Bramshott CP. P. Ch e, m, r, v. Sch pe.
Many famous people from Edward II
onwards have stayed at Royal Anchor Inn.

LISKEARD Cornwall
186 SX 2564 11m E of Bodmin. MB, 5,255.
P. Bdmn CC.

LISS Hants
181 SU 7728 4m NE of Petersfield.
CP, 3,283. Ptrsfld RD. P. Ch e, v3. Sch p.
Ptrsfld CC. See also E Lss.

LISSETT Yorks (E)
99 TA 1458 6m SSW of Bridlington. Loc,
Ulrome CP. Ch e.

LISS FOREST Hants
169, 181 SU 7828 4m NE of Petersfield.
Loc, Lss CP. P Lss.

LISSINGTON Lincs (L)
104 TF 1083 4m S of Mkt Rasen. CP, 145.
Caistor RD. P LINCOLN. Ch e, m.
Gainsborough CC.

LISTON Essex
149 TL 8544 1m SW of Long Melford.
CP, 70. Halstead RD. Ch e. Saffron
Walden CC.

LITCHAM Norfolk
125 TF 8817 7m NE of Swaffham. CP, 624.
Mitford and Launditch RD. P King's Lynn.
Ch e, m. Sch p, s. SW Nflk CC.

LITCHBOROUGH Northants
145, 146 SP 6354 5m NW of Towcester.
CP, 222. Tcstr RD. P Tcstr. Ch e, b. Sch pe.
Daventry CC (S Nthnts).

LITCHFIELD Hants
168 SU 4653 4m N of Whitchurch.
CP(Ltchfld and Woodcott), 231. Kingsclere
and Whtchch RD. Ch e. Basingstoke CC. On
Beacon Hill to NW and Ladle Hill to NE,
Iron Age hill forts, Bronze Age barrows.

LITHERLAND Lancs
100 SJ 3397 4m N of Liverpool.
UD, 23,670. P LVPL 21. Bootle BC
(Crosby).

LITLINGTON Cambs
147 TL 3142 3m WNW of Royston.
CP, 608. S Cambs RD. P Rstn, Herts.
Ch e, v. Sch pe. Cambs CC.

LITLINGTON Sussex (E)
183 TQ 5201 3m ENE of Seaford. CP, 117.
Hailsham RD. P,Polegate. Ch e. Lewes CC
(Eastbourne). Flint vllge on Cuckmere river
in S Downs.

LITTLE ABINGTON Cambs
148 TL 5349 7m N of Saffron Walden.
CP, 321. S Cambs RD. Ch e, c. Cambs CC.
Joined on to Gt A.

LITTLE ADDINGTON Northants
134 SP 9573 4m N of Rushden. CP, 208.
Oundle and Thrapston RD. P Kettering.
Ch e, m. Wellingborough CC
(Peterborough).

LITTLE ALNE Warwicks
131 SP 1361 6m NW of Stratford. Loc,
Aston Cantlow CP.

LITTLE AMWELL Herts
148, 161 TL 3511 2m SSW of Ware.
CP, 982. Hertford RD. Ch e. Htfd and
Stevenage CC (Htfd).

LITTLE ASBY Westm
83 NY 6909 7m S of Appleby. Loc,
Asby CP. N Westm RD. Ch c. Westm CC.

LITTLE ASTON Staffs
120 SK 0900 3m NW of Sutton Coldfield.
Loc, Shenstone CP. Ch e. Sch p.

LITTLE ATHERFIELD IOW
180 SZ 4680 6m SSW of Newport. Loc,
Shorwell CP.

LITTLE AYTON Yorks (N)
86 NZ 5710 5m SW of Guisborough.
CP, 108. Stokesley RD. Richmond CC.

LITTLE BADDOW Essex
162 TL 7807 4m E of Chelmsford.
CP, 1,125. Chlmsfd RD. P Chlmsfd. Ch e, v.
Chlmsfd CC. Ch: 14c oak effigies; monmts.

LITTLE BADMINTON Glos
156 ST 8084 8m W of Malmesbury. Loc,
Hawkesbury CP. Ch e.

LITTLE BAMPTON Cumb
75 NY 2755 4m NNE of Wigton. Loc,
Kirkbampton CP.

LITTLE BARDFIELD Essex
148 TL 6530 3m E of Thaxted. CP, 246.
Dunmow RD. Ch e. Saffron Walden CC. Ch:
massive Saxon twr.

LITTLE BARFORD Beds
134 TL 1856 2m S of St Neots. CP, 68.
Bedford RD. P HUNTINGDON. Ch e.
Mid-Beds CC.

LITTLE BARNINGHAM Norfolk
125 TG 1333 5m SE of Holt. CP, 116.
Erpingham RD. P NORWICH, NOR 19Y.
Ch e, v. N Nflk CC.

LITTLE BARRINGTON Glos
144 SP 2012 3m W of Burford. Loc,
Brrngtn CP. Northleach RD. Ch e. Sch pe.
Cirencester and Tewkesbury CC. Grn
traversed by stream in pleasing Cotswold
vllge.

LITTLE BARROW Ches
109 SJ 4670 5m ENE of Chester. Loc,
Brrw CP. Chstr RD. City of Chstr CC.

LITTLE BARUGH Yorks (N)
92 SE 7679 4m SW of Pickering. CP(Brgh,
Gt and Lit), 153. Pckrng RD.
Scarborough CC (Thirsk and Malton).

LITTLE BAVINGTON Nthmb
77 NY 9878 9m N of Corbridge. Loc,
Bvngtn CP. Bellingham RD. Hexham CC.

LITTLE BEALINGS Suffolk (E)
150 TM 2347 3m WSW of Woodbridge.
CP, 412. Deben RD. Ch e. Sch p. Sudbury
and Wdbrdge CC. Pleasant suburban vllge.
Commuters' hses in woods towards
Martlesham.

LITTLE BEDWYN Wilts
158 SU 2966 4m WSW of Hungerford.
CP, 345. Marlborough and Ramsbury RD.
P Mlbrgh. Ch e, v. Sch pe. Devizes CC. See
also Chisbury.

LITTLE BENTLEY Essex
150 TM 1125 4m S of Manningtree.
CP, 260. Tendring RD. P Colchester.
Ch e, m. Harwich CC.

LITTLE BERKHAMSTED Herts
160 TL 2907 4m E of Hatfield. CP, 567.
Hertford RD. P HTFD. Ch e. Htfd and
Stevenage CC (Htfd). See also Epping Grn.
Red brick folly twr erected 1789 by
Admiral Stratton for viewing ships in
R Thames; distance c 40 miles.

LITTLE BILLING Northants
133 SP 8061 3m E of Northampton. Loc,
Bllng CP. Nthmptn RD. Ch e. Daventry CC
(S Nthnts). 'Aquadrome', camping and
amusement area.

LITTLE BIRCH Herefs
142 SO 5131 5m S of Hereford. CP, 203.
Hrfd RD. Ch e, m. Hrfd CC.

LITTLE BLAKENHAM Suffolk (E)
150 TM 1048 5m NW of Ipswich. CP, 185.
Gipping RD. Ch e. Eye CC.

LITTLE BLENCOW Cumb
83 NY 4532 4m WNW of Penrith. Loc,
Greystoke CP. Ch m. B. Hall, 16c.

LITTLE BOOKHAM Surrey
170 TQ 1254 3m WSW of Leatherhead.
Loc, Lthrhd UD. P Gt Bkhm, Lthrhd.

LITTLEBOROUGH Lancs
95, 101 SD 9316 3m ENE of Rochdale.
UD, 11,987. P. Heywood and Royton CC.
See also Calderbrook, Summit. Textile tn.
To E at Blackstone Edge, section of paved
Roman rd over Pennines.

LITTLEBOROUGH Notts
104 SK 8182 5m S of Gainsborough. Loc,
Sturton le Steeple CP. Ch e. Small Nmn ch.
Site of Roman ford across R Trent, used by
King Harold on way to Hastings.

LITTLEBOURNE Kent
173 TR 2057 4m E of Canterbury.
CP, 1,104. Bridge-Blean RD. P Cntrbry.
Ch e, c. Sch pe. Cntrbry CC.

LITTLE BOURTON Oxon
145 SP 4544 2m N of Banbury. Loc,
Btn CP. Bnbry RD. Ch m. Bnbry CC.

LITTLE BOWDEN Leics
133 SP 7487 just E of Mkt Harborough.
Loc, Mkt Hbrgh UD. P Mkt Hbrgh.

LITTLE BRADLEY Suffolk (W)
148 TL 6852 4m N of Haverhill. CP, 90.
Clare RD. Ch e. Bury St Edmunds CC.

LITTLE BRAXTED Essex
149, 162 TL 8314 just E of Witham.
CP, 131. Maldon RD. Ch e. Mldn CC.

LITTLEBREDY Dorset
177, 178 SY 5889 6m W of Dorchester.
CP, 101. Dchstr RD. P Dchstr. Ch e.
W Dst CC.

LITTLE BRICKHILL Bucks
146 SP 9032 2m ESE of Bletchley. CP, 381.
Newport Pagnell RD. P Bltchly. Ch e, m.
Sch pe. Buckingham CC.

LITTLE BRIDGEFORD Staffs
119 SJ 8727 4m NW of Stafford. Loc,
Seighford CP.

LITTLE BRINGTON Northants
132, 133 SP 6663 6m WNW of
Northampton. Loc, Brngtn CP.
Brixworth RD. Ch b. Sch p.
Daventry (Kettering). The Washingtons of
Sulgrave (qv) moved here, to Wshngtn Hse,
in 1660. Two are buried at Gt Brngtn; the
stars and stripes of their arms on
gravestones.

LITTLE BROMLEY Essex
149 TL 0928 2m SSW of Manningtree.
CP, 256. Tendring RD. P Mnnngtree.
Ch e, m. Harwich CC.

LITTLE BUDWORTH Ches
109 SJ 5965 4m W of Winsford. CP, 508.
Northwich RD. P Tarporley. Ch e, m.
Nthwch CC. To W, Oulton Pk motor racing
circuit.

LITTLE BURSTEAD Essex
161 TQ 6692 2m S of Billericay. Loc,
Basildon UD. P Bllrcy.

LITTLEBURY Essex
148 TL 5139 2m NW of Saffron Walden.
CP, 511. Sffrn Wldn RD. P Sffrn Wldn.
Ch e. Sch pe. Sffrn Wldn CC. See also
Lttlbry Grn.

Littlebury Green

LITTLEBURY GREEN Essex
148 TL 4838 3m W of Saffron Walden. Loc,
Lttlbry CP.

LITTLE BYTHAM Lincs (K)
123 TF 0118 5m WSW of Bourne. CP, 298.
S Kesteven RD. P Grantham. Ch e, m.
Sch p. Rutland and Stamford CC.

LITTLE CARLTON Lincs (L)
105 TF 4085 5m ESE of Louth. CP, 83.
Lth RD. Ch e. Lth CC.

LITTLE CASTERTON Rutland
123 TF 0109 2m NNW of Stamford.
CP, 184. Ketton RD. Ch e, m. Rtlnd and
Stmfd CC.

LITTLE CAWTHORPE Lincs (L)
105 TF 3583 3m SE of Louth. CP, 109.
Lth RD. Ch e. Lth CC.

LITTLE CHALFONT Bucks
159, 160 SU 9997 2m E of Amersham. Loc,
Amrshm CP. P Amrshm. Ch m, r. Sch p.

LITTLE CHART Kent
172, 184 TQ 9446 2m SSW of Charing.
CP, 282. W Ashford RD. P Ashfd. Ch e.
Ashfd CC.

LITTLE CHESTERFORD Essex
148 TL 5141 3m NNW of Saffron Walden.
CP, 213. Sffrn Wldn RD. P Sffrn Wldn.
Ch e, m. Sffrn Wldn CC. Mnr hse, 13c:
timber-framed great hall, solar wing; later
additions. Ch also 13c.

LITTLE CHEVERELL Wilts
167 ST 9953 5m S of Devizes. CP(Chvrll
Parva), 153. Dvzs RD. Ch e. Dvzs CC.

LITTLE CHISHILL Cambs
148 TL 4137 4m ESE of Royston. Loc, Gt
and Lit Chshll CP. S Cambs RD. Ch e, c.
Cambs CC. Transferred from Essex in 1895.

LITTLE CLACTON Essex
150 TM 1618 3m N of Clacton on Sea.
CP, 1,647. Tendring RD. P Clctn-on-Sea.
Ch e, m. Sch p. Harwich CC.

LITTLE CLIFTON Cumb
82 NY 0528 3m E of Workington. CP, 421.
Cockermouth RD. Ch e. Sch p. Wkngtn CC.

LITTLE COMBERTON Worcs
143, 144 SO 9643 2m SE of Pershore.
CP, 227. Pshre RD. P Pshre. Ch e.
S Worcs CC.

LITTLE COMMON Sussex (E)
183, 184 TQ 7107 2m W of Bexhill. Loc,
Bexhill MB. P Bxhll-on-Sea.

LITTLE COMPTON Warwicks
144 SP 2630 4m ESE of Moreton-in-Marsh.
CP, 286. Shipston on Stour RD.
P Mtn-in-Msh, Glos. Ch e, b. Sch p.
Stratford-on-Avon CC (Strtfd).

LITTLE CORNARD Suffolk (W)
149 TL 9039 2m SE of Sudbury. CP, 289.
Melford RD. Ch e. Sdbry and
Woodbridge CC.

LITTLE COWARNE Herefs
142, 143 SO 6051 4m SW of Bromyard.
CP, 105. Brmyd RD. Ch e. Leominster CC.

LITTLE COXWELL Berks
158 SU 2893 10m NE of Swindon. CP, 185.
Faringdon RD. P Frngdn. Ch e, b.
Abingdon CC.

LITTLE CRANSLEY Northants
133 SP 8276 3m WSW of Kettering. Loc,
Crnsly CP. Kttrng RD. Ch e. Kttrng CC.

LITTLE CRESSINGHAM Norfolk
136 TF 8700 3m W of Watton. CP, 253.
Swaffham RD. P Thetford. Ch e.
SW Nflk CC.

LITTLE CUBLEY Derbys
120 SK 1637 6m SSW of Ashbourne. Loc,
Cbly CP. Ashbne RD. Ch e. W Derbys CC.

LITTLE DALBY Leics
122 SK 7714 4m SSE of Melton Mowbray.
Loc, Burton and Dlby CP. Mltn and
Belvoir RD. Ch e. Mltn CC.

LITTLEDEAN Glos
142, 143 SO 6713 1m E of Cinderford.
CP, 1,378. E Dean RD. P Cndrfd. Ch e, v.
Sch pe. W Glos CC. Motte and bailey to E.

LITTLE DEWCHURCH Herefs
142 SO 5331 5m SSE of Hereford. CP, 320.
Hrfd RD. P HRFD. Ch e. Sch pe. Hrfd CC.

LITTLE DUNHAM Norfolk
125 TF 8612 4m NE of Swaffham. CP, 182.
Mitford and Launditch RD. P King's Lynn.
Ch e, m. SW Nflk CC.

LITTLE DUNMOW Essex
148 TL 6521 2m E of Dunmow. CP, 359.
Dnmw RD. P Dnmw. Ch e. Saffron
Walden CC. Orig home of 'Dnmw Flitch'
ceremony (see Dnmw).

LITTLE EASTON Essex
148 TL 6023 2m NW of Dunmow. CP, 327.
Dnmw RD. P Dnmw. Ch e. Saffron
Walden CC. See also Butcher's Pasture. Ch:
wall-paintings, tombs, monmts.

LITTLE EATON Derbys
120, 121 SK 3641 3m N of Derby. CP.
SE Derbys RD. P DBY. Ch c, m. Sch p.
SE Derbys CC.

LITTLE ECCLESTON Lancs
94 SD 4139 7m ENE of Blackpool. CP(Lit
Ecclstn-w-Larbreck), 288. Fylde RD.
S Flde CC.

LITTLE ELLINGHAM Norfolk
136 TM 0099 4m NW of Attleborough.
CP, 210. Wayland RD. P Attlbrgh. Ch e.
Sch p. S Nflk CC.

LITTLE END Essex
161 TL 5400 2m SSW of Ongar. Loc,
Stanford Rivers CP.

LITTLE EVERDON Northants
132, 133 SP 5958 3m SSE of Daventry.
Loc, Evrdn CP.

LITTLE EVERSDEN Cambs
148 TL 3753 6m SW of Cambridge.
CP, 295. S Cambs RD. Ch e. Cambs CC.

LITTLE FAKENHAM Suffolk (W)
136 TL 9076 5m SSE of Thetford. Loc,
Fknhm Magna CP. Thingoe RD.
P Thtfd, Norfolk. Ch e. Bury
St Edmunds CC. Honington Airfield to E.

LITTLE FARINGDON Oxon
157 SP 2201 1m NNE of Lechlade. CP, 101.
Witney RD. Ch e. Mid-Oxon CC (Banbury).

LITTLE FENTON Yorks (W)
97 SE 5235 6m SSE of Tadcaster. CP, 85.
Tdcstr RD. Barkston Ash CC.

LITTLE FRANSHAM Norfolk
125 TF 9011 6m W of E Dereham. Loc,
Frnshm CP. Mitford and Launditch RD.
P Drhm. Ch e. Sch p. SW Nflk CC.

LITTLE GADDESDEN Herts
147, 159, 160 SP 9913 4m N of
Berkhamsted. CP, 1,095. Bkhmstd RD.
P Bkhmstd. Ch e, m. Sch pe. Hemel
Hempstead CC. See also Ringshall. Mnr hse*
dates from 16c. John o' Gddsdn's Hse, 15c.
To S, Ashridge, early 19c by Wyatt, now
management college. Much NT property in
area, incl Ashrdge Pk*.

LITTLE GARWAY Herefs
142 SO 4424 8m NNW of Monmouth. Loc,
Garway CP.

LITTLE GIDDING Hunts
134 TL 1281 7m SE of Oundle. CP, 31.
Huntingdon RD. Ch e. Hunts CC.

LITTLE GLEMHAM Suffolk (E)
137 TM 3458 4m SW of Saxmundham.
CP, 209. Blyth RD. P Woodbridge. Ch e.
Eye CC. Isolated ch has life-size seated
statue of Dudley North, 1749–1829. G.
Hall* in pk on E side of A12 rd; mixture of
architectural styles.

LITTLE GRANSDEN Cambs
134 TL 2755 6m ESE of St Neots. CP, 235.
S Cambs RD. P Sandy, Beds. Ch e.
Cambs CC.

LITTLE HABTON Yorks (N)
92 SE 7477 4m NW of Malton. CP, 59.
Mltn RD. Thirsk and Mltn CC.

LITTLE HADHAM Herts
148 TL 4322 3m WNW of Bishop's
Stortford. CP, 858. Braughing RD. P Much
Hdhm. Ch e, c. Sch p, s. E Herts CC. See
also Bury Grn, Hdhm Ford. Attractive vllge
with several timbered cottages. Part of Elizn
H. Hall still stands.

LITTLE HALE Lincs (K)
113, 123 TF 1441 5m SE of Sleaford.
CP, 176. E Kesteven RD. Ch m. Sch pe.
Grantham CC.

LITTLE HALLINGBURY Essex
148 TL 5017 2m SSE of Bishop's Stortford.
CP, 1,025. Dunmow RD. P Bshp's
Sttfd, Herts. Ch e, v. Sch pe. Saffron
Walden CC. To W, Wallbury Camp, rems of
Iron Age settlement.

LITTLEHAM Devon
163 SS 4323 2m SSW of Bideford. CP, 266.
Bdfd RD. P Bdfd. Ch e, m. N Dvn CC
(Torrington).

LITTLEHAM Devon
176 SY 0281 2m E of Exmouth. Loc,
Exmth UD. P Exmth.

LITTLE HAMPDEN Bucks
159 SP 8603 3m E of Princes Risborough.
CP(Gt and Lit Hmpdn), 331. Wycombe RD.
Ch e. Aylesbury CC (Wcmbe).

LITTLEHAMPTON Sussex (W)
181, 182 TQ 0202 7m W of Worthing.
UD, 18,621. P. Arundel CC (Arndl and
Shoreham). See also Wick. Coastal resort at
mouth of R Arun. Sands.

LITTLE HARROWDEN Northants
133 SP 8671 3m NNW of Wellingborough.
CP, 758. Wllngbrgh RD. P Wllngbrgh.
Ch e, m. Sch p. Wllngbrgh CC.

LITTLE HASELEY Oxon
158, 159 SP 6400 5m SW of Thame. Loc,
Gt Hsly CP. Hsly Ct gdns* (12 acres).

LITTLE HAUTBOIS Norfolk
126 TG 2521 4m NW of Wroxham. Loc,
Buxton w Lammas CP.

LITTLE HAY Staffs
120 SK 1202 4m S of Lichfield. Loc,
Shenstone CP. P Lchfld.

LITTLE HAYWOOD Staffs
120 SK 0021 3m NW of Rugeley. Loc,
Colwich CP. P STAFFORD.

LITTLEHEMPSTON Devon
188 SX 8162 2m NNE of Totnes. CP, 203.
Ttns RD. Ch e. Ttns CC. To NW, Old Mnr,
14c, covenanted to NT.

LITTLE HEREFORD Herefs
129 SO 5568 3m W of Tenbury Wells.
CP, 346. Leominster and Wigmore RD.
P Ludlow, Salop. Ch e. Lmnstr CC. See also
Middleton.

LITTLE HINTON Wilts
157 SU 2383 5m E of Swindon. See Hinton
Parva.

LITTLE HORKESLEY Essex
149 TL 9632 5m NNW of Colchester.
CP, 253. Lexden and Winstree RD.
P Clchstr. Ch e. Clchstr CC. Ch rebuilt in
1957 after destruction by bombs in 1940;
has mdvl effigies and brasses from old ch.

LITTLE HORMEAD Herts
148 TL 4029 7m NW of Bishop's Stortford.
Loc, Hrmd CP. Braughing RD. Ch e.
E Herts CC.

LITTLE HORSTED Sussex (E)
183 TQ 4718 2m S of Uckfield. CP, 224.
Uckfld RD. Ch e. Sch pe. E Grinstead CC.

LITTLE HORWOOD Bucks
146 SP 7930 6m ESE of Buckingham.
CP, 260. Winslow RD. P Bletchley. Ch e, v.
Bcknghm CC.

LITTLE HOUGHTON Northants
133 SP 8059 3m E of Northampton.
CP, 409. Nthmptn RD. P NTHMPTN.
Ch e, m. Sch pe. Daventry CC (S Nthnts).

LITTLEHOUGHTON Nthmb
71 NU 2316 3m NE of Alnwick. Loc,
Longhoughton CP. L. Twr, 17c–18c hse
incorporating mdvl twr.

LITTLE HOUGHTON Yorks (W)
103 SE 4205 5m E of Barnsley. CP, 1,008.
Hemsworth RD. P Bnsly. Hmswth CC.

LITTLE HUCKLOW Derbys
111 SK 1678 7m NNW of Bakewell. CP, 96.
Bkwll RD. W Derbys CC. See also Coplow
Dale.

LITTLE HULTON Lancs
101 SD 7203 3m S of Bolton. Loc,
Worsley UD. P Wsly, MANCHESTER.

LITTLE HUNGERFORD Berks
169 SU 7571 3m ESE of Reading. Loc,
Woodley and Sandford CP.

LITTLE IRCHESTER Northants
133 SP 9066 1m SSE of Wellingborough.
Loc, Irchstr CP. P Wllngbrgh.

LITTLE KIMBLE Bucks
159 SP 8207 3m NNE of Princes
Risborough. CP(Gt and Lit Kmble), 807.
Wycombe RD. P Aylesburyy Ch e, v.
Aylesbury CC (Wcmbe).

LITTLE KINGSHILL Bucks
159 SU 8998 4m NNE of High Wycombe.
Loc, Amersham RD. P Gt Missenden. Ch b.
Sch p. Chesham and Amrshm CC
P Aylesbury.

LITTLE LANGDALE Westm
88, 89 NY 3103 4m W of Ambleside. Loc,
Lakes UD. P Amblsde. Westm CC. To W,
Wrynose Pass.

LITTLE LANGFORD Wilts
167 SU 0436 7m NW of Salisbury. Loc,l
Steeple Lngfd CP. Ch e.

LITTLE LAVER Essex
161 TL 5409 4m N of Ongar. CP, 95.
Epping and Ongr RD. Ch e. Brentwood and
Ongr CC (Chigwell).

LITTLE LAWFORD Warwicks
132 SP 4777 2m NW of Rugby. CP, 26.
Rgby RD. Rgby CC.

LITTLE LEIGH Ches
101 SJ 6176 3m WNW of Northwich.
CP, 449. Nthwch RD. P Nthwch. Ch e, b.
Sch p. Nthwch CC.

LITTLE LEIGHS Essex
148, 149, 162 TL 7116 5m SSW of
Braintree. CP(Gt and Lit Lghs), 1,018.
Chelmsford RD. Ch e. Brntree CC
(Chlmsfd).

LITTLE LEVER Lancs
101 SD 7507 3m ESE of Bolton.
UD, 9,124. P Bltn. Farnworth BC (CC).

LITTLE LINFORD Bucks
146 SP 8444 2m W of Newport Pagnell.
CP(Haversham-cum-Lit Lnfd), 795. Npt
Pgnll RD. Ch e. Buckingham CC.

LITTLE LONDON Hants
168 SU 3749 3m NNE of Andover. Loc,
Smannell CP.

LITTLE LONDON Hants
168 SU 6259 5m N of Basingstoke. Loc,
Pamber CP. Bsngstke RD. P Bsngstke. Ch m.
Bsngstke CC.

LITTLE LONDON Lincs (H)
123 TF 2421 1m SSW of Spalding. Loc,
Spldng UD. P Spldng.

LITTLE LONDON Sussex (E)
183 TQ 5719 1m SSW of Heathfield. Loc,
Waldron CP. P Hthfld. Ch v.

LITTLE LONGSTONE Derbys
111 SK 1871 3m NW of Bakewell. CP, 127.
Bkwll RD. Ch c. W Derbys CC.

LITTLE MALVERN Worcs
143 SO 7740 3m S of Malvern. CP, 72.
Upton upon Severn RD. Ch e, r.
S Worcs CC. Rems of 15c Benedictine
priory incorporated in ch and Ct.

LITTLE MAPLESTEAD Essex
149 TL 8233 2m NNE of Halstead. CP, 214.
Hlstd RD. P Hlstd. Ch e, c. Saffron
Walden CC. Round early 14c ch.

LITTLE MARCLE Herefs
142, 143 SO 6736 3m W of Ledbury.
CP, 107. Ldbry RD. P Ldbry. Ch e.
Leominster CC.

LITTLE MARLOW Bucks
159 SU 8787 2m NE of Marlow. CP, 1,103.
Wycombe RD. P Mlw. Ch e. Sch pe.
Wcmbe CC. Jcbn mnr hse.

LITTLE MASSINGHAM Norfolk
125 TF 7924 9m WSW of Fakenham.
CP, 110. Freebridge Lynn RD. Ch e.
NW Nflk CC (King's Lynn).

LITTLE MELTON Norfolk
126 TG 1606 4m WSW of Norwich.
CP, 402. Forehoe and Henstead RD.
P NRWCH, NOR 45X. Ch e, v. Sch p.
S Nflk CC (Central Nflk).

LITTLE MILTON Oxon
158 SP 6100 7m SE of Oxford. CP, 234.
Bullingdon RD. P OXFD. Ch e, m. Sch ie.
Henley CC.

LITTLE MISSENDEN Bucks
159 SU 9298 3m WNW of Amersham.
CP, 3,348. Amrshm RD. P Amrshm.
Ch e, m, v. Sch pe. Chesham and
Amrshm CC (Aylesbury). See also Holmer
Grn, Hyde Hth. 17c mnr hse.

LITTLEMORE Oxon
158 SP 5302 3m SSE of Oxford. CP, 8,259.
Bullingdon RD. P OXFD. Ch e, b, r.
Sch je, p, s. Henley CC.

LITTLE MUSGRAVE Westm
84 NY 7613 3m NNW of Kirkby Stephen.
Loc, Msgrve CP. N Westm RD. Westm CC.

LITTLE NESS Shrops
118 SJ 4019 7m NW of Shrewsbury. CP, 220.
Atcham RD. P Shrsbry. Ch e. Shrsbry CC
(Oswestry). Shrsbry CC.

LITTLE NEWSHAM Co Durham
84 NZ 1217 5m E of Barnard Cstle. Loc,
Winston CP.

LITTLE OAKLEY Essex
150 TM 2129 3m SW of Harwich. CP, 978.
Tendring RD. P Hrwch. Ch e, m. Sch ie.
Hrwch CC.

LITTLE OAKLEY Northants
133 SP 8985 2m S of Corby. Loc, Newton
CP. Ch e.

LITTLE OFFLEY Herts
147 TL 1328 3m W of Hitchin. Loc,
Offley CP. Htchn RD. Htchn CC.

LITTLE ORTON Cumb
76 NY 3555 3m W of Carlisle. Loc,
Ortn CP. Border RD. Penrith and the
Bdr CC.

LITTLE OUSEBURN Yorks (W)
91 SE 4460 5m SE of Boroughbridge.
CP, 173. Nidderdale RD. Ch e, m.
Harrogate CC.

LITTLE PACKINGTON Warwicks
131 SP 2184 3m SSE of Coleshill. CP, 68.
Meriden RD. Ch e. Mrdn CC. Gt Pckngtn
(no vllge) to E with P. Old Hall, 17c, P. Hall
17c—18c, large pk (Capability Brown), and
imp-essive 18c ch.

LITTLE PAXTON Hunts
134 TL 1862 2m N of St Neots. CP, 436.
St Nts RD. P HUNTINGDON. Ch e.
Hunts CC.

LITTLE PETHERICK Cornwall
185 SW 9172 2m S of Padstow. Loc,
St Issey CP. P Wadebridge. Ch e.

LITTLE PLUMPTON Lancs
94 SD 3832 5m ESE of Blackpool. Loc,
Westby-w-Plmptns CP.

LITTLE PLUMSTEAD Norfolk
126 TG 3112 3m SSE of Wroxham. CP(Gt
and Lit Plmstd), 1,695. Blofield and
Flegg RD. P NORWICH, NOR 52Z. Ch e.
Sch pe. Yarmouth CC (Central Nflk).

LITTLE PONTON Lincs (K)
113, 122 SK 9232 2m SSE of Grantham.
CP (Lit Pntn and Stroxton), 255.
W Kesteven RD. P Grnthm. Ch e. Sch pe.
Rutland and Stamford CC.

LITTLEPORT Cambs
135 TL 5686 5m NNE of Ely. CP, 5,291.
Ely RD. P Ely. Ch e2, m2, s, v2. Sch p2, s.
Isle of Ely CC. Fenland tn on R Ouse.

LITTLE PRESTON Yorks (W)
96 SE 3830 6m ESE of Leeds. CP(Gt and
Lit Prstn), 1,078. Tadcaster RD. Sch j.
Normanton CC.

LITTLE RAVELEY Hunts
134 TL 2579 5m N of Huntingdon. Loc,
Upwood and the Raveleys CP. Ch e.

LITTLE RIBSTON Yorks (W)
96 SE 3853 3m SE of Knaresborough.
CP, 183. Wetherby RD. P Wthrby. Ch m.
Barkston Ash CC.

LITTLE RISSINGTON Glos
144 SP 1919 4m S of Stow-on-the-Wold.
CP, 1,306. N Cotswold RD. P Cheltenham.
Ch e. Sch p. Cirencester and
Tewkesbury CC. Above vllge to E, not in
sight, RAF airfield and rash of hses.

LITTLE RYBURGH Norfolk
125 TF 9628 3m ESE of Fakenham. CP, 59.
Walsingham RD. NW Nflk CC (N Nflk).

LITTLE RYLE Nthmb
71 NU 0211 6m NNW of Rothbury. Loc,
Alnham CP.

LITTLE SALKELD Cumb
83 NY 5636 5m NE of Penrith. Loc,
Hunsonby CP. To N, Long Meg and her
Daughters, and Lit Meg: see Glassonby.

LITTLE SAMPFORD Essex
148 TL 6533 3m NE of Thaxted. CP, 266.
Saffron Walden RD. Ch e. Sffrn Wldn CC.
To W, Tewes*, 15c moated hse with gdns.

LITTLE SANDHURST Berks
169 SU 8262 3m NW of Camberley. Loc,
Sndhst CP. P Cmbrly, Surrey.

LITTLE SAREDON Staffs
119 SJ 9407 3m SW of Cannock. Loc,
Srdn CP. Cnnck RD. SW Staffs CC (Cnnck).

LITTLE SAXHAM Suffolk (W)
136 TL 7963 3m W of Bury St Edmunds.
CP, 92. Thingoe RD. Ch e. Bury St Eds CC.
Ch has arcaded round Nmn twr.

LITTLE SHELFORD Cambs
148 TL 4551 4m S of Cambridge. CP, 717.
Chesterton RD. P CMBRDGE. Ch e, v.
Sch pe. Cambs CC.

LITTLE SILVER Devon
176 SS 9109 3m SW of Tiverton. Loc,
Cadeleigh CP. Ch m.

LITTLE SINGLETON Lancs
94 SD 3739 5m ENE of Blackpool. Loc,
Sngltn CP.

LITTLE SMEATON Yorks (W)
103 SE 5216 6m ESE of Pontefract.
CP, 262. Hemsworth RD. Hmswth CC.

LITTLE SNORING Norfolk
125 TF 9532 3m NE of Fakenham.
CP, 341. Walsingham RD. P Fknhm.
Ch e, m. Sch p. NW Nflk CC (N Nflk). Ch:
detached round twr, Nmn font.

LITTLE SODBURY Glos
156 ST 7583 11m SW of Tetbury. CP, 132.
Sdbry RD. Ch e, b. S Glos CC. Lit Sdbry
Mnr, 15c.

LITTLE SOMBORNE Hants
168 SU 3832 7m WNW of Winchester.
CP, 57. Romsey and Stockbridge RD. Ch e.
Wnchstr CC.

LITTLE SOMERFORD Wilts
157 ST 9684 3m SE of Malmesbury.
CP, 232. Mlmsbry RD. P Chippenham. Ch e.
Sch pe. Chppnhm CC.

LITTLE STAINTON Co Durham
85 NZ 3420 5m NE of Darlington. CP, 95.
Dlngtn RD. Bishop Auckland CC
(Sedgefield).

LITTLE STANNEY Ches
109 SJ 4174 2m S of Ellesmere Port. CP.
Chester RD. P CHSTR. City of Chstr CC.

LITTLE STAUGHTON Beds
134 TL 1062 5m WNW of St Neots.
CP, 224. Bedford RD. P BDFD. Ch e, b.
Sch i. Bdfd CC.

LITTLE STEEPING Lincs (L)
114 TF 4362 8m W of Skegness. CP, 176.
Spilsby RD. P Splsby. Ch e, m.
Horncastle CC.

LITTLESTONE-ON-SEA Kent
184 TR 0824 11m ENE of Rye. Loc, New
Romney MB. P(Lttlstne), New Rmny.
Holiday resort.

LITTLE STONHAM Suffolk (E)
136 TM 1160 4m E of Stowmarket.
CP(Stnhm Parva), 311. Gipping RD.
P Stwmkt. Ch e, b. Sch p. Eye CC.

LITTLE STRETTON Leics
121, 122 SK 6600 6m ESE of Leicester.
CP, 79. Billesdon RD. Ch e. Harborough CC
(Melton).

LITTLE STRETTON Shrops
129 SO 4491 1m SSW of Ch Strttn. Loc,
Ch Strttn CP. P Ch Strttn. Ch e. Some old
timber-framed hses; ch also t-f, but of 1903.

LITTLE STRICKLAND Westm
83 NY 5619 7m SSE of Penrith. CP, 88.
N Westm RD. P Pnrth, Cumberland. Ch e.
Sch p. Westm CC.

LITTLE STUKELEY Hunts
134 TL 2075 3m NNW of Huntingdon. Loc,
The Stukeleys CP. Hntngdn RD.
P HNTNGDN. Ch e, b. Hunts CC.

LITTLE SUTTON Ches
100, 109 SJ 3776 2m W of Ellesmere Port.
Loc, Ellesmre Pt MB. P Wirral.

LITTLE SUTTON Shrops
129 SO 5182 5m N of Ludlow. Loc,
Diddlebury CP.

LITTLE SWINBURNE Nthmb
77 NY 9477 8m N of Hexham. Loc,
Chollerton CP. Beside Lit Swnbne
Reservoir, and near the much larger
reservoirs of Colt Crag (NW) and
Hallington (SE).

LITTLE TEW Oxon
145 SP 3828 5m ENE of Chipping Norton.
CP, 169. Chppng Ntn RD. P OXFORD.
Ch e, b. Banbury CC.

LITTLE THETFORD Cambs
135 TL 5376 2m S of Ely. Loc, Thtfd CP.
Ely RD. P Ely. Ch e, b. Isle of Ely CC.

LITTLE THORNTON Lancs
94 SD 3541 4m SSE of Fleetwood. Loc,
Thntn Cleveleys UD.

LITTLETHORPE Leics
132 SP 5496 6m SSW of Leicester. Loc,
Narborough CP.

LITTLETHORPE Yorks (W)
91 SE 3269 2m SSE of Ripon. CP, 435.
Rpn and Pateley Br RD. Ch e. Rpn CC.

LITTLE THURLOW Suffolk (W)
148 TL 6750 3m N of Haverhill. CP, 231.
Clare RD. Ch e. Sch pe. Bury
St Edmunds CC. Fine modern sch. Ch has
lurid gargoyles in nave.

LITTLE THURROCK Essex
161, 171 TQ 6277 2m NNW of Tilbury.
Loc, Thrrck UD. P Grays. Thrrck BC (CC).
To N by Southend rd, Hangman's Wd, with
numerous deep pits and underground
chambers called Dane or Dene holes, origin
and purpose unknown.

LITTLETON Ches
109 SJ 4466 2m E of Chester. CP, 522.
Chstr RD. P CHSTR. City of Chstr CC.

LITTLETON Hants
168 SU 4532 3m NW of Winchester.
CP, 985. Wnchstr RD. P Wnchstr. Ch e.
Wnchstr CC.

LITTLETON Som
165 ST 4930 6m S of Glastonbury. Loc,
Compton Dundon CP. Langport RD.
Yeovil CC.

LITTLETON Surrey
170 TQ 0768 3m SE of Staines. Loc,
Sunbury-on-Thames UD. Among reservoirs
S of London Airpt (Heathrow).

LITTLETON DREW Wilts
156 ST 8380 7m NW of Chippenham. Loc,
Grittleton CP. P Chppnhm. Ch e, v.

LITTLETON PANNELL Wilts
167 SU 0053 5m S of Devizes. Loc,
W Lavington CP. Ch m. Alternative spelling:
Littleton Panell.

LITTLETON-UPON-SEVERN Glos
155, 156 ST 5990 11m N of Bristol. Loc,
Aust CP. P BRSTL. Ch e.

LITTLE TORRINGTON Devon
163 SS 4916 2m S of Gt Trrngtn. CP, 281.
Trrngtn RD. Ch e. W Dvn CC (Trrngtn).
See also Taddiport.

LITTLE TOTHAM Essex
162 TL 8811 4m NE of Maldon. CP, 237.
Mldn RD. P Mldn. Ch e, v. Sch pe. Mldn CC.

LITTLETOWN Co Durham
85 NZ 3443 4m E of Durham. Loc,
Pittington CP. Ch m.

LITTLE TOWN Cumb
82 NY 2319 3m SW of Keswick. Loc,
Above Derwent CP. Cockermouth RD.
Workington CC.

LITTLE URSWICK Lancs
88 SD 2673 3m SSW of Ulverston. Loc,
Urswck CP. N Lonsdale RD. P Ulvstn.
Sch pe. Morecambe and Lnsdle CC.

LITTLE WAKERING Essex
162 TQ 9388 4m ENE of Southend. Loc,
Barling Magna CP. Ch e, m2. To NE,
Defence Dept prohibited area (Army).

LITTLE WALDEN Essex
148 TL 5441 2m N of Saffron Walden. Loc,
Sffrn Wldn RD. Sffrn Wldn CC.

LITTLE WALDINGFIELD Suffolk (W)
149 TL 9245 3m S of Lavenham. CP, 228.
Melford RD. P Sudbury. Ch e, m. Sdbry and
Woodbridge CC. 15c ch underwent
extensive 20c repainting in pink and blue.
Jcbn plpt. Brasses.

LITTLE WALSINGHAM Norfolk
125 TF 9336 4m S of Wells. CP, 686.
Wlsnghm RD. Ch e, m, r. Sch p.
NW Nflk CC (N Nflk). Place of pilgrimage of
European repute in Middle Ages. Rems of
priory* in grnds of 18c and later abbey.
Parish ch, mainly Perp, restored after fire of
1961. Shrine of Our Lady blt 1930s,
possibly on site of mdvl original.

LITTLE WALTHAM Essex
148, 149, 161, 162 TL 7012 4m N of
Chelmsford. CP, 1,019. Chlmsfd RD.
P Chlmsfd. Ch e, c. Sch pe. Braintree CC
(Chlmsfd).

LITTLE WARLEY Essex
161 TQ 6090 2m S of Brentwood. Loc,
Brntwd UD. Essex Regimental museum and
chpl. Modern offices of Ford Motor Co.
Much new housing; new shopping centre.

LITTLE WASHBOURNE Glos
143, 144 SO 9933 6m E of Tewkesbury.
Loc, Teddington CP. Ch e.

LITTLE WEIGHTON Yorks (E)
98 SE 9833 5m SW of Beverley. Loc,
Rowley CP. P Hull. Ch m. Sch pe.

LITTLE WELDON Northants
133 SP 0289 2m E of Corby. Loc, Wldn CP.
Kettering RD. Ch v. Sch pe. Kttrng CC.

LITTLE WELNETHAM Suffolk (W)
136 TL 8960 3m SE of Bury St Edmunds.
CP(Lit Whelnetham), 111. Thingoe RD.
Ch e. Bury St Eds CC.

LITTLE WENHAM Suffolk (E)
149 TM 0839 4m SE of Hadleigh. CP(Wnhm
Parva), 51. Samford RD. Ch e. Sudbury and
Woodbridge CC. Lit Wnhm Hall, 13c, oldest
brick-blt hse in England.

LITTLE WENLOCK Shrops
118, 119 SJ 6407 3m S of Wellington. CP.
Wllngtn RD. P Telford. Ch e. The
Wrekin CC (part: Ludlow). See also Aston.

LITTLE WHITTINGHAM GREEN Suffolk
(E)
137 TM 2877 7m W of Halesworth. Loc,
Fressingfield CP.

LITTLEWICK GREEN Berks
159 SU 8380 3m W of Maidenhead. Loc,
Hurley CP. P Mdnhd. Ch e. Sch ie.

LITTLE WILBRAHAM Cambs
135 TL 5458 6m E of Cambridge. CP, 388.
Chesterton RD. P CMBRDGE. Ch e.
Cambs CC. See also Six Mile Bottom.

LITTLE WITCOMBE Glos
143, 144 SO 9115 5m SW of Cheltenham.
Loc, Badgeworth CP.
P(Wtcmbe), GLOUCESTER.

LITTLE WITLEY Worcs
130 SO 7863 5m SSW of Stourport.
CP, 176. Martley RD. P WORCESTER.
Ch e. Kidderminster CC.

LITTLE WITTENHAM Berks
158 SU 5693 3m NE of Didcot. CP, 77.
Wallingford RD. Ch e. Abingdon CC.

LITTLE WOLFORD Warwicks
144 SP 2635 3m S of Shipston on Stour.
CP, 133. Shpstn on Str RD.
Stratford-on-Avon CC (Strtfd). 16c–17c
mnr hse.

LITTLE WOOLSTONE Bucks
146 SP 8739 3m N of Bletchley. Loc,
Wlstne-cum-Willen CP. Newport Pagnell RD.
Ch e. Buckingham CC.

LITTLEWORTH Berks
158 SU 3197 2m NE of Faringdon. CP, 217.
Frngdn RD. P Frngdn. Ch e, m.
Abingdon CC.

LITTLEWORTH Staffs
120 SK 0112 3m ENE of Cannock. Loc,
Cnnck UD. P Cnnck. Cnnck CC.

LITTLEWORTH Worcs
143, 144 SO 8850 4m SE of Worcester.
Loc, Norton juxta Kempsey CP. Ch m.

LITTLE WRATTING Suffolk (W)
148 TL 6847 1m NE of Haverhill. CP, 158.
Clare RD. Ch e. Bury St Edmunds CC.

LITTLE WYMONDLEY Herts
147 TL 2127 2m SE of Hitchin. Loc,
Wmndly CP. Htchn RD. P Htchn. Ch e, b.
Sch p. Htchn CC.

LITTLE WYRLEY Staffs
120 SK 0105 3m SE of Cannock. Loc,
Cnnck UD. Cnnck CC (Walsall N BC).

LITTLE WYTHEFORD Shrops
118 SJ 5619 6m NE of Shrewsbury. Loc,
Shawbury CP.

LITTLE YELDHAM Essex
149 TL 7739 4m S of Clare. CP, 265.
Halstead RD. P Hlstd. Ch e. Saffron
Walden CC.

LITTON Derbys
111 SK 1675 5m NW of Bakewell. CP, 590.
Bkwll RD. P Buxton. Ch m. Sch p, pe.
W Derbys CC.

LITTON Som
165, 166 ST 5954 6m NNE of Wells.
CP, 197. Clutton RD. P Bath. Ch e.
N Som CC.

LITTON Yorks (W)
90 SD 9074 9m NE of Settle. CP, 53.
Sttle RD. P Skipton. Skptn CC.

LITTON CHENEY Dorset
177, 178 SY 5590 6m ESE of Bridport.
CP, 216. Brdpt RD. Ch e, m. Sch pe.
W Dst CC.

LIVERMERE, GREAT Suffolk (W)
136 TL 8871 5m NNE of Bury St Edmunds.
See Gt Lvrmre.

LIVERPOOL Lancs
100 SJ 3490 178m NW of London.
CB, 606,834. P(LVPL). BCs: Edge Hill,
Garston, Kirkdale, Scotland Exchange,
Toxteth, Walton, Wavertree, W Derby.
(Sctlnd and Exchnge separate.) See also
Speke. Major port and indstrl city.
University. Anglican and RC cathedrals. Rd
tunnels under R Mersey to Birkenhead. Airpt
at Speke.

LIVERSEDGE Yorks (W)
96, 102 SE 2023 3m WNW of Dewsbury.
Loc, Spenborough MB. P. Brighouse and
Spnbrgh BC. Wool textile tn.

LIVERTON Devon
176, 188 SX 8075 4m NW of Newton
Abbot. Loc, Ilsington CP. P Ntn Abbt.

LIVERTON Yorks (N)
86 NZ 7115 2m SSW of Loftus. Loc,
Lfts UD.

LIVERTON MINES Yorks (N)
86 NZ 7117 just SW of Loftus. Loc,
Lfts UD. P Saltburn-by-the-Sea.

LIZARD Cornwall
189, 190 SW 7012 10m SSE of Helston.
Loc, Landewednack CP. Ch m.

LLANCLOUDY Herefs
142 SO 4920 5m N of Monmouth. Loc,
Llangarron CP. P HEREFORD. Ch m.

LLANDINABO Herefs
142 SO 5128 6m WNW of Ross-on-Wye.
CP, 59. Rss and Whitchurch RD. Ch e.
Hereford CC.

LLANFAIR WATERDINE Shrops
128 SO 2476 4m NW of Knighton. CP, 231.
Clun and Bishop's Cstle RD.
P Knghtn, Radnor. Ch e, m. Ludlow CC.
Stone vllge in Teme valley.

LLANGARRON Herefs
142 SO 5321 5m WSW of Ross-on-Wye.
CP, 754. Rss and Whitchurch RD.
P Rss-on-Wye. Ch e. Sch ie. Hereford CC.
See also Llancloudy, Llangrove.

LLANGROVE Herefs
142 SO 5219 4m NNE of Monmouth. Loc,
Llangarron CP. P Ross-on-Wye. Ch e, c, m.
Sch je.

LLANROTHAL Herefs
142 SO 4718 4m NNW of Monmouth.
CP, 97. Ross and Whitchurch RD. Ch e.
Hereford CC.

LLANVEYNOE Herefs
142 SO 3031 14m WSW of Hereford.
CP, 108. Dore and Bredwardine RD. Ch e.
Hrfd CC.

LLANWARNE Herefs
142 SO 5028 6m WNW of Ross-on-Wye.
CP, 308. Rss and Whitchurch RD. Ch e.
Hereford CC.

LLANYBLODWEL Shrops
117 SJ 2422 5m SSW of Oswestry. CP, 768.
Oswstry RD. P Oswstry. Ch e. Oswstry CC.
See also Llynclys. Ch, vicarage, sch all
designed by mid-19c vicar.

LLANYMYNECH Shrops
117 SJ 2620 6m SSW of Oswestry.
CP(Llanymynech and Pant), 763.
Oswstry RD. P Montgomeryshire. Ch e.
Sch pe. Oswstry CC. Below rocky hill with
quarries. Half the vllge is in Wales.

LLAWNT Shrops
117 SJ 2430 3m WNW of Oswestry. Loc,
Oswstry RD. Oswstry CC.

LLYNCLYS Shrops
118 SJ 2824 4m S of Oswestry. Loc,
Llanyblodwel CP. P Oswstry. Ch m.

LOBSCOMBE CORNER Wilts
167 SU 2435 7m ENE of Salisbury.
Alternative spelling for Lopcombe
Corner, qv.

LOCKENGATE Cornwall
185, 186 SX 0361 4m SSW of Bodmin. Loc,
Luxulyan CP.

LOCKERIDGE Wilts
157 SU 1467 3m WSW of Marlborough.
Loc, W Overton CP. P Mlbrgh.

LOCKERLEY Hants
168 SU 2926 5m NW of Romsey. CP, 618.
Rmsy and Stockbridge RD. P Rmsy.
Ch e, b2, m. Sch pe. Winchester CC. See also
Carter's Clay.

LOCKING Som
165 ST 3659 3m ESE of Weston. CP, 3,291.
Axbridge RD. P Wstn-super-Mare. Ch e.
Sch p. W-s-M CC.

LOCKINGE Berks
158 SU 4287 2m E of Wantage. CP, 254.
Wntge RD. P(E Lcknge), Wntge. Ch e.
Sch pe. Abingdon CC. Vctrn model vllge.

LOCKINGTON Leics
121 SK 4628 4m SSW of Long Eaton.
CP(Lckngtn-Hemington), 529. Cstle Donington RD. P DERBY. Ch e. Loughborough CC.

LOCKINGTON Yorks (E)
98 SE 9947 5m NNW of Beverley. CP, 507.
Bvrly RD. P Driffield. Ch e, m. Sch pe.
Haltemprice CC. See also Aike, Thorpe.

LOCKLEYWOOD Shrops
119 SJ 6928 4m SSE of Mkt Drayton. Loc,
Hinstock CP.

LOCK'S HEATH Hants
180 SU 5107 4m WNW of Fareham. Loc,
Frhm UD. P SOUTHAMPTON.

LOCKTON Yorks (N)
86, 92 SE 8489 5m NE of Pickering. CP, 234.
Pckrng RD. P Pckrng. Ch e, m2.
Scarborough CC (Scbrgh and Whitby).

LODDINGTON Leics
122 SK 7902 5m WNW of Uppingham.
CP, 83. Billesdon RD. Ch e. Harborough CC
(Melton). 1½m N, Launde Abbey, rems of
12c priory acquired by Thomas Cromwell at
Dissolution, 1538. Large 16c—17c hse blt
on site.

LODDINGTON Northants
133 SP 8178 3m W of Kettering. CP, 387.
Kttrng RD. P Kttrng. Ch e, c. Sch pe.
Kttrng CC.

LODDISWELL Devon
187, 188 SX 7248 3m NNW of Kingsbridge.
CP, 637. Kngsbrdge RD. P Kngsbrdge.
Ch e, c. Sch p. Totnes CC.

LODDON Norfolk
137 TM 3698 6m NNE of Bungay.
CP, 1,242. Lddn RD.
P NORWICH, NOR 21W. Ch e, m. Sch p, s.
S Nflk CC.

LODE Cambs
135 TL 5362 6m ENE of Cambridge.
CP, 607. Newmarket RD. P CMBRDGE.
Ch e, b. Sch p. Cambs CC. Anglesey Abbey
(NT)*, 17c hse blt over 13c abbey; gdns.

LODERS Dorset
177 SY 4994 2m ENE of Bridport. CP, 414.
Brdpt RD. P Brdpt. Ch e, m. Sch pe.
W Dst CC.

LODSWORTH Sussex (W)
181 SU 9223 3m ENE of Midhurst.
CP, 526. Mdhst RD. P Petworth. Ch e.
Chichester CC (Horsham). See also Lickfold.

LOFTHOUSE Yorks (W)
91 SE 1073 6m NW of Pateley Br. Loc,
Fountains Earth CP. Ripon and Ptly Br RD.
P Harrogate.Ch m. Sch pe. Rpn CC.

LOFTHOUSE Yorks (W)
96, 102 SE 3326 3m N of Wakefield. Loc,
Rothwell UD. P Wkfld.

LOFTHOUSE GATE Yorks (W)
96, 102 SE 3324 2m N of Wakefield. Loc,
Rothwell UD. P Wkfld.

LOFTUS Yorks (N)
86 NZ 7218 4m ESE of Saltburn.
UD, 7,706. P Sltbn-by-the-Sea. Cleveland
and Whitby CC (Clvlnd). See also Boulby,
Easington, Liverton, Lvtn Mines, Scaling,
Skinningrove. Mining area, with iron and
steel wks.

LOGGERHEADS Staffs
110, 119 SJ 7335 4m ENE of Mkt Drayton.
Loc, Newcastle-under-Lyme RD. P Mkt
Drtn, Salop. N-u-L BC.

LOLWORTH Cambs
135 TL 3664 6m NW of Cambridge.
CP, 123. Chesterton RD. P CMBRDGE.
Ch e. Cambs CC.

LONDESBOROUGH Yorks (E)
98 SE 8645 2m NNW of Mkt Weighton.
CP, 219. Pocklington RD. P YORK. Ch e.
Sch pe. Howden CC. L. Pk, early 19c
mansion in large grnds.

LONDON
160 TQ 3079 130m E of Cardiff, 330m SSE
of Edinburgh. County (Greater
Lndn), 7,379,014. Political, commercial and
cultural capital of England. Financial capital

of sterling area. Important port (R Thames).
Intntl airpts. Consists of 32 boroughs and
the City of Lndn, each with its own council;
the whole administered by the Grtr Lndn
Cncl.

LONDON AIRPORT (Gatwick)
170, 182 TQ 2841 1m S of Horley. See
Gatwick.

LONDON AIRPORT (Heathrow)
160, 170 TQ 0775 14m WSW of Charing
Cross. See Heathrow.

LONDON APPRENTICE Cornwall
185, 186, 190 SX 0050 2m S of St Austell.
Loc, St Astll w Fowey MB. P St Astll.
Truro CC.

LONDON, CITY OF
160 TQ 3281 2m NE of Westminster. See
City of London.

LONDON COLNEY Herts
160 TL 1704 3m SE of St Albans. CP, 8,651.
St Albns RD. P St Albns. Ch e, b, r, v.
Sch p2, s. S Herts CC (St Albns).

LONDONDERRY Yorks (N)
91 SE 3087 2m E of Bedale. Loc, Exelby,
Leeming and Newton CP. P Northallerton.

LONDONTHORPE Lincs (K)
113, 123 SK 9537 3m ENE of Grantham.
CP (Lndnthpe and Harrowby
Without), 1,948. W Kesteven RD.
P Grnthm. Ch e. Grnthm CC. Estate vllge.

LONG ASHTON Som
155, 156, 165 ST 5570 2m SW of Bristol.
CP, 4,504. Lng Ashtn RD. P BRSTL.
Ch e, c, v2. Sch p, pe. N Som CC. See also
Leighwoods. L. A. Ct, in large pk, is one of
longest hses in county (300ft). Mostly
Vctrn, round 15c and later core.

LONG BENNINGTON Lincs (K)
113 SK 8344 7m NW of Grantham.
CP, 851. W Kesteven RD. P Newark, Notts.
Ch e, m. Sch pe. Grnthm CC.

LONGBENTON Nthmb
78 NZ 2668 3m NNE of Newcastle.
UD, 48,970. P NCSTLE UPON TYNE 7.
Wallsend BC. See also Annitsford, Burradon,
Camperdown, Dudley, Killingworth, Seaton
Burn, W Allotment, Wide Open.

LONGBOROUGH Glos
144 SP 1729 2m SW of Moreton-in-Marsh.
CP, 435. N Cotswold RD. P Mtn-in-Msh.
Ch e, v. Sch pe. Cirencester and
Tewkesbury CC. Entirely stone-blt Ctswld
vllge. Ch: effigies, font.

LONG BREDY Dorset
177, 178 SY 5690 7m ESE of Bridport.
CP, 208. Dorchester RD. P Dchstr. Ch e, m.
W Dst CC.

LONGBRIDGE Warwicks
131 SP 2662 2m SW of Warwick. Loc,
Wrwck MB.

LONGBRIDGE DEVERILL Wilts
166 ST 8640 3m S of Warminster. CP, 723.
Wmnstr and Westbury RD. P Wmnstr.
Ch e, b, m. Sch pe. Wstbry CC. See also
Crockerton, Shear Cross. Riverside vllge;
17c almshouses. Watercress beds.

LONG BUCKBY Northants
132, 133 SP 6267 5m NE of Daventry.
CP, 2,368. Dvntry RD. P RUGBY.
Ch e, b, r, v. Sch p. Dvntry CC (S Nthnts).

LONG BUCKBY WHARF Northants
132, 133 SP 6165 3m NE of Daventry. Loc,
Lng Bckby CP. Rly, M1 motorway, and
Grand Union Canal with locks.

LONGBURTON Dorset
178 ST 6412 3m S of Sherborne. CP, 233.
Shbne RD. P Shbne. Ch e, m. W Dst CC.

LONG CLAWSON Leics
122 SK 7227 5m NNW of Melton Mowbray.
Loc, Clsn and Harby CP. Mltn and
Belvoir RD. P Mltn Mbry. Ch e, b, m2.
Sch pe. Mltn CC.

LONGCLIFFE Derbys
111 SK 2255 5m SW of Matlock. Loc,
Brassington CP.

LONG COMMON Hants
180 SU 5014 4m SW of Bishop's Waltham.
Loc, Botley CP.

LONG COMPTON Staffs
119 SJ 8522 4m W of Stafford. Loc,
Ranton CP.

LONG COMPTON Warwicks
145 SP 2832 4m NNW of Chipping Norton.
CP, 531. Shipston on Stour RD. P Shpstn

on Str. Ch e, m, v. Sch p. Stratford-on-Avon CC (Strtfd). Cotswold vllge in corner of county.

LONGCOT Berks
157 SU 2790 8m ENE of Swindon. CP, 337. Faringdon RD. P Frngdn. Ch e, m. Sch pe. Abingdon CC.

LONG CRENDON Bucks
159 SP 6908 2m NNW of Thame. CP, 1,498. Aylesbury RD. P Aylesbury. Ch e, b. Sch p. Aylesbury CC. Several old hses, incl Ct Hse (NT)*, 14c, and mnr hse with stone gatehouse. 2m E, Notley Abbey, 15c, with dovecote nearby.

LONG CRICHEL Dorset
179 ST 9710 6m ENE of Blandford. CP, 99. Wimborne and Cranborne RD. P Wmbne. Ch e. N Dst CC.

LONGDEN Shrops
118 SJ 4406 5m SW of Shrewsbury. Loc, Pontesbury CP. P Shrsbry. Ch e, m. Sch pe.

LONG DITTON Surrey
170 TQ 1666 2m SSW of Kingston. Loc, Esher UD. P Thames Dttn.

LONGDON Staffs
120 SK 0814 3m SE of Rugeley. CP, 1,009. Lichfield RD. P Rgly. Ch e. Sch pe. Lchfld and Tamworth CC. See also Gentleshaw, Upr Lngdn.

LONGDON Worcs
143 SO 8336 4m NW of Tewkesbury. CP, 427. Upton upon Severn RD. P Tksbry, Glos. Ch e. Sch pe. S Worcs CC.

LONGDON UPON TERN Shrops
118, 119 SJ 6115 3m NW of Wellington. CP, 126. Wllngtn RD. P Telford. Ch e. The Wrekin CC. Shrops Union Canal carried over R Tern on cast iron aqueduct by Telford (1794). L. Hall is Tdr, with impressive chimneys.

LONGDOWN Devon
176 SX 8691 4m W of Exeter. Loc, St Thomas RD. P Extr. Ch m. Tiverton CC.

LONG DOWNS Cornwall
190 SW 7434 4m W of Falmouth. Loc, Kerrier RD. P Penryn. Flmth and Camborne CC.

LONG DRAX Yorks (W)
97, 98 SE 6828 5m ESE of Selby. CP, 91. Slby RD. Skipton CC.

LONG DUCKMANTON Derbys
112 SK 4471 4m E of Chesterfield. Loc, Sutton cum Dckmntn CP. Chstrfld RD. P(Dckmntn), Chstrfld. NE Derbys CC.

LONG EATON Derbys
112, 121 SK 4933 9m E of Derby. UD, 33,694. P NOTTINGHAM. SE Derbys CC. See also Sawley. Indstrl tn; prosperity originally founded on lace-making, but now on various industries.

LONGFIELD Kent
171 TQ 6069 4m SW of Gravesend. CP, 1,807. Dartford RD. P Dtfd. Ch e. Sch pe, s. Sevenoaks CC (Dtfd). See also Lngfld Hill.

LONGFIELD HILL Kent
171 TQ 6268 4m SSW of Gravesend. Loc, Lngfld CP. P Dartford.

LONGFORD Derbys
120 SK 2137 6m SSE of Ashbourne. CP, 297. Ashbne RD. P DERBY. Ch e, m. Sch pe. W Derbys CC. Ch: monmts. Hall, orig Tdr, partly remodelled c 1700, burnt out 1942, now restored.

LONGFORD Glos
143 SO 8320 1m N of Gloucester. CP, 1,303. Glcstr RD. P GLCSTR. W Glos CC.

LONGFORD London
160, 170 TQ 0476 4m NNE of Staines. Loc, Hillingdon LB. P: W Drayton, Middx. Hayes and Harlington BC (Uxbridge CC). The Far West of Lndn beyond Heathrow Airpt.

LONGFORD Shrops
110, 118, 119 SJ 6434 2m W of Mkt Drayton. Loc, Moreton Say CP.

LONGFORD Shrops
119 SJ 7218 1m WSW of Newport. CP, 102. Wellington RD. Ch e. The Wrekin CC.

LONGFRAMLINGTON Nthmb
71 NU 1301 5m E of Rothbury. CP, 575. Rthbry RD. P Morpeth. Ch e, v. Berwick-upon-Tweed CC.

LONG GREEN Ches
109 SJ 4770 5m ENE of Chester. Loc, Barrow CP. Chstr RD. City of Chstr CC.

LONGHAM Dorset
179 SZ 0698 5m NNW of Bournemouth. L o c, H a m p r e s t o n C P. P Ferndown, Wimborne. Ch c.

LONGHAM Norfolk
125 TF 9415 3m NW of Dereham. CP. Mitford and Launditch RD. P Drhm. Ch e, m. SW Nflk CC.

LONG HANBOROUGH Oxon
145 SP 4214 2m SW of Woodstock. Loc, Hnbrgh CP. Witney RD. P OXFORD. Ch m. Sch ie, p. Mid-Oxon CC (Banbury).

LONGHIRST Nthmb
78 NZ 2289 3m NE of Morpeth. CP, 521. Mpth RD. P Mpth. Ch e. Mpth CC.

LONGHOPE Glos
143 SO 6818 4m NNE of Cinderford. CP, 1,041. E Dean RD. P. Ch e, b. Sch p, pe. W Glos CC.

LONGHORSLEY Nthmb
78 NZ 1494 6m NW of Morpeth. CP, 488. Mpth RD. P Mpth. Ch e, r, v. Sch pe. Mpth CC.

LONGHOUGHTON Nthmb
71 NU 2415 4m ENE of Alnwick. CP, 1,116. Alnwck RD. P Alnwck. Ch e. Sch pe. Berwick-upon-Tweed CC. See also Boulmer, Howick, Littlehoughton.

LONG ITCHINGTON Warwicks
132 SP 4165 2m N of Southam. CP, 1,679. Sthm RD. P Rugby. Ch e, c, m. Sch pe. Stratford-on-Avon CC (Strtfd). Some old half-timbered hses.

LONG LAWFORD Warwicks
132 SP 4776 2m W of Rugby. CP, 2,761. Rgby RD. P Rgby. Ch e, m. Sch p. Rgby CC.

LONGLEVENS Glos
143 SO 8520 NE distr of Gloucester. Loc, Glcster CB; CP, 6,966. Glcstr RD. P GLCSTR. Glcstr BC, W Glos CC. (W Glos CC.)

LONGLEY GREEN Worcs
143 SO 7350 4m NW of Malvern. Loc, Suckley CP.

LONG LOAD Som
177 ST 4623 4m W of Ilchester. CP, 200. Yeovil RD. P Langport. Ch e. Yvl CC.

LONG MARSTON Herts
146 SP 8915 3m NNW of Tring. Loc, Trng Rural CP. Berkhamsted RD. P Trng. Ch e, b, m. Sch pe. Hemel Hempstead CC.

LONG MARSTON Warwicks
144 SP 1548 5m SW of Stratford. CP, 611. Strtfd-on-Avon RD. P Strtfd-upon-Avn. Ch e, m. Strtfd-on-Avon CC (Strtfd).

LONG MARSTON Yorks (W)
97 SE 5051 6m W of York. CP, 302. Wetherby RD. Ch e, m. Sch pe. Barkston Ash CC. 1m NW, Mstn Moor, site of Civil War battle 1644.

LONG MARTON Westm
83 NY 6624 3m NNW of Appleby. CP, 692. N Westm RD. P Appleby. Ch e, m. Sch p. Westm CC. See also Knock.

LONG MELFORD Suffolk (W)
149 TL 8645 3m N of Sudbury. CP, 2,416. Mlfd RD. P Sdbry. Ch e, m, v2. Sch pe. Sdbry and Woodbridge CC. See also Br St. Famous beautiful vllge or small tn. Splendid Perp ch. Melford Hall (NT)* and Kentwell Hall are Elizn. Many other old hses.

LONGMOOR CAMP Hants
169, 181 SU 7930 6m NNE of Petersfield. Loc, Whitehill CP. P Liss. Sch i.

LONG NEWNTON Glos
156, 157 ST 9092 1m SE of Tetbury. CP, 210. Ttbry RD. P Ttbry. Ch e. Sch pe. Stroud CC.

LONG NEWTON Co Durham
85 NZ 3816 4m WSW of Teesside (Stockton). CP, 429. Stcktn RD. P STCKTN-ON-TEES, Tssde. Ch m. Easington CC (Sedgefield).

LONGNEY Glos
143 SO 7612 6m SW of Gloucester. CP, 248. Glcstr RD. P GLCSTR. Ch e, c. Sch pe. Stroud CC.

LONGNOR Shrops
118 SJ 4800 7m S of Shrewsbury. CP, 257. Atcham RD. P Shrsbry. Ch e. Sch pe. Shrsbry CC. Tiny EE ch with Ggn furnishings. 17c hall in red brick.

LONGNOR Staffs
111 SK 0864 6m SSE of Buxton. CP, 381.
Leek RD. P Bxtn, Derbyshire. Ch e, m.
Sch pe. Lk CC. Moorland vllge between
rivers Dove and Manifold. Construction of
reservoir in Mnfld valley immediately S of
vllge proposed by Trent River
Authority 1970.

LONGPARISH Hants
168 SU 4344 4m E of Andover. CP, 266.
Andvr RD. P Andvr. Ch e, m. Sch pe.
Winchester CC (Basingstoke). See also
Middleton.

LONG PRESTON Yorks (W)
95 SD 8358 4m SSE of Settle. CP, 616.
Sttle RD. P Skipton. Ch e, b, m. Sch pe.
Skptn CC.

LONGRIDGE Lancs
94, 95 SD 6037 6m NE of Preston.
UD, 6,507. P Prstn. Clitheroe CC.

LONG RISTON Yorks (E)
99 TA 1242 6m ENE of Beverley. Loc,
Rstn CP. Holderness RD. P Hull. Ch e, m.
Sch pe. Bridlington CC.

LONGROCK Cornwall
189 SW 5031 2m ENE of Penzance. Loc,
Ludgvan CP. P Pnznce.

LONGSDON Staffs
110 SJ 9654 2m WSW of Leek. CP, 639.
Lk RD. P Stoke-on-Trent. Ch e, m. Sch pe.
Lk CC.

LONGSHAW COMMON Lancs
100 SD 5302 4m SW of Wigan. Loc, Billinge
and Winstanley UD. P(Lngshw), Wgn.

LONGSLOW Shrops
110, 118, 119 SJ 6535 2m NW of Mkt
Drayton. Loc, Moreton Say CP.

LONG STANTON Cambs
135 TL 3966 6m NNW of Cambridge.
CP, 1,723. Chesterton RD. P CMBRDGE.
Ch e2, m. Sch p. Cambs CC. Main ch (All
Saints') has monmts to Hatton family, who
bought mnr from Elizabeth I. St Michael's,
thatched, used only occasionally.

LONGSTOCK Hants
168 SU 3537 5m S of Andover. CP, 524.
Romsey and Stockbridge RD. P Stckbrdge.
Ch e, m. Winchester CC.

LONGSTONE, GREAT Derbys
111 SK 2071 2m NNW of Bakewell. See Gt
Lngstne.

LONGSTOWE Cambs
134/147 TL 3055 8m ESE of St Neots.
CP, 218. S Cambs RD. P CAMBRIDGE.
Ch e. Cambs CC.

LONG STRATTON Norfolk
137 TM 1992 8m SE of Wymondham.
CP, 888. Depwade RD.
P NORWICH, NOR 72W. Ch e, c, m2.
Sch pe, s. S Nflk CC. See also Strttn
St Michael.

LONG STREET Bucks
146 SP 7947 5m NNW of Wolverton. Loc,
Hanslope CP.

LONG SUTTON Hants
169 SU 7347 5m NNE of Alton. CP, 743.
Hartley Wintney RD. P Basingstoke. Ch e.
Sch pe. Bsngstke CC (Aldershot). See also
Well. Agricultural college. 13c ch.

LONG SUTTON Lincs (H)
124 TF 4322 5m ESE of Holbeach.
CP, 2,794. E Elloe RD. P Spalding.
Ch e, b, v. Sch p, s. Holland w Boston CC.
See also Sutton Crosses. 14c-15c ch; twr
has rare 13c lead spire. To E, six-sailed twr
windmill.

LONG SUTTON Som
177 ST 4625 4m NW of Ilchester. CP, 712.
Langport RD. P Lngpt. Ch e, f. Sch pe.
Yeovil CC.

LONGTHORPE Hunts
134 TL 1698 2m W of Peterborough. Loc,
Ptrbrgh MB. L. Twr (A.M.), fortified mdvl
hse; wall-paintings.

LONGTON Lancs
94 SD 4725 5m WSW of Preston. CP, 3,884.
Prstn RD. P Prstn. Ch e, m, r. Sch p, pr.
S Fylde CC. See also New Lngtn.

LONGTON Staffs
110, 119 SJ 9043 SE distr of
Stoke-on-Trent. Loc, Stke-on-Trnt CB.
P Stke-on-Trnt. S-on-T S BC. Pottery distr.
One of Arnold Bennett's *Five Towns*
('Longshaw').

LONGTOWN Cumb
76 NY 3868 8m N of Carlisle. Loc,

Arthuret CP. Border RD. P Clsle.
Ch e, m, r, v2. Sch i, j, s. Penrith and the
Border CC. On the old, orig Roman, rd from
Clsle to Glasgow until 1830.

LONGTOWN Herefs
142 SO 3229 9m N of Abergavenny.
CP, 437. Dore and Bredwardine RD.
P HEREFORD. Ch e, b, m. Sch p. Hrfd CC.
See also Clodock. Rems of Nmn cstle.

LONGVILLE IN THE DALE Shrops
129 SO 5493 5m E of Ch Stretton. Loc,
Rushbury CP. P(Lngvlle), Much Wenlock.
Below Wnlck Edge. To S, Wilderhope
(NT)*, late 16c stone mnr hse, now youth
hostel.

LONGWELL GREEN Glos
156 ST 6571 5m ESE of Bristol. Loc,
Warmley RD. P BRSTL. Ch e, m. Sch p.
Kingswood CC (S Glos).

LONG WHATTON Leics
121 SK 4723 4m NW of Loughborough.
CP, 1,247. Cstle Donington RD. P Lghbrgh.
Ch e, b, m. Lghbrgh CC. See also Diseworth.

LONGWICK Bucks
159 SP 7805 2m NW of Princes Risborough.
CP(Lngwck-cum-Ilmer), 640. Wycombe RD.
P Aylesbury. Ch m. Sch pe. Aylesbury CC
(Wcmbe). See also Horsenden, Meadle,
Owlswick.

LONG WITTENHAM Berks
158 SU 5493 3m NNE of Didcot. CP, 694.
Wallingford RD. P Abingdon. Ch e. Sch pe.
Abngdn CC. Pendon Museum houses model
rly and exhibition of rly relics.

LONGWITTON Nthmb
77, 78 NZ 0788 8m WNW of Morpeth. Loc,
Netherwitton CP. P Mpth.

LONGWOOD Shrops
118, 119 SJ 6007 4m SW of Wellington.
Loc, Leighton CP.

LONGWORTH Berks
158 SU 3999 7m W of Abingdon. CP, 773.
Faringdon RD. P Abngdn. Ch e, c. Sch pu.
Abngdn CC. Bthplce of R.D. Blackmore,
author of *Lorna Doone* .

LOOE Cornwall
186 SX 2553 7m S of Liskeard. UD, 4,051.
P. Bodmin CC. See also St Martin. Resort

and fishing tn divided by river into E and
W Looe; E Looe older and quainter.

LOOSE Kent
172 TQ 7552 2m S of Maidstone. CP.
Mdstne RD. P Mdstne. Ch e, b, v. Sch p.
Mdstne CC. 15c Wool Hse (NT).

LOOSLEY ROW Bucks
159 SP 8100 2m SSE of Princes
Risborough. Loc, Lacey Grn CP.
P Aylesbury. Ch b.

LOPCOMBE CORNER Wilts
167 SU 2435 7m ENE of Salisbury. Loc,
Winterslow CP. P Slsbry.

LOPEN Som
177 ST 4214 3m NNW of Crewkerne.
CP, 221. Chard RD. P: S Petherton. Ch e.
Yeovil CC.

LOPPINGTON Shrops
118 SJ 4729 3m W of Wem. CP, 496.
N Shrops RD. P Shrewsbury. Ch e, m.
Sch pe. Oswestry CC. See also Burlton,
Noneley. Outside Dickin Arms, bull-baiting
ring, a rare example.

LOPSCOMBE CORNER Wilts
167 SU 2435 7m ENE of Salisbury.
Alternative spelling for Lopcombe
Corner, qv.

LOSCOE Derbys
112 SK 4247 2m SE of Ripley. Loc,
Heanor UD. P DERBY.

LOSTOCK GRALAM Ches
101/110 SJ 6974 2m ENE of Northwich.
CP, 2,008. Nthwch RD. P Nthwch.
Ch e, m2. Nthwch CC.

LOSTOCK JUNCTION Lancs
101 SD 6708 3m W of Bolton. Loc,
Bltn CB. P Bltn. Aero-engineering plant.

LOSTWITHIEL Cornwall
186 SX 1059 5m SSE of Bodmin.
CP, 1,955. St Austell RD. P. Ch e, m.
Sch p, pe. Bdmn CC. Mkt tn on R Fowey
(crossed by mdvl br, A.M.), with several old
bldngs. 1m N, ruins of the Nmn Restormel
Cstle (A.M.).

LOTHERSDALE Yorks (W)
95 SD 9646 4m SSW of Skipton. CP, 349.
Skptn RD. P Keighley. Ch e, m. Sch p.
Skptn CC.

LOTTISHAM Som
165, 166 ST 5734 5m ESE of Glastonbury.
Loc, W Bradley CP. Ch e.

LOUDWATER Bucks
159 SU 9090 3m W of Beaconsfield. Loc,
Chepping Wycombe CP. Wcmbe RD. P High
Wcmbe. Ch e, b. Sch p. Wcmbe CC.

LOUGHBOROUGH Leics
121 SK 5319 10m NNW of Leicester.
MB, 45,863. P. Lghbrgh CC. See also
Hathern, Nanpantan, Thorpe Acre,
Woodthorpe. Indstrl tn specialising in
hosiery and engineering, incl bell-founding
(Taylors of Loughborough). Carillon Twr,
blt 1922 as war memorial, has 47 bells.
University of Technology.

LOUGHTON Bucks
146 SP 8337 2m SSE of Wolverton.
CP, 402. Newport Pagnell RD. P Bletchley.
Ch e, b. Buckingham CC.

LOUGHTON Essex
161 TQ 4296 4m SSW of Epping. Loc,
Chigwell UD. P. Many modern public and
indstrl bldngs, incl Bank of England printing
wks.

LOUGHTON Shrops
129, 130 SO 6183 8m NE of Ludlow. Loc,
Wheathill CP. Ch e.

LOUND Lincs (K)
123 TF 0618 2m SW of Bourne. CP(Toft
w Lnd and Manthorpe), 153.
S Kesteven RD.   Rutland and Stamford CC.

LOUND Notts
103 SK 6986 3m N of Retford. CP, 418.
E Rtfd RD. P Rtfd. Ch e, m. Sch pe.
Bassetlaw CC.

LOUND Suffolk (E)
137 TM 5099 5m NNW of Lowestoft.
CP, 336. Lothingland RD. P Lwstft.
Ch e, m. Sch pe, s. Lwstft CC.

LOUNT Leics
120, 121 SK 3819 3m NE of Ashby de la
Zouch. Loc, Staunton Harold CP.

LOUTH Lincs (L)
105 TF 3287 14m SSE of Grimsby.
MB, 11,746. P. Lth CC. 295ft twr of ch is
landmark for miles. Many pleasant 18c and

early 19c hses. Large modern malting
factory.

LOVE CLOUGH Lancs
95 SD 8127 4m SSW of Burnley. Loc,
Rawtenstall MB. P Rossendale.

LOVER Wilts
167 SU 2120 7m SSE of Salisbury. Loc,
Redlynch CP. P Slsbry.

LOVERSALL Yorks (W)
103 SK 5798 3m S of Doncaster. CP, 140.
Dncstr RD. Ch e. Don Valley CC.

LOVES GREEN Essex
161 TL 6404 4m WSW of Chelmsford. Loc,
Highwood CP. Chlmsfd RD. Chlmsfd CC.

LOVINGTON Som
165, 166 ST 5930 6m WSW of Bruton.
CP, 156. Wincanton RD. Ch e, m. Sch pe.
Wells CC. See also Wheathill.

LOW ACKWORTH Yorks (W)
103 SE 4417 3m S of Pontefract. Loc,
Ackwth CP. Hemsworth RD. Hmswth CC.
To W, 18c Friends' Sch.

LOW ANGERTON Nthmb
77, 78 NZ 0984 7m W of Morpeth. Loc,
Hartburn CP.

LOW BRADFIELD Yorks (W)
102 SK 2692 6m WNW of Sheffield. Loc,
Brdfld CP. Sch p.

LOW BRADLEY Yorks (W)
96 SE 0048 2m SSE of Skipton. Loc, Brdlys
Both CP. Skptn RD. Ch m. Sch p.
Skptn CC.

LOW BRAITHWAITE Cumb
83 NY 4242 9m S of Carlisle. Loc,
Skelton CP.

LOW BRUNTON Nthmb
77 NY 9270 4m NNW of Hexham. Loc,
Wall CP. Up the rd at B. Bank, exposed
section of Roman Wall (A.M.).

LOW BURNHAM Lincs (L)
104 SE 7802 1m S of Epworth. Loc,
Haxey CP. Ch m.

LOWCA Cumb
82 NX 9821 2m N of Whitehaven.
CP, 1,099. Ennerdale RD. P Whthvn.
Ch m2. Sch p. Whthvn CC.

LOW CATTON Yorks (E)
97, 98 SE 7053 6m E of York. Loc, Cttn CP. Pocklington RD. Ch e. Howden CC.

LOW CONISCLIFFE Co Durham
85 NZ 2413 3m W of Darlington. CP, 321. Dlngtn RD. Bishop Auckland CC (Sedgefield).

LOW CROSBY Cumb
76 NY 4459 4m NE of Carlisle. Loc, Stanwix Rural CP. Border RD. Ch e. Penrith and the Bdr CC.

LOWDHAM Notts
112 SK 6646 7m NE of Nottingham. CP, 1,734. Southwell RD. P NTTNGHM. Ch e, m2. Sch pe. Newark CC.

LOW DINSDALE Co Durham
85 NZ 3411 4m SE of Darlington. CP, 840. Dlngtn RD. Ch e. Bishop Auckland CC (Sedgefield).

LOW EGGBOROUGH Yorks (W)
97 SE 5623 6m SSW of Selby. Loc, Eggbrgh CP. Osgoldcross RD. Ch m. Sch p. Goole CC.

LOWER ARNCOTT Oxon
145, 146 SP 6118 3m SSE of Bicester. Loc, Arnctt CP. Ploughley RD. Mid-Oxon CC (Henley).

LOWER ASHTON Devon
176 SX 8484 7m SW of Exeter. Loc, Ashtn CP. St Thomas RD. P Extr. Tiverton CC.

LOWER ASSENDON Oxon
159 SU 7484 1m NW of Henley. Loc, Bix CP.

LOWER BEEDING Sussex (W)
182 TQ 2227 4m SE of Horsham. CP, 1,570. Hshm RD. P Hshm. Ch e. Sch pe. Hshm and Crawley CC (Hshm). See also Colgate, Crabtree.

LOWER BENTHAM Yorks (W)
89 SD 6569 6m SSE of Kirkby Lonsdale. Loc, Bnthm CP. Settle RD. Ch e, f, m. Sch p, pe. Skipton CC.

LOWER BENTLEY Worcs
130, 131 SO 9865 3m SSE of Bromsgrove.

Loc, Bntly Pauncefoot CP. Brmsgrve RD. Brmsgrve and Redditch CC (Brmsgrve).

LOWER BOCKHAMPTON Dorset
178 SY 7290 2m E of Dorchester. Loc, Stinsford CP. P(Bckhmptn), Dchstr.

LOWER BODDINGTON Northants
145 SP 4852 7m NNE of Banbury. Loc, Bddngtn CP. Brackley RD. P Rugby, Warwickshire. Ch m. Daventry CC (S Nthnts). To E, lake with sailing boats.

LOWER BRAILES Warwicks
145 SP 3139 4m ESE of Shipston on Stour. Loc, Brls CP. Shpstn on Str RD. P(Brls), Banbury, Oxon. Ch e, m. Sch pe. Stratford-on-Avon CC (Strtfd). Large Perp ch with 120ft twr.

LOWER BROADHEATH Worcs
130 SO 8157 3m WNW of Worcester. Loc, Brdhth CP. Martley RD. P WCSTR. Ch e. Kidderminster CC.

LOWER BULLINGHAM Herefs
142 SO 5238 1m SE of Hereford. CP, 670. Hrfd RD. P HRFD. Ch r, v. Hrfd CC. Industrialised suburb of Hrfd.

LOWER CAM Glos
156 SO 7500 2m N of Dursley. Loc, Cm CP. Ch e, m.

LOWER CATESBY Northants
132 SP 5159 4m WSW of Daventry. Loc, Ctsby CP. Dvntry RD. Ch e. Dvntry CC (S Nthnts).

LOWER CHUTE Wilts
168 SU 3153 6m NNW of Andover. Loc, Pewsey RD. Ch m. Devizes CC.

LOWER CUMBERWORTH Yorks (W)
102 SE 2209 4m NNW of Penistone. Loc, Denby Dale UD. P Huddersfield.

LOWER DARWEN Lancs
94, 95 SD 6825 S distr of Blackburn. Loc, Blckbn CB. P Dwn. Dwn CC.

LOWER DEAN Beds
134 TL 0569 6m ENE of Rushden. Loc, Dn and Shelton CP. Bedford RD. Ch m. Bdfd CC.

LOWER DUNSFORTH Yorks (W)
91, 97 SE 4464 3m ESE of Boroughbridge.

Loc, Dnsfths CP. Nidderdale RD. Ch e. Harrogate CC.

LOWER EGLETON Herefs
142, 143 SO 6245 7m NW of Ledbury. Loc, Eggltn CP. Ldbry RD. Leominster CC.

LOWER FAILAND Som
155, 165 ST 5173 5m W of Bristol. Loc, Wraxall CP.

LOWER FROYLE Hants
169 SU 7644 4m NE of Alton. Loc, Frle CP. P Altn. Ch e, m.

LOWER GRAVENHURST Beds
147 TL 1135 5m ESE of Ampthill. Loc, Grvnhst CP. Ampthll RD. Ch e. Mid-Beds CC.

LOWER GREEN Norfolk
125 TF 9837 6m SE of Wells. Loc, Hindringham CP.

LOWER HALSTOW Kent
172 TQ 8567 4m NW of Sittingbourne. CP, 484. Swale RD. Ch e. Sch p. Faversham CC. On creek of Medway estuary.

LOWER HARDRES Kent
173 TR 1553 3m S of Canterbury. CP, 323. Bridge-Blean RD. P Cntrbry. Ch e. Sch pe. Cntrbry CC. See also Nackington.

LOWER HARTSHAY Derbys
111 SK 3851 1m WNW of Ripley. Loc, Rply UD. P DERBY.

LOWER HAYTON Shrops
129 SO 5080 4m N of Ludlow. Loc, Stanton Lacy CP.

LOWER HERGEST Herefs
128 SO 2755 2m SW of Kington. Loc, Kngtn Rural CP. Kngtn RD. Leominster CC.

LOWER HEYFORD Oxon
145 SP 4824 6m WNW of Bicester. CP, 447. Ploughley RD. Ch e, m. Sch pe. Banbury CC (Henley). See also Caulcott.

LOWER HORDLEY Shrops
118 SJ 3929 4m S of Ellesmere. Loc, N Shrops RD. Oswestry CC.

LOWER KINGSWOOD Surrey
170 TQ 2453 2m N of Reigate. Loc, Banstead UD. P Tadworth.

LOWER KINNERTON Ches
109 SJ 3462 5m SW of Chester. CP, 128. Chstr RD. City of Chstr CC.

LOWER LANGFORD Som
165 ST 4660 3m SSE of Congresbury. Loc, Churchill CP. Ch e, c.

LOWER LEMINGTON Glos
144 SP 2134 2m NE of Moreton-in-Marsh. Loc, Batsford CP. Ch e.

LOWER LYE Herefs
129 SO 4066 6m ENE of Presteigne. Loc, Aymestrey CP. Ch e.

LOWER MAES-COED Herefs
142 SO 3430 12m SW of Hereford. Loc, Newton CP. Ch m.

LOWER MAYLAND Essex
162 TL 9101 5m SE of Maldon. Loc, Mlnd CP. Mldn RD. P (Mlnd), Chelmsford. Ch e. Sch p. Mldn CC. Holiday bungalows.

LOWER MOOR Worcs
143, 144 SO 9747 2m ENE of Pershore. Loc, Hill and Moor CP. Pshre RD. P Pshre. Ch e. S Worcs CC.

LOWER NAZEING Essex
161 TL 3906 3m N of Waltham Abbey. Loc, Nzng CP. P Wltham Abbey. Surrounded by mkt gdns and glasshouses.

LOWER PENN Staffs
130 SO 8696 3m WSW of Wolverhampton. CP. Seisdon RD. P Wlvrhmptn. SW Staffs CC (Brierley Hill).

LOWER PENNINGTON Hants
180 SZ 3193 2m S of Lymington. Loc, Lmngtn MB.

LOWER PEOVER Ches
110 SJ 7474 3m SSW of Knutsford. Loc, Bucklow RD, Northwich RD. P Kntsfd. Ch e. Sch pe. Kntsfd CC, Nthwch CC. Black and white half-timbered ch; early 18c schoolhouse.

LOWER QUINTON Warwicks
144 SP 1847 5m SSW of Stratford. Loc, Quntn CP. Strtfd-on-Avon RD. P Strtfd-upon-Avn. Ch e. Sch p. Strtfd-on-Avn CC (Strtfd). Ch: board bearing royal arms of Elizabeth I.

Lower Rochford

LOWER ROCHFORD Worcs
129, 130 SO 6268 2m E of Tenbury Wells.
Loc, Rchfd CP. Tnbry RD. Ch e.
Kidderminster CC.

LOWER SAPEY Worcs
130 SO 6960 4m NE of Bromyard. CP, 172.
Martley RD. Ch m. S Worcs CC. See also
Harpley.

LOWER SEAGRY Wilts
157 ST 9580 4m SSE of Malmesbury. Loc,
Sutton Benger CP.

LOWER SHELTON Beds
147 SP 9942 5m SSW of Bedford. Loc,
Marston Moretaine CP. Sch p.

LOWER SHIPLAKE Oxon
159 SU 7779 2m SSE of Henley. Loc,
Shplke CP. P Hnly-on-Thames.

LOWER SHUCKBURGH Warwicks
132 SP 4862 5m E of Southam. CP, 74.
Sthm RD. P Daventry, Northants. Ch e.
Stratfordd-on-Avon CC (Strtfd).

LOWER SLAUGHTER Glos
144 SP 1622 3m SW of Stow-on-the-Wold.
CP, 210. N Cotswold RD. P Cheltenham.
Ch e. Cirencester and Tewkesbury CC.
Famous Cotswold beauty spot. Mostly blt
round grn. Stream crossed by several stone
footbridges.

LOWER STANTON ST QUINTIN Wilts
156, 157 ST 9180 4m S of Malmesbury.
Loc, Stntn St Quntn CP. Ch m. On edge of
disused airfield.

LOWER STOKE Kent
172 TQ 8375 7m NE of Rochester. Loc,
Stke CP. P Rchstr. Ch m.

LOWER STONDON Beds
147 TL 1535 4m NNW of Hitchin. Loc,
Shillington CP. P Henlow. Ch e, b. Sch p.

LOWER STREET Norfolk
126 TG 2635 3m NNW of N Walsham. Loc,
Southrepps CP.

LOWER STRENSHAM Worcs
143, 144 SO 9040 5m N of Tewkesbury.
Loc, Strnshm CP. Pershore RD. Ch e.
S Worcs CC. Ch: 15c painted scrn;
14c–16c brasses; other monmts.

LOWER SWANWICK Hants
180 SU 4909 5m WNW of Fareham. Loc,
Frhm UD.

LOWER SWELL Glos
144 SP 1725 1m W of Stow-on-the-Wold.
Loc, Swll CP. N Cotswold RD.
P Cheltenham.1. Ch e. Sch pe. Cirencester
and Tewkesbury CC. Picturesque Ctswld
vllge.

LOWER TEAN Staffs
120 SK 0138 3m S of Cheadle. Loc,
Checkley CP.

LOWER THURNHAM Lancs
95 SD 4555 4m SSW of Lancaster. Loc,
Thnhm CP. Lncstr RD. Lncstr CC.

LOWER TOWN St Martin's, Isles of Scilly
189 SV 9116. Loc, St Mtn's CP.

LOWER TYSOE Warwicks
145 SP 3445 8m WNW of Banbury. Loc,
Tysoe CP. Shipston on Stour RD.
Stratford-on-Avon (Strtfd).

LOWER UPHAM Hants
180 SU 5219 2m NW of Bishop's Waltham.
Loc, Uphm CP. P SOUTHAMPTON.

LOWER UPNOR Kent
172 TQ 7671 2m NNE of Rochester. Loc,
Strood RD. Gravesend CC. On Medway
estuary. Up river, U. Cstle (A.M.), where
Elizabeth I reviewed fleet in 1581.

LOWER WEARE Som
165 ST 4053 3m W of Cheddar. Loc,
Weare CP. P(Weare), Axbridge.
Ambleside*, water gdns, aviaries.

LOWER WHITLEY Ches
101 SJ 6179 4m NW of Northwich. Loc,
Whtly CP. Runcorn RD. Ch e. Rncn CC.

LOWER WIELD Hants
168, 169 SU 6340 5m W of Alton. Loc,
Wld CP.

LOWER WINCHENDON Bucks
146, 159 SP 7312 4m NNE of Thame.
CP, 143. Aylesbury RD. Ch e. Sch pe.
Aylesbury CC. Thatched cottages. Nether
W. Hse*, 16c–18c, with gdns. Ch has
three-decker plpt.

LOWER WOODFORD Wilts
167 SU 1235 4m NNW of Salisbury. Loc, Wdfd CP. Amesbury RD. Slsbry CC.

LOWER WRAXALL Dorset
177, 178 ST 5700 9m NE of Bridport. Loc, Wrxll CP. Beaminster RD. Ch e. W Dst CC.

LOWESBY Leics
122 SK 7207 7m SSW of Melton Mowbray. CP, 93. Billesdon RD. Ch e. Sch pe. Harborough CC (Mltn). Site of one of Leics' many vanished vllges.

LOWESTOFT Suffolk (E)
137 TM 5493 38m NE of Ipswich. MB, 52,182. P. Lwstft CC. See also Kirkley, Oulton Broad, Pakefield. Fishing port. Resort. Coach-building. Most easterly tn in England.

LOWESTOFT END Suffolk (E)
137 TM 5394 1m NNW of Lowestoft. Loc, Lwstft MB.

LOWESWATER Cumb
82 NY 1421 6m S of Cockermouth. CP, 174. Cckrmth RD. P Cckrmth. Ch e. Workington CC. See also Mockerkin.

LOW ETHERLEY Co Durham
85 NZ 1628 3m W of Bishop Auckland. Loc, Ethrly CP. Barnard Cstle RD. P(Ethrly Dene), Bshp Aucklnd. Bshp Auckland CC.

LOWFIELD HEATH Surrey
170, 182 TQ 2740 2m N of Crawley. Loc, Charlwood CP. P Crly, Sussex. Ch e. On the S edge of London (Gatwick) Airpt.

LOW GATE Nthmb
77 NY 9064 2m W of Hexham. Loc, Hxhm UD.

LOWGILL Lancs
89 SD 6564 9m SSE of Kirkby Lonsdale. Loc, Tatham CP. Ch m.

LOWGILL Westm
89 SD 6297 4m NW of Sedbergh. Loc, Dillicar CP. S Westm RD. P Kendal. Westm CC.

LOW HAM Som
177 ST 4329 7m NW of Ilchester. Loc, High Ham CP. Ch e, c. Roman villa excavated 1945.

LOW HAUXLEY Nthmb
71 NU 2802 2m SE of Amble. Loc, Hxly CP.

LOW HESKET Cumb
83 NY 4646 7m SSE of Carlisle. Loc, Hskt CP. Penrith RD. P Clsle. Ch m. Pnrth and the Border CC.

LOW HESLEYHURST Nthmb
71 NZ 0897 3m SE of Rothbury. Loc, Brinkburn CP. Rthbry RD. Berwick-upon-Tweed CC.

LOW HUTTON Yorks (N)
92 SE 7667 3m SW of Malton. Loc, Httns Ambo CP. Mltn RD. P(Httns Ambo), YORK. Ch m. Thirsk and Mltn CC.

LOWICK Lancs
88 SD 2986 5m N of Ulveston. CP, 223. N Lonsdale RD. Ch e. Sch pe. Morecambe and Lnsdle CC. See also Lwck Grn.

LOWICK Northants
134 SP 9780 2m NW of Thrapston. CP, 312. Oundle and Thrpstn RD. P Kettering. Ch e. Wellingborough CC (Peterborough). See also Slipton. Ch: 15c twr with octagonal lantern; monmts to Greenes and other owners of Drayton Hse, mansion of all periods 14c–18c in well laid out grnds.

LOWICK Nthmb
64, 71 NU 0139 7m NNE of Wooler. CP, 666. Glendale RD. P BERWICK-UPON-TWEED. Ch e, m, r, v2. Sch p. Brwck-upn-Twd CC. See also Holburn.

LOWICK GREEN Lancs
88 SD 2985 5m N of Ulverston. Loc, Lwck CP. P Ulvstn.

LOW LORTON Cumb
82 NY 1525 4m SE of Cockermouth. Loc, Ltn CP. Cckrmth RD. Ch e. Sch p. Workington CC.

LOW MARISHES Yorks (N)
92 SE 8177 4m NNE of Malton. Loc, Mrshs CP. Pickering RD. Scarborough CC (Scbrgh and Whitby).

LOW MARNHAM Notts
113 SK 8069 11m W of Lincoln. Loc, Mnhm CP. E Retford RD. Ch e. Bassetlaw CC.

Low Mill

LOW MILL Yorks (N)
86, 92 SE 6795 6m NNW of
Kirkbymoorside. Loc, Farndale W CP.
Kbmsde RD. P YORK. Sch pe. Thirsk and
Malton CC.

LOW MOOR Lancs
95 SD 7341 just W of Clitheroe. Loc,
Clthroe MB.

LOW MOORSLEY Co Durham
85 NZ 3446 2m S of Houghton-le-Spring.
Loc, Hetton UD. P Httn-le-Hole.

LOW NEWTON-BY-THE-SEA Nthmb
71 NU 2424 8m NNE of Alnwick. Loc,
Ntn-by-the-Sea CP. Alnwck RD.
Berwick-upon-Tweed CC.

LOW REDFORD Co Durham
84 NZ 0730 6m SSW of Tow Law. Loc,
S Bedburn CP. Barnard Cstle RD. Bishop
Auckland CC.

LOW ROW Cumb
76 NY 5863 4m ENE of Brampton. Loc,
Nether Denton CP. Border RD. P Brmptn.
Ch m. Penrith and the Bdr CC.

LOW ROW Yorks (N)
90 SD 9897 13m WSW of Richmond. Loc,
Melbecks CP. Reeth RD. P Rchmnd.
Ch e, c, m. Rchmnd CC.

LOWSONFORD Warwicks
131 SP 1868 6m WNW of Warwick. Loc,
Rowington CP. P Solihulll. Ch e.

LOW STREET Norfolk
126 TG 3423 6m SE of N Walsham. Loc,
Smallburgh CP.

LOWTHER Westm
83 NY 5323 4m SSE of Penrith. CP, 379.
N Westm RD. Ch e. Sch pe. Westm CC. The
present cstle, ruined early 19c mansion, is
the second on the site. L. Newtown blt 17c;
L. Vllge, to E, 18c.

LOWTHORPE Yorks (E)
99 TA 0860 4m ENE of Driffield. Loc,
Harpham CP. Ch e.

LOW THURLTON Norfolk
137 TM 4299 6m N of Beccles. Loc,
Thltn CP.

LOWTON Lancs
101 SJ 6197 6m N of Warrington. Loc,
Golborne UD. P Wrrngtn.

LOWTON Som
164 ST 1918 4m SE of Wellington. Loc,
Pitminster CP. P Taunton.

LOWTON COMMON Lancs
101 SJ 6397 6m NNE of Warrington. Loc,
Golborne UD.

LOW WALWORTH Co Durham
85 NZ 2417 4m NW of Darlington. Loc,
Wlwth CP.

LOW WESTWOOD Co Durham
77, 78 NZ 1156 3m N of Consett. Loc,
Cnstt UD.

LOW WORSALL Yorks (N)
85 NZ 3910 7m SSW of Teesside
(Stockton). CP, 151. Stokesley RD.
Ch e, m. Richmond CC.

LOW WRAY Lancs
88, 89 NY 3701 2m S of Ambleside. Loc,
Claife CP. N Lonsdale RD. Ch e. Morecambe
and Lnsdle CC. On W shore of Lake
Windermere, Wray Cstle, blt 1840s, all
turrets, twrs, and battlements.

LOXBEARE Devon
164 SS 9116 3m NW of Tiverton. CP, 162.
Tvtn RD. Ch e, m. Tvtn CC. See also
Calverleigh.

LOXHORE Devon
163 SS 6138 5m NE of Barnstaple. CP, 141.
Bnstple RD. Ch e, m. N Dvn CC.

LOXLEY Warwicks
144 SP 2552 4m ESE of Stratford. CP, 244.
Strtfd-on-Avon RD. P WARWICK. Ch e, v.
Sch pe. Strtfd-on-Avn CC (Strtfd).

LOXLEY Yorks (W)
102 SK 3089 3m WNW of Sheffield. Loc,
Bradfield CP. P SHFFLD. Ch c. Sch p.

LOXTON Som
165 ST 3755 5m SE of Weston. CP, 187.
Axbridge RD. P Axbrdge. Ch e.
Wstn-super-Mare CC. See also Christon.

LOXWOOD Sussex (W)
182 TQ 0331 5m NW of Billingshurst.

CP, 898. Petworth RD. P Bllngshst. Ch e, v. Sch p. Chichester CC (Horsham). See also Roundstreet Cmmn.

LUBENHAM Leics
133 SP 7087 2m W of Mkt Harborough. CP, 690. Mkt Hbrgh RD. P Mkt Hbrgh. Ch e, v. Sch pe. Hbrgh CC.

LUCCOMBE Som
164 SS 9144 4m WSW of Minehead. CP, 189. Williton RD. P Mnhd. Ch e. Bridgwater CC. See also Stoke Pero. Colour-washed thatched cottages beside Horner Water, in deep wooded valley, mostly NT (Holnicote estate).

LUCCOMBE VILLAGE IOW
180 SZ 5879 1m S of Shanklin. Loc, Sandown-Shnkln UD. 1m SW, Landslip, undercliff ravine caused by landslip in 1818.

LUCKER Nthmb
71 NU 1530 4m SE of Belford. CP(Adderstone w Lckr), 303. Blfd RD. P Blfd. Ch e. Berwick-upon-Tweed CC.

LUCKETT Cornwall
186 SX 3873 3m NE of Callington. Loc, Stokeclimsland CP. P Cllngtn. Ch m.

LUCKINGTON Wilts
156 ST 8383 7m WSW of Malmesbury. CP, 466. Mlmsbry RD. P Chippenham. Ch e, b, m. Sch p. Chppnhm CC. See also Alderton.

LUCKWELL BRIDGE Som
164 SS 9038 6m SW of Minehead. Loc, Cutcombe CP. Ch m.

LUCTON Herefs
129 SO 4364 5m NW of Leominster. CP, 113. Lmnstr and Wigmore RD. Ch e. Lmnstr CC. L. Sch founded 1708; much bldng of that date.

LUDBOROUGH Lincs (L)
105 TF 2995 6m NNW of Louth. CP, 184. Lth RD. P Grimsby. Ch e, m. Lth CC.

LUDDENDEN Yorks (W)
96, 102 SE 0426 3m W of Halifax. Loc, Hlfx CB, Sowerby Br UD. P Luddendenfoot, Hlfx. Hlfx BC, Sby CC.

LUDDENDENFOOT Yorks (W)
96, 102 SE 0324 3m W of Halifax. Loc, Sowerby Br UD. P Hlfx.

LUDDESDOWN Kent
171 TQ 6766 5m SSE of Gravesend. CP, 257. Strood RD. P Grvsnd. Ch e. Grvsnd CC. L. Ct, Nmn mnr, possibly oldest continuously inhabited hse in Britain.

LUDDINGTON Lincs (L)
104 SE 8216 4m NE of Crowle. CP, 414. Isle of Axholme RD. P Scunthorpe. Ch e, m, r. Sch p. Gainsborough CC.

LUDDINGTON Warwicks
144 SP 1652 3m WSW of Stratford. CP, 425. Strtfd-on-Avon RD. Ch e, m. Strtfd-on-Avn CC (Strtfd).

LUDDINGTON IN THE BROOK Northants
134 TL 1083 5m SE of Oundle. CP(Lddngtn), 64. Oundle and Thrapston RD. Ch e. Wellingborough CC (Peterborough).

LUDFORD Lincs (L)
105 TF 1989 6m E of Mkt Rasen. CP, 358. Louth RD. P LINCOLN. Ch e, m. Sch pe. Lth CC.

LUDFORD Shrops
129 SO 5173 just S of Ludlow. CP, 220. Ldlw RD. Ch e. Ldlw CC. Connected to Ldlw across R Teme by well known mdvl br.

LUDGERSHALL Bucks
145, 146, 159 SP 6617 6m ESE of Bicester. CP, 281. Aylesbury RD. P Aylesbury. Ch e, m. Sch pe. Aylesbury CC. John Wycliffe was vicar here. Brass in ch commemorates woman who lived in nine reigns.

LUDGERSHALL Wilts
167 SU 2650 7m WNW of Andover. CP, 2,217. Pewsey RD. P Andvr, Hants. Ch e, v. Sch p, sg. Devizes CC. Military tn. Rems of cstle (A.M.).

LUDGVAN Cornwall
189 SW 5033 3m NE of Penzance. CP, 2,213. W Penwith RD. P Pnznce. Ch e, m. Sch p. St Ives CC. See also Crowlas, Lelant Downs, Longrock.

LUDHAM Norfolk
126 TG 3818 6m E of Wroxham. CP, 886. Smallburgh RD. P Gt Yarmouth. Ch e, b, m2. Sch p. N Nflk CC. See also Johnson's St. In Broads country; boatyards. Many 18c hses round mkt place.

LUDLOW Shrops
129 SO 5174 24m S of Shrewsbury.
C P , 6 , 7 9 6 . L d l w R D . P .
Ch e2, b, c, m3, r, s, v3. Sch i, ie, j, je, s, se.
Ldlw CC. Busy old mkt tn on hill beside
R Teme. 11c cstle*. Huge parish ch, mainly
15c. Half-timbered Feathers Inn, 16c.

LUDWELL Wilts
166, 167 ST 9122 3m E of Shaftesbury.
L o c , Donhead S t Mary C P .
P Shftsbry, Dorset. Sch p.

LUDWORTH Co Durham
85 NZ 3641 4m W of Peterlee. Loc,
Shadforth CP. P DRHM. Sch p.

LUFFINCOTT Devon
174 SX 3394 6m S of Holsworthy. CP, 69.
Hlswthy RD. Ch e. W Dvn CC (Tavistock).

LUGWARDINE Herefs
142 SO 5541 2m E of Hereford. CP, 660.
Hrfd RD. P HRFD. Ch e, v. Sch p, sr.
Leominster CC. See also Hagley.

LULHAM Herefs
142 SO 4041 6m W of Hereford. Loc,
Madley CP.

LULLINGTON Derbys
120 SK 2513 7m S of Burton-on-Trent.
CP, 158. Repton RD. P Btn-on-Trnt, Staffs.
Ch e. Belper CC.

LULLINGTON Som
166 ST 7851 3m N of Frome. CP, 211.
Frme RD. P Frme. Ch e. Wells CC. See also
Laverton. Nmn ch. To SW, Orchardleigh,
Vctrn mansion in terraced grnds* with lake,
and ch on small island.

LULSGATE BOTTOM Som
155, 165 ST 5165 6m SW of Bristol. Loc,
Wrington CP. On edge of Brstl Airpt.

LULSLEY Worcs
130 SO 7455 7m W of Worcester. CP, 120.
Martley RD. Ch e. Kidderminster CC.

LUMB Yorks (W)
96, 102 SE 0221 5m SW of Halifax. Loc,
Sowerby Br UD.

LUMBY Yorks (W)
97 SE 4830 4m NE of Castleford. Loc,
S Milford CP.

LUMLEY, GREAT Co Durham
85 NZ 2949 2m SE of Chester-le-Street. See
Gt Lmly.

LUND Yorks (E)
97, 98 SE 6532 2m E of Selby. Loc,
Cliffe CP.

LUND Yorks (E)
98 SE 9748 7m NE of Weighton. CP, 279.
Beverley RD. P Driffield. Ch e, m.
Haltemprice CC.

LUNDY Devon
163 SS 1344 11m NNW of Hartland Point.
CP, 32. Bideford RD. Ch e. N Dvn CC
(Torrington). Granite island in Bristol
Channel, NT since 1969. Puffins abound;
seals often seen. Hmlt at S end, incl rems of
Marisco Cstle. Regular boat service from
Bdfd.

LUNSFORD'S CROSS Sussex (E)
183, 184 TQ 7210 2m NW of Bexhill. Loc,
Ninfield CP.

LUNT Lancs
100 SD 3401 5m SE of Formby. Loc,
Sefton CP.

LUPPITT Devon
176 ST 1606 4m N of Honiton. CP, 442.
Hntn RD. P Hntn. Ch e. Hntn CC. See also
Beacon.

LUPTON Westm
89 SD 5581 4m WNW of Kirkby Lonsdale.
CP, 181. S Westm RD. Sch pe. Westm CC.

LURGASHALL Sussex (W)
181 SU 9327 4m NW of Petworth. CP, 495.
Midhurst RD. P Ptwth. Ch e. Chichester CC
(Horsham). Picturesque vllge under Blackdown.

LUSBY Lincs (L)
114 TF 3367 5m ESE of Horncastle.
CP, 68. Hncstle RD. Ch e. Hncstle CC.

LUSTLEIGH Devon
175 SX 7881 4m SE of Moretonhampstead.
CP, 590. Newton Abbot RD. P Ntn Abbt.
Ch e, r. Totnes CC. To W, L. Cleave,
wooded valley of R Bovey and well known
beauty spot.

LUSTON Herefs
129 SO 4863 3m N of Leominster. CP, 327.
Lmnstr and Wigmore RD. P Lmnstr.
Ch m, v. Sch p. Lmnstr CC.

LUTON Beds
147 TL 0921 28m NNW of London.
CB, 161,178. P. BCs: Ltn E, Ltn W. (Ltn).
See also Stopsley, Sundon Pk. Mnfg tn: cars,
general. Largest brewery in Europe. Intntl
airpt, 2m E. Ltn Hoo*, hse designed by
Adam, restored, 2m S, with Wernher
Collection of art treasures.

LUTON Devon
176, 188 SX 9076 4m NE of Newton
Abbot. Loc, Bishopsteignton CP. Ch e.

LUTTERWORTH Leics
132 SP 5484 6m NNE of Rugby. CP, 3,729.
Lttrwth RD. P RGBY. Ch e, m, r, v2.
Sch i, je, p, s. Blaby CC (Harborough). 19c
obelisk to John Wycliffe, who was rector of
L. and died here in 1384.

LUTTON Devon
187 SX 5959 3m NW of Ivybridge. Loc,
Cornwood CP. P(Lttn Cnwd), Ivybridge.
Ch c.

LUTTON Lincs (H)
124 TF 4325 2m N of Long Sutton.
CP, 796. E Elloe RD. P Spalding. Ch e, m.
Sch p. Holland w Boston CC.

LUTTON Northants
134 TL 1187 8m SW of Peterborough.
CP, 167. Oundle and Thrapston RD.
P PTRBRGH. Ch e. Wellingborough CC
(Ptrbrgh).

LUXBOROUGH Som
164 SS 9737 5m S of Minehead. CP, 182.
Williton RD. P Watchet. Ch e, m. Sch p.
Bridgwater CC. See also Kingsbridge.

LUXULYAN Cornwall
185, 186 SX 0558 4m NE of St Austell.
CP, 861. St Astll RD. P Bodmin. Ch e, m3.
Sch p. Bdmn CC. See also Lockengate.
Former tin-mining and granite-(luxulyanite-)
quarrying vllge. China clay mines to N
and W.

LYDBURY NORTH Shrops
129 SO 3586 2m SE of Bishop's Cstle.
CP, 568. Clun and Bp's Cstle RD. P.
Ch e, m. Sch pe. Ludlow CC. See also
Acton, Brockton, Choulton, Plowden.
Walcot, 18c hse blt for Clive of India. In
World War II, home of the emperor Haile
Selassie.

LYDCOTT Devon
163 SS 6936 7m N of S Molton. Loc, High
Bray CP.

LYDD Kent
184 TR 0420 8m E of Rye. MB, 4,301.
P Romney Marsh. Folkestone and
Hythe CC. See also Dungeness, Ldd-on-Sea.
Once minor Cinque port, but sea now over
2m away. Large ch; some old hses. Airpt
and army camp.

LYDDEN Kent
173 TR 2645 4m NW of Dover. CP, 507.
Dvr RD. P Dvr. Ch e, m. Sch p. Dvr and
Deal CC (Dvr).

LYDDINGTON Rutland
133 SP 8797 2m SSE of Uppingham.
CP, 286. Uppnghm RD. P Uppnghm.
Ch e, m. Rtlnd and Stamford CC. Bede
Hse (A.M.), former home of Bishops of
Lincoln, converted to hsptl 1602. Ch: Perp
arcades.

LYDD-ON-SEA Kent
184 TR 0820 10m E of Rye. Loc,
Lydd MB.

LYDEARD ST LAWRENCE Som
164 ST 1232 8m SE of Watchet. CP, 362.
Taunton RD. P Tntn. Ch e, c. Sch p.
Tntn CC. See also Tarr.

LYDFORD Devon
175 SX 5184 7m NNE of Tavistock.
CP, 2,059. Tvstck RD. P Okehampton.
Ch e, m2. Sch p. W Dvn CC (Tvstck). See
also Hexworthy, Postbridge, Princetown,
Two Bridges. Largest CP in England. To SW,
L. Gorge(NT), famous beauty spot.

LYDGATE Yorks (W)
95 SD 9225 1m NW of Todmorden. Loc,
Tdmdn MB. P Tdmdn, Lancs.

LYDHAM Shrops
129 SO 3391 2m NNE of Bishop's Cstle.
CP, 239. Clun and Bp's Cstle RD. Ch e.
Ludlow CC.

LYDIARD MILLICENT Wilts
157 SU 0985 4m W of Swindon. CP, 958.
Cricklade and Wootton Bassett RD.
P Swndn. Ch e, m2. Sch pe.
Chippenham CC.

LYDIARD TREGOZE Wilts
157 SU 1084 3m W of Swindon. CP, 525.
Cricklade and Wootton Bassett RD.
Ch e, m2. Chippenham CC. See also Hook.
Ch: ornate 17c monmts to St John family
of L. Pk*, Ggn hse which replaced earlier
one. Now conference centre.

LYDIATE Lancs
100 SD 3604 4m SW of Ormskirk.
C P , 4 , 6 6 7 . W L a n c s R D .
P Maghull, LIVERPOOL. Ch e, r2.
Sch i, j, pe, pr2. Ormskk CC. Scotch Piper
Inn, 14c, thatched.

LYDLINCH Dorset
178 ST 7413 7m ESE of Sherborne.
CP, 393. Sturminster RD. P Stmnstr
Newton. Ch e. N Dst CC. See also Kingstag.

LYDNEY Glos
155, 156 SO 6303 9m NE of Chepstow.
CP, 5,041. Ldny RD. P. Ch e, b, c, m, v2.
Sch p, pe2, s, sb, sg. W Glos CC. See also
Purton. 14c vllge cross. 1m W, rems of
Roman temple.

LYE Worcs
130, 131 SO 9284 1m E of Stourbridge.
Loc, Stbrdge MB. P Stbrdge.

LYE GREEN Bucks
159, 160 SP 9703 2m NE of Chesham. Loc,
Chshm UD.

LYFORD Berks
158 SU 3994 4m N of Wantage. CP, 75.
Abingdon RD. Abngdn CC. Scene of
capture in 1581 of Edmund Campion, the
Jesuit, who was later hanged for treason.

LYMBRIDGE GREEN Kent
173 TR 1243 6m NNW of Hythe. Loc,
Stowting CP.

LYME REGIS Dorset
177 SY 3492 20m SW of Yeovil. MB, 3,394.
P. W Dst CC. Small mainly Ggn resort blt
into steep cliffs. Duke of Monmouth landed
on Cobb, 1685. Jane Austen visited the tn.
To W, cliff walk to Seaton (qv) by Dowlands
Landslip.

LYMINGE Kent
173 TR 1641 4m N of Hythe. CP, 1,794.
Elham RD. P Folkestone. Ch e, m. Sch pe.
Flkstne and Hthe CC. See also Etchinghill.
Site of one of earliest Christian communities

in England (633). Parts of orig abbey bldngs
incorporated in present ch.

LYMINGTON Hants
180 SZ 3295 15m E of Bournemouth.
MB, 35,644. P. Christchurch and
Lmngtn BC (New Forest CC). See also
Barton-on-Sea, Bashley, Downton, Everton,
Hordle, Keyhaven, Lr Pennington, Lymore,
Milford-on-Sea, New Milton, Wootton.
Yachting centre nd rsdntl tn. Car ferry to
Yarmouth, IOW.

LYMINSTER Sussex (W)
181, 182 TQ 0204 2m N of Littlehampton.
CP, 283. Worthing RD. P Lttlhmptn. Ch e.
Sch p. Arundel CC (Arndl and Shoreham).

LYMM Ches
101 SJ 6887 5m E of Warrington.
UD, 10,458. P. Runcorn CC. See also
Broomedge, Heatley. Astride Bridgewater
Canal.

LYMORE Hants
180 SZ 2992 3m SW of Lymington. Loc,
Lmngtn MB.

LYMPNE Kent
173 TR 1134 3m W of Hythe. CP, 715.
Elham RD. P Hythe. Ch e. Sch pe.
Folkestone and Hthe CC. Pronounced 'lim'.
Once a Roman port. L. Cstle*, 14c fortified
mnr hse, restored 1905; terraced gdns with
views of Romney Marsh and sea. Royal
Military Canal to S, airpt to N.

LYMPSHAM Som
165 ST 3354 5m S of Weston. CP, 509.
Axbridge RD. P Wstn-super-Mare. Ch e, m.
Sch pe. W-s-M CC. See also Eastertown.

LYMPSTONE Devon
176 SX 9984 2m N of Exmouth. CP, 1,620.
St Thomas RD. P Exmth. Ch e, m, r. Sch pe.
Honiton CC.

LYNCH Som
164 SS 9047 4m W of Minehead. Loc,
Selworthy CP. Colour-washed cottages; chpl
of former mnr hse. Most NT (Holnicote
estate).

LYNDHURST Hants
180 SU 2908 4m N of Brockenhurst.
CP, 2,931. New Forest RD. P. Ch e, b, r.
Sch pe. Nw Frst CC. See also Bank. 'Capital
of Nw Frst'. Old Verderers' ct hse still in use.

LYNDON Rutland
122 SK 9004 4m SE of Oakham. CP, 79.
Oakhm RD. P Oakhm. Ch e. Rtlnd and
Stamford CC.

LYNE Surrey
169, 170 TQ 0166 2m W of Chertsey. Loc,
Chtsy UD. P Chtsy.

LYNEAL Shrops
118 SJ 4433 3m ESE of Ellesmere. Loc,
Ellesmre Rural. N Shrops RD. Ch e. Sch pe.
Oswestry CC.

LYNEHAM Oxon
144 SP 2720 5m SSW of Chipping Norton.
CP, 155. Chppng Ntn RD. P OXFORD.
Ch m. Banbury CC.

LYNEHAM Wilts
157 SU 0279 5m N of Calne. CP, 3,688.
Cricklade and Wootton Bassett RD.
P Chippenham. Ch e, b, m2. Sch i, j.
Chppnhm CC. See also Bradenstoke, Ch
End, Preston. RAF stn.

LYNEMOUTH Nthmb
78 NZ 2991 7m ENE of Morpeth.
CP, 2,618. Mpth RD. P Mpth. Ch e, m.
Sch p. Mpth CC.

LYNG Norfolk
125 TG 0617 6m ENE of E Dereham.
CP, 378. Mitford and Launditch RD.
P NORWICH, NOR 63X. Ch e, m. Sch pe.
SW Nflk CC. See also Primrose Grn.

LYNG Som
177 ST 3328 7m ENE of Taunton. CP, 291.
Bridgwater RD. Ch e. Brdgwtr CC.

LYNMOUTH Devon
163 SS 7249 by Lynton. Loc, Lntn UD. P.
Small resort with harbour at foot of combe
between high cliffs. Cliff rly up to Lynton.

LYNSTED Kent
172 TQ 9460 3m SE of Sittingbourne.
CP, 1,022. Swale RD. P Sttngbne.
Ch e, m, s. Sch p. Faversham CC.

LYNTON Devon
163 SS 7149 12m E of Ilfracombe.
UD, 1,981. P. N Dvn CC. See also Barbrook,
Furzehill, Lynmouth. Small tn on cliff
above Lnmth. To W, Valley of the Rocks,
popular beauty spot.

LYONSHALL Herefs
129 SO 3355 3m E of Kington. CP, 619.
Kngtn RD. P Kngtn. Ch e, b, m.
Leominster CC. See also Holme Marsh. To
SW, section of Offa's Dyke.

LYTCHETT MATRAVERS Dorset
179 SY 9495 5m NNE of Wareham.
CP, 1,335. Wrhm and Purbeck RD. P Poole.
Ch e, m, s. Sch p. S Dst CC.

LYTCHETT MINSTER Dorset
179 SY 9692 4m WNW of Poole. CP, 3,203.
Wareham and Purbeck RD. P Poole.
Ch e, c, m. S Dst CC. See also Organford,
Slepe, Upton.

LYTHAM Lancs
94 SD 3627 7m SE of Blackpool. Loc,
Lthm St Anne's MB.

LYTHAM ST ANNE'S Lancs
94 SD 3427 6m SSE of Blackpool.
MB, 40,089. P. S Fylde CC. See also Lthm;
St Anne's. Resort; windmill on sea front.
Aero-engineering wks. Blckpl Airpt is within
borough.

LYTHE Yorks (N)
86 NZ 8413 4m WNW of Whitby. CP, 635.
Whtby RD. P Whtby. Ch e. Sch pe.
Cleveland and Whtby CC (Scarborough and
Whtby). See also Goldsborough, Kettleness,
Sandsend. To S, Mulgrave Cstle, 18c to 19c
mansion in fine grnds laid out by Repton.

M

MABE BURNTHOUSE Cornwall
190 SW 7634 3m WNW of Falmouth. Loc,
Mabe CP. Kerrier RD. P Penryn. Ch m.
Sch pe. Flmth and Camborne CC. Granite
quarries to W.

MABLETHORPE Lincs (L)
105 TF 5085 21m SE of Grimsby.
UD(Mblthpe and Sutton), 6,156. P.
Horncastle CC. See also Sandilands, Thorpe,
Trusthorpe. Resort with caravans, chalets,
concrete sea defences.

MACCLESFIELD Ches
110 SJ 9173 10m S of Stockport.
MB, 44,240. P. Mcclsfld CC. See also
Broken Cross, Tytherington. Former centre
of silk mnftre; now also other textiles,
clothing, pharmaceuticals. Commuting distr
for Manchester.

MACCLESFIELD FOREST Ches
110 SJ 9772 4m ESE of Macclesfield.
CP, 98. Mcclsfld RD. Ch e. Mcclsfld CC. In
Peak Distr National Pk. 2m E, Cat and
Fiddle Inn, 1600ft up (on O.S. sheet 111).

MACKWORTH Derbys
120, 121 SK 3137 3m WNW of Derby. CP.
Belper RD. P DBY. Ch e. Blpr CC. Scant
rems of cstle: part of 15c gatehouse.

MADEHURST Sussex (W)
181 SU 9810 3m NW of Arundel. CP, 129.
Chichester RD. Ch e. Arndl CC (Chchstr).
19c estate vllge.

MADELEY Shrops
119 SJ 6904 4m S of Oakengates. Loc,
Dawley UD. P Telford. The Wrekin CC
(Ludlow). Indstrl; mainly Vctrn. Many
chpls. Ch designed by Telford. Rems of
M. Ct, 16c.

MADELEY Staffs
110, 119 SJ 7744 5m W of
Newcastle-under-Lyme. CP, 3,444.
Ncstle-under-Lme RD. P Crewe, Cheshire.
Ch e, m3, v. Sch p, pe, s. N-u-L BC. See also
Onneley. Old Hall, 17c. 1½m N, slight rems
of Heighley Cstle.

MADINGLEY Cambs
135 TL 3960 4m WNW of Cambridge.
CP, 262. Chesterton RD. P CMBRDGE.
Ch e. Sch pe. Cambs CC. American World
War II cemetery. Hall, Tdr and later; grnds
open to members of public on foot.

MADLEY Herefs
142 SO 4138 6m W of Hereford. CP, 960.
Dore and Bredwardine RD. P HRFD.
Ch e, m. Sch p. Hrfd CC. See also Canon Br,
Lulham, Shenmore. Outstanding, large,
13c–14c ch. Enormous font.

MADRESFIELD Worcs
143 SO 8047 2m NE of Malvern. CP, 215.
Upton upon Severn RD. P Mlvn. Ch e.
Sch pe. S Worcs CC. M. Ct, Tdr, moated,
much altered in 19c; seat of Lygon family
from 14c.

MADRON Cornwall
189 SW 4531 2m NW of Penzance.
CP, 1,420. W Penwith RD. P Pnznce.
Ch e, m2. Sch pe. St Ives CC. See also
Newmill. To SW, Trengwainton Gdns
(NT)*. Antiquities in area incl St Mdrn's Wll
and Baptistry; Chysauster Ancient
Vllge (A.M.); Lanyon Quoit (cromlech, NT);
Men-an-Tol, Men Scryfs, Nine Maidens
(stones); Ding-Dong Mine.

MAER Staffs
110, 119 SJ 7938 6m SW of
Newcastle-under-Lyme. CP, 577.
Ncstle-undr-Lme RD. Ch e. Sch pe.
N-u-L BC. See also Aston, Blackbrook.

MAESBROOK GREEN Shrops
118 SJ 3021 5m S of Oswestry. Loc,
Kinnerley CP. P(Msbrk), Llanymynech,
Montgomeryshire. Ch e, m2.

MAESBURY Shrops
118 SJ 3025 3m SSE of Oswestry. Loc,
Oswstry Rural CP. Oswstry RD. Ch c, m.
Sch p. Oswstry CC.

MAESBURY MARSH Shrops
118 SJ 3125 3m SSE of Oswestry. Loc,
Oswstry Rural CP. Oswstry RD. P Oswstry.
Oswstry CC.

MAGDALEN LAVER Essex
161 TL 5108 4m NW of Ongar. CP, 282.
Epping and Ongr RD. Ch e. Harlow CC
(Eppng).

MAGGOTS END Essex
148 TL 4727 4m N of Bishop's Stortford.
Loc, Manuden CP.

MAGHAM DOWN Sussex (E)
183 TQ 6011 2m NE of Hailsham. Loc,
Hlshm CP. P Hlshm.

MAGHULL Lancs
100 SD 3702 4m SW of Ormskirk.
CP, 16,379. W Lancs RD. P LIVERPOOL.
Ch e, b, m, r, v. Sch ir, jr, p4, pe, s3.
Crosby BC (Ormskk CC).

MAIDA VALE London
160 TQ 2582 3m WNW of Charing Cross.
Loc, City of Westminster LB.
Paddington BC (Pddngtn N).

MAIDEN BRADLEY Wilts
166 ST 8039 6m SW of Warminster.
CP(Mdn Brdly w Yarnfield), 417. Mere and
Tisbury RD. P Wmnstr. Ch e, c.
Westbury CC.

MAIDENCOMBE Devon
188 SX 9268 3m N of Torquay. Loc,
Torbay CB. P Tquay.

MAIDENHEAD Berks
159 SU 8881 5m W of Slough. MB, 45,306.
P. Windsor and Mdnhd CC (Wndsr). Largely
rsdntl distr. 18c rd br over Thames, and 19c
rly by Brunel with exceptionally low and
wide brick arches.

MAIDEN LAW Co Durham
85 NZ 1749 1m NNE of Lanchester. Loc,
Lnchstr RD. NW Drhm CC.

MAIDEN NEWTON Dorset
177, 178 SY 5997 8m NW of Dorchester.
CP, 680. Dchstr RD. P Dchstr. Ch e, m.
Sch pe. W Dst CC.

MAIDFORD Northants
145, 146 SP 6052 6m WNW of Towcester.
CP, 147. Tcstr RD. P Tcstr. Ch e, m. Sch pe.
Daventry CC (S Nthnts).

MAIDS MORETON Bucks
146 SP 7035 1m NNE of Buckingham.
CP, 147. Bcknghm RD. P BCKNGHAM.
Ch e. Sch pe. Bcknghm CC. Notable Perp
ch.

MAIDSTONE Kent
172 TQ 7655 32m ESE of London.
MB, 70,918. P. Mdstne CC. See also
Shepway. County tn, on R Medway.
Industries incl brewing, paper-making,
engineering. 2m NW, moated Allington
Cstle*, 13c with later additions.

MAIDWELL Northants
133 SP 7476 6m S of Mkt Harborough.
CP, 161. Brixworth RD.
P NORTHAMPTON. Ch e. Sch p.
Daventry CC (Kettering).

MAINSFORTH Co Durham
85 NZ 3131 3m NW of Sedgefield. CP, 229.
Sdgfld RD. Drhm CC (Sdgfld).

MAINSTONE Shrops
128 SO 2787 3m W of Bishop's Cstle.
CP, 110. Clun and Bp's Cstle RD. Ch e, m.
Ludlow CC. Stone and slate settlement in
steep remote valley.

MAISEMORE Glos
143 SO 8121 2m NW of Gloucester. CP, 447.
Glcstr RD. P GLCSTR. Ch e. Sch pe.
W Glos CC.

MAJOR'S GREEN Worcs
131 SP 1077 6m SSE of Birmingham. Loc,
Wythall CP. Bromsgrove and Redditch CC
(Solihull CC).

MALBOROUGH Devon
187, 188 SX 7039 3m SSW of Kingsbridge.
CP, 793. Kngsbrdge RD. P Kngsbrdge.
Ch e, b. Sch pe. Totnes CC. Parish incl
spectacular coastal stretch (NT) from Bolt
Head to Blt Tail. Ch spire is well known
landmark.

MALDEN RUSHETT London
170 TQ 1761 5m S of Kingston. Loc,
Kngstn upon Thames LB. Surbiton BC.

MALDON Essex
162 TL 8507 9m E of Chelmsford.
MB, 13,840. P. Mldn CC. See also
Heybridge, Hbrdge Basin. Ancient tn at
head of Blackwater estuary. Site of battle
with Vikings, 991. Old bldngs incl 15c moot
hall. To W, Beeleigh Abbey*, rems of 12c
abbey incorporated in hse.

MALHAM Yorks (W)
90 SD 9062 5m E of Settle. CP, 135.
Sttle RD. P Skipton. Ch m. Skptn CC. In
limestone Craven distr on Pennine Way. To
NW, M. Cove, 300ft escarpment from foot
of which flows R Aire. 2m N, M. Tarn (NT,
with surrounding moorland); Field Studies
Centre. 1m NE, Gordale Scar: canyon with
waterfalls.

MALMESBURY Wilts
157 ST 9387 9m N of Chippenham.
MB, 2,526. P. Chppnhm CC. Par ch is rems
of 12c and later abbey. Mkt cross. Old hses,
inns, almshouses.

MALPAS Ches
109 SJ 4847 5m NW of Whitchurch.
CP, 1,310. Tarvin RD. P. Ch e, m3, r, v.
Sch pe, s. Nantwich CC. Bthplce of Reginald
Heber, 1783–1826, writer of well-known
hymns; became Bishop of Calcutta 1822.
See also Hodnet, Shrops.

MALPAS Cornwall
190 SW 8442 2m SE of Truro. Loc,
Truro MB. P Truro.

MALTBY Yorks (N)
85 NZ 4613 4m SSE of Teesside
(Stockton). CP. Stokesley RD.
Richmond CC.

MALTBY Yorks (W)
103 SK 5292 6m E of Rotherham.
UD, 14,050. P Rthrhm. Rother Valley CC.
1½m SW, Roche Abbey (A.M.), 12c
Cistercian abbey in grnds laid out in 18c by
Capability Brown.

MALTBY LE MARSH Lincs (L)
105 TF 4681 4m SW of Mablethorpe.
CP, 217. Louth RD. P Alford. Ch e, b, m.
Lth CC. Twr windmill.

MALTING GREEN Essex
149, 162 TL 9720 3m SSW of Colchester.
Loc, Layer-de-la-Haye CP.

MALTON Yorks (N)
92 SE 7871 17m NE of York. UD, 3,980. P.
Thirsk and Malton CC. See also Old Mltn,
Wykeham. Mkt tn, on site of Roman stn.
Roman museum. Racing stables.

MALVERN Worcs
143 SO 7745 7m SW of Worcester.
UD, 29,004. P. S Worcs CC. See also Upr
Welland, W Mlvn, Wyche. On steep E slope
of M. Hills, which rise to 1,395ft from plain
below and provide popular recreational area.
M. developed as spa 19c. Priory ch: 15c
stained glass. Shaw Drama Festival.

MALVERN LINK Worcs
143 SO 7948 2m NE of Malvern. Loc,
Mlvn UD. P Mlvn.

MALVERN WELLS Worcs
143 SO 7742 2m S of Malvern. Loc,
Mlvn UD. P Mlvn.

MAMBLE Worcs
130 SO 6871 7m WSW of Bewdley.
CP, 204. Tenbury RD. P Kidderminster.
Ch e. Kddrmnstr CC.

MAMHEAD Devon
176 SX 9380 7m S of Exeter. CP, 148.
St Thomas RD. Ch e. Tiverton CC. Ch in pk
of M. Hse. Pk laid out by Capability
Brown, 1779; hse by Salvin, 1830, in Tdr
style.

MANACCAN Cornwall
190 SW 7624 7m ESE of Helston. CP, 361.
Kerrier RD. P Hlstn. Ch e, m. Sch p.
St Ives CC. See also Helford.

MANATON Devon
175 SX 7481 3m S of Moretonhampstead.
CP, 424. Newton Abbot RD. P Ntn Abbt.
Ch e. Totnes CC. Becka Falls, ½m S,
popular beauty spot.

MANBY Lincs (L)
105 TF 3986 4m E of Louth. CP, 887.
Lth RD. P Lth. Ch e, m. Lth CC. RAF
college and air stn.

MANCETTER Warwicks
132 SP 3296 1m SE of Atherstone.
CP, 2,759. Athrstne RD. P Athrstne.
Ch e, m. Sch pe. Meriden CC. See also Ridge
Lane. Half-timbered 14c mnr hse.

MANCHESTER Lancs
101 SJ 8398 164m NW of London.
CB, 541,468. P(MNCHSTR). BCs: Ardwick,
Blackley, Central, Gorton, Moss Side,
Openshaw, Withington, Wythenshawe.
(Same plus Cheetham and Exchange, minus
Central.) Important commercial centre and
port; outlet to sea via M. Ship Canal.
University. Cathedral, formerly parish ch.
Intntl airpt (Ringway).

MANEA Cambs
135 TL 4889 6m ENE of Chatteris.
CP, 1,393. N Witchford RD. P March.
Ch e2, m. Sch p. Isle of Ely CC. See also
Purls Br, Welches Dam.

MANFIELD Yorks (N)
85 NZ 2213 4m W of Darlington. CP. 212.
Croft RD. P Dlngtn, Co Durham. Ch e.
Sch pe. Richmond CC.

MANGOTSFIELD Glos
155, 156 ST 6676 5m NE of Bristol.
UD, 23,269. P BRSTL. Kingswood CC
(Brstl NE BC).

MANKINHOLES Yorks (W)
95 SD 9623 2m ESE of Todmorden. Loc,
Tdmdn MB.

MANLEY Ches
109 SJ 5071 7m ENE of Chester. CP, 706.
Runcorn RD. P WARRINGTON. Ch m.
Sch p. Rncn CC.

MANNINGFORD ABBOTS Wilts
167 SU 1458 2m SW of Pewsey. Loc,
Mnngfd CP. Psy RD. Ch e. Devizes CC.

MANNINGFORD BOHUNE Wilts
167 SU 1357 2m SW of Pewsey. Loc,
Mnngfd CP. Psy RD. Ch e, b. Devizes CC.

MANNINGFORD BRUCE Wilts
167 SU 1359 2m WSW of Pewsey. Loc,
Mnngfd CP. Psy RD. P Psy. Ch e. Sch pe.
Devizes CC.

MANNINGS HEATH Sussex (W)
182 TQ 2028 2m SE of Horsham. Loc,
Nuthurst CP. P Hshm. Ch m.

MANNINGTON Dorset
179 SU 0606 5m W of Ringwood. Loc,
Wimborne and Cranborne RD. N Dst CC.

MANNINGTREE Essex
150 TM 1031 8m NE of Colchester.
CP, 524. Tendring RD. P. Ch e, m, r, s.
Sch pe, pm, s. Harwich CC. Some recent
rsdntl development. Ggn bldngs remain
from 18c attempt to develop M. as model
port (see Mistley).

MANSELL GAMAGE Herefs
142 SO 3944 8m WNW of Hereford. CP, 65.

Weobley RD. Ch e. Leominster CC. To S,
Garnons, 19c hse in grnds landscaped late
18c by Repton.

MANSELL LACY Herefs
142 SO 4245 6m NW of Hereford. CP, 136.
Weobley RD. P HRFD. Ch e.
Leominster CC.

MANSERGH Westm
89 SD 6082 3m NNW of Kirkby Lonsdale.
CP, 119. S Westm RD. Ch e. Westm CC.

MANSFIELD Notts
112 SK 5361 14m N of Nottingham. MB,
57,598. P. Mnsfld CC. Coal-mining; hosiery-
mnfg. Tall rly viaduct above tn centre.

MANSFIELD WOODHOUSE Notts
112 SK 5363 2m N of Mansfield. UD,
24,787. P Mnsfld. Mnsfld CC. See also Forest
Tn. Coal mines; quarries.

MANSRIGGS Lancs
88 SD 2980 2m N of Ulverston. CP, 33.
N Lonsdale RD. Morecambe and Lnsdle CC.

MANSTON Dorset
178 ST 8115 6m SW of Shaftesbury.
CP, 188. Sturminster RD. P Stmnstr
Newton. Ch e. Sch pe. N Dst CC.

MANSTON Kent
173 TR 3466 2m WNW of Ramsgate. Loc,
Rmsgte MB. P Rmsgte. Airpt.

MANSWOOD Dorset
179 ST 9708 5m NNW of Wimborne. Loc,
Moor Crichel CP. P Wmbne.

MANTHORPE Lincs (K)
113, 122 SK 9237 1m NNE of Grantham.
CP (Belton and Mnthpe), 214.
W Kesteven RD. P Grnthm. Ch e.
Grnthm CC.

MANTHORPE Lincs (K)
123 TF 0716 3m SW of Bourne. CP(Toft
w Lound and Mnthpe), 153. S Kesteven RD.
Ch m. Rutland and Stamford CC.

MANTON Lincs (L)
104 SE 9302 5m SW of Brigg. CP, 105.
Glanford Brgg RD. Ch e. Brgg and
Scunthorpe CC (Brgg).

MANTON Rutland
122 SK 8804 3m SSE of Oakham. CP, 301.

Oakhm RD. P Oakhm. Ch e. Rtlnd and Stamford CC. Vllge with several 17c–18c hses.

MANTON Wilts
157 SU 1768 1m W of Marlborough. Loc, Mlbrgh MB. P Mlbrgh.

MANUDEN Essex
148 TL 4926 3m N of Bishop's Stortford. CP, 500. Saffron Walden RD. P Bshp's Sttfd, Herts. Ch e. Sch p. Sffrn Wldn CC. See also Maggots End.

MAPERTON Som
166 ST 6726 3m WSW of Wincanton. CP, 108. Wncntn RD. Ch e. Wells CC.

MAPLEBECK Notts
112 SK 7160 5m SE of Ollerton. CP, 66. Southwell RD. Ch e. Newark CC.

MAPLE CROSS Herts
160 TQ 0392 2m SW of Rickmansworth. Loc, Rckmnswth UD. P Rckmnswth.

MAPLEDURHAM Oxon
158, 159 SU 6776 4m NW of Reading. CP, 2,042. Henley RD. P Rdng, Berks. Ch e, r. Sch pe. Hnly CC. Thames-side vllge with Tdr mnr hse* and 17c almshouses.

MAPLEDURWELL Hants
169 SU 6851 3m E of Basingstoke. CP(Mpldrwll and Up Nately), 322. Bsngstke RD. P Bsngstke. Ch e. Bsngstke CC.

MAPLEHURST Sussex (W)
182 TQ 1824 4m SSE of Horsham. Loc, Hshm RD. Ch c. Hshm and Crawley CC (Hshm).

MAPLESTEAD, GREAT Essex
149 TL 8034 2m N of Halstead. See Gt Mplstd.

MAPLETON Derbys
111 SK 1648 1m NW of Ashbourne. CP, 165. Ashbne RD. Ch e. W Derbys CC. Ch twr topped by octagonal dome.

MAPPERLEY Derbys
112, 121 SK 4343 2m WNW of Ilkeston. CP, 374. Belper RD. P DERBY. Ch e, m. Sch p. Blpr CC.

MAPPERTON Dorset
177 SY 5099 5m NNE of Bridport. CP, 21. Beaminster RD. Ch e. W Dst CC. M. Mnr, 16c and later; terraced gdns*.

MAPPLEBOROUGH GREEN Warwicks
131 SP 0866 3m ESE of Redditch. Loc, Studley CP. P Stdly. Ch e, m. Sch pe.

MAPPLETON Yorks (E)
99 TA 2243 3m SSE of Hornsea. CP, 290. Holderness RD. P Hnsea. Ch e, m. Bridlington CC. See also Gt Cowden, Rolston.

MAPPLEWELL Yorks (W)
102 SE 3209 3m NNW of Barnsley. Loc, Darton UD. P Bnsly.

MAPPOWDER Dorset
178 ST 7306 9m W of Blandford. CP, 185. Sturminster RD. P Stmnstr Newton. Ch e. N Dst CC.

MARAZION Cornwall
189 SW 5130 3m E of Penzance. CP, 1,352. W Penwith RD. P. Ch e, f, m2. Sch p. St Ives CC.

MARBURY Ches
109 SJ 5645 3m NNE of Whitchurch. CP(Mbry cum Quoisley), 276. Nantwich RD. P Whtchch, Salop. Ch e. Sch pe. Nntwch CC.

MARCH Cambs
135 TL 4196 14m E of Peterborough. UD, 14,268. P. Isle of Ely CC. See also Westry. There are large rly marshalling yards. St Wendreda's ch has double-hammerbeam angel roof.

MARCHAM Berks
158 SU 4596 3m W of Abingdon. CP, 835. Abngdn RD. P Abngdn. Ch e. Sch pe. Abngdn CC.

MARCHAMLEY Shrops
118 SJ 5929 5m E of Wem. Loc, Hodnet CP. P Shrewsbury.

MARCHINGTON Staffs
120 SK 1330 3m ESE of Uttoxeter. CP, 785. Uttxtr RD. P Uttxtr. Ch e, m, r. Sch pe. Burton CC. See also Gorsty Hill, Mchngtn Woodlands.

MARCHINGTON WOODLANDS Staffs
120 SK 1128 3m SSE of Uttoxeter. Loc, Mchngtn CP. Ch e. Sch pe.

MARCHWOOD Hants
180 SU 3810 6m NW of Fawley. CP, 1,767.
New Forest RD. P SOUTHAMPTON.
Ch e, b, v. Sch pe. Nw Frst CC. See also
Pooksgreen. Power stn; electricity research
establishment.

MARDEN Herefs
142 SO 5147 4m N of Hereford. CP, 783.
Hrfd RD. P HRFD. Ch e. Sch p.
Leominster CC. See also Urdimarsh, Vauld,
Walker's Grn.

MARDEN Kent
171, 172, 184 TQ 7444 7m S of Maidstone.
CP, 2,590. Mdstne RD. P Tonbridge.
Ch e, m2, v3. Sch p. Mdstne CC. See also
Chainhurst, Milebush. Apple growing and
marketing centre.

MARDEN Wilts
167 SU 0857 5m WSW of Pewsey. CP, 115.
Devizes RD. Ch e. Dvzs CC.

MARE GREEN Som
177 ST 3326 7m E of Taunton. Loc, Stoke
St Gregory CP.

MAREHAM LE FEN Lincs (L)
114 TF 2761 5m SSE of Horncastle.
CP, 704. Hncstle RD. P Boston. Ch e.
Sch pe. Hncstle CC.

MAREHAM ON THE HILL Lincs (L)
114 TF 2867 2m SE of Horncastle. CP, 101.
Hncstle RD. Ch e. Hncstle CC.

MARESFIELD Sussex (E)
183 TQ 4624 2m N of Uckfield. CP, 3,403.
Uckfld RD. P Uckfld. Ch e. Sch pe.
E Grinstead CC. See also Duddleswell,
Fairwarp, Nutley.

MARGARET MARSH Dorset
178 ST 8218 4m SW of Shaftesbury.
CP, 46. Shftsbry RD. Ch e. N Dst CC.

MARGARET RODING Essex
148, 161 TL 5912 6m SSW of Dunmow.
CP, 193. Dnmw RD. Ch e. Saffron
Walden CC. One of eight Rodings,
pronounced 'roothing'.

MARGARETTING Essex
161 TL 6701 4m SW of Chelmsford.
CP, 891. Chlmsfd RD. P Ingatestone. Ch e.
Sch pe. Chlmsfd CC.

MARGATE Kent
173 TR 3570 15m ENE of Canterbury.
MB, 50,145. P. Thanet W BC (Isle of
Thnt CC). See also Birchington, Westgate on
Sea. Resort, with large harbour. S side of tn,
Salmestone Grange*, restored 14c monastic
bldng.

MARHAM Norfolk
124 TF 7009 7m NE of Downham Mkt.
CP, 3,021. Dnhm RD. P King's Lynn.
Ch e, m. Sch i, p. SW Nflk CC.

MARHAMCHURCH Cornwall
174 SS 2203 2m SSE of Bude. CP, 473.
Stratton RD. P Bde. Ch e, m. Sch pe.
N Cnwll CC. See also Budd's Titson. Ch
contains rare example of a cresset stone —
see also Lewannick.

MARHOLM Hunts
123 TF 1402 3m NW of Peterborough.
CP, 205. Ptrbrgh RD. Ch e. Ptrbrgh BC (CC).
Topiary figure of a man outside Fitzwilliam
Arms.

MARIANSLEIGH Devon
163 SS 7422 3m SE of S Molton. CP, 153.
S Mltn RD. Ch e. N Dvn CC.

MARISTOW Devon
187 SX 4764 6m N of Plymouth. Loc,
Bickleigh CP. Ch e.

MARK Som
165 ST 3847 5m E of Burnham. CP, 851.
Axbridge RD. P Highbridge. Ch e, b. Sch pe.
Weston-super-Mare CC. See also
Mk Causeway.

MARKBEECH Kent
171 TQ 4742 3m SE of Edenbridge. Loc,
Sevenoaks RD. P Ednbrdge. Ch e. Svnks CC.

MARKBY Lincs (L)
105 TF 4878 3m NE of Alford. CP, 52.
Spilsby RD. P Alfd. Ch e. Horncastle CC.
Only thatched ch in Lincs.

MARK CAUSEWAY Som
165 ST 3547 3m ESE of Burnham. Loc,
Mark CP. P Highbridge. Ch m.

MARK CROSS Sussex (E)
183 TQ 5831 5m S of Tunbridge Wells. Loc,
Uckfield RD. P Crowborough. Ch e. Sch pe.
E Grinstead CC.

MARKET BOSWORTH Leics
121 SK 4003 6m NNW of Hinckley.
CP, 1,253. Mkt Bswth RD. P Nuneaton,
Warwickshire. Ch e, r, v. Sch pe, s2.
Bswth CC. Ancient mkt tn. Bswth Field
battle was fought 2m S in 1485 (see Sutton
Cheney).

MARKET DEEPING Lincs (K)
123 TF 1310 7m ENE of Stamford.
CP, 1,935. S Kesteven RD.
P PETERBOROUGH. Ch e. Sch pe. Rutland
and Stmfd CC. 13c—14c rectory*, possibly
oldest in England still in use.

MARKET DRAYTON Shrops
110, 118, 199 SJ 6734 14m WSW of
Stoke-on-Trent. CP, 5,859. Mkt Drtn RD. P.
Ch e, m3, r, v. Sch i, j, s. Oswestry CC.
Centre of important agricultural distr.

MARKET HARBOROUGH Leics
133 SP 7387 10m NW of Kettering.
UD, 14,527. P. Hbrgh CC. See also
Gt Bowden, Lit Bdn. Ancient mkt tn and
hunting centre, with many old bldngs. Ch
has fine twr and spire. Timber-framed
former grammar sch of 1614.

MARKET LAVINGTON Wilts
167 SU 0154 5m S of Devizes. CP, 1,148.
Dvzs RD. P Dvzs. Ch e, v. Sch pe, s.
Dvzs CC.

MARKET OVERTON Rutland
122 SK 8816 5m NNE of Oakham. CP, 409.
Oakhm RD. P Oakhm. Ch e. Rtlnd and
Stamford CC. On site of Roman settlement.
Ironstone quarries in vicinity. Airfield
to SE.

MARKET RASEN Lincs (L)
104 TF 1089 14m NE of Lincoln.
UD, 2,430. P. Gainsborough CC. Mkt tn.
Racecourse.

MARKET STAINTON Lincs (L)
105 TF 2280 7m NNW of Horncastle.
CP, 65. Hncstle RD. P LINCOLN. Ch e.
Hncstle CC.

MARKET STREET Norfolk
126 TG 2921 3m N of Wroxham. Loc,
Tunstead CP.

MARKET WEIGHTON Yorks (E)
98 SE 8741 10m W of Beverley. CP, 2,185.
Pocklington RD. P YORK. Ch e, c, m2, r.
Sch pe, pr, s. Howden CC.

MARKET WESTON Suffolk (W)
136 TL 9877 8m W of Diss. CP, 182.
Thingoe RD. P Dss, Norfolk. Ch e, m.
Bury St Edmunds CC.

MARKFIELD Leics
121 SK 4810 5m SE of Coalville. CP, 2,455.
Mkt Bosworth RD. P LEICESTER.
Ch e, c2, m. Sch p, s. Bswth CC. See also
Copt Oak, Stanton under Bardon.

MARKINGTON Yorks (W)
91 SE 2864 4m SSW of Ripon. CP(Mkngtn
w Wallerthwaite), 540. Rpn and
Pateley Br RD. P Harrogate. Ch e, m.
Sch pe. Rpn CC. 1½m NE, Markenfield
Hall*, moated 14c hse.

MARKSBURY Som
166 ST 6662 5m N of Radstock. CP, 339.
Bathavon RD. P Bath. Ch e, m. Sch pe.
N Som CC. See also Hunstrete, Stanton
Prior.

MARKS TEY Essex
149, 162 TL 9123 5m W of Colchester.
CP, 978. Lexden and Winstree RD.
P Clchstr. Ch e, m. Sch pe. Clchstr CC.
Model vllge development.

MARKWELL Cornwall
186 SX 3658 4m W of Saltash. Loc,
Landrake w St Erney CP.

MARKYATE Herts
147 TL 0616 4m SSW of Luton. CP, 2,242.
Hemel Hempstead RD. P St Albans.
Ch e, b, m. Sch p. Hml Hmpstd CC.

MARLBOROUGH Wilts
157 SU 1869 10m S of Swindon.
MB, 6,031. P. Devizes CC. See also Manton.
Mainly Ggn tn amid downs. Wide main st;
ch at each end. Boys' public sch.

MARLDON Devon
188 SX 8663 3m W of Torquay. CP.
Totnes RD. P Paignton. Ch e, c. Sch pe.
Ttns CC. See also Compton.

MARLESFORD Suffolk(E)
137 TM 3258 4m SE of Framlingham.
CP, 285. Blyth RD. P Woodbridge. Ch e.
Eye CC.

MARLEY HILL Co Durham
78 NZ 2057 5m SW of Gateshead.
Loc, Whickham UD. P NEWCASTLE UPON
TYNE.

MARLEY MOUNT Hants
179 SZ 2698 4m WNW of Lymington.
Loc, Sway CP.

MARLINGFORD Norfolk
125 TG 1309 5m NNE of Wymondham.
CP, 309. Foreshore and Henstead RD.
P NORWICH, NOR 40X. Ch e. S Nflk CC
(Central Nflk). See also Colton. Picturesque
water mill.

MARLOW Bucks
159 SU 8586 4m NNW of Maidenhead.
UD, 11,706. P. Wcmbe CC. Riverside tn
with 19c suspension br and weir.

MARLOW Herefs
129 SO 3976 5m SSW of Cravens Arms.
Loc, Leintwardine CP.

MARLPIT HILL Kent
171 TQ 4447 1m N of Edenbridge.
Loc, Ednbrdge CP.

MARNHULL Dorset
178 ST 7818 9m E of Sherborne. CP,1,293.
Sturminster RD. P Stmnstr Newton.
Ch e, c, m2, r. Sch pe, pr. N Dst CC.

MARPLE Ches
101 SJ 9588 4m ESE of Stockport.
UD, 23,217. P Stckpt. Hazel Grove BC
(Cheadle CC). See also High Lane, Mellor.
Bthplce of John Bradshaw, president of
court which sentenced Charles I to death.

MARR Yorks (W)
103 SE 5105 4m WNW of Doncaster.
CP, 137. Dncstr RD. P Dncstr. Ch e. Don
Valley CC.

MARRICK Yorks (N)
90 SE 0798 6m WSW of Richmond.
CP, 107. Reeth RD. P Rchmnd. Ch e, m2.
Rchmnd CC. See also Washfold.

MARSDEN Co Durham
78 NZ 4064 3m SE of Shields.
Loc, Boldon UD. The impressive M. Rock
stands offshore across the sands.

MARSDEN Yorks (W)
102 SE 0411 7m WSW of Huddersfield.
Loc, Colne Valley UD. P Hddsfld. Clne
Vlly CC.

MARSETT Yorks (N)
90 SD 9086 3m SE of Hawes.
Loc, Bainbridge CP. Ch m.

MARSH Devon
177 ST 2510 5m WNW of Chard.
Loc, Yarcombe CP.

MARSHALL MEADOWS Nthmb
64 NT 9856 3m NNW of
Berwick-upon-Tweed.
Loc, Brwck-upn-Twd MB. Over M.M. Bay,
with main line rly between. Most northerly
place in England.

MARSHALL'S HEATH Herts
147 TL 1514 2m E of Harpenden.
Loc, Wheathampstead CP.

MARSHAM Norfolk
126 TG 1924 2m S of Aylsham. CP, 633.
St Faith's and Aylshm RD. P NORWICH,
NOR O6Y. Ch e, m. Sch p. N Nflk CC
(Central Nflk).

MARSH BALDON Oxon
158 SU 5699 SE of Oxford. CP, 333.
Bullingdon RD. Ch e. Sch pe. Henley CC.

MARSHBROOK Shrops
129 SO 4489 3m S of Ch Stretton.
Loc, Wistanstow CP.

MARSH CHAPEL Lincs (L)
105 TF 3699 7m SSE of Cleethorpes.
CP, 546. Louth RD. P Grimsby. Ch e, m.
Sch p. Lth CC.

MARSHFIELD Glos
156 ST 7873 6m NNE of Bath. CP, 1,167.
Sodbury RD. P Chippenham, Wilts.
Ch e, b, c, v. Sch pe. S Glos CC. 2½m SSE,
Three Shire Stone, 19c 'cromlech', marks
boundary of Glos, Som, Wilts.

MARSHGATE Cornwall
174 SX 1591 6m NE of Camelford.
Loc, Cmlfd RD. P Cmlfd. N Cnwll CC.

MARSH GIBBON Bucks
145, 146 SP 6423 4m E of Bicester.
Cp, 545. Buckingham RD. P Bcstr, Oxon.
Ch e, c. Sch pe. Bcknghm CC.

MARSH GREEN Devon
176 SY 0493 8m E of Exeter.
Loc, Rockbeare CP. Ch c.

MARSH GREEN Kent
171 TQ 4344 1m S of Edenbridge.
Loc, Ednbrdge CP. P Ednbrdge. Ch v.

MARSH GREEN Shrops
118, 119 SJ 6014 3m WNW of Wellington.
Loc, Rodington CP. Ch m.

MARSH GREEN Staffs
110 SJ 8859 3m SSE of Congleton. Loc,
Biddulph UD.

MARSHLANE Derbys
103 SK 4079 6m SSE of Sheffield. Loc,
Eckington CP. P SHFFLD. Sch p.

MARSHWOOD Dorset
177 SY 3899 5m NE of Lyme Regis.
CP, 303. Beaminster RD. P Bridport.
Ch e, v. Sch pe. W Dst CC.

MARSKE Yorks (N)
91 NZ 1000 4m W of Richmond. CP, 124.
Rchmnd RD. P Rchmnd. Ch e. Rchmnd CC.

MARSKE-BY-THE-SEA Yorks (N)
86 NZ 6322 9m E of Teesside
(Middlesborough). UD(Saltburn and
Mske-by-the-Sea), 19,562.
P REDCAR, Tssde. Cleveland and
Whitby CC (Clvlnd). Resort; good sands.

MARSTON Ches
101 SJ 6775 1m NE of Northwich. CP, 693.
Nthwch RD. Ch e. Nthwch CC.

MARSTON Herefs
129 SO 3657 4m E of Kington. Loc,
Pembridge CP. Ch m.

MARSTON Lincs (K)
113 SK 8943 5m NNW of Grantham.
CP, 228. W Kesteven RD. P Grnthm.
Ch e, m. Sch pe. Grnthm CC. Tudor and 18c
mnr hse*, orig seat of Thorold family.
Modern gazebo in gdn.

MARSTON Oxon
158 SP 5208 2m NNE of Oxford.
CP, 3,560. Bullingdon RD. P OXFD. Ch e.
Sch s. Mid-Oxon CC (Henley).

MARSTON Staffs
119 SJ 8314 7m ESE of Newport. Loc,
Ch Eaton CP.

MARSTON Staffs
119 SJ 9227 3m N of Stafford. CP, 157.
Stffd RD. Ch e. Sch p. Stffd and Stone CC.
See also Yarlet.

MARSTON Warwicks
131 SO 2094 4m N of Coleshill. Loc, Lea
Mstn CP.

MARSTON Wilts
167 ST 9656 4m SW of Devizes. CP, 123.
Dvzs RD. Ch e, m. Dvzs CC.

MARSTON BIGOT Som
166 ST 7545 2m SW of Frome. Loc,
Trudoxhill CP. Ch e.

MARSTON GREEN Warwicks
131 SP 1785 3m SW of Coleshill. Loc,
Bickenhill CP. P BIRMINGHAM 37. Ch e, b.
Sch p.

MARSTON MAGNA Som
166, 177 ST 5922 5m NNE of Yeovil.
CP, 337. Yvl RD. P Yvl. Ch e. Yvl CC.

MARSTON MEYSEY Wilts
157 SU 1297 7m ESE of Cirencester.
CP(Mstn Maisey), 178. Cricklade and
Wootton Bassett RD. P Swndn. Ch e.
Chippenham CC.

MARSTON MONTGOMERY Derbys
120 SK 1337 4m NE of Uttoxeter. CP, 274.
Ashbourne RD. P Ashbne. Ch e, m. Sch p.
W Derbys CC.

MARSTON MORETAINE Beds
147 SP 9941 3m NW of Ampthill.
CP, 1,928. Ampthll RD. P BEDFORD.
Ch e, m2, r. Sch p. Mid-Beds CC. See also Lr
Shelton, Upr Shltn. In brickfield area. Ch
has detached twr.

MARSTON ON DOVE Derbys
120 SK 2329 4m N of Burton-on-Trent.
CP, 50. Repton RD. Ch e. Belper CC. Ch
has oldest bell in county (1366), with 'Hail
Mary' inscription.

MARSTON ST LAWRENCE Northants
145 SP 5342 5m E of Banbury. CP, 184.
Brackley RD. P Bnbry, Oxon. Ch e. Sch pe.
Daventry CC (S Nthnts).

MARSTON STANNETT Herefs
129 SO 5755 5m ESE of Leominster. Loc,
Pencombe w Grendon Warren CP.

MARSTON TRUSSELL Northants
133 SP 6985 3m WSW of Mkt Harborough.
CP, 198. Brixworth RD. P Mkt
Hbrghh, Leics. Ch e. Daventry CC
(Kettering).

MARSTOW Herefs
142 SO 5519 4m SW of Ross-on-Wye.
CP, 345. Rss and Whitchurch RD.
Hereford CC. See also Glewstone, Pencraig.

MARSWORTH Bucks
146, 159 SP 9114 2m N of Tring. CP, 570.
Wing RD. P Trng, Herts. Ch e. Sch pe.
Buckingham CC.

MARTEN Wilts
168 SU 2860 6m SW of Hungerford. Loc,
Grafton CP. Marlborough and
Ramsbury RD. Devizes CC.

MARTHALL Ches
101 SJ 7975 3m ESE of Knutsford.
CP, 171. Bucklow RD. Ch e. Kntsfd CC.

MARTHAM Norfolk
126 TG 4518 8m NNW of Yarmouth.
CP, 1,143. Blofield and Flegg RD.
P Gt Ymth. Ch e, b, m. Sch p, s. Ymth CC.

MARTIN Hants
179 SU 0619 6m WNW of Fordingbridge.
CP, 364. Ringwood and Fdngbrdge RD.
P Fdngbrdge. Ch e, m. New Forest CC. See
also Mtn Drove End. Bronze Age earthworks:
Grim's Ditch, Bokerley Dyke.

MARTIN Kent
173 TR 3347 4m NNE of Dover. Loc,
Langdon CP. Dvr RD. P(Mtn Mill Stn), Dvr.
Dvr and Deal CC (Dvr).

MARTIN Lincs (K)
113 TF 1259 5m WSW of Woodhall Spa.
CP, 760. E Kesteven RD. P LINCOLN.
Ch e, m. Sch pe. Grantham CC.

MARTIN Lincs (L)
114 TF 2366 2m SSW of Horncastle. Loc,
Roughton CP. Ch e.

MARTIN DROVE END Hants
167 SU 0521 8m SW of Salisbury. Loc,
Mtn CP.

MARTINHOE Devon
163 SS 6648 3m W of Lynton. CP, 149.
Barnstaple RD. Ch e. N Dvn CC.

MARTIN HUSSINGTREE Worcs
130, 131 SO 8860 2m SSW of Droitwich.
CP, 226. Drtwch RD. Ch e. Worcester BC.

MARTINSCROFT Lancs
101 SJ 6589 3m E of Warrington. Loc,
Woolston CP. Ch m, r.

MARTINSTOWN Dorset
178 SY 6488 3m WSW of Dorchester. Loc,
Winterborne St Martin CP. Dchstr RD.
P Dchstr. Ch m. Sch pe. W Dst CC.

MARTLESHAM Suffolk (E)
150 TM 2547 2m SW of Woodbridge.
CP, 1,521. Deben RD. P Wdbrdge. Ch e.
Sch p. Sudbury and Wdbrdge CC. Red Lion
Inn on A12 rd has red ship's-figurehead sign,
prob 17c. Airfield.

MARTLEY Worcs
130 SO 7559 7m WNW of Worcester.
CP, 949. Mtly RD. P WCSTR. Ch e, v.
Sch pe, s. Kidderminster CC.

MARTOCK Som
177 ST 4619 4m SW of Ilchester. CP, 2,230.
Yeovil RD. P. Ch e, m, v2. Sch ie, je.
Yvl CC. See also Coat, Stapleton. Ch: richly
carved 16c roof. Mdvl Treasurer's Hse. Ggn
tn hall.

MARTON Ches
110 SJ 8568 3m N of Congleton. CP, 236.
Macclesfield RD. P Mcclsfld. Ch e, m.
Sch pe. Mcclsfld CC. 14c ch, largely
wooden. Famous old oak tree.

MARTON Lincs (L)
104 SK 8481 5m SSE of Gainsborough.
CP, 420. Gnsbrgh RD. P Gnsbrgh. Ch e, m.
Sch p. Gnsbrgh CC.

MARTON Shrops
118 SJ 2802 5m ESE of Welshpool. Loc,
Chirbury CP. P Wlshpl, Montgomeryshire.
Ch e, c. Sch ie.

MARTON Shrops
118 SJ 4423 5m WSW of Wem. Loc,
Myddle CP.

MARTON Warwicks
132 SP 4068 5m N of Southam. CP, 412.
Rugby RD. P Rgby. Ch e, c. Sch pe.
Rgby CC.

MARTON Yorks (E)
93 TA 2069 2m NE of Bridlington. Loc,
Brdlngtn MB.

MARTON Yorks (E)
99 TA 1839 6m SSW of Hornsea. Loc,
Burton Constable CP. Ch r. Sch p.

MARTON Yorks (N)
92 SE 7383 4m W of Pickering. CP, 127.
Pckrng RD. P YORK. Ch m. Sch pe.
Scarborough CC (Thirsk and Malton).

MARTON Yorks (W)
91, 97 SE 4162 3m SSE of Boroughbridge.
CP(Mtn cum Grafton), 344. Nidderdale RD.
Ch e. Sch pe. Harrogate CC.

MARTON-IN-THE-FOREST Yorks (N)
92 SE 6068 11m N of York. Loc,
Mtn-cum-Moxby CP. Easingwold RD. Ch e.
Thirsk and Malton CC.

MARTON-LE-MOOR Yorks (N)
91 SE 3770 3m NNW of Boroughbridge.
CP, 154. Wath RD. P Ripon. Ch e, m. Thirsk
and Malton CC.

MARTYR WORTHY Hants
168 SU 5132 3m NE of Winchester. Loc,
Itchen Valley CP. Wnchstr RD. Ch e.
Wnchstr CC.

MARWOOD Devon
163 SS 5437 3m NNW of Barnstaple.
CP, 584. Bnstple RD. P Bnstple. Ch e, m2.
Sch p. N Dvn CC. See also Middle Mwd,
Muddiford. Ch: scrn with part of rood loft.

MARYLEBONE London
160 TQ 2881 2m NW of Charing Cross. See
St Marylebone.

MARYPORT Cumb
81, 82 NY 0336 5m NNE of Workington.
UD, 11,615. P. Wkngtn CC. See also
Flimby. Developed as coal port in 18c but
came to nothing. Sands. To N, Roman fort.

MARYSTOW Devon
175 SX 4382 6m NNW of Tavistock.
CP, 193. Tvstck RD. Ch e. W Dvn CC
(Tvstck).

MARY TAVY Devon
175, 187 SX 5079 4m NNE of Tavistock.
CP, 763. Tvstck RD. P Tvstck. Ch e, m2.
Sch p. W Dvn CC (Tvstck). See also
Horndon. Former mining vllge on edge of
Dartmoor.

MASHAM Yorks (N)
91 SE 2280 8m NW of Ripon. CP, 884.
Mshm RD. P Rpn. Ch e, b, m, r. Sch pe.
Richmond CC. Small mkt tn above R Ure.

blt round large square. Fine ch
mainly 14c–15c.

MASHBURY Essex
148, 161 TL 6511 5m NW of Chelmsford.
CP, 109. Chlmsfd RD. Ch e, s. Braintree CC
(Chlmsfd).

MASON Nthmb
78 NZ 2073 3m E of Ponteland. Loc,
Dinnington CP. Ch m.

MASONGILL Yorks (W)
89 SD 6675 4m SE of Kirkby Lonsdale.
Loc, Thornton in Lnsdle CP.

MASSINGHAM, GREAT Norfolk
125 TF 7922 9m WSW of Fakenham. See
Gt Mssnghm.

MASTIN MOOR Derbys
103 SK 4575 8m ENE of Chesterfield. Loc,
Staveley UD. P Chstrfld.

MATCHING Essex
148, 161 TL 5211 5m ENE of Harlow.
CP, 697. Epping and Ongar RD. Ch e.
Hlw CC (Eppng). See also Mtchng Tye. Rare
15c 'marriage feast' room beside ch.

MATCHING GREEN Essex
148, 161 TL 5311 6m E of Harlow. Loc,
Epping and Ongar RD. P Hlw. Sch pe.
Brentwood and Ongr CC, Hlw CC.
(Chigwell CC, Eppng CC.)

MATCHING TYE Essex
148, 161 TL 5111 3m E of Harlow. Loc,
Mtchng CP. P Hlw. Ch c.

MATFEN Nthmb
77 NZ 0371 5m NNE of Corbridge.
CP, 432. Cstle Ward RD. P NEWCASTLE
UPON TYNE. Ch e, m. Sch p. Hexham CC.
See also Fenwick, Ingoe, Ryal. Ch has spire,
unusual for the district.

MATFIELD Kent
171 TQ 6541 5m ESE of Tonbridge. Loc,
Brenchley CP. P Tnbrdge. Ch e, b. Blt round
large grn with duck pond. 1m N, Crittenden
Hse; gdn* incl several ornamental ponds
formerly iron workings.

MATHON Herefs
143 SO 7345 3m W of Malvern. CP(Mthn
Rural), 345. Ledbury RD. P Mlvn, Worcs.
Ch e. Leominster CC.

MATLASK Norfolk
126 TG 1534 5m S of Sheringham. CP, 195.
Erpingham RD. P NORWICH NOR 21Y.
Ch e, m. N Nflk CC.

MATLOCK Derbys
111 SK 2960 9m SW of Chesterfield.
UD, 19,575. P. W Derbys CC. See also
Bonsall, Brightgate, Cromford, Tansley,
Two Dales, Upr Hackney, Wensley. Spa in
steep-sided limestone section of Derwent,
valley.

MATLOCK BATH Derbys
111 SK 2958 1m S of Matlock. Loc,
Mtlck UD. P Mtlck.

MATTERDALE END Cumb
83 NY 3923 9m SW of Penrith. Loc,
Mttrdle CP. Pnrth RD. Pnrth and the
Border CC.

MATTERSEY Notts
103 SK 6889 5m N of Retford. CP, 878.
E Rtfd RD. P Doncaster, Yorkshire.
Ch e, m. Sch p. Bassetlaw CC. Rems of 12c
priory to E beside R Idle.

MATTINGLEY Hants
169 SU 7357 10m S of Reading. CP, 534.
Hartley Wintney RD. P Basingstoke. Ch e.
Bsngstke CC (Aldershot). See also Hazeley,
Hound Grn. 15c timber-framed ch; rare 17c
altar frontal.

MATTISHALL Norfolk
125 TG 0511 4m ESE of E Dereham.
CP, 940. Mitford and Launditch RD.
P Drhm. Ch e, c, m, v. Sch p. SW Nflk CC.
See also Mttshll Burgh.

MATTISHALL BURGH Norfolk
125 TG 0511 4m ESE of E Dereham. Loc,
Mttshll CP. Ch e. Ch has 18c barrel organ
still in use.

MAUGERSBURY Glos
144 SP 2025 just SE of Stow-on-the-Wold.
CP, 183. N Cotswold RD. Cirencester and
Tewkesbury CC.

MAULDEN Beds
147 TL 0538 1m E of Ampthill. CP, 1,618.
Ampthll RD. P BEDFORD. Ch e, b, m.
Sch p. Mid-Beds CC.

MAULDS MEABURN Westm
83 NY 6216 5m SW of Appleby. Loc,
C r o s b y   R a v e n s w o r t h   C P.
P Penrith, Cumberland. Ch m.

MAUNBY Yorks (N)
91 SE 3586 5m SSW of Northallerton.
CP, 121. Thirsk RD. P Thsk. Ch e, m. Thsk
and Malton CC.

MAUND BRYAN Herefs
142 SO 5650 7m NNE of Hereford. Loc,
Bodenham CP.

MAUTBY Norfolk
126 TG 4812 4m NW of Yarmouth.
CP, 404. Blofield and Flegg RD. Ch e.
Ymth CC. See also Runham, Thrigby.

MAVESYN RIDWARE Staffs
120 SK 0816 3m ESE of Rugeley. CP, 527.
L i c h f i e l d R D.   Ch e.   Lchfld   and
Tamworth CC. See also Hill Rdwre, Pipe
Rdwre. Restored 14c gatehouse of former
mnr hse.

MAVIS ENDERBY Lincs (L)
114 TF 3666 7m ESE of Horncastle.
CP, 81. Spilsby RD. Ch e, m. Hncstle CC.

MAWBRAY Cumb
81, 82 NY 0846 5m SSW of Silloth. Loc,
Holme St Cuthbert CP. P Maryport. Ch m.

MAWDESLEY Lancs
100 SD 4914 6m WSW of Chorley.
CP, 1,128. Chly RD. P Ormskirk. Ch e, m, r.
Sch pe, pm, pr. Chly CC.

MAWGAN Cornwall
189, 190 SW 7025 4m ESE of Helston.
CP (Mgn-in-Meneage), 1,644. Kerrier RD.
P Hlstn.   Ch e.   St Ives CC.   1m SE,
Trelowarren, 15c, ancestral home of the
Vyvyans; on the estate, Halligey fogou.

189, 190 SW 7045 2m N of Redruth. Lc
St Agnes CP. Ch m2.

MAWNAN Cornwall
190 SW 7827 4m SSW of Falmouth.
CP, 999. Kerrier RD. Ch e. Sch pe. Flmth
and Camborne CC.

MAWNAN SMITH Cornwall
190 SW 7728 3m SSW of Falmouth. Loc,
Mnn CP. P Flmth.   Ch m2, r.   To SW,

Glendurgan Hse; grnds* (NT, with wooded valley down to Helford River).

MAXEY Hunts
123 TF 1208 6m E of Stamford. CP, 379. Peterborough RD. P PTRBRGH. Ch e, v. Sch p. Ptrbrgh BC (CC). Nmn ch, by gravel pits.

MAXSTOKE Warwicks
131 SP 2386 3m SE of Coleshill. CP, 277. Meriden RD. Ch e. Mrdn CC. Moated 14c cstle.

MAXWORTHY Cornwall
174 SX 2593 7m NW of Launceston. Loc, N Petherwin CP. P Lncstn. Ch m.

MAYFIELD Staffs
111 SK 1545 1m WSW of Ashbourne. CP, 1,362. Uttoxeter RD. P Ashbne, Derbyshire. Ch e, m. Sch pe. Burton CC. On R Dove. Ch, Nmn and later (Perp twr), is S of vllge, on O.S. sheet 120.

MAYFIELD Sussex (E)
183 TQ 5826 8m S of Tunbridge Wells. CP, 3,344. Uckfield RD. P. Ch e, b, c, r2, v. Sch pe. E Grinstead CC. See also Five Ashes. Attractive vllge. Middle Hse, 16c, and other old hses. RC convent incorporates rems of mdvl palace of Archbishops of Canterbury.

MAYFORD Surrey
169, 170 SU 9956 2m SSW of Woking. Loc, Wkng UD. P Wkng.

MAYPOLE GREEN Norfolk
137 TM 4195 3m N of Beccles. Loc, Toft Monks CP. Ch m.

MEADLE Bucks
159 SP 8005 2m N of Princes Risborough. Loc, Longwick-cum-Ilmer CP.

MEADOWBANK Ches
110 SJ 6568 1m N of Winsford. Loc, Wnsfd UD. P Wnsfd.

MEADOWTOWN Shrops
118 SJ 3101 7m ESE of Welshpool. Loc, Worthen CP. Ch m.

MEAL BANK Westm
89 SD 5495 3m NE of Kendal. Loc, S Westm RD. Westm CC.

MEALSGATE Cumb
82 NY 2042 5m SW of Wigton. Loc, Boltons CP. Wgtn RD. P Carlisle. Ch e, m. Penrith and the Border CC.

MEARBECK Yorks (W)
90 SD 8160 2m S of Settle. Loc, Sttle CP.

MEARE Som
165 ST 4541 3m WNW of Glastonbury. CP, 910. Wells RD. P Glstnbry. Ch e, m, v. Sch p. Wlls CC. See also Westhay. Formerly beside large lake which supplied monks of Glstnbry with fish. Abbot's Fish Hse (A.M.). Site of lake vllge (see also Godney, Ulrome).

MEARE GREEN Som
177 ST 2922 5m ESE of Taunton. Loc, W Hatch CP.

MEARS ASHBY Northants
133 SP 8366 3m W of Wellingborough. CP, 410. Wllngbrgh RD. P NORTHAMPTON. Ch e, m. Sch pe. Wllngbrgh CC.

MEASHAM Leics
120, 121 SK 3312 3m SSW of Ashby de la Zouch. CP, 2,728. Ashby de la Zch RD. P Burton-on-Trent, Staffs. Ch e, b, m, r. Sch je, pr. Loughborough CC.

MEATH GREEN Surrey
170, 182 TQ 2743 4m S of Reigate. Loc, Horley CP. Sch p.

MEATHOP Westm
89 SD 4380 3m NE of Grange-over-Sands. CP(Mthp and Ulpha), 189. S Westm RD. Westm CC.

MEAVY Devon
187 SX 5467 6m SE of Tavistock. CP, 527. Tvstck RD. P Yelverton. Ch e. Sch pe. W Dvn CC (Tvstck). See also Dousland, Hoo Mvy.

MEDBOURNE Leics
133 SP 7993 6m NE of Mkt Harborough. CP, 374. Mkt Hbrgh RD. P Mkt Hbrgh. Ch e, v. Sch pe. Hbrgh CC.

MEDDON Devon
174 SS 2717 8m NNE of Bude. Loc, Hartland CP. Ch m.

MEDMENHAM Bucks
159 SU 8084 3m WSW of Marlow.
CP, 1,241. Wycombe RD. P Mlw. Ch e.
Sch p, pe. Wcmbe CC. Lush Thames-side
place. Fragments of Nmn abbey
incorporated in Jcbn hse.

MEDOMSLEY Co Durham
77, 78 NZ 1154 2m NNE of Consett. Loc,
Cnstt UD. P Cnstt.

MEDSTEAD Hants
168, 169 SU 6537 4m WSW of Alton.
CP, 1,383. Altn RD. P Altn. Ch e. Sch pe.
Petersfield CC. See also Hattingley,
Soldridge, S Tn.

MEERBROOK Staffs
110 SJ 9960 3m N of Leek. Loc,
Leekfrith CP. Lk RD. P Lk. Ch e, m. Lk CC.

MEER END Warwicks
131 SP 2474 6m NNW of Warwick. Loc,
Balsall CP. Meriden RD. Mrdn CC.

MEESDEN Herts
148 TL 4332 7m SE of Royston. CP, 135.
Braughing RD. Ch e. E Herts CC.

MEETH Devon
175 SS 5408 9m NNW of Okehampton.
CP, 133. Okhmptn RD. P Okhmptn. Ch e.
W Dvn CC (Torrington).

MEIRHEATH Staffs
110, 119 SJ 9240 5m SE of Stoke-on-Trent.
Loc, Stone RD. Ch e. Sch i. Stafford and
Stne CC.

MELBOURN Cambs
148 TL 3844 3m NNE of Royston.
CP, 1,832. S Cambs RD. P Rstn, Herts.
Ch e, c. Sch p, s. Cambs CC.

MELBOURNE Derbys
120, 121 SK 3825 7m SSE of Derby.
CP, 3,640. SE Derbys RD. P DBY.
Ch e, b, c, m, r, v. Sch i, j, s. SE Derbys CC.
Large ch with impressive Nmn interior. M.
Hall*, 18c hse with formal gdns*.

MELBOURNE Yorks (E)
97, 98 SE 7544 4m SW of Pocklington.
CP, 420. Pcklngtn RD. P YORK. Ch e, m.
Sch p. Howden CC.

MELBURY ABBAS Dorset
166, 167 ST 8820 2m SE of Shaftesbury.

CP, 293. Shftsbry RD. P Shftsbry. Ch e.
Sch pe. N Dst CC.

MELBURY BUBB Dorset
177, 178 ST 5906 6m SSE of Yeovil.
CP, 80. Sherborne RD. Ch e. W Dst CC.

MELBURY OSMOND Dorset
177, 178 ST 5707 5m S of Yeovil. CP, 251.
Beaminster RD. P Dorchester. Ch e, v.
Sch pe. W Dst CC.

MELBURY SAMPFORD Dorset
177, 178 ST 5706 6m S of Yeovil. CP, 50.
Beaminster RD. Ch e. W Dst CC. Nothing
but the ch and M. Hse*, 16c and later; gdns.

MELCHBOURNE Beds
134 TL 0265 4m E of Rushden.
CP (Mlchbne and Yielden), 342.
Bedford RD. P BEDFORD. Ch e. Bdfd CC.

MELCOMBE REGIS Dorset
178 SY 6880 just N of Weymouth.
MB (Wmth and Mlcmbe Rgs), 42,120.
P(Wmth). S Dst CC. Merged with Wmth
since 17c; now a suburb.

MELDON Devon
175 SX 5692 3m SW of Okehampton. Loc,
Okehamptonn Hmlts CP. Okhmptn RD.
W Dvn CC (Torrington). Extensive quarries
and famous rly viaduct. Reservoir.

MELDON Nthmb
77, 78 NZ 1183 5m WSW of Morpeth.
CP, 250. Mpth RD. Ch e. Mpth CC. See also
Throphill. 13c ch.

MELDRETH Cambs
148 TL 3746 4m NNE of Royston. CP, 893.
S Cambs RD. P Rstn, Herts. Ch e, m. Sch p.
Cambs CC. Ch has good ring of eight bells.

MELKINTHORPE Westm
83 NY 5525 4m SE of Penrith. Loc,
Lowther CP. N Westm RD. Westm CC.

MELKRIDGE Nthmb
77 NY 7363 2m E of Haltwhistle. CP, 235.
Hltwhstle RD. Ch m2. Hexham CC.

MELKSHAM Wilts
166, 167 ST 9063 6m S of Chippenham.
UD, 9,803. P. Westbury CC. Mainly
indstrl. Rubber and associated factories.

MELLING Lancs
89 SD 5971 5m S of Kirkby Lonsdale.
CP(Mllng-w-Wrayton), 180. Lunesdale RD.
Ch e. Sch pe. Lancaster CC.

MELLING Lancs
100 SD 3900 5m NE of Bootle. CP, 1,713.
W Lancs RD. P Maghull, LIVERPOOL.
Ch e, r. Sch p, pe. Ormskirk CC.

MELLIS Suffolk (E)
136 TM 0974 3m W of Eye. CP, 314.
Hartismere RD. P Eye. Ch e, m. Sch pe.
Eye CC. Vast vllge grn.

MELLOR Ches
101 SJ 9888 6m E of Stockport. Loc,
Marple UD. P Stckpt. Transferred from
Derbys 1936. Ch on rocky eminence has
14c plpt carved from single block of oak.

MELLOR Lancs
94, 95 SD 6530 2m NW of Blackburn.
CP, 1,387. Blckbn RD. P Blckbn. Ch e, m.
Sch pe. Darwen CC.

MELLOR BROOK Lancs
94, 95 SD 6431 3m NW of Blackburn. Loc,
Blckbn RD, Preston RD. P Blckbn.
Darwen CC, S Fylde CC.

MELLS Som
166 ST 7249 3m W of Frome. CP, 717.
Frme RD. P Frme. Ch e. Sch pe. Wells CC.
See also Vobster. Ch with 104ft twr beside
Tdr mnr hse. To E, several large prehistoric
camps.

MELMERBY Cumb
83 NY 6137 8m NE of Penrith. Loc,
Ousby CP. P Pnrth. Ch e, m. Sch pe.

MELMERBY Yorks (N)
90 SE 0785 4m SW of Leyburn. CP, 60.
Lbn RD. Ch m. Richmond CC.

MELMERBY Yorks (N)
91 SE 3376 4m NNE of Ripon. CP, 224.
Wath RD. P Rpn. Ch m. Thirsk and
Malton CC.

MELPLASH Dorset
177 SY 4898 4m NNE of Bridport. Loc,
Netherbury CP. P Brdpt. Ch e. M. Ct, Tdr,
once home of Sir Thomas More.

MELSONBY Yorks (N)
85 NZ 1908 5m NNE of Richmond.

CP, 418. Rchmnd RD. P Rchmnd. Ch e, m.
Sch pm. Rchmnd CC.

MELTHAM Yorks (W)
102 SE 1010 5m SW of Huddersfield.
UD, 6,595. P Hddsfld. Colne Valley CC. See
also Wilshaw.

MELTON Suffolk (E)
150 TM 2850 1m NE of Woodbridge.
CP, 2,557. Deben RD. P Wdbrdge. Ch e, v2.
Sch p. Sudbury and Wdbrdge CC. Joined to
Wdbrdge.

MELTON Yorks (E)
98 SE 9726 8m WSW of Hull. Loc,
Welton CP. Ch e.

MELTONBY Yorks (E)
97, 98 SE 7952 2m N of Pocklington. Loc,
Yapham CP. Ch e.

MELTON CONSTABLE Norfolk
125 TG 0433 4m SSW of Holt. CP, 670.
Walsingham RD. P. Ch e. Sch p, s.
NW Nflk CC (N Nflk). Ch: Astley family
pew, 1681. M.C. Hall, late 17c Wren-style
hse in fine grnds with lake.

MELTON, GREAT Norfolk
125 TG 1206 4m NNE of Wymondham. See
Gt Mltn.

MELTON MOWBRAY Leics
122 SK 7519 14m NE of Leicester.
UD, 19,932. P. Mltn CC. Old mkt tn and
hunting centre; many large 19c hses
previously hunting lodges. Fine 13c–14c ch.
Tn is famous for production of Stilton
cheese and pork pies.

MELTON ROSS Lincs (L)
104 TA 0610 5m ENE of Brigg. CP, 212.
Glanford Brgg RD. P Barnetby. Ch e, m.
Sch pe. Brgg and Scunthorpe CC (Brgg). See
also New Barnetby.

MELVERLEY Shrops
118 SJ 3316 9m SSE of Oswestry. CP, 129.
Oswstry RD. Ch e, m. Oswstry CC. See also
Mlvly Grn. Curious half-timbered ch, above
R Vyrnwy.

MELVERLEY GREEN Shrops
118 SJ 3218 8m SSE of Oswestry. Loc,
Mlvrly CP. P Llanymynech, Montgomeryshire.

MEMBURY Devon
177 ST 2703 3m NNW of Axminster.
CP, 491. Axmnstr RD. P Axmnstr. Ch e.
Sch p. Honiton CC.

MENDHAM Suffolk (E)
137 TM 2782 6m SW of Bungay. CP, 378.
Hartismere RD. P Harleston, Norfolk. Ch e.
Sch p. Eye CC. See also Withersdale St.

MENDLESHAM Suffolk (E)
136 TM 1065 5m NE of Stowmarket.
CP, 933. Hartismere RD. P Stmkt. Ch e.
Sch p. Eye CC. See also Mndlshm Grn.

MENDLESHAM GREEN Suffolk (E)
136 TM 0963 4m NE of Stowmarket. Loc,
Mndlshm CP. P Stmkt.

MENHENIOT Cornwall
186 SX 2862 3m SE of Liskeard. CP, 1,095.
Lskd RD. P Lskd. Ch e, m2. Sch pe.
Bodmin CC. See also Merrymeet.

MENSTON Yorks (W)
96 SE 1643 2m WSW of Otley. Loc,
Ilkley UD. P Ilkley. County mental hsptl.

MENTMORE Bucks
146 SP 9019 4m SSW of Leighton Buzzard.
CP, 210. Wing RD. P Lghtn Bzzd, Beds.
Ch e. Buckingham CC. See also Ledburn.
Large 19c mansion in spacious pk.

MEOLE BRACE Shrops
118 SJ 4810 1m SSW of Shrewsbury. Loc,
Shrsbry MB. P Shrsbry. Ch has stained glass
by Morris and Burne-Jones.

MEONSTOKE Hants
168/180 SU 6120 4m ENE of Bishop's
Waltham. CP(Corhampton and
Mnstke), 629. Droxford RD.
P SOUTHAMPTON. Ch e. Sch ie.
Petersfield CC. 2m E, Old Winchester Hill:
Iron Age hill fort, numerous bowl barrows.

MEOPHAM Kent
171 TQ 6466 5m S of Gravesend. CP.
Strood RD. P Grvsnd. Ch e, b, r, v. Sch p.
Grvsnd CC. See also Culverstone Grn,
Harvel. Pronounced 'meppm'. Grn, famous
for cricket, with well preserved smock-mill
(1801).

MEOPHAM STATION Kent
171 TQ 6467 4m S of Gravesend. Loc,
Mphm CP.

MEPAL Cambs
135 TL 4480 4m SE of Chatteris. CP, 441.
Ely RD. P Ely. Ch e, b. Sch pe. Isle
of Ely CC.

MEPPERSHALL Beds
147 TL 1336 5m NNW of Hitchin. CP, 725.
Biggleswade RD. P Shefford. Ch e, m.
Sch pe. Mid-Beds CC.

MERE Ches
101 SJ 7281 3m NW of Knutsford. CP, 661.
Bucklow RD. P Kntsfd. Kntsfd CC.

MERE Wilts
166 ST 8132 7m NNW of Shaftesbury.
CP, 1,920. Mre and Tisbury RD.
Ch e, c2, f, m, r. Sch p, s. Westbury CC.

MERE BROW Lancs
100 SD 4118 5m E of Southport. Loc,
Tarleton CP. P Preston. Ch m2. Sch pe.

MERE CLOUGH Lancs
95 SD 8730 3m ESE of Burnley. Loc,
Cliviger CP. Bnly RD. Clitheroe CC.

MEREWORTH Kent
171 TQ 6653 6m W of Maidstone.
CP, 1,263. Malling RD. P Mdstne. Ch e.
Sch p. Tonbridge and Mllng CC (Sevenoaks).
Vllge rebuilt 18c when old one replaced by
M. Cstle, vast Palladian edifice in finely
wooded pk. Ch reminiscent of
St Martin-in-the-Fields, London.

MERIDEN Warwicks
131 SP 2482 6m WNW of Coventry.
CP, 2,076. Mrdn RD. P Cvntry. Ch e, m.
Sch pe. Mrdn CC. Held by some to be centre
of England.

MERRIOTT Som
177 ST 4412 2m N of Crewkerne.
CP, 1,361. Chard RD. P. Ch e, bc, m, v2.
Sch p. Yeovil CC.

MERRIVALE Devon
175, 187 SX 5475 4m E of Tavistock. Loc,
Whitchurch CP. P(Merrivale Br), Yelverton.

MERRYMEET Cornwall
186 SX 2766 2m ENE of Liskeard. Loc,
Menheniot CP. P Lskd. Ch e, m.

MERSHAM Kent
172, 173, 184 TR 0539 3m SE of Ashford.
CP, 787. E Ashfd RD. P Ashfd. Ch e, m.

Merstham

Sch p. Ashfd CC. NE of vllge, M. Hatch*, 18c mansion blt by Adam for Knatchbull family, now used by Caldecott Community for homeless children.

MERSTHAM Surrey
170 TQ 2953 3m NE of Reigate. Loc, Rgte MB. P Redhill. Ch: brasses; cornerstone from former old London Br.

MERSTON Sussex (W)
181 SU 8903 2m ESE of Chichester. Loc, Oving CP. Ch e.

MERSTONE IOW
180 SZ 5285 3m SSE of Newport. Loc, S Arreton CP. Isle of Wight RD and CC. Ch m.

MERTHER Cornwall
190 SW 8644 2m E of Truro across river. Loc, St Michael Penkevil CP. Ch e, m.

MERTON Devon
163, 175 SS 5212 5m SSE of Torrington. CP, 292. Trrngtn RD. P Okehampton. Ch e, m. Sch pe. W Dvn CC (Trrngtn).

MERTON London
170 TQ 2569 3m S of Wandsworth. LB, 176,524. BCs: Mitcham and Morden, Wimbledon (Mtn and Mdn, Mtchm, Wmbldn). See also Mtchm, Mdn, Motspur Pk, Raynes Pk, Wmbldn.

MERTON Norfolk
136 TL 9098 8m SE of Swaffham. CP. Wayland RD. Ch e. S Nflk CC.

MERTON Oxon
145, 146 SP 5717 3m S of Bicester. CP, 188. Ploughley RD. P Bcstr. Ch e. Mid-Oxon CC (Henley).

MESHAW Devon
163 SS 7519 5m SSE of S Molton. CP, 118. S Mltn RD. P: S Mltn. Ch e, m. N Dvn CC.

MESSING Essex
149, 162 TL 8918 2m N of Tiptree. CP(Mssng-cum-Inworth), 363. Lexden and Winstree RD. P Colchester. Ch e, v. Sch p. Clchstr CC.

MESSINGHAM Lincs (L)
104 SE 8904 4m S of Scunthorpe. CP, 1,436. Glanford Brigg RD. P Scnthpe. Ch e, m. Sch p. Brgg and Scnthpe CC (Brgg).

Water-filled sandpits haunted by gulls. Ch: furnishings and glass filched by 19c rector from other chs.

METFIELD Suffolk (E)
137 TM 2980 6m WNW of Halesworth. CP, 256. Hartismere RD. P Harleston, Norfolk. Ch e, m. Eye CC.

METHERELL Cornwall
187 SX 4069 3m E of Callington. Loc, Calstock CP. P Cllngtn. Ch b.

METHERINGHAM Lincs (K)
113 TF 0661 9m SE of Lincoln. CP, 1,679. N Kesteven RD. P LNCLN. Ch e, m2, v. Sch p. Grantham CC. See also Sots Hole.

METHLEY Yorks (W)
96, 102 SE 3926 5m NE of Wakefield. Loc, Rothwell UD. P LEEDS.

METHWOLD Norfolk
135 TL 7394 6m NNW of Brandon. CP, 1,560. Downham RD. P Thetford. Ch e, m. Sch pe, s. SW Nflk CC. Ch: angel hammerbeam roof; 14c life-size brass.

METHWOLD HYTHE Norfolk
135 TL 7194 7m NW of Brandon. Loc, Mthwld CP. Ch m.

METTINGHAM Suffolk (E)
137 TM 3690 2m E of Bungay. CP, 236. Wainford RD. P Bngy. Ch e. Lowestoft CC. Rems of 14c cstle; gatehouse lone ruin, remainder hidden among farm bldngs.

METTON Norfolk
126 TG 2037 3m SSW of Cromer. Loc, Sustead CP. Ch e.

MEVAGISSEY Cornwall
190 SX 0144 5m S of St Austell. Loc, St Astll w Fowey MB. P St Astll. Truro CC. Double-harboured fishing vllge; canning, tourism. Folk museum on E Quay.

MEXBOROUGH Yorks (W)
103 SK 4799 5m NNE of Rotherham. UD, 15,946. P. Dearne Valley CC. Colliery tn.

MEYSEY HAMPTON Glos
157 SU 1199 6m ESE of Cirencester. CP(Maiseyhampton), 327. Crncstr RD. P Crncstr. Ch e, b. Sch pe. Crncstr and Tewkesbury CC.

MICHAELCHURCH Herefs
142 SO 5225 5m W of Ross-on-Wye.
CP(Tretire w Mchlchch), 79. Rss and
Whitchurch RD. Ch e. Hereford CC. Tiny
ch: Roman altar used as holy water stoup;
traces of 13c wall-paintings.

MICHAELCHURCH ESCLEY Herefs
142 SO 3134 13m WSW of Hereford.
CP, 185. Dore and Bredwardine RD.
P HRFD. Ch e, m. Sch p. Hrfd CC. Ch has
wall-paintings of Christ of the Trades, a rare
subject.

MICHAELSTOW Cornwall
185, 186 SX 0878 3m SSW of Camelford.
CP, 204. Cmlfd RD. Ch e, m2. Sch p.
N Cnwll CC. See also Treveighan.

MICHELDEVER Hants
168 SU 5139 6m NNE of Winchester.
CP, 1,091. Wnchstr RD. P Wnchstr.
Ch e, m2. Sch p. Wnchstr CC. See also
E Stratton.

MICHELMERSH Hants
168 SU 3425 3m N of Romsey. CP, 645.
Rmsy and Stockbridge RD. P Rmsy. Ch e.
Eastleigh CC. See also Timsbury.

MICKFIELD Suffolk (E)
136 TM 1361 6m ENE of Stowmarket.
CP, 140. Gipping RD. P Stmkt. Ch e, v.
Eye CC.

MICKLEBRING Yorks (W)
103 SK 5194 6m E of Rotherham. Loc,
Braithwell CP.

MICKLEBY Yorks (N)
86 NZ 8013 6m WNW of Whitby. CP, 127.
Whtby RD. P Saltburn-by-the-Sea. Ch c.
Cleveland and Whtby CC (Scarborough and
Whtby).

MICKLEFIELD Yorks (W)
97 SE 4432 5m N of Castleford. CP, 1,860.
Tadcaster RD. P LEEDS. Ch e, m. Sch pe.
Barkston Ash CC.

MICKLEHAM Surrey
170 TQ 1753 2m S of Leatherhead. Loc,
Dorking UD. P Dkng. Mole valley vllge with
bypass, below N Downs. To S, Juniper Hall
(NT), field study centre.

MICKLETON Glos
144 SP 1643 3m NNE of Chipping
Campden. CP, 940. N Cotswold RD.
P Chppng Cmpdn. Ch e, m. Sch p.
Cirencester and Tewkesbury CC. Medford
Hse, late 17c, in Ctswld stone.

MICKLETON Yorks (N)
84 NY 9623 2m SE of Middleton in
Teesdale. CP, 405. Startforth RD. P Barnard
Cstle, Co Durham. Ch m2. Sch pe.
Richmond CC.

MICKLE TRAFFORD Ches
109 SJ 4469 3m NE of Chester. CP.
Chstr RD. P CHSTR. Ch m. Sch p. City
of Chstr CC.

MICKLEY Yorks (W)
91 SE 2576 5m NW of Ripon. Loc,
Azerley CP. P Rpn. Ch e, m.

MICKLEY SQUARE Nthmb
77, 78 NZ 0762 1m WSW of Prudhoe. Loc,
Prdhoe UD. P Stocksfield.

MIDDLE ASTON Oxon
145 SP 4727 7m WNW of Bicester. CP, 82.
Banbury RD. Bnbry CC.

MIDDLE BARTON Oxon
145 SP 4325 6m N of Woodstock. Loc,
Steeple Btn CP. P OXFORD. Ch m. Sch p.

MIDDLE CHINNOCK Som
177 ST 4713 3m NE of Crewkerne. Loc,
W Chinnock CP. Ch e.

MIDDLE CLAYDON Bucks
146 SP 7225 6m SSE of Buckingham.
CP, 177. Bcknghm RD. P Bletchley. Ch e.
Bcknghm CC. C. Hse (NT)*, 18c, with
gdns*.

MIDDLE DUNTISBOURNE Glos
157 SO 9806 4m NW of Cirencester. Loc,
Dntsbne Rouse CP. Farm, cottages, ford.

MIDDLEHAM Yorks (N)
91 SE 1287 2m SSE of Leyburn. CP, 663.
Lbn RD. P Lbn. Ch e, m2. Sch pe.
Richmond CC. Extensive rems of 12c—15c
cstle (A.M.). 1½m SW, Braithwaite Hall
(NT)*, 17c hse now farm. Racing stables.

MIDDLE HANDLEY Derbys
103 SK 4078 6m NE of Chesterfield. Loc,
Unstone CP. P SHEFFIELD.

MIDDLE LAMBROOK Som
177 ST 4218 5m NE of Ilminster. See Mid Lambrook.

MIDDLE LITTLETON Worcs
144 SP 0747 3m NE of Evesham. CP(N and Mddle Lttltn), 601. Eveshm RD. Ch e. S Worcs CC.

MIDDLE MAES-COED Herefs
142 SO 3333 11m WSW of Hereford. Loc, Newton CP.

MIDDLEMARSH Dorset
178 ST 6706 6m SSE of Sherborne. Loc, Minterne Magna CP. Ch m.

MIDDLE MARWOOD Devon
163 SS 5338 4m NNW of Barnstaple. Loc, Mrwd CP.

MIDDLE RASEN Lincs (L)
104 TF 0989 1m W of Mkt Rasen. CP, 916. Caistor RD. P Mkt Rsn. Ch e, m. Sch p. Gainsborough CC.

MIDDLESBROUGH Yorks (N)
85 NZ 4920 13m ENE of Darlington. Loc, Teesside CB. P(MDDLSBRGH, Tssde). Tssde, Mddlsbrgh BC. Iron and steel mnfg tn developed on rectangular plan in 19c. Transporter br over R Tees, largest of its type in the world.

MIDDLESMOOR Yorks (W)
90 SE 0974 7m NW of Pateley Br. Loc, Stonebeck Up CP. Ripon and Ptly Br RD. P Harrogate. Ch e, m. Sch pe. Rpn CC.

MIDDLES, THE Co Durham
78 NZ 2051 4m W of Chester-le-Street. Loc, Stanley UD. P Craghead, Stnly.

MIDDLESTONE Co Durham
85 NZ 2531 1m S of Spennymoor. Loc, Bishop Auckland UD.

MIDDLESTONE MOOR Co Durham
85 NZ 2432 just SW of Spennymoor. Loc, Spnnmr UD. P Spnnmr.

MIDDLE STOUGHTON Som
165 ST 4249 3m SW of Cheddar. Loc, Wedmore CP.

MIDDLESTOWN Yorks (W)
96, 102 SE 2617 5m WSW of Wakefield. Loc, Sitlington CP. Wkfld RD. P Wkfld. Ch e, m. Sch p. Wkfld BC.

MIDDLE TAPHOUSE Cornwall
186 SX 1763 5m W of Liskeard. Loc, Broadoak CP.

MIDDLE TEMPLE London
160 TR 3180 just ENE of Charing Cross. See Temples, Inner and Middle.

MIDDLETON Derbys
111 SK 1963 3m SSW of Bakewell. CP(Mddltn and Smerrill), 151. Bkwll RD. Ch e, v. Sch pe. W Derbys CC.

MIDDLETON Derbys
111 SK 2756 3m SSW of Matlock. Loc, Wirksworth UD. P DERBY.

MIDDLETON Essex
149 TL 8739 1m S of Sudbury. CP, 101. Halstead RD. Ch e. Saffron Walden CC.

MIDDLETON Hants
168 SU 4243 4m ESE of Andover. Loc, Longparish CP. Ch e.

MIDDLETON Herefs
129 SO 5469 3m WNW of Tenbury Wells. Loc, Lit Hereford CP. Ch m.

MIDDLETON Lancs
94 SD 4258 4m S of Morecambe. CP, 547. Lancaster RD. P Mcmbe. Ch m. Lncstr CC.

MIDDLETON Lancs
101 SD 8605 5m NNE of Manchester. MB, 53,419. P MNCHSTR. Mddltn and Prestwich BC (CC). See also Birch, Rhodes, Slattocks, Top of Hebers. Large ch in dominating position. 17c half-timbered inn, The Boar's Head. Industries incl tobacco, foam-rubber, textiles.

MIDDLETON Norfolk
124 TF 6616 4m SE of King's Lynn. CP, 976. Freebridge Lynn RD. P K's Lnn. Ch e. Sch pe. NW Nflk CC (K's Lnn). See also Blackborough End.

MIDDLETON Northants
133 SP 8389 4m W of Corby. CP. Kettering RD. Ch c. Kttrng CC.

MIDDLETON Nthmb
64, 71 NU 1035 1m NNW of Belford. CP, 233. Blfd RD. Berwick-upon-Tweed CC. See also Detchant, Elwick, Ross.

MIDDLETON Nthmb
77, 78 NZ 0685 9m W of Morpeth. Loc,
Wallington Demesne CP. Mpth RD. P Mpth.
Ch v. Mpth CC.

MIDDLETON Shrops
129 SO 2999 5m ENE of Montgomery. Loc,
Chirbury CP. Ch e.

MIDDLETON Shrops
129 SO 5377 2m NE of Ludlow. Loc,
Bitterley CP. P Ldlw. Ch e.

MIDDLETON Suffolk (E)
137 TM 4267 4m NE of Saxmundham.
CP, 410. Blyth RD. P Sxmndhm. Ch e, m.
Sch p. Eye CC.

MIDDLETON Warwicks
131 SP 1798 4m ENE of Sutton Coldfield.
CP. Meriden RD. P Tamworth, Staffs. Ch e.
Sch p. Mrdn CC.

MIDDLETON Yorks (N)
86, 92 SE 7885 1m NW of Pickering.
CP, 225. Pckrng RD. P Pckrng. Ch e, m.
Scarborough CC (Thirsk and Malton).

MIDDLETON Yorks (W)
96 SE 1249 1m NNE of Ilkley. CP, 389.
Wharfedale RD. Ripon CC.

MIDDLETON CHENEY Northants
145 SP 4941 3m ENE of Banbury.
CP, 1,784. Brackley RD. P Bnbry, Oxon.
Ch e, b, m. Sch p. Daventry CC (S Nthnts).
See also Overthorpe. Ch has windows by
various pre-Raphaelites.

MIDDLETON GREEN Staffs
110, 119 SJ 9935 5m SSW of Cheadle. Loc,
Leigh CP. Uttoxeter RD. Sch pe.
Burton CC.

MIDDLETON IN TEESDALE Co Durham
84 NY 9425 8m NW of Barnard Cstle.
CP, 1,539. Bnd Cstle RD. P Bnd Cstle.
Ch e, m2, r. Sch p, s. Bishop Auckland CC.
Modern ch has detached 16c belfry.

MIDDLETON ONE ROW Co Durham
85 NZ 3512 4m ESE of Darlington. Loc,
Mddltn St George CP. P Dlngtn. Ch v.

MIDDLETON-ON-SEA Sussex (W)
181, 182 SU 9700 3m E of Bognor.
CP, 2,623. Chichester RD. P Bgnr Regis.

Ch e. Arundel CC (Chchstr). See also
Ancton.

MIDDLETON ON THE HILL Herefs
129 SO 5464 4m NE of Leominster. CP,
224. Lmnstr and Wigmore RD. Ch e.
Lmnstr CC. See also Layster's Pole, Miles
Hope.

MIDDLETON-ON-THE-WOLDS Yorks (E)
98 SE 9449 7m NE of Mkt Weighton.
CP(Mddltn), 494. Driffield RD. P Drffld.
Ch e, m. Sch pe. Howden CC. 3m SW on
Mddltn Wld, possibly oldest racecourse in
England.

MIDDLETON PRIORS Shrops
129, 130 SO 6290 6m WSW of Bridgnorth.
Loc, Ditton Priors CP. Ch r.

MIDDLETON QUERNHOW Yorks (N)
91 SE 3378 5m NNE of Ripon. CP, 70.
Wath RD. Thirsk and Malton CC.

MIDDLETON ST GEORGE Co Durham
85 NZ 3412 4m ESE of Darlington.
CP, 2,337. Dlngtn RD. P Dlngtn. Ch e, m.
Sch p. Bishop Auckland CC (Sedgefield).
See also Mddltn One Row, W Mddltn.

MIDDLETON SCRIVEN Shrops
130 SO 6887 4m SSW of Bridgnorth.
CP, 76. Brdgnth RD. P Brdgnth. Ch e.
Ludlow CC.

MIDDLETON STONEY Oxon
145 SP 5323 3m WNW of Bicester. CP, 242.
Ploughley RD. P Bcstr. Ch e. Banbury CC
(Henley).

MIDDLETON TYAS Yorks (N)
85 NZ 2205 5m NE of Richmond. CP, 477.
Rchmnd RD. P Rchmnd. Ch e, m. Sch pe.
Rchmnd CC.

MIDDLE TOWN St Martin's, Isles of Scilly
189 SV 9216. Loc, St Mtn's CP.

MIDDLE TYSOE Warwicks
145 SP 3344 8m WNW of Banbury. Loc,
Tysoe CP. Shipston on Stour RD.
P(Tysoe), WARWICK. Ch e, m, v. Sch pe.
Stratford-on-Avon CC (Strtfd).

MIDDLE WALLOP Hants
168 SU 2937 7m SW of Andover. Loc,
Romsey and Stockbridge RD. P Stckbrdge.
Winchester CC.

MIDDLEWICH Ches
110 SJ 7066 6m SE of Northwich.
UD, 7,783. P. Nantwich CC. One of the
county's salt tns. Salt is extracted from
brine springs.

MIDDLE WINTERSLOW Wilts
167 SU 2333 6m ENE of Salisbury. Loc,
Wntrslw CP. Ch v.

MIDDLE WOODFORD Wilts
167 SU 1136 4m NNW of Salisbury. Loc,
Wdfd CP. Amesbury RD. P(Wdfd), Slsbry.
Ch e. Sch pe. Slsbry CC.

MIDDLEWOOD GREEN Suffolk (E)
136 TM 0961 3m ENE of Stowmarket. Loc,
Stonham Earl CP. Gipping RD.. Eye CC.

MIDDLEZOY Som
165 ST 3733 5m ESE of Bridgwater.
CP, 533. Brdgwtr RD. P Brdgwtr. Ch e, m.
Sch p. Brdgwtr CC.

MIDDRIDGE Co Durham
85 NZ 2556 3m SE of Bishop Auckland.
Loc, Shildon UD. P Shldn.

MIDFORD Som
166 ST 7560 3m S of Bath. Loc,
Southstoke CP. Ch m. To W, M. Cstle, 18c.
Shape said to represent ace of clubs by
which owner scored great gambling success.

MIDGE HALL Lancs
94 SD 5123 4m SSW of Preston. Loc,
Leyland UD. P Prstn.

MIDGEHOLME Cumb
76 NY 6458 7m ESE of Brampton. CP, 114.
Border RD. Penrith and the Bdr CC.

MIDGHAM Berks
158 SU 5567 5m E of Newbury. CP, 365.
Nbry RD. Ch e. Nbry CC.

MIDGLEY Yorks (W)
96, 102 SE 0326 4m W of Halifax. Loc,
Sowerby Br UD. P Hlfx.

MIDHOPESTONES Yorks (W)
102 SK 2399 2m SSW of Penistone. Loc,
Bradfield CP. P SHEFFIELD. Ch e. Large
reservoir for Shffld.

MIDHURST Sussex (W)
181 SU 8821 8m S of Haslemere. CP, 1,880.
Mdhst RD. P. Ch e, m, r. Sch pe, s.

Chichester CC (Horsham). Twisty tn in
Rother valley N of Downs. Ruins of
Cowdray Hse*, burnt in 1793. Modern hse
nearby. Polo and golf in pk.

MID LAMBROOK Som
177 ST 4218 5m NE of Ilminster. Loc,
Kingsbury Episcopi CP. Ch v.

MID LAVANT Sussex (W)
181 SU 8508 3m N of Chichester. Loc,
Lvnt CP. Chchstr RD. P(Lvnt), Chchstr.
Ch e. Chchstr CC.

MIDSOMER NORTON Som
166 ST 6654 8m NW of Frome.
UD(Norton-Radstock), 15,232. P Bath.
N Som CC. See also Clandown,
Writhlington. In N Som coalfield.

MIDVILLE Lincs (L)
114 TF 3857 9m NNE of Boston. CP, 244.
Spilsby RD. Ch e. Horncastle CC.

MILBORNE PORT Som
178 ST 6718 3m NE of Sherborne.
CP, 1,570. Wincanton RD. P Shbne, Dorset.
Ch e, m, v. Sch je, p. Wells CC. See also
Mlbne Wick.

MILBORNE ST ANDREW Dorset
178 SY 8097 8m ENE of Dorchester.
CP, 526. Blandford RD. P Blndfd Forum.
Ch e, m. Sch p. N Dst CC.

MILBORNE WICK Som
166 ST 6620 3m NNE of Sherborne. Loc,
Milborne Port CP.

MILBOURNE Nthmb
77, 78 NZ 1175 3m WNW of Ponteland.
Loc, Pntlnd CP. Ch m.

MILBURN Westm
83 NY 6529 6m NNW of Appleby. CP, 175.
N Westm RD. P Penrith, Cumberland.
Ch e, m. Sch p. Westm CC.

MILBURY HEATH Glos
155, 156 ST 6690 6m E of Severn Rd Br.
Loc, Thornbury CP. Ch m.

MILCOMBE Oxon
145 SP 4134 5m SW of Banbury. CP, 415.
Bnbry RD. P Bnbry. Ch e, b. Bnbry CC.

MILDEN Suffolk (W)
149 TL 9546 3m SE of Lavenham. CP, 129.
Cosford RD. Ch e. Sudbury and
Woodbridge CC.

MILDENHALL Suffolk (W)
135 TL 7174 8m NNE of Newmarket.
CP, 7,132. Mldnhll RD. P Bury St Edmunds.
Ch e, b, m. Sch p2, pe, s. Bury St Eds CC.
See also Beck Row, Holywell Row,
Kennyhill, Thistley Grn, W Row. Small mkt
tn on edge of Fens. EE to Perp ch: 113ft
twr, angel roof. 'Mldnhll Treasure' found
1946, now in British Museum. Airfield
to NW.

MILDENHALL Wilts
157 SU 2169 1m ENE of Marlborough.
CP, 421. Mlbrgh and Ramsbury RD.
P Mlbrgh. Ch e. Devizes CC. Mdvl ch with
Ggn Gothic furnishings.

MILEBUSH Kent
172, 184 TQ 7545 6m S of Maidstone. Loc,
Marden CP.

MILE ELM Wilts
157 ST 9969 1m S of Calne. Loc, Clne
Without CP. Clne and Chippenham RD.
Chppnhm CC.

MILE END Essex
149 TL 9927 2m N of Colchester. Loc,
Clchstr MB. P Clchstr.

MILEHAM Norfolk
125 TF 9119 6m NW of E Dereham.
CP, 341. Mitford and Launditch RD.
P King's Lynn. Ch e, m. Sch p. SW Nflk CC.

MILES GREEN Staffs
110 SJ 8049 4m NW of
Newcastle-under-Lyme. Loc, Audley
Rural CP. Ch m.

MILES HOPE Herefs
129 SO 5764 3m SW of Tenbury Wells. Loc,
Middleton on the Hill CP.

MILFIELD Nthmb
64, 71 NT 9333 5m NW of Wooler. CP, 268.
Glendale RD. P Wlr. Ch m. Sch p.
Berwick-upon-Tweed CC.

MILFORD Derbys
111 SK 3545 1m S of Belper. Loc, Blpr UD.
P DERBY. Prosperity dates from c 1780
when Jedediah Strutt blt cotton mills.

MILFORD Staffs
119 SJ 9721 4m ESE of Stafford. Loc,
Baswich CP. P STFFD.

MILFORD Surrey
169 SU 9442 2m SW of Godalming. Loc,
Witley CP. P Gdlmng. Ch e, c. Sch i, pe.

MILFORD-ON-SEA Hants
180 SZ 2891 4m SW of Lymington. Loc,
Lmngtn MB. P Lmngtn. Resort and rsdntl
tn. 13c ch. 2m SE along narrow shingle
bank, Hurst Cstle (A.M.), coastal defence
cstle blt by Henry VIII; Charles I
imprisoned there, 1648.

MILKWALL Glos
155, 156 SO 5809 5m ESE of Monmouth.
Loc, W Dean CP. W Dn RD. P Coleford.
W Glos CC.

MILLAND Sussex (W)
169, 181 SU 8328 5m SW of Haslemere.
Loc, Trotton CP. P Liphook. Ch e.

MILL BANK Yorks (W)
96, 102 SE 0321 4m SW of Halifax. Loc,
Sowerby Br UD. P Triangle, Hlfx.

MILLBRIDGE Surrey
169 SU 8442 3m S of Farnham. Loc,
Frensham CP.

MILLBROOK Beds
147 TL 0138 1m W of Ampthill. CP, 145.
Ampthll RD. Ch e, m. Sch p. Mid-Beds CC.

MILLBROOK Cornwall
187 SX 4252 2m SSW of Torpoint.
CP, 1,600. St Germans RD.
P Plymouth, Devon. Ch e, m. Sch pe.
Bodmin CC.

MILL COMMON Suffolk (E)
137 TM 4181 3m NNE of Halesworth. Loc,
Westhall CP. P Hlswth.

MILLCORNER Sussex (E)
184 TQ 8223 6m WNW of Rye. Loc,
Northiam CP.

MILL END Bucks
159 SU 7885 2m NE of Henley. Loc,
Hambleden CP.

MILL END Herts
147 TL 3332 5m SSW of Royston. Loc,
Sandon CP.

MILLER'S DALE Derbys
111 SK 1473 5m E of Buxton. Loc,
Tideswell CP. Ch e. Steep-sided valley of
R Wye; limestone cliffs.

MILL GREEN Essex
161 TL 6301 5m NE of Brentwood. Loc,
Ingatestone and Fryering CP. P Ingtstne.
Ch v.

MILLHALF Herefs
141 SO 2748 5m NE of Hay-on-Wye. Loc,
Whitney CP.

MILLHEAD Lancs
89 SD 4971 just N of Carnforth. Loc,
Warton CP.

MILL HILL London
160 TQ 2292 9m NW of Charing Cross. Loc,
Barnet LB. Hendon N BC. Boys' public sch.

MILLHOLME Westm
89 SD 5690 3m ESE of Kendal. Loc, New
Hutton CP.

MILLHOUSE Yorks (W)
102 SE 2203 2m W of Penistone. Loc,
Pnstne UD. P(Mllhse Grn), SHEFFIELD.

MILLINGTON Yorks (E)
98 SE 8351 3m NE of Pocklington.
CP, 188. Pcklngtn RD. P YORK. Ch e, m.
Howden CC. See also Gt Givendale.

MILL LANE Hants
169 SU 7850 4m NW of Farnham. Loc,
Crondall CP.

MILLMEECE Staffs
110, 119 SJ 8333 4m W of Stone. Loc,
Eccleshall CP.

MILLOM Cumb
88 SD 1780 27m SSE of Whitehaven.
CP, 7,955. Mllm RD. P. Ch e, b, m, r, s, v3.
Sch i, pb, pg, pr, s. Whthvn CC. See also
Haverigg. Rems of cstle. There are large
ironworks.

MILLPOOL Cornwall
186 SX 1270 4m NE of Bodmin. Loc,
Cardinham CP. Ch m.

MILL STREET Norfolk
125 TG 0118 5m NE of E Dereham. Loc,
Swanton Morley CP.

MILLTHROP Yorks (W)
89 SD 6691 just S of Sedbergh. Loc,
Sdbgh CP. Ch m.

MILLTOWN Derbys
111 SK 3561 4m E of Matlock. Loc,
Ashover CP. P Ashovr, Chesterfield. Ch m.

MILLWALL London
161, 171 TQ 3779 3m ESE of Lndn Br.

Loc, Twr Hmlts LB. Stepney and Poplar BC
(Pplr). On the Isle of Dogs, qv. Docks.

MILNROW Lancs
101 SD 9212 2m E of Rochdale.
UD, 10,329. P Rchdle. Heywood and
Royton CC. See also Firgrove, New Hey.

MILNTHORPE Westm
89 SD 4981 7m S of Kendal. CP, 1,675.
S Westm RD. P. Ch e, m, r. Sch p, s.
Westm CC.

MILSON Shrops
129, 130 SO 6373 4m NE of Tenbury Wells.
CP, 73. Ludlow RD. P Kidderminster,
Worcs. Ch e. Ldlw CC.

MILSTEAD Kent
172 TQ 9058 3m S of Sittingbourne.
CP, 179. Swale RD. P Sttngbne. Ch e.
Sch pe. Faversham CC.

MILSTON Wilts
167 SU 1645 3m N of Amesbury. CP, 251.
Amesbury RD. Ch e. Salisbury CC. In Army
dominated area.

MILTON Berks
158 SU 4892 3m NW of Didcot. CP, 888.
Abingdon RD. P Abngdn. Ch e, m, r.
Sch pe. Abngdn CC. See also Mltn Hill. M.
Mnr*, 17c hse with walled gdn.

MILTON Cambs
135 TL 4762 3m NNE of Cambridge.
CP, 857. Chesterton RD. P CMBRDGE.
Ch e, b. Sch pe. Cambs CC. Virtually suburb
of Cmbrdge.

MILTON Cumb
76 NY 5560 2m ESE of Brampton. Loc,
Brmptn CP. Ch m.

MILTON Derbys
120, 121 SK 3226 5m ENE of
Burton-on-Trent. Loc, Repton CP.
P DERBY.

MILTON Northants
133 SP 7355 3m S of Northampton.
CP(Mltn Malsor), 658. Nthmptn RD.
P NTHMPTN. Ch e, b, m. Sch pe.
Daventry CC (S Nthnts).

MILTON Notts
112 SK 7173 5m S of Retford. Loc,
W Markham CP. Ch e.

MILTON Oxon
145 SP 4535 3m S of Banbury. CP, 203.
Bnbry RD. P Bnbry. Ch e. Bnbry CC.

MILTON Wilts
166 ST 8731 5m N of Shaftesbury. Loc,
E Knoyle CP.

MILTON ABBAS Dorset
178 ST 8001 6m WSW of Blandford.
CP, 558. Blndfd RD. P Blndfd Forum.
Ch e, m. Sch pe. N Dst CC. 18c vllge blt by
Earl of Dorchester; he considered former
one too near his hse, now itself part of Mltn
Abbey Sch. 14c—15c abbey ch* alongside.

MILTON ABBOT Devon
175, 187 SX 4079 6m NW of Tavistock.
CP, 614. Tvstck RD. P Tvstck. Ch e, m.
Sch p. W Dvn CC (Tvstck). See also
Chillaton.

MILTON BRYAN Beds
147 SP 9730 6m NNW of Dunstable.
CP, 146. Ampthill RD. P Bletchley Bucks.
Ch e. Sch pe. Mid-Beds CC. Also known as
M. Bryant. Bthplce of Paxton, designer of
Crystal Palace, London, for the Great
Exhibition of 1851.

MILTON CLEVEDON Som
166 ST 6637 2m NW of Bruton. CP, 91.
Shepton Mallet RD. Ch e. Wells CC.

MILTONCOMBE Devon
187 SX 4866 5m S of Tavistock. Loc,
Buckland Monachorum CP. P Yelverton.
Ch m.

MILTON DAMEREL Devon
174 SS 3810 5m NNE of Holsworthy.
CP, 388. Hlswthy RD. P Hlswthy. Ch e, m2.
Sch p. W Dvn CC (Tavistock).

MILTON ERNEST Beds
134 TL 0156 4m NNW of Bedford. CP, 373.
Bdfd RD. P BDFD. Ch e, m. Sch pe.
Bdfd CC.

MILTON, GREAT Oxon
158 SP 6202 8m ESE of Oxford. See
Gt Mltn.

MILTON GREEN Ches
109 SJ 4658 6m SE of Chester. Loc,
Handley CP.

MILTON HILL Berks
158 SU 4790 3m W of Didcot. Loc,
Mltn CP. Sch p.

MILTON KEYNES Bucks
146 SP 8839 3m S of Newport Pagnell.
CP, 159. Npt Pgnll RD. P Npt Pgnll. Ch e.
Buckingham CC. Large new tn development.
(Pop. 1971: 46,473.)

MILTON LILBOURNE Wilts
167 SU 1960 2m E of Pewsey. CP, 513.
Psy RD. P Psy. Ch e, m. Sch p. Devizes CC.

MILTON ON STOUR Dorset
166 ST 8028 1m NNW of Gillingham. Loc,
Gllnghm CP. P Gllnghm. Ch e. Sch pe.

MILTON-UNDER-WYCHWOOD Oxon
144 SP 2618 4m N of Burford. CP, 953.
Chipping Norton RD. P OXFORD.
Ch e, b2, m. Sch p. Banbury CC.

MILVERTON Som
164 ST 1225 3m N of Wellington.
CP, 1,426. Wllngtn RD. P Tntn. Ch e, c, m.
Sch p. Tntn CC. Ch: carved bench-ends.

MILWICH Staffs
110, 119 SJ 9732 5m ESE of Stone.
CP, 412. Stne RD. P STAFFORD. Ch e.
Sch p. Stffd and Stne CC. See also Coton,
Garshall Grn.

MINCHINHAMPTON Glos
156 SO 8700 3m SSE of Stroud. CP, 4,318.
Strd RD. P Strd. Ch e, b, m. Strd CC. See
also Amberley, Box, Hyde. A 'wool' vllge.
To N, M. Cmmn (NT).

MINDRUM Nthmb
64, 70 NT 8432 4m S of Coldstream. Loc,
Carham CP. P.

MINEHEAD Som
164 SS 9746 21m NW of Taunton.
UD, 8,063. P. Bridgwater CC. Resort with
extensive sands, small harbour, holiday
camp. Approached by precipitous rds.

MINETY Wilts
157 SU 0290 6m ENE of Malmesbury.
CP, 790. Mlmsbry RD. P Mlmsbry.
Ch e, b, m. Sch pe. Chippenham CC. See
also Upr Mnty.

MININGSBY Lincs (L)
114 TF 3264 5m SE of Horncastle. CP, 55.
Hncstle RD. Ch e. Hncstle CC.

MINIONS Cornwall
186 SX 2671 4m N of Liskeard. Loc,
Linkinhorne CP. P Lskd. Ch m. To W, The
Hurlers, three stone circles. 1m N, The
Cheesewring, curious granite pile.

MINSKIP Yorks (W)
91 SE 3864 1m SSW of Boroughbridge.
Loc, Brghbrdge CP. P YORK. Ch m.

MINSTEAD Hants
180 SU 2811 8m SW of Romsey. CP, 792.
New Forest RD. P Lyndhurst. Ch e.
NW Frst CC. See also Newtown, Stoney
Cross.

MINSTER Kent
172 TQ 9573 7m NNE of Sittingbourne.
Loc, Queenborough-in-Sheppey MB. On a
ridge; sea to N, flat plain to S. Ch has 14c
brasses.

MINSTER Kent
173 TR 3064 5m W of Ramsgate.
CP, 2,703. Eastry RD. P Rmsgte.
Ch e, m, r, s. Sch pe. Thanet W BC (Isle of
Thnt CC). Overshadowed by Richborough
Power Stn. Abbey Hse* dates partly
from 11c.

MINSTERACRES Nthmb
77 NZ 0255 6m NW of Consett. Loc,
Healey CP. Ch r.

MINSTERLEY Shrops
118 SJ 3705 9m WSW of Shrewsbury.
CP, 909. Atcham RD. P Shrsbry. Ch e, m, v.
Sch p. Shrsbry CC. See also Ploxgreen.
Maidens' garlands in late 17c ch.

MINSTER LOVELL Oxon
145 SP 3111 3m WNW of Witney. CP, 708.
Wtny RD. P OXFORD. Ch e, m2. Sch pe.
Mid-Oxon CC (Banbury). See also
Charterville Allotments. Cotswold vllge on
R Windrush. 15c Old Swan Inn. Perp ch:
tomb in S transept. Ruins of 15c mnr
hse (A.M.).

MINSTERWORTH Glos
143 SO 7717 4m W of Gloucester. CP, 497.
Glcstr RD. P GLCSTR. Ch e, m. Sch pe.
W Glos CC.

MINTERNE MAGNA Dorset
178 ST 6504 8m S of Sherborne. CP, 217.
Dorchester RD. Ch e. W Dst CC. See also
Middlemarsh. Ch: monmts.

MINTING Lincs (L)
113 TF 1873 5m NW of Horncastle.
CP, 173. Hncstle RD. P Hncstle. Ch e.
Hncstle CC.

MIREHOUSE Cumb
82 NX 9815 2m SSE of Whitehaven. Loc,
Whthvn MB. P Whthvn.

MIRFIELD Yorks (W)
96, 102 SE 2019 3m WSW of Dewsbury.
UD, 16,871. P. Dsbry BC. See also Upr
Hopton. Indstrl tn. College of the
Community of the Resurrection is here.

MISERDEN Glos
157 SO 9308 7m NW of Cirencester.
CP, 451. Stroud RD. P Strd. Ch e. Sch pe.
Strd CC. See also Camp, Sudgrove,
Whiteway. Misarden Pk, partly Tdr; gdns*.

MISSENDEN, GREAT Bucks
159 SP 8901 4m W of Chesham. See Gt
Mssndn.

MISSON Notts
103 SK 6995 9m N of Retford. CP, 710.
E Rtfd RD. P Doncaster, Yorkshire.
Ch e, m2. Sch p. Bassetlaw CC.

MISTERTON Leics
132 133 SP 5583 1m ESE of Lutterworth.
CP, 442. Lttrwth RD. Ch e. Blaby CC
(Harborough). See also Walcote.

MISTERTON Notts
104 SK 7694 4m NW of Gainsborough.
CP, 1,529. E Retford RD.
P Doncaster, Yorkshire Ch e, m. Sch p, s.
Bassetlaw CC.

MISTERTON Som
177 ST 4508 1m SE of Crewkerne. CP, 569.
Chard RD. P Crkne. Ch e, b. Sch pe.
Yeovil CC.

MISTLEY Essex
150 TM 1231 1m E of Manningtree.
CP, 2,115. Tendring RD. P Mnnngtree.
Ch e, m. Sch pe. Harwich CC. See also
Horsleycross St. Beside Stow estuary; swans,

sailing boats. Partly developed in 18c as model port, hence many Ggn bldngs, incl M. Twrs (A.M.), rems of ch by Adam. Extensive maltings.

MITCHAM London
170 TQ 2768 4m SSE of Wandsworth. Loc, Merton LB P Surrey. Mtchm and Morden BC (Mtchm).

MITCHELDEAN Glos
142, 143 SO 6618 3m N of Cinderford. CP, 1,931. E Dean RD. P. Ch e, m, v. Sch p, pe, s. W Glos CC. Much new building.

MITCHELL Cornwall
185, 190 SW 8654 5m SE of Newquay. Loc, Newlyn CP. Truro RD. P Nquay. Ch m. Truro CC.

MITFORD Nthmb
78 NZ 1786 2m W of Morpeth. CP, 357. Mpth RD. P Mpth. Ch e. Sch pe. Mpth CC. See also Tranwell. In wooded Wansbeck valley. Ruined cstle and 17c mnr hse. Spired ch of many periods.

MITHIAN Cornwall
185, 190 SW 7450 6m NNE of Redruth. Loc, St Agnes CP. P St Agnes. Ch e, m. Sch p.

MITTON Staffs
119 SJ 8815 6m SSW of Stafford. Loc, Penkridge CP.

MITTON, GREAT Yorks (W)
95 SD 7139 3m SW of Clitheroe. See Gt Mttn.

MIXBURY Oxon
145, 146 SP 6033 2m SE of Brackley. CP, 216. Ploughley RD. P Brckly, Northants. Ch e. Banbury CC (Henley).

MIXON Staffs
111 SK 0457 4m E of Leek. Loc, Onecote CP.

MOBBERLEY Ches
101 SJ 7879 2m ENE of Knutsford. CP, 2,295. Bucklow RD. P Kntsfd. Ch e, c m, v Sch pe. Kntsfd CC. See also Knolls Grn. Bthplce of George Mallory, mountain climber who died on Everest in 1924.

MOCCAS Herefs
142 SO 3542 8m E of Hay-on-Wye. CP, 106. Weobley RD. P HEREFORD. Ch e. Leominster CC. Nmn ch in pk, laid out by Capability Brown, of M. Ct, 18c hse by Adam; lodges by Nash.

MOCKERKIN Cumb
82 NY 0923 5m SSW of Cockermouth. Loc Loweswater CP.

MODBURY Devon
187, 188 SX 6551 3m SSE of Ivybridge. CP, 1,077 Kngsbrdge RD. P Ivybrdge. Ch e, b, m, r. Sch p. Totnes CC. See also Brownston.

MODDERSHALL Staffs
110, 119 SJ 9236 2m NE of Stone. Loc, Stne Rural CP. Stne RD. P Stne. Stafford and Stne CC.

MOGGERHANGER Beds
147 TL 1449 2m SW of Sandy. CP (Mogerhanger), 561. Biggleswade RD. P BEDFORD. Ch e, m. Sch p. Mid-Beds CC.

MOIRA Leics
120, 121 SK 3115 3m W of Ashby de la Zouch. Loc, Ashby Woulds UD. P Burton-on-Trent, Staffs. Loughborough CC. Coal mining tn.

MOLASH Kent
172, 173 TR 0251 5m ENE of Charing. CP, 224. E Ashford RD. P Cntrbry. Ch e. Ashfd CC.

MOLEHILL GREEN Essex
148 TL 5624 4m WNW of Dunmow. Loc, Takeley CP. P Tkly, Bishop's Stortford, Herts.

MOLESCROFT Yorks (E)
99 TA 0240 1m NW of Beverley. CP, 1,453. Bvrly RD. Haltemprice CC.

MOLESWORTH Hunts
134 TL 0775 5m ESE of Thrapston. CP(Brington and Mlswth), 635. Huntingdon RD. P HNTNGDN. Ch e. Hunts CC.

MOLLAND Devon
164 SS 8028 6m ENE of S Molton. CP, 242. S Mltn RD. P(Mllnd-Botreaux): S Mltn. Ch e, m2. N Dvn CC. Ch: unrestored 18c interior; Nmn font.

MOLLAND CROSS Devon
163 SS 7133 5m N of S Molton. Loc,
N Mltn CP. Ch m.

MOLLINGTON Ches
109 SJ 3870 3m NNW of Chester. CP, 481.
Chstr RD. Sch pe. City of Chstr CC.

MOLLINGTON Oxon
145 SP 4447 4m N of Banbury. CP, 167.
Bnbry RD.   P Bnbry. Ch e. Sch pe.
Bnbry CC.

MONEWDEN Suffolk (E)
137 TM 2458 6m NNW of Woodbridge.
CP, 114. Deben RD. P Wdbrdge. Ch e.
Eye CC.

MONGEHAM, GREAT Kent
173 TR 3451 2m W of Deal. Loc, D1 MB.
P D1.

MONKEN HADLEY London
160 TQ 2597 1m N of Barnet. Loc, Bnt LB.
Chipping Bnt BC (Bnt CC). Site of Battle of
Bnt, 1471.

MONK FRYSTON Yorks (W)
97 SE 5029 5m ENE of Castleford. CP, 581.
Osgoldcross RD. P LEEDS. Ch e, m.
Goole CC. M.F. Hall, partly dating from
mdvl period, now hotel. Picturesque grnds.

MONK HESLEDEN Co Durham
85 NZ 4537 3m SSE of Peterlee. CP, 7,775.
Easington RD. Ch e. Easngtn CC. See also
Blackhall Colliery. Hsldn, High Hsldn.

MONKHOPTON Shrops
129, 130 SO 6293 6m W of Bridgnorth.
CP, 206.   Brdgnth RD. P Brdgnth. Ch e.
Sch pe. Ludlow CC.

MONKLAND Herefs
129 SO 4557 3m WSW of Leominster.
CP, 169.   Lmnstr and Wigmore RD.
P Lmnstr. Ch e. Lmnstr CC.

MONKLEIGH Devon
163 SS 4520 3m WNW of Torrington.
CP 323. Bideford RD. P Bdfd. Ch e, m2.
Sch p. N Dvn CC (Trrngtn). See also
Saltrens.

MONKOKEHAMPTON Devon
175 SS 5805 6m N of Okehampton.
CP, 120. Okhmptn RD. P Winkleigh.
Ch e, m. W Dvn CC (Torrington).

MONKSEATON Nthmb
78 NZ 3472 just W of Whitley Bay. Loc,
Whtly Bay MB. P Whtly Bay.

MONKS ELEIGH Suffolk (W)
149 TL 9647 3m ESE of Lavenham.
CP, 415. Cosford RD. P Ipswich. Ch e, v.
Sch pe. Sudbury and Woodbridge CC. Vllge
grn and cottages leading up to ch with noble
twr.

MONKS' HEATH Ches
110 SJ 8474 5m W of Macclesfield. Loc,
Nether Alderley CP. P Mcclsfld.

MONK SHERBORNE Hants
168 SU 6056 3m NNW of Basingstoke.
CP, 338. Bsngstke RD. P Bsngstke. Ch e.
Sch p. Bsngstke CC. Nmn ch.

MONKSILVER Som
164 ST 0737 4m S of Watchet. CP, 101.
Williton RD.   P Taunton.   Ch e, m.
Bridgwater CC.

MONKS KIRBY Warwicks
132 SP 4683 6m NNW of Rugby. CP, 394.
Rgby RD. P Rgby. Ch e, r. Sch pe, pr
Rgby CC.

MONK SOHAM Suffolk (E)
137 TM 2165 4m WNW of Framlingham.
CP, 184. Hartismere RD. P Woodbridge.
Ch e. Eye CC.

MONKS RISBOROUGH Bucks
159 SP 8104 just N of Princes Risborough.
Loc, Prncs Rsbrgh CP. Ch e. Sch pe.

MONKTON Devon
176 ST 1803 2m NE of Honiton. CP, 233.
Hntn RD. Ch e. Hntn CC. 1m NW,
Dumpdon Hill, Iron Age fort.

MONKTON Kent
173 TR 2865 6m W of Ramsgate CP, 404.
Eastry RD. P Rmsgte. Ch e, m. Sch pe.
Thanet W BC (Isle of Thnt CC).

MONKTON COMBE Som
166 ST 7762 2m SE of Bath. CP, 2,330.
Bathavon RD. P Bth. Ch e, v. Sch pe.
N Som CC. Large RC boys' public sch here.

MONKTON DEVERILL Wilts
166 ST 8537 5m SSW of Warminster. Loc
Kingston Deverill CP. Ch e. Watercress beds.

MONKTON FARLEIGH Wilts
156 ST 8065 4m E of Bath. CP, 452.
Bradford and Melksham RD.
P Brdfd-on-Avon. Ch e. Sch pe.
Westbury CC.

MONKTON HEATHFIELD Som
177 ST 2526 3m NE of Taunton. Loc,
W Monkton CP.

MONKTON UP WIMBORNE Dorset
179 SU 0113 9m N of Wimborne. Loc,
Wmbne St Giles CP.

MONKTON WYLD Dorset
177 SY 3396 3m N of Lyme Regis. Loc,
Wootton Fitzpaine CP. Ch e.

MONKWEARMOUTH Co Durham
78 NZ 4058 N distr of Sunderland. Loc,
Sndrlnd CB. Sndrlnd N BC. Parish ch
incorporates rems of monastery founded
in 675.

MONKWOOD Hants
168, 169 181 SU 6630 6m SSW of Alton.
Loc, Ropley CP. P Alresford.

MONNINGTON ON WYE Herefs
142 SO 3743 9m WNW of Hereford. CP, 64.
Weobley RD. Ch e. Leominster CC.

MONTACUTE Som
177 ST 4916 4m W of Yeovil. CP, 806.
Yvl RD. P. Ch e, b. Sch pe. Yvl CC. Estate
vllge of Ham stone. M. Hse (NT)*, Elizn hse
with gdns of contemporary design.

MONTFORD Shrops
118 SJ 4114 5m WNW of Shrewsbury.
CP, 558. Atcham RD. P(Mntfd Br), Shrsbry.
Ch e. Shrsbry CC. See also Ensdon,
Forton, Shrawardine. Br over R Severn to
E is by Telford.

MONXTON Hants
168 SU 3144 3m W of Andover. CP, 281.
Andvr RD. Ch e. Winchester CC
(Basingstoke).

MONYASH Derbys
111 SK 1566 4m WSW of Bakewell.
CP, 300. Bkwll RD. P Bkwll. Ch e, m.
Sch pe. W Derbys CC.

MOORBY Lincs (L)
114 TF 2964 4m SSE of Horncastle. CP, 50.
Hncstle RD. Ch e. Hncstle CC.

MOORCOT Herefs
129 SO 3555 4m E of Kington. Loc,
Pembridge CP. Ch e.

MOOR CRICHEL Dorset
179 ST 9908 6m N of Wimborne. CP, 250.
Wmbne and Cranborne RD. Ch e. Sch pe.
N Dst CC. See also Manswood. C. Hse,
imposing 18c mansion; 19c ch alongside.

MOORE Ches
100, 109 SJ 5784 4m ENE of Runcorn. CP.
Rncn RD. P WARRINGTON. Ch m. Sch p.
Rncn CC.

MOORENDS Yorks (W)
103 SE 6915 1m NNE of Thorne. Loc,
Thne CP. P Doncaster. Ch e, m, r, v. Sch i, j.

MOORHALL Derbys
111 SK 3074 5m WNW of Chesterfield. Loc,
Barlow CP. P Bakewell.

MOORHAMPTON Herefs
142 SO 3847 9m NW of Hereford. Loc,
Yazor CP. P HRFD.

MOORHOUSE Cumb
76 NY 3356 4m W of Carlisle. Loc, Burgh
by Sands CP.

MOORHOUSE Notts
112 SK 7566 6m E of Ollerton. Loc,
Laxton CP.

MOORLAND Som
165 ST 3332 4m SE of Bridgwater.
Alternative name for Northmoor Grn, qv.

MOORLINCH Som
165 ST 3936 6m E of Bridgwater. CP, 191.
Brdgwtr RD. P Brdgwtr. Ch e. Brdgwtr CC.

MOOR MONKTON Yorks (W)
97 SE 5056 7m WNW of York. CP, 152.
Nidderdale RD. P YK. Ch e, m. Barkston
Ash CC.

MOOR ROW Cumb
82 NY 0014 3m SE of Whitehaven. Loc,
Egremont CP. P. Ch m. Sch p.

MOORSHOLM Yorks (N)
86 NZ 6814 3m SW of Loftus. Loc, Skelton
and Brotton UD. P Saltburn-by-the-Sea.

MOOR, THE Kent
184 TQ 7529 just S of Hawkhurst. Loc,
Hkhst CP. P Hkhst. Ch e.

MOORTOWN IOW
180 SZ 4283 6m SW of Newport. Loc,
Brighstone CP.

MOORTOWN Lincs (L)
104 TF 0799 3m WSW of Caistor. Loc,
S Kelsey CP. Ch m.

MORBORNE Hunts
134 TL 1391 6m SW of Peterborough.
CP, 62. Norman Cross RD. Ch e. Hunts CC.

MORCHARD BISHOP Devon
175 SS 7707 6m NNW of Crediton.
CP, 780. Crdtn RD. P Crdtn. Ch e, m.
Sch pe. Tiverton CC (Torrington).

MORCOMBELAKE Dorset
177 SY 4094 4m W of Bridport. Loc,
Whitechurch Canonicorum CP. P Brdpt.
Ch e, v.

MORCOTT Rutland
122 SK 9200 4m E of Uppingham. CP, 317.
Uppnghm RD. P Uppnghm. Ch e. Rtlnd and
Stamford CC. Ch predominantly Nmn.

MORDA Shrops
118 SJ 2827 1m S of Oswestry. Loc,
Oswstry Rural CP. Oswstry RD. P Oswstry.
Ch m. Sch pe. Oswstry CC.

MORDEN Dorset
178, 179 SY 9195 5m N of Wareham.
CP, 411. Wrhm and Purbeck RD. P Wrhm.
Ch e, m. S Dst CC.

MORDEN London
170 TQ 2567 4m S of Wandsworth. Loc,
Merton LB. P Surrey. Mitcham and Mdn BC
(Mtn and Mdn). Rsdntl distr. M. Hall (NT),
several bldngs in R Wandle valley, incl old
snuff mill; deer pk* and bird sanctuary.

MORDIFORD Herefs
142 SO 5737 4m ESE of Hereford. CP, 527.
Hrfd RD. P HRFD. Ch e, v2. Sch pe.
Hrfd CC.

MORDON Co Durham
85 NZ 3326 8m NW of Teesside (Stockton).
CP, 138. Sedgefield RD. Ch m. Drhm CC
(Sdgfld).

MORE Shrops
129 SO 3491 2m NNE of Bishop's Cstle.
CP, 125. Clun and Bp's Cstle RD. Ch e.
Ludlow CC. To N, Linley Hall, 18c

Palladian hse with mile-long avenue
running SSE.

MOREBATH Devon
164 SS 9524 2m N of Bampton. CP, 399.
Tiverton RD. P Tvtn. Ch e. Tvtn CC.

MORECAMBE Lancs
89, 94 SD 4364 3m NW of Lancaster.
MB (Mcmbe and Heysham), 41,863. P.
Mcmbe and Lonsdale CC. Resort. Views of
Lake District hills across M. Bay.

MORELEIGH Devon
187, 188 SX 7652 5m SSW of Totnes.
CP, 112. Ttns RD. P Ttns. Ch e. Ttns CC.

MORESBY Cumb
82 NX 9921 2m NNE of Whitehaven.
CP, 968. Ennerdale RD. Ch e, v. Sch p.
Whthvn CC.

MORESBY PARKS Cumb
82 NX 9919 2m ENE of Whitehaven. Loc,
Msby CP. P Whthvn. Ch m, r.

MORESTEAD Hants
168 SU 5025 3m SE of Winchester. Loc,
Owslebury CP. Ch e.

MORETON Dorset
178 SY 8089 7m E of Dorchester. CP, 327.
Wareham and Purbeck RD. P Dchstr. Ch e.
S Dst CC. Burial place of T.E.
Lawrence, d 1935. Ch: etched glass, 1950.

MORETON Essex
161 TL 5307 3m NNW of Ongar. CP, 350.
Epping and Ongr RD. P Ongr. Ch e. Sch pe.
Brentwood and Ongr CC (Chigwell).
Extensive gravel wks.

MORETON Oxon
159 SP 6904 1m SW of Thame. Loc,
Thme UD.

MORETON Staffs
119 SJ 7917 3m ESE of Newport. Loc,
Gnosall CP. P Npt, Salop. Ch e. Sch pe.

MORETON CORBET Shrops
118 SJ 5523 5m SE of Wem. CP, 257.
N Shrops RD. Ch e. Oswestry CC. See also
Preston Brockhurst. M.C. Cstle* — keep,
gatehouse, Elizn mansion — in ruins.

MORETONHAMPSTEAD Devon
175 SX 7586 11m WSW of Exeter.

CP, 1,541. Newton Abbot RD. P Ntn Abbt. Ch e, b, c, m, v. Sch p. Totnes CC. See also Doccombe. Small mkt tn. Almshouses of 1637 (NT): granite with thatched roof, over open colonnade.

MORETON-IN-MARSH Glos
144 SP 2032 8m NW of Chipping Norton. CP, 1,935. N Cotswold RD. P. Ch e, c, v. Sch pe. Cirencester and Tewkesbury CC. Situated on the Roman Fosse Way (A46 at this point). Blt of Ctswld stone.

MORETON JEFFRIES Herefs
142, 143 SO 6048 5m SW of Bromyard. CP, 33. Brmyd RD. Ch e. Leominster CC.

MORETON MORRELL Warwicks
132 SP 3155 6m S of Leamington. CP, 419. Stratford-on-Avon RD. P WARWICK. Ch e, m, r. Sch pe. Strtfd-on-Avn CC (Strtfd).

MORETON ON LUGG Herefs
142 SO 5045 4m N of Hereford. CP, 94. Hrfd RD. Ch e. Leominster CC.

MORETON PINKNEY Northants
145, 146 SP 5749 8m N of Brackley. CP, 256. Brckly RD. P Rugby, Warwickshire. Ch e, b. Sch pe. Daventry CC (S Nthnts).

MORETON SAY Shrops
110, 118, 119 SJ 6234 3m W of Mkt Drayton. CP, 627. Mkt Drtn RD. Ch e. Sch pe. Oswestry CC. See also Bletchley, Longford, Longslow, Ternhill.

MORETON VALENCE Glos
156 SO 7809 5m NW of Stroud. CP, 208. Gloucester RD. Ch e. Strd CC.

MORGAN'S VALE Wilts
167 SU 1921 7m SSE of Salisbury. Loc, Redlynch CP. Ch e, m. Sch pe.

MORLAND Westm
83 NY 5922 6m WNW of Appleby. CP, 280. N Westm RD. P Penrith, Cumberland. Ch e, m. Sch pe. Westm CC. Ch: Saxon twr; 16c palimsest brass.

MORLEY Derbys
120, 121 SK 3941 4m NE of Derby. CP. SE Derbys RD. P DBY. Ch e, m. Sch p. SE Derbys CC. Ch Nmn and later; monmts, glass.

MORLEY Yorks (W)
96, 102 SE 2627 4m SSW of Leeds. MB, 44,340. P LDS. Batley and Mly BC. See also Ardsley E, Churwell, Drighlington, Gildersome, Tingley. Textile tn; also general industry.

MORLEY GREEN Ches
101 SJ 8282 2m WNW of Wilmslow. Loc, Wlmslw UD. P(Mly), Wlmslw.

MORLEY ST BOTOLPH Norfolk
136 TM 0799 3m WSW of Wymondham. CP(Mly), 521. Forehoe and Henstead RD. P Wndhm. Ch e2, m. Sch pe. S Nflk CC (Central Nflk).

MORNING THORPE Norfolk
137 TM 2192 8m WNW of Bungay. CP, 264. Depwade RD. Ch e. S Nflk CC. See also Fritton.

MORPETH Nthmb
78 NZ 1986 14m NNW of Newcastle. MB, 14,055. P. Mpth CC. Mkt tn near edge of mining area. Large 14c ch. Annual miners' gala in pk beside Wansbeck.

MORREY Staffs
120 SK 1318 6m N of Lichfield. Loc, Yoxall CP.

MORSTON Norfolk
125 TG 0043 5m NW of Holt. CP, 141. Walsingham RD. P Hlt. Ch e. NW Nflk CC (N Nflk).

MORTEHOE Devon
163 SS 4545 4m WSW of Ilfracombe. CP, 1,289. Barnstaple RD. P Woolacombe. Ch e, m. N Dvn CC. See also Wlcmbe. Ch: roof, bench-ends, tomb in S transept. To W, Morte Point (NT).

MORTHEN Yorks (W)
103 SK 4789 4m SE of Rotherham. Loc, Whiston CP.

MORTIMER Berks
168, 169 SU 6664 7m SSW of Reading. Alternative name for Stratfield Mortimer, qv.

MORTIMER COMMON Berks
168, 169 SU 6564 7m SSW of Reading. Loc, Stratfield Mtmr CP. P Rdng.

MORTIMER'S CROSS Herefs
129 SO 4263 5m NW of Leominster. Loc,
Lmnstr and Wigmore RD. Lmnstr CC. Site
of Wars of the Roses battle, 1461.

MORTIMER WEST END Hants
168, 169 SU 6363 7m N of Basingstoke.
CP, 608. Bsngstke RD. P Reading, Berks.
Ch e, v. Bsngstke CC.

MORTLAKE London
160, 170 TQ 2075 3m W of Wandsworth.
Loc, Richmond upon Thames LB.
Rchmnd BC. On S bank of Thames. Once
known for its tapestry industry, but now for
its brewery and the finish of the Boat Race
(see Barnes).

MORTON Derbys
112 SK 4060 3m N of Alfreton. CP, 1,021.
Chesterfield RD. P DERBY. Ch e. Sch p.
NE Derbys CC.

MORTON Glos
155, 156 ST 6490 5m E of Severn Rd Br.
Loc, Thornbury CP. Ch b.

MORTON Lincs (K)
123 TF 0924 2m N of Bourne. CP, 992.
S Kesteven RD. P Bne. Ch e, b, m. Sch pe.
Rutland and Stamford CC. See also
Hanthorpe.

MORTON Lincs (L)
104 SK 8091 1m NNW of Gainsborough.
CP, 854. Gnsbrgh RD. P Gnsbrgh. Ch e, m.
Sch p. Gnsbrgh CC. Ch has Burne-Jones
windows.

MORTON Norfolk
125 TG 1217 9m NW of Norwich. CP(Mtn
on the Hill), 88. St Faith's and
Aylsham RD. Ch e. N Nflk CC (Central
Nflk).

MORTON Notts
112 SK 7251 5m WSW of Newark.
CP(Fiskerton cum Mtn), 353.
Southwell RD. Ch e. Nwk CC.

MORTON BAGOT Warwicks
131 SP 1164 5m ESE of Redditch. CP, 83.
Alcester RD. Ch e. Stratford-on-Avon CC
(Strtfd).

MORTON-ON-SWALE Yorks (N)
91 SE 3292 3m WSW of Northallerton.
CP, 230. Nthlltn RD. Ch m. Richmond CC.

MORTON TINMOUTH Co Durham
85 NZ 1821 5m SSW of Bishop Auckland.
CP, 16. Barnard Cstle RD. Bshp
Aucklnd CC.

MORVAH Cornwall
189 SW 4035 6m NW of Penzance. CP, 65.
W Penwith RD. Ch e, m. St Ives CC. 1m S,
Chun Cstle, Iron Age fort, and Chun Quoit,
ancient stone chamber.

MORVAL Cornwall
186 SX 2656 2m N of Looe. CP, 475.
Liskeard RD. Ch e. Bodmin CC. See also
Sandplace, Widegates.

MORVILLE Shrops
129, 130 SO 6694 3m W of Bridgnorth.
CP, 377. Brdgnth RD. P Brdgnth. Ch e.
Sch pe. Ludlow CC. M. Hall (NT), 18c hse.

MORWELLHAM Devon
187 SX 4469 4m SW of Tavistock. Loc,
Tvstck Hmlts CP. Tvstck RD. Ch m.
W Dvn CC (Tvstck). On R Tamar. Former
important copper-mining centre.
Reclamation of vllge put in hand 1970.

MORWENSTOW Cornwall
174 SS 2015 6m N of Bude. CP, 569.
Stratton RD. P Bde. Ch e. Sch pe.
N Cnwll CC. See also Cleave Camp,
Coombe, Eastcott, Gooseham, Shop,
W Youlstone, Woodford, Woolley. Famous
as living of Revd Stephen Hawker from
1835 to 1875.

MOSELEY Worcs
130 SO 8159 4m NW of Worcester. Loc,
Grimley CP.

MOSS Yorks (W)
103 SE 5914 6m W of Thorne. CP, 208.
Doncaster RD. P Dncstr. Ch e, m. Sch p.
Don Valley CC.

MOSS, GREAT Lancs
100 SD 5203 4m WSW of Wigan. Loc,
Billinge-and-Winstanley UD.

MOSSLEY Lancs
101 SD 9702 4m SE of Oldham.
MB, 10,055. P Ashton-under-Lyne.
Ashtn-undr-Lne BC. Textiles.

MOSS SIDE Lancs
94 SD 3830 6m SE of Blackpool. Loc,
Fylde RD. S Flde CC.

MOSSY LEA Lancs
100 SD 5312 4m SW of Chorley. Loc,
Wrightington CP. Wigan RD. P Wgn. Ch v.
Sch p. Westhoughton CC.

MOSTERTON Dorset
177 ST 4505 3m SSE of Crewkerne.
CP, 177. Beaminster RD. P Bmnstr. Ch e, v.
Sch pe. W Dst CC.

MOTCOMBE Dorset
166 ST 8525 2m NNW of Shaftesbury.
CP, 719. Shftsbry RD. P Shftsbry. Ch e, m2.
Sch pe. N Dst CC.

MOTHECOMBE Devon
187, 188 SX 6047 5m SSW of Ivybridge.
Loc, Holbeton CP.

MOTSPUR PARK London
170 TQ 2267 3m ESE OF Kingston. Loc.
Kngstn upon Thames LB, Merton LB.
P New Malden, Surrey. Kngstn
upn Thms BC, Wimbledon BC (Kngstn
upn Thms BC, Mtn and Morden BC). Sports
grnds.

MOTTINGHAM London
161, 171 TQ 4172 3m SE of Lewisham.
Loc, Bromley LB. Chislehurst BC (CC).

MOTTISFONT Hants
168 SU 3226 4m NNW of Romsey. CP, 402.
Rmsy and Stockbridge RD. P Rmsy.
Ch e, b. Sch pe. Winchester CC.
Trout-fishing in R Test. M. Abbey (NT)*,
rems of 12c priory incorporated in 18c hse.
Ch has much 15c glass.

MOTTISTONE IOW
180 SZ 4083 7m WSW of Newport. Loc,
Brighstone CP. Ch e. 16c mnr hse, buried by
a landslide for c 150 years.

MOTTRAM IN LONGDENDALE Ches
101 SJ 9995 3m WNW of Glossop. Loc,
Lngdndle UD. P (Mttrm), Hyde. Ch e.
Stalybridge and Hde CC.

MOULDSWORTH Ches
109 SJ 5171 7m ENE of Chester. CP, 277.
Tarvin RD. Ch m, r. Northwich CC.

MOULSFORD Berks
158 SU 5983 4m S of Wallingford. CP, 376.
Wllngfd RD. P Wllngfd. Ch e. Sch pe.
Abingdon CC.

MOULSOE Bucks
146 SP 9041 2m SE of Newport Pagnell.
CP, 206. Npt Pgnll RD. P Npt Pgnll. Ch e.
Sch p. Buckingham CC.

MOULTON Ches
110 SJ 6569 3m S of Northwich. CP, 1,512.
Nthwch RD. P Nthwch. Ch e, m, v. Sch p.
Nthwch CC.

MOULTON Lincs (H)
123 TF 3024 3m W of Holbeach. CP, 2,445.
Spalding RD. P Spldng. Ch e, m2. Sch p.
Holland w Boston CC. See also Mltn Chpl,
Mltn Seas End.

MOULTON Northants
133 SP 7866 4m NNE of Northampton. CP.
Brixworth RD. P NTHMPTN. Ch e, b, m.
Sch p, s. Daventry CC (Kettering).

MOULTON Suffolk (W)
135 TL 6964 3m E.of Newmarket. CP, 624.
Mildenhall RD. P Nmkt. Ch e, m. Sch pe.
Bury St Edmunds CC.

MOULTON Yorks (N)
91 NZ 2303 4m ENE of Richmond.
CP, 163. Rchmnd RD. P Rchmnd.
Rchmnd CC. M. Hall (NT), mid-17c hse.

MOULTON CHAPEL Lincs (H)
123 TF 2918 4m SE of Spalding. Loc,
Mltn CP. P Spldng. Ch e, m. Sch p.

MOULTON ST MARY Norfolk
126 TG 3907 8m W of Yarmouth. Loc,
Beighton CP. P NORWICH, NOR 63Z. Ch e.

MOULTON ST MICHAEL Norfolk
137 TM 1690 7m NNE of Diss. Loc, Gt
Mltn CP. Depwade RD. Ch e, b. S Nflk CC.

MOULTON SEAS END Lincs (H)
123 TF 3227 3m NW of Holbeach. Loc,
Mltn CP. P Spalding. Ch m.

MOUNT Cornwall
186 SX 1468 5m E of Bodmin. Loc,
Warleggan CP. P Bdmn.

MOUNT AMBROSE Cornwall
189, 190 SW 7043 1m NE of Redruth. Loc,
Camborne-Rdrth UD. P Rdrth.

MOUNT BURES Essex
149 TL 9032 6m SSE of Sudbury. CP, 180.
Lexden and Winstree RD. Ch e, b.
Colchester CC.

MOUNT EDGCUMBE Cornwall
187 SX 4552 2m WSW of Plymouth. Loc,
Maker-with-Rame CP. St Germans RD.
Bodmin CC. Estate of Earls of
Mt Edgcumbe. 16c hse burnt out in World
War II; since rebuilt. Large pk*.

MOUNTFIELD Sussex (E)
183, 184 TQ 7320 3m N of Battle. CP, 543.
Bttle RD. P Robertsbridge. Ch e, m. Sch pe.
Rye CC. 1m WSW, gypsum mine; gypsum
discovered here in 19c during unsuccessful
search for coal.

MOUNT HAWKE Cornwall
190 SW 7147 4m NNE of Redruth. Loc,
St Agnes CP. P Truro. Ch e, m. Sch p.

MOUNTJOY Cornwall
185 SW 8760 4m E of Newquay. Loc,
Colan CP.

MOUNTNESSING Essex
161 TQ 6397 3m NE of Brentwood.
CP, 1,413. Chelmsford RD. P Brntwd.
Ch e, c. Sch pe. Chlmsfd CC. To N, scant
rems of 12c priory. Post-mill.

MOUNT PLEASANT Suffolk (E)
137 TM 5077 1m NNW of Southwold. Loc,
Reydon CP. Ch m.

MOUNTSORREL Leics
121, 122 SK 5815 4m SE of Loughborough.
CP, 4,032. Barrow upon Soar RD.
P Lghbrgh. Ch e, m2. Sch ie, je. Melton CC.
Famous granite quarries.

MOUSEHOLE Cornwall
189 SW 4626 3m S of Penzance. Loc,
Pnznce MB. P Pnznce. Fishing vllge, esp for
pilchard; resort.

MOW COP Ches and Staffs
110 SJ 8557 4m S of Congleton. Loc, Odd
Rode CP, Cngltn RD; Kidsgrove UD. P Stoke-
on-Trent, Staffs. Ch e, m, v. Sch pe.
Knutsford CC, Leek CC. On hill (NT) is
artificial ruin blt in 1750; views over Ches
Plain.

MOWSLEY Leics
132, 133 SP 6489 6m W of Mkt
Harborough. CP, 141. Mkt Hbrgh RD.
P Rugby, Warwickshire. Ch e, m, v. Sch pe.
Hbrgh CC.

MUCH BIRCH Herefs
142 SO 5030 6m S of Hereford. CP, 747.
Hrfd RD. P HRFD. Ch e. Sch pe. Hrfd CC.

MUCH COWARNE Herefs
142, 143 SO 6147 5m SSW of Bromyard.
CP, 365. Brmyd RD. Ch e. Sch pe.
Leominster CC. Ch: monmts.

MUCH DEWCHURCH Herefs
142 SO 4831 6m SSW of Hereford. CP, 468.
Hrfd RD. Ch e. Sch p. Hrfd CC. See also
Kingsthorne.

MUCHELNEY Som
177 ST 4224 6m WNW of Ilchester.
CP, 164. Langport RD. P Lngpt. Ch e.
Yeovil CC. Rems of abbey (A.M.), founded
10c. Priest's Hse (NT), small late mdvl hse
with thatched roof.

MUCH HADHAM Herts
148 TL 4219 4m WSW of Bishop's
Stortford. CP, 1,946. Braughing RD. P.
Ch e, r. Sch pe. E Herts CC. See also Hdhm
Cross, Perry Grn. Large embattled ch. Long
main st with Ggn hses and 16c and 17c
cottages.

MUCH HOOLE Lancs
94 SD 4622 6m SW of Preston. CP, 745.
Prstn RD. P Prstn. Ch e, m. Sch pe.
S Fylde CC.

MUCHLARNICK Cornwall
186 SX 2156 3m NW of Looe. Loc,
Pelynt CP.

MUCH MARKLE Herefs
142, 143 SO 6532 5m SW of Ledbury.
CP, 621. Ldbry RD. P Ldbry. Ch e, m2.
Sch pe. Leominster CC. See also Rushall.
Ch 13c−15c; monmts. To N, Hellens*,
mainly Jcbn hse.

MUCH WENLOCK Shrops
129, 130 SO 6299 7m NW of Bridgnorth.
CP. Brdgnth RD. P. Ch e, m, r. Sch p, s.
Ludlow CC. See also Bourton, Homer,
Presthope. At NE end of Wnlck Edge and
known to readers of A.E. Housman. Ruined
priory (A.M.). Half-timbered guildhall*.

MUCKING Essex
161 TQ 6881 5m NE of Tilbury. Loc,
Thurrock UD. Thrrck BC (CC).

MUCKLESTONE Staffs
110, 119 SJ 7237 4m ENE of Mkt Drayton.
CP, 409. Newcastle-under-Lyme RD. P Mkt
Drtn, Salop. Ch e, m. Sch pe. N-u-L BC. See
also Knighton.

MUCKLETON Shrops
118 SJ 5921 7m SE of Wem. Loc,
Shawbury CP.

MUCKTON Lincs (L)
105 TF 3781 5m SE of Louth. CP, 51.
Lth RD. Ch e, m. Lth CC.

MUDDIFORD Devon
163 SS 5638 3m N of Barnstaple. Loc,
Marwood CP. P Bnstple. Ch c.

MUDEFORD Hants
179 SZ 1892 2m E of Christchurch. Loc,
Chrstchch MB.

MUDFORD Som
177, 178 ST 5719 3m NNE of Yeovil.
CP, 633. Yvl RD. P Yvl. Ch e, m. Yvl CC.

MUDGLEY Som
165 ST 4445 6m W of Wells. Loc,
Wedmore CP.

MUGGINGTON Derbys
120, 121 SK 2843 6m NW of Derby. Loc,
Weston Underwood CP. Ch e. Sch pe.

MUGGLESWICK Co Durham
77, 78/84 NZ 0450 4m W of Consett.
CP, 150. Lanchester RD. Ch e.
NW Drhm CC. See also Waskerley.

MUKER Yorks (N)
90 SD 9197 6m NNE of Hawes. CP, 386.
Reeth RD. P Richmond. Ch e, m. Sch pe.
Rchmnd CC. See also Keld, Thwaite. On
Pennine Way in Swaledale. 3½m W, Gt
Shunner Fell, 2,340ft.

MULBARTON Norfolk
137 TG 1901 5m SSW of Norwich. CP, 735.
Forehoe and Henstead RD.
P NRWCH, NOR 93W. Ch e, m. Sch p.
S Nflk CC (Central Nflk). Very large vllge
grn.

MULLION Cornwall
189 SW 6719 5m S of Helston. CP, 1,166.
Kerrier RD. P Hlstn. Ch e, m, r. Sch p.
St Ives CC. See also Porth Mellin. 1m inland
from coast of rocks and coves, mainly NT.

1m W, Marconi Memorial (NT),
commemorating first transatlantic radio
transmission in 1901.

MUMBY Lincs (L)
114 TF 5174 4m ESE of Alford. CP, 206.
Spilsby RD. P Alfd. Ch e, m. Sch pe.
Horncastle CC.

MUNDERFIELD ROW Herefs
142, 143 SO 6451 2m S of Bromyard. Loc,
Avenbury CP. Brmyd RD. Leominster CC.

MUNDERFIELD STOCKS Herefs
142, 143 SO 6550 3m S of Bromyard. Loc,
Avenbury CP. Brmyd RD.
P(Mndrfld), Brmyd. Leominster CC.

MUNDESLEY Norfolk
126 TG 3136 4m NNE of N Walsham.
CP, 1,558. Erpingham RD.
P NORWICH, NOR 33Y. Ch e, bv, m. Sch p.
N Nflk CC. Twr windmill.

MUNDFORD Norfolk
136 TL 8093 5m NNE of Brandon. CP, 461.
Swaffham RD. P Thetford. Ch e, m. Sch pe.
SW Nflk CC.

MUNDHAM Norfolk
137 TM 3397 5m N of Bungay. CP, 164.
Loddon RD. Ch e, m. S Nflk CC.

MUNDON HILL Essex
162 TL 8702 3m SSE of Maldon. Loc,
Mndn CP. Mldn RD. P(Mndn), Mldn. Ch e, m.
Mldn CC.

MUNGRISDALE Cumb
83 NY 3630 9m W of Penrith. CP, 336.
Pnrth RD. P Pnrth. Ch e. Pnrth and the
Border CC. See also Hutton Roof. Cottage-
like 18c ch with box pews and three-decker
plpt.

MUNSLEY Herefs
142, 143 SO 6640 4m NW of Ledbury.
CP, 159. Ldbry RD. Ch e. Leominster CC.

MUNSLOW Shrops
129 SO 5287 6m ENE of Craven Arms.
CP, 402. Ludlow RD. P Crvn Arms. Ch e.
Sch pe. Ldlw CC. See also Broadstone,
Hungerford, Mnslw Aston. The White Hse*,
orig 14c—16c mnr hse with later additions;
museum of country crafts.

MUNSLOW ASTON Shrops
129 SO 5186 6m ENE of Craven Arms. Loc,
Mnslw CP. Ch m.

MURCOTT Oxon
145, 146 SP 5815 4m S of Bicester.
CP(Fencott and Mctt), 134. Ploughley RD.
Ch m. Mid-Oxon CC (Henley).

MURROW Cambs
124 TF 3707 6m WSW of Wisbech. Loc,
Wsbch RD. P Wsbch. Ch e, m. Sch p. Isle
of Ely CC.

MURSLEY Bucks
146 SP 8128 5m WSW of Bletchley.
CP, 402. Winslow RD. P Bltchly. Ch e, b.
Sch pe. Buckingham CC.

MURTON Co Durham
85 NZ 3947 3m SW of Seaham. Loc,
E Mtn CP. Easington RD. P Shm.
Ch m 3, r 2, s, v 3. Sch p, pr, s.
Houghton-le-Spring CC (Easngtn).

MURTON Nthmb
78 NZ 3270 2m NW of Tynemouth. Loc,
Whitley Bay MB.

MURTON Westm
83 NY 7221 3m ENE of Appleby. CP, 313.
N Westm RD. Ch e, m. Sch pe. Westm CC.
See also Hilton.

MURTON Yorks (N)
97, 98 SE 6552 3m E of York. CP, 350.
Flaxton RD. Ch e, m. Thirsk and
Malton CC.

MUSBURY Devon
177 SY 2794 3m SSW of Axminster.
CP, 477. Axmnstr RD. P Axmnstr. Ch e, v.
Sch p. Honiton CC.

MUSCOATES Yorks (N)
92 SE 6880 5m ESE of Helmsley. CP, 23.
Kirkbymoorside RD. Thirsk and Malton CC.

MUSGRAVE, GREAT Westm
84 NY 7613 3m N of Kirkby Stephen. See
Gt Msgrve.

MUSTON Leics
113, 122 SK 8237 6m WNW of Grantham.
Loc, Bottesford CP. P NOTTINGHAM.
Ch e, m.

MUSTON Yorks (E)
93 TA 0979 1m WSW of Filey. CP, 300.
Bridlington RD. P Filey. Ch e, m.
Brdlngtn CC.

MUSTOW GREEN Worcs
130 SO 8774 3m SE of Kidderminster. Loc,
Kddrmnstr RD. Kddrmnstr CC.

MUSWELL HILL London
160 TQ 2989 6m N of Charing Cross. Loc,
Haringey LB. Hornsey BC. To NE,
Alexandra Palace, Alxndra Pk TV
transmitting stn; racecourse.

MUTFORD Suffolk (E)
137 TM 4888 4m ESE of Beccles. CP, 381.
Lothingland RD. P Bccls. Ch e. Sch p.
Lowestoft CC.

MUTTERTON Devon
176 ST 0205 7m SE of Tiverton. Loc,
Cullompton CP.

MYDDLE Shrops
118 SJ 4623 4m SW of Wem. CP, 745.
N Shrops RD. P Shrewsbury. Ch e. Sch pe.
Oswestry CC. See also Harmerhill, Marton.
Slight rems of 13c cstle.

MYLOR Cornwall
190 SW 8235 2m E of Penryn. CP, 2,080.
Truro RD. Ch e. Truro CC. See also
Flushing, Mlr Br. Hamlet at mouth of Mlr
Creek.

MYLOR BRIDGE Cornwall
190 SW 8036 2m NE of Penryn. Loc,
Mlr CP. P Falmouth. Ch m. Sch p.

MYNDTOWN Shrops
129 SO 3989 4m E of Bishop's Cstle.
CP, 94. Clun and Bp's Cstle RD. Ch e.
Ludlow CC. See also Asterton. Below the
Longmynd.

MYTCHETT Surrey
169 SU 8855 3m NNE of Aldershot. Loc,
Frimley and Camberley UD. P Cmbrly.

MYTHOLM Yorks (W)
95 SD 9827 just W of Hebden Br. Loc,
Hbdn Royd UD, Hepton RD. Sowerby CC.

MYTHOLMROYD Yorks (W)
96, 102 SE 0126 5m W of Halifax. Loc,
Hebden Royd UD. P Hlfx. Sowerby CC.

MYTON-ON-SWALE Yorks (N)
91 SE 4366 3m E of Boroughbridge.
CP, 132. Easingwold RD. Ch e. Thirsk and
Malton CC.

MYTTON Shrops
118 SJ 4417 4m NW of Shrewsbury. Loc,
Pimhill CP. Atcham RD. Shrsbry CC.

NABURN Yorks (E)
97 SE 5945 4m S of York. CP, 473.
Derwent RD. P YK. Ch e, m. Sch pe.
Howden CC.

NACKINGTON Kent
173 TR 1554 2m S of Canterbury. Loc, Lr
Hardres CP. Ch e.

NACTON Suffolk (E)
150 TM 2240 5m SE of Ipswich. CP, 677.
Deben RD. P Ipswch. Ch e. Sch pe. Sudbury
and Woodbridge CC. On Orwell estuary.
Orwell Pk, 18c, now boys' boarding sch.

NAFFERTON Yorks (E)
99 TA 0559 2m ENE of Driffield.
CP, 1,318. Drffld RD. P Drffld. Ch e, m.
Sch p. Howden CC.

NAILSEA Som
155, 165 SU 4770 7m W of Bristol.
CP, 4,173. Long Ashton RD. P BRSTL.
Ch e2, c, m2, v. Sch i2, j, je, s. N Som CC.
See also St Mary's Grove. N. Ct, mainly
Elizn.

NAILSTONE Leics
121 SK 4107 5m S of Coalville. CP, 580.
Mkt Bosworth RD. P Nuneaton, Warwickshire. Ch e. Sch i. Bswth CC. Coal mines
and brickworks.

NAILSWORTH Glos
156 ST 8499 4m S of Stroud. UD, 3,947.
P Strd. Strd CC. Wool tn with steep streets.

NANCEGOLLAN Cornwall
189 SW 6332 3m NNW of Helston. Loc,
Kerrier RD. P Hlstn. Ch m. Falmouth and
Camborne CC, St Ives CC.

NANCLEDRA Cornwall
189 SW 4936 3m SSW of St Ives. Loc,
W Penwith RD. P Penzance. Ch m2. Sch p.
St Ives CC.

NANPANTAN Leics
121 SK 5017 2m SW of Loughborough.
Loc, Lghbrgh MB.

NANPEAN Cornwall
185 SW 9656 4m NW of St Austell. Loc,
St Stephen-in-Brannel CP. St Astll RD.
P St Astll. Ch m. Sch p. Truro CC.

NANSTALLON Cornwall
185, 186 SX 0367 2m W of Bodmin. Loc,
Lanivet CP. P Bdmn. Ch e, m. Sch p.

NANTMAWR Shrops
117 SJ 2524 4m SSW of Oswestry. Loc,
Oswstry RD. P Oswstry. Ch c. Sch p.
Oswstry CC.

NANTWICH Ches
110 SJ 6552 4m WSW of Crewe.
UD, 11,666. P. Nntwch CC. Old salt and
cheese tn with many black and white hses,
esp Welsh Row. Churche's Mansion*, 1577.

NAPHILL Bucks
159 SU 8596 3m NNW of High Wycombe.
Loc, Hughenden CP. Wcmbe RD. P Hgh
Wcmbe. Ch m. Sch p. Wcmbe CC.

NAPTON ON THE HILL Warwicks
132 SP 4661 3m E of Southam. CP, 769.
Sthm RD. P WARWICK. Ch e, m, v. Sch pe.
Stratford-on-Avon CC (Strtfd).

NARBOROUGH Leics
132 SP 5397 5m SW of Leicester. CP, 3,479.
Blaby RD. P LCSTR. Ch e, c, r. Sch p.
Blby CC (Harborough).

NARBOROUGH Norfolk
124 TF 7413 5m NW of Swaffham.
CP, 423. Swffhm RD. P King's Lynn.
Ch e, m. Sch pe. SW Nflk CC. Ch: 15c–16c
brasses. To E, Narford Hall and ch, 18c with
Vctrn alterations, in large pk with lake and
temple.

NASEBY Northants
133 SP 6878 6m SSW of Mkt Harborough.
C P , 3 4 4 . B r i x w o r t h R D .
P Rugby, Warwickshire. Ch e, m. Sch pe.
Daventry CC (Kettering). Site of final defeat
of Royalists in Civil War, 1645.

NASH Bucks
146 SP 7834 4m S of Stony Stratford.

CP, 214. Winslow RD. P Bletchley.
Ch e, b, v. Buckingham CC.

NASH Herefs
129 SO 3062 1m S of Presteigne. CP(Rodd,
Nsh and Lit Brampton), 74. Kington RD.
Leominster CC.

NASH Shrops
129, 130 SO 6071 2m N of Tenbury Wells.
CP, 367. Ludlow RD. P Ldlw. Ch e.
Ldlw CC.

NASSINGTON Northants
134 TL 0696 5m NNE of Oundle. CP, 478.
Oundle and Thrapston RD.
P PETERBOROUGH. Ch e, m, v. Sch p.
Wellingborough CC (Ptrbrgh).

NASTY Herts
148 TL 3524 6m N of Ware. Loc,
Gt Munden CP. Ware RD. E Herts CC.

NATEBY Lancs
94 SD 4644 10m S of Lancaster. CP, 269.
Garstang RD. P Prstn. Sch p. N Fylde CC.

NATEBY Westm
84 TY 7706 1m S of Kirkby Stephen.
CP, 112. N Westm RD. Ch m. Sch p.
Westm CC.

NATLAND Westm
89 SD 5289 2m S of Kendal. CP, 351.
S Westm RD. P Kndl. Ch e. Sch pe.
Westm CC.

NAUGHTON Suffolk (W)
149 TM 0248 4m N of Hadleigh. CP(Nedging-
w-Nghtn), 278. Cosford RD. Ch e. Sudbury
and Woodbridge CC. See also Ndgng Tye.

NAUNTON Glos
144 SP 1123 5m WSW of Stow-on-the-Wold.
CP, 298. N Cotswold RD. P Cheltenham.
Ch e, b. Sch p. Cirencester and
Tewkesbury CC.

NAUNTON Worcs
143 SO 8739 4m N of Tewkesbury. Loc,
Ripple CP.

NAUNTON BEAUCHAMP Worcs
143, 144 SO 9652 7m ESE of Worcestcr.
CP, 102. Pershore RD. Ch e. S Worcs CC.

NAVENBY Lincs (K)
113 SK 9857 9m S of Lincoln. CP, 812.

N Kesteven RD. P LNCLN. Ch e, m. Sch pe.
Grantham CC.

NAVESTOCK Essex
161 TQ 5397 4m NW of Brentwood.
CP, 613. Epping and Ongar RD. P Romford.
Ch e. Brntwd and Ongr CC (Chigwell).

NAVESTOCK SIDE Essex
161 TQ 5697 3m NW of Brentwood. Loc,
Nvstck CP. P Brntwd.

NAWTON Yorks (N)
92 SE 6584 3m ENE of Helmsley. CP, 401.
Kirkbymoorside RD. P YORK. Ch e, m, r.
Sch p, s. Thirsk and Malton CC.

NAYLAND Suffolk (W)
149 TL 9734 6m N of Colchester.
CP(Nlnd-w-Wissington), 960. Melford RD.
P Colchester, Essex. Ch e, c, r. Sch p.
Sudbury and Woodbridge CC. Stour valley
vllge. Perp ch contains Constable painting.
Old hses.

NAZEING Essex
161 TL 4106 3m SW of Harlow. CP, 3,880.
Eppng and Ongar RD. P Waltham Abbey.
Ch e, v. Sch p. Hlw CC (Eppng). See also
Bumble's Grn, Lr Nzng. Surrounded by mkt
gdns and glasshouses.

NEACROFT Hants
179 SZ 1896 3m NE of Christchurch. Loc,
Chrstchch E CP. Ringwood and
Fordingbridge RD. Ch v. New Forest CC.

NEAR COTTON Staffs
111 SK 0646 4m NE of Cheadle. Loc,
Cttn CP. Chdle RD. Ch m, r. Leek CC.

NEAR SAWREY Lancs
88, 89 SD 3695 4m ESE of Coniston. Loc,
Claife CP. N Lonsdale RD. Morecambe and
Lnsdle CC. Hill Top (NT)*, former home of
Beatrix Potter.

NEASDEN London
160 TQ 2086 2m SW of Hendon. Loc,
Brent LB. Brnt E BC (Willesden W). Indstrl
distr by N Circular Rd (A406). To N, Brnt
Reservoir.

NEASHAM Co Durham
85 NZ 3210 4m SSE of Darlington.
CP, 285. Dlngtn RD. P Dlngtn. Bishop
Auckland CC (Sedgefield).

NEATISHEAD Norfolk
126 TG 3421 3m NE of Wroxham. CP, 470.
Smallburgh RD. P NORWICH, NOR 37Z.
Ch e, b, m. Sch pe. N Nflk CC.

NECTON Norfolk
125 TF 8709 4m E of Swaffham. CP, 763.
Swffhm RD. P Swffhm. Ch e, b. Sch pe.
SW Nflk CC. Ch has hammerbeam roof with
angels and figures.

NEDDERTON Nthmb
78 NZ 2382 3m SE of Morpeth. Loc,
Bedlingtonshire UD. P Bedlington. Blyth BC.

NEDGING Suffolk (W)
149 TL 9948 4m NNW of Hadleigh.
CP(Ndgng-w-Naughton), 278. Cosford RD.
Ch e. Sudbury and Woodbridge CC. See also
Ndgng Tye.

NEDGING TYE Suffolk (W)
149 TM 0149 5m N of Hadleigh. Loc,
Ndgng-w-Naughton CP. P Ipswich.

NEEDHAM Norfolk
137 TM 2281 7m E of Diss. CP, 241.
Depwade RD. P Harleston. Ch e. S Nflk CC.

NEEDHAM MARKET Suffolk (E)
149 TM 0855 3m SE of Stowmarket.
CP, 1,674. Gipping RD. P Ipswich.
Ch e, c, m, v. Sch p, s. Eye CC.

NEEDINGWORTH Hunts
134 TL 3472 2m E of St Ives.
CP(Holywell-cum-Ndngwth), 753.
St Ives RD. P HUNTINGDON. Ch b, m.
Sch pe. Hunts CC.

NEEN SAVAGE Shrops
129, 130 SO 6777 1m N of Cleobury
Mortimer. CP, 495. Bridgnorth RD. Ch e.
Ludlow CC. Restored Nmn ch. Ruined
paper mills.

NEEN SOLLARS Shrops
129, 130 SO 6672 5m ENE of Tenbury
Wells. CP, 123. Ludlow RD.
P Kidderminster, Worcs. Ch e. Ldlw CC. In
steep wooded valley. Ch: Conyngsby
monmt.

NEENTON Shrops
129, 130 SO 6387 6m SW of Bridgnorth.
CP, 100. Brdgnth RD. P Brdgnth. Ch e.
Ludlow CC.

NELSON Lancs
95 SD 8537 4m NNE of Burnley.

MB, 31,225. P. Nlsn and Colne BC.
Textile tn.

NELSON VILLAGE Nthmb
78 NZ 2577 4m SW of Blyth. Loc, Seaton
Valley UD. P Cramlington. Blth BC.

NEMPNETT THRUBWELL Som
165, 166 ST 5360 9m SSW of Bristol.
CP, 184. Clutton RD. Ch e. N Som CC.

NENTHEAD Cumb
84 NY 7843 4m ESE of Alston. Loc, Alstn
w Garrigill CP. P Alstn. Ch e, m. Sch p. In
former lead-mining area high up on
Co Durham border. Was blt early 19c as
model vllge.

NESBIT Nthmb
64, 71 NT 9833 6m N of Wooler. Loc,
Doddington CP.

NESFIELD Yorks (W)
96 SE 0949 2m NW of Ilkley. CP(Nsfld
w Langbar), 175. Wharfedale RD.
Ripon CC.

NESS Ches
100, 109 SJ 3076 6m W of Ellesmere Port.
Loc, Neston UD. Liverpool University
Botanic Gdns: esp alpines, heather gdn.

NESSCLIFF Shrops
118 SJ 3819 8m NW of Shrewsbury. Loc,
Gt Ness CP. P Shrsbry. Sch pe. Main rd vllge
in red sandstone below wooded cliff of the
same, containing Kynaston's Cave, hideout
of 15c outlaw.

NESS, GREAT Shrops
118 SJ 3918 7m NW of Shrewsbury. See
Gt Nss.

NESTON Ches
100, 109 SJ 2977 7m SSW of Birkenhead.
UD, 16,848. P Wirral. Wrrl CC. See also
Burton, Ness, Parkgate, Willaston.

NESTON Wilts
156 ST 8668 5m SW of Chippenham. Loc,
Corsham CP. P Hawthorn. Ch e. Sch p

NETHER ALDERLEY Ches
101 SJ 8476 3m S of Wilmslow. CP, 608.
Macclesfield RD. Ch e. Sch p. Mcclsfld CC.
See also Monk's Heath. A. Old Mill (NT)*,
15c corn mill, working up to 1939. Old
wheels, machinery.

NETHERAVON Wilts
167 SU 1448 5m N of Amesbury.
CP, 1,075. Pewsey RD. P Salisbury.
Ch e, b, m. Devizes CC. In Army dominated
area. Ch partly Saxon. In grnds of Nthrvn
Hse, dovecote (A.M.).

NETHER BROUGHTON Leics
122 SK 6925 6m NW of Melton Mowbray.
Loc, Brghtn and Old Dalby CP. Mltn and
Belvoir RD. P Mltn Mbry. Ch e, m. Mltn CC.

NETHER BURROW Lancs
89 SD 6175 2m S of Kirkby Lonsdale. Loc,
Brrw-w-Brrw CP. Lunesdale RD.
Lancaster CC.

NETHERBURY Dorset
177 SY 4799 4m N of Bridport. CP, 1,072.
Beaminster RD. P Brdpt. Ch e. Sch pe.
W Dst CC. See also Melplash, Salwayash.

NETHERBY Yorks (W)
96 SE 3346 5m WSW of Wetherby.
CP(Kearby w Nthrby), 143. Wthrby RD.
Barkston Ash CC.

NETHER CERNE Dorset
178 SY 6798 5m N of Dorchester. CP, 33.
Dchstr RD. Ch e. W Dst CC.

NETHER COMPTON Dorset
177, 178 ST 5917 3m ENE of Yeovil.
CP, 224. Sherborne RD. P Shbne. Ch e.
Sch pe. W Dst CC.

NETHEREND Glos
155, 156 SO 5900 5m NE of Chepstow.
Loc, Woolaston CP. P Lydney.

NETHER EXE Devon
176 SS 9300 5m N of Exeter. CP, 56.
St Thomas RD. Ch e. Tiverton CC.

NETHERFIELD Sussex (E)
183, 184 TQ 7118 3m NE of Battle. Loc,
Bttle CP. P Bttle. Ch e, c. Sch pe.

NETHERHAMPTON Wilts
167 SU 1029 3m W of Salisbury. CP, 167.
Slsbry and Wilton RD. Slsbry CC.

NETHER HAUGH Yorks (W)
103 SK 4196 3m NNW of Rotherham. Loc,
Wentworth CP.

NETHER HEAGE Derbys
111 SK 3650 2m W of Ripley. Loc,
Rply UD. P DERBY.

NETHER HEYFORD Northants
132, 133 SP 6558 6m W of Northampton.
CP, 733. Nthmptn RD. P NTHMPTN.
Ch e, b, m. Sch pe. Daventry CC (S Nthnts).

NETHER KELLET Lancs
89 SD 5068 2m SSE of Carnforth. CP, 320.
Lunesdale RD. P Cnfth. Ch v2. Sch p.
Lancaster CC.

NETHER LANGWITH Notts
112 SK 5270 6m N of Mansfield. CP, 530.
Worksop RD. Ch m. Bassetlaw CC.

NETHER PADLEY Derbys
111 SK 2578 7m NNE of Bakewell.
CP, 201. Bkwll RD. W Derbys CC.

NETHER POPPLETON Yorks (W)
97 SE 5654 3m NW of York. CP, 597.
Nidderdale RD. Ch e. Barkston Ash CC.

NETHERSEAL Derbys
120, 121 SK 2813 5m WSW of Ashby de la
Zouch. CP, 837. Repton RD.
P Burton-on-Trent, Staffs. Ch e, m. Sch pe.
Belper CC.

NETHER SILTON Yorks (N)
91 SE 4592 6m ESE of Northallerton.
CP, 118. Nthlltn RD. P Thirsk. Ch e, m.
Sch pe. Richmond CC.

NETHER STOWEY Som
164 ST 1939 8m ESE of Watchet. CP, 688.
Bridgwater RD. P Brdgwtr. Ch e, c. Sch pe.
Brdgwtr CC. Coleridge's cottage (NT)*,
home of the poet 1797–1800.

NETHERSTREET Wilts
157 ST 9865 4m SSW of Calne. Loc,
Bromham CP.

NETHERTHONG Yorks (W)
102 SE 1309 4m S of Huddersfield. Loc,
Holmfirth UD. P Hlmfth, Hddsfld.

NETHERTON Devon
176, 188 SX 8971 2m E of Newton Abbot.
Loc, Haccombe w Combe CP. Ntn Abbt RD.
Totnes CC.

NETHERTON Lancs
100 SD 3500 4m NNE of Bootle. CP.
W Lancs RD. P BTLE 10. Ch e, r.
Ormskirk CC.

NETHERTON Nthmb
71 NT 9807 6m NW of Rothbury. CP, 200.
Rthbry RD. P Morpeth. Sch p.

Berwick-upon-Tweed CC. See also Burradon.

NETHERTON Worcs
143, 144 SO 9941 3m SW of Evesham. CP, 41. Pershore RD. S Worcs CC.

NETHERTON Yorks (W)
96, 102 SE 2716 4m SW of Wakefield. Loc, Sitlington CP. Wkfld RD. P Wkfld. Ch e, m. Sch p. Wkfld BC.

NETHERTON COLLIERY Nthmb
78 NZ 2482 3m SE of Morpeth. Loc, Bedlingtonshire UD. Blyth BC.

NETHERTOWN Cumb
82 NZ 9907 7m S of Whitehaven. Loc, Lowside Quarter CP. Ennerdale RD. Whthvn CC.

NETHER WALLOP Hants
168 SU 3036 6m SW of Andover. CP, 858. Romsey and Stockbridge RD. P Stckbrdge. Ch e, m. Sch p. Winchester CC. Ch: 15c wall-paintings. 1½m NE, Danebury Camp, hill fort with three lines of ramparts. Long barrows nearby.

NETHER WESTCOTE Glos
144 SP 2220 4m E of Bourton-on-the-Water. Loc, Wstcte CP.

NETHER WHITACRE Warwicks
131 SP 2392 3m NE of Coleshill. CP, 828. Meriden RD. Ch e, m. Sch pe. Mrdn CC. See also Whtcre Hth.

NETHERWITTON Nthmb
77, 78 NZ 1090 7m WNW of Morpeth. CP, 253. Mpth RD. P Mpth. Ch e. Mpth CC. See also Longwitton, Stanton.

NETHER WORTON Oxon
145 SP 4230 7m SSW of Banbury. Loc, Wtn CP. Chipping Norton RD. Ch e. Bnbry CC.

NETLEY Hants
180 SU 4508 3m SE of Southampton. Loc, Hound CP. P(Ntly Abbey), STHMPTN. Ch m, r. Sch i. Vctrn vllge which grew up round large military hsptl (now demolished). Henry VIII's coastal cstle converted into Vctrn mansion. Rems of 13c abbey (A.M.).

NETLEY MARSH Hants
180 SU 3312 4m NE of Lyndhurst. CP, 2,618. New Forest RD. Ch e. Sch pe. Nw Frst CC (Eastleigh). See also Ower, Woodlands.

NETTLEBED Oxon
159 SU 7086 5m NW of Henley. CP, 758. Hnly RD. P Hnly-on-Thames. Ch e, r, v. Sch p. Hnly CC.

NETTLEBRIDGE Som
166 ST 6448 4m NNE of Shepton Mallet. Loc, Shptn Mllt RD. Wells CC.

NETTLECOMBE Dorset
177 SY 5195 4m ENE of Bridport. Loc, Powerstock CP. Ch m.

NETTLECOMBE Som
164 ST 0537 4m SSW of Watchet. CP, 201. Williton RD. Ch e. Bridgwater CC. Nttlcmbe Ct, gabled Elizn hse in red sandstone.

NETTLEDEN Herts
147, 159, 160 TL 0210 2m NE of Berkhamsted. CP(Nttldn w Potten End), 1,199. Bkhmstd RD. Ch e. Hemel Hempstead CC.

NETTLEHAM Lincs (L)
104 TF 0075 4m NE of Lincoln. CP. Welton RD. P LNCLN. Ch e, m. Sch pe. Gainsborough CC. Several grns; stream flows through. Large 13c ch, restored.

NETTLESTEAD Kent
171 TQ 6852 5m WSW of Maidstone. CP, 660. Mdstne RD. P Mdstne. Ch e. Sch p. Mdstne CC. See also Nttlstd Grn.

NETTLESTEAD Suffolk (E)
149 TM 0849 6m NW of Ipswich. CP, 123. Gipping RD. Ch e. Eye CC.

NETTLESTEAD GREEN Kent
171 TQ 6850 6m SW of Maidstone. Loc, Nttlstd CP.

NETTLESTONE IOW
180 SZ 6290 2m SE of Ryde. Loc, Rde MB. P Seaview.

NETTLESWORTH Co Durham
85 NZ 2547 3m SSW of Chester-le-Street. Loc, Plawsworth CP. Ch m. Sch i.

NETTLETON Lincs (L)
104 TA 1100 just SW of Caistor. CP, 568.
Cstr RD. P LINCOLN. Ch e, m. Sch p.
Gainsborough CC. Iron mines nearby.

NETTLETON Wilts
156 ST 8178 7m NW of Chippenham.
CP, 570. Calne and Chppnhm RD. Ch e, b.
Sch pe. Chppnhm CC. See also Burton,
W Kington. Ch is at Btn.

NEVENDON Essex
161, 162 TQ 7391 2m N of Basildon. Loc,
Bsldn UD.

NEW ADDINGTON London
171 TQ 3862 4m SE of Croydon. Loc,
Crdn LB. Crdn Central BC (Crdn S).
Somewhat isolated rsdntl area on windswept
plateau attaining height of 500ft.

NEWALL Yorks (W)
96 SE 2046 just N of Otley. CP(Nwll
w Clifton)), 197. Wharfedale RD. P Otley.
Ripon CC.

NEW ALRESFORD Hants
168 SU 5832 7m ENE of Winchester.
CP, 2,159. Wnchstr RD. P(Alrsfd).
Ch e, m, v. Sch i, j, s. Wnchstr CC. New
in 1200.

NEW ANNESLEY Notts
112 SK 5053 5m SSW of Mansfield. Loc,
Kirkby in Ashfield UD, Basford RD.
P(Annesley), NOTTINGHAM. Ashfld CC.

NEWARK-ON-TRENT Notts
112/113 SK 7953 16m SW of Lincoln.
MB(Nwk), 24,631. P(Nwk). Nwk CC. Rems
of cstle*, 12c–13c. King John died
here, 1216. Superb EE to Perp ch with tall
spire. Mkt square.

NEWBALD Yorks (E)
98 SE 9136 4m SSE of Mkt Weighton.
CP, 695. Beverley RD. P(N Nbld), YORK.
Ch e. Sch p.

NEW BARNETBY Lincs (L)
104 TA 0710 5m ENE of Brigg. Loc,
Melton Ross CP.

NEW BEWICK Nthmb
71 NU 0620 7m SE of Wooler. Loc,
Bwck CP. Glendale RD.
Berwick-upon-Tweed CC.

NEWBIGGIN Co Durham
84 NY 9127 3m NW of Middleton in
Teesdale. CP, 206. Barnard Cstle RD. P Bnd
Cstle. Ch m2. Bishop Auckland CC.

NEWBIGGIN Cumb
83 NY 4729 3m W of Penrith. Loc,
Dacre CP. P Pnrth. Ch m.

NEWBIGGIN Cumb
83 NY 5549 8m SSE of Brampton. Loc,
Ainstable CP. Ch m.

NEWBIGGIN Lancs
88 SD 2669 4m E of Barrow. Loc,
Aldingham CP.

NEWBIGGIN Nthmb
84 NY 9549 9m S of Hexham. Loc,
Blanchland CP.

NEWBIGGIN Westm
83 NY 6228 6m NW of Appleby. CP, 107.
N Westm RD. P Penrith, Cumberland.
Ch e, m. Westm CC.

NEWBIGGIN Yorks (N)
90 SD 9591 4m NW of Aysgarth. Loc,
Askrigg CP.

NEWBIGGIN Yorks (N)
90 SD 9985 2m S of Aysgarth. CP, 52.
Aysgth RD. Richmond CC.

NEWBIGGIN-BY-THE-SEA Nthmb
78 NZ 3087 7m E of Morpeth.
UD, 10,661. P. Mpth CC. See also
N Seaton, N Stn Colliery. Mining, fishing,
caravanning.

NEWBIGGIN ON LUNE Westm
83 NY 7005 5m WSW of Kirkby Stephen.
Loc, Ravenstonedale CP. P Kby Stphn.
Ch e, m. Sch pe.

NEWBOLD Derbys
111 SK 3773 2m NNW of Chesterfield. Loc,
Chstrfld MB. P Chstrfld.

NEWBOLD Leics
121 SK 4018 3m NNW of Coalville. Loc,
Worthington CP. Sch pe.

NEWBOLD ON AVON Warwicks
132 SP 4877 2m NNW of Rugby. Loc,
Rgby MB. P Rgby.

NEWBOLD ON STOUR Warwicks
144 SP 2446 6m SSE of Stratford. Loc,
Tredington CP. P Strtfd-upon-Avon.
Ch e, m. Sch pe.

NEWBOLD PACEY Warwicks
132 SP 2957 5m S of Warwick. CP, 349.
Strtfd-on-Avon RD. Ch e.
Strtfd-on-Avon CC (Strtfd). See also
Ashorne.

NEWBOLD VERDON Leics
121 SK 4403 7m N of Hinckley. CP, 2,253.
Mkt Bosworth RD. P LEICESTER.
Ch e, b, m, v. Sch p. Bswth CC.

NEW BOLINGBROKE Lincs (L)
114 TF 3058 9m N of Boston. Loc,
Carrington CP. P Bstn. Ch e, m.

NEWBOROUGH Hunts
123 TF 2006 5m N of Peterborough.
CP, 719. Ptrbrgh RD. P PTRBRGH. Ch e.
Sch pe. Ptrbrgh BC (CC).

NEWBOROUGH Staffs
120 SK 1325 6m SSE of Uttoxeter.
CP, 459. Uttxtr RD. P Burton-on-Trent.
Ch e, m. Sch pe. Btn CC.

NEWBOTTLE Co Durham
78 NZ 3351 1m N of Houghton-le-Spring.
Loc, Htn-le-Sprng UD. P Htn-le-Sprng.

NEWBOTTLE Northants
145 SP 5236 4m W of Brackley. CP, 376.
Brckly RD. Ch e. Daventry CC (S Nthnts).
See also Charlton.

NEWBOURN Suffolk (E)
150 TM 2743 4m S of Woodbridge.
CP, 310. Deben RD. P Wdbrdge. Ch e, m.
Sudbury and Wdbrdge CC.

NEW BRANCEPETH Co Durham
85 NZ 2241 3m W of Durham. Loc,
Brandon and Byshottles UD. P DRHM.

NEWBRIDGE Cornwall
189 SW 4231 3m WNW of Penzance. Loc,
W Penwith RD. P Pnznce. Ch m. St Ives CC.

NEWBRIDGE Hants
180 SU 2915 5m SW of Romsey. Loc,
Copythorne CP.

NEWBRIDGE IOW
180 SZ 4187 4m ESE of Yarmouth. Loc,
Shalfleet CP. P Newport. Ch m.

NEW BRINSLEY Notts
112 SK 4650 4m E of Ripley. Loc,
Brnsly CP. P NOTTINGHAM. Ch m.

NEWBROUGH Nthmb
77 NY 8767 3m NE of Haydon Br. CP, 607.
Hexham RD. Ch e. Sch pe. Hxhm CC. Near
site of Roman fort above N bank of S Tyne
and on line of Roman rd.

NEW BUCKENHAM Norfolk
136 TM 0890 4m SE of Attleborough.
CP, 375. Wayland RD. Ch e, m. S Nflk CC.
Scanty rems of 12c cstle. To SW, Banham
Zoo*.

NEWBUILDINGS Devon
175 SS 7903 3m NW of Crediton. Loc,
Sandford CP. Ch m.

NEWBURGH Lancs
100 SD 4810 4m ENE of Ormskirk. Loc,
Ormskk UD. P Wigan.

NEWBURN Nthmb
78 NZ 1665 5m W of Newcastle.
UD, 39,379. P NCSTLE UPON TYNE 5.
Ncstle upn Tne W BC. See also Lemington,
N Walbottle, Throckley, Thrckly Bank Top,
Wlbttle, Westerhope. Mining and indstrl tn.

NEWBURY Berks
158 SU 4767 16m WSW of Reading.
MB, 23,696. P. Nbry CC. Busy tn on
R Kennet, here crossed by 18c br. Its long
prosperity only once faintly interrupted, by
Civil War (Battle of Newbury, 1644). Now
increased by considerable commuting pop.

NEWBY Westm
83 NY 5921 6m W of Appleby. CP, 172.
N Westm RD. P Penrith, Cumberland. Ch m.
Westm CC.

NEWBY Yorks (N)
85 NZ 5012 3m NW of Stokesley. CP.
Stokesley RD. Ch m. Sch p. Richmond CC.

NEWBY Yorks (W)
90 SD 7270 7m NW of Settle. CP(Clapham
cum Nby), 536. Sttle RD. Ch m. Sch p.
Skipton CC. Blt round large grn.

NEWBY BRIDGE Lancs
88, 89 SD 3686 7m NE of Ulverston. Loc,
Staveley CP. P Ulvstn. 17c br over R Leven;
18c inn. 1m NE, S end of Lake Windermere.

NEWBY EAST Cumb
76 NY 4758 5m ENE of Carlisle. Loc,
Irthington CP.

NEWBY WEST Cumb
76 NY 3653 3m SW of Carlisle. Loc,
Cummersdale CP.

NEWBY WISKE Yorks (N)
91 SE 3687 4m S of Northallerton. CP, 289.
Thirsk RD. P Nthlltn. Ch m. Sch p. Thsk
and Malton CC. Largely 18c estate vllge.

NEWCASTLE Shrops
128 SO 2482 4m WNW of Clun. Loc,
Cln CP. P Craven Arms. Ch e, m. Sch pe.
Well defined stretch of Offa's Dyke to E.

NEWCASTLE-UNDER-LYME Staffs
110 SJ 8445 2m W of Stoke-on-Trent.
MB, 76,970. P(Ncstle). N-u-L BC. See also
Clayton, Red St, Silverdale.

NEWCASTLE UPON TYNE Nthmb
78 NZ 2464 80m N of Leeds. CB, 222,153.
P(NCSTLE UPN TNE). BCs: Central, E,
N, W. See also Jesmond, Scotswood, Walker.
Cultural and commercial capital of the North
East. Port. Shipbuilding. Various mnfctres.
Cathedral, formerly par ch. University. Airpt.
Notable early 19c architecture and layout
of central area. Three fine brs span R Tyne.
12c cstle keep* (restored); 13c Black Gate*.

NEWCHAPEL Staffs
110 SJ 8654 6m N of Stoke-on-Trent. Loc,
Kidsgrove UD. P Stke-on-Trnt.

NEW CHAPEL Surrey
171 TQ 3642 3m NW of E Grinstead. Loc,
Godstone RD. Ch v. E Srry CC (Reigate).
Mormon temple, with gdns*.

NEWCHURCH IOW
180 SZ 5685 3m WNW of Sandown.
CP, 1,122. Isle of Wight RD and CC.
P Sndn. Ch e, c. Sch p. See also Apse Hth,
Branstone.

NEWCHURCH Kent
173, 184 TR 0531 7m WSW of Hythe.

CP, 258. Romney Marsh RD. P Rmny Msh.
Ch e. Folkstone and Hthe CC.

NEWCHURCH Lancs
95 SD 8239 2m WNW of Nelson. Loc,
Bnly RD. Ch e. Sch pe. Clitheroe CC.

NEWCHURCH Staffs
120 SK 1423 6m W of Burton-on-Trent.
Loc, Yoxall CP. Ch e.

NEW CLIPSTONE Notts
112 SK 5863 3m ENE of Mansfield. Loc,
Clpstne CP.

NEW COSTESSEY Norfolk
126 TG 1810 3m WNW of Norwich. Loc,
Cstssy CP. Ch m2.

NEW CROFTON Yorks (W)
96, 102, 103 SE 3817 4m SE of Wakefield.
Loc, Crftn CP. P Wkfld.

NEW CROSS London
161, 171 TQ 3677 3m SE of Lndn Br. Loc,
Lewisham LB. Deptford BC.

NEW DELAVAL Nthmb
78 NZ 3079 2m SW of Blyth. Loc, Blth MB.

NEWDIGATE Surrey
170, 182 TQ 1942 5m SSE of Dorking.
CP, 1,394. Dkng and Horley RD. P Dkng.
Ch e, c. Sch pe. Dkng CC. See also Parkgate.
Some half-timbered hses.

NEW DUSTON Northants
133 SP 7162 3m NW of Northampton. Loc,
Nthmptn CB. P NTHMPTN. Nthmptn S BC
(S Nthnts CC).

NEW EARSWICK Yorks (N)
97, 98 SE 6155 2m N of York. CP, 2,001.
Flaxton RD. P YK. Ch m. Sch p, s. Thirsk
and Malton CC. Gdn suburb blt early 20c by
Joseph Rowntree Village Trust.

NEW EDLINGTON Yorks (W)
103 SK 5398 4m SW of Doncaster. Loc,
Edlngtn CP. Dncstr RD. P(Edlngtn), Dncstr.
Ch e, r. Sch i, j, p, pr, s. Don Valley CC.

NEW ELLERBY Yorks (E)
99 TA 1639 6m SSW of Hornsea. Loc,
Burton Constable CP. Ch m.

NEWELL GREEN Berks
169 SU 8871 1m NE of Bracknell. Loc,
Warfield CP.

NEW END Worcs
131 SP 0560 5m S of Redditch. Loc,
Inkberrow CP.

NEWENDEN Kent
184 TQ 8327 5m SW of Tenterden.
CP, 168. Tntdn RD. P Hawkhurst. Ch e.
Ashfd CC.

NEWENT Glos
143 SO 7226 8m NW of Gloucester.
CP, 3,167. Nwnt RD. P. Ch e, m, r, v3.
Sch s. W Glos CC. See also Kilcot. 16c mkt
hall, timber-framed, on 'stilts'.

NEWFIELD Co Durham
78 NZ 2452 2m WNW of Chester-le-Street.
Loc, Pelton CP. P Chstr-le-Strt. Ch s.

NEWFIELD Co Durham
85 NZ 2033 1m SSE of Willington. Loc,
Bishop Auckland UD. P Bshp Aucklnd.

NEW FISHBOURNE Sussex (W)
181 SU 8404 1m W of Chichester. Loc,
Chchstr MB. P(Fshbne), Chchstr.

NEWGATE Norfolk
125 TG 0443 3m NW of Holt. Loc, Cley
next the Sea CP.

NEWGATE STREET Herts
160 TL 3005 4m WNW of Cheshunt. Loc,
Hatfield CP.

NEW GRIMBSY Tresco, Isles of Scilly
189 SV 8815. Loc, Tresco CP. P(Trsco).

NEWHALL Ches
110 SJ 6045 5m SSW of Nantwich. CP, 672.
Nntwch RD. Ch m. Nntwch CC. See also
Aston.

NEWHALL Derbys
120, 121 SK 2820 3m SE of
Burton-on-Trent. Loc, Swadlincote UD.
P Btn-on-Trnt, Staffs.

NEWHAM Nthmb
71 NU 1728 5m SE of Belford. Loc,
Ellingham CP.

NEW HARTLEY Nthmb
78 NZ 3076 3m S of Blyth. Loc, Seaton
Valley UD. P Whitley Bay. Blth BC.

NEWHAVEN Sussex (E)
183 TQ 4401 9m ESE of Brighton.
UD, 9,977. P. Lewes CC. See also Denton.
Cross-channel port.

NEW HEATON Nthmb
63, 64 NT 8840 3m E of Coldstream. Loc,
Cornhill-on-Tweed CP.

NEW HERRINGTON Co Durham
78 NZ 3352 2m N of Houghton-le-Spring.
Loc, Htn-le-Sprng UD. P Htn-le-Sprng.

NEW HEY Lancs
101 SD 9311 3m ESE of Rochdale. Loc,
Milnrow UD. P Rchdle.

NEW HOLLAND Lincs (L)
99 TA 0823 3m ENE of
Barton-upon-Humber. Loc,
Barrow-upn-Hmbr CP. P Brrw-on-Hmbr.
Ch e. Sch pem. Ferry to Hull.

NEWHOLM Yorks (N)
86 NZ 8610 2m W of Whitby.
CP(Nhlm-cum-Dunsley), 206. Whtby RD.
P Whtby. Ch m. Cleveland and Whtby CC
(Scarborough and Whtby).

NEW HOUGHTON Derbys
112 SK 4965 4m NW of Mansfield. Loc,
Pleasley CP. P Mnsfld, Notts. Ch e.

NEW HOUGHTON Norfolk
125 TF 7927 8m W of Fakenham. Loc,
Hghtn CP. Docking RD. P(Hghtn), King's
Lynn. Ch e, m. NW Nflk CC (K's Lnn).
Vllge rebuilt 18c at gates of great hse blt for
Sir Robert Walpole c 1730 by Kent.

NEWHOUSES Nthmb
77 NZ 0083 10m SE of Otterburn. Loc,
Kirkwhelpington CP.

NEW HOUSES Yorks (W)
90 SD 8073 6m N of Settle. Loc, Horton in
Ribblesdale CP.

NEW HUTTON Westm
89 SD 5691 3m ESE of Kendal. CP, 208.
S Westm RD. Ch e. Westm CC. See also
Millholme.

NEW HYTHE Kent
171, 172 TQ 7159 4m NW of Maidstone.
Loc, E Malling and Larkfield CP. P Mdstne.
Ch e.

NEWICK Sussex (E)
183 TQ 4121 4m W of Uckfield. CP, 1,299. Chailey RD. P Lewes. Ch e, b, v. Sch pe. Lws CC.

NEWINGTON Kent
172 TQ 8564 3m WNW of Sittingbourne. CP, 1,822. Swale RD. P Sttngbne. Ch e, m. Sch pe. Faversham CC.

NEWINGTON Kent
173 TR 1837 3m WNW of Folkestone. CP, 338. Elham RD. Ch e. Flkstne and Hythe CC.

NEWINGTON Oxon
158 SU 6096 5m N of Wallingford. CP, 137. Bullingdon RD. Ch e. Henley CC.

NEWINGTON BAGPATH Glos
156 ST 8194 5m WNW of Tetbury. Loc, Kingscote CP. Ch e.

NEW INVENTION Shrops
129 SO 2976 3m N of Knighton. Loc, Clun CP. Ch m.

NEW LAMBTON Co Durham
78 NZ 3150 2m WNW of Houghton-le-Spring. Loc, Bournmoor CP. P Htn-le-Sprng. Ch m2. Sch p.

NEWLAND Glos
155, 156 SO 5509 4m SE of Monmouth. CP, 963. W Dean RD. P Coleford. Ch e. W Glos CC. See also Clearwell, Redbrook, Trow Grn.

NEWLAND Worcs
143 SO 7948 2m NE of Malvern. CP, 248. Upton upon Severn RD. Ch e. S Worcs CC.

NEWLAND Yorks (W)
97, 98 SE 6924 3m WNW of Goole. CP, 165. Selby RD. Barkston Ash CC.

NEWLANDS Nthmb
77, 78 NZ 0955 3m NNW of Consett. Loc, Shotley Low Quarter CP. Hexham RD. Hxhm CC.

NEW LANE Lancs
100 SD 4212 3m NNE of Ormskirk. Loc, Ormskk UD.

NEW LEAKE Lincs (L)
114 TF 4057 9m NNE of Boston. CP, 417.

Spilsby RD. P Bstn. Ch e, m. Sch p. Horncastle CC.

NEW LONGTON Lancs
94 SD 5025 3m SW of Preston. Loc, Lngtn CP. P Prstn. Ch e, m. Sch pe.

NEWLYN Cornwall
189 SW 4628 1m SSW of Penzance. Loc, Pnznce MB. P Pnznce. Fishing vllge, artists' haunt.

NEWLYN EAST Cornwall
185 SW 8256 4m SSE of Newquay. Loc, Nln CP. Truro RD. Ch e, m. Sch pe. Truro CC.

NEW MALDEN London
170 TQ 2168 2m E of Kingston. Loc, Kngstn upon Thames LB. P Surrey. Kngstn upn Thms BC.

NEWMARKET Suffolk (W)
135 TL 6463 12m ENE of Cambridge. UD, 12,934. P. Bury St Edmunds CC. See also Exning. HQ of English horse-racing. Racecourses. National Stud*, 1½m SW. Tn has wide main st; Ggn hses.

NEW MARSKE Yorks (N)
86 NZ 6221 8m E of Teesside (Middlesborough). Loc, Saltburn and Mske-by-the-Sea UD. P REDCAR, Tssde.

NEW MARTON Shrops
118 SJ 3334 4m W of Ellesmere. Loc, Ellesmre Rural CP. N Shrops RD. Oswestry CC.

NEWMILL Cornwall
189 SW 4534 3m NNW of Penzance. Loc, Madron CP. P Pnznce.

NEW MILL Herts
146, 159 SP 9212 just NNE of Tring. Loc, Trng UD.

NEW MILL Yorks (W)
102 SE 1608 5m SSE of Huddersfield. Loc, Holmfirth UD. P Hddsfld.

NEW MILLS Cornwall
185, 190 SW 8952 7m NE of Truro. Loc, Ladock CP. Ch m.

NEW MILLS Derbys
101/102/111 SK 0085 6m SSW of Glossop.

UD, 9,165. P Stockport, Cheshire. High Peak CC. See also Newtown. Textile printing, engineering, paper-mnfg, etc.

NEW MILTON Hants
179 SZ 2495 6m ENE of Christchurch. Loc, Lymington MB. P.

NEWNHAM Glos
143 SO 6911 3m ESE of Cinderford. CP, 1,118. Gloucester RD. P. Ch e, v. Sch pe. W Glos CC. On Severn estuary.

NEWNHAM Hants
169 SU 7053 5m ENE of Basingstoke. CP, 340. Bsngstke RD. P Bsngstke. Ch e, m. Bsngstke CC.

NEWNHAM Herts
147 TL 2437 2m N of Baldock. CP, 153. Hitchin RD. P Bldck. Ch e. Htchn CC.

NEWNHAM Kent
172 TQ 9557 5m SW of Faversham. CP, 291. Swale RD. Ch e. Fvrshm CC.

NEWNHAM Northants
132, 133 SP 5759 2m S of Daventry. CP, 358. Dvntry RD. P Dvntry. Ch e, c. Sch p. Dvntry CC (S Nthnts).

NEWNHAM BRIDGE Worcs
129, 130 SO 6469 3m E of Tenbury Wells. Loc, Knighton on Teme CP. P Tnbry Wlls.

NEWPORT Devon
163 SS 5632 1m SE of Barnstaple. Loc, Bnstple MB.

NEWPORT Essex
148 TL 5234 3m SSW of Saffron Walden. CP, 1,154. Sffrn Wldn RD. P Sffrn Wldn. Ch e, v. Sch p, s. Sffrn Wldn CC. Many old hses with good pargetting.

NEWPORT Glos
156 ST 6997 10m NE of Severn Rd Br. Loc, Alkington CP. Thornbury RD. Ch v. S Glos CC.

NEWPORT IOW
180 SZ 4989 6m WSW of Ryde. MB, 22,286. P. Isle of Wight CC. See also Bowcombe, Carisbrooke, Downend, Parkhurst, Staplers, Wootton Br, Wttn Cmmn. Capital of IOW. To N, Parkhurst Prison. To S, Roman villa*.

NEWPORT Norfolk
126 TG 5016 6m N of Yarmouth. Loc, Hemsby CP.

NEWPORT Shrops
119 SJ 7419 8m NE of Wellington. UD, 6,919. P. The Wrekin CC (The Wrkn CC, Stafford and Stone CC). Pleasing small tn with long High St.

NEWPORT Yorks (E)
98 SE 8530 7m S of Mkt Weighton. CP, 924. Howden RD. P Brough. Ch e, m2, r. Sch p. Hdn CC.

NEWPORT PAGNELL Bucks
146 SP 8743 6m N of Bletchley. UD, 6,337. P. Buckingham CC.

NEWPOUND COMMON Sussex (W)
182 TQ 0627 2m WNW of Billingshurst. Loc, Wisborough Grn CP.

NEWQUAY Cornwall
185 SW 8161 11m N of Truro. UD, 14,963. P. N Cnwll CC. See also Crantock, Pentire, St Columb Minor, W Pentire. Resort with many fine beaches.

NEW ROMNEY Kent
184 TR 0624 10m ENE of Rye. MB, 3,414. P. Folkestone and Hythe CC. See also Greatstone-on-Sea, Littlestone-on-Sea. Orig Cinque Port, not now on sea. Fine ch with brasses. At stn, museum of narrow-gauge rly and models.

NEW ROSSINGTON Yorks (W)
103 SK 6197 4m SE of Doncaster. Loc, Rssngtn CP. P Dncstr. Ch v. Sch i, j2, p.

NEW SARUM Wilts
167 SU 1430 21m NW of Southampton. See Salisbury.

NEWSHAM Lancs
94 SD 5136 5m NNW of Preston. Loc, Barton CP. Ch r. Sch pr.

NEWSHAM Nthmb
78 NZ 3079 1m SW of Blyth. Loc, Blth MB. P Blth.

NEWSHAM Yorks (N)
84 NZ 1010 5m SE of Barnard Cstle. CP, 220. Richmond RD. P Rchmnd. Ch m. Rchmnd CC.

NEWSHOLME Yorks (E)
97, 98 SE 7129 4m NNW of Goole. Loc, Wressle CP.

NEWSTEAD Notts
112 SK 5252 5m S of Mansfield. CP, 2,569.
Basford RD. P (Nstd Colliery), NOTTING-
HAM. Ch e, m, v. Sch i, p. Charlton CC
(Ashfield). The 12c abbey* (correctly
'priory') was given to Ld Byron's ancestors
by Henry VIII at the Dissolution and
converted to private residence. Byron relics.

NEWSTEAD Nthmb
71 NU 1527 5m SSE of Belford. Loc,
Adderstone w Lucker CP.

NEWTHORPE YORKS (W)
97 SE 4732 5m NNE of Castleford.
CP(Huddleston w Nthpe), 102.
Tadcaster RD. Ch m. Barkston Ash CC.

NEWTON Cambs
124 TF 4314 4m NNW of Wisbech. CP, 729.
Wsbch RD. P Wsbch. Ch e, m. Sch p. Isle of
Ely CC. See also Fitton End.

NEWTON Cambs
148 TL 4349 6m S of Cambridge. CP, 306.
Chesterton RD. P CMBRDGE. Ch e.
Cambs CC.

NEWTON Ches
109 SJ 5059 8m SE of Chester. CP(Ntn
by Tattenhall), 148. Tarvin RD.
Nantwich CC.

NEWTON Ches
109 SJ 5375 5m S of Runcorn. Loc,
Kingsley CP. Sch p, pe.

NEWTON Derbys
112 SK 4459 3m NE of Alfreton. Loc,
Blackwell CP. P DERBY. Ch m. Sch p.

NEWTON Herefs
142 SO 3433 11m WSW of Hereford.
CP, 123. Dore and Bredwardine RD.
Ch e, m. Hrfd CC. See also Lr Maes-coed,
Middle Ms-Cd.

NEWTON Herefs
142 SO 5053 3m S of Leominster. CP, 56.
Lmnstr and Wigmore RD. Lmnstr CC.

NEWTON Lancs
88 SD 2371 3m NE of Barrow. Loc,
Dalton-in-Furness UD.
P(Ntn-in-Fnss), Brrw-in-Fnss.

NEWTON Lancs
89 SD 5974 3m SSW of Kirkby Lonsdale.
Loc, Whittington CP.

NEWTON Lancs
94 SD 3436 2m E of Blackpool. Loc,
Staining CP.

NEWTON Lancs
94 SD 4430 6m W of Preston. CP(Ntn-w-
Clifton), 1,785. Fylde RD. Sch pe. S Flde CC.
See also Scales.

NEWTON Lincs (K)
113, 123 TF 0436 6m SSW of Sleaford.
CP(Ntn and Haceby), 134. E Kesteven RD.
P Slfd. Ch e. Sch pe. Rutland and
Stamford CC.

NEWTON Norfolk
125 TF 8315 4m N of Swaffham. CP(Ntn
by Cstle Acre), 50. Swffm RD. Ch e.
SW Nflk CC.

NEWTON Northants
133 SP 8883 3m N of Kettering. CP.
Kttrng RD. Ch e. Kttrng CC. See also Lit
Oakley.

NEWTON Notts
112, 122 SK 6841 7m E of Nottingham.
Loc, Shelford CP.

NEWTON Nthmb
77, 78 NZ 0364 3m E of Corbridge. Loc,
Bywell CP. Hexham RD. P Stocksfield.
Ch m. Hxhm CC. Bywell has two chs and a
cstle in a bend of R Tyne 2m SSE.

NEWTON Staffs
120 SK 0325 5m N of Rugeley. Loc,
Blithfield CP. Uttoxeter RD. Burton CC. At
NW end of Blthfld Reservoir.

NEWTON Suffolk (W)
149 TL 9140 3m E of Sudbury. CP, 331.
Melford RD. Ch e. Sdbry and
Woodbridge CC. Vast vllge grn contains
Sdbry golf course. Large 14c ch; chancel
only in use.

NEWTON Warwicks
132 SP 5378 3m NE of Rugby. CP(Ntn and
Biggin), 263. Rgby RD. P Rgby. Ch e.
Rgby CC.

NEWTON Wilts
167 SU 2322 7m SE of Salisbury. Loc,
Whiteparish CP.

NEWTON Yorks (E)
92, 93 SE 8872 6m E of Malton. Loc, Wintringham CP.

NEWTON Yorks (N)
86 NZ 5713 6m SE of Teesside (Middlesbrough). Loc, Guisborough UD. To E, Roseberry Topping, conical hill and landmark, 1,057ft.

NEWTON Yorks (W)
94, 95 SD 6950 6m NNW of Clitheroe. CP, 249. Bowland RD. Ch v. Skipton CC.

NEWTON ABBOT Devon
176, 188 SX 8571 14m SSW of Exeter. UD, 19,367. P. Totnes CC. See also Highweek. Mkt tn and rly junction. St Leonard's Twr remains from former ch in tn centre.

NEWTON ARLOSH Cumb
75 NY 1955 2m WSW of Kirkbride. Loc, Holme East Waver CP. Wigton RD. Ch e. Sch p. Penrith and the Border CC. Ch has fortified twr of early 14c.

NEWTON AYCLIFFE Co Durham
85 NZ 2724 6m N of Darlington. Loc, Gt Ayclffe CP. Dlngtn RD. P Dlngtn. Ch e, m, r, v. Sch i, j2, jr, p3, pr, s2. Bishop Auckland CC (Sedgefield). New tn developed since World War II. (Pop. in 1971: 20,190.) Ayclffe Indstrl Estate to S.

NEWTON BEWLEY Co Durham
85 NZ 4626 5m NNE of Teesside (Stockton). CP. Stcktn RD. Easington CC (Sedgefield).

NEWTON BLOSSOMVILLE Bucks
146 SP 9251 2m E of Olney. CP, 171. Newport Pagnell RD. P BEDFORD. Ch e. Sch pe. Buckingham CC.

NEWTON BROMSHOLD Northants
134 SP 9965 3m E of Rushden. CP, 62. Wellingborough RD. Ch e. Wllngbrgh CC.

NEWTON BURGOLAND Leics
120, 121 SK 3709 5m SW of Coalville. Loc, Swepstone CP. P LEICESTER. Ch v. Sch p.

NEWTON BY TOFT Lincs (L)
104 TF 0587 4m WSW of Mkt Rasen. Loc, Tft Ntn CP. Caistor RD. Ch e, m. Gainsborough CC.

NEWTON FERRERS Devon
187 SX 5448 6m SE of Plymouth. CP(Newton and Noss), 1,842. Plympton St Mary RD. P Plmth. Ch e. Sch pe. W Dvn CC (Tavistock). Old vllge of slate and thatch with many new hses. Boating.

NEWTON FLOTMAN Norfolk
137 TM 2198 7m S of Norwich. CP, 327. Forehoe and Henstead RD. P NRWCH, NOR 59W. Ch e. Sch pe. S Nflk CC (Central Nflk).

NEWTON HARCOURT Leics
132, 133 SP 6396 6m SE of Leicester. Loc, Wistow CP. Billesdon RD. P LCSTR. Ch e. Harborough CC (Melton).

NEWTON KYME Yorks (W)
97 SE 4645 2m NW of Tadcaster. CP(Ntn Kme cum Toulston), 236. Tdcstr RD. P Tdcstr. Ch e. Barkston Ash CC.

NEWTON-LE-WILLOWS Lancs
100 SK 5995 5m E of St Helens. UD, 22,380. P. Ntn CC. See also Earlestown. Rly wks. Coal-mining.

NEWTON-LE-WILLOWS Yorks (N)
91 SE 2189 3m WNW of Bedale. CP, 288. Leyburn RD. P Bdle. Ch m2. Sch pe. Richmond CC.

NEWTON LONGVILLE Bucks
146 SP 8431 2m SW of Bletchley. CP, 871. Winslow RD. P Bltchly. Ch e, b, m. Sch pe. Buckingham CC. Mnr hse incorporates rems of Nmn priory.

NEWTON MORRELL Yorks (N)
85 NZ 2309 4m SW of Darlington. CP, 49. Croft RD. Richmond CC.

NEWTON MULGRAVE Yorks (N)
86 NZ 7815 5m ESE of Loftus. CP, 63. Whitby RD. Cleveland and Whtby CC (Scarborough and Whtby).

NEWTON-ON-OUSE Yorks (N)
97 SE 5160 8m NW of York. CP, 371. Easingwold RD. P YK. Ch e, m. Sch pe. Thirsk and Malton CC.

NEWTON-ON-RAWCLIFFE Yorks (N)
86, 92 SE 8190 4m NNE of Pickering. CP(Ntn), 197. Pckrng RD. P Pckrng. Ch e, m2. SCARBOROUGH CC (Scbrgh and Whitby).

NEWTON-ON-THE-MOOR Nthmb
71 NU 1705 5m S of Alnwick. CP, 492.
Alnwck RD. P Felton, Morpeth. Sch p.
Berwick-upon-Tweed CC. See also Swarland,
Swlnd Estate.

NEWTON ON TRENT Lincs (L)
113 SK 8374 9m WNW of Lincoln. CP, 251.
Gainsborough RD. P LNCLN. Ch e, m.
Sch pe. Gnsbrgh CC. To W, toll br over
R Trent to Notts.

NEWTON POPPLEFORD Devon
176 SY 0889 3m NW of Sidmouth. Loc,
Harpford CP. P Sdmth. Ch e, m. Sch p.

NEWTON PURCELL Oxon
145, 146 SP 6230 5m SE of Brackley.
CP(Ntn Pcll w Shelswell), 91. Ploughley RD.
P BUCKINGHAM. Ch e. Banbury CC
(Henley).

NEWTON REGIS Warwicks
120 SK 2707 5m ENE of Tamworth.
CP, 402. Atherstone RD. P Tmwth, Staffs.
Ch e. Sch pe. Meriden CC. See also No Man's
Hth.

163, 175 SS 4112 7m SW of Torrington.
83 NY 4731 2m WNW of Penrith. Loc,
Catterlen CP. P Pnrth. Ch e.

NEWTON ST CYRES Devon
176 SX 8897 3m ESE of Crediton. CP, 758.
Crdtn RD. P Exeter. Ch e. Sch p.
Tiverton CC (Torrington). See also
Sweetham.

NEWTON ST FAITH Norfolk
126 TG 2117 5m N of Norwich.
CP(Horsham St Fth and Ntn St Fth).
St Fth's and Aylsham RD.
P NRWCH, NOR 86X. N Nflk CC (Central
Nflk).

NEWTON ST LOE Som
166 ST 7064 3m W of Bath. CP, 242.
Bathavon RD. P Bth. Ch e. Sch pe.
N Som CC. Ntn Pk, 18c mansion now
training college.

NEWTON ST PETROCK Devon
163, 175 SS 4112 7m SW OF Torrington
CP, 143. Bideford RD. Ch e, b. N Dvn CC
(Trrngtn).

NEWTON SOLNEY Derbys
120, 121 SK 2825 3m ENE of Burton-on-
Trent. CP, 430. Repton RD. P Btn-on-Trnt,
Staffs. Ch e. Sch ie. Belper CC.

NEWTON STACEY Hants
168 SU 4140 4m SE of Andover. Loc,
Barton Stcy CP.

NEWTON TONEY Wilts
167 SU 2140 4m ESE of Amesbury.
CP, 342. Amesbury RD. P Salisbury.
Ch e, m. Sch pe. Slsbry CC.

NEWTON TRACEY Devon
163 SS 5226 5m SSW of Barnstaple. CP, 92.
Bnstple RD. P Bnstple. Ch e. Sch p. N Dvn CC.

NEWTON UPON DERWENT Yorks (E)
97, 98 SE 7249 5m W of Pocklington. Loc,
Wilberfoss CP. Ch m.

NEWTON VALENCE Hants
169, 181 SU 7232 4m S of Alton. CP, 264.
Altn RD. P Altn. Ch e. Petersfield CC.

NEWTOWN Ches
110 SJ 6248 3m SSW of Nantwich. Loc,
Sound CP. Nntwch RD. P(Snd), Nntwch.
Nntwch CC.

NEWTOWN Cornwall
190 SW 7423 6m SE of Helston. Loc,
St Martin-in-Meneage CP. Kerrier RD.
St Ives CC.

NEWTOWN Cumb
76 NY 5062 2m NW of Brampton. Loc,
Irthington CP. P Carlisle.

NEWTOWN Cumb
81, 82 NY 0948 3m SSW of Silloth. Loc,
Holme St Cuthbert CP.

NEWTOWN Derbys
101 SJ 9984 6m SSW of Glossop. Loc, New
Mills UD. P Nw Mlls, Stockport, Cheshire.

NEWTOWN Devon
163 SS 7625 3m E of S Molton. Loc,
Bishop's Nympton CP. Ch m.

NEWTOWN Glos
155, 156 SO 6701 6m WNW of Dursley.
Loc, Hinton CP. P Berkeley.

NEWTOWN Hants
168 SU 3023 3m NW of Romsey. Loc,
Rmsy and Stockbridge RD. Eastleigh CC,
Winchester CC.

NEWTOWN Hants
168 SU 4763 2m S of Newbury. CP, 250.
Kingsclere and Whitchurch RD. P Nbry,
Berks. Ch e. Bsngstke CC.

NEW TOWN Hants
168 SU 5962 7m NNW of Basingstoke. Loc,
Tadley CP.

NEWTOWN Hants
179 SU 2710 3m NW of Lyndhurst. Loc,
Minstead CP.

NEWTOWN Hants
180 SU 6113 5m NNE of Fareham. Loc,
Soberton CP. P Frhm. Ch e. Sch p.

NEWTOWN Herefs
142, 143 SO 6144 7m ENE of Hereford.
Loc, Yarkhill CP.

NEWTOWN IOW
180 SZ 4290 4m E of Yarmouth. Loc,
Calbourne CP. Ch e. Tn hall* dates from
18c, when tn was a busy port. Whole
area NT.

NEWTOWN Lancs
100 SD 5118 4m W of Chorley. Loc,
Chly RD. Chly CC.

NEWTOWN Nthmb
64, 71 NT 9631 3m NW of Wooler. Loc,
E w a r t CP. G l e n d a l e R D .
Berwick-upon-Tweed CC.

NEWTOWN Nthmb
71 NU 0300 1m WSW of Rothbury. Loc,
T o s s o n CP. R t h b r y R D .
Berwick-upon-Tweed CC. Tweeds formerly
made here in now deserted mill.

NEWTOWN Nthmb
71 NU 0425 4m SE of Wooler. Loc,
L i l b u r n CP. G l e n d a l e R D .
Berwick-upon-Tweed CC.

NEWTOWN Shrops
118 SJ 4731 3m NW of Wem. Loc, Wm
Rural. N Shrops RD. Ch e. Sch pe.
Oswestry CC.

NEWTOWN Staffs
110 SJ 9060 3m ESE of Congleton. Loc,
Rushton CP. Leek RD. Lk CC.

NEWTOWN Wilts
166, 167 ST 9129 5m NE of Shaftesbury.
Loc, W Tisbury CP. Mere and Tisbury RD.

Ch e. Westbury CC. To SW, Pyte Hse*, late
Ggn.

NEWTOWN LINFORD Leics
121 SK 5110 6m NW of Leicester. CP.
Barrow upon Soar RD. P LCSTR. Ch e.
Sch p. Melton CC. To E, Bradgate Pk*,
grnds of now ruined 15c–16c hse of Grey
family; home of Lady Jane Grey, executed
1554. Old John's Twr, folly of 1786,
memorial ,to old family retainer.

NEW TUPTON Derbys
111 SK 3965 3m S of Chesterfield. Loc,
Tptn CP. Chstrfld RD. P Chstrfld. Ch m2.
Sch p. NE Derbys CC.

NEW WALTHAM Lincs (L)
105 TA 2804 3m S of Grimsby. CP.
Grmsby RD. P Grmsby. Ch m. Sch p.
Louth CC.

NEW WHITTINGTON Derbys
103, 111 SK 3975 3m NNE of Chesterfield.
Loc, Chstrfld MB. P Chstrfld.

NEW WIMPOLE Cambs
147 TL 3449 6m N of Royston. Loc,
Wmple CP. S Cambs RD. Cambs CC. To
NW is Wmple Hall; see Arrington.

NEW YATT Oxon
145 SP 3713 2m NNE of Witney. Loc,
Wtny RD. Ch m. Mid-Oxon CC (Banbury).

NEW YORK Lincs (L)
114 TF 2455 6m SE of Woodhall Spa. Loc,
Wildmore CP. Horncastle RD. P LINCOLN.
Sch p. Hncstle CC.

NEW YORK Nthmb
78 NZ 3270 NW distr of Tynemouth. Loc,
Tnmth CP. P: N Shields.

NIBLEY Glos
156 ST 6982 9m NE of Bristol. Loc,
Westerleigh CP.

NICHOLASHAYNE Devon
164 ST 1016 4m SW of Wellington. Loc,
Culmstock CP.

NIDD Yorks (W)
91 SE 3060 4m N of Harrogate. CP, 106.
Nidderdale RD. Ch e. Hrrgte CC.

NINE ASHES Essex
161 TL 5902 3m E of Ongar. Loc, High
Ongr CP.

NINEBANKS Nthmb
77 NY 7853 6m NE of Alston. Loc,
W Allen CP. Hexham RD. P Hxhm. Ch e.
Hxhm CC.

NINE ELMS London
160, 170 TQ 2977 3m NE of Wandsworth.
Loc, Wndswth LB. Battersea N BC. On S
bank of Thames. Rly goods depot. Gas wks.
Proposed location of fruit and vegetable
mkt now at Covent Gdn (½m N of Charing
Cross rly stn).

NINFIELD Sussex (E)
183, 184 TQ 7012 4m NW of Bexhill.
CP, 1,163. Hailsham RD. P Battle.
Ch e, m2, v. Sch pe. Rye CC. See also
Lunsford's Cross. Cast-iron stocks to N
of ch.

NINGWOOD IOW
180 SZ 3989 3m E of Yarmouth. Loc,
Shalfleet CP.

NITON IOW
180 SZ 5076 4m W of Ventnor. CP, 1,300.
Isle of Wight RD and CC. P Vntnr.
Ch e, b, m, r, v. Sch p. See also Bierley,
Whitwell. 1m SW, St Catherine's Point
Lighthouse*.

NOAK HILL London
161 TQ 5493 3m W of Brentwood. Loc,
Havering LB. Upminster BC (Romford).

NOBOTTLE Northants
132, 133 SP 6763 5m WNW of
Northampton. Loc, Brington CP.
Brixworth RD. Daventry CC (Kettering).

NOCTON Lincs (K)
113 TF 0564 7m SE of Lincoln. CP, 990.
N Kesteven RD. P LNCLN. Ch e. Sch p.
Grantham CC. Largely Vctrn stone vllge.
Sumptuous ch by Sir Gilbert Scott.

NOKE Oxon
145 SP 5413 5m NNE of Oxford. CP, 87.
Ploughley RD. Ch e. Mid-Oxon CC
(Henley).

NO MAN'S HEATH Glos
109 SJ 5148 4m NNW of Whitchurch. Loc,
Tarvin RD. P Malpas. Ch m. Nantwich CC.

NO MAN'S HEATH Warwicks
120, 121 SK 2908 6m ENE of Tamworth.
Loc, Newton Regis CP. Ch e.

NOMANSLAND Devon
164, 176 SS 8313 7m W of Tiverton. Loc,
Thelbridge CP. P Tvtn. Ch c.

NOMANSLAND Wilts
179 SU 2517 7m ENE of Fordingbridge.
Loc, Redlynch CP. P Salisbury. Ch m.
Sch pe.

NONELEY Shrops
118 SJ 4827 2m W of Wem. Loc,
Loppington CP.

NONINGTON Kent
173 TR 2552 6m SW of Sandwich. CP, 614.
Eastry RD. P Dover. Ch e, b, v. Sch pe. Dvr
and Deal CC (Dvr). See also Easole St. In
mining area.

NORBURY Ches
109 SJ 5547 4m NNE of Whitchurch.
CP, 218. Nantwich RD. Ch c, m.
Nntwch CC.

NORBURY Derbys
120 SK 1242 5m SW of Ashbourne.
CP(Nbry and Roston), 280. Ashbne RD.
Sch pe. W Derbys CC. Ch: monmts, glass.

NORBURY London
170 TQ 3169 3m NNW of Croydon. Loc,
Crdn LB. Crdn NW BC.

NORBURY Shrops
129 SO 3692 4m NE of Bishop's Cstle.
CP, 117. Clun and Bp's Cstle RD. Ch e, m.
Sch p. Ludlow CC.

NORBURY Staffs
119 SJ 7823 4m NE of Newport. CP, 321.
Stafford RD. P STFFD. Ch e. Sch pe. Stffd
and Stone CC. See also Weston Jones. To S,
series of locks on Shrops Union Canal; Nbry
Junction, canal junction to SE.

NORCOTT BROOK Ches
101 SJ 6180 5m S of Warrington. Loc,
Whitley CP. Runcorn RD. P WRRNGTN.
Rncn CC.

NORDELPH Norfolk
124 TF 5501 4m WSW of Downham Mkt.
CP, 445. Dnhm RD. P Dnhm Mkt. Ch e, m.
SW Nflk CC.

NORDEN HEATH Dorset
179 SY 9483 3m SSE of Wareham. Loc,
Corfe Cstle CP.

NORDLEY Shrops
130 SO 6996 3m NNW of Bridgnorth. Loc,
Astley Abbotts CP. P Brdgnth.

NORHAM Nthmb
64 NT 9047 7m SW of Berwick-upon-Tweed.
CP, 553. Nrhm and Islandshires RD.
P BRWCK-UPN-TWD. Ch e, v. Sch p.
Brwck-upn-Twd CC. Ruins of 12c cstle keep
(A.M.) above R Tweed.

NORLAND TOWN Yorks (W)
96, 102 SE 0722 2m SW of Halifax. Loc,
Sowerby Br UD. P Swby Br.

NORLEY Ches
109 SJ 5772 5m W of Northwich. CP, 841.
Runcorn RD. P WARRINGTON. Ch e, m3.
Sch pe. kncn CC. See also Hatchmere.

NORLEYWOOD Hants
180 SZ 3597 2m ENE of Lymington. Loc,
Boldre CP.

NORMANBY Lincs (L)
104 SE 8816 4m N of Scunthorpe. Loc,
Burton upon Strather CP. P Scnthpe. Ch m.
Estate vllge. Nmnby Pk*, classical hse
formerly seat of Sheffield family.

NORMANBY Lincs (L)
104 TF 0088 7m W of Mkt Rasen.
CP(Nmnby by Spital), 248. Welton RD.
P(Nmnby by Sptl), LINCOLN. Ch e. Sch p.
Gainsborough CC.

NORMANBY Yorks (N)
92 SE 7381 4m WSW of Pickering. CP, 111.
Pckrng RD. Ch e, m. Scarborough CC
(Thirsk and Malton).

NORMANBY LE WOLD Lincs (L)
104 TF 1295 4m NNE of Mkt Rasen.
CP, 87. Caistor RD. Ch e. Gainsborough CC.
Views.

NORMAN CROSS Hunts
134 TL 1690 5m SSW of Peterborough.
Loc, Nmn Crss RD. Hunts CC. Column
erected 1914 commemorates French
soldiers imprisoned here in Napoleonic wars.

NORMANDY Surrey
169 SU 9251 4m E of Aldershot. CP, 2,434.
Guildford RD. P Gldfd. Ch c. Woking CC.
See also Flexford, Willey Grn, Wyke.

NORMAN'S GREEN Devon
176 ST 0503 7m WNW of Honiton. Loc,
Plymtree CP. Ch c.

NORMANTON Leics
113, 122 SK 8140 7m WNW of Grantham.
Loc, Bottesford CP. P Grnthm, Lincs.

NORMANTON Lincs (K)
113 SK 9446 7m NNE of Grantham.
CP, 104. W Kesteven RD. P Grnthm. Ch e.
Grnthm CC.

NORMANTON Notts
112 SK 7054 6m W of Newark. Loc,
Southwell CP.

NORMANTON Yorks (W)
96, 103 SE 3822 4m ENE of Wakefield.
UD, 17,656. P. Nmntn CC. See also Altofts.
Colliery tn.

NORMANTON LE HEATH Leics
120, 121 SK 3712 3m SSE of Ashby de la
Zouch. CP, 102. Ashby de la Zch RD.
P LEICESTER. Ch e, m. Loughborough CC.

NORMANTON ON SOAR Notts
121 SK 5123 3m NNW of Loughborough.
CP, 291. Basford RD. P Lghbrgh, Leics.
Chh e, b. Sch p. Rushcliffe CC.

NORMANTON ON THE WOLDS Notts
112, 121, 122 SK 6232 6m SE of
Nottingham. CP, 1,010. Bingham RD. Ch m.
Rushcliffe CC (Carlton).

NORMANTON ON TRENT Notts
112 SK 7968 9m N of Newark. CP, 175.
E Retford RD. P Nwk. Ch e, m. Sch pe.
Bassetlaw CC.

NORMOSS Lancs
94 SD 3437 3m ENE of Blackpool. Loc,
Poulton-le-Fylde UD. P Blckpl.

NORNEY Surrey
169 SU 9444 2m WNW of Godalming. Loc,
Shackleford CP.

NORRINGTON COMMON Wilts
166, 167 ST 8864 5m NNE of Trowbridge.
Loc, Broughton Gifford CP.

NORRIS HILL Leics
120, 121 SK 3216 2m W of Ashby de la
Zouch. Loc, Ashby Woulds UD.
Loughborough CC.

NORTHALLERTON Yorks (N)
91 SE 3693 14m SSE of Darlington.
UD, 8,750. P. Richmond CC. Administrative
capital of N Riding. Old coaching tn.

NORTHAM Devon
163 SS 4529 2m N of Bideford. UD, 8,082.
P Bdfd. N Dvn CC (Torrington). See also
Appledore, Westward Ho! Almost joined to
Bdfd. To N, Nthm Burrows, with golf
course (see Appldre).

NORTHAMPTON Northants
133 SP 7560 6m NW of London.
CB, 126,608. P(NTHMPTN). BCs: Nthmptn N,
Nthmptn S(Nthmptn.) See also Buttock's
Booth, Duston, New Dstn, Weston Favell.
County tn; footwear mnfg, etc. Interesting
bldngs incl round ch of 12c and RC cathedral
by Pugin. Large central square. Many pks.
New tn designated, 1967.

NORTH ASHTON Lancs
100 SD 5500 4m SSW of Wigan. Loc,
Astn-in-Makerfield UD. P Wgn.

NORTH ASTON Oxon
145 SP 4729 7m S of Banbury. CP, 193.
Bnbry RD. P OXFORD. Ch e. Bnbry CC.

NORTHAW Herts
160 TL 2702 2m ENE of Potters Bar.
CP, 5,389. Hatfield RD. Ch e, r. Sch pe.
Welwyn and Htfld CC (Hertford). See also
Cuffley.

NORTH BADDESLEY Hants
168 SU 4020 3m E of Romsey. CP, 2,175.
Rmsy and Stockbridge RD.
P SOUTHAMPTON. Ch e, b, v. Sch j, p.
Eastleigh CC.

NORTH BARROW Som
166 ST 6029 6m SW of Bruton. CP, 79.
Wincanton RD. P Yeovil. Ch e. Wells CC.

NORTH BARSHAM Norfolk
125 TF 9134 3m N of Fakenham. Loc,
Bshm CP. Walsingham RD. Ch e.
NW Nflk CC (N Nflk).

NORTH BENFLEET Essex
162 TQ 7589 2m NE of Basildon. Loc,
Bsldn UD. P Wickford.

NORTH BOARHUNT Hants
180 SU 6010 3m NE of Fareham. Loc,
Brhnt CP. P Frhm. Ch m.

NORTHBOROUGH Hunts
123 TF 1507 6m NNW of Peterborough.
CP, 615. Ptrbrgh RD. P PTRBRGH.
Ch e, m. Sch p. Ptrbrgh BC (CC). At S end
of vllge, 14c mnr hse, once home of
Cromwell's son-in-law. Crmwll's widow
buried in the ch.

NORTHBOURNE Kent
173 TR 3352 3m W of Deal. CP, 786.
Eastry RD. P Dl. Ch e, m. Sch pe. Dover and
Dl CC (Dvr). See also Betteshanger, Ham. In
mining area. N. Ct has Elizn gdn*.

NORTH BOVEY Devon
175 SX 7483 2m SSW of
Moretonhampstead. CP, 391. Newton
Abbot RD. P Ntn Abbt. Ch e. Totnes CC.
Thatched granite hses and granite ch on
edge of Dartmoor.

NORTH BRADLEY Wilts
166 ST 8555 2m S of Trowbridge. CP, 925.
Warminster and Westbury RD. P Trwbrdge.
Ch e, b. Sch pe. Wstbry CC.

NORTH BRENTOR Devon
175 SX 4881 4m N of Tavistock. Loc,
Brentor CP. Tvstck RD. P(Brentor), Tvstck.
Ch e, m2. W Dvn CC (Tvstck).

NORTH BREWHAM Som
166 ST 7236 3m NE of Bruton. Loc,
Brhm CP. Wincanton RD. Ch b. Wells CC.

NORTH BUCKLAND Devon
163 SS 4840 2m NNW of Braunton. Loc,
Georgeham CP.

NORTH BURLINGHAM Norfolk
126 TG 3610 6m SE of Wroxham. Loc,
Blnghm CP. Blofield and Flegg RD. Ch e.
Yarmouth CC.

NORTH CADBURY Som
166 ST 6327 5m W of Wincanton. CP, 707.
Wncntn RD. P Yeovil. Ch e, m. Sch pe.
Wells CC. See also Galhampton. Stone vllge;
fine ch and Elizn mansion.

NORTH CARLTON Lincs (L)
104 SK 9477 5m NNW of Lincoln. CP, 99.
Welton RD. Ch e. Gainsborough CC.

NORTH CAVE Yorks (E)
98 SE 8932 6m S of Mkt Weighton.
CP, 1,524. Howden RD. P Brough. Ch e, m.
Sch pe. Hdn CC.

NORTH CERNEY Glos
157 SP 0208 4m N of Cirencester. CP, 499.
Crncstr RD. P Crncstr. Ch e, m. Sch pe.
Crncstr and Tewkesbury CC. See also
Calmsden. Cotswold vllge of charm. Ch:
Nmn to Perp. In churchyard, 14c cross.

NORTHCHAPEL Sussex (W)
169, 181, 182 SU 9529 5m NNW of
Petworth. CP, 674. Ptwth RD. P Ptwth.
Ch e, v. Sch p. Chichester CC (Horsham).
See also Fisher St.

NORTH CHARFORD Hants
179 SU 1919 4m NE of Fordingbridge. Loc,
Hale CP.

NORTH CHARLTON Nthmb
71 NU 1622 6m N of Alnwick. Loc,
Eglingham CP. P Chathill.

NORTH CHERITON Som
166 ST 6925 2m SW of Wincanton.
CP, 157. Wncntn RD. P Templecombe.
Ch e. Sch pe. Wells CC.

NORTH CHIDEOCK Dorset
177 SY 4294 3m W of Bridport. Loc,
Chdck CP.

NORTHCHURCH Herts
159, 160 SP 9708 1m NW of Berkhamsted.
CP, 1,147. Bkhmstd RD. P Bkhmstd. Ch e, b.
Hemel Hempstead CC. To W in this CP,
stretches of Grim's Dyke, Saxon boundary
line consisting of ditch and bank.

NORTH CLIFFE Yorks (E)
98 SE 8737 3m S of Mkt Weighton. Loc,
S Clffe CP. Ch e.

NORTH CLIFTON Notts
113 SK 8272 9m W of Lincoln. CP, 149.
Newark RD. P Nwk. Ch e, m. Sch p.
Nwk CC.

NORTH COATES Lincs (L)
105 TA 3500 7m SE of Grimsby. CP, 764.
Louth RD. P Grmsby. Ch e, m. Sch pe.
Lth CC.

NORTH COCKERINGTON Lincs (L)
105 TF 3790 4m ENE of Louth. CP, 178.
Lth RD. Ch e, m. Sch pe. Lth CC. Ch shares
churchyard with Alvingham, qv.

NORTH COKER Som
177, 178 ST 5313 2m SW of Yeovil. Loc,
E Coker CP.

NORTH COLLINGHAM Notts
113 SK 8362 6m NNE of Newark.
CP, 1,149. Nwk RD. P(Cllnghm), Nwk.
Ch e, b, m. Sch p, s. Nwk CC.

NORTH COMMON Sussex (E)
183 TQ 3921 7m N of Lewes. Loc,
Chailey CP. P(N Chly), Lewes. Windmill.
Heritage Crafts Sch for handicapped
children.

NORTHCOTT Devon
174 SX 3392 5m N of Launceston. CP, 22.
Holsworthy RD. W Dvn CC (Tavistock).

NORTH COVE Suffolk (E)
137 TM 4689 3m E of Beccles. CP, 202.
Wainford RD. P Bccls. Ch e. Sch p.
Lowestoft CC.

NORTH COWTON Yorks (N)
91 NZ 2803 7m S of Darlington. CP, 376.
Richmond RD. P Northallerton. Ch m.
Sch p. Rchmnd CC.

NORTH CRAWLEY Bucks
146 SP 9244 3m E of Newport Pagnell.
CP, 465. Npt Pgnll RD. P Npt Pgnll. Ch e, c.
Sch pe. Buckingham CC.

NORTH CREAKE Norfolk
125 TF 8538 5m SW of Wells. CP, 520.
Docking RD. P Fakenham. Ch e, m. Sch p.
NW Nflk CC (King's Lynn). 1m N, rems of
13c abbey (A.M.).

NORTH CURRY Som
177 ST 3125 6m E of Taunton. CP, 1,228.
Tntn RD. P Tntn. Ch e, b, m. Sch pe.
Tntn CC. See also Knapp, Wrantage.

NORTH DALTON Yorks (E)
98 SE 9352 6m SW of Driffield. CP, 363.
Drffld RD. P Drffld. Ch e, m. Howden CC.

NORTH DEAN Bucks
159 SU 8498 4m NNW of High Wycombe.
Loc, Hughenden CP. Wcmbe RD.
Wcmbe CC.

NORTH DEIGHTON Yorks (W)
96 SE 3951 2m NNW of Wetherby. CP, 117.
Wthrby RD. Barkston Ash CC.

NORTH DUFFIELD Yorks (E)
97, 98 SE 6837 5m ENE of Selby. CP, 356.
Derwent RD. P Slby. Ch m. Sch p.
Howden CC.

NORTH ELKINGTON Lincs (L)
105 TF 2890 3m NW of Louth. CP, 55.
Lth RD. Ch e. Lth CC.

NORTH ELMHAM Norfolk
125 TF 9820 5m N of E Dereham. CP, 964.
Mitford and Launditch RD.
P(Elmhm), Drhm. Ch e, m2. Sch pe.
SW Nflk CC. Rems of Saxon cathedral and
bishop's cstle (A.M.).

NORTH ELMSALL Yorks (W)
103 SE 4712 6m SSE of Pontefract.
CP, 3,543. Hemsworth RD. Ch e. Sch i.
Hmswth CC.

NORTHEND Bucks
159 SU 7392 6m NNW of Henley. Loc,
Turville CP. P Hnly-on-Thames, Oxon.

NORTH END Hants
168 SU 4162 5m SW of Newbury. Loc,
E Woodhay CP. P Nbry, Berks.

NORTH END Som
155, 165 ST 4167 2m NNW of
Congresbury. Loc, Yatton CP.

NORTH END Sussex (W)
182 TQ 1209 5m NNW of Worthing. Loc,
Findon CP.

NORTHEND Warwicks
145 SP 3952 6m SSW of Southam. Loc,
Burton Dassett CP. P Leamington Spa.
Ch m. Sch p.

NORTHEND WOODS Bucks
159 SU 9089 3m W of Beaconfield. Loc,
Chepping Wycombe CP. Wcmbe RD.
Wcmbe CC.

NORTH FAMBRIDGE Essex
162 TQ 8597 6m S of Maldon. CP, 240.
Mldn RD. P Chelmsford. Ch e. Mldn CC.

NORTH FERRIBY Yorks (E)
98 SE 9825 7m WSW of Hull. CP, 2,450.
Beverley RD. P. Ch e, m. Sch pe.
Haltemprice CC. Wide view across Humber
to S Frrby in Lincs.

NORTHFLEET Kent
161, 171 TQ 6274 2m W of Gravesend.
UD, 26,679. P Grvsnd. Grvsnd CC.
Thames-side indstrl. World's largest cement
works.

NORTH FRODINGHAM Yorks (E)
99 TA 1053 6m ESE of Driffield. CP, 551.
Drffld RD. P Drffld. Ch e, c, m. Sch p.
Howden CC.

NORTH GORLEY Hants
179 SU 1611 2m SSE of Fordingbridge.
Loc, Fdngbrdge CP.

NORTH GRIMSTON Yorks (E)
92 SE 8467 4m SE of Malton. Loc,
Birdsall CP. P Mltn. Stream-side vllge; partly
Nmn ch.

NORTH HAYLING Hants
181 SU 7303 3m SSE of Havant. Loc, Hvnt
and Waterloo UD.

NORTH HAZELRIGG Nthmb
64, 71 NU 0533 4m W of Belford. Loc,
Chatton CP.

NORTH HEATH Sussex (W)
182 TQ 0621 2m NE of Pulborough. Loc,
Plbrgh CP. Sch pe.

NORTH HILL Cornwall
186 SX 2776 6m SW of Launceston.
CP, 665. Lncstn RD. P Lncstn. Ch e, m2.
N Cnwll CC. See also Bathpool, Coad's Grn,
Congdon's Shop, Trebartha. High-standing
vllge. Ch mainly 15c; monmts.

NORTH HINKSEY Bucks
158 SP 4905 1m W of Oxford. CP, 4,452.
Abingdon RD. Ch e, m. Sch pe. Abngdn CC.
See also Botley.

NORTH HOLMWOOD Surrey
170 TQ 1647 1m S of Dorking. Loc,
Dkng UD. P Dkng.

NORTH HUISH Devon
187, 188 SX 7156 5m E of Ivybridge.
CP, 355. Totnes RD. Ch e. Ttns CC. See also
Avonwick.

NORTH HYKEHAM Lincs (K)
113 SK 9465 4m SSW of Lincoln.
CP, 5,308. N Kesteven RD. P LNCLN.
Ch e, m2. Sch p, pe, s2. Grantham CC.

NORTHIAM Sussex (E)
184 TQ 8224 7m WNW of Rye. CP, 1,445.
Battle RD. P Rye. Ch e, m. Sch pe. Rye CC.
See also Millcorner. Elizabeth I said to have
dined under oak tree on grn. To SE, Brick-
wall*, Jcbn hse now a sch. To NW, Gt
Dixter*, 15c half-timbered hse with large
gdn.

NORTHILL Beds
147 TL 1446 2m SW of Sandy. CP, 1,446.
Biggleswade RD. P Bgglswde. Ch e, m.
Sch pe. Mid-Beds CC. See also Hatch,
Ickwell Grn, Upr Caldecote. Bthplce of
Thomas Tompion, clockmaker, 1639.

NORTHINGTON Hants
168 SU 5637 7m NE of Winchester.
CP, 205. Wnchstr RD. P Alresford. Ch e.
Wnchstr CC.

NORTH KELSEY Lincs (L)
104 TA 0401 4m SE of Brigg. CP, 743.
Caistor RD. P LINCOLN. Ch e, m2. Sch p.
Gainsborough CC. See also N Klsy Moor.

NORTH KELSEY MOOR Lincs (L)
104 TA 0602 3m W of Caistor. Loc,
N Klsy CP. P LINCOLN. Ch e.

NORTH KILLINGHOLME Lincs (L)
104 TA 1417 3m NW of Immingham.
CP, 215. Glanford Brigg RD. Ch e. Brgg and
Scunthorpe CC (Brgg). At foot of Lindsey
Oil Refinery.

NORTH KILVINGTON Yorks (N)
91 SE 4285 2m N of Thirsk. CP, 38.
Thsk RD. Thsk and Malton CC.

NORTH KILWORTH Leics
132, 133 SP 6183 5m E of Lutterworth.
C P , 3 9 4 . L t t r w t h R D .
P Rugby, Warwickshire. Ch e, bv. Sch pe.
Blaby CC (Harborough).

NORTH KYME Lincs (K)
113 TF 1552 7m SSW of Woodhall Spa.
CP, 555. E Kesteven RD. P LINCOLN.
Ch e, m. Sch p. Grantham CC.

NORTH LANCING Sussex (W)
182 TQ 1805 3m NE of Worthing. See
Lancing.

NORTHLANDS Lincs (L)
114 TF 3453 6m N of Bcston. Loc,
Sibsey CP. P Bstn.

NORTHLEACH Glos
144 SP 1114 10m NE of Cirencester.
CP(Nthlch w Eastington), 1,248.
Nthlch RD. P Cheltenham. Ch e, v.

Sch pe, s. Crncstr and Tewkesbury CC.
Typical Cotswold small tn. Perp 'wool' ch:
font, brasses. 1½m NE, rems of Roman vlla.

NORTH LEE Bucks
159 SP 8308 3m SSE of Aylesbury. Loc,
Ellesborough CP.

NORTHLEIGH Devon
176 SY 1995 4m SSE of Honiton. CP, 121.
Hntn RD. P Colyton. Ch e. Hntn CC.

NORTH LEIGH Oxon
145 SP 3813 3m NE of Witney. CP, 1,197.'
Wtny RD. P Wtny. Ch e, m, v. Sch pe.
Mid-Oxon CC (Banbury). See also E End.
Ch: Saxon twr; Perrott and Wilcote chpls.
1m NW, N Lgh Roman villa (A.M.).

NORTH LEVERTON WITH
HABBLESTHORPE Notts
104 SK 7882 5m SSW of Gainsborough.
CP, 348. E Retford RD. P(N Lvtn), Rtfd.
Ch e, m. Sch pe. Bassetlaw CC. H. Mnr is
early 17c, brick. Two dovecotes at N Lvtn.

NORTHLEW Devon
175 SX 5099 6m WNW of Okehampton.
CP, 499. Okhmptn RD. P Okhmptn.
Ch e, m2. Sch pe. W Dvn CC (Torrington).

NORTH LITTLETON Worcs
144 SP 0847 4m NE of Evesham. CP(N
and Middle Lttltn), 601. Eveshm RD.
P Eveshm. S Worcs CC.

NORTH LOPHAM Norfolk
136 TM 0382 5m WNW of Diss. CP, 461.
Wayland RD. P Dss. Ch e, m. Sch p.
S Nflk CC.

NORTH LUFFENHAM Rutland
122 SK 9303 5m ENE of Uppingham.
CP, 425. Uppnghm RD. P Oakham. Ch e, m.
Rtlnd and Stamford CC. Limestone vllge
commanding wide views. Handsome ch with
14c twr and spire.

NORTH MARDEN Sussex (W)
181 SU 8016 6m SE of Petersfield. Loc,
Mdn CP. Chichester RD. Ch e. Chchstr CC.
Farm and simple Nmn ch.

NORTH MARSTON Bucks
146 SP 7722 6m NNW of Aylesbury.
CP, 454. Winslow RD. P Bletchley. Ch e, m.
Sch pe. Buckingham CC.

NORTH MIDDLETON Nthmb
71 NU 0024 2m S of Wooler. Loc, Ilderton CP.

NORTH MOLTON Devon
163 SS 7329 3m NE of S Molton. CP, 855. S Mltn RD. P: S Mltn. Ch e, m. Sch p. N Dvn CC. See also Heasley Mill, Molland Cross, N Radworthy. S Rdwthy. Small vllge, large parish.

NORTHMOOR Oxon
158 SP 4202 4m S of Eynsham. CP, 292. Witney RD. P OXFORD. Ch e. Sch pe. Mid-Oxon CC (Banbury). Fine 13c ch.

NORTHMOOR GREEN Som
165 ST 3332 4m SE of Bridgwater. Loc, N Petherton CP. P(Moorland), Brdgwtr. Ch e. Sch p.

NORTH MORETON Berks
158 SU 5689 3m W of Wallingford. CP, 232. Wllngfd RD. P. Didcot. Ch e, m. Abingdon CC.

NORTH MUNDHAM Sussex (W)
181 SU 8702 2m SE of Chichester. CP, 887. Chchstr RD. P Chchstr. Ch e. Sch p. Chchstr CC. See also Runcton, S Mndhm.

NORTH MUSKHAM Notts
112 SK 7958 3m N of Newark. CP, 525. Southwell RD. P Nwk. Ch e, m. Nwk CC Trentside vllge.

NORTH NEWINGTON Oxon
145 SP 4239 2m W of Banbury. CP, 265. Bnbry RD. P Bnbry. Ch e, v. Sch pe. Bnbry CC.

NORTH NEWNTON Wilts
167 SU 1257 3m SW of Pewsey. CP, 321. Psy RD. Ch e. Devizes CC.

NORTH NEWTON Som
165 ST 2931 4m S of Bridgwater. Loc, N Petherton CP. P Brdgwtr. Ch e2, v. Sch p. Second ch is St Michael Ch, ½m S.

NORTH NIBLEY Glos
156 ST 7495 9m SW of Stroud. CP, 714. Dursley RD. P Dsly. Ch e, c. Sch pe. Strd CC. Bthplce of William Tyndale, 1484, who translated the Bible into English and was martyred for his pains; commemorated by column on Nbly Knoll.

NORTH OAKLEY Hants
168 SU 5354 7m WNW of Basingstoke. Loc, Kingsclere CP.

NORTH OCKENDON London
161 TQ 5884 5m S of Brentwood. Loc, Havering LB. P Upminster, Essex. Upmnstr BC (Hornchurch). Lndn's Far East.

NORTHOLT London
160 TQ 1384 3m SSW of Harrow. Loc, Ealing LB. P Middx. Ealng N BC. The airfield formerly Lndn's main airpt, superseded by Heathrow.

NORTH ORMSBY Lincs (L)
105 TF 2893 4m NNW of Louth. CP, 65. Lth RD. Ch e. Lth CC.

NORTHORPE Lincs (K)
123 TF 0917 2m S of Bourne. Loc, Thurlby CP.

NORTHORPE Lincs (L)
104 SK 8997 7m NE of Gainsborough. CP, 149. Gnsbrgh RD. P Gnsbrgh. Ch e, m. Gnsbrgh CC.

NORTH OTTERINGTON Yorks (N)
91 SE 3689 3m S of Northallerton. CP, 43. Nthlltn RD. Ch e. Richmond CC.

NORTHOVER Som
177 ST 5223 just N of Ilchester. Loc Ilchstr CP. Ch e.

NORTH OWERSBY Lincs (L)
104 TF 0694 4m NW of Mkt Rasen. Loc, Owrsby CP. Caistor RD. P Mkt Rsn. Ch e, m. Sch pe. Gainsborough CC.

NORTH PERROTT Som
177 ST 4709 2m E of Crewkerne. CP, 224. Yeovil RD. P Crkne. Ch e. Yvl CC.

NORTH PETHERTON Som
165 ST 2833 3m S of Bridgwater. CP, 3,769. Brdgwtr RD. P Brdgwtr. Ch e, m, v2. Sch i, j. Brdgwtr CC. See also Huntworth, Northmoor Grn, N Newton. Ch: fine 109ft twr.

NORTH PETHERWIN Cornwall
174, 186 SX 2889 4m NW of Launceston. CP, 537. Lncstn RD. P Lncstn. Ch e, m2. Sch p. N Cnwll CC (Tavistock). See also Maxworthy, S Wheatley.

NORTH PICKENHAM Norfolk
125 TF 8606 3m ESE of Swaffham.
CP, 466. Swffhm RD. P Swffhm. Ch e.
Sch pe. SW Nflk CC.

NORTH PIDDLE Worcs
143, 144 SO 9654 7m E of Worcester.
CP, 110. Pershore RD. Ch e. S Worcs CC.

NORTH POORTON Dorset
177 SY 5198 5m NE of Bridport. CP, 22.
Beaminster RD. Ch e. W Dst CC.

NORTH RADWORTHY Devon
163 SS 7534 6m NNE of S Molton. Loc,
N Mltn CP.

NORTH RAUCEBY Lincs (K)
113 TF 0246 3m W of Sleaford. CP, 183.
E Kesteven RD. Ch e, m. Sch pe.
Grantham CC.

NORTHREPPS Norfolk
126 TG 2439 2m SE of Cromer. CP, 672.
Erpingham RD. P Crmr. Ch e. Sch p.
N Nflk CC. See also Crossdale St.

NORTH RESTON Lincs (L)
105 TF 3883 4m SE of Louth. CP, 36.
Lth RD. Ch e. Lth CC.

NORTH RIGTON Yorks (W)
96 SE 2749 4m SSW of Harrogate. CP, 365.
Wetherby RD. P LEEDS. Ch e, m. Sch pe.
Barkston Ash CC.

NORTH RODE Ches
110 SJ 8966 3m NE of Congleton. CP, 195.
Macclesfield RD. P Cngltn. Sch pe.
Mcclsfld CC.

NORTH RUNCTON Norfolk
124 TF 6415 3m SSE of King's Lynn.
CP, 383. Freebridge Lynn RD. P K's Lnn.
Ch e. Sch pe. NW Nflk CC (K's Lnn). Early
18c ch in classical style.

NORTH SCALE Lancs
88 SD 1869 on Walney Is. just W of Barrow.
Loc, Brrw-in-Furness CB. P Brrw-in-Fnss.

NORTH SCARLE Lincs (K)
113 SK 8466 8m WSW of Lincoln. CP, 464.
N Kesteven RD. P LNCLN. Ch e, m2. Sch p.
Grantham CC.

NORTH SEATON Nthmb
78 NZ 2986 6m E of Morpeth. Loc,
Newbiggin-by-the-Sea UD.

NORTH SEATON COLLIERY Nthmb
78 NZ 2985 6m E of Morpeth. Loc,
Newbiggin-by-the-Sea UD. P Ashington.

NORTH SHIELDS Nthmb
78 NZ 3568 central distr of Tynemouth.
Loc, Tnmth CB. P.

NORTH SIDE Hunts
134 TL 2799 5m E of Peterborough. Loc,
Thorney CP. On N bank of R Nene.

NORTH SKELTON Yorks (N)
86 NZ 6718 2m SSE of Saltburn. Loc, Skltn
and Brotton UD. P Skltn-in-Cleveland,
Sltburn-by-the-Sea.

NORTH SOMERCOTES Lincs (L)
105 TF 4296 8m NE of Louth. CP, 1,132.
Lth RD. P Lth. Ch e, m. Sch pe, s. Lth CC.
Annual pancake race against Bodiam,
Sussex.

NORTH STAINLEY Yorks (W)
91 SE 2877 4m NNW of Ripon. CP(N Stnly
w Sleningford), 389. Rpn and Pateley
Br RD. P Rpn. Ch e, m. Sch pe. Rpn CC.

NORTH STAINMORE Westm
84 NY 8315 2m E of Brough. Loc,
Stnmre CP. N Westm RD. Ch e. Westm CC.

NORTH STOKE Oxon
158 SU 6186 2m S of Wallingford. Loc,
Crowmarsh CP. Henley RD. P OXFORD.
Ch e. Hnly CC. Ch has mdvl wall-paintings.

NORTH STOKE Som
156 ST 7069 4m NW of Bath. CP, 113.
Bathavon RD. Ch e, c. N Som CC.

NORTH STOKE Sussex (W)
181, 182 TQ 0210 3m N of Arundel. Loc,
Amberley CP. Ch e. On loop of R Arun;
views. Ch has curiously placed wooden
belfry.

NORTH STREET Hants
168, 169, 181 SU 6433 6m SW of Alton.
Loc, Ropley CP.

NORTH SUNDERLAND Nthmb
71 NU 2131 3m SE of Bamburgh.
CP, 1,625. Belford RD. P Seahouses.
Ch e, v. Sch p. Berwick-upon-Tweed CC. See
also Seahouses.

NORTH TAMERTON Cornwall
174 SX 3197 4m SSW of Holsworthy.
CP, 259. Stratton RD. P Hlswthy, Devon.
Ch e, m. N Cnwll CC.

NORTH TAWTON Devon
175 SS 6601 6m NE of Okehampton.
CP, 1,098. Okhmptn RD. P. Ch e, c, m, v.
Sch p. W Dvn CC (Torrington).

NORTH THORESBY Lincs (L)
105 TF 2998 6m S of Cleethorpes. CP, 667.
Louth RD. P Grimsby. Ch e, m. Sch p.
Lth CC.

NORTH TIDWORTH Wilts
167 SU 2349 8m WNW of Andover.
CP, 2,824. Pewsey RD. P Tdwth, Hants.
Ch e. Sch i, j, sb. Devizes CC. Army tn.

NORTH TOGSTON Nthmb
71 NU 2502 1m SW of Amble. Loc,
Tgstn CP.

NORTH TUDDENHAM Norfolk
125 TG 0314 3m E of E Dereham. CP, 240.
Mitford and Launditch RD. P Drhm. Ch e.
Sch pe. SW Nflk CC.

NORTH WALBOTTLE Nthmb
78 NZ 1767 5m WNW of Newcastle. Loc,
Newburn UD. P NCSTLE UPON TYNE 5.

NORTH WALSHAM Norfolk
126 TG 2830 14m NNE of Norwich.
UD, 6,357. P. N Nflk CC. See also Spa
Cmmn.

NORTH WALTHAM Hants
168 SU 5646 6m SW of Basingstoke.
CP, 359. Bsngstke RD. P Bsngstke. Ch e, m.
Sch p. Bsngstke CC.

NORTH WARNBOROUGH Hants
169 SU 7351 6m E of Basingstoke. Loc,
Odiham CP. P Bsngstke. Ch m. To NW, 13c
octagonal keep*, sole rems of Odhm Cstle.

NORTH WEALD BASSETT Essex
161 TL 4904 3m W of Ongar. CP, 3,957.
Epping and Ongr RD. P (N Wld), Eppng.
Ch e, m. Sch pe. Harlow CC (Eppng). See
also Foster St, Hastingwood, Thornwood
Cmmn. RAF and radio stn.

NORTH WHEATLEY Notts
104 SK 7585 4m SW of Gainsborough.
CP, 334. E Retford RD. P Rtfd. Ch e, m.

Sch pe. Bassetlaw CC. Old Hall, 1673, with
interesting brickwork.

NORTH WHILBOROUGH Devon
188 SX 8766 3m S of Newton Abbot. Loc,
Kerswells CP. Ntn Abbt RD. Totnes CC.

NORTHWICH Ches
110 SJ 6573 10m SSE of Warrington.
UD, 18,109. P. Nthwch CC. Tn blt on salt;
important salt industry. Salt museum.

NORTHWICK Glos
155, 156 ST 5686 9m N of Bristol. Loc,
Olveston CP.

NORTH WIDCOMBE Som
165, 166 ST 5758 8m N of Wells. Loc,
W Harptree CP.

NORTH WILLINGHAM Lincs (L)
105 TF 1688 4m E of Mkt Rasen. CP, 95.
Caistor RD. P Mkt Rsn. Ch e.
Gainsborough CC.

NORTH WINGFIELD Derbys
112 SK 4165 4m SSE of Chesterfield.
CP, 8,012. Chstrfld RD. P Chstrfld.
Ch e, m, v2. Sch p, s. NE Derbys CC.

NORTH WITHAM Lincs (K)
122 SK 9221 9m S of Grantham. CP, 142.
W Kesteven RD. Ch e. R Rutland and
Stamford CC. Ch: monmts to Sherard
family.

NORTHWOLD Norfolk
136 TL 7597 7m NNW of Brandon.
CP, 902. Downham RD. P Thetford.
Ch e, m. Sch pe. SW Nflk CC. See also
Whitington.

NORTHWOOD IOW
180 SZ 4893 2m SSW of Cowes. Loc,
Cowes UD.

NORTHWOOD London
160 TQ 0991 3m SE of Rickmansworth.
Loc, Hillingdon LB. P Middx.
Ruislip-Nthwd BC.

NORTHWOOD Shrops
118 SJ 4633 4m ESE of Ellesmere. Loc,
Wem Rural CP. N Shrops RD.
P Shrewsbury. Ch m. Oswestry CC.

NORTHWOOD GREEN Glos
143 SO 7216 4m ENE of Cinderford. Loc,
Westbury-on-Severn CP. P Wstbry-on-Svn.

NORTH WOOTTON Dorset
178 ST 6514 2m SE of Sherborne. CP, 51.
Shbne RD. Ch e. W Dst CC.

NORTH WOOTTON Norfolk
124 TF 6424 3m NNE of King's Lynn.
CP, 531. Freebridge Lynn RD. P K's Lnn.
Ch e. Sch pe. NW Nflk CC (K's Lnn).

NORTH WOOTTON Som
165, 166 ST 5641 3m SSE of Wells.
CP, 219. Wlls RD. P Shepton Mallet. Ch e.
Wlls CC.

NORTH WRAXALL Wilts
156 ST 8175 6m W of Chippenham.
CP, 304. Calne and Chppnhm RD.
P Chppnhm. Ch e, c. Chppnhm CC. See also
Ford, Upr Wrxll.

NORTH WROUGHTON Wilts
157 SU 1481 2m S of Swindon. Loc,
Wrghtn CP. P Swndn.

NORTON Ches
100, 109 SJ 5582 3m E of Runcorn. Loc,
Rncn UD.

NORTON Glos
143 SO 8524 4m NNE of Gloucester.
CP, 314. Glcstr RD. P GLCSTR. Ch e.
Sch pe. W Glos CC.

NORTON Herts
147 TL 2334 1m NE of Letchworth. Loc,
Ltchwth UD. P Ltchwth.

NORTON IOW
180 SZ 3489 just W of Yarmouth. Loc,
Freshwater CP.

NORTON Northants
132, 133 SP 6063 2m ENE of Daventry.
CP, 243. Dvntry RD. P Dvntry. Ch e, m.
Dvntry CC (S Nthnts).

NORTON Notts
112 SK 5771 5m S of Worksop. CP, 190.
Wksp RD. Bassetlaw CC.

NORTON Shrops
119 SJ 7200 5m N of Bridgnorth. Loc,
Stockton CP. P Shifnal. Ch e. Sch pe. Vctrn
sch looks like a ch. Stocks and whipping
post on grn.

NORTON Suffolk (W)
136 TL 9565 6m E of Bury St Edmunds.
CP, 683. Thedwastre RD. P Bury St Eds.
Ch e, b, s. Sch pe. Bury St Eds CC. See also
Stanton St.

NORTON Sussex (W)
181 SU 9206 4m ENE of Chichester. Loc,
Aldingbourne CP.

NORTON Wilts
156, 157 ST 8884 4m SW of Malmesbury.
CP, 148. Mlmsbry RD. Ch e.
Chippenham CC. See also Foxley.

NORTON Worcs
143 SO 8751 3m SE of Worcester. CP(Ntn
juxta Kempsey), 959. Pershore RD.
P WCSTR. Ch e. Sch pe. S Worcs CC. See
also Littleworth.

NORTON Worcs
144 SP 0447 3m N of Evesham. CP(Ntn
and Lenchwick), 803. Eveshm RD. P Eveshm.
Ch e. Sch pe. S Worcs CC.

NORTON Yorks (E)
92 SE 7971 just SE of Malton. UD, 5,410.
P Mltn. Howden CC.

NORTON Yorks (W)
103 SE 5415 7m ESE of Pontefract.
CP, 3,282. Doncaster RD. P Dncstr. Ch m2.
Sch p. Don Valley CC. See also Campsall,
Sutton.

NORTON BAVANT Wilts
166, 167 ST 9043 3m ESE of Warminster.
CP, 121. Wmnstr and Westbury RD. Ch e.
Wstbry CC.

NORTON BRIDGE Staffs
110, 119 SJ 8730 3m SW of Stone. Loc,
Chebsey CP. P Stne. To S beside Meece
Brook and main line rly, Shallowford*,
restored cottage now museum, once home
of Izaac Walton.

NORTON CANES Staffs
120 SK 0107 3m SE of Cannock. Loc,
Cnnck UD. P Cnnck. Cnnck CC
(Walsall N BC). Mining distr N of A5.

NORTON CANON Herefs
142 SO 3847 9m NW of Hereford. CP, 219.
Weobley RD. P HRFD. Ch e, m. Sch pe.
Leominster CC. See also Calver Hill.

NORTON DISNEY Lincs (K)
113 SK 8859 6m NE of Newark. CP, 196.
N Kesteven RD. Ch e. Grantham CC. Ch:
monmts and brasses to Disney family,
ancestors of famous cartoon and film
maker.

NORTON FERRIS Wilts
166 ST 7936 7m S of Frome. Loc,
Kilmington CP.

NORTON FITZWARREN Som
164/177 ST 1925 2m WNW of Taunton.
CP, 1,812. Tntn RD. P Tntn. Ch e, v.
Sch pe. Tntn CC. See also Heathfield. Ch
has richly carved scrn and bench-ends.

NORTON GREEN IOW
180 SZ 3388 1m SW of Yarmouth. Loc,
Freshwater CP. P Frshwtr.

NORTON HAWKFIELD Som
165, 166 ST 5964 5m S of Bristol. Loc,
Norton Malreward CP.

NORTON HEATH Essex
161 TL 6004 3m ENE of Ongar. Loc, High
Ongr CP. Ch c.

NORTON IN HALES Shrops
110, 119 SJ 7038 3m NE of Mkt Drayton.
CP, 508. Mkt Drtn RD. P Mkt Drtn. Ch e.
Sch pe. Oswestry CC. See also Betton.
Bradling Stone on grn formerly used to
punish those who worked after noon on
Shrove Tuesday. Ch: Cotton monmt.

NORTON JUXTA TWYCROSS Leics
120, 121 SK 3206 6m N of Atherstone.
Loc, Twcrss CP. P Athrstne, Warwickshire.
Ch e.

NORTON-LE-CLAY Yorks (N)
91 SE 4071 3m N of Boroughbridge.
CP, 100. Thirsk RD. Ch e, m. Thsk and
Malton CC.

NORTON LINDSEY Warwicks
131 SP 2263 4m WSW of Warwick. CP, 204.
Wrwck RD. P WRWCK. Ch e. Wrwck and
Leamington CC.

NORTON MALREWARD Som
155, 156 ST 6065 5m S of Bristol. CP, 185.
Clutton RD. Ch e. N Som CC. See also Ntn
Hawkfield. To N, Maes Knoll Camp, large
prehistoric earthwork incorporating section
of Wansdyke (see also Stanton Prior).

NORTON ST PHILIP Som
166 ST 7755 5m N of Frome. CP, 699.

Frme RD. P Bath. Ch e, b, r. Sch pe.
Wells CC. See also Farleigh Hungerford. The
George, 15c inn.

NORTON SUBCOURSE Norfolk
137 TM 4198 5m N of Beccles. CP, 302.
Loddon RD. Ch e, m. Sch pe. S Nflk CC.

NORTON SUB HAMDON Som
177 ST 4715 5m W of Yeovil. CP, 568.
Yvl RD. P Stoke sb Hmdn. Ch e. Sch pe.
Yvl CC. Stone vllge; fine ch, with round
dovecote alongside.

NORWELL Notts
112 SK 7761 5m NNW of Newark. CP, 322.
Southwell RD. P Nwk. Ch e, m. Sch pe.
Nwk CC. See also Nrwll Woodhouse. Ch:
14c monmt to a lady.

NORWELL WOODHOUSE Notts
112 SK 7462 6m NNW of Newark. Loc,
Nrwll CP. Ch m.

NORWICH Norfolk
126 TG 2208 98m NE of London.
CB, 121,688. P. BCs: Nrwch N, Nrwch S.
(Nrwch N BC, Nrwch S BC, Central
Nflk CC.) County capital and cathedral city.
Once centre of cloth trade; now many
industries, esp footwear. Interesting bldngs
incl the partly Nmn cthdrl, Nmn cstle, 15c
guildhall, numerous chs, modern city hall.
University of E Anglia.

NORWOOD Derbys
103 SK 4681 8m ESE of Sheffield. Loc,
Killamarsh CP.

NORWOOD London
160, 170 TQ 3370 4m N of Croydon. Loc,
Croydon LB, Lambeth LB. Crdn NW BC,
Nwd BC.

NORWOOD GREEN Yorks (W)
96, 102 SE 1426 3m ENE of Halifax. Loc,
Brighouse MB. P Hlfx.

NORWOOD HILL Surrey
170, 182 TQ 2443 3m W of Horley. Loc,
Dorking and Hly RD. P Hly. Dkng CC.

NOSS MAYO Devon
187 SX 5447 6m SE of Plymouth.
CP(Newton and Nss), 1,842. Plympton
St Mary RD. P Plmth. Ch e, m. W Dvn CC
(Tavistock). Boating.

NOSTERFIELD Yorks (N)
91 SE 2780 3m E of Masham. Loc,
W Tanfield CP. Ch m.

NOTGROVE Glos
144 SP 1020 3m N of Northleach. CP, 158.
Nthlch RD. P Cheltenham. Ch e. Cirencester
and Tewkesbury CC. To NW, long barrow;
Neolithic pottery, skeletons, etc now in
Chltnhm Museum.

NOTTINGHAM Notts
112, 121, 122 SK 5740 108m NNW of
London. CB, 299,758. P(NOTTINGHAM).
BCs: Nttnghm E, N, W. (Central, N, S, W.)
Busy commercial and indstrl tn (hosiery,
lace, tobacco, chemicals, etc) on R Trent.
17c cstle*, with art gallery and museum.
University. Repertory theatre. Trent Br
Cricket Ground (test matches). Wollaton
Hall*, Elizn mansion, now museum.

NOTTON Wilts
156, 157 ST 9169 3m S of Chippenham.
Loc, Lacock CP.

NOTTON Yorks (W)
102 SE 3413 4m N of Barnsley. CP, 721.
Wakefield RD. P Wkfld. Wkfld BC.

NOUNSLEY Essex
162 TL 7910 3m SW of Witham. Loc,
Hatfield Peverel CP.

NOUTARD'S GREEN Worcs
130 SO 7966 3m S of Stourport. Loc,
Shrawley CP.

NUFFIELD Oxon
158, 159 SU 6687 4m ESE of Wallingford.
CP, 633. Henley RD. P Hnly-on-Thames.
Ch e. Sch p. Hnly CC.

NUNBURNHOLME Yorks (E)
98 SE 8448 3m ESE of Pocklington.
CP, 196. Pcklngtn RD. P YORK. Ch e, m.
Howden CC. See also Kilnwick Percy.

NUNCARGATE Notts
112 SK 5054 5m SSW of Mansfield. Loc,
Kirkby in Ashfield UD. P Kkby
in Ashfld, NOTTINGHAM.

NUNEATON Warwicks
132 SP 3691 8m NNE of Coventry.
MB, 66,979. P. Nntn BC (CC). See also
Galley Cmmn. Mnfg tn in coal-mining distr.
Tn centre re-designed by Sir F. Gibberd.

NUNEHAM COURTENAY Oxon
158 SU 5599 5m SSE of Oxford. CP, 221.
Bullingdon RD. P OXFD. Ch e. Henley CC.

18c vllge moved from former site and
rebuilt here. 18c mnr hse.

NUNHEAD London
161, 171 TQ 3575 4m SSE of Lndn Br.
Loc, Lewisham LB, Southwark LB.
Deptford BC, Dulwich BC. Large cemetery.

NUN MONKTON Yorks (W)
97 SE 5057 7m NW of York. CP, 222.
Nidderdale RD. P YK. Ch e, r. Sch pe.
Harrogate CC. Blt round grn with trees,
pond, maypole. Ch nave all that survives of
orig nunnery.

NUNNEY Som
166 ST 7345 3m WSW of Frome. CP, 910.
Frme RD. P Frme. Ch e, m. Sch p. Wells CC.
Rems of 14c moated cstle (A.M.).

NUNNINGTON Yorks (N)
92 SE 6679 4m SE of Helmsley. CP, 213.
Kirkbymoorside RD. P YORK. Ch e, m.
Sch pe. Thirsk and Malton CC. Nnnngtn
Hall (NT)*, 16c–17c hse.

NUNNYKIRK Nthmb
77, 78 NZ 0892 6m SSE of Rothbury.
CP, 182. Rthbry RD.
Berwick-upon-Tweed CC. See also Wingates.

NUNTHORPE Yorks (N)
86 NZ 5314 4m SSE of Teesside
(Middlesbrough). Loc, Tssde CB;
CP, Stokesley RD. P(Nnthpe
Stn), MDDLSBRGH, Tssde. Ch e.
Tssde, Mddlsbrgh BC; Richmond CC.
(Rchmnd CC.)

NUNTON Wilts
167 SU 1526 3m SSE of Salisbury. Loc,
Odstock CP. Ch e.

NUPEND Glos
156 SO 7806 4m WNW of Stroud. Loc,
Eastington CP. P Stonehouse.

NURSLING Hants
180 SU 3616 4m NW of Southampton.
CP(Nslng and Rownhams), 2,584. Romsey
and Stockbridge RD. P STHMPTN. Ch e, m.
Sch pe. Eastleigh CC. See also Toot Hill,
Upton. 14c ch dedicated to St Boniface,
who set out from monastery here to convert
Germans in 8c.

NURSTED Hants
181 SU 7621 2m SE of Petersfield. Loc,
Buriton CP.

NUTBOURNE Sussex (W)
181 SU 7705 5m W of Chichester. Loc,
Southbourne CP. P Chchstr. Ch m, r.

NUTBOURNE Sussex (W)
182 TQ 0718 2m E of Pulborough. Loc,
Plbrgh CP. P Plbrgh.

NUTFIELD Surrey
170 TQ 3050 3m E of Reigate. CP, 2,597.
Godstone RD. P Redhill. Ch e, v. Sch pe.
E Srry CC (Rgte). See also S Ntfld.

NUTHALL Notts
112, 121 SK 5144 4m NW of Nottingham.
CP, 3,721. Basford RD. P NTTNGHM.
Ch e, m. Sch p2. Beeston CC (Rushcliffe).

NUTHAMPSTEAD Herts
148 TL 4034 5m SE of Royston. CP, 108.
Hitchin RD. Htchn CC.

NUTHURST Sussex (W)
182 TQ 1926 3m SSE of Horsham.
CP, 1,111. Hshm RD. Ch e. Sch pe. Hshm
and Crawley CC (Hshm). See also Copsale,
Mannings Hth.

NUTHURST Warwicks
131 SP 1571 5m S of Solihull. Loc,
Tanworth CP. Ch b.

NUTLEY Hants
168 SU 6044 5m SSW of Basingstoke.
CP, 119. Bsngstke RD. Bsngstke CC.

NUTLEY Sussex (E)
183 TQ 4427 5m NNW of Uckfield. Loc,
Maresfield CP. P Uckfld. Ch e, v. Sch pe.

NYETIMBER Sussex (W)
181 SZ 8998 3m W of Bognor. Loc, Pagham
CP. P Bgnr Regis. Ntmbr Barton, partly 12c.

NYEWOOD Sussex (W)
181 SU 8021 4m ESE of Petersfield. Loc,
Harting CP. Midhurst RD. P Ptrsfld. Chichester CC (Horsham).

NYMET ROWLAND Devon
175 SS 7108 9m NW of Crediton. CP, 111.
Crdtn RD. Ch e. Tiverton CC (Torrington).

NYMET TRACEY Devon
175 SS 7200 7m W of Crediton. Loc,
Bow CP. Ch e.

NYMPSFIELD Glos
156 SO 8000 3m ENE of Dursley. CP, 364.
Dsley RD. P Stonehouse. Ch e, r. Sch pr.
Stroud CC.

NYNEHEAD Som
164 ST 1322 1m N of Wellington. CP, 310.
Wllngtn RD. P Wllngtn. Ch e. Sch pe.
Taunton CC.

NYTON Sussex (W)
181 SU 9305 5m E of Chichester. Loc,
Aldingbourne CP.

O

OADBY Leics
121, 122 SK 6200 3m SE of Leicester.
UD, 19,530. P LCSTR. Harborough CC
(Lcstr SE BC). Several halls of residence of
University of Lcstr. Mnr High Sch, first
purpose-blt 'middle' sch in Europe for
pupils aged 11–14.

OAD STREET Kent
172 TQ 8762 2m WSW of Sittingbourne.
Loc, Borden CP. Ch m.

OAKAMOOR Staffs
120 SK 0544 3m ENE of Cheadle. CP, 784.
Chdle RD. P Stoke-on-Trent. Ch e, m, v.
Sch p, pr. Leek CC.

OAKE Som
164 ST 1525 3m NNE of Wellington.
CP, 551. Wllngtn RD. P Taunton. Ch e, m.
Sch p. Tntn CC. See also Hillfarance.

OAKEN Staffs
119 SJ 8502 4m NW of Wolverhampton.
Loc, Codsall CP. P Wlvrhmptn.

OAKENCLOUGH Lancs
94 SD 5347 10m SSE of Lancaster. Loc,
Garstang RD. Ch e. N Fylde CC. The ch of
Calder Vale.

OAKENGATES Shrops
119 SJ 7010 13m E of Shrewsbury. UD,

16,684. P Telford. The Wrekin CC. See also Priorslee, Trench. Iron and coal tn.

OAKENSHAW Co Durham
85 NZ 2037 1m N of Willington. Loc, Crook and Wllngtn UD. P Crk.

OAKENSHAW Yorks (W)
96, 102 SE 1727 3m S of Bradford. Loc, Spenborough MB. P Brdfd. Brighouse and Spnbrgh BC.

OAKFORD Devon
164 SS 9121 3m W of Bampton. CP, 316. Tiverton RD. P Tvtn. Ch e. Sch pe. Tvtn CC. See also Esworthy.

OAKHAM Rutland
122 SK 8608 9m SE of Melton Mowbray. UD, 6,411. P. Rtlnd and Stamford CC. County tn. Large ch with 14c twr and spire. 12c great hall* survives from fortified hse of the Ferrers family. Mkt place with butter cross.

OAKHANGER Hants
169 SU 7635 4m SE of Alton. Loc, Selborne CP. P Bordon. Ch e.

OAKHILL Som
166 ST 6347 3m NNE of Shepton Mallet. Loc, Ashwick CP. P Bath. Ch e, c, m. Sch pe.

OAKINGTON Cambs
135 TL 4164 4m NW of Cambridge. CP, 698. Chesterton RD. P CMBRDGE. Ch e, b, m. Sch pe. Cambs CC. Airfield at N end.

OAKLE STREET Glos
143 SO 7517 5m W of Gloucester. Loc, Churcham CP.

OAKLEY Beds
147 TL 0053 3m NW of Bedford. CP, 624. Bdfd RD. P BDFD. Ch e, m. Sch p, s. Bdfd CC.

OAKLEY Bucks
145, 146, 159 SP 6312 6m NW of Thame. CP, 496. Aylesbury RD. P Aylesbury. Ch e. Sch pe. Aylesbury CC.

OAKLEY Hants
168 SU 5650 5m W of Basingstoke. CP, 336. Bsngstke RD. P Bsngstke. Ch e. Sch pe. Bsngstke CC. See also E Oakley.

OAKLEY Suffolk (E)
137 TM 1678 3m NNE of Eye. CP, 204. Hartismere RD. P Diss, Norfolk. Ch e. Eye CC.

OAKLEY, GREAT Essex
150 TM 1927 6m ESE of Manningtree. See Gt Oakley, Essex.

OAKLEY, GREAT Northants
133 SP 8785 3m SW of Corby. Loc, Cby UD. P Cby.

OAKLEY GREEN Berks
159 SU 9276 2m W of Windsor. Loc, Bray CP. P Wndsr.

OAKMERE Ches
109 SJ 5769 6m WSW of Northwich. CP, 583. Nthwch RD. Nthwch CC.

OAKRIDGE LYNCH Glos
156, 157 SO 9103 7m W of Cirencester. Loc, Bisley-w-Lypiatt CP. P Stroud. Ch e, m. Sch pe.

OAKSEY Wilts
157 ST 9993 5m NE of Malmesbury. CP, 446. Mlmsbry RD. P Mlmsbry. Ch e, m. Sch pe. Chippenham CC. Ch: 15c wall-paintings.

OAKTHORPE Leics
120, 121 SK 3213 3m SW of Ashby de la Zouch. CP (Oakthpe and Donisthorpe), 2,435. Ashby de la Zch RD. P Burton-on-Trent, Staffs. Ch m. Sch p. Loughborough CC.

OAKWOODHILL Surrey
170, 182 TQ 1337 5m NNW of Horsham. Loc, Abinger CP. P Dorking. Ch e. Remote 13c ch to NW; glass, 15c brass.

OAKWORTH Yorks (W)
96 SE 0338 2m SW of Keighley. Loc, Kghly MB. P Kghly.

OARE Kent
172 TR 0063 1m NNW of Faversham. CP, 542. Swale RD. P Fvrshm. Ch e. Fvrshm CC. See also Uplees.

OARE Som
164 SS 8047 5m ESE of Lynton. CP, 86. Williton RD. Ch e. Bridgwater CC. See also Culbone. Ch in which R.D. Blackmore's 'Lorna Doone' was married and died.

OARE Wilts
167 SU 1563 2m N of Pewsey. Loc,
Wilcot CP. P Marlborough. Ch e, m. Sch pe.

OASBY Lincs (K)
113, 123 TF 0039 6m ENE of Grantham.
Loc, Haydor CP. W Kesteven RD.
P Grnthm. Grnthm CC.

OBORNE Dorset
178 ST 6518 2m NE of Sherborne. CP, 115.
Shbne RD. P Shbne. Ch e. Sch pe.
W Dst CC.

OCKBROOK Derbys
112, 121 SK 4236 4m E of Derby. CP.
SE Derbys RD. P DBY. Ch e, m, v. Sch p.
SE Derbys CC. See also Borrowash.

OCKHAM Surrey
170 TQ 0756 5m ESE of Woking. CP, 532.
Guildford RD. P Wkng. Ch e. Dorking CC.

OCKLEY Surrey
170, 182 TQ 1439 5m E of Cranleigh.
CP, 855. Dorking and Horley RD. P Dkng.
Ch e. Sch pe. Dkng CC. Wide grn; on Roman
Stane St, A29.

OCLE PYCHARD Herefs
142 SO 5946 7m NE of Hereford. CP, 271.
Bromyard RD. Ch e. Sch pe.
Leominster CC.

OCCOLD Suffolk (E)
137 TM 1570 2m SSE of Eye. CP, 282.
Hartismere RD. P Eye. Ch e, b. Sch p.
Eye CC.

ODCOMBE Som
177 ST 5015 3m W of Yeovil. CP, 574.
Yvl RD. P Yvl. Ch e, m. Sch pe. Yvl CC.

ODDINGLEY Worcs
130, 131 SO 9159 3m SSE of Droitwich.
CP, 171. Drtwch RD. P Drtwich. Ch e.
Worcester BC.

ODDINGTON Glos
144 SP 2325 3m E of Stow-on-the-Wold.
CP, 411. N Cotswold RD.
P Moreton-in-Marsh. Ch e. Sch pe.
Cirencester and Tewkesbury CC.

ODDINGTON Oxon
145, 146 SP 5514 5m SSW of Bicester.
CP, 86. Ploughley RD. Ch e. Mid-Oxon CC
(Henley).

ODELL Beds
134 SP 9657 6m S of Rushden. CP, 241.
Bedford RD. P BDFD. Ch e, m. Sch pe.
Bdfd CC. Sometimes called Woodhill. Cstle
rems on mound beside R Ouse; hse on site -
gdns open.

ODIHAM Hants
169 SU 7351 6m E of Basingstoke.
CP, 3,416. Hartley Wintney RD. P Bsngstke.
Ch e, b, c. Sch p, s. Bsngstke CC
(Aldershot). See also N Warnborough.
Mainly Ggn tn. Partly 14c ch: brasses.
Almshouses. Old stocks, whipping post.

ODSTOCK Wilts
167 SU 1426 2m S of Salisbury. CP, 561.
Slsbry and Wilton RD. Ch e. Sch p.
Slsbry CC. See also Bodenham Nunton.

ODSTONE Leics
120, 121 SK 3907 4m SSW of Coalville.
Loc, Shackerstone CP.

OFFCHURCH Warwicks
132 SP 3565 3m E of Leamington. CP, 288.
Warwick RD. P Lmngtn Spa. Ch e, r. Sch pe.
Wrwck and Lmngtn CC.

OFFENHAM Worcs
144 SP 0546 2m NE of Evesham. CP, 892.
Eveshm RD. P Eveshm. Ch e. Sch je, p.
S Worcs CC.

OFFHAM Kent
171 TQ 6557 7m W of Maidstone. CP, 731.
Malling RD. P Mdstne. Ch e, m. Sch p.
Tonbridge and Mllng CC (Sevenoaks). On
vllge grn is only surviving quintain, or
tilting-post, in England.

OFFHAM Sussex (E)
183 TQ 4012 2m NW of Lewes. Loc,
Hamsey CP. P Lewes. Ch e.

OFFHAM Sussex (W)
181, 182 TQ 0208 1m NNE of Arundel.
Loc, S Stoke CP.

OFFLEY, GREAT Herts
147 TL 1427 3m WSW of Hitchin. See Gt
Offley.

OFFLEYHAY Staffs
119 SJ 8029 7m NNE of Newport. Loc,
Eccleshall CP. Sch pe. Small lake of Cop
Mere to N of hmlt.

OFFORD CLUNY Hunts
134 TL 2167 3m SSW of Huntingdon.
CP, 321. St Neots RD. Ch e. Hunts CC.
Joined on to O. Darcy, but each has ch
hard by main Kings Cross-Edinburgh line.

OFFORD DARCY Hunts
134 TL 2166 4m SSW of Huntingdon.
CP, 295. St Neots RD. P HNTNGDN.
Ch e, b. Sch p. Hunts CC. Rly curves
re-aligned 1970 for E coast speed-up,
necessitating new embankment on top of
R Ouse.

OFFTON Suffolk (E)
149 TM 0649 5m NE of Hadleigh. CP, 226.
Gipping RD. P Ipswich. Ch e. Eye CC.

OFFWELL Devon
176 SY 1999 2m ESE of Honiton. CP, 453.
Hntn RD. P Hntn. Ch e. Sch pe. Hntn CC.

OGBOURNE MAIZEY Wilts
157 SU 1871 2m N of Marlborough. Loc,
Ogbne St Andrew CP.

OGBOURNE ST ANDREW Wilts
157 SU 1872 2m N of Marlborough.
CP, 339. Mlbrgh and Ramsbury RD.
P Mlbrgh. Ch e, r. Sch pe. Devizes CC. See
also Ogbne Maizey, Rockley.

OGBOURNE ST GEORGE Wilts
157 SU 2974 3m N of Marlborough.
CP, 421. Mlbrgh and Ramsbury RD.
P Mlbrgh. Ch e, m. Sch pe. Devizes CC.
Army camp on hills to W.

OGLE Nthmb
78 NZ 1378 4m NNW of Ponteland. Loc,
Whalton CP.

OGWELL Devon
176, 188 SX 8270, 8370 2m SW of Newton
Abbot. CP, 508. Ntn Abbt RD. Ch e.
Totnes CC. See also E Ogwll, W Ogwll.

OKEFORD FITZPAINE Dorset
178 ST 8010 6m NW of Blandford. CP, 619.
Sturminster RD. P Blndfd Forum. Ch e.
Sch pe. N Dst CC. See also Belchalwell.

OKEHAMPTON Devon
175 SX 5895 2m W of Exeter. MB, 3,908.
P. W Dvn CC (Torrington). Mkt tn and chief
tn of central Dvn. To S, rems of cstle on

mound in wooded valley. Military camp and
artillery ranges on moor to S.

OKEOVER Staffs
111 SK 1548 2m NW of Ashbourne. CP, 52.
Uttoxeter RD. Ch e. Burton CC. Ch and
hall; deer pk.

OLD Northants
133 SP 7873 6m WSW of Kettering.
CP, 287. Brixworth RD.
P NORTHAMPTON. Ch e, v. Daventry CC
(Kttrng).

OLD ALRESFORD Hants
168 SU 5833 7m ENE of Winchester.
CP, 527. Wnchstr RD. P Alrsfd. Ch e, r.
Sch pe. Wnchstr CC.

OLD BARNS Nthmb
71 NU 2405 1m NW of Amble. Loc,
Warkworth CP.

OLDBERROW Warwicks
131 SP 1265 5m E of Redditch. CP, 68.
Alcester RD. Ch e. Stratford-on-Avon CC
(Strtfd).

OLD BEWICK Nthmb
71 NU 0621 6m SE of Wooler. Loc,
Bwck CP. Glendale RD. P Alnwick. Ch e.
Berwick-upon-Tweed CC. Nmn ch ½m N.
Large prehistoric camp on hill to E.

OLD BOLINGBROKE Lincs (L)
114 TF 3564 6m SE of Horncastle.
CP(Blngbrke), 264. Spilsby RD. P Splsby.
Ch e, m. Sch pe. Hncstle CC. Ch blt by John
of Gaunt, late 14c. Slight rems of cstle*,
birthplace of Henry IV.

OLD BRAMPTON Derbys
111 SK 3371 3m W of Chesterfield.
CP(Brmptn), 932. Chstrfld RD. Ch e.
NE Derbys CC.

OLD BUCKENHAM Norfolk
136 TM 0691 3m SSE of Attleborough.
CP, 854. Wayland RD. P Attlbrgh.
Ch e, b, m. Sch p, s. S Nflk CC.

OLD BURGHCLERE Hants
168 SU 4757 5m S of Newbury. Loc,
Bghclre CP. P Nbry, Berks.

OLDBURY Shrops
130 SO 7191 1m SW of Bridgnorth. Loc,
Brdgnth CP. Ch e.

OLDBURY Warwicks
132 SP 3194 2m S of Atherstone. CP, 82.
Athrstne RD. Meriden CC.

OLDBURY Worcs
130, 131 SO 9989 3m E of Dudley. Loc,
Warley CB. P Wly. Wly W BC (Oldbury and
Halesowen).

OLDBURY ON THE HILL Glos
156 ST 8188 6m SW of Tetbury. Loc,
Didmarton CP. Ch e. 1m NW, Nan Tow's
Tump, large round barrow.

OLDBURY-UPON-SEVERN Glos
155, 156 ST 6192 3m NE of Severn Rd Br.
CP, 519. Thornbury RD. P BRISTOL.
Ch e, m. Sch pe. S Glos CC. See also
Sheperdine. To NE, Iron Age fort; 1m N,
nuclear power stn.

OLD BYLAND Yorks (N)
86, 92 SE 5585 4m WNW of Helmsley.
CP, 68. Hlmsly RD. Ch e, m. Thirsk and
Malton CC. Blnd Abbey: see Wass.

OLD CASSOP Co Durham
85 NZ 3339 4m ESE of Durham. Loc,
Cssp-cum-Quarrington CP. Drhm RD.
Drhm CC.

OLD CLEEVE Som
164 ST 0341 2m WSW of Watchet.
CP, 1,429. Williton RD. P Minehead.
Ch e, m. Sch pe. Bridgwater CC. See also
Blue Anchor, Washford.

OLDCOTES Notts
103 SK 5888 6m N of Worksop. CP(Styrrup
w Oldcts), 430. Wksp RD. P Wksp. Ch m, r.
Bassetlaw CC.

OLD DALBY Leics
121, 122 SK 6723 6m WNW of Melton
Mowbray. CP(Broughton and Old
Dlby), 1,303. Mltn and Belvoir RD. P Mltn
Mbry. Ch e, m. Sch pe. Mltn CC.

OLD EDLINGTON Yorks (W)
103 SK 5397 5m SW of Doncaster. Loc,
Edlngtn CP. Dncstr RD. Don Valley CC.

OLD ELDON Co Durham
85 NZ 2427 3m SE of Bishop Auckland.
Loc, Shildon UD.

OLD ELLERBY Yorks (E)
99 TA 1637 7m NE of Hull. Loc, Ellrby CP.
Holderness RD. Bridlington CC.

OLDFIELD Worcs
130 SO 8464 6m N of Worcester. Loc,
Ombersley CP.

OLD FISHBOURNE Sussex (W)
181 SU 8304 2m W of Chichester. Loc,
Bosham CP. P(Fshbne), Chchstr. Rems of
Roman palace*, largest in Britain; mosaic
pavements.

OLD FLETTON Hunts
134 TL 1997 1m S of Peterborough.
UD, 13,660. P PTRBRGH. Hunts CC. See
also Stanground. Brickworks abound.

OLD GRIMSBY Tresco, Isles of Scilly
189 SV 8915. Loc, Tresco CP.

OLDHAM Lancs
101 SD 9305 7m NE of Manchester.
CB, 105,705. P. BCs: Oldhm E, Oldhm W.
Blt orig on cotton. Industries now incl
additionally aero-engineering, mining,
paper-making, tanning.

OLD HEATH Essex
149, 162 TM 0122 2m SE of Colchester.
Loc, Clchstr MB.

OLD HEATHFIELD Sussex (E)
183 TQ 5920 1m SE of Heathfield. Loc,
Hthfld CP. P Hthfld. Ch e.

OLD HURST Hunts
134 TL 3077 2m S of Warboys. CP, 269.
St Ives RD. P HUNTINGDON. Hunts CC.

OLD HUTTON Westm
89 SD 5688 4m SE of Kendal. CP(Old Httn
and Holmescales), 258. S Westm RD. P Kndl.
Ch e. Sch pe. Westm CC.

OLD KEA Cornwall
190 SW 8441 2m SSE of Truro across river.
Loc, Kea CP. 15c twr of old ch stands above
creek.

OLD KNEBWORTH Herts
147 TL 2320 3m S of Stevenage. Loc,
Knbwth CP. P Knbwth. Ch e. K. Hse*, 16c
and 19c, former home of Bulwer Lytton;
collection of portraits, furniture.

OLDLAND Glos
155, 156 ST 6671 6m E of Bristol.
CP, 5,516. Warmley RD. P(Oldlnd
Cmmn), BRSTL. Ch e, c, m4, v4.
Sch p2, pe, sb. Kingswood CC (S Glos).

OLD LEAKE Lincs (H)
114 TF 4050 6m NE of Boston. CP, 1,557.
Bstn RD. P Bstn. Ch e. Sch p, s. Holland and
Bstn CC. See also Lke Cmmn Side.

OLD MALDEN London
170 TQ 2166 3m SE of Kingston. Loc,
Kngstn upon Thames LB. P Worcester Pk,
Surrey. Kngstn upn Thms BC.

OLD MALTON Yorks (N)
92 SE 7972 1m NE of Malton. Loc,
Mltn UD. P Mltn.

OLD MILVERTON Warwicks
132 SP 2967 2m NNE of Warwick. CP, 272.
Wrwck RD. Ch e. Wrwck and
Leamington CC.

OLD NEWTON Suffolk (E)
136 TM 0562 3m N of Stowmarket. CP(Old
Ntn w Dagworth), 591. Gipping RD.
P Stmkt. Ch e, m. Sch pe. Eye CC. See also
Ward Grn.

OLDPARK Shrops
119 SJ 6909 1m SW of Oakengates. Loc,
Dawley UD. P Telford. The Wrekin CC.

OLD QUARRINGTON Co Durham
85 NZ 3237 4m SE of Durham. Loc,
Cassop-cum-Qurrngtn CP. Drhm RD.
Drhm CC.

OLDRIDGE Devon
176 SX 8296 3m S of Crediton. Loc, Whitestone CP. Ch e.

OLD ROMNEY Kent
184 TR 0325 8m ENE of Rye. CP, 251.
Rmny Marsh RD. P Rmny Msh. Ch e.
Folkestone and Hythe CC.

OLD SODBURY Glos
156 ST 7581 10m N of Bath. Loc,
Sdbry CP. Sdbry RD. P BRISTOL. Ch e, b.
Sch pe. S Glos CC.

OLD SOMERBY Lincs (K)
113, 123 SK 9633 3m ESE of Grantham.
CP, 213. W Kesteven RD. P Grnthm. Ch e.
Sch pe. Rutland and Stamford CC.

OLDSTEAD Yorks (N)
92 SE 5380 6m WSW of Helmsley. CP, 66.
Hlmsly RD. Ch m. Thirsk and Malton CC.
Observatory twr, disused, on hill to E
commemorates Queen Victoria's
coronation, 1838.

OLD STRATFORD Northants
146 SP 7741 just NW of Stony Stratford.
CP, 909. Towcester RD.
P Wolverton, Bucks. Ch e. Sch p.
Daventry CC (S Nthnts). See also
Passenham.

OLD THORNVILLE Yorks (W)
97 SE 4554 5m NE of Wetherby.
CP(Thnvlle), 20. Nidderdale RD.
Harrogate CC.

OLD TOWN Nthmb
77 NY 8891 1m S of Otterburn. Loc,
Ottrbn CP.

OLD WARDEN Beds
147 TL 1343 5m W of Biggleswade. CP, 457.
Bgglswde RD. P Bgglswde. Ch e. Sch pe.
Mid-Beds CC. Thatched cottages. 1m NE,
Bgglswde or Old Wdn airfield; exhibition of
old aircraft and cars.

OLD WESTON Hunts
134 TL 0977 6m E of Thrapston. CP, 207.
Huntingdon RD. P HNTNGDN. Ch e, m.
Hunts CC.

OLD WINDSOR Berks
159, 160, 170 SU 9874 2m SE of Windsor.
CP, 5,344. Wndsr RD. P Wndsr. Ch e, m, r2.
Sch p, pe. Wndsr and Maidenhead CC
(Wndsr). Downstream from Wndsr
(R Thames); separated therefrom by Home
Pk of Wndsr Cstle.

OLD WIVES LEES Kent
172, 173 TR 0754 5m WSW of Canterbury.
Loc, Chilham CP. P Cntrbry. Ch m.

OLIVER'S BATTERY Hants
168 SU 4527 2m SW of Winchester.
CP, 747. Wnchstr RD. Wnchstr CC. Vantage
point whence Cromwell bombarded
Wnchstr.

OLLERTON Ches
101 SJ 7776 2m SE of Knutsford. CP, 314.
Bucklow RD. P Kntsfd. Ch m. Sch pe.
Kntsfd CC.

OLLERTON Notts
112 SK 6567 8m ENE of Mansfield.
CP, 5,529. Southwell RD. P Newark.
Ch e2, b, m2, r, s, v2. Sch p2, s. Nwk CC.

OLLERTON Shrops
118, 119 SJ 6525 6m SSW of Mkt Drayton.
Loc, Stoke upon Tern CP.

OLNEY Bucks
146 SP 8851 5m N of Newport Pagnell.
CP, 2,384. Npt Pgnll RD. P. Ch e, b, r, v.
Sch p, s. Buckingham CC. On R Ouse.
Home of Cowper, 18c poet. Annual pancake
race on Shrove Tuesday.

OLVESTON Glos
155, 156 ST 6087 3m SE of Severn Rd Br.
CP, 1,287. Thornbury RD. P BRISTOL.
Ch e, m. Sch pe. S Glos CC. See also
Awkley, Ingst, Northwick, Tockington.

OMBERSLEY Worcs
130 SO 8463 5m N of Worcester. CP, 2,259.
Droitwich RD. P Drtwch. Ch e, c. Sch pe.
Wcstr BC. See also Dunhampton, Hawford,
Oldfield, Sytchampton. Vllge of
half-timbered thatched cottages. O. Ct, early
18c; Rgncy facade.

OMPTON Notts
112 SK 6865 3m SE of Ollerton. CP, 38.
Southwell RD. Ch m. Newark CC.

ONECOTE Staffs
111 SK 0455 4m ESE of Leek. CP, 229.
Lk RD. P Lk. Ch e, m. Sch p. Lk CC. See
also Mixon.

ONEHOUSE Suffolk (E)
136 TM 0259 2m WNW of Stowmarket.
CP, 357. Gipping RD. Ch e. Eye CC.

ONGAR Essex
161 TL 5502 6m NNW of Brentwood. CP.
Epping and Ongr RD. P. Ch e, c, r.
Sch i, j, s. Brntwd and Ongr CC (Chigwell).
See also Greensted, Shelley. Old mkt tn
busy with traffic. Rems of moated Nmn
cstle.

ONGAR HILL Norfolk
124 TF 5824 4m NNW of King's Lynn. Loc,
Terrington St Clement CP.

ONGAR STREET Herefs
129 SO 3967 5m ENE of Presteigne. Loc,
Wigmore CP.

ONIBURY Shrops
129 SO 4579 3m SSE of Craven Arms.
CP, 272. Ludlow RD. P Crvn Arms. Ch e.
Sch pe. Ldlw CC.

ONNELEY Staffs
110, 119 SJ 7543 6m WSW of
Newcastle-under-Lyme. Loc, Madeley CP.

ONSLOW VILLAGE Surrey
169, 170 SU 9749 1m W of Guildford. Loc,
Gldfd MB. P Gldfd.

OPENWOODGATE Derbys
111 SK 3647 1m E of Belper. Loc, Blpr UD,
Blpr RD. P DERBY.

ORBY Lincs (L)
114 TF 4967 5m WNW of Skegness.
CP, 249. Spilsby RD. P Skgnss. Ch e, m.
Sch p. Horncastle CC.

ORCHARD PORTMAN Som
177 ST 2421 2m SSE of Taunton. CP, 161.
Tntn RD. Ch e. Tntn CC. See also
Thurlbear.

ORCHESTON Wilts
167 SU 0545 7m WNW of Amesbury.
CP, 388. Amesbury RD. P Salisbury.
Ch e2. Slsbry CC.

ORCOP Herefs
142 SO 4726 9m SSW of Hereford. CP, 387.
Dore and Bredwardine RD. P HRFD. Ch e.
Hrfd CC. See also Bagwy Llydiart, Garway
Hill, Orcp Hill.

ORCOP HILL Herefs
142 SO 4728 8m SSW of Hereford. Loc,
Orcp CP.

ORE Sussex (E)
184 TQ 8311 NE distr of Hastings. Loc,
Hstngs CB. P Hstngs.

OREHAM COMMON Sussex (W)
182 TQ 2213 1m S of Henfield. Loc,
Hnfld CP.

ORETON Shrops
129, 130 SO 6580 3m NNW of Cleobury
Mortimer. Loc, Farlow CP.
P Kidderminster, Worcs.

ORFORD Suffolk (E)
150 TM 4249 9m E of Woodbridge.
CP, 697. Deben RD. P Wdbrdge. Ch e, m.
Sch pe. Eye CC. Sailing, fishing. Rems of
12c cstle (A.M.).

ORGANFORD Dorset
179 SY 9392 3m NNE of Wareham. Loc,
Lytchett Minster CP. P Poole.

ORGREAVE Staffs
120 SK 1516 5m NNE of Lichfield. Loc,
Alrewas CP.

ORLESTONE Kent
184 TR 0034 5m S of Ashford. CP, 664.
E Ashfd RD. Ch e. Sch p. Ashfd CC. See
also Hamstreet.

ORLETON Herefs
129 SO 4967 5m N of Leominster. CP, 445.
Lmnstr and Wigmore RD. P Ludlow, Salop.
Ch e, m2. Sch pe. Lmnstr CC.

ORLETON Worcs
130 SO 6966 6m E of Tenbury Wells.
CP(Stanford w Orletn) 169. Tnbry RD.
Ch e. Kidderminster CC.

ORLINGBURY Northants
133 SP 8672 3m NNW of Wellingborough.
CP, 248. Wllngbrgh RD. P Kettering. Ch e.
Wllngbrgh CC.

ORMESBY Yorks (N)
86 NZ 5317 3m SE of Teesside
(Middlesbrough). Loc, Tssde CB.
P MDDLSBRGH, Tssde. Tssde, Redcar BC.
O. Hall (NT)*, 18c mansion by Carr of
York.

ORMESBY ST MARGARET Norfolk
126 TG 4914 5m NNW of Yarmouth.
CP(O St M w Scratby), 1,357. Blofield and
Flegg RD. P(Ormesby), Gt Ymth. Ch e, m.
Sch p. Ymth CC. See also California, E End.

ORMESBY ST MICHAEL Norfolk
126 TG 4814 5m NNW of Yarmouth.
CP, 321. Blofield and Flegg RD.   Ch e.
Ymth CC.

ORMSIDE, GREAT Westm
83 NY 7017 2m SSE of Appleby. See Gt
Ormsde.

ORMSKIRK Lancs
100 SD 4108 7m SE of Southport.
UD, 27,618. P. Ormskk CC. See also
Burscough, Bscgh Br, Newburgh, New Lane,
Scarth Hill, Tarlscough, Westhead.

ORPINGTON London
171 TQ 4666 4m ESE of Bromley. Loc,

Brmly LB.   P Kent.   Orpngtn BC (CC).
Rsdntl distr.

ORRELL Lancs
100 SD 5203 4m WSW of Wigan.
UD, 14,015. P Wgn. Ince BC. See also
Gathurst.

ORSETT Essex
161 TQ 6482 4m N of Tilbury. Loc,
Thurrock UD. P Grays. Thrrck BC (CC).

ORSLOW Staffs
119 SJ 8015 4m ESE of Newport. Loc,
Blymhill CP.

ORSTON Notts
112, 122 SK 7741 8m SSW of Newark.
CP, 374. Bingham RD. P NOTTINGHAM.
Ch e, m. Rushcliffe CC (Carlton).

ORTON Northants
133 SP 8079 4m W of Kettering. CP, 62.
Kttrng RD. Ch e. Kttrng CC.

ORTON Westm
83 NY 6208 9m SSW of Appleby. CP, 626.
N Westm RD.   P Penrith, Cumberland.
Ch e, m. Sch p, pe. Westm CC. See also
Greenholme, Raisbeck.

ORTON, GREAT Cumb
75 NY 3254 5m WSW of Carlisle. See Gt
Ortn.

ORTON LONGUEVILLE Hunts
134 TL 1696 2m SW of Peterborough.
CP, 1,256. Norman Cross RD. P PTRBRGH.
Ch e. Sch j, pe, s2. Hunts CC.

ORTON ON THE HILL Leics
120, 121 SK 3003 4m N of Atherstone.
Loc, Twycross CP. P Athrstne, Warwickshire.
Ch e.

ORTON WATERVILLE Hunts
134 TL 1596 3m SW of Peterborough.
CP, 371. Norman Cross RD. P PTRBRGH.
Ch e, m. Hunts CC.

ORWELL Cambs
148 TL 3650 8m SW of Cambridge.
CP, 619.   S Cambs RD.   P Royston, Herts.
Ch e, m. Sch pe. Cambs CC.

OSBALDESTON Lancs
94, 95 SD 6431 3m NW of Blackburn.
CP, 223. Blckbn RD. Ch r. Sch pr.
Darwen CC.

Osbaldwick

OSBALDWICK Yorks (N)
97, 98 SE 6351 2m E of York. CP.
Flaxton RD. P YK. Ch e. Sch p. Thirsk and
Malton CC.

OSBASTON Leics
121 SK 4204 6m S of Coalville. CP, 160.
Mkt Bosworth RD. Bswth CC.

OSBOURNBY Lincs (K)
113, 123 TF 0738 5m S of Sleaford.
CP, 348. E Kesteven RD. P Slfd. Ch e, m.
Sch p. Rutland and Stamford CC.

OSCROFT Ches
109 SJ 5066 6m E of Chester. Loc,
Tarvin CP. Ch m. Northwich CC.

OSGATHORPE Leics
121 SK 4319 4m N of Coalville. CP. Ashby
de la Zouch RD. P Loughborough. Ch e.
Lghbrgh CC. Sch and almshouses of 1670.

OSGODBY Lincs (L)
104 TF 0792 3m NW of Mkt Rasen. CP, 532.
Caistor RD. P Mkt Rsn. Ch e, m. Sch p.
Gainsborough CC. See also Kirkby, Usselby.
Private RC chpl, 18c, in wing of farmhouse,
marked by white cross on gable end.

OSGODBY Yorks (E)
97, 98 SE 6433 2m ENE of Selby. Loc,
Barlby CP.

OSGODBY Yorks (N)
93 TA 0584 3m SSE of Scarborough. Loc,
Scbrgh MB, Scbrgh RD. Scbrgh CC (Scbrgh
and Whitby).

OSMASTON Derbys
120 SK 1943 2m SE of Ashbourne.
CP, 216. Ashbne RD. P Ashbne. Ch e.
Sch pe. W Derbys CC.

OSMINGTON Dorset
178 SY 7283 4m NE of Weymouth.
CP, 539. Dorchester RD. P Wmth. Ch e, m.
S Dst CC. John Constable spent honeymoon
here. 1m NNW, chalk figure of George III
on horseback cut in turf of hillside.

OSMINGTON MILLS Dorset
178 SY 7381 6m SSE of Dorchester. Loc,
Osmngtn CP. Famous for lobsters.

OSMOTHERLEY Yorks (N)
91 SE 4597 6m ENE of Northallerton.
CP, 578. Nthlltn RD. P Nthlltn.

Ch e, f, m, r2. Sch p. Richmond CC. Stone
vllge round grn. Stone table used by Wesley
as pulpit. 1m NW, Mt Grace Priory (A.M.),
rems of 14c Carthusian priory, and 17c
hse (NT)*.

OSPRINGE Kent
172 TR 0060 1m SW of Faversham. Loc,
Fvrshm MB; CP, 470, Swale RD. P Fvrshm.
Fvrshm CC. Maison Dieu (A.M.), 15c
timber-framed hse; contains museum of
Roman pottery.

OSSETT Yorks (W)
96, 102 SE 2720 3m W of Wakefield.
MB, 17,181. P. Dewsbury BC.

OSSINGTON Notts
112 SK 7564 7m NNW of Newark. CP, 141.
Southwell RD. Ch e. Nwk CC. Classical 18c
ch; contains two worldly statues of William
and Robert Denison.

OSTEND Essex
162 TQ 9397 1m NW of
Burnham-on-Crouch. Loc,
Bnhm-on-Crch UD.

OSWALDKIRK Yorks
92 SE 6279 3m SSE of Helmsley. CP, 207.
Hlmsly RD. P YORK. Ch e, r. Thirsk and
Malton CC.

OSWALDTWISTLE Lancs
95 SD 7327 2m WSW of Accrington.
UD, 14,015. P Accrngtn. Accrngtn BC. See
also Belthorn. Mainly textiles.

OSWESTRY Shrops
118 SJ 2929 16m NW of Shrewsbury.
CP, 11,215. Oswstry RD. P.
Ch e2, b3, c2, f, m3, r, s, v5.
Sch i, je, p, pr, sb2, sg2. Oswstry CC. Busy
Welsh-border tn. Large ch, mostly Vctrn. To
N, Old O., extensive Iron Age fort (A.M.).

OTFORD Kent
171 TQ 5259 3m N of Sevenoaks.
CP, 3,179. Svnks RD. P Svnks. Ch e, m.
Sch p. Svnks CC. Blt round grn with pond.
Rems of Archbishop's Palace.

OTHAM Kent
172 TQ 7953 3m ESE of Maidstone.
CP, 340. Mdstne RD. P Mdstne. Ch e.
Mdstne CC. Among hop gdns and orchards.
Stoneacre (NT)*, 15c half-timbered Kentish
yeoman's hse.

OTHERY Som
165 ST 3831 6m SE of Bridgwater. CP, 498.
Brdgwtr RD. P Brdgwtr. Ch e, v. Sch p.
Brdgwtr CC.

OTLEY Suffolk (E)
150 TM 2055 6m NW of Woodbridge.
CP, 502. Deben RD. P Ipswich. Ch e, b.
Sch p. Eye CC.

OTLEY Yorks (W)
96 SE 2045 8m NNE of Bradford.
UD, 13,254. P. Ripon CC. Ancient mkt tn.
Engineering and textile wks.

OTTERBOURNE Hants
168 SU 4522 3m N of Eastleigh. CP, 809.
Winchester RD. P Wnchstr. Ch e, v. Sch pe.
Wnchstr CC. Home of Charlotte Yonge,
Vctrn novelist. Parts of Netley Abbey (see
Ntly) re-erected in grnds of late 18c
Cranbury Pk, 1m W.

OTTERBURN Nthmb
77 NY 8893 19m N of Hexham. CP, 555.
Bellingham RD. P NEWCASTLE
UPON TYNE. Ch e, m, r, v. Sch p.
Hxhm CC. See also Old Tn. O. tweeds made
here, although main factory elsewhere. 2m
N, military camp.

OTTERBURN Yorks (W)
95 SD 8857 8m WNW of Skipton. CP, 40.
Settle RD. Skptn CC.

OTTERFORD Som
177 ST 2214 6m S of Taunton. CP, 281.
Tntn RD. Ch e, v. Tntn CC. See also
Bishop's Wd, Fyfet.

OTTERHAM Cornwall
174 SX 1690 6m NE of Camelford.CP, 206.
Cmlfd RD. Ch e. Sch p. N Cnwll CC.

OTTERHAMPTON Som
165 ST 2443 5m NW of Bridgwater.
CP 442. Brdgwtr RD. Ch e. Sch p.
Brdgwtr CC. See also Combwich, Steart.

OTTERSHAW Surrey
169, 170 TQ 0263 3m NNE of Woking.
Loc, Chertsey UD. P Chtsy.

OTTERTON Devon
176 SY 0885 3m WSW of Sidmouth.
CP, 611. St Thomas RD. P Budleigh
Salterton. Ch e, m. Sch pe. Honiton CC.

Colourwash, cob, thatch; wide main street.
1m E, Ladram Bay, beauty spot with
caravan site.

OTTERY ST MARY Devon
176 SY 0995 5m NNW of Sidmouth.
UD, 5,824. P. Honiton CC. See also
Alfington, Fairmile, Fenny Bridges, Tipton
St John, W Hill, Wiggaton. Bthplce of
Coleridge, 1772. Large ch mainly 14c.

OTTRINGHAM Yorks (E)
99 TA 2624 5m WSW of Withernsea.
CP, 560. Holderness RD. P Hull. Ch e, m.
Bridlington CC. Ch has very tall stone spire.

OUGHTERSIDE Cumb
82 NY 1140 6m ENE of Maryport.
CP (Oughtrsde and Allerby), 604.
Cockermouth RD. P Carlisle. Ch m. Sch p.
Workington CC.

OUGHTIBRIDGE Yorks (W)
102 SK 3093 5m NW of Sheffield. Loc,
Bradfield CP. P SHFFLD. Ch e, c, m, v.
Sch p.

OULSTON Yorks (N)
92 SE 5474 3m NNE of Easingwold.
CP, 130. Easngwld RD. P YORK. Thirsk
and Malton CC.

OULTON Cumb
75 NY 2450 2m NNW of Wigton. Loc,
Woodside CP. Wgtn RD. P Wgtn. Sch pe.
Penrith and the Border CC.

OULTON Norfolk
125 TG 1328 4m WNW of Aylsham.
CP, 263. St Faith's and Aylshm RD.
P NORWICH, NOR 10Y. Ch e, c, v.
N Nflk CC (Central Nflk). See also Oultn St.

OULTON Staffs
110, 119 SJ 9135 1m NE of Stone. Loc,
Stne Rural CP. Stne RD. P Stne. Ch e.
Sch pe. Stafford and Stne CC.

OULTON Suffolk (E)
137 TM 5294 2m NW of Lowestoft. CP, 369.
Lothingland RD. P Lwstft. Ch e. Lwstft CC.

OULTON Yorks (W)
96, 102 SE 3628 5m NNE of Wakefield.
Loc, Rothwell UD.

OULTON BROAD Suffolk (E)
137 TM 5292 2m W of Lowestoft. Loc,
Lwstft MB. P Lwstft.

OULTON STREET Norfolk
126 TG 1527 3m W of Aylsham. Loc,
Oultn CP.

OUNDLE Northants
134 TL 0388 12m NE of Kettering.
UD, 3,741. P PETERBOROUGH.
Wellingborough CC (Ptrbrgh). Stone tn with
many old hses and inns. Ch has fine twr and
spire. Boys' public sch, founded 1556.

OUSBY Cumb
83 NY 6234 7m ENE of Penrith. CP, 384.
Pnrth RD. P Pnrth. Ch e, m. Sch pe. Pnrth
and the Border CC. See also Melmerby.

OUSDEN Suffolk (W)
135 TL 7459 7m ESE of Newmarket.
CP, 213. Clare RD. P Nmkt. Ch e, m.
Sch pe. Bury St Edmunds CC.

OUSEBURN, GREAT Yorks (W)
91, 97 SE 4461 5m SE of Boroughbridge.
See Gt Ousebn.

OUSEFLEET Yorks (W)
98 SE 8223 5m E of Goole. CP, 167.
Gle RD. Sch p. Gle CC.

OUSTON Co Durham
78 NZ 2554 2m NNW of Chester-le-Street.
CP, 1,181. Chstr-le-Strt RD. P Chstr-le-Strt.
Ch r. Sch i, j. Chstr-le-Strt CC.

OUT GATE Lancs
88, 89 SD 3599 3m SSW of Ambleside. Loc,
Hawkshead CP. P Amblsde, Westmorland.

OUTHGILL Westm
90 NY 7801 5m S of Kirkby Stephen. Loc,
Mallerstang CP. N Westm RD. P Kby Stphn.
Ch m. Westm CC.

OUT NEWTON Yorks (E)
99 TA 3821 5m SSE of Withernsea. Loc,
Easington CP. Sea encroaching.

OUT RAWCLIFFE Lancs
94 SD 4041 7m NE of Blackpool. CP, 603.
Garstang RD. Ch e. Sch pe. N Fylde CC.

OUTWELL Cambs and Norfolk
124 TF 5103 5m SE of Wisbech. CP, 604,
Wsbch RD; CP, 1,132, Marshland RD.
P Wsbch, Cambs. Ch e, m. Sch p. Isle
of Ely CC, King's Lynn CC.

OUTWOOD Surrey
170 TQ 3245 3m NE of Horley. Loc,
Burstow CP. P Redhill. Ch e. Sch p.
Post-mill of 1665*.

OUTWOOD Yorks (W)
96, 102 SE 3223 2m N of Wakefield. Loc,
Stanley UD. P Wkfld.

OUTWOODS Staffs
119 SJ 7818 3m ESE of Newport. Loc,
Gnosall CP.

OVER Cambs
135 TL 3770 4m E of St Ives. CP, 908.
Chesterton RD. P CAMBRIDGE. Ch e, b, m.
Sch p. Cambs CC.

OVER Glos
155, 156 ST 5882 6m N of Bristol. Loc,
Almondsbury CP.

OVER BURROW Lancs
89 SD 6175 2m S of Kirkby Lonsdale. Loc,
Brrw-w-Brrw CP. Lunesdale RD.
Lancaster CC.

OVERBURY Worcs
143, 144 SO 9537 5m NE of Tewkesbury.
CP, 281. Evesham RD. P Tksbry, Glos. Ch e.
Sch pe. S Worcs CC. Under Bredon Hill.
O. Ct, Ggn; landscaped gdns. Restored partly
Nmn ch.

OVER COMPTON Dorset
177, 178 ST 5916 2m E of Yeovil. CP, 103.
Sherborne RD. Ch e. Sch pe. W Dst CC.

OVER HADDON Derbys
111 SK 2066 2m SW of Bakewell. CP, 193.
Bkwll RD. P Bkwll. Ch e, v. W Derbys CC.

OVER KELLET Lancs
89 SD 5270 1m E of Carnforth. CP, 530.
Lunesdale RD. P Cnfth. Ch e, m. Sch pe.
Lancaster CC. See also Capernwray.

OVER KIDDINGTON Oxon
145 SP 4022 4m NW of Woodstock. Loc,
Kddngtn w Asterleigh CP. 1½m WSW,
Ditchley Pk*, early 18c hse by James Gibbs.
Gibbs. Now Anglo-American conference
centre.

OVER NORTON Oxon
145 SP 3128 just N of Chipping Norton.
CP, 428. Chppng Ntn RD. P Chppng Ntn.
Ch e. Banbury CC. Ch is St John's Chpl
one room in a hse.

OVERSEAL Derbys
120, 121 SK 2915 4m W of Ashby de la
Zouch. CP, 2,042. Repton RD.
P Burton-on-Trent, Staffs. Ch b, m. Sch p.
Belper CC.

OVER SILTON Yorks (N)
91 SE 4593 5m E of Northallerton. CP, 37.
Nthlltn RD. Ch e. Richmond CC.

OVERSTONE Northants
133 SP 8066 5m NE of Northampton. CP.
Brixworth RD. P NTHMPTN. Ch e. Sch p.
Daventry CC (Kettering).

OVER STOWEY Som
164 ST 1838 8m ESE of Watchet. CP, 447.
Bridgwater RD. Ch e. Sch pe. Brdgwtr CC.

OVERSTRAND Norfolk
126 TG 2440 2m ESE of Cromer. CP, 796.
Erpingham RD. P Crmr. Ch e, m, r. Sch pe.
N Nflk CC.

OVER STRATTON Som
177 ST 4315 5m E of Ilminster. Loc,
S Petherton CP. P: S Pthrtn. Ch m.

OVER TABLEY Ches
101 SJ 7279 2m WNW of Knutsford.
CP(Tbly Superior), 382. Bucklow RD.
P Kntsfd. Ch e. Kntsfd CC.

OVERTHORPE Northants
145 SP 4840 2m E of Banbury. Loc,
Middleton Cheney CP.

OVERTON Hants
168 SU 5149 8m WSW of Basingstoke.
CP, 2,036. Kingsclere and Whitchurch RD.
P Bsngstke. Ch e, m. Sch pe. Bsngstke CC.
See also Quidhampton.

OVERTON Lancs
94 SD 4358 4m S of Morecambe. CP, 551.
Lancaster RD. P Mcmbe. Ch e, m. Sch pe.
Lncstr CC. See also Sunderland.

OVERTON Yorks (N)
97 SE 5555 4m NW of York. CP, 48.
Easingwold RD. Thirsk and Malton CC.

OVERTON GREEN Ches
110 SJ 7960 3m E of Sandbach. Loc,
Smallwood CP.

OVER WALLOP Hants
168 SU 2838 7m SW of Andover.
CP, 1,501. Romsey and Stockbridge RD.
Ch e, b. Winchester CC. See also Palestine.

OVER WHITACRE Warwicks
131 SP 2491 3m ENE of Coleshill. CP, 369.
Meriden RD. Ch e. Mrdn CC.

OVER WORTON Oxon
145 SP 4329 7m SSW of Banbury. Loc,
Wtn CP. Chipping Norton RD. Ch e.
Bnbry CC.

OVERY STAITHE Norfolk
125 TF 8444 4m W of Wells. Loc,
Burnham Overy CP. P King's Lynn. Ch m.
Small yachting centre. Twr windmill and
water mill, both NT.

OVING Bucks
146 SP 7821 5m NNW of Aylesbury.
CP, 340. Aylesbury RD. P Aylesbury.
Ch e, m. Aylesbury CC.

OVING Sussex (W)
181 SU 9005 3m E of Chichester. CP, 952.
Chchstr RD. P Chchstr. Ch e, r. Chchstr CC.
See also Colworth, Merston. On S side of
Tangmere airfield.

OVINGHAM Nthmb
77, 78 NZ 0863 just NW of Prudhoe.
CP, 556. Hexham RD. P Prdhoe. Ch e.
Sch pe. Hxhm CC.

OVINGTON Essex
149 TL 7642 2m S of Clare. CP, 55.
Halstead RD. Ch e. Saffron Walden CC.

OVINGTON Hants
168 SU 5631 5m ENE of Winchester.
CP(Itchen Stoke and Ovngtn), 253.
Wnchstr RD. Ch e. Wnchstr CC.

OVINGTON Norfolk
125 TF 9202 1m NNE of Watton. CP, 198.
Wayland RD. Ch e, m. S Nflk CC.

OVINGTON Nthmb
77, 78 NZ 0663 2m WNW of Prudhoe.
CP, 411. Hexham RD. P Prdhoe. Ch m.
Hxhm CC.

OVINGTON Yorks (N)
85 NZ 1314 5m ESE of Barnard Cstle.
CP, 145. Startforth RD. P Richmond.
Rchmnd CC.

OWER Hants
180 SU 3216 4m SSW of Romsey. Loc, Netley Marsh CP. P Rmsy.

OWERMOIGNE Dorset
178 SY 7685 6m SE of Dorchester. CP, 599. Dchstr RD. P Dchstr. Ch e, m. Sch pe. S Dst CC.   See also Crossways, Holworth. Moigne Ct*, 13c hse, formerly moated. Opening limited.

OWLPEN Glos
156 ST 7998 5m SSW of Stroud. CP, 56. Dursley RD. Ch e. Strd CC. O. Mnr,* beautiful old Cotswold hse.

OWLSWICK Bucks
159 SP 7806 2m NNW of Princes Risborough. Loc, Longwick-cum-Ilmer CP.

OWMBY Lincs (L)
104 TA 0705 3m NW of Caistor. CP(Searby cum Ownby), 166.Cstr RD. Gainsborough CC.

OWMBY Lincs (L)
104 TF 0087 7m W of Mkt Rasen. CP, 271. Welton RD. Ch e, m. Gainsborough CC.

OWSLEBURY Hants
168 SU 5123 4m SSE of Winchester. CP, 717. Wnchstr RD. P Wnchstr. Ch e, m2. Sch p. Wnchstr CC. See also Morestead. Bottom Pond Farm, site of large Belgic (late Iron Age) vllge; many finds of pottery, jewellery, etc.

OWSTON Leics
122 SK 7707 5m W of Oakham. CP(Owstn and Newbold), 94. Billesdon RD. Ch e. Harborough CC (Melton).

OWSTON Yorks (W)
103 SE 5511 5m NNW of Doncaster. CP, 167. Dncstr RD. Ch e. Sch s. Don Valley CC.

OWSTON FERRY Lincs (L)
104 SE 8000 7m N of Gainsborough. CP, 1,066. Isle of Axholme RD. P Doncaster, Yorkshire. Ch e, m2. Sch pe. Gnsbrgh CC.

OWSTWICK Yorks (E)
99 TA 2732 5m NW of Withernsea. Loc, Roos CP. Ch m.

OWTHORPE Notts
112, 121, 122 SK 6733 7m SE of Nottingham. CP, 98. Bingham RD. Ch e. Rushcliffe CC (Carlton).

OXBOROUGH Norfolk
124 TF 7401 7m SW of Swaffham. CP, 195. Swffhm RD. P King's Lynn. Ch e, r. Sch pe. SW Nflk CC. O. Hall (NT)*, moated 15c and later hse with splendid gate twr. Seat of Bedingfield family since 1482. RC ch by Pugin in grnds.

OXCOMBE Lincs (L)
105 TF 3177 6m NNE of Horncastle. Loc, Maidenwell CP. Louth RD. Ch e. Lth CC.

OXENDON, GREAT Northants
133 SP 7383 2m S of Mkt Harborough. See Gt Oxndn.

OXENHALL Glos
143 SO 7126 just NW of Newent. CP, 256. Nwnt RD. Ch e. W Glos CC.

OXENHOLME Westm
89 SD 5390 2m SE of Kendal. Loc, Kndl MB.

OXENHOPE Yorks (W)
96 SE 0335 4m SSW of Keighley. Loc, Kghly MB. P Kghly.

OXEN PARK Lancs
88, 89 SD 3187 6m NNE of Ulverston. Loc, Colton CP. P Ulvstn.

OXENTON Glos
143, 144 SO 9531 4m E of Tewkesbury. CP, 154. Cheltenham RD. Ch e. Cirencester and Tksbry CC.

OXENWOOD Wilts
168 SU 3059 6m SSW of Hungerford. Loc, Shalbourne CP. P Marlborough.

OXFORD Oxon
158 SP 5106 52m WNW of London. CB, 108,564. P(OXFD). Oxfd BC. See also Cowley, Headington. City on R Thames, famous for ancient university. Cathedral is chpl of Christ Ch College. Busy commercial centre.

OXHILL Warwicks
145 SP 3145 5m NE of Shipton on Stour. CP, 181. Shpstn on Str RD. Ch e, m. Stratford-on-Avon CC (Strtfd).

OXNEAD Norfolk
126 TG 2324 3m SE of Aylsham. Loc, Brampton CP. Ch e. O. Hall was principal seat of Paston family until early 18c. Only one wing of orig hse remains.

OXNEY GREEN, GREAT Essex
161 TL 6606 3m W of Chelmsford. See Gt Oxney Grn.

OXSHOTT Surrey
170 TQ 1460 3m NNW of Leatherhead. Loc, Esher UD. P Lthrhd.

OXSPRING Yorks (W)
102 SE 2602 2m ESE of Penistone. CP, 745. Pnstne RD. P SHEFFIELD. Sch p. Pnstne CC.

OXTED Surrey
171 TQ 3952 9m N of E Grinstead. CP, 8,094. Godstone RD. P. Ch e, c, f, r, v2. Sch p, pe, s. E Srry CC (Reigate). See also Holland, Hurst Grn.

OXTON Notts
112 SK 6251 8m NNE of Nottingham. CP, 575. Southwell RD. P Sthwll. Ch e, m. Sch pe. Nwk CC.

OXWICK Norfolk
125 TF 9125 3m S of Fakenham. Loc, Colkirk CP.

OZLEWORTH Glos
156 ST 7993 4m SE of Dursley. CP, 115. Tetbury RD. Ch e. Stroud CC. Ch has hexagonal Nmn twr (cf Swindon, Glos).

P

PACKINGTON Leics
120, 121 SK 3614 1m S of Ashby de la Zouch. CP, 433. Ashby de la Zch RD. P Ashby de la Zch. Ch e, m. Sch pe. Loughborough CC.

PADBURY Bucks
146 SP 7130 3m SE of Buckingham. CP, 467. Bcknghm RD. P BCKNGHM. Ch e, m. Sch pe. Bcknghm CC. Old half-timbered cottages.

PADDINGTON London
160 TQ 2581 3m WNW of Charing Cross. Loc, City of Westminster LB. Pddngtn BC (Pddngtn N, Pddngtn S). Contains wharves on Grand Union Canal; Pddngtn (rly) Stn; Little Venice (basin in canal).

PADDLESWORTH Kent
173 TR 1939 3m NW of Folkestone. CP, 35. Elham RD. Ch e, r. Flkstne and Hythe CC. High on downs.

PADDOCK WOOD Kent
171 TQ 6645 5m E of Tonbridge. CP, 2,856. Tnbrdge RD. P Tnbrdge. Ch e, m, r, v. Sch p, s. Royal Tunbridge Wells CC (Tnbrdge). Centre of hop-growing industry.

PADIHAM Lancs
95 SD 7933 3m WNW of Burnley. UD, 10,192. P Bnly. Clitheroe CC. Textiles, engineering. 1m E, Gawthorpe Hall*, early 17c.

PADSIDE Yorks (W)
96 SE 1659 4m S of Pateley Br. CP(Thornthwaite w Pdsde), 136. Ripon and Ptly Br RD. Rpn CC.

PADSTOW Cornwall
185 SW 9175 11m WNW of Bodmin. CP, 2,640. Wadebridge and Pdstw RD. P. Ch e, m, r. Sch p. N Cnwll CC. See also Crugmeer, Trevone. Resort of narrow twisty streets down to harbour. Hobby Horse dance on May Day involves grotesque costumes and music.

PADWORTH Berks
158 SU 6166 9m E of Newbury. CP, 432. Bradfield RD. P Reading. Ch e. Sch pe. Nbry CC.

PAGE BANK Co Durham
85 NZ 2335 2m E of Willington. Loc, Crook and Wllngtn UD. P Spnnmr.

PAGHAM Sussex (W)
181 SZ 8897 3m WSW of Bognor. CP, 1,772. Chichester RD. P Bgnr Regis.

Ch e. Arundel CC (Chchstr). See also Nyetimber.

PAGLESHAM Essex
162 TQ 9293 4m ENE of Rochford. CP, 302. Rchfd RD. P Rchfd. Ch e, c. Sch p. Maldon CC (SE Essx). See also Eastend. Yachting and yacht-building.

PAIGNTON Devon
188 SX 8960 2m SW of Torquay. Loc, Torbay CB. P. An urban distr, pop. over 30,000, until absorbed into Tby CB. Resort, with harbour and sands. Kirkham Hse (A.M.).

PAILTON Warwicks
132 SP 4781 5m NNW of Rugby. CP, 440. Rgby RD. P Rgby. Ch e. Rgby CC.

PAINSHAWFIELD Nthmb
77, 78 NZ 0660 3m SW of Prudhoe. Loc, Broomley and Stocksfield CP. Hexham RD. Ch b. Hxhm CC.

PAINSTHORPE Yorks (E)
98 SE 8158 6m N of Pocklington. Loc, Kirby Underdale CP.

PAINSWICK Glos
156 SO 8609 3m NNE of Stroud. CP, 2,844. Strd RD. P Strd. Ch e, b, c3, f, m, r. Sch p, pe. Strd CC. See also Sheepscombe, Slad. 15c ch; in churchyard, clipped yews, table tombs. Ct Hse*, c1600. Many bldngs of interest in this Cotswold stone tn.

PAKEFIELD Suffolk (E)
137 TN 5290 2m SSW of Lowestoft. Loc, Lwstft MB.

PAKENHAM Suffolk (W)
136 TL 9267 5m ENE of Bury St Edmunds. CP, 862. Thingoe RD. P Bury St Eds. Ch e, m. Sch pe. Bury St Eds CC. Twr windmill*.

PALESTINE Hants
167 SU 2640 7m WSW of Andover. Loc, Over Wallop CP.

PALEY STREET Berks
159 SU 8776 3m SSW of Maidenhead. Loc, White Waltham CP. Ch v.

PALGRAVE Suffolk (E)
136 TM 1178 1m S of Diss. CP, 596.

Hartismere RD. P Dss, Norfolk. Ch e. Sch pe. Eye CC.

PALMARSH Kent
173 TR 1333 2m WSW of Hythe. Loc, Hythe MB. P(Plmsh Estate), Hythe.

PALMER'S GREEN London
160 TQ 3193 2m SSW of Enfield. Loc, Enfld LB. Southgate BC.

PALTERTON Derbys
112 SK 4768 6m ESE of Chesterfield. Loc, Scarcliffe CP. P Chstrfld. Ch m. Sch p.

PAMBER END Hants
168 SU 6158 4m NNW of Basingstoke. Loc, Pmbr CP. Bsngstke RD. Ch e. Bsngstke CC. Ch is sole rems of 12c priory.

PAMBER GREEN Hants
168 SU 6059 5m NNW of Basingstoke. Loc, Pmbr CP. Bsngstke RD. Bsngstke CC.

PAMBER HEATH Hants
168 SU 6162 7m N of Basingstoke. Loc, Pmbr CP. Bsngstke RD. P Bsngstke. Ch v. Bsngstke CC.

PAMPHILL Dorset
179 ST 9900 1m W of Wimborne. CP, 679. Wmbne and Cranborne RD. Ch e. Sch pe. N Dst CC. See also Hillbutts. 1m NW, Kingston Lacy*, 17c and later hse. Beech avenue on main rd beside pk.

PAMPISFORD Cambs
148 TL 4948 7m SSE of Cambridge. CP, 295. S Cambs RD. P CMBRDGE. Ch e. Cambs CC. Tympanum of Nmn doorway to ch dedicated to John the Baptist tells story of his death in gruesome detail.

PANCRASWEEK Devon
174 SS 2905 3m WNW of Holsworthy. CP, 209. Hlswthy RD. Ch e, m. W Dvn CC (Tavistock).

PANFIELD Essex
148, 149 TL 7325 2m NW of Braintree. CP, 358. Brntree RD. P Brntree. Ch e, v. Brntree CC (Maldon).

PANGBOURNE Berks
158, 159 SU 6376 5m WNW of Reading. CP, 1,953. Bradfield RD. P Rdng. Ch e, c, m, r. Sch p. Newbury CC. 1m SW, nautical college.

PANNAL Yorks (W)
96 SE 3051 2m S of Harrogate. Loc,
Hrrgte MB; CP, 265. Nidderdale RD.
P Hrrgte. Ch e. Hrrgte CC. See also
Beckwithshaw.

PANT Shrops
117 SJ 2722 5m SSW of Oswestry.
CP(Llanymynech and Pnt), 763.
Oswstry RD. P Oswstry. Ch c, m.
Oswstry CC.

PANTON Lincs (L)
105 TF 1778 8m SE of Mkt Rasen. CP, 67.
Horncastle RD. Hncstle CC.

PANXWORTH Norfolk
126 TG 3413 4m SE of Wroxham. Loc,
Woodbastwick CP. Ch e.

PAPCASTLE Cumb
82 NY 1031 1m NW of Cockermouth.
CP, 311. Cckrmth RD. P Cckrmth.
Workington CC. To N, Roman fort.

PAPPLEWICK Notts
112 SK 5451 6m S of Mansfield. CP, 585.
Basford RD. P NOTTINGHAM. Ch e.
Carlton CC (Ashfield).

PAPWORTH EVERARD Cambs
134 TL 2862 6m SSE of Huntingdon.
CP, 1,130. Chesterton RD. P CAMBRIDGE.
Ch e, m, r. Sch p. Cambs CC. Originally
created as settlement for tuberculosis
sufferers, now available for other sick
people.

PAPWORTH ST AGNES Cambs
134 TL 2664 5m SSE of Huntingdon.
CP, 63. Chesterton RD. Ch e. Cambs CC.
Tiny place down dead-end lane.

PAR Cornwall
185, 186, 190 SX 0753 4m E of St Austell.
Loc, St Astll w Fowey MB. P. Truro CC.
Port for china clay exports; sands: caravan
camp; rly junction for Newquay.

PARBOLD Lancs
100 SD 4910 5m ENE of Ormskirk.
CP, 974. Wigan RD. P Wgn.   Ch r.
Sch pe, pr. Westhoughton CC.

PARBROOK Som
165, 166 ST 5636 5m ESE of Glastonbury.
Loc, W Bradley CP. P Glstnbry. Ch m.

PARDSHAW Cumb
82 NY 0924 4m SSW of Cockermouth. Loc,
Dean CP. Ch f, m. Friends' Meeting Hse at
P. Hall to NE.

PARHAM Suffolk (E)
137 TM 3060 2m SE of Framlingham.
CP, 285. Blyth RD. P Woodbridge. Ch e.
Sch pe. Eye CC. Tdr Ch Farm in centre of
vllgc. P. Hall, Vctrn, now flats. P. Old Hall,
Tdr chimneys. Moat Hall, 15c moated mnr
hse, now farm.

PARK CORNER Oxon
159 SU 6988 6m NW of Henley. Loc,
Swyncombe CP. Hnly RD. Hnly CC.

PARKEND Glos
155, 156 SO 6108 3m NNW of Lydney.
Loc, W Dean CP. W Dn RD. P Ldny. Ch e, b.
Sch p. W Glos CC.

PARKESTON Essex
150 TM 2332 2m W of Harwich. Loc,
Ramsey CP. P Hrwch. Ch e, m. Sch p.
Terminal of Continental passenger and
freight ferries.

PARKFIELD Bucks
159 SP 8002 just S of Princes Risborough.
Loc, Prncs Rsbrgh CP.

PARKGATE Ches
100, 108, 109 SJ 2778 7m SSW of
Birkenhead. Loc, Neston UD.
P Nstn, Wirral. On Dee estuary; former port
for Chester.

PARKGATE Ches
110 SJ 7874 3m SSE of Knutsford. Loc,
Peover Superior CP. Bucklow RD. P(Over
Pvr), Kntsfd. Kntsfd CC. To SW across pk,
Pvr Hall, Elizn, restored.

PARK GATE Hants
180 SU 5108 4m WNW of Fareham. Loc,
Frhm UD. P SOUTHAMPTON.

PARKGATE Surrey
170, 182 TQ 2043 4m SSE of Dorking. Loc,
Newdigate CP.

PARKHAM Devon
174 SS 3821 5m SW of Bideford. CP, 568.
Bdfd RD.   P Bdfd. Ch e, m2. Sch p.
N Dvn CC (Torrington). See also
Goldworthy, Horns Cross, Pkhm Ash.

PARKHAM ASH Devon
174 SS 3620 7m SW of Bideford. Loc,
Pkhm CP. P Bdfd.

PARKHURST IOW
180 SZ 4991 1m N of Newport. Loc,
Npt MB. P Npt. HM Prison.

PARK ROYAL London
160 TQ 1982 2m NE of Ealing. Loc,
Brent LB. Brnt S BC (Willesden W).

PARKSTONE Dorset
179 SZ 0391 3m W of Bournemouth. Loc,
Poole MB. P Ple. Mainly rsdntl suburb.

PARLEY CROSS Dorset
179 SZ 0898 4m N of Bournemouth. Loc,
W Parley CP. P Ferndown, Wimborne.
Sch p.

PARLINGTON Yorks (W)
97 SE 4236 6m SW of Tadcaster. CP, 141.
Tdcstr RD. Barkston Ash CC.

PARNDON, GREAT Essex
161 TL 4308 1m SW of Harlow. Loc,
Hlw UD. P Hlw.

PARRACOMBE Devon
163 SS 6644 4m SW of Lynton. CP, 309.
Barnstaple RD. P Bnstple. Ch e, m, v.
Sch pe. N Dvn CC.

PARSON DROVE Cambs
124 TF 3708 6m W of Wisbech. CP, 926.
Wsbch RD. P Wsbch. Ch e, m, s. Sch p. Isle
of Ely CC. See also Church End.

PARTINGTON Ches
101 SJ 7191 7m ENE of Warrington.
CP, 6,514. Bucklow RD.
P Urmston, MANCHESTER. Ch e, c, m, r, v.
Sch i2, j, p, pr, s. Knutsford CC.

PARTNEY Lincs (L)
114 TF 4168 6m SW of Alford. CP, 202.
Spilsby RD. P Splsby. Ch e, m. Sch pe.
Horncastle CC.

PARTON Cumb
82 NX 9820 2m N of Whitehaven.
CP, 1,124. Ennerdale RD. P Whthvn. Ch m.
Sch pe. Whthvn CC.

PARTON Glos
143 SO 8820 4m ENE of Gloucester. Loc,
Churchdown CP. Sch j.

PARTRIDGE GREEN Sussex (W)
182 TQ 1919 3m NNW of Henfield. Loc,
W Grinstead CP. P Horsham. Ch e, m.

PARWICH Derbys
111 SK 1854 5m N of Ashbourne. CP, 480.
Ashbne RD. P Ashbne. Ch e, m. Sch p.
W Derbys CC.

PASSENHAM Northants
146 SP 7839 just SW of Stony Stratford.
Loc, Old Stratford CP. Ch e.

PASTON STREET Norfolk
126 TG 3134 4m NE of N Walsham. Loc,
Pstn CP. Smallburgh RD. Ch e, m.
N Nflk CC. Orig seat of Paston family
famous for 'Paston Letters'.

PATCHING Sussex (W)
182 TQ 0806 5m NE of Littlehampton.
CP, 272. Worthing RD. P Wthng. Ch e.
Arundel CC (Arndl and Shoreham).

PATCHOLE Devon
163 SS 6142 7m ESE of Ilfracombe. Loc,
Kentisbury CP.

PATCHWAY Glos
155, 156 ST 6081 6m N of Bristol.
CP, 6,861. Thornbury RD. P BRSTL.
Ch e, b, r. Sch i2, j2, p, pe, s. S Glos CC.
Aero-engine factory.

PATELEY BRIDGE Yorks (W)
91 SE 1565 11m NW of Harrogate. Loc,
High and Low Bishopside CP. Ripon and
Ptly Br RD. P Hrrgte. Ch e, m, r, s, v.
Sch i, s. Rpn CC. In steep-sided valley.
Disused lead mines on hills and rems of
Bronze Age settlements. 5m SW, Stump
Cross caverns*.

PATNEY Wilts
167 SU 0758 5m ESE of Devizes. CP, 131.
Dvzs RD. Ch e. Dvzs CC.

PATRICK BROMPTON Yorks (N)
91 SE 2290 3m WNW of Bedale. CP, 118.
Leyburn RD. P Bdle. Ch e. Richmond CC.

PATRINGTON Yorks (E)
99 TA 3122 4m SSW of Withernsea.
CP, 1,724. Holderness RD. P Hull. Ch e, m4.
Sch pe. Bridlington CC. See also Haven Side,
Winestead. Magnificent 14c cruciform ch
known as 'Queen of Holderness'. (Hedon ch
is 'King'.)

PATRIXBOURNE Kent
173 TR 1855 3m SE of Canterbury.
CP, 245. Bridge-Blean RD. Ch e.
Cntrbry CC. Stream flows through vllge.
Famous Nmn ch.

PATTERDALE Westm
83 NY 3915 8m NNE of Ambleside. Loc,
Lakes UD. P Penrith, Cumberland.
Westm CC. Centre for walking and climbing
on surrounding fells.

PATTINGHAM Staffs·
130 SO 8299 6m W of Wolverhampton.
CP, 1,382. Seisdon RD. P Wlvhmptn. Ch e.
Sch pe. SW Staffs CC (Brierley Hill).

PATTISHALL Northants
145, 146 SP 6754 4m NNW of Towcester.
CP, 733. Tcstr RD. P Tcstr. Ch e. Sch pe.
Daventry CC (S Nthnts). See also Astcote,
Eastcote.

PAUL Cornwall
189 SW 4627 2m S of Penzance. Loc,
Pnznce MB. P(Pl Church Town), Pnznce.
Burial place of Dolly Pentreath, d 1777,
said to be last speaker of Cornish.

PAULERSPURY Northants
146 SP 7145 3m SE of Towcester. CP, 791.
Tcstr RD. P Tcstr. Ch e, v. Sch pe.
Daventry CC (S Nthnts). See also Pury End.
Kennels of Grafton Hunt.

PAULL Yorks (E)
99 TA 1626 4m ESE of Hull. CP, 629.
Holderness RD. P Hll. Ch e, m. Sch p.
Bridlington CC. Fine early 15c ch.

PAULTON Som
166 ST 6556 3m WNW of Radstock.
CP, 2,790. Clutton RD. P BRISTOL.
Ch e, b, m2, r. Sch p, s. N Som CC. See also
Withy Mills. In mining area.

PAUPERHAUGH Nthmb
71 NZ 1099 3m ESE of Rothbury. Loc,
Brinkburn CP. Rthbry RD. P Morpeth.
Berwick-upon-Tweed CC.

PAVENHAM Beds
134 SP 9955 5m NW of Bedford. CP, 456.
Bdfd RD. P BDFD. Ch e. Sch p. Bdfd CC.
On R Ouse; ch and vllge considered outstanding.

PAWLETT Som
165 ST 2942 4m N of Bridgwater. CP, 672.
Brdgwtr RD. P Brdgwtr. Ch e, m. Sch p.
Brdgwtr CC. See also Stretcholt. The
surrounding flat pastures, P. Hams, famous
for grazing and dairy cattle.

PAWSTON Nthmb
64, 70 NT 8532 4m S of Coldstream. Loc,
Kilham CP.

PAXFORD Glos
144 SP 1837 2m ESE of Chipping
Campden. Loc, Blockley CP. P Chppng
Cmpdn. Ch e, b.

PAXTON, GREAT Hunts
134 TL 2063 3m NE of St Neots. See Gt
Pxtn.

PAYHEMBURY Devon
176 ST 0801 5m W of Honiton. CP, 443.
Hntn RD. P Hntn. Ch e. Sch pe. Hntn CC.

PAYTHORNE Yorks (W)
95 SD 8351 8m S of Settle. CP, 98.
Bowland RD. Ch m. Sch p.

PEACEHAVEN Sussex (E)
183 TQ 4100 2m W of Newhaven.
CP, 4,786. Chailey RD. P Nhvn. Ch e, r, v2.
Sch i. Lewes CC. Large rash of hses bisected
by Greenwich meridian.

PEACHLEY Worcs
130 SO 8057 3m WNW of Worcester. Loc,
Broadheath CP. Martley RD.
Kidderminster CC.

PEAK DALE Derbys
111 SK 0976 3m NE of Buxton. Loc,
Wormhill CP. P Bxtn. Ch e.

PEAK FOREST Derbys
111 SK 1179 5m NE of Buxton. CP, 318.
Chapel en le Frith RD. P Bxtn. Ch e, m.
Sch pe. High Pk CC. To N on Eldon Hill,
Eldn Hole, 200ft deep pothole.

PEAKIRK Hunts
123 TF 1606 5m NNW of Peterborough.
CP, 238. Ptrbrgh RD. P PTRBRGH. Ch e.
Sch pe. Ptrbrgh BC (CC). Ch mainly Nmn;
wall-paintings. Waterfowl Gdns*, large
collection of live wildfowl.

PEASEDOWN ST JOHN Som
166 ST 7057 2m NNE of Radstock.
CP, 3,238. Bathavon RD. P Bath.
Ch e, b, m, r. Sch p. N Som CC. See also
Carlingcott. In mining and indstrl area.

PEASEMORE Berks
158 SU 4577 6m N of Newbury. CP, 169.
Wantage RD. P Nbry. Ch e. Abingdon CC.

PEASENHALL Suffolk (E)
137 TM 3569 4m NNW of Saxmundham.
CP, 543. Blyth RD. P Sxmndhm. Ch e, v2.
Sch p. Eye CC. Stream runs down side of
main st.

PEASLAKE Surrey
170, 182 TQ 0844 4m NNE of Cranleigh.
Loc, Shere CP. P Guildford. Ch e, v. Sch pe.

PEASMARSH Sussex (E)
184 TQ 8823 3m NW of Rye. CP, 783.
Battle RD. P Rye. Ch e, m. Sch pe. Rye CC.

PEATLING MAGNA Leics
132, 133 SP 5992 8m S of Leicester.
CP, 135. Lutterworth RD. P LCSTR. Ch e.
Blaby CC (Harborough).

PEATLING PARVA Leics
132, 133 SP 5889 4m NE of Lutterworth.
CP, 137. Lttrwth RD.
P Rugby, Warwickshire. . Ch e. Blaby CC
(Harborough).

PEATON Shrops
129 SO 5384 6m N of Ludlow. Loc,
Diddlebury CP. Ch m.

PEBMARSH Essex
149 TL 8533 3m NE of Halstead. CP, 373.
Hlstd RD. P Hlstd. Ch e, v. Sch pe. Saffron
Walden CC. Ch has 14c brass.

PEBWORTH Worcs
144 SP 1346 6m ENE of Evesham. CP, 373.
Eveshm RD. P Stratford-upon-Avon,
Warwickshire. Ch e, m. Sch p. S Worcs CC.
See also Broad Marston.

PECKET WELL Yorks (W)
95 SD 9929 2m N of Hebden Br. Loc,
Wadsworth CP. Hepton RD. Sowerby CC.

PECKFORTON Ches
109 SJ 5356 8m WNW of Nantwich. CP, 114.
Nntwch RD. Nntwch CC. On hill to N, P.

Cstle, 19c, looking across to Beeston Cstle,
13c; see Beeston.

PECKHAM London
160, 170 TQ 3476 3m SSE of Lndn Br.
Loc, Southwark LB. Dulwich BC, Pckhm BC.

PECKLETON Leics
121 SK 4701 5m NNE of Hinckley.
CP, 717. Mkt Bosworth RD. Ch e.
Bswth CC. See also Kirkby Mallory,
Stapleton.

PEDMORE Worcs
130, 131 SO 9182 1m SSE of Stourbridge.
Loc, Stbrdge MB. P Stbrdge.

PEDWELL Som
165 ST 4236 5m WSW of Glastonbury. Loc,
Ashcott CP. Ch m.

PEEL COMMON Hants
180 SU 5703 2m S of Fareham. Loc,
Frhm UD. P Frhm.

PEGSDON Beds
147 TL 1130 4m W of Hitchin. Loc,
Shillington CP. Ch m.

PEGSWOOD Nthmb
78 NZ 2287 2m NE of Morpeth. CP, 2,590.
Mpth RD. P(Pgswd Colliery), Mpth. Ch m, r.
Sch p. Mpth CC.

PELDON Essex
149, 162 TL 9916 5m S of Colchester.
CP, 400. Lexden and Winstree RD. P Clchstr.
Ch e, m. Clchstr CC.

PELSALL Staffs
120 SK 0203 3m N of Walsall. Loc,
Aldridge-Brownhills UD. P Wlsll. A−B BC
(Wlsll S).

PELTON Co Durham
78 NZ 2553 2m NW of Chester-le-Street.
CP, 5,880. Chstr-le-Strt RD. P Chstr-le-Strt.
Ch e, m. Sch p2, s2. Chstr-le-Strt CC. See
also Grange Villa, Newfield, Perkinsville.

PELTON FELL Co Durham
78 NZ 2552 1m W of Chester-le-Street. Loc,
Chstr-le-Strt UD. P Chstr-le-Strt.

PELYNT Cornwall
186 SX 2055 3m WNW of Looe. CP, 475.
Liskeard RD. P Looe. Ch e, m. Sch pe.
Bodmin CC. See also Muchlarnick. Home
(Trelawne) of Bishop Trelawny, one of

seven bshps imprisoned by James II and subject of Hawker's famous ballad 'And shall Trelawny die...'.

PEMBRIDGE Herefs
129 SO 3958 6m E of Kington. CP, 809. Kngtn RD. P Leominster. Ch e, m2. Sch pe. Lmnstr CC. See also Broxwood, Marston, Moorcot. Many timbered hses; tmbrd mkt hall. Ch has detached belfry. 'New'Inn is early 16c.

PEMBURY Kent
171 TQ 6240 3m ENE of Tunbridge Wells. CP, 3,592. Tonbridge RD. P Tnbrdge Wlls. Ch e2, bc, m. Sch p. Royal Tnbrdge Wlls CC (Tnbrdge).

PENARE Cornwall
190 SW 9940 8m SSW of St Austell. Loc, St Goran CP. St Astll RD. Truro CC.

PENCOMBE Herefs
142 SO 5952 8m SE of Leominster. CP(Pncmbe w Grendon Warren), 257. Bromyard RD. P Brmyd. Ch e. Sch pe. Lmnstr CC. See also Hegdon Hill, Marston Stannett.

PENCOYD Herefs
142 SO 5126 5m WNW of Ross-on-Wye. CP, 144. Rss and Whitchurch RD. Ch e. Hereford CC.

PENCRAIG Herefs
142 SO 5620 3m SW of Ross-on-Wye. Loc, Marstow CP. P Rss-on-Wye.

PENDEEN Cornwall
189 SW 3834 6m WNW of Penzance. Loc, St Just UD. P Pnznce. Ch e. Mid-19c ch, copy of Iona Cathedral blt by unemployed miners.

PENDLEBURY Lancs
101 SD 7802 4m NW of Manchester. MB(Swinton and Pndlbry), 40,124. P Swntn, MNCHSTR. Eccles BC.

PENDLETON Lancs
95 SD 7539 2m SSE of Clitheroe. CP, 251. Clthroe RD. P Clthroe. Ch e. Sch pe. Clthroe CC. Picturesque vllge; stream runs along main st.

PENDOCK Worcs
143 SO 7832 6m ESE of Ledbury. CP, 224. Upton upon Severn RD. Ch e, m. Sch pe. S Worcs CC. See also Sledge Grn.

PENDOGGETT Cornwall
185, 186 SX 0279 5m NNE of Wadebridge. Loc, St Kew CP. P Bodmin. Ch m.

PENDOMER Som
177 ST 5210 4m SW of Yeovil. Loc, Closworth CP. Ch e.

PENGE London
170 TQ 3469 3m W of Bromley. Loc, Brmly LB. Beckenham BC. Rsdntl area S of Crystal Palace Pk.

PENHALLOW Cornwall
185, 190 SW 7651 5m NW of Truro. Loc, Perranzabuloe CP. P Truro.

PENHALVEAN Cornwall
190 SW 7137 3m SSE of Redruth. Loc, Stithians CP.

PENHURST Sussex (E)
183 TQ 6916 3m W of Battle. CP, 29. Bttle RD. Ch e. Rye CC. To NW, Ashburnham Furnace, last iron-smelting wks in Sussex.

PENISTONE Yorks (W)
102 SE 2403 7m WSW of Barnsley. UD, 8,182. P SHEFFIELD. Pnstne CC. See also Hoyland Swaine, Millhouse, Thurlstone. Steel mnfg tn in wild moorland setting.

PENKETH Lancs
100, 109 SJ 5687 3m W of Warrington. CP, 5,220. Wrrngtn RD. P Wrrngtn. Ch m, r. Sch i, p, pr, s. Newton CC.

PENKRIDGE Staffs
119 SJ 9214 4m NW of Cannock. CP, 3,383. Cnnck RD. P STAFFORD. Ch e, m. Sch i, pe, s. SW Staffs CC (Cnnck). See also Gailey, Levedale, Mitton, Whiston. Rly, canal, motorway. Ch: wrought-iron scrn; monmts.

PENN Bucks
159 SU 9193 3m E of High Wycombe. CP, 3,112. Amersham RD. P Hgh Wcmbe. Ch e, v. Chesham and Amrshm CC (S Bucks). See also Forty Grn, Knotty Corner, Winchmore Hill. Once home of Penn family, famous member of which was the Quaker William, founder of Pennsylvania.

PENNERLEY Shrops
129 SO 3599 7m NNE of Bishop's Cstle.
Loc, Worthen CP. P Shrewsbury. Ch m.

PENNINGTON Lancs
88 SD 2677 2m WSW of Ulverston.
CP, 1,333. N Lonsdale RD. P Ulvstn.
Ch e, m. Sch pe. Morecambe and Lnsdle CC.
P. Reservoir 1m N.

PENN STREET Bucks
159 SU 9296 2m WSW of Amersham. Loc,
Pnn CP. P Amrshm. Ch e. Sch pe.

PENNY BRIDGE Lancs
88, 89 SD 3083 3m NNE of Ulverston. Loc,
Egton w Newland CP. N Lonsdale RD. Ch e.
Sch pe. Morecambe and Lnsdle CC. Ch is
that of Egtn.

PENNYMOOR Devon
164, 176 SS 8611 6m W of Tiverton. Loc,
Cruwys Morchard CP. P Tvtn. Ch v.

PENPILLICK Cornwall
185, 186 SX 0856 3m SSW of Lostwithiel.
Loc, St Austell w Fowey MB. Truro CC.

PENPOLL Cornwall
186 SX 1454 4m SSE of Lostwithiel. Loc,
St Veep CP.

PENPOLL Cornwall
190 SW 8139 4m SSW of Truro. Loc,
Feock CP. Ch m.

PENRITH Cumb
83 NY 5130 18m SSE of Carlisle.
UD, 11,299. P. Pnrth and the Border CC.
Mkt tn. Rems. of 14c cstle (A.M.). M6
motorway passes to W.

PENROSE Cornwall
185 SW 8770 4m SW of Padstow. Loc,
St Ervan CP. P Wadebridge. Ch m.

PENRUDDOCK Cumb
83 NY 4227 6m WSW of Penrith. Loc,
Hutton CP. P Pnrth. Ch e, v. Sch p.

PENRYN Cornwall
190 SW 7834 2m NW of Falmouth.
MB, 5,082. P. Flmth and Camborne CC.
Granite tn adjoining Flmth. Older than
Flmth but has no old bldngs. Grnte
quarries at Mabe, 1m W.

PENSAX Worcs
130 SO 7269 6m WSW of Stourport.
CP, 272. Tenbury RD. P WORCESTER.
Ch e. Sch pe. Kidderminster CC.

PENSBY Ches
100, 108, 109 SJ 2683 5m SW of
Birkenhead. Loc, Wirral UD.
P Heswall. Wirral. Wrrl CC.

PENSELWOOD Som
166 ST 7531 3m NE of Wincanton.
CP, 216. Wncntn RD. P Wncntn. Ch e.
Wells CC.

PENSFORD Som
166 ST 6163 6m SSE of Bristol. Loc,
Publow CP. P BRSTL. Ch e, m, v. Sch p.

PENSHAW Co Durham
78 NZ 3253 3m ENE of Chester-le-Street.
Loc, Houghton-le-Spring UD. Monmt to 1st
Earl of Drhm, 1844; reminiscent of (but
unmistakably different from) the
Parthenon.

PENSHURST Kent
171 TQ 5243 4m WSW of Tonbridge.
CP, 1,895. Sevenoaks RD. P Tnbrdge.
Ch e, c. Sch pe. Svnks CC. See also
Fordcombe. Typical Kentish vllge. P.
Place*, 14c mnr hse, home of Sidney
family, much visited by Tdr royalty.

PENSILVA Cornwall
186 SX 2969 4m NE of Liskeard. Loc,
St Ive CP. P Lskd. Ch m s. Sch p.

PENTEWAN Cornwall
186, 190 SX 0147 3m S of St Austell. Loc,
St Astll w Fowey MB. P St Astll. Truro CC.
Has large sandy beach backed by camp site
and whitened by stream from china clay
workings to N.

PENTIRE Cornwall
185 SW 7961 1m W of Newquay. Loc,
Nquay UD. P Nquay. Faces N over Fistral
Bay and S over Gannel estuary.

PENTIREGLAZE Cornwall
185 SW 9379 5m NW of Wadebridge. Loc,
St Minver Highlands CP. Wdbrdge and
Padstow RD. N Cnwll CC.

PENTLOW Essex
149 TL 8146 5m NW of Sudbury. CP, 160.
Halstead RD. Ch e. Saffron Walden CC. Ch
has round Nmn twr, rare in Essex.

PENTNEY Norfolk
124 TF 7213 7m ESE of King's Lynn.
CP, 351. Freebridge Lnn RD. P K's Lnn.
Ch e, b. NW Nflk CC (K's Lnn).

PENTON GRAFTON Hants
168 SU 3247 2m NW of Andover. CP, 514.
Andvr RD. Ch e. Winchester CC
(Basingstoke). See also Clanville, Weyhill.

PENTON MEWSEY Hants
168 SU 3347 2m NW of Andover. CP, 286.
Andvr RD. P Andvr. Ch e. Winchester CC
(Basingstoke).

PENTONVILLE London
160 TQ 3183 2m NNE of Charing Cross.
Loc, Islington LB. Islngtn S and
Finsbury BC (Islngtn SW, Shoreditch and
Fnsbry). To N, on E side of Caledonian Rd,
P. Prison. Sir Roger Casement hanged
here, 1916.

PENTRE Shrops
118 SJ 3617 9m WNW of Shrewsbury. Loc,
Kinnerley CP. P Shrsbry.

PENTRICH Derbys
111 SK 3952 1m NNW of Ripley. CP, 163.
Belper RD. Ch e. Sch p. Blpr CC.

PENTRIDGE Dorset
179 SU 0317 10m SW of Salisbury.
CP, 168. Wimborne and Cranborne RD.
P Slsbry, Wilts. Ch e. N Dst CC. See also
Woodyates.

PENWITHICK STENTS Cornwall
185, 186 SX 0256 3m N of St Austell. Loc,
St Astll w Fowey MB. P(Pnwthck), St Astll.
Truro CC.

PENZANCE Cornwall
189 SW 4730 24m WSW of Truro.
MB, 19,352. P. St Ives CC. See also Gulval,
Heamoor, Mousehole, Newlyn, Paul,
Tredavoe, Trevarrack. Resort and port with
Ggn and Rgncy hses; mainland terminus of
steamer and helicopter services to Scillies.

PEOPLETON Worcs
143, 144 SO 9350 6m ESE of Worcester.
CP, 265. Pershore RD. P Pshre. Ch e.
S Worcs CC.

PEOVER HEATH Ches
110 SJ 7973 4m SE of Knutsford. Loc, Pvr
Superior CP. Bucklow RD. Ch m. Sch pe.
Kntsfd CC. See Parkgate.

PEPER HAROW Surrey
69 SU 9344 2m W of Godalming. CP, 271.
Hambledon RD. Ch e. Farnham CC.

PEPLOW Shrops
118, 119 SJ 6324 7m SSW of Mkt Drayton.
Loc, Hodnet CP. P Mkt Drtn. Ch e.

PERIVALE London
160 TQ 1682 1m N of Ealing. Loc,
Ealng LB. Ealng N BC. Rsdntl distr to N of
R Brent and Western Avenue (A40). Ch has
weatherboarded twr.

PERKINSVILLE Co Durham
78 NZ 2553 2m NW of Chester-le-Street.
Loc, Pelton CP. Ch m.

PERLETHORPE Notts
112 SK 6471 2m N of Ollerton. CP(Plthpe
cum Budby), 332. Southwell RD. P Newark.
Ch e. Sch pe. Nwk CC. To W, Thoresby,
Vctrn pile blt for Ld Manvers by Salvin in
pk laid out in 17c–18c. P. Ch also by
Salvin.

PERRANARWORTHAL Cornwall
190 SW 7738 5m SW of Truro. CP, 998.
Truro RD. P Truro. Ch e. Sch p. Truro CC.
See also Perranwell.

PERRANPORTH Cornwall
185, 190 SW 7554 6m SW of Newquay.
Loc, Perranzabuloe CP. P. Ch e, m, r.
Sch p. Resort with extensive sands to N.
Behind sands, St Piran's Ch (A.M.). 1m E,
St P's Round (A.M.), ancient amphitheatre.

PERRANUTHNOE Cornwall
189 SW 5329 4m E of Penzance. CP, 868.
W Penwith RD. P Pnznce. Ch e, m.
St Ives CC. See also Goldsithney. 1½m SE,
Prussia Cove - see Rosudgeon.

PERRANWELL Cornwall
190 SW 7739 5m SW of Truro. Loc,
Perranarworthal CP. P Truro. Ch m2.

PERRANZABULOE Cornwall
185, 190 SW 7752 7m SSW of Newquay.
CP, 3,623. Truro RD. Ch e, m. Truro CC.

Perry

See also Bolingey, Callestick, Goonhavern, Penhallow, Perranporth, Rose.

PERRY Hunts
134 TL 1466 5m NNW of St Neots. Loc, St Neots RD. P(W Prry), HUNTINGDON. Hunts CC.

PERRY GREEN Herts
148 TL 4317 4m SW of Bishop's Stortford. Loc, Much Hadham CP. Ch e.

PERSHORE Worcs
143, 144 SO 9445 6m WNW of Evesham. CP, 5,181. Pshre RD. P. Ch e2, b, r. Sch i, j, p, pr, s. S Worcs CC. In centre of fruit-growing area; gives name to type of plum. Mainly Ggn tn. Two 13c–15c chs, one an abbey.

PERTENHALL Beds
134 TL 0865 7m NW of St Neots. CP, 181. Bedford RD. P BDFD. Ch e. Bdfd CC. Late 16c mnr hse.

PERTHY Shrops
118 SJ 3633 2m WSW of Ellesmere. Loc, Ellesmre Rural CP. N Shrops RD. Ch m. Oswestry CC.

PERTON Staffs
130 SO 8598 4m W of Wolverhampton. Loc, Wrottesley CP.

PERTWOOD Wilts
166, 167 ST 8835 6m S of Warminster. Loc, E Knoyle CP. Ch e.

PETERBOROUGH Hunts
134 TL 1998 73m N of London. MB, 70,021. P(PTRBRGH). Ptrbrgh BC (CC). See also Longthorpe, Newark, Werrington. Indstrl city; many brickworks in vicinity. Nmn and later cathedral. Guildhall of 1671. New Tn designated, 1967. Pop. 1971: 87,493.

PETERCHURCH Herefs
142 SO 3438 10m W of Hereford. CP, 581. Dore and Bredwardine RD. P HRFD. Ch e, b, m. Sch p, s. Hrfd CC. See also Snodhill. Nmn ch. Wellbrook Mnr, 14c, with great hall and solar.

PETERLEE Co Durham
85 NZ 4341 5m S of Seaham. CP. Easington RD. P. Ch e, m, r, v. Sch p6, pr, s4. Easngtn CC. See also Shotton. New tn; pop. 1971: 21,836.

PETERSFIELD Hants
181 SU 7423 16m NNE of Portsmouth. UD, 8,958. P. Ptrsfld CC. See also Sheet, Stroud. Nmn ch. 3m SW on Butser Hill, 889ft, many prehistoric barrows, banks, and field systems.

PETER'S GREEN Herts
147 TL 1419 3m N of Harpenden. Loc, Kimpton CP. P Luton, Beds.

PETERS MARLAND Devon
163, 175 SS 4713 4m SSW of Torrington. CP, 253. Trrngtn RD. Ch e, m. W Dvn CC (Trrngtn). See also Winswell.

PETERSTOW Herefs
142 SO 5624 2m W of Ross-on-Wye. CP, 271. Rss and Whitchurch RD. P Rss-on-Wye. Ch e. Hereford CC.

PETER TAVY Devon
175, 187 SX 5177 3m NE of Tavistock. CP, 291. Tvstck RD. P Tvstck. Ch e, m. W Dvn (Tvstck). See also Cudlipptown. Former mining vllge.

PETHAM Kent
173 TR 1251 4m SSW of Canterbury. CP, 625. Bridge-Blean RD. P Cntrbry. Ch e, v. Sch p. Cntrbry CC.

PETROCKSTOW Devon
175 SS 5109 9m SSE of Torrington. CP, 305. Trrngtn RD. P Okehampton. Ch e, m. W Dvn CC (Trrngtn).

PETT Sussex (E)
184 TQ 8713 5m ENE of Hastings. CP, 639. Battle RD. P Hstngs. Ch e, m. Rye CC. See also Cliff End.

PETTAUGH Suffolk (E)
137 TM 1659 8m WSW of Framlingham. CP, 179. Gipping RD. P Stowmarket. Ch e. Eye CC.

PETTISTREE Suffolk (E)
150 TM 2954 4m NNE of Woodbridge. CP, 216. Deben RD. Ch e. Eye CC.

PETTON Devon
164 ST 0024 4m ENE of Bampton. Loc, Bmptn CP. Ch e.

PETTON Shrops
118 SJ 4326 5m WSW of Wem. CP, 99.
N Shrops RD. Ch e. Oswestry CC.

PETTS WOOD London
171 TQ 4467 1m NW of Orpington. Loc,
B r o m l e y L B . P Orpngtn, Kent.
Orpngtn BC (CC). Rsdntl distr. About 100
acres of the wd owned by NT.

PETWORTH Sussex (W)
181, 182 SU 9721 5m WNW of Pulborough.
CP, 2,347. Ptwth RD. P. Ch e, b2, c, r.
Sch pe, s. Chichester CC (Horsham). See also
Byworth. Small tn of much charm. Old
hses. Narrow twisty streets. Traffic. P. Hse
(NT)*, 17c—19c hse with large pk.

PEVENSEY Sussex (E)
183 TQ 6404 4m NE of Eastbourne. CP,
2,151. Hailsham RD. P. Ch e. Eastbne CC.
The Roman *Anderida*. Landing place of
William I, 1066. Nmn cstle within walls of
Roman fort (A.M.).

PEVENSEY BAY Sussex (E)
183 TQ 6504 4m NE of Eastbourne. Loc,
Pvnsy CP. P Pvnsy. Ch b, r. 20c
development with shingle beach. Martello
twrs to SW.

PEWSEY Wilts
167 SU 1660 6m SSW of Marlborough.
CP, 2,542. Psy RD. P. Ch e, m, r. Sch p, s.
Devizes CC. Small mkt tn on branch of
R Avon. 1m S, White Horse cut in
hillside 1937.

PEWSHAM Wilts
157 ST 9570 3m SE of Chippenham.
CP, 541. Calne and Chppnhm RD. Ch m.
Chppnhm CC. See also W Tytherton.

PHILADELPHIA Co Durham
7 8 N Z 3 3 5 2 2 m N N W o f
Houghton-le-Spring. Loc, Htn-le-Sprng UD.
P Htn-le-Sprng.

PHILHAM Devon
174 SS 2522 11m NNE of Bude. Loc,
Hartland CP.

PHILLACK Cornwall
189 SW 5638 5m W of Camborne. Loc,
Hayle CP. Ch e, m2.

PHILLEIGH Cornwall
190 SW 8739 4m NNE of St Mawes. CP, 268.
Truro RD. P Truro. Ch e, m. Truro CC.

PHOCLE GREEN Herefs
142, 143 SO 6226 2m NE of Ross-on-Wye.
Loc, Upton Bishop CP.

PHOENIX GREEN Hants
169 SU 7555 8m ENE of Basingstoke. Loc,
Hartley Wintney CP. P Bsngstke.

PICA Cumb
82 NY 0222 4m NE of Whitehaven. Loc,
Distington CP. P Workington.

PICCOTTS END Herts
160 TL 0509 1m N of Hemel Hempstead.
Loc, Hml Hmpstd MB. 15c hall hse* with
mdvl wall-paintings.

PICKERING Yorks (N)
92 SE 7984 15m WSW of Scarborough.
UD, 4,544. P. Scbrgh CC (Scbrgh and
Whitby). See also Stape. Old mkt tn. Nmn
cstle (A.M.). Ch also largely Nmn, with 15c
wall-paintings. P. Vale Museum and Arts
Centre*.

PICKET PIECE Hants
168 SU 3846 2m ENE of Andover. Loc,
Andvr MB. P Andvr.

PICKET POST Hants
179 SU 1906 3m E of Ringwood. Loc,
Burley CP.

PICKHILL Yorks (N)
91 SE 3483 6m SE of Bedale. CP(Pckhll
w Roxby), 272. Thirsk RD. P Thsk.
Ch e, m. Sch pe. Thsk and Malton CC.

PICKMERE Ches
101 SJ 6977 3m NE of Northwich. CP, 371.
Bucklow RD. P Knutsford. Ch m.
Kntsfd CC.

PICKWELL Devon
163 SS 4540 3m NW of Braunton. Loc,
Georgeham CP.

PICKWELL Leics
122 SK 7811 5m SSE of Melton Mowbray.
Loc, Somerby CP. Ch e.

PICKWORTH Lincs (K)
113, 123 TF 0433 8m E of Grantham.
CP, 90. W Kesteven RD. P Sleaford. Ch e.
Sch p. Rutland and Stamford CC. Ch: 14c
wall-paintings.

PICKWORTH Rutland
123 SK 9913 5m NNW of Stamford. CP, 113.
Ketton RD. Ch e, m. Rtlnd and Stmfd CC.

PICTON Ches
109 SJ 4371 4m NE of Chester. CP.
Chstr RD. City of Chstr CC.

PICTON Yorks (N)
85 NZ 4107 7m SSW of Teesside
(Stockton). CP, 106. Stokesley RD. Ch m.
Richmond CC.

PIDDINGHOE Sussex (E)
183 TQ 4303 2m NNW of Newhaven.
CP, 197. Chailey RD. P Nhvn. Ch e.
Lewes CC. Ch with Nmn round twr.

PIDDINGTON Bucks
159 SU 8094 4m W of High Wycombe. Loc,
W Wcmbe Rural CP. Wcmbe RD. P Hgh
Wcmbe. Ch m. Wcmbe CC. Ch has Nmn
round twr.

PIDDINGTON Northants
146 SP 8054 5m SE of Northampton. Loc,
Hackleton CP. P NTHMPTN. Ch e, v.

PIDDINGTON Oxon
145, 146, 159 SP 6417 5m SE of Bicester.
CP, 376. Ploughley RD. P Bcstr.   Ch e.
Mid-Oxon CC (Henley).

PIDDLEHINTON Dorset
178 SY 7197 4m NNE of Dorchester.
CP, 616. Dchstr RD. P Dchstr. Ch e. Sch pe.
W Dst CC. Formerly known as Honey
Puddle.

PIDDLETRENTHIDE Dorset
178 SY 7099 6m N of Dorchester. CP, 540.
Dchstr RD. P Dchstr. Ch e, b, m. Sch pe.
W Dst CC. See also Plush, White Lackington.
Ch: twr.

PIDLEY Hunts
134 TL 3377 2m SE of Warboys. CP (Pdly
cum Fenton), 376. St Ives RD.
P HUNTINGDON. Ch e, b. Hunts CC.

PIERCEBRIDGE Co Durham
85 NZ 2115 5m W of Darlington. CP, 157.
Dlngtn RD. P Dlngtn. Ch e, m. Bishop
Auckland CC (Sedgefield). Vllge with large
grn and 18c br over R Tees. Roman rems.

PIGDON Nthmb
78 NZ 1588 3m WNW of Morpeth. Loc,
Meldon CP. Mpth RD. Mpth CC.

PIKEHALL Derbys
111 SK 1959 7m W of Matlock. Loc,
Ashbourne RD. W Derbys CC.

PILGRIMS' HATCH Essex
161 TQ 5795 2m NW of Brentwood. Loc,
Brntwd UD. P Brntwd.

PILHAM Lincs (L)
104 SK 8693 4m NE of Gainsborough.
CP, 39. Gnsbrgh RD. Ch e. Gnsbrgh CC.

PILL Som
155 ST 5275 5m NW of Bristol. Loc,
Easton-in-Gordano CP. P BRSTL. Ch e, s.
Sch i, je. Wharves, ferries, factories.

PILLATON Cornwall
186 SX 3664 3m S of Callington. CP, 279.
St Germans RD. P Saltash. Ch e, m2.
Bodmin CC.

PILLERTON HERSEY Warwicks
145 SP 2948 7m ESE of Stratford. CP, 91.
Shipston on Stour RD. Ch e.
Strtfd-on-Avon CC (Strtfd).

PILLERTON PRIORS Warwicks
145 SP 2947 7m SE of Stratford. CP, 150.
Shipston on Stour RD. P WARWICK. Ch m.
Strtfd-on-Avon CC (Strtfd).

PILLEY Yorks (W)
102 SE 3300 4m S of Barnsley. Loc,
Tankersley CP.

PILLING Lancs
94 SD 4048 4m E across river from
Fleetwood. CP, 1,461. Garstang RD.
P Preston. Ch e, m, r. Sch pe. N Fylde CC.
See also Egland Hill, Stakepool.

PILLING LANE Lancs
94 SD 3749 2m ENE across river from
Fleetwood. Loc, Preesall UD.

PILNING Glos
155, 156 ST 5684 3m S of Severn rd Br.
CP(Plnng and Svn Beach). Thornbury RD.
P BRISTOL. Ch e. Sch p. S Glos CC. See
also Cross Hands, Redwick.

PILSLEY Derbys
111 SK 2471 2m NE of Bakewell. CP, 170.
Bkwll RD. P Bkwll. Sch ie. W Derbys CC.

PILSLEY Derbys
112 SK 4262 6m SSE of Chesterfield.
CP, 2,607. Chstrfld RD. P Chstrfld.
Ch e, m3, v. Sch p2. NE Derbys CC.

PILSDON Dorset
177 SY 4199 5m NW of Bridport. CP, 44.
Beaminster RD. Ch e. W Dst CC. 1m N, Iron
Age fort on P. Pen, 908ft and highest point
in Dorset.

PILTDOWN Sussex (E)
183 TQ 4422 2m WNW of Uckfield. Loc,
Uckfld RD. P Uckfld. Ch b. E Grinstead CC.
Skull of P. Man 'discovered' here in 1912;
pronounced a hoax over 40 years later.

PILTON Northants
134 TL 0284 3m SSW of Oundle. CP, 73.
Oundle and Thrapston RD. Ch e.
Wellingborough CC (Peterborough).

PILTON Rutland
122 SK 9102 4m NE of Uppingham. CP, 15.
Uppnghm RD. Ch e. Rtlnd and
Stamford CC. Large ironstone quarries.

PILTON Som
165, 166 ST 5840 3m SW of Shepton
Mallet. CP, 808. Shptn Mllt RD. P Shptn
Mllt. Ch e, m2. Wells CC. See also
W Compton. Ch has carved angel roof.
Glastonbury Abbey tithe barn nearby.

PIMLICO London
160, 170 TQ 2978 1m SSW of Charing
Cross. Loc, City of Westminster LB. The
City of Lndn and Wstmnstr S BC (The Cities
of Lndn and Wstmnstr). Rsdntl area S of
Victoria rly stn.

PIMPERNE Dorset
178, 179 ST 9009 2m NNE of Blandford.
CP, 1,119. Blndfd RD. P Blndfd Forum.
Ch e, m. Sch pe. N Dst CC.

PINCHBECK Lincs (H)
123 TF 2425 2m N of Spalding. CP, 3,826.
Spldng RD. P Splndg. Ch e, b, m, v. Sch pe.
Holland w Boston CC. See also Pnchbck
Bars, Pnchbck W. Amid bulb fields.

PINCHBECK BARS Lincs (H)
123 TF 1925 4m WNW of Spalding. Loc,
Pnchbck CP. P Spldng. Ch m.

PINCHBECK WEST Lincs (H)
123 TF 2024 3m NW of Spalding. Loc,
Pnchbck CP. Ch e. Sch pe.

PINFOLD Lancs
100 SD 3911 3m NW of Ormskirk. Loc,
Scarisbrick CP.

PINHOE Devon
176 SX 9694 NE distr of Exeter. Loc,
Extr CB. P Extr. Extr BC (Tiverton CC).

PINKNEY Wilts
156 ST 8686 4m W of Malmesbury.
Alternative name for Sherston Parva, qv.

PIN MILL Suffolk (E)
150 TM 2037 5m SE of Ipswich. Loc,
Chelmondiston CP. On Orwell estuary. Old
inn is former haunt of smugglers.

PINNER London
160 TQ 1289 2m WNW of Harrow. Loc,
Hrrw LB. P Middx. Hrrw W BC.

PINVIN Worcs
143, 144 SO 9548 2m N of Pershore.
CP, 546. Pshre RD. P Pshre. Ch e. Sch pe.
S Worcs CC.

PINXTON Derbys
112 SK 4554 3m E of Alfreton. CP, 4,556.
Blackwell RD. P NOTTINGHAM.
Ch e, m2, v. Sch i2, j. Bolsover CC.

PIPE AND LYDE Herefs
142 SO 5044 3m N of Hereford. CP, 296.
Hrfd RD. Ch e. Leominster CC.

PIPE GATE Shrops
110, 119 SJ 7340 6m NE of Mkt Drayton.
Loc, Woore CP. P Mkt Drtn.

PIPE RIDWARE Staffs
120 SK 0917 3m E of Rugeley. Loc,
Mavesyn Rdwre CP. Ch e. On R Trent.

PIPERS POOL Cornwall
186 SX 2684 5m W of Launceston. Loc,
Trewen CP. P Lncstn. Ch m.

PIPEWELL Northants
133 SP 8485 4m WSW of Corby. Loc,
Kettering RD. Kttrng CC.

PIPPACOTT Devon
163 SS 5237 3m NW of Barnstaple. Loc,
Braunton CP.

PIRBRIGHT Surrey
169 SU 9455 4m WSW of Woking.
CP, 3,325. Guildford RD. P Wkng. Ch e.
Sch i, j. Wkng CC. See also Fox Corner.

PIRTON Herts
147 TL 1431 3m NW of Hitchin. CP, 882. Htchn RD. P Htchn. Ch e. Sch p. Htchn CC. Several old hses.

PIRTON Worcs
143 SO 8847 5m SSE of Worcester. CP, 118. Pershore RD. P WCSTR. Ch e. S Worcs CC. Ch 12c—15c; half-timbered bell twr.

PISHILL Oxon
159 SU 7289 5m NNW of Henley. CP(Pshll w Stonor), 306. Hnly RD. Ch e. Hnly CC.

PITCHCOMBE Glos
156 SO 8508 2m N of Stroud. CP, 298. Strd RD. P Strd. Ch e. Strd CC. Picturesque hillside vllge.

PITCHCOTT Bucks
146 SP 7720 5m NNW of Aylesbury. CP, 27. Aylesbury RD. Ch e. Aylesbury CC.

PITCHFORD Shrops
118 SJ 5303 6m SSE of Shrewsbury. CP, 130. Atcham RD. Ch e. Shrsbry CC. P. Hall, large 16c black-and-white hse, perhaps best example in county.

PITCH GREEN Bucks
159 SP 7703 2m W of Princes Risborough. Loc, Bledlow-cum-Saunderton CP.

PITCH PLACE Surrey
169, 170 SU 9752 2m NNW of Guildford. Loc, Worplesdon CP. P Gldfd.

PITCOMBE Som
166 ST 6733 1m SW of Bruton. CP, 536. Wincanton RD. Ch e, m. Wells CC. See also Cole.

PITMINSTER Som
177 ST 2219 3m S of Taunton. CP, 1,418. Tntn RD. P Tntn. Ch e, v. Sch p. Tntn CC. See also Angersleigh, Blagdon, Lowton.

PITNEY Som
177 ST 4428 6m NW of Ilchester. CP, 192. Langport RD. P Lngpt. Ch e, c. Yeovil CC.

PITSEA Essex
161, 162 TQ 7488 1m E of Basildon. Loc, Bsldn UD. P Bsldn.

PITSFORD Northants
133 SP 7568 5m N of Northampton. CP, 822. Brixworth RD. P NTHMPTN. Ch e.

Sch p. Daventry CC (Kettering). Large reservoir to N.

PITSTONE Bucks
146, 159 SP 9315 3m NNE of Tring. CP, 766. Wing RD. Ch e. Buckingham CC.

PITTINGTON Co Durham
85 NZ 3244 4m ENE of Durham. CP, 1,260. Drhm RD. P DRHM. Ch e, m, s. Sch p. Drhm CC. See also Hallgarth, Hetton le Hill, Littletown. Ch has impressive Nmn work.

PITTON Wilts
167 SU 2131 4m E of Salisbury. CP(Pttn and Farley), 534. Slsbry and Wilton RD. P Slsbry. Ch e, m. Sch pe. Slsbry CC.

PITY ME Co Durham
85 NZ 2645 2m NNW of Durham. Loc, Framwellgate Moor CP.

PIXLEY Herefs
142, 143 SO 6638 3m W of Ledbury. CP, 214. Ldbry RD. Ch e. Leominster CC. See also Trumpet.

PLAISTOW Sussex (W)
169, 181, 182 TQ 0030 6m NW of Billingshurst. CP, 1,038. Petworth RD. P Bllngshst. Ch e. Sch p. Chichester CC (Horsham). See also Ifold.

PLAITFORD Hants
179 SU 2719 5m W of Romsey. CP(Melchet Pk and Pltfd), 369. Rmsy and Stockbridge RD. Ch e. Eastleigh CC (Winchester).

PLASHETTS Nthmb
76 NY 6690 12m WNW of Bellingham. Loc, Falstone CP. P Hexham. Ch v.

PLASTOW GREEN Hants
168 SU 5361 5m SE of Newbury. Loc, Kingsclere CP. Ch m.

PLATT Kent
171 TQ 6257 6m E of Sevenoaks. CP, 1,111. Malling RD. P(St Mary's Pltt), Svnks. Ch e. Sch pe. Tonbridge and Mllng CC (Svnks). See also Wrotham Hth.

PLATTS COMMON Yorks (W)
102, 103 SE 3701 3m SSE of Barnsley. Loc, Hoyland Nether UD. P Bnsly.

PLATT'S HEATH Kent
172 TQ 8750 5m W of Charing. Loc,
Lenham CP. Sch p.

PLAWSWORTH Co Durham
85 NZ 2648 2m SSW of Chester-le-Street.
CP, 1,570. Chstr-le-Strt RD.
Chstr-le-Strt CC. See also Nettlesworth.

PLAXTOL Kent
171 TQ 6053 5m E of Sevenoaks.
CP, 1,015. Malling RD. P Svnks. Ch e, m.
Sch p. Tonbridge and Mllng CC (Svnks). See
also Claygate Cross. Hilltop vllge. 1m NE,
Old Soar (A.M. and NT)*, rems of 13c mnr
hse.

PLAYDEN Sussex (E)
184 TQ 9121 1m N of Rye. CP, 359.
Battle RD. Ch e. Sch pe. Rye CC.

PLAYFORD Suffolk (E)
150 TM 2147 4m NE of Ipswich. CP, 213.
Deben RD. P Ipswch. Ch e. Sudbury and
Woodbridge CC. Small vllge enlarged by
several modern hses. P. Hall, 16c, moated,
down by br and screened by trees.

PLAY HATCH Oxon
159 SU 7476 2m NE of Reading. Loc, Eye
and Dunsden CP. Henley RD. Hnly CC.

PLAYING PLACE Cornwall
190 SW 8141 2m SSW of Truro. Loc,
Kea CP. P Truro.

PLAYLEY GREEN Glos
143 SO 7631 5m SE of Ledbury. Loc,
Redmarley D'Abitot CP.

PLEALEY Shrops
118 SJ 4206 6m SW of Shrewsbury. Loc,
Pontebury CP. Ch m.

PLEASINGTON Lancs
94, 95 SD 6426 3m WSW of Blackburn.
CP, 528. Blckbn RD. P Blckbn. Ch r. Sch pr.
Darwen CC. RC ch is a prominent, am-
bitious bldng of 1816—19.

PLEASLEY Derbys
112 SK 5064 3m NW of Mansfield.
CP, 2,754. Blackwell RD. P Mnsfld, Notts.
Ch e, m, v. Sch p. Bolsover CC. See also
New Houghton.

PLENMELLER Nthmb
76 NY 7163 just SE of Haltwhistle.
CP (Plnmllr w Whitfield), 304.
Hltwhstle RD. Hexham CC. See also
Bearsbridge.

PLESHEY Essex
148, 161 TL 6614 5m SSE of Dunmow. CP.
Chelmsford RD. P Chlmsfd. Ch e, v.
Braintree CC (Chlmsfd). Vllge surrounded
by vast Nmn earthworks. Rems of cstle
keep*. 15c br across moat.

PLOUGHFIELD Herefs
142 SO 3841 8m W of Hereford. Loc,
Preston on Wye CP. Ch m.

PLOWDEN Shrops
129 SO 3887 4m E of Bishop's Cstle. Loc,
Lydbury N CP. Ch r. Half-timbered mainly
Elizn hse, P. Hall, contains RC chpl.

PLOXGREEN Shrops
118 SJ 3603 9m WSW of Shrewsbury. Loc,
Minsterley CP.

PLUCKLEY Kent
172, 184 TQ 9245 3m SW of Charing.
CP, 957. W Ashford RD. P Ashfd. Ch e, m.
Sch pe. Ashfd CC.

PLUMBLAND Cumb
82 NY 1539 7m E of Maryport. CP, 457.
Cockermouth RD. Ch e. Sch pe.
Workington CC. See also Arkleby.

PLUMLEY Ches
101 SJ 7175 3m SW of Knutsford. CP, 840.
Bucklow RD. P Kntsfd. Ch m. Kntsfd CC.

PLUMPTON Northants
145, 146 SP 5948 7m N of Brackley. Loc,
Weston and Weedon CP. Ch e.

PLUMPTON Sussex (E)
183 TQ 3613 4m NW of Lewes. CP, 865.
Chailey RD. P Lws. Ch e, c. Sch p. Lws CC.
See also Plmptn Grn. Downland vllge.
Racecourse to N.

PLUMPTON, GREAT Lancs
94 SD 3833 5m ESE of Blackpool. Loc,
Westby-w-Plmptns CP.

PLUMPTON GREEN Sussex (E)
183 TQ 3616 5m NW of Lewes. Loc,
Plmptn CP. Ch e. P. Racecourse to S.

PLUMPTON WALL Cumb
83 NY 4937 4m NNW of Penrith. Loc,
Hesket CP. Pnrth RD. P(Plmptn), Pnrth.
Ch e. Sch p. Pnrth and the Border CC.

PLUMSTEAD London
161, 171 TQ 4478 8m ESE of Lndn Br.
Loc, Greenwich LB. Woolwich E BC. To N,
P. Marshes and stretch of Thames (Barking
Reach).

PLUMSTEAD Norfolk
125 TG 1334 4m SE of Holt. CP, 136.
Erpingham RD. P NORWICH, NOR 20Y.
Ch e, v. N Nflk CC.

PLUMSTEAD, GREAT Norfolk
126 TG 3009 5m E of Norwich. See Gt
Plmstd.

PLUMTREE Notts
112, 121, 122 SK 6133 5m SSE of
Nottingham. CP, 210. Bingham RD.
P NTTNGHM. Ch e. Sch pe. Rushcliffe CC
(Carlton).

PLUNGAR Leics
112, 122 SK 7633 9m N of Melton
Mowbray. Loc, Redmile CP.
P NOTTINGHAM. Ch e, m.

PLUSH Dorset
178 ST 7102 7m NNE of Dorchester. Loc,
Piddletrenthide CP. Ch e.

PLYMOUTH Devon
187 SX 4754 100m SW of Bristol.
CB, 239,314. P. BCs: Plmth, Devonport;
Plmth, Drake; Plmth, Sutton.
(Plmth, Dvnpt; Plmth, Sttn.) See also
Dvnpt, Elburton, Plympton, Plymstock,
Staddiscombe, Tamerton Foliot. Port and
commercial city; naval dockyards at Dvnpt.
Centre rebuilt since World War II. Drake
played bowls on Hoe, 1588. Mayflower
sailed from Sttn Pool, 1620.

PLYMPTON Devon
187 SX 5456 4m E of Plymouth. Loc,
Plmth CB. P Plmth. Plmth, Sutton BC
(Tavistock CC). Rems of Nmn cstle. 1½m
W, Saltram (NT)*, Tdr hse with 18c
additions; gdns.

PLYMSTOCK Devon
187 SX 5153 2m ESE of Plymouth. Loc,
Plmth CB. P Plmth. Plmth, Sutton BC
(Tavistock CC).

PLYMTREE Devon
176 ST 0502 7m WNW of Honiton.
CP, 305. Hntn RD. P Cullompton. Ch e.
Sch pe. Hntn CC. See also Norman's Grn.
Ch: scrn.

POCKLEY Yorks (N)
86, 92 SE 6386 2m NE of Helmsley.
CP, 110. Hlmsly RD. P YORK. Ch e, m.
Thirsk and Malton CC.

POCKLINGTON Yorks (E)
98 SK 8049 13m E of York. CP, 3,452.
Pcklngtn RD. P YK. Ch e, c, m, r, s.
Sch ie, p, pr, s. Howden CC. Boys' public
sch at which William Wilberforce, slavery
abolitionist, was educated.

PODE HOLE Lincs (H)
123 TF 2122 2m W of Spalding. Loc,
Spldng UD, Spldng RD. P Spldng.
Holland w Boston CC.

PODIMORE Som
166, 177 ST 5425 2m NE of Ilchester. Loc,
Yeovilton CP. Ch e.

PODINGTON Beds
133 SP 9462 3m SSW of Rushden. CP, 423.
Bedford RD. P Wellingborough, Northants.
Ch e, m. Sch pe. Bdfd CC. See also
Farndish, Hinwick.

POINTON Lincs (K)
113, 123 TF 1131 7m N of Bourne.
CP(Pntn and Sempringham), 505.
S Kesteven RD. P Sleaford. Ch e, m. Sch pe.
Rutland and Stamford CC. To W around
Nmn parish ch stood monastery of
St Gilbert of Sempringham, founder in
1130s of only English monastic order.

POLAPIT TAMAR Cornwall
174, 186 SX 3389 3m N of Launceston.
Loc, Werrington CP.

POLBATHIC Cornwall
186 SX 3456 6m WNW of Torpoint. Loc,
St Germans RD. P Tpnt. Ch m. Bodmin CC.

POLEBROOK Northants
134 TL 0687 2m ESE of Oundle. CP, 302.
Oundle and Thrapston RD.
P PETERBOROUGH. Ch e. Sch pe.
Wellingborough CC (Ptrbrgh). See also
Armston.

POLEGATE Sussex (E)
183 TQ 5804 4m NNW of Eastbourne.
CP, 5,208. Hailsham RD. P. Ch e, c, r.
Sch p. Eastbne CC. Early 19c twr-mill*,
85ft high; orig machinery.

POLELANE ENDS Ches
101 SJ 6479 4m NNW of Northwich. Loc,
Antrobus CP. Runcorn RD. Ch f. Rncn CC.

POLE MOOR Yorks (W)
96, 102 SE 0616 5m W of Huddersfield.
Loc, Colne Valley UD. Clne Vlly CC.

POLESWORTH Warwicks
120 SK 2602 4m ESE of Tamworth. CP.
Atherstone RD.   P Tmwth, Staffs.
Ch e, b, m, v. Sch i, j, pe, s. Meriden CC. See
also Warton.

POLGOOTH Cornwall
185, 190 SW 9950 2m SW of St Austell.
Loc, St Astll RD. P St Astll. Truro CC.

POLING Sussex (W)
182 TQ 0404 2m NNE of Littlehampton.
CP, 159. Worthing RD. Ch e. Arundel CC
(Arndl and Shoreham). See also Plng
Corner.

POLING CORNER Sussex (W)
182 TQ 0405 2m ESE of Arundel. Loc,
Plng CP. P Arndl.

POLKERRIS Cornwall
185, 186, 190 SX 0952 2m W of Fowey.
Loc, St Austell w Fwy MB. P Par. Truro CC
(Bodmin).

POLLINGTON Yorks (W)
103 SE 6119 6m NW of Thorne. CP, 659.
Goole Rd. P Gle. Ch e, m. Gle CC.

POLMASSICK Cornwall
190 SW 9745 8m SW of St Austell. Loc,
St Ewe CP. Ch m.

POLPERRO Cornwall
186 SX 2051 3m WSW of Looe. Loc,
Lansallos CP. P Looe. Ch e, m. Sch p.
Narrow-streeted fishing resort with rugged
cliffs (NT) to E and W.

POLRUAN Cornwall
186 SX 1250 just S of Fowey across river.
Loc, Lanteglos CP. Liskeard RD. P Fwy.
Ch e, m. Sch p. Bodmin CC. Foot-passenger
ferry to Fowey.

POLSHAM Som
165 ST 5142 3m SW of Wells. Loc,
St Cuthbert Out CP. Wlls RD. Wlls CC.

POLSTEAD Suffolk (W)
149 TL 9938 4m SW of Hadleigh. CP, 556.
Cosford RD. P Colchester, Essex. Ch e, b, m.
Sch p. Sudbury and Woodbridge CC.

POLTIMORE Devon
176 SX 9696 4m NE of Exeter. CP, 311.
St Thomas RD. P Extr. Ch e. Sch pe.
Tiverton CC.

POLYPHANT Cornwall
186 SX 2682 5m WSW of Launceston. Loc,
Lewannick CP. P Lncstn. Ch m.

POLZEATH Cornwall
185 SW 9378 5m NW of Wadebridge.
Loc, Wdbrdge and Padstow RD. P Wdbrdge.
Ch m. N Cnwll CC. Small resort with
extensive sands; surfing.

PONDERSBRIDGE Cambs
134 TL 2692 6m SE of Peterborough. Loc,
Whittlesey UD. P HUNTINGDON.

PONDERS END London
161 TQ 3595 2m E of Enfield. Loc,
Enfld LB. P Enfld, Middx. Enfld N BC
(Enfld E). Indstrl distr. To E, R Lee
reservoirs   and Lee Valley Regional Pk
development.

PONSANOOTH Cornwall
190 SW 7537 4m NW of Falmouth. Loc,
Kerrier RD. P Truro. Ch e, m. Flmth and
Camborne CC.

PONSWORTHY Devon
175, 187, 188 SX 7073 4m NW of
Ashburton. Loc, Widecombe
-in-the-Moor CP. P Newton Abbot.

PONTEFRACT Yorks (W)
97 SE 4521 8m E of Wakefield.
MB, 31,335. P. Pntfrct and Castleford BC
(Pntfrct). Mining and mnfg tn. Racecourse.
Much of historical interest. Rems of Nmn
castle* where Richard II died, and which
was thrice besieged in Civil War. Tn gives
name to liquorice sweets known as 'Pomfret
cakes'.

PONTELAND Nthmb
78 NZ 1672 7m NW of Newcastle.
CP, 6,050. Cstle Ward CP. P NCSTLE
UPON TYNE. Ch e, m, r, v. Sch p2, s.
Hexham CC. See also Berwick Hill, High
Callerton, Milbourne, Prestwick. Suburban.
12c–14c ch; 14c–16c mnr hse, now an
inn.

PONTESBURY Shrops
118 SJ 4006 7m WSW of Shrewsbury.
CP, 3,039. Atcham RD. P Shrsbry.
Ch e, b, m3. Sch pe, s. Shrsbry CC. See also
Asterley, Cruckmeole, Cruckton, Edge,
Habberley, Lea, Longden, Plealey,
Pontesford.

PONTESFORD Shrops
118 SJ 4106 6m WSW of Shrewsbury. Loc,
Pontesbury CP. Ch c. Gives name to 1,047ft
hill to S.

PONTON, GREAT Lincs (K)
113, 122 SK 9230 4m S of Grantham. See
Gt Pntn.

PONTRILAS Herefs
142 SO 3927 10m NNE of Abergavenny.
Loc, Kentchurch CP. P HEREFORD. P. Ct,
Elizn; gdn* beside R Monnow.

PONTSHILL Herefs
142, 143 SO 6321 3m ESE of Ross-on-Wye.
Loc, Weston under Penyard CP.
P Rss-on-Wye.

POOKSGREEN Hants
180 SU 3710 5m ENE of Lyndhurst.
Loc, Marchwood CP.

POOL Cornwall
189 SW 6641 2m NE of Camborne. Loc,
Cmbne-Redruth UD. P Rdrth.

POOL Yorks (W)
96 SE 2445 3m E of Otley. CP, 1,470.
Wharfedale RD. P(Pl-in-Whfdle), Otley.
Ch e, m. Sch pe. Ripon CC.

POOLE Dorset
179 SZ 0291 4m W of Bournemouth.
MB, 106,697. P. Ple BC. See also Bearwood,
Branksome, Broadstone, Hamworthy,
Parkstone, Sandbanks. Port and mnfg tn;
resort and yachting centre. Several Ggn
bldngs. In P. Harbour, Brownsea
Island (NT), with nature reserve.

POOLE GREEN Ches
110 SJ 6355 3m NNW of Nantwich. Loc,
Poole CP. Nntwch RD. Ch m. Nntwch CC.

POOLE KEYNES Glos
157 SU 0095 4m S of Cirencester. CP, 126.
Crncstr RD. Ch e. Crncstr and
Tewkesbury CC.

POOLEY BRIDGE Westm
83 NY 4724 5m SW of Penrith. Loc,
Barton CP. P Pnrth, Cumberland. Ch e.

POOLFOLD Staffs
110 SJ 8959 3m SE of Congleton. Loc,
Biddulph UD. P Stoke-on-Trent.

POOL HEY Lancs
100 SD 3615 2m SE of Southport. Loc,
Scarisbrick CP.

POOLHILL Glos
143 SO 7329 6m S of Ledbury. Loc,
Newent RD. P Nwnt. Sch pe. W Glos CC.

POOLSBROOK Derbys
112 SK 4473 4m ENE of Chesterfield. Loc,
Staveley UD. P Chstrfld.

POOL STREET Essex
149 TL 7637 5m NW of Halstead. Loc,
Gt Yeldham CP.

POPESWOOD Berks
169 SU 8469 2m W of Bracknell. Loc,
Binfield CP. P Brcknell.

POPHAM Hants
168 SU 5543 7m SW of Basingstoke.
CP, 67. Bsngstke RD. Ch e. Bsngstke CC.

POPLAR London
161 TQ 3781 5m E of Charing Cross. Loc,
Twr Hmlts LB. Stepney and Pplr BC (Pplr).
To E, R Lee; to S, docks and R Thames. Rd
tunnels under river at Blackwall, qv.

PORCHFIELD IOW
180 SZ 4491 4m SW of Cowes. Loc,
Calbourne CP. P Newport. Ch e, m.

PORKELLIS Cornwall
189 SW 6933 4m NNE of Helston. Loc,
Wendron CP. P Hlstn. Ch e, m.

PORLOCK Som
164 SS 8846 5m W of Minehead. CP, 1,307.
Williton RD. P Mnhd. Ch e, m. Sch pe.
Bridgwater CC. Small tn and resort at foot
of precipitous hill. Large stony beach;
submarine forest visible at low tide. To W,
P. Weir; tiny harbour, colour-washed
cottages.

PORTBURY Som
155 ST 4975 6m WNW of Bristol. CP, 375.
Long Ashton RD. P BRSTL. Ch e. Sch pe.
N Som CC.

PORT CARLISLE Cumb
75 NY 2462 4m NNE of Kirkbride. Loc,
Bowness CP. Wigton RD. P Csle. Ch m.
Penrith and the Border CC. Blt in 19c as
outlet to sea for Clsle, with connecting
canal; unsuccessful.

PORTCHESTER Hants
180 SU 6105 2m E of Fareham. Loc,
Frhm UD. P Frhm. Nmn cstle (A.M.), blt
within walls of Roman fort. Nmn ch in cstle
precincts.

PORTESHAM Dorset
178 SY 6085 6m WSW of Dorchester.
CP, 412. Dchstr RD. P Weymouth. Ch e, m.
Sch pe. W Dst CC. 1¼m NE on Black Down,
(Admiral) Hardy Monmt, erected 1844.

PORTGATE Devon
175 SX 4185 6m E of Launceston. Loc,
Stowford CP. Ch m.

PORTGAVERNE Cornwall
185, 186 SX 0080 just E of Port Isaac. Loc,
St Endellion CP. Hmlt at head of small cove
owned by NT.

PORTHALLOW Cornwall
190 SW 7923 9m ESE of Helston. Loc,
St Keverne CP. P St Kvne, Hlstn. Ch m.
Boating vllge.

PORTHCOTHAN BAY Cornwall
185 SW 8572 4m WSW of Padstow. Loc,
St Eval CP. P Pdstw. Hmlt at head of narrow
inlet (P. Beach).

PORTHCURNO Cornwall
189 SW 3822 7m SW of Penzance. Loc,
St Levan CP. P Pnznce. At W end of beach,
Minack open-air theatre; at E end, Logan
Rock. Cliffs to E of cove are NT.

PORTHLEVEN Cornwall
189 SW 6225 2m WSW of Helston. Loc,
Hlstn MB. P Hlstn. Ch e. Large vllge with
harbour; fishing and shipbuilding.

PORTH MELLIN Cornwall
189 SW 6617 6m S of Helston. Loc,
Mullion CP. Mullion Cove and
harbour (NT).

PORTHMEOR Cornwall
189 SW 4337 5m NW of Penzance. Loc,
Zennor CP.

PORTH NAVAS Cornwall
190 SW 7527 5m SW of Falmouth. Loc,
Constantine CP. Oyster farm.

PORTHOLLAND Cornwall
190 SW 9541 8m SSW of St Austell. Loc,
St Astll RD. Truro RD. Ch m. Truro CC.
Fishing vllge with sand and rock cove.

PORTHOUSTOCK Cornwall
190 SW 8021 10m ESE of Helston. Loc,
St Keverne CP. Ch m. Shingle beach flanked
by quarry bldngs.

PORTHPEAN Cornwall
185, 186, 190 SX 0350 2m SE of St Austell.
Loc, St Astll w Fowey MB. P St Astll.

PORTHSCATHO Cornwall
190 SW 8735 3m NE of St Mawes across
river. Loc, Gerrans CP. Fishing hmlt with
tiny harbour. Sailing.

PORTHTOWAN Cornwall
189 SW 6947 4m N of Redruth. Loc,
St Agnes CP. P Truro. Ch m. Vllge in
narrow combe leading to large sandy beach.
Derelict mines scattered about.

PORTINGTON Yorks (E)
97, 98 SE 7830 5m NNE of Goole. Loc,
Eastrington CP. John Wesley often stayed at
the hall.

PORT ISAAC Cornwall
185 SW 9980 5m N of Wadebridge. Loc,
St Endellion CP. P. Ch e, m2. Sch p. Small
place with harbour; old, but much enlarged
of late up hill to E.

PORTISHEAD Som
155 ST 4676 8m WNW of Bristol.
UD, 9,015. P BRSTL. N Som CC. Formerly
port, now rsdntl and holiday resort.
14c–15c ch. Spring equinox tides rise to
45ft, some of highest in world. Wansdyke
(see Stanton Prior) ends here.

PORTLAND Dorset
178 SY 6972 S of Weymouth. UD, 12,306.
P. S Dst CC. See also Easton, Fortuneswell,
Grove, Southwell, Weston. Limestone
peninsula with very narrow neck and
forbidding aspect. Provides famous bldng
stone. Former prison is a Borstal institute.

PORTLOE Cornwall
190 SW 9339 7m NE of St Mawes. Loc,
Veryan CP. P Truro. Ch m. Fishing,
boat-building, tourism.

PORTMORE Hants
180 SZ 3397 1m NE of Lymington. Loc,
Boldre CP.

PORT MULGRAVE Yorks (N)
86 NZ 7917 5m E of Loftus. Loc,
Hinderwell CP.

PORTON Wilts
167 SU 1936 5m NE of Salisbury. Loc,
Idmiston CP. P Slsbry. Ch e. Sch p.

PORTQUIN Cornwall
185 SW 9780 5m NNW of Wadebridge. Loc,
Wdbrdge and Padstow RD. N Cnwll CC.
Semi-derelict vllge overlooked by 18c folly.

PORTREATH Cornwall
189 SW 6545 3m NW of Redruth. Loc,
Camborne-Rdrth UD. P Rdrth. Resort with
large sandy beach; the port still handles
coal.

PORTSEA Hants
180 SU 6300 W distr of Portsmouth. Loc,
Ptsmth CB. P Ptsmth. Ptsmth N BC
(Ptsmth W). Gives name to island on which
oldest part of Ptsmth is blt.

PORTSLADE-BY-SEA Sussex (E)
182 TQ 2605 3m W of Brighton.
UD, 18,150. P(Ptslde), Brghtn. Hove BC.
Refinery. Power Stns. Much recent housing
development.

PORTSMOUTH Hants
180, 181 SU 6400 65m SW of London.
CB, 196,973. P. BCs: Ptsmth N, Ptsmth S.
See also Cosham, Fratton, Portsea, Southsea.
Chief naval base; extensive docks and service
bldngs. Nelson's flagship HMS Victory*. Boat
and hovercraft ferries to IOW. Cathedral.
On Portsdown Hill, six Palmerston forts blt
mid-19c for defence against French (see also
Gosport); Nelson monmt.

PORTSMOUTH Yorks (W)
95 SD 9026 3m WNW of Todmorden. Loc,
Tdmdn MB. P Tdmdn, Lancs.

PORT SUNLIGHT Ches
100, 109 SJ 3484 3m SSE of Birkenhead.
Loc, Bebington MB. P Wirral. Model 'village'
blt by Mr Lever, later Lord Leverhulme,
founder of soap firm. Lady Lever Art
Gallery.

PORTWAY Herefs
142 SO 4845 4m N of Hereford. Loc,
Burghill CP. Ch v.

PORTWAY Warwicks
131 SP 0872 4m NE of Redditch. Loc,
Tanworth CP. P BIRMINGHAM.

PORTWRINKLE Cornwall
186 SX 3553 5m W of Torpoint. Loc,
Sheviock CP. Two beaches of sand and
rocks.

POSBURY Devon
176 SX 8197 2m SW of Crediton. Loc,
Crdtn Hmlts CP. Crdtn RD. Ch e.
Tiverton CC (Torrington).

POSLINGFORD Suffolk (W)
149 TL 7748 2m N of Clare. CP, 187.
Clre RD. P Sudbury. Ch e. Bury
St Edmunds CC.

POSTBRIDGE Devon
175, 187, 188 SX 6579 8m SW of Moretonhampstead. Loc, Lydford CP. P Yelverton.
Ch e, m. Famous clapper br of uncertain
date.

POSTCOMBE Oxon
159 SU 7099 4m S of Thame. Loc,
Lewknor CP. P OXFORD.

POSTLING Kent
173 TR 1439 3m NNW of Hythe. CP, 163.
Elham RD. Ch e. Folkestone and Hthe CC.

POSTWICK Norfolk
126 TG 2907 4m E of Norwich. CP, 479.
B l o f i e l d   a n d   F l e g g   R D .
P NRWCH, NOR 88Z. Ch e. Yarmouth CC
(Central Nflk). See also Whitton.

POTSGROVE Beds
147 SP 9529 4m NE of Leighton Buzzard.
CP, 69. Ampthill RD. Ch e. Mid-Beds CC.

POTTEN END Herts
159, 160 TL 0109 2m ENE of
Berkhamsted. CP(Nettleden w Pttn
End), 1,199. Bkhmstd RD. P Bkhmstd.
Ch e, b. Sch pe. Hemel Hempstead CC.

POTTER BROMPTON Yorks (E)
93 SE 9777 9m WSW of Filey. Loc,
Ganton CP.

POTTERHANWORTH Lincs (K)
113 TF 0566 6m SE of Lincoln. CP, 535.
N Kesteven RD. P LNCLN. Ch e, m. Sch pe.
Grantham CC.

POTTER HEIGHAM Norfolk
126 TG 4119 8m E of Wroxham. CP, 513.
Smallburgh RD. P Gt Yarmouth. Ch e, m.
Sch p. N Nflk CC. Broads yachting centre.

POTTERNE Wilts
167 ST 9958 2m SSW of Devizes.
CP, 1,218. Dvzs RD. P Dvzs. Ch e. Sch pe.
Dvzs CC. Cruciform EE ch. Porch Hse*, 15c
half-timbered.

POTTERNE WICK Wilts
167 ST 9957 2m S of Devizes. Loc,
Pttne CP.

POTTERS BAR Herts
160 TL 2401 3m N of Barnet. UD, 24,583.
P. S Herts CC (Enfield W BC). See also
S Mimms. Rsdntl district.

POTTERS BROOK Lancs
94 SD 4852 6m S of Lancaster. Loc,
Garstang RD, Lncstr RD. N Fylde CC,
Lncstr CC.

POTTER'S CROSS Staffs
130 SO 8484 4m W of Stourbridge. Loc,
Kinver CP. P Stbrdge, Worcs. Ch m.

POTTERS MARSTON Leics
132 SP 4996 5m ENE of Hinckley. CP, 45.
Blaby RD. Ch e. Blby CC (Harborough).

POTTERSPURY Northants
146 SP 7543 3m NW of Stony Stratford.
CP, 771. Towcester RD. P Tcstr. Ch e, v.
Sch p. Daventry CC (S Nthnts). See also
Furtho.

POTTER STREET Essex
161 TL 4608 1m S of Harlow. Loc,
Hlw UD.

POTTO Yorks (N)
91 NZ 4703 9m NE of Northallerton.
CP, 144. Stokesley RD. Richmond CC.

POTTON Beds
147 TL 2249 3m NE of Biggleswade.
CP, 2,070. Bgglswde RD. P Sandy.
Ch e, b, m, s v. Sch p. Mid-Beds CC.

POTT ROW Norfolk
124 TF 7021 5m E of King's Lynn. Loc,
Grimston CP. P K's Lnn. Ch m.

POTT SHRIGLEY Ches
101 SJ 9479 4m NNE of Macclesfield.
CP, 376 Mcclsfld RD. Ch e, m, r. Sch pe.
Mcclsfld CC.

POUGHILL Cornwall
174 SS 2207 1m NE of Bude. Loc,
Bde-Stratton UD. P Bde. Ch e. Ch has 78
carved bench ends.

POUGHILL Devon
176 SS 8508 5m NNE of Crediton. CP, 176.
Crdtn RD. P Crdtn. Ch e, c. Sch pe.
Tiverton CC (Torrington).

POULSHOT Wilts
167 ST 9759 3m WSW of Devizes. CP, 320.
Dvzs RD. P Dvzs. Ch e, m. Sch pe. Dvzs CC.

POULTON Glos
157 SP 1000 5m E of Cirencester. CP, 340.
Crncstr RD. P Crncstr. Ch e, m. Sch pe.
Crncstr and Tewkesbury CC.

POULTON-LE-FYLDE Lancs
94 SD 3439 3m NE of Blackpool.
UD, 16,401. P Blckpl. N Fylde CC. See also
Carleton, Normoss. Stocks and whipping
post in mkt place.

POUND BANK Worcs
130 SO 7373 3m W of Bewdley. Loc,
Rock CP.

POUND HILL Sussex (W)
170, 182 TQ 2936 2m E of Crawley. Loc,
Crly UD. P Crly.

POUNDON Bucks
145, 146 SP 6425 4m ENE of Bicester.
CP, 59. Buckingham RD. Ch e.
Bcknghm CC.

POUNDSGATE Devon
175, 187, 188 SX 7072 4m WNW of Ashburton. Loc, Widecombe in the Moor CP.
P Newton Abbot. Ch m.

POUNDSTOCK Cornwall
174 SX 2099 4m S of Bude. CP, 621.
Stratton RD. P Bde. Ch e, m. Sch p. See also
Bangors, Coppathorne, Widemouth. The 14c
guildhall, now parish room, stands next ch.
1¼m E, Penfound*, England's oldest
inhabited mnr hse.

POWBURN Nthmb
71 NU 0616 9m SSE of Wooler. Loc,
Hedgeley CP. Alnwick RD. P Alnwick.
Berwick-upon-Tweed CC.

POWDERHAM Devon
176 SX 9684 6m SSE of Exeter. CP, 98.
St Thomas RD. Ch e. Tiverton CC. Cstle*,
home of the Courtenays since 14c but now
mainly 18c and later.

POWERSTOCK Dorset
177 SY 5196 4m ENE of Bridport. CP, 440.
Beaminster RD. P Brdpt. Ch e. Sch pe.
W Dst CC. See also Nettlecombe, S Poorton,
W Milton.

POWICK Worcs
143 SO 8351 3m SSW of Worcester.
CP, 3,102. Upton upon Severn RD.
P WCSTR. Ch e. Sch pe. S Worcs CC. See
also Bowling Grn, Callow End. Large mental
hsptl.

POXWELL Dorset
178 SY 7484 5m SE of Dorchester. CP, 54.
Dchstr RD. Ch e. S Dst CC.

POYLE Surrey
160, 170 TQ 0376 3m N of Staines. Loc,
Stns UD.

POYNINGS Sussex (E)
182 TQ 2612 6m NNW of Brighton.
CP, 300. Cuckfield RD. P Brghtn. Ch e, b.
Mid-Sx CC (Lewes). Picturesque vllge under
S Downs.

POYNTINGTON Dorset
166, 178 ST 6520 2m NNE of Sherborne.

CP, 136. Shbne RD. Ch e. W Dst CC.

POYNTON Ches
101 SJ 9283 4m SSE of Stockport.
CP (Pntn-w-Worth), 7,750.
Macclesfield RD. P Stckpt. Ch e, b, m2, r.
Sch p3, s. Mcclsfld CC.

POYNTON GREEN Shrops
118 SJ 5618 6m NE of Shrewsbury. Loc,
Ercall Magna CP. Wellington RD. Ch m. The
Wrekin CC.

POYS STREET Suffolk (E)
137 TM 3570 5m SSW of Halesworth. Loc,
Sibton CP.

POYSTREET GREEN Suffolk (W)
136 TL 9858 4m W of Stowmarket. Loc,
Rattlesden CP.

PRAA SANDS Cornwall
189 SW 5828 5m W of Helston. Loc,
Breage CP. P Penzance.

PRATT'S BOTTOM London
171 TQ 4762 3m S of Orpington. Loc,
Bromley LB. Orpngtn BC (CC).

PRAZE Cornwall
189 SW 5735 5m WSW of Camborne. See
St Erth Praze.

PRAZE-AN-BEEBLE Cornwall
189 SW 6335 3m S of Camborne. Loc,
Crowan CP. P Cmbne. Ch m.

PREES Shrops
118 SJ 5533 4m NE of Wem. CP, 2,128.
N Shrops RD. P Whitchurch. Ch e, m, v.
Sch pe. Oswestry CC. See also Darliston,
Faulsgreen, Preesgreen, Prs Hr Hth,
Prs Lr Hth. Red sandstone ch; brick Ggn
hall opposite.

PREESALL Lancs
94 SD 3647 2m ESE across river from
Fleetwood. UD, 4,066. P Blackpool.
N Fylde CC. See also Knott End-on-Sea,
Pilling Lane.

PREESGREEN Shrops
118 SJ 5631 4m ENE of Wem. Loc,
Prees CP. P Whitchurch. Ch m.

PREESGWEENE Shrops
118 SJ 2936 4m N of Oswestry. Loc, Weston
Rhyn CP. P Wstn Rhn, Oswestry.

PREES HIGHER HEATH Shrops
118 SJ 5636 4m SSE of Whitchurch. Loc,
Prs CP. P(Hr Hth), Whtchch.

PREES LOWER HEATH Shrops
118 SJ 5732 5m ENE of Wem. Loc, Prs CP.
Sch pe.

PRENDWICK Nthmb
71 NU 0012 7m NNW of Rothbury. Loc,
Alnham CP.

PRESCOT Lancs
100 SJ 4692 4m WSW of St Helens.
UD, 12,590. P. Huyton CC. Indstrl, incl
cable-mnfg.

PRESCOTT Devon
164, 176 ST 0814 5m SW of Wellington.
Loc, Culmstock CP. Ch b.

PRESCOTT Glos
143, 144 SO 9829 5m NNE of Cheltenham.
CP, 90. Chltnhm RD. Cirencester and
Tewkesbury CC. A few scattered bldngs
with no nucleus.

PRESCOTT Shrops
118 SJ 4221 7m NW of Shrewsbury. Loc,
Baschurch CP.

PRESSEN Nthmb
64, 70 NT 8335 2m SSW of Coldstream.
Loc, Carham CP.

PRESTBURY Ches
101 SJ 9077 2m NNW of Macclesfield.
CP, 2,159. Mcclsfld RD. P Mcclsfld.
Ch e, m. Sch pe. Mcclsfld CC. Show vllge,
with black and white hses, esp former
vicarage with gallery above porch.

PRESTBURY Glos
143, 144 SO 9723 2m ENE of Cheltenham.
CP, 4,325. Chltnhm RD. P Chltnhm.
Ch e, c. Sch pe. Cirencester and
Tewkesbury CC. Rsdntl suburb of Chltnhm.

PRESTHOPE Shrops
129 SO 5897 3m WSW of Much Wenlock.
Loc, Mch Wnlck CP. Ch m.

PRESTON Devon
176, 188 SX 8574 2m N of Newton Abbot.
Loc, Kingsteignton CP.

PRESTON Dorset
178 SY 7083 3m NNE of Weymouth. Loc,
Wmth and Melcombe Regis MB. Caravan
sites. Ch: sundial, effigy.

PRESTON Glos
142, 143 SO 6734 3m SW of Ledbury. Loc,
Dymock CP. Ch e.

PRESTON Glos
157 SP 0400 1m SE of Cirencester. CP, 238.
Crncstr RD. Ch e. Crncstr and
Tewkesbury CC.

PRESTON Herts
147 TL 1824 3m S of Hitchin. CP, 374.
Htchn RD. P Htchn. Ch b. Sch pe.
Htchn CC.

PRESTON Kent
172, 173 TR 0260 just SE of Faversham.
Loc, Fvshm MB.

PRESTON Kent
173 TR 2560 5m WNW of Sandwich.
CP, 589. Eastry RD. P Canterbury. Ch e, v.
Sch p. Dover and Deal CC (Dvr). See also
Elmstone.

PRESTON Lancs
94 SD 5429 27m NW of Manchester.
CB, 97,365. P. BCs: Prstn N, Prstn S. Large
textiles and engineering tn on R Ribble. To
S, New Tn designated. (Central Lancashire,
pop. 1971: 234,721.)

PRESTON Nthmb
71 NU 1825 7m SE of Belford. Loc, Ellingham CP.

PRESTON Rutland
122 SK 8702 2m N of Uppingham. CP, 183.
Uppnghm RD. P Uppnghm. Ch e. Rtlnd and
Stamford CC. Jcbn mnr hse.

PRESTON Suffolk (W)
149 TL 9450 2m ENE of Lavenham.
CP(Prstn St Mary), 201. Cosford RD.
P(Prstn St Mary), Sudbury. Ch e. Sdbry and
Woodbridge CC.

PRESTON Wilts
157 SU 0377 5m NNE of Calne. Loc,
Lyneham CP. Ch m.

PRESTON Yorks (E)
99 TA 1830 6m E of Hull. CP, 1,938.
Holderness RD. P Hll. Ch e, m. Sch p.

Preston Bagot

Bridlington CC. 15c ch twr impressive landmark.

PRESTON BAGOT Warwicks
131 SP 1765 7m W of Warwick. CP, 158. Stratford-on-Avon RD. Ch e. Strtfd-on-Avn CC (Strtfd).

PRESTON BISSETT Bucks
145, 146 SP 6529 3m SW of Buckingham. CP, 233. Bcknghm RD. P BCKNGHM. Ch e. Sch pe. Bcknghm CC.

PRESTON BROCKHURST Shrops
118 SJ 5324 3m SSE of Wem. Loc, Moreton Corbet CP. P Shrewsbury. Black-and-white hses surround vllge grn.

PRESTON BROOK Ches
100, 109 SJ 5680 3m ESE of Runcorn. Loc, Rncn UD; CP, Rncn RD. P WARRINGTON. Rncn CC. See also Prstn on the Hill.

PRESTON CANDOVER Hants
168 SU 6041 7m SSW of Basingstoke. CP, 359. Bsngstke RD. P Bsngstke. Ch e. Sch pe. Bsngstke CC.

PRESTON CAPES Northants
145, 146 SP 5754 5m S of Daventry. C P , 1 6 2 . D v n t r y R D . P Rugby, Warwickshire. Ch e. Dvntry CC (S Nthnts).

PRESTON, GREAT Yorks (W)
97 SE 4029 3m NNW of Castleford. See Gt Prstn.

PRESTON GUBBALS Shrops
118 SJ 4919 4m N of Shrewsbury. Loc, Pimhill CP. Atcham RD. Ch e. Shrsbry CC. To N on main rd, Lea Hall, Elizn brick hse.

PRESTON ON STOUR Warwicks
144 SP 2049 3m S of Stratford. CP, 203. Strtfd-on-Avon RD. P Strtfd-upon-Avn. Ch e. Sch pe. Strtfd-on-Avn CC (Strtfd). 18c ch with Perp twr. To NE across R Stour, Alscot Pk, Gothic Revival hse.

PRESTON ON THE HILL Ches
100, 109 SJ 5780 4m ESE of Runcorn. Loc, Prstn Brook CP. Ch m.

PRESTON ON WYE Herefs
142 SO 3842 8m WNW of Hereford. CP, 151. Weobley RD. P HRFD. Ch e, b. Leominster CC. See also Ploughfield.

PRESTON PLUCKNETT Som
177, 178 ST 5316 1m W of Yeovil. Loc, Yvl MB. P Yvl. Yvl CC.

PRESTON-UNDER-SCAR Yorks (N)
90 SE 0791 3m W of Leyburn. CP, 179. Lbn RD. P Lbn. Ch m. Richmond CC.

PRESTON UPON THE WEALD MOORS Shrops
119 SJ 6815 3m NE of Wellington. CP, 173. Wllngtn RD. P(Prstn), Telford. Ch e. Sch pe. The Wrekin CC. Early Ggn hsptl.

PRESTON WYNNE Herefs
142 SO 5547 5m NE of Hereford. CP, 171. Hrfd RD. P HRFD. Ch e. Leominster CC.

PRESTWICH Lancs
101 SD 8203 4m N of Manchester. MB, 32,838. P MNCHSTR. Middleton and .'rstwch BC (CC). Textiles. To E, Heaton Hall*, Ggn hse by James Wyatt, in pk.

PRESTWICK Nthmb
78 NZ 1872 1m ESE of Ponteland. Loc, Pntlnd CP.

PRESTWOOD Bucks
159 SP 8700 5m N of High Wycombe. Loc, Gt Missenden CP. P Gt Mssndn. Ch e, b, m. Sch p.

PRICKWILLOW Cambs
135 TL 5982 4m ENE of Ely. Loc, Ely UD. P Ely.

PRIDDY Som
165 ST 5251 4m NNW of Wells. CP, 250. Wlls RD. P Wlls. Ch e. Sch p. Wlls CC. Lonely Mendip vllge with large grn, once at centre of lead-mining area. To E, Priddy Nine Barrows, Bronze Age round barrows, most spectacular of many prehistoric earthworks in area.

PRIEST HUTTON Lancs
89 SD 5373 3m NE of Carnforth. CP, 178. Lancaster RD. P Cnfth. Sch pe. Morecambe and Lonsdale CC. See also Tewitfield.

PRIESTWESTON Shrops
129 SO 2997 6m NNW of Bishop's Cstle. Loc, Chirbury CP. P MONTGOMERY.

PRIMETHORPE Leics
132 SP 5293 8m SSW of Leicester. Loc, Broughton Astley CP. P LCSTR.

PRIMROSE GREEN Norfolk
125 TG 0616 5m ENE of E Dereham. Loc,
Lyng CP.

PRIMROSE HILL Cambs
135 TL 3889 2m N of Chatteris. Loc,
Doddington CP.

PRIMROSEHILL Herts
160 TL 0702 3m SSE of Hemel Hempstead.
Loc, Abbots Langley CP.

PRINCES RISBOROUGH Bucks
159 SP 8003 7m S of Aylesbury. CP, 6,484.
Wycombe RD. P Aylesbury. Ch e, b, m, r.
Sch i, j, p, s. Aylesbury CC (Wcmbe). See
also Askett, Monks Rsbrgh, Parkfield. Mnr
Hse (NT)*, near ch.

PRINCETHORPE Warwicks
132 SP 4070 6m NE of Leamington.
CP, 465. Rugby RD. P Rgby. Ch e, r2.
Sch pr. Rgby CC.

PRINCETOWN Devon
175, 187 SX 5873 7m E of Tavistock. Loc,
Lydford CP. P Yelverton. Ch e, m. Sch p.
Mid-Dartmoor tn blt round prison originally
founded to accommodate French prisoners
in Napoleonic wars.

PRINSTED Sussex (W)
181 SU 7605 3m E of Havant. Loc,
Southbourne CP. Picturesque cottages
running down to mooring on Thorney
Channel.

PRIORS HARDWICK Warwicks
132 SP 4756 5m SE of Southam. CP, 143.
Sthm RD. P Rugby. Ch e. Rgby CC.

PRIORSLEE Shrops
119 SJ 7009 just S of Oakengates. Loc,
Oakngts UD. P Telford.

PRIORS MARSTON Warwicks
132 SP 4857 6m WSW of Daventry.
CP, 466. Southam RD. P Rugby. Ch e, m, v.
Sch pe. Stratford-on-Avon CC (Strtfd).

PRIORY WOOD Herefs
141 SO 2545 3m NE of Hay-on-Wye. Loc,
Clifford CP. Ch m.

PRISTON Som
166 ST 6960 4m N of Radstock. CP, 212.
Bathavon RD. P Bath. Ch e. Sch pe.
N Som CC.

PRIVETT Hants
168, 181 SU 6726 5m WNW of Petersfield.
Loc, Froxfield CP. Ptrsfld RD. P Alton.
Ch e. Sch p. Ptrsfld CC.

PROBUS Cornwall
190 SW 8947 5m ENE of Truro. CP, 1,244.
Truro RD. P Truro. Ch e, m. Sch p.
Truro CC. Ch has 'best tower in Cornwall'.

PRUDHOE Nthmb
77, 78 NZ 0962 10m W of Newcastle.
UD, 11,015. P. Hexham CC. See also
Eltringham, High Mickley, Mckly Square,
W Wylam. Indstrl. Mining district. 12c–14c
cstle* overlooking R Tyne.

PUBLOW Som
166 ST 6264 6m SSE of Bristol. CP, 990.
Clutton RD. Ch e. N Som CC. See also
Pensford.

PUCKERIDGE Herts
148 TL 3823 6m NNE of Ware. Loc,
Standon CP. P Ware. Ch r, v. Sch pe.

PUCKINGTON Som
177 ST 3718 3m NNE of Ilminster. CP, 91.
Langport RD. P Ilmnstr. Ch e. Yeovil CC.

PUCKLECHURCH Glos
156 ST 6976 7m ENE of Bristol. CP, 1,471.
Sodbury RD. P BRSTL. Ch e, m2, v. Sch pe.
S Glos CC.

PUDDINGTON Ches
109 SJ 3273 6m NW of Chester. CP, 325.
Chstr RD. City of Chstr CC.

PUDDINGTON Devon
164, 176 SS 8310 8m W of Tiverton.
CP, 126. Crediton RD. Ch e, c. Tvtn CC
(Torrington).

PUDDLETOWN Dorset
178 SY 7594 5m ENE of Dorchester.
CP, 795. Dchstr RD. P Dchstr. Ch e, c.
Sch pe, se. W Dst CC. Ch mainly 15c; font,
woodwork, side-chpl. 1½m WNW, Waterston
Mnr*, Elizn, with large gdns; limited
opening.

PUDLESTON Herefs
129 SO 5659 4m E of Leominster.
CP (Pudlestone), 211. Lmnstr and
Wigmore RD. P Lmnstr. Ch e. Sch pe.
Lmnstr CC. See also Whyle.

PUDSEY Yorks (W)
96 SE 2233 4m E of Bradford. MB, 38,127.
P. Pdsy BC. See also Calverley, Farsley.

PULBOROUGH Sussex (W)
182 TQ 0418 11m SW of Horsham.
CP, 2,809. Chanctonbury RD. P. Ch e, c, r.
Sch pe. Shoreham CC (Arundel and Shrhm).
See also N Hth, Nutbourne.

PULFORD Ches
109 SJ 3758 5m SSW of Chester. CP, 313.
Chstr RD. P CHSTR. Ch e. Sch pe. City
of Chstr CC.

PULHAM Dorset
178 ST 7008 7m SE of Sherborne. CP, 196.
Sturminster RD. P Dorchester. Ch e.
N Dst CC.

PULHAM MARKET Norfolk
137 TM 1986 6m NE of Diss. CP, 866.
Depwade RD. P Dss. Ch e. Sch pe.
S Nflk CC.

PULHAM ST MARY Norfolk
137 TM 2185 7m NE of Diss. CP, 636.
Depwade RD. P Dss. Ch e, m3, v. Sch pe.
S Nflk CC.

PULLOXHILL Beds
147 TL 0633 3m SE of Ampthill. CP, 648.
Ampthll RD. P BEDFORD. Ch e. Sch p.
Mid-Beds CC.

PUNCKNOWLE Dorset
177, 178 SY 5388 5m ESE of Bridport.
CP, 269. Brdpt RD. P Dorchester. Ch e, m.
W Dst CC. See also W Bexington. Partly
Nmn ch. 15c mnr hse.

PUNNETT'S TOWN Sussex (E)
183 TQ 6220 3m E of Heathfield. Loc,
Hailsham RD. P Hthfld. Sch p. Rye CC. On
500ft ridge commanding fine views.

PURBROOK Hants
180, 181 SU 6708 3m WNW of Havant.
Loc, Hvnt and Waterloo UD. P Portsmouth.

PURFLEET Essex
161, 171 TQ 5578 6m W of Tilbury. Loc,
Thurrock UD. P. Thrrck BC (CC). Chemical
and other industries.

PURITON Som
165 ST 3241 3m NNE of Bridgwater.
CP, 991. Brdgwtr RD. P Brdgwtr. Ch e, v.
Sch p. Brdgwtr CC. See also Dunball. Large
explosives factory.

PURLEIGH Essex
162 TL 8402 3m S of Maldon. CP, 914.
Mldn RD. P Chelmsford. Ch e. Sch p.
Mldn CC. See also Cock Clarks.

PURLEY Berks
158, 159 SU 6576 1m E of Pangbourne.
CP, 1,868. Bradfield RD. P Reading. Ch e.
Sch p, pe. Newbury CC.

PURLEY Surrey
170 TQ 3161 3m SSW of Croydon. Loc,
Crdn LB. P Surrey. Crdn S BC (E Srry CC,
Crdn S BC).

PURLOGUE Shrops
129 SO 2877 3m N of Knighton. Loc,
Clun CP.

PURLS BRIDGE Cambs
135 TL 4787 5m E of Chatteris. Loc,
Manea CP.

PURSE CAUNDLE Dorset
178 ST 6917 4m E of Sherborne. CP, 119.
Shbne RD. Ch e. W Dst CC. Mdvl mnr hse*.

PURSTON JAGLIN Yorks (W)
103 SE 4319 2m SW of Pontefract. Loc,
Featherstone UD. P Fthstne, Pntfrct.

PURTON Glos
155, 156 SO 6704 3m ENE of Lydney. Loc,
Ldny CP.

PURTON Glos
156 SO 6904 6m NW of Dursley. Loc,
Hinton CP. P Berkeley. Ch e.

PURTON Wilts
157 SU 0987 4m NW of Swindon.
CP, 3,295. Cricklade and Wootton Bassett RD.
P Swndn. Ch e, m3. Sch pe, s.
Chippenham CC. See also Ptn Stoke.
Cruciform 13c–14c ch: two twrs, mdvl
glass, wall-paintings.

PURTON STOKE Wilts
157 SU 0990 6m NW of Swindon. Loc,
Ptn CP. P Swndn. Sch p.

PURY END Northants
146 SP 7045 2m SSE of Towcester. Loc,
Paulerspury CP. P Tcstr. Ch m.

PUSEY Berks
158 SU 3596 5m E of Faringdon. CP, 96.
Frngdn RD. Ch e. Sch pe. Abingdon CC.
Limestone estate vllge called after family of
same name.

PUTLEY Herefs
142, 143 SO 6437 4m W of Ledbury.
CP, 193. Ldbry RD. P Ldbry. Ch e.
Leominster CC. Among hop gdns.

PUTLOE Glos
156 SO 7809 5m NW of Stroud. Loc,
Gloucester RD. Strd CC.

PUTNEY London
160, 170 TQ 2475 1m WNW of
Wandsworth. Loc, Wndswth LB. Ptny BC.
High st leads up from P. Br over Thames to
P. Hth and Wimbledon Cmmn.

PUTTENHAM Herts
146, 159 SP 8814 3m NW of Tring. Loc,
Trng Rural CP. Berkhamsted RD. Ch e.
Hemel Hempstead CC.

PUTTENHAM Surrey
169 SU 9347 4m W of Guildford. CP, 615.
Gldfd RD. P Gldfd. Ch e. Sch pe. Gldfd CC.
On line of Pilgrims' Way below Hog's Back,
chalk ridge commanding long views.

PUXTON Som
165 ST 4063 2m W of Congresbury.
CP, 206. Axbridge RD. Ch e, m.
Weston-super-Mare CC.

PYECOMBE Sussex (E)
182 TQ 2812 6m NNW of Brighton.
CP, 280. Cuckfield RD. P Brghtn. Ch e.
Mid-Sx CC (Lewes). Downland vllge. 1m
NW, Newtimber Place*, moated
17c—18c hse.

PYE GREEN Staffs
119 SJ 9914 3m NNE of Cannock. Loc,
Cnnck UD. P Cnnck. Cnnck CC. At S edge
of Cnnck Chase.

PYLE IOW
180 SZ 4779 6m SSW of Newport. Loc,
Chale CP.

PYLLE Somerset
166 ST 6038 3m S of Shepton Mallet.
CP, 169. Shptn Mllt RD. P Shptn Mllt. Ch e.
Wells CC. See also Street on the Fosse.

PYMORE Cambs
135 TL 4986 4m W of Littleport. Loc,
Downham CP. P Ely. Ch m. Sch pe.

PYMORE Dorset
177 SY 4794 1m NNE of Bridport. Loc,
Brdpt RD. W Dst CC.

PYRFORD Surrey
170 TQ 0458 2m E of Woking. Loc,
Wkng UD. P Wkng.

PYRTON Oxon
159 SU 6895 6m S of Thame. CP, 190.
Bullingdon RD. Ch e. Henley CC.

PYTCHLEY Northants
133 SP 8574 2m S of Kettering. CP, 484.
Kttrng RD. P Kttrng. Ch e, m. Sch pe.
Kttrng CC. Gives name to famous hunt.
Kennels now at Brixworth.

PYWORTHY Devon
174 SS 3102 2m W of Holsworthy. CP, 467.
Hlswthy RD. P Hlswthy. Ch e, m2. Sch pe.
W Dvn CC (Tavistock). See also Derrill.

Q

QUADRING Lincs (H)
114, 123 TF 2233 7m N of Spalding.
CP, 1,060. Spldng RD. P Spldng. Ch e, m3.
Sch p, pe. Holland w Boston CC.

QUAINTON Bucks
146 SP 7420 6m NW of Aylesbury. CP, 820.
Aylesbury RD. P Aylesbury. Ch e, b.
Sch pe. Aylesbury CC. Mkt cross, almshses,
windmill.

QUARLEY Hants
167 SU 2743 6m W of Andover. CP, 167.
Andvr RD. P Andvr. Ch e. Winchester CC
(Basingstoke).

QUARNDON Derbys
120, 121 SK 3341 3m NNW of Derby. CP.
Belper RD. P DBY. Ch e. Sch pe. Blpr CC.

Quarrington

QUARRINGTON Lincs (K)
113, 123 TF 0544 1m SW of Sleaford. Loc,
Slfd UD.

QUARRINGTON HILL Co Durham
85 NZ 3337 5m SE of Durham. Loc,
Drhm RD. P DRHM. Ch e, m2. Drhm CC.

QUARRYBANK Ches
109 SJ 5465 7m W of Winsford. Loc,
Utkinton CP. Northwich RD.
P(Utkntn), Tarporley. Ch m. Sch pe.
Nthwch CC.

QUARRY, THE Glos
156 ST 7399 8m WSW of Stroud. Loc,
Cam CP. Ch v.

QUATFORD Shrops
130 SO 7390 2m SE of Bridgnorth. Loc,
Brdgnth CP. Ch e.

QUATT Shrops
130 SO 7588 4m SE of Bridgnorth.
CP(Quatt Malvern), 254. Brdgnth RD.
P Brdgnth. Ch e. Ludlow CC. See also
Hampton Loade.

QUEBEC Co Durham
85 NZ 1843 3m SSE of Lanchester. Loc,
Esh CP. P DRHM. Ch m.

QUEDGELEY Glos
143 SO 8114 3m SSW of Gloucester.
CP, 1,121. Glcstr RD. P GLCSTR. Ch e, m.
Sch pe, s. Stroud CC.

QUEEN ADELAIDE Cambs
135 TL 5681 2m ENE of Ely. Loc, Ely UD.
P Ely.

QUEENBOROUGH-IN-SHEPPEY Kent
172 TQ 9072 5m N of Sittingbourne.
MB, 31,541. P(Qunbrgh). Faversham CC.
See also Eastchurch, Halfway Hses,
Leysdown-on-Sea, Minster, Sheerness,
Warden. Chemical wks, foundries, potteries.

QUEEN CAMEL Som
166, 177 ST 5924 5m ENE of Ilchester.
CP, 536. Wincanton RD. P Yeovil. Ch e.
Sch p. Wells CC. Stone vllge on R Cam.

QUEEN CHARLTON Som
155, 156 ST 6367 5m SE of Bristol. Loc,
Compton Dando CP. Ch e.

QUEENHILL Worcs
143 SO 8636 3m NW of Tewkesbury.
CP, 67. Upton upon Severn RD. Ch e.
S Worcs CC.

QUEEN OAK Dorset
166 ST 7730 5m ENE of Wincanton. Loc,
Bourton CP.

QUEENSBURY Yorks (W)
96 SE 1030 4m WSW of Bradford.
UD(Qunsbry and Shelf), 10,603. P Brdfd.
Brdfd S BC. See also Ambler Thorn,
Catharine Slack, Shibden Head, Stone Chair.

QUEEN'S HEAD Shrops
118 SJ 3426 4m ESE of Oswestry. Loc,
Oswstry Rural CP. Oswstry RD.
P: W Felton. Oswstry. Oswestry CC.

QUEEN STREET Kent
171 TQ 6845 6m E of Tonbridge. Loc,
Maidstone RD, Tnbrdge RD. P Tnbrdge.
Mdstne CC, Royal Tunbridge Wells CC.
(Mdstne CC, Tnbrdge CC.)

QUENDON Essex
148 TL 5130 5m SSW of Saffron Walden.
CP(Qundn and Rickling), 508. Sffrn
Wldn RD. P Sffrn Wldn. Ch e. Sffrn
Wldn CC.

QUENIBOROUGH Leics
121, 122 SK 6412 6m NE of Leicester.
CP, 1,727. Barrow upon Soar RD. P LCSTR.
Ch e, m. Sch pe. Melton CC. Ch has fine twr
and spire.

QUENINGTON Glos
157 SP 1404 5m NW of Lechlade. CP, 481.
Cirencester RD. P Crncstr. Ch e, v. Sch pe.
Crncstr and Tewkesbury CC. Ch: Nmn N
and S doorways, richly carved. 17c hses.

QUERNMORE Lancs
89, 94 SD 5160 3m ESE of Lancaster.
CP, 592. Lunesdale RD. P Lncstr. Ch e, f, m.
Sch pe. Lncstr CC.

QUETHIOCK Cornwall
186 SX 3164 4m E of Liskeard. CP, 317.
St Germans RD. P Lskd. Ch e, m2. Sch pe.
Bodmin CC.

QUIDENHAM Norfolk
136 TM 0287 5m SSW of Attleborough.
CP, 515. Wayland RD.
P NORWICH, NOR 07X. Ch e. S Nflk CC.
See also Eccles Rd, Wilby.

QUIDHAMPTON Hants
168 SU 5150 8m W of Basingstoke. Loc,
Overton CP.

QUIDHAMPTON Wilts
167 SU 1131 2m WNW of Salisbury.
CP, 307. Slsbry and Wilton RD. P Slsbry.
Slsbry CC.

QUINTON Northants
146 SP 7754 4m SSE of Northampton.

CP, 183. Nthmptn RD. Ch e, m.
Daventry CC (S Nthnts).

QUORNDON Leics
121, 122 SK 5616 3m SE of Loughborough.
CP, 3,355. Barrow upon Soar RD.
P(Quorn), Lghbrgh. Ch e, b, m. Sch pe, sg.
Melton CC. Q. Hall, now part of Lghbrgh
University, is former home of Meynell,
founder of Quorn hunt.

R

RABY Ches
100, 109 SJ 3179 6m S of Birkenhead. Loc,
Bebington MB.

RACKENFORD Devon
164 SS 8518 7m WNW of Tiverton.
CP, 291. S Molton RD. P Tvtn. Ch e, m.
Sch pe. N Dvn CC.

RACKHAM Sussex (W)
182 TQ 0513 3m S of Pulborough. Loc,
Parham CP. Chanctonbury RD. Ch e.
Shoreham CC (Arundel and Shrhm). On W
edge of pk of Prhm Hse*, Tdr hse among
downs. Ch is that of Prhm par, also in pk.

RACKHEATH Norfolk
126 TG 2814 2m SW of Wroxham. CP, 998.
St Faith's and Aylsham RD. P Norwich.
Ch e. Sch p. N Nflk CC (Central Nflk). See
also Slipper's Bottom.

RADBOURNE Derbys
120, 121 SK 2836 4m W of Derby. CP.
Repton RD. Ch e. Belper CC.

RADCLIFFE Lancs
101 SD 7807 2m SSW of Bury. MB, 29,320.
P MANCHESTER. Bury and Rdclffe BC.
See also Ainsworth, Black Lane. Textiles,
engineering, paper-mnfg, paint-mnfg.

RADCLIFFE Nthmb
71 NU 2602 1m S of Amble. Loc,
Hauxley CP. P Morpeth. Ch m. Sch p.

RADCLIFFE ON TRENT Notts
112, 121, 122 SK 6439 5m E of
Nottingham. CP, 6,468. Bingham RD.
P NTTNGHM. Ch e, m, r. Sch j, p, s.
Rushcliffe CC (Carlton).

RADCLIVE Bucks
145, 146 SP 6734 1m W of Buckingham.
CP(Rdclve-cum-Chackmore), 231.
Bcknghm RD. Ch e. Bcknghm CC.

RADCOT Oxon
158 SU 2899 3m N of Faringdon.
CP(Grafton and Rdct), 63. Witney RD.
Mid-Oxon CC (Banbury). 14c br over
R Thames — the oldest to cross this river.

RADFORD SEMELE Warwicks
132 SP 3464 2m ESE of Leamington.
CP, 1,273. Warwick RD. P Lmngtn Spa.
Ch e, b. Sch pe. Wrwck and Lmngtn CC.

RADLETT Herts
160 TQ 1699 5m S of St Albans. Loc,
Aldenham CP. P. Ch e, c, m, r, v. Sch ie, j, p.
Rsdntl; much larger than Aldnhm, which
gives name to parish.

RADLEY Berks
158 SU 5298 2m NE of Abingdon.
CP, 1,675. Abngdn RD. P Abngdn. Ch e.
Sch pe. Abngdn CC. Well-known public
school here.

RADNAGE Bucks
159 SU 7897 6m NW of High Wycombe.
CP, 609. Wcmbe RD. P Hgh Wcmbe.
Ch e, m. Sch pe. Aylesbury CC (Wcmbe).
See also City, The.

RADSTOCK Som
166 ST 6854 7m NW of Frome.
UD(Norton-Radstock), 15,232. P Bath.
N Som CC. See also Clandown,
Writhlington. Centre of Som coal-mining
area. Industries incl mnftre of gloves, tools,
electrical equipment, paper, prefabricated
farm bldngs.

RADSTONE Northants
145, 146 SP 5840 2m N of Brackley.
CP, 73. Brckly RD. Ch e. Daventry CC
(S Nthnts).

RADWAY Warwicks
145 SP 3748 7m NW of Banbury. CP, 231.
Southam RD. P WARWICK. Ch e, m.
Stratford-on-Avon CC (Strtfd).

RADWAY GREEN Ches
110 SJ 7754 5m E of Crewe. Loc,
Barthomley CP.

RADWELL Herts
147 TL 2335 1m NNW of Baldock. CP, 87.
Hitchin RD. Ch e. Htchn CC.

RADWINTER Essex
148 TL 6037 4m E of Saffron Walden.
CP, 511. Sffrn Wldn RD. P Sffrn Wldn.
Ch e, c. Sch pe. Sffrn Wldn CC.

RAGDALE Leics
121, 122 SK 6619 6m W of Melton
Mowbray. Loc, Hoby w Rotherby CP. Ch e.

RAGNALL Notts
113 SK 8073 11m W of Lincoln. CP, 128.
E Retford RD. Ch e. Bassetlaw CC.

RAINFORD Lancs
100 SD 4701 4m NW of St Helens.
UD, 8,381. P St Hlns. Ormskirk CC. See also
Crank.

RAINHAM Kent
172 TQ 8165 3m ESE of Gillingham. Loc,
Gllnghm MB. P Gllnghm.

RAINHAM London
161 TQ 5282 2m ESE of Dagenham. Loc,
Havering LB. P Essex. Hornchurch BC. To
S, Rnhm Marshes, reservoirs, and R Thames.
To W beside Ingrebourne River, Rnhm Hall
(NT), early Ggn hse.

RAINHILL Lancs
100 SJ 4991 3m SSW of St Helens.
CP, 7,913. Whiston RD. P Prescot.
Ch e, c, m, r, v. Sch ie, je, p2. Widnes CC.
See also Rnhll Stoops.

RAINHILL STOOPS Lancs
100 SJ 5090 3m SSW of St Helens. Loc,
Rnhll CP.

RAINOW Ches
101 SJ 9475 2m NE of Macclesfield.
CP, 1,005. Mcclsfld RD. P Mcclsfld.
Ch e, m2. Sch pe, pm. Mcclsfld CC.

RAINTON Yorks (N)
91 SE 3775 4m NE of Ripon. CP(Rntn
w Newby), 436. Wath RD. P Thirsk. Ch m.
Thsk and Malton CC.

RAINWORTH Notts
112 SK 5958 4m ESE of Mansfield. Loc,
Southwell RD. P Mnsfld. Ch e, m, r.
Sch i, p, s. Newark CC.

RAISBECK Westm
83 NY 6407 8m SSW of Appleby. Loc,
Orton CP.

RAITHBY Lincs (L)
105 TF 3184 2m SSW of Louth. CP(Rthby
cum Maltby), 85. Lth RD. Ch e. Lth CC.

RAITHBY Lincs (L)
114 TF 3767 7m ESE of Horncastle.
CP, 109. Spilsby RD. P Splsby. Ch e, m.
Hncstle CC.

RAKE Hants and Sussex (W)
181 SU 8027 5m NE of Petersfield. Loc,
Ptrsfld RD, Midhurst RD. P Liss, Hants.
Sch pe. Ptrsfld CC, Chichester CC
(Horsham).

RAME Cornwall
187 SX 4249 4m S of Torpoint. CP(Maker-
w-Rame), 1,441. St Germans RD. Ch e.
Bodmin CC. 1m SW, Rme Head, with ruined
mdvl chpl; views.

RAME Cornwall
190 SW 7233 5m W of Falmouth. Loc,
Wendron CP. P(Rme Cross), Penryn.

RAM LANE Kent
172, 184 TQ 9646 2m SSE of Charing. Loc,
Westwell CP.

RAMPISHAM Dorset
177, 178 ST 5602 8m NE of Bridport.
CP, 151. Beaminster RD. P Dorchester.
Ch e. W Dst CC.

RAMPSIDE Lancs
88 SD 2466 3m SE of Barrow. Loc,
Brrw-in-Furness CB. P Brrw-in-Fnss.

RAMPTON Cambs
135 TL 4268 6m NNW of Cambridge.
CP, 256. Chesterton RD. P CMBRDGE.
Ch e, bv. Cambs CC.

RAMPTON Notts
104 SK 7978 6m ESE of Retford.
CP, 1,875. E Rtfd RD. P Rtfd. Ch e, m.
Sch p. Bassetlaw CC. See also Woodbeck.

RAMSBOTTOM Lancs
95, 101 SD 7916 4m N of Bury.
UD, 15,872. P Bury. Rossendale BC. See
also Chatterton, Edenfield, Holcombe,
Stubbins, Summerseat. Textiles.

RAMSBURY Wilts
157 SU 2771 5m WNW of Hungerford.
CP, 1,468. Marlborough and Rmsbry RD.
P Mlbrgh. Ch e, m. Sch p. Devizes CC. See
also Axford, Whittonditch. 14c—15c ch:
partly Saxon foundations, Saxon carved
stones, 17c—18c monmts. Trout-fishing in
R Kennet.

RAMSDEAN Hants
181 SU 7022 3m WSW of Petersfield. Loc,
Langrish CP.

RAMSDELL Hants
168 SU 5857 4m NW of Basingstoke. Loc,
Wootton St Lawrence CP. P Bsngstke.
Sch p.

RAMSDEN Oxon
145 SP 3515 3m N of Witney. CP, 351.
Wtny RD. P OXFORD. Ch e. Sch pe.
Mid-Oxon CC (Banbury).

RAMSDEN BELLHOUSE Essex
161, 162 TQ 7294 3m E of Billericay. Loc,
Basildon UD. P Bllrcy.

RAMSDEN HEATH Essex
161, 162 TQ 7195 3m ENE of Billericay.
Loc, S Hanningfield CP. P Bllrcy. Ch c.

RAMSEY Essex
150 TM 2130 3m WSW of Harwich.
CP, 2,276. Tendring RD. P Hrwch. Ch e, m.
Sch p. Hrwch CC. See also Parkeston.
Post-mill.

RAMSEY Hunts
134 TL 2885 9m NNE of Huntingdon.
UD, 5,646. P HNTNGDN. Hunts CC. See
also Forty Feet Br, Rmsy St Mary's. 15c
abbey gatehouse (NT)*.

RAMSEY ISLAND Essex
162 TL 9505 6m E of Maldon. Loc,
St Lawrence CP.

RAMSEY ST MARY'S Hunts
134 TL 2588 3m NW of Ramsey. Loc,
Rmsy UD. P HUNTINGDON.

RAMSGATE Kent
173 TR 3864 15m ENE of Canterbury.
MB, 39,482. P. Thanet E BC(Isle of
Thnt CC). See also Manston. Orig a Cinque
port, now resort; large harbour, many schs.
Airpt at Mnstn. SE, Pegwell Bay,
traditionally landing place of Saxon
conquerors Hengist and Horsa AD 449 and
St Augustine AD 597. Now hovercraft
terminal.

RAMSGATE STREET Norfolk
125 TG 0933 4m SSE of Holt. Loc,
Edgefield CP.

RAMSGILL Yorks (W)
91 SE 1171 4m NW of Pateley Br. Loc,
Stonebeck Down CP. Ripon and
Ptly Br RD. Ch e. Rpn CC.

RAMSHOLT Suffolk (E)
150 TM 3041 5m SSE of Woodbridge.
CP, 53. Deben RD. Ch e. Sudbury and
Wdbrdge CC. On Deben estuary.

RAMSHORN Staffs
111 SK 0845 5m ENE of Cheadle. CP, 65.
Uttoxeter RD. Burton CC.

RANBY Lincs (L)
105 TF 2378 6m NNW of Horncastle.
CP, 56. Hncstle RD. Ch e. Hncstle CC.

RANBY Notts
103 SK 6581 3m W of Retford. Loc,
Babworth CP. P Rtfd. Sch pe.

RAND Lincs (L)
104 TF 1078 6m S of Mkt Rasen. CP, 46.
Welton RD. Ch e. Gainsborough CC.

RANDWICK Glos
156 SO 8206 2m NW of Stroud. CP, 836.
Strd RD. P Strd. Ch e, m. Sch pe. Strd CC.

RANGEMORE Staffs
120 SK 1822 4m W of Burton-on-Trent.
Loc, Tatenhill CP. P Btn-on-Trnt. Ch e.
Sch pe.

RANGEWORTHY Glos
156 ST 6886 8m ESE of Severn Rd Br.
CP 299. Thornbury RD. P BRISTOL.
Ch e, m. Sch pe. S Glos CC.

RANMORE COMMON Surrey
170 TQ 1450 2m NW of Dorking. Loc,
Wotton CP. P Dkng. Ch e. Sch pe.

RANN Lancs
95 SD 7124 3m SE of Blackburn. Loc,
Blckbn RD, Oswaldtwistle UD. Darwen CC,
Accrington BC.

RANSKILL Notts
103 SK 6587 5m NNW of Retford. CP, 552.
E Rtfd RD. P Rtfd. Ch e, m. Sch p.
Bassetlaw CC.

RANTON Staffs
119 SJ 8524 4m W of Stafford. CP, 239.
Stffd RD. P STFFD. Ch e. Sch pe. Stffd and
Stone CC. See also Long Compton.

RANWORTH Norfolk
126 TG 3514 4m ESE of Wroxham. Loc,
Woodbastwick CP. P NORWICH, NOR 55Z.
Ch e. By Rnwth Broad. Outstanding mdvl
ch.

RASKELF Yorks (N)
91 SE 4971 7m ENE of Boroughbridge.
CP, 335. Easingwold RD. P YORK. Ch e, m.
Sch pe. Thirsk and Malton CC. Curious
pyramidal wooden ch twr.

RASTRICK Yorks (W)
96, 102 SE 1321 3m N of Huddersfield.
Loc, Brighouse MB. P Brghse.

RATBY Leics
121 SK 5105 5m WNW of Leicester.
CP, 2,182. Mkt Bosworth RD. P LCSTR.
Ch e, m. Sch p. Bswth CC. To W, Bury
Camp, Roman earthwork.

RATCLIFFE CULEY Leics
132 SP 3299 2m NE of Atherstone. Loc,
Witherley CP. P Athrstne, Warwickshire.
Ch e.

RATCLIFFE ON SOAR Notts
121 SK 4928 3m S of Long Eaton. CP, 82.
Basford RD. Ch e. Rushcliffe CC. Ch:
alabaster monmts to the Sacheverells.

RATCLIFFE ON THE WREAKE Leics
121, 122 SK 6314 7m NNE of Leicester.
CP, 155. Barrow upon Soar RD. P LCSTR.
Ch e. Melton CC. RC college by Pugin,
1844.

RATHMELL Yorks (W)
95 SD 8059 3m SSW of Settle. CP, 196.
Sttle RD. P Sttle. Ch e, m. Sch pe.
Skipton CC.

RATLEY Hants
168 SU 3223 2m WNW of Romsey. Loc,
Sherfield English CP.

RATLEY Warwicks
145 SP 3847 6m NW of Banbury. CP(Rtly
and Upton), 369. Southam RD. P Bnbry,
Oxon. Ch e, m. Sch pe.
Stratford-on-Avon CC (Strtfd).

RATLINGHOPE Shrops
129 SO 4096 4m NW of Ch Stretton.
CP, 136. Clun and Bishop's Cstle RD.
P Shrewsbury. Ch e. Ludlow CC. In the
valley of Darnford Brook, tributary of the
E Onny, among bracken-covered hills.

RATTERY Devon
187, 188 SX 7461 3m S of Buckfastleigh.
CP, 371. Totnes RD. P: S Brent. Ch e, r.
Ttns CC.

RATTLESDEN Suffolk (W)
136 TL 9758 4m W of Stowmarket.
CP, 739. Thedwastre RD.
P Bury St Edmunds. Ch e, b. Sch pe.
Bury St Eds CC. See also Poystreet Grn.

RAUGHTON HEAD Cumb
83 NY 3745 7m SSW of Carlisle. Loc,
Dalston CP. Ch e. Sch pe. 1m NW,
Rose Cstle, residence of the Bishops of Clsle
since 13c.

RAUNDS Northants
134 SP 9972 4m NNE of Rushden.
UD, 5,945. P Wellingborough.
Wllngbrgh CC. See also Stanwick. Footwear
mnfg. Ch has 15c wall-paintings.

RAVELEY, GREAT Hunts
134 TL 2581 3m SW of Ramsey. Loc,
Upwood and the Raveleys CP.

RAVENFIELD Yorks (W)
103 SK 4895 4m ENE of Rotherham.
CP, 995. Rthrhm RD. P Rthrhm. Ch e.
Sch p. Rother Valley CC.

RAVENGLASS Cumb
88 SD 0896 4m SE of Seascale. Loc,
Muncaster CP. Millom RD. P.
Whitehaven CC. Former port; W terminus of
narrow gauge (15 in.) rly up Eskdale. Views
of Lakes fells to E.

RAVENINGHAM Norfolk
137 TM 3996 4m NNW of Beccles. CP, 236.
Loddon RD. Ch e. S Nflk CC.

RAVENSCAR Yorks (N)
93 NZ 9801 8m SE of Whitby. Loc,
Stainton Dale CP. P Scarborough. Ch e. On
some of the highest cliffs in Yorkshire.
Raven Hall Hotel on site of Roman signal
stn.

RAVENSDEN Beds
147 TL 0754 3m NNE of Bedford. CP.
Bdfd RD. P BDFD. Ch e, b. Sch pe.
Bdfd CC.

RAVENSMOOR Ches
110 SJ 6250 2m WSW of Nantwich. Loc,
Burland CP. Ch m.

RAVENSTHORPE Northants
132, 133 SP 6670 8m NW of Northampton.
CP, 315. Brixworth RD. P NTHMPTN.
Ch e, b. Daventry CC (Kettering). See also
Coton.

RAVENSTONE Bucks
146 SP 8450 3m W of Olney. CP, 185.
Newport Pagnell RD. P Olney. Ch e.
Buckingham CC.

RAVENSTONE Leics
121 SK 4013 1m W of Coalville.
CP(Rvnstne w Snibstone), 1,393. Ashby de
la Zouch RD. P Clvlle, LEICESTER.
Ch e, m. Sch p. Loughborough CC. 18c–19c
almshouses.

RAVENSTONEDALE Westm
90 NY 7204 4m SW of Kirkby Stephen.
CP, 590. N Westm RD. P Kby Stphn.
Ch e, c, m2. Sch pe. Westm CC. See also
Newbiggin on Lune.

RAVENSWORTH Yorks (N)
85 NZ 1407 5m NNW of Richmond.
CP, 185. Rchmnd RD. P Rchmnd. Ch m.
Sch pe. Rchmnd CC.

RAW Yorks (N)
93 NZ 9305 4m SE of Whitby. Loc,

Fylingdales CP. Whtby RD. Cleveland and
Whtby CC (Scarborough and Whtby).

RAWCLIFFE Yorks (N)
97 SE 5855 2m NNW of York. CP, 2,722.
Flaxton RD. Sch i. Thirsk and Malton CC.

RAWCLIFFE Yorks (W)
97, 98 SE 6822 4m W of Goole. CP, 2,324.
Gle RD. P Gle. Ch e, m, v. Sch p. Gle CC.
See also Rclffe Br.

RAWCLIFFE BRIDGE Yorks (W)
97, 98 SE 6921 3m WSW of Goole. Loc,
Rclffe CP. P Gle. Ch m. Sch p.

RAWDON Yorks (W)
96 SE 2039 5m NNE of Bradford. Loc,
Aireborough UD. P LEEDS. Pudsey BC.

RAWMARSH Yorks (W)
103 SK 4396 2m N of Rotherham.
UD, 19,884. P Rthrhm. Rother Valley CC.

RAWNSLEY Staffs
120 SK 0212 3m ENE of Cannock. Loc,
Cnnck UD. P Cnnck. Cnnck CC.

RAWRETH Essex
162 TQ 7893 5m NE of Basildon. Loc,
Rayleigh UD.

RAWTENSTALL Lancs
95 SD 8122 6m SSW of Burnley.
MB, 21,404. P Rossendale. Rssndle BC. See
also Crawshaw Booth, Love Clough, Water,
Waterfoot. Textiles, footwear. Declining
pop.

RAYDON Suffolk (E)
149 TM 0538 3m SSE of Hadleigh. CP, 382.
Samford RD. P Ipswich. Ch e, s. Sch p.
Sudbury and Woodbridge CC.

RAYLEIGH Essex
162 TQ 8090 6m NW of Southend.
UD, 26,265. P. SE Essx CC. See also
Battlesbridge, Rawreth. R. Mt (NT)*, rems
of early Nmn cstle.

RAYMOND'S HILL Devon
177 SY 3296 2m SE of Axminster. Loc,
Axmnstr CP. P Axmnstr.

RAYNE Essex
148, 149, 162 TL 7222 2m W of Braintree.
CP, 760. Brntree RD. P Brntree. Ch e, c.
Sch p. Brntree CC(Maldon).

RAYNES PARK London
170 TQ 2369 4m E of Kingston. Loc,
Merton LB. Wimbledon BC (Mtn and
Morden). Sports grnds.

REACH Cambs
135 TL 5666 5m WNW of Newmarket.
CP, 269. Nmkt RD. P CAMBRIDGE.
Ch e, v. Cambs CC.

READ Lancs
95 SD 7634 5m WNW of Burnley. CP, 869.
Bnly RD. P Bnly. Ch e, c. Sch pc, pe.
Clitheroe CC.

READING Berks
159, 169 SU 7173 36m W of London. CB,
132,023. P. Rdng N BC, Rdng S CC.
(Rdng BC). See also Caversham, Whitley.
Indstrl tn and important rly centre. University. Rems of Nmn abbey. Oscar Wilde
wrote *De Profundis* in R. gaol, 1897.

READING STREET Kent
184 TQ 9230 3m SE of Tenterden. Loc,
Tntdn MB.

REAGILL Westm
83 NY 6017 5m WSW of Appleby. Loc,
Crosby Ravensworth CP.

REARSBY Leics
121, 122 SK 6514 7m WSW of Melton
Mowbray. CP, 677. Barrow upon Soar RD.
P LEICESTER. Ch e, m. Sch pe. Mltn CC.
Mdvl packhorse br.

RECULVER Kent
173 TR 2269 3m E of Herne Bay. Loc, Hne
Bay UD. Roman fort of Saxon shore (A.M.)
surrounded by caravan sites.

REDBOURN Herts
147, 160 TL 1012 2m SW of Harpenden.
CP, 3,835. St Albans RD. P St Albns.
Ch e, b, m, r, v. Sch s. St Albns CC (Hemel
Hempstead). Partly Nmn ch and several old
hses. 1m SW, Iron Age fort, The Aubreys.

REDBOURNE Lincs (L)
104 SK 9799 5m SSW of Brigg. CP, 348.
Glanford Brgg RD. P Gainsborough. Ch e.
Sch p. Brgg and Scunthorpe CC (Brgg).

REDBROOK Glos
142/155, 156 SO 5310 2m SE of
Monmouth. Loc, Newland CP. P MNMTH.
Ch e, m. Sch pe. On the wooded banks of
the R Wye.

REDBROOK STREET Kent
172, 184 TQ 9336 3m ENE of Tenterden.
Loc, Woodchurch CP.

REDCAR Yorks (N)
86 NZ 6025 8m ENE of Teesside
(Middlesbrough). Loc, Tssde CB. P(RDCR,
Tssde). Tssde, Rdcr BC. Steel-mnfg plant.
Resort with extensive firm sands.
Racecourse. At The Lakes, interesting
modern housing development.

REDCLIFF BAY Som
155 ST 4475 9m WNW of Bristol. Loc,
N Weston CP. Long Ashton RD.
P Portishead, BRSTL. N Som CC.

RED DIAL Cumb
82 NY 2546 2m S of Wigton. Loc,
Westward CP.

REDDITCH Worcs
131 SP 0467 12m S of Birmingham.
UD, 40,775. P. Bromsgrove and Rddtch CC
(Brmsgrve). See also Astwood Bank,
Bradley, Crabbs Cross, Feckenham, Ham
Grn, Headless Cross, Hunt End, Webheath.
Manfg tn, largely 19c but with modern
development. Needles made here.

REDE Suffolk (W)
149 TL 8055 7m NNE of Clare. CP, 136.
Thingoe RD. Ch e, b. Bury St Edmunds CC.

REDENHALL Norfolk
137 TM 2684 6m SW of Bungay. CP(Rdnhll
w Harleston), 1,809. Depwade RD. Ch e.
Sch je, s. S Nflk CC.

REDESMOUTH Nthmb
77 NY 8682 2m ESE of Bellingham. Loc,
Bllnghm RD. Hexham CC. Where R Rede
runs into the N Tyne.

REDGRAVE Suffolk (E)
136 TM 0478 5m WSW of Diss. CP, 449.
Hartismere RD. P Dss, Norfolk. Ch e.
Sch pe. Eye CC. R. Hall demolished;
Capability Brown's large lake survives in pk.
At br to N, sources of rivers Lit Ouse
(flows W) and Waveney (E).

REDHILL Som
165 ST 4963 8m SW of Bristol. Loc,
Wrington CP. P BRSTL. Ch e. Sch pe. Brstl
Airpt to N.

REDHILL Surrey
170 TQ 2850 2m E of Reigate. Loc,
Rgte MB. P. Rsdntl tn at foot of N Downs;
growth due to rly.

REDISHAM Suffolk (E)
137 TM 4084 4m SSW of Beccles. CP, 130.
Wainford RD. Ch e. Lowestoft CC.

REDLINGFIELD Suffolk (E)
137 TM 1871 3m SE of Eye. CP, 100.
Hartismere RD. Ch e. Eye CC.

REDLYNCH Som
166 ST 7033 2m SE of Bruton. Loc,
Brtn CP. Ch e.

REDLYNCH Wilts
167 SU 2021 7m SSE of Salisbury.
CP, 2,148. Slsbry and Wilton RD. P Slsbry.
Ch e2, m. Sch pe. Slsbry CC. See also
Hamptworth, Lover, Morgan's Vale,
Nomansland, Woodfalls.

REDMARLEY D'ABITOT Glos
143 SO 7531 5m SSE of Ledbury. CP, 739.
Newent RD. P(Rdmly), GLOUCESTER.
Ch e, m. Sch pe. W Glos CC. See also
Playley Grn. Half-timbered hses.

REDMARSHALL Co Durham
85 NZ 3821 4m WNW of Teesside
(Stockton). CP. Stcktn RD. Ch e. Sch pe.
Easington CC (Sedgefield). Ch Nmn to Perp.

REDMILE Leics
112, 122 SK 7935 7m W of Grantham.
CP, 656. Melton and Belvoir RD.
P NOTTINGHAM. Ch e, m. Sch pe.
Mltn CC. See also Barkestone, Plungar.

REDMIRE Yorks (N)
90 SE 0491 4m W of Leyburn. CP, 208.
Lbn RD. P Lbn. Ch e, m. Sch pe.
Richmond CC.

RED ROCK Lancs
100 SD 5809 3m N of Wigan. Loc,
Haigh CP. Sch pe.

RED ROW Nthmb
71 NZ 2599 3m SSW of Amble. Loc,
E Chevington CP. P Morpeth. Ch m, v.
Sch p.

REDRUTH Cornwall
189 SW 6942 8m WSW of Truro.
UD(Camborne-Rdrth), 42,029. P. Falmouth

and Cmbne CC. Former centre of mining
industry.

RED STREET Staffs
110 SJ 8251 5m NW of Stoke-on-Trent.
Loc, Newcastle-under-Lyme MB. P Ncstle.

REDWICK Glos
155, 156 ST 5486 9m N of Bristol. Loc,
Pilning and Severn Beach CP. Sch pe.

REDWORTH Co Durham
85 NZ 2423 4m SSE of Bishop Auckland.
Loc, Heighington CP.

REED Herts
148 TL 3636 3m S of Royston. CP, 217.
Hitchin RD. P Rstn. Ch e, v. Sch p.
Htch CC.

REEDHAM Norfolk
126/137 TG 4201 8m WSW of Yarmouth.
CP, 908. Blofield and Flegg RD.
P NORWICH, NOR 69Z. Ch e, m. Sch p.
Ymth CC.

REEDNESS Yorks (W)
97, 98 SE 7923 3m E of Goole. CP, 381.
Gle RD. P Gle. Ch m. Sch p. Gle CC.

REEPHAM Lincs (L)
113 TF 0373 4m ENE of Lincoln. CP, 704.
Welton RD. P LNCLN. Ch e, m. Sch pe.
Gainsborough CC.

REEPHAM Norfolk
125 TG 1022 6m WSW of Aylsham.
CP, 1,276. St Faith's and Aylshm RD.
P NORWICH, NOR 69X. Ch e2. Sch p, s.
N Nflk CC (Central Nflk). Two chs and
ruins of a third in one churchyard.

REETH Yorks (N)
90 SE 0399 8m W of Richmond. CP(Rth,
Fremington and Healaugh), 540. Rth RD.
P Rchmnd. Ch c, m. Sch p. Rchmnd CC.
Stone vllge round large grn. Rems of lead
mines on hills.

REIGATE Surrey
170 TQ 2550 10m SSW of Croydon.
MB, 56,088. P. Rgte BC (CC). See also
Gatton, Merstham, Redhill. Rsdntl tn and
shopping centre below N Downs. Early 18c
mkt hse.

REIGHTON Yorks (E)
93 TA 1375 3m SSE of Filey. CP, 503.

Bridlington RD. P Filey. Ch e, m. Sch p. Brdlngtn CC. See also Speeton.

REJERRAH Cornwall
185 SW 8055 4m S of Newquay. Loc, Newlyn CP. Truro RD. Ch m.

RELUBBUS Cornwall
189 SW 5631 6m WNW of Helston. Loc, St Hilary CP. P Penzance. Ch m.

REMENHAM Berks
159 SU 7784 1m NNE of Henley. CP, 596. Wokingham RD. Ch e. Wknghm CC. See also Aston.

REMENHAM HILL Berks
159 SU 7882 1m E of Henley. Loc, Rnmhm CP. P Hnly-on-Thames, Oxon.

REMPSTONE Notts
121, 122 SK 5724 4m NE of Loughborough. CP, 254. Basford RD. P Lghbrgh, Leics. Ch e. Sch p. Rushcliffe CC.

RENDCOMB Glos
157 SP 0109 5m N of Cirencester. CP, 214. Crncstr RD. P Crncstr. Ch e. Crncstr and Tewkesbury CC.

RENDHAM Suffolk (E)
137 TM 3464 2m WNW of Saxmundham. CP, 338. Blyth RD. P Sxmndhm. Ch e, v. Sch p. Eye CC.

RENDLESHAM Suffolk (E)
150 TM 3253 4m NE of Woodbridge. CP, 1,337. Deben RD. Ch e, v. Eye CC. Two fantastic 19c gatehouses of old R. Hse still stand.

RENHOLD Beds
147 TL 0852 3m NE of Bedford. CP. Bdfd RD. P BDFD. Ch e, bc. Sch pe. Mid-Beds CC. See also Salph End.

RENISHAW Derbys
103 SK 4477 8m E of Sheffield. Loc, Eckington CP. P SHFFLD. Ch e, m. Sch p. R. Hall, 17c and later, seat of Sitwells.

RENNINGTON Nthmb
71 NU 2118 4m NNE of Alnwick. CP, 382. Alnwck RD. P Alnwck. Ch e. Sch pe. Berwick-upon-Tweed CC. See also Rock, Stamford.

RENWICK Cumb
83 NY 5943 8m WSW of Alston. Loc, Kirkoswald CP. P Penrith. Ch e, m. Sch p.

REPPS Norfolk
126 TG 4117 8m E of Wroxham. CP(Rpps v Bastwick), 347. Blofield and Flegg RD. P Gt Yarmouth. Ch e, m. Sch p. Ymth CC.

REPTON Derbys
120, 121 SK 3026 5m NE of Burton-on-Trent. CP, 1,850. Rptn RD. P DERBY. Ch e, c. Sch p. Belper CC. See also Milton. Ch: Saxon crypt. Public sch incorporates rems of former priory.

RETFORD Notts
103 SK 7081 18m WNW of Lincoln. See E Rtfd.

RETIRE Cornwall
185, 186 SX 0064 4m WSW of Bodmin. Loc, Withiel CP. Ch m.

RETTENDON Essex
162 TQ 7698 7m SSE of Chelmsford. CP, 1,406. Chlmsfd RD. P(Rttndn Cmmn), Chlmsfd. Ch e. Sch p. Chlmsfd CC.

REVESBY Lincs (L)
114 TF 2961 6m SSE of Horncastle. CP, 305. Hncstle RD. P Boston. Ch e. Sch pe. Hncstle CC. Estate vllge blt round grn. R. Abbey was home of Sir Joseph Banks, naturalist who accompanied Captain Cook to S Pacific.

REWE Devon
176 SX 9499 5m NNE of Exeter. CP, 320. St Thomas RD. Ch e. Tiverton CC. See also Up Exe.

REXON Devon
175 SX 4188 6m ENE of Launceston. Loc, Broadwoodwidger CP. Ch m.

REYDON Suffolk (E)
137 TM 4978 1m NW of Southwold. CP, 1,527. Lothingland RD. P Sthwld. Ch e. Sch i, s. Lowestoft CC. See also Blackwater, Mt Pleasant.

REYMERSTON Norfolk
125 TG 0206 5m SSE of E Dereham. Loc, Garvestone CP. P NORWICH, NOR 28X. Ch e.

REZARE Cornwall
186 SX 3677 5m SSE of Launceston. Loc,
Lezant CP. P Lncstn.

RHODES Lancs
101 SD 8505 5m N of Manchester. Loc,
Middleton MB. P Mddltn, MNCHSTR.

RHODES MINNIS Kent
173 TR 1543 5m N of Hythe. Loc,
Elham RD. Ch m. Folkestone and Hthe CC.

RHYDD Worcs
143 SO 8345 4m E of Malvern. Loc, Upton
upon Severn RD. S Worcs CC.

RIBBESFORD Worcs
130 SO 7874 just S of Bewdley. CP, 183.
Kidderminster RD. Ch e. Kddrmnstr CC.

RIBBY Lancs
94 SD 4031 7m ESE of Blackpool.
CP(Rbby-w-Wrea), 949. Fylde RD. Ch e.
Sch pe. S Flde CC. See also Wrea Grn.

RIBCHESTER Lancs
94, 95 SD 6535 5m NNW of Blackburn.
CP, 1,356. Preston RD. P Prstn. Ch e, r, v.
Sch pe, pr. Clitheroe CC. See also
Knowle Grn. Former Roman stn on
R Ribble. Rems of fort (NT)*. Early 18c
inn in vllge centre. 1m E, Rbchstr Br, 18c.

RIBY Lincs (L)
105 TA 1807 5m W of Grimsby. CP, 193.
Caistor RD. P Grmsby. Ch e.
Gainsborough CC.

RICCALL Yorks (E)
97, 98 SE 6237 3m N of Selby. CP, 783.
Derwent RD. P YORK. Ch e, m. Sch p.
Howden CC.

RICHARD'S CASTLE Herefs and Shrops
129 SO 4970 3m SSW of Ludlow.
CP(Herefs), 212, Leominster and
Wigmore RD; CP(Shrops), 347, Ldlw RD.
P Ldlw, Salop. Ch e, m. Sch p. Lmnstr CC,
Ldlw CC. See also Woofferton (Shrops). Ch
Nmn and later. Rems of Nmn cstle.

RICHMOND London
160, 170 TQ 1774 8m WSW of Charing
Cross. LB(Rchmnd upon Thames), 173,592.
P Surrey. BCs: Rchmnd, Twickenham. See
also Barnes, Ham, Hampton, Hmptn Wick,
Kew, Mortlake, Teddington, Twcknhm.

Thames-side borough; Rchmnd and
Twcknhm Brs. To S, Rchmnd Pk; To N,
Kew Gdns. White Lodge* in pk.

RICHMOND Yorks (N)
91 NZ 1701 11m SW of Darlington.
MB, 7,245. P. Rchmnd CC. Blt on steep
hillside overlooking R Swale. Many mdvl
bldngs. Large mkt square. Rems of huge
cstle (A.M.) and twr of Franciscan monastic
chpl (Greyfriars). Ggn theatre*. Green
Howards Museum. Racecourse.

RICKFORD Som
165 ST 4859 4m NNE of Cheddar. Loc,
Blagdon CP.

RICKINGHALL INFERIOR Suffolk (W)
136 TM 0375 6m WSW of Diss. CP, 312.
Thedwastre RD. P Dss. Ch e.
Bury St Edmunds CC. Apparently all one
with R. Superior (and Botesdale), but
divided from them by administrative county
boundary.

RICKINGHALL SUPERIOR Suffolk (E)
136 TM 0475 5m WSW of Diss. CP, 369.
Hartismere RD. P Dss, Norfolk. Ch e.
Sch pe. Eye CC.

RICKLING Essex
148 TL 4931 5m SSW of Saffron Walden.
CP(Quendon and Rcklng), 508. Sffn
Wldn RD. Ch e. Sch pe. Sffrn Wldn CC.

RICKMANSWORTH Herts
160 TQ 0594 3m WSW of Watford.
UD, 29,510. P. SW Herts CC. See also
Croxley Grn, Eastbury, Heronsgate, Maple
Cross, W Hyde. Rsdntl tn. Moor Park GC
to SE has 18c Palladian mansion* for
clubhouse.

RIDDLECOMBE Devon
163,175 SS 6114 8m ESE of Torrington.
Loc, Ashreigney CP. P Chulmleigh.

RIDDLESDEN Yorks (W)
96 SE 0742 1m NE of Keighley. Loc,
Kghly MB. P Kghly. E Rddlsdn Hall (NT)*,
stone 17c hse with wheel windows.

RIDGE Dorset
179 SY 9386 1m SE of Wareham. Loc,
Arne CP.

RIDGE Herts
160 TL 2100 3m W of Potters Bar. CP, 270.
Elstree RD. Ch e. S Herts CC (Barnet). 15c
ch N of grn.

RIDGEHILL Som
165, 166 ST 5362 7m SSW of Bristol. Loc,
Winford CP.

RIDGE LANE Warwicks
132 SP 2995 2m SSW of Atherstone. Loc,
Mancetter CP. P Nuneaton.

RIDGEWAY Derbys
103 SK 4081 5m SE of Sheffield. Loc,
Eckington CP. P SHFFLD. Ch e, m. Sch p.

RIDGEWAY CROSS Herefs
143 SO 7247 4m WNW of Malvern. Loc,
Cradley CP. P Mlvn, Worcs.

RIDGEWELL Essex
148, 149 TL 7340 5m SE of Haverhill.
CP, 378. Halstead RD. P Hlstd. Ch e, v.
Sch pe. Saffron Walden CC.

RIDGEWOOD Sussex (E)
183 TQ 4719 1m S of Uckfield. Loc,
Uckfld CP. P Uckfld.

RIDGMONT Beds
147 SP 9736 4m WSW of Ampthill.
CP, 808. Ampthll RD. P BEDFORD.
Ch e, b. Sch p. Mid-Beds CC.

RIDING MILL Nthmb
77 NZ 0161 3m SE of Corbridge. Loc,
Broomhaugh and Rdng CP. P. Ch m.

RIDLEY Kent
171 TQ 6163 7m SSW of Gravesend. Loc,
Ash-cum-Rdly CP. Dartford RD. Ch e.
Sevenoaks CC (Dtfd).

RIDLINGTON Norfolk
126 TG 3430 4m E of N Walsham. Loc,
Witton CP. Ch e.

RIDLINGTON Rutland
122 SK 8402 2m NNW of Uppingham.
CP, 180. Uppnghm RD. P Uppnghm. Ch e.
Rtlnd and Stamford CC.

RIDSDALE Nthmb
77 NY 9084 5m E of Bellingham. Loc,
Corsenside CP. Bllnghm RD. P Hexham.
Hxhm CC.

RIEVAULX Yorks (N)
86, 92 SE 5785 3m WNW of Helmsley.
CP, 140. Hlmsly RD. Ch e, m. Thirsk and
Malton CC. Rems of 12c—13c Cistercian
abbey (A.M.); just SE, R. Terrace*,
landscaped grnds with classical temples, part
of Duncombe Pk (see Hlmsly).

RILEY GREEN Lancs
94, 95 SD 6225 4m WSW of Blackburn.
Loc, Hoghton CP.

RILLA MILL Cornwall
186 SX 2973 5m NW of Callington. Loc,
Linkinhorne CP. P Cllngtn. Ch m.

RILLINGTON Yorks (E)
92 SE 8574 5m ENE of Malton. CP, 725.
Norton RD. Mltn. Ch m 2. Sch p.
Howden CC.

RIMINGTON Yorks (W)
95 SD 8145 5m ENE of Clitheroe. CP, 310.
Bowland RD. P Clthroe, Lancs. Ch v.
Skipton CC.

RIMPTON Som
166 ST 6021 4m NNW of Sherborne.
CP, 192. Yeovil RD. P Yvl. Ch e. Yvl CC.

RIMSWELL Yorks (E)
99 TA 3128 2m WNW of Withernsea.
CP, 216. Holderness RD. Ch e.
Bridlington CC. See also Waxholme.

RINGLAND Norfolk
125 TG 1314 7m NW of Norwich. CP, 156.
St Faith's and Aylsham RD.
P NRWCH, NOR 56X. Ch e. N Nflk CC
(Central Nflk).

RINGMER Sussex (E)
183 TQ 4512 3m ENE of Lewes. CP, 2,208.
Chailey RD. P Lws. Ch e. Sch p, s. Lws CC.

RINGMORE Devon
176, 188 SX 9272 4m E of Newton Abbot.
Loc, Teignmouth UD.

RINGMORE Devon
187, 188 SX 6545 6m S of Ivybridge.
CP, 201. Kingsbridge RD. P Kngsbrdge.
Ch e. Totnes CC.

RING'S END Cambs
123 TF 3903 6m SW of Wisbech. Loc,
Wsbch RD. Ch m. Isle of Ely CC.

RINGSFIELD Suffolk (E)
137 TM 4088 2m SW of Beccles. CP, 259.
Wainford RD. Ch e. Sch pe. Lowestoft CC.
See also Rngsfld Corner.

RINGSFIELD CORNER Suffolk (E)
137 TN 4087 2m SSW of Beccles. Loc,
Rngsfld CP. P(Rngsfld Common), Bccls.

RINGSHALL Herts
147, 159, 160 SP 9814 4m N of
Berkhamsted. Loc, Lit Gaddesden CP.

RINGSHALL Suffolk (E)
149 TM 0452 4m S of Stowmarket.
CP, 1,425. Gipping RD. P Stmkt. Ch e, v.
Sch p. Eye CC. See also Charles Tye,
Rngshll Stocks. Aircraft noise.

RINGSHALL STOCKS Suffolk (E)
149 TM 0551 4m S of Stowmarket. Loc,
Rngshll CP.

RINGSTEAD Norfolk
124 TF 7040 2m E of Hunstanton. CP, 447.
Docking RD. P King's Lynn. Ch e, m.
Sch pe. NW Nflk CC (K's Lnn).

RINGSTEAD Northants
134 SP 9875 2m S of Thrapston. CP, 907.
Oundle and Thrpstn RD. P Kettering.
Ch e, b, m. Sch pe. Wellingborough CC
(Peterborough).

RINGWAY Ches
101 SJ 8184 3m NW of Wilmslow. CP, 239.
Bucklow RD. Ch e. Knutsford CC.
Manchester Airpt.

RINGWOOD Hants
179 SU 1405 10m NNE of Bournemouth.
CP, 7,971. Rngwd and Fordingbridge RD. P.
Ch e, b, m2, r, s, v4. Sch ie, j, s. New
Forest CC. See also Kingston. Ch: brass
of 1400.

RINGWOULD Kent
173 TR 3548 3m SSW of Deal. CP, 1,154.
Dover RD. P Dl. Ch e. Sch pe. Dvr and
Dl CC (Dvr). See also Kingsdown.

RINSEY Cornwall
189 SW 5927 4m W of Helston. Loc,
Breage CP.

RIPE Sussex (E)
183 TQ 5110 5m W of Hailsham. CP, 369.

Hlshm RD. P Lewes. Ch e. Lws CC
(Eastbourne).

RIPLEY Derbys
111/112 SK 3950 10m NNE of Derby.
UD, 17,825. P DBY. Ilkeston CC. See also
Ambergate, Heage, Lr Hartshay, Nether
Heage, Upr Hartshay. Coal-mining distr.

RIPLEY Hants
179 SZ 1698 4m N of Christchurch. Loc,
Sopley CP. Ch c.

RIPLEY Surrey
170 TQ 0556 3m ESE of Woking.
CP, 2,038. Guildford RD. P Wkng.
Ch e, b, m. Sch pe. Dorking CC. Handsome
vllge on Portsmouth rd (A3); some old hses
and inns.

RIPLEY Yorks (W)
91 SE 2860 4m NNW of Harrogate. CP, 171.
Nidderdale RD. P Hrrgte. Ch e. Sch pe.
Hrrgte CC. 18c estate vllge. R. Cstle*, rebuilt
16c—18c; gatehouse c 1450.

RIPLINGHAM Yorks (E)
98 SE 9631 7m SW of Beverley. Loc,
Rowley CP.

RIPON Yorks (W)
91 SE 3171 10m N of Harrogate.
MB, 10,987. P. Rpn CC. See also Bishopton,
Ure Bank. Cathedral. Many interesting old
bldngs. Curfew still rung, and sounded on
Wakeman's horn at 9 pm. Wakeman's Hse*,
13c, now museum. Racecourse.

RIPPINGALE Lincs (K)
123 TF 0927 5m N of Bourne. CP, 593.
S Kesteven RD. P Bne. Ch e, m. Sch pe.
Rutland and Stamford CC.

RIPPLE Kent
173 TR 3450 2m SW of Deal. CP, 265.
Eastry RD. P Dl. Ch e. Sch p. Dover and
Dl CC (Dvr).

RIPPLE Worcs
143 SO 8737 3m NNW of Tewkesbury.
CP, 616. Upton upon Severn RD. Ch e.
S Worcs CC. See also Naunton.

RIPPONDEN Yorks (W)
96, 102 SE 0319 5m SW of Halifax.
UD, 4,782. P Hlfx. Sowerby CC. See also
Barkisland, Rishworth.

RISBURY Herefs
129/142 SO 5455 4m SE of Leominster.
Loc, Humber CP. Lmnstr and Wigmore RD.
P Lmnstr. Ch m. Lmnstr CC.

RISBY Lincs (L)
104 SE 9314 4m NE of Scunthorpe.
CP(Roxby cum Rsby), 416. Glanford
Brigg RD. Ch e. Brgg and Scnthpe CC
(Brgg).

RISBY Suffolk (W)
136 TL 7966 4m WNW of Bury St Edmunds.
CP, 464. Thingoe RD. P Bury St Eds. Ch e.
Sch pe. Bury St Eds CC.

RISE Yorks (E)
99 TA 1542 5m SW of Hornsea. CP, 132.
Holderness RD. Ch e. Bridlington CC.

RISEGATE Lincs (H)
123 TF 2129 5m NNW of Spalding. Loc,
Gosberton CP. P(Gsbtn Rsgte), Spldng.
Ch m. Sch p.

RISELEY Beds
134 TL 0462 6m ESE of Rushden. CP, 554.
Bedford RD. P BDFD. Ch e, m, v. Sch pe, s.
Bdfd CC. Thatched and half-timbered hses.

RISELEY Berks
169 SU 7263 7m S of Reading. Loc,
Swallowfield CP. P Rdng. Sch pe.

RISHANGLES Suffolk (E)
137 TM 1668 3m SSE of Eye. CP, 94.
Hartismere RD. Ch e, b. Eye CC.

RISHTON Lancs
95 SD 7230 3m ENE of Blackburn.
UD, 6,010. P Blckbn. Accrington BC.

RISHWORTH Yorks (W)
96, 102 SE 0318 6m SW of Halifax. Loc,
Ripponden UD. P Hlfx.

RISINGHURST Oxon
158 SP 5607 3m E of Oxford. CP(Rsnghst
and Sandhills), 3,271. Bullingdon RD.
Mid-Oxon CC (Henley).

RISLEY Derbys
112, 121 SK 4635 4m S of Ilkeston.
CP, 767. SE Derbys RD. P DERBY. Ch e.
Sch je. SE Derbys CC. Early 18c Latin Hse
and schools.

RISSINGTON, GREAT Glos
144 SP 1917 5m NW of Burford. See Gt
Rssngtn.

RIVAR Wilts
168 SU 3161 5m SSW of Hungerford. Loc,
Shalbourne CP.

RIVENHALL END Essex
149, 162 TL 8316 2m NE of Witham. Loc,
Wthm UD. P Wthm.

RIVER BANK Cambs
135 TL 5368 8m WNW of Newmarket. Loc,
Swaffham Prior CP.

RIVERHEAD Kent
171 TQ 5156 1m NW of Sevenoaks.
CP, 1,762. Svnks RD. P Svnks. Ch e.
Svnks CC.

RIVINGTON Lancs
101 SD 6214 3m SE of Chorley. CP, 148.
Chly RD. P Horwich, Bolton. Ch e, v.
Sch pe. Chly CC. On E shore of the large
Rvngtn Reservoir (for Liverpool).

ROADE Northants
146 SP 7551 4m ENE of Towcester.
CP, 1,534. Northampton RD. P NTHMPTN.
Ch e, b, m, r. Sch p, s. Daventry CC
(S Nthnts).

ROADWATER Som
164 ST 0338 4m SW of Watchet. Loc,
Williton RD. P Wtcht. Ch m2.
Bridgwater CC.

ROA ISLAND Lancs
88 SD 2364 3m SE of Barrow. Loc,
Brrw-in-Furness CB.

ROBERTSBRIDGE Sussex (E)
183, 184 TQ 7323 5m N of Battle. Loc,
Salehurst CP. P. Ch b, c. Sch s.

ROBERTTOWN Yorks (W)
96, 102 SE 1922 3m W of Dewsbury. Loc,
Spenborough MB. P Liversedge. Brighouse
and Spnbrgh BC.

ROBIN HOOD Yorks (W)
96, 102 SE 3227 4m SSE of Leeds. Loc,
Rothwell UD. P Wakefield.

ROBIN HOOD'S BAY Yorks (N)
93 NZ 9505 5m SE of Whitby. Loc,
Fylingdales CP. Whtby RD. P Whtby.
Ch e2, c, m, r. Cleveland and Whtby CC
(Scarborough and Whtby). Fishing vllge blt

down side of cliffs, a maze of steep narrow streets. Coast erosion.

ROBOROUGH Devon
163 SS 5717 5m ESE of Torrington. CP, 208. Trrngtn RD. P Winkleigh. Ch e, m. W Dvn CC (Trrngtn). See also Villavin.

ROBOROUGH Devon
187 SX 5062 5m NNE of Plymouth. Loc, Bickleigh CP. P Plmth. Ch m. Gdns* of Bickham Hse.

ROBY Lancs
100 SJ 4391 6m E of Liverpool. UD(Huyton-w-Rby), 66,629. P Htn, LVPL. Htn CC.

ROBY MILL Lancs
100 SD 5107 4m WNW of Wigan. Loc, Skelmersdale and Holland UD. P Wgn.

ROCESTER Staffs
120 SK 1039 4m NNE of Uttoxeter. CP, 1,345. Uttxtr RD. P Uttxtr. Ch e, m. Sch p, s. Burton CC. Site of Roman tn at confluence of rivers Dove and Churnet.

ROCHDALE Lancs
101 SD 8913 10m NNE of Manchester. CB, 91,344. P. Rchdle BC. See also Firgrove, Smallbridge. Mainly textiles tn, but some recent diversification. Impressive tn hall.

ROCHE Cornwall
185 SW 9860 5m NNW of St Austell. CP, 1,701. St Astll RD. P St Astll. Ch e, m2. Truro CC. See also Belowda, Bilberry, Victoria. To S, a group of rocks; on tallest, ruined 14c chpl.

ROCHESTER Kent
171, 172 TQ 7468 27m ESE of London. MB, 55,460. P. Rchstr and Chthm BC. See also Strood. Ancient port, cathedral, and now commercial city on Medway estuary.

ROCHESTER Nthmb
70 NY 8398 5m NW of Otterburn. CP, 554. Bellingham RD. P NEWCASTLE UPOŃ TYNE. Ch v. Hexham CC. See also Byrness, Horsley. On main (A68) rd to Scottish border at Carter Bar in area of camps — prehistoric, Roman, and modern (Redesdale Camp).

ROCHFORD Essex
162 TQ 8790 3m N of Southend. CP, 7,806. Rchfd RD. P. Ch e, b, c, m, v. Sch j, p, s. Maldon CC (SE Essx). Sthnd airpt to S.

ROCK Cornwall
185 SW 9375 just E of Padstow across river. Loc, St Minver Lowlands CP. \ Wadebridge and Pdstw RD. P Wdbrdge. Ch m. N Cnwll CC.

ROCK Nthmb
71 NU 2020 5m NNE of Alnwick. Loc, Rennington CP. P Alnwck. Ch e. 16c–19c Hall, now a youth hostel.

ROCK Worcs
130 SO 7371 4m SW of Bewdley. CP, 1,948. Kidderminster RD. P Kddrmnstr. Ch e. Sch p. Kddrmnstr CC. See also Bliss Gate, Buckridge, Callow Hill, Far Forest, Lem Hill, Pound Bank.

ROCKBEARE Devon
176 SY 0195 6m ENE of Exeter. CP, 553. St Thomas RD. Ch e. Sch pe. Hntn CC. See also Marsh Grn.

ROCKBOURNE Hants
179 SU 1118 3m NW of Fordingbridge. CP, 384. Ringwood and Fdngbrdge RD. P Fdngbrdge. Ch e, b. Sch pe. New Forest CC. To S, large Roman vlla*.

ROCKCLIFFE Cumb
76 NY 3661 4m NW of Carlisle. CP, 747. Border RD. P Clsle. Ch e. Sch pe. Penrith and the Bdr CC. See also Harker, Todhills.

ROCKHAMPTON Glos
155, 156 ST 6593 6m ENE of Severn Rd Br. CP, 124. Thornbury RD. P Berkeley. Ch e. S Glos CC.

ROCKINGHAM Northants
133 SP 8691 3m NW of Corby. CP, 135. Kettering RD. P Mkt Harborough, Leics. Ch e. Kttrng CC. Vllge of stone and thatch climbs hill; dominated by R. Cstle*, Nmn with Elizn alterations.

ROCKLAND ALL SAINTS Norfolk
136 TL 9996 4m WNW of Attleborough. Loc, Rocklands CP. Wayland RD. P Attlbrgh. Ch e. Sch p. S Nflk CC.

ROCKLAND ST MARY Norfolk
126 TG 3104 6m ESE of Norwich. CP, 451. Forehoe and Henstead RD.

P NRWCH, NOR 08W. Ch e. Sch p.
S Nflk CC (Central Nflk).

ROCKLAND ST PETER Norfolk
136 TL 9997 4m WNW of Attleborough.
Loc, Rocklands CP. Wayland RD. Ch e, m.
S Nflk CC.

ROCKLEY Wilts
157 SU 1671 3m NW of Marlborough. Loc,
Ogbourne St Andrew CP. Ch e.

ROCKWELL END Bucks
159 SU 7988 4m WNW of Marlow. Loc,
Hambleden CP.

RODBOROUGH Glos
156 SO 8404 just S of Stroud. Loc,
Strd UD; CP, 1,485. Strd RD. P Strd.
Strd CC.

RODBOURNE Wilts
157 ST 9383 2m S of Malmesbury. Loc,
St Paul Mlmsbry Without CP. Mlmsbry RD.
Ch e. Sch pe. Chippenham CC. Ch has
William Morris E window.

RODD Herefs
129 SO 3262 1m SE of Presteigne. CP(Rdd,
Nash and Lit Brampton), 74. Kington RD.
Leominster CC.

RODDAM Nthmb
71 NU 0220 5m SSE of Wooler. CP, 116.
Glendale RD. Berwick-upon-Tweed CC. See
also Roseden, Wooperton.

RODDEN Dorset
178 SY 6184 5m NW of Weymouth. Loc,
Abbotsbury CP.

RODE Som
166 ST 8053 4m NNE of Frome. CP, 594.
Frme RD. P Bath. Ch e2, b, m. Sch pm.
Wells CC. Lake and tree-dotted pk* with
aviaries of tropical birds.

RODE HEATH Ches
110 SJ 8057 4m SE of Sandbach. Loc, Odd
R o d e C P . C o n g l e t o n R D .
P Stoke-on-Trent, Staffs. Ch m. Sch pe.
Knutsford CC.

RODEN Shrops
118 SJ 5716 6m ENE of Shrewsbury. Loc,
Ercall Magna CP. Wellington RD. P Telford.
The Wrekin CC.

RODHUISH Som
164 ST 0139 4m SW of Watchet. Loc,
Withycombe CP. Ch e.

RODINGTON Shrops
118 SJ 5814 4m WNW of Wellington.
CP, 553. Wllngtn RD. P Shrewsbury.
Ch e, m. Sch pe. The Wrekin CC. See also
Marsh Grn. Shrops Union Canal here passes
over R Roden.

RODLEY Glos
143 SO 7411 6m E of Cinderford. Loc,
Westbury-on-Severn CP.

RODMARTON Glos
157 ST 9497 5m NE of Tetbury. CP, 318.
Cirencester RD. P Crncstr. Ch e. Crncstr and
Tewkesbury CC. See also Tarlton.

RODMELL Sussex (E)
183 TQ 4106 3m S of Lewes. CP, 327.
Chailey RD. P Lws. Ch e. Sch pe. Lws CC.

RODMERSHAM Kent
172 TQ 9261 2m SE of Sittingbourne.
CP, 349. Swale RD. Ch e. Sch p.
Faversham CC. See also Rdmshm Grn.

RODMERSHAM GREEN Kent
172 TQ 9161 2m SSE of Sittingbourne.
Loc, Rdmshm CP. P Sttngbne.

RODNEY STOKE Som
165 ST 4850 3m SE of Cheddar. CP, 751.
Wells RD. P Chddr. Ch e, b. Wlls CC. See
also Draycott. Ch full of Rodney monmts.

RODSLEY Derbys
120 SK 2040 4m SSE of Ashbourne.
CP, 79. Ashbne RD. Ch m. W Derbys CC.

ROECLIFFE Yorks (W)
91 SE 3765 1m WSW of Boroughbridge.
CP, 227. Nidderdale RD. Ch e. Sch pe.
Harrogate CC.

ROEHAMPTON London
160, 170 TQ 2273 2m WSW of
Wandsworth. Loc, Wndswth LB. Putney BC.
Rsdntl distr at N edge of Wimbledon Cmmn.

ROFFEY Sussex (W)
182 TQ 1932 2m NE of Horsham. Loc,
Hshm UD, Hshm RD. P Hshm. Hshm and
Crawley CC (Hshm).

ROGATE Sussex (W)
181 SU 8023 4m E of Petersfield.
CP, 1,394. Midhurst RD. P Ptrsfld, Hants.
Ch e. Sch pe. Chichester CC (Horsham). See
also Hillbrow, Rake.

ROKER Co Durham
78 NZ 4059 N distr of Sunderland. Loc,
Sndrlnd CB. P Sndrlnd. Sndrlnd N BC.
Interesting early 20c ch (St Andrew). Sands.
Rkr Pk: Sndrlnd FC grnd.

ROLLESBY Norfolk
126 TG 4416 7m NW of Yarmouth.
CP, 533. Blofield and Flegg RD. P Gt Ymth.
Ch e, m. Sch p. Ymth CC.

ROLLESTON Leics
122 SK 7300 8m N of Mkt Harborough.
CP, 55. Billesdon RD. Ch e. Hbrgh CC
(Melton).

ROLLESTON Notts
112 SK 7452 4m W of Newark. CP, 173.
Southwell RD. P Nwk. Ch e. Nwk CC.

ROLLESTON Staffs
120 SK 2327 3m N of Burton-on-Trent.
CP, 2,162. Tutbury RD. P Btn-on-Trnt.
Ch e, m. Sch j, p, s. Btn CC.

ROLLRIGHT, GREAT Oxon
145 SP 3231 3m N of Chipping Norton. See
Gt Rllrght.

ROLSTON Yorks (E)
99 TA 2145 2m SSE of Hornsea. Loc,
Mappleton CP.

ROLVENDEN Kent
184 TQ 8431 3m WSW of Tenterden.
CP, 1,288. Tntdn RD. P Cranbrook. Ch e.
Sch p. Ashford CC. In orchard and hop
country. To S, Gt Maytham*, Lutyens
mansion in fine grnds. To NW, restored
post-mill, and Hole Pk gdns*. To NE, old rly
stn museum.

ROLVENDEN LAYNE Kent
184 TQ 8530 3m SW of Tenterden. Loc,
Rlvndn CP. P Cranbrook. Ch m.

ROMALDKIRK Yorks (N)
84 NY 9922 5m NW of Barnard Cstle.
CP, 154. Startforth RD. P Bnd
Cstle, Co Durham. Ch e, m. Richmond CC.
Picturesque stone vllge with large grn and
trees.

ROMANBY Yorks (N)
91 SE 3693 just SW of Northallerton.
CP, 2,059. Nthlltn RD. P Nthlltn. Ch e, m.
Sch p. Richmond CC.

ROMANSLEIGH Devon
163 SS 7220 3m S of S Molton. CP, 103.
S Mltn RD. Ch e. N Dvn CC.

ROMILEY Ches
101 SJ 9490 3m E of Stockport.
UD(Bredbury and Rmly), 28,472. P Stckpt.
Hazel Grove BC (Cheadle CC).

ROMSEY Hants
168 SU 3521 7m NW of Southampton.
MB, 10,057. P. Eastleigh CC (Winchester).
Abbey ch 10c–12c. King John's hunting
box, 13c hse, now museum. 1m SE,
Broadlands, 18c mansion formerly home of
Ld Palmerston, now of Mountbatten family.

ROMSLEY Shrops
130 SO 7882 8m SSE of Bridgnorth.
CP, 101. Brdgnth RD. Ludlow CC.

ROMSLEY Worcs
130, 131 SO 9679 6m N of Bromsgrove.
CP, 1,572. Brmsgrve RD. P Halesowen.
Ch e, m2. Sch pe. Brmsgrve and
Redditch CC (Brmsgrve). Ancient ch;
Burne-Jones window.

ROOKHOPE Co Durham
84 NY 9342 4m NW of Stanhope. Loc,
Stnhpe CP. P Bishop Auckland. Ch e, m.

ROOKLEY IOW
180 SZ 5084 3m S of Newport. Loc, Isle
of Wight RD and CC. P Ventnor. Ch m.

ROOKS BRIDGE Som
165 ST 3652 7m SSE of Weston. Loc,
E Brent CP. P Axbridge. Ch b.

ROOS Yorks (E)
99 TA 2930 4m WNW of Withernsea.
CP, 631. Holderness RD. P Hull. Ch e, m2.
Sch pe. Bridlington CC. See also Hilston,
Owstwick, Tunstall.

ROPLEY Hants
168, 169, 181 SU 6431 6m SW of Alton.
CP, 1,210. Altn RD. P Alresford. Ch e, m.
Sch pe. Petersfield CC. See also Monkwood,
N St, Rply Dean.

ROPLEY DEAN Hants
168 SU 6332 7m SW of Alton. Loc, Rply CP.

ROPSLEY Lincs (K)
113, 123 SK 9934 5m E of Grantham. CP (Rpsly and Humby), 571. W Kesteven RD. P Grnthm. Ch e, m. Sch pe. Rutland and Stamford CC.

RORRINGTON Shrops
118 SJ 3000 6m SE of Welshpool. Loc, Chirbury CP. P MONTGOMERY.

ROSE Cornwall
185, 190 SW 7754 SSW of Newquay. Loc, Perranzabuloe CP. P Truro. Ch m.

ROSEACRE Lancs
94 SD 4336 8m E of Blackpool. CP(Treales, Rscre and Wharles), 348. Fylde RD. S Flde CC.

ROSE ASH Devon
163 SS 7821 5m ESE of S Molton. CP, 268. S Mltn RD. P: S Mltn. Ch e, m. N Dvn CC.

ROSEDALE ABBEY Yorks (N)
86, 92 SE 7296 9m NW of Pickering. Loc, Rsdle East Side CP. Pckrng RD. P Pckrng. Ch e, m. Sch p. Scarborough CC (Thirsk and Malton). Rems of 12c priory in wild moorland valley. Disused lead mines.

ROSEDEN Nthmb
71 NU 0321 5m SE of Wooler. Loc, Roddam CP.

ROSEMARY LANE Devon
164, 176 ST 1514 4m SSE of Wellington. Loc, Clayhidon CP.

ROSENANNON Cornwall
185 SW 9566 4m SSW of Wadebridge. Loc, St Wenn CP. Ch m.

ROSGILL Westm
83 NY 5316 9m S of Penrith. Loc, Shap Rural CP. N Westm RD. Westm CC.

ROSLEY Cumb
82 NY 3245 5m ESE of Wigton. Loc, Westward CP. Ch e. Sch pe.

ROSLISTON Derbys
120 SK 2416 4m S of Burton-on-Trent. CP, 417. Repton RD. P Btn-on-Trnt, Staffs. Ch e, m. Sch pe. Belper CC.

ROSS Nthmb
64, 71 NU 1337 3m NE of Belford. Loc, Middleton CP.

ROSSINGTON Yorks (W)
103 SK 6298 4m SE of Doncaster. CP, 10,190. Dncstr RD. P Dncstr. Ch e, m, r, s2, v2. Sch i, pe. Don Valley CC. See also New Rssngtn. Colliery tn.

ROSS-ON-WYE Herefs
142 SO 6024 11m SSE of Hereford. UD, 6,399. P. Hrfd CC. Mkt tn, bypassed by M50 motorway; old mkt hall, many old hses. The Prospect, public riverside gdn laid out in 1700. Ch 14c–15c; monmts, impressive spire.

ROSTHERNE Ches
101 SJ 7483 3m SSW of Altrincham. CP, 195. Bucklow RD. P Knutsford. Ch e. Sch pe. Knutsford CC. To N is the large R. Mere, national nature reserve.

ROSTHWAITE Cumb
82 NY 2514 6m S of Keswick. Loc, Borrowdale CP. P Kswck.

ROSTON Derbys
120 SK 1340 5m SW of Ashbourne. CP(Norbury and Rstn), 280. Ashbne RD. P Ashbne. Ch m. W Derbys CC.

ROSUDGEON Cornwall
189 SW 5529 7m WNW of Helston. Loc, W Penwith RD. P Penzance. Ch m. St Ives CC. 1m S, Prussia Cove, named after 'The King of Prussia', the smuggler John Carter who here vainly defied the revenue men.

ROTHBURY Nthmb
71 NU 0501 11m SW of Alnwick. CP, 1,784. Rthbry RD. P Morpeth. Ch e, c, r. Sch p, se. Berwick-upon-Tweed CC. Stone-blt small mkt tn on R Coquet among hills collectively known as Rthbry Forest. Ch has font with Saxon stem and 17c bowl. Grnds* of Cragside, Vctrn mansion 1m E.

ROTHERBY Leics
121, 122 SK 6716 5m WSW of Melton Mowbray. CP(Hoby w Rthrby), 585. Mltn and Belvoir RD. P Mltn Mbry. Ch e. Sch pe. Mltn CC.

ROTHERFIELD Sussex (E)
183 TQ 5529 3m E of Crowborough.
CP, 2,852. Uckfield RD. P Crbrgh. Ch e.
Sch p. E Grinstead CC. See also Boarshead.
Vllge on ridge; shingled ch spire is prominent landmark, as is windmill at Argos Hill, 1¼m SE.

ROTHERFIELD GREYS Oxon
159 SU 7282 2m W of Henley. CP, 382.
Hnly RD. P Hnly-on-Thames. Ch e2.
Hnly CC. EE ch: brass, tombs. To N, Greys Ct (NT)*, gabled Elizn hse.

ROTHERFIELD PEPPARD Oxon
159 SU 7181 3m W of Henley. CP, 1,241.
Hnly RD. Ch e, v. Sch pe. Hnly CC.

ROTHERHAM Yorks (W)
103 SK 4292 6m NE of Sheffield.
CB, 84,646. P. Rthrhm BC. See also Greasbrough, Thorpe Hesley. Iron and steel mnfg centre. Coal mines. Clifton Pk*, by Carr of York, now municipal museum. 15c toll chpl on br, cf Bradford-on-Avon; St Ives, Hunts; Wakefield.

ROTHERHITHE London
161, 171 TQ 3579 2m ESE of Lndn Br.
Loc, Southwark LB. Bermondsey BC.
Dockland on S bank of Thames. Rthrhthe (rd) Tunnel under river to Stepney.

ROTHERSTHORPE Northants
133 SP 7156 3m SW of Northampton.
CP, 230. Nthmptn RD. P NTHMPTN.
Ch e, b. Sch pe. Daventry CC (S Nthnts).

ROTHERWICK Hants
169 SU 7156 5m ENE of Basingstoke.
CP, 667. Hartley Wintney RD. P Bsngstke.
Ch e. Sch pe. Bsngstke CC (Aldershot).

ROTHLEY Leics
121, 122 SK 5812 5m N of Leicester.
CP, 3,033. Barrow upon Soar RD.
P LCSTR. Ch e, b, m2, r. Sch pe.
Melton CC. R. Temple, mdvl, Elizn, and 19c hse, incorporates 13c chpl of Knights Templar.

ROTHLEY Nthmb
77, 78 NZ 0488 10m W of Morpeth.
CP, 138. Rothbury RD.
Berwick-upon-Tweed CC. See also High Hartington.

ROTHWELL Lincs (L)
104/105 TF 1599 2m SE of Caistor.
CP, 214. Cstr RD. P LINCOLN. Ch e, m.
Sch p. Gainsborough CC.

ROTHWELL Northants
133 SP 8181 4m WNW of Kettering.
UD, 4,762. P Kttrng. Kttrng CC. Ancient mkt tn with much new development. Elizn mkt hall blt by Sir Thomas Tresham (see Rushton).

ROTHWELL Yorks (W)
96, 102 SE 3428 4m SE of Leeds.
UD, 28,353. P LDS. Normanton CC. See also Carlton, Lofthouse, Lfthse Gate, Methley, Oulton, Robin Hood, Woodlesford.

ROTTINGDEAN Sussex (E)
183 TQ 3702 E distr of Brighton. Loc, Brghtn CB. P Brghtn. Brghtn, Kemptown BC. The Grange, Ggn hse altered by Lutyens, now a museum incl Kipling relics and a collection of toys.

ROTTINGTON Cumb
82 NX 9613 3m SSW of Whitehaven.
CP, 92. Ennerdale RD. Whthvn CC.

ROUD IOW
180 SZ 5180 4m NW of Ventnor. Loc, Godshill CP. Ch b.

ROUGHAM Norfolk
125 TF 8320 7m N of Swaffham. CP, 204.
Mitford and Launditch RD. P King's Lynn.
Ch e, m. SW Nflk CC. Ch: 15c and 16c brasses.

ROUGHAM GREEN Suffolk (W)
136 TL 9061 4m ESE of Bury St Edmunds.
Loc, Rghm CP. Thingoe RD.
P(Rghm), Bury St Eds. Ch e, b. Sch pe.
Bury St Eds CC.

ROUGH CLOSE Staffs
110, 119 SJ 9239 5m SE of Stoke-on-Trent.
Loc, Stone Rural CP. Stne RD.
P Stke-on-Trnt. Ch m. Sch pe. Stafford and Stne CC.

ROUGHLEE Lancs
95 SD 8440 2m NNW of Nelson. Loc, Rghlee Booth CP. Burnley RD. Sch pe.
Clitheroe CC.

ROUGHTON Lincs (L)
114 TF 2464 3m SSW of Horncastle.
CP, 341. Hncstle RD. Ch e. Hncstle CC. See
also Dalderby, Martin.

ROUGHTON Norfolk
126 TG 2137 3m S of Cromer. CP, 517.
Erpingham RD. P NORWICH, NOR 29Y.
Ch e, m. Sch pe. N Nflk CC.

ROUGHTON Shrops
130 SO 7594 3m ENE of Bridgnorth. Loc,
Worfield CP.

ROUNDSTREET COMMON Sussex (W)
182 TQ 0528 3m NW of Billingshurst. Loc,
Loxwood CP.

ROUNDWAY Wilts
167 SU 0163 1m NNE of Devizes.
CP, 2,400. Dvzs RD. P Dvzs. Dvzs CC.
Army tn.

ROUSDON Devon
177 SY 2991 3m W of Lyme Regis.
CP (Combpyne Rousdon), 268.
Axmnstr RD. P Lme Rgs, Dorset. Ch e.
Honiton CC.

ROUSHAM Oxon
145 SP 4824 5m NNE of Woodstock.
CP, 74. Chipping Norton RD. Ch e.
Banbury CC. R. Hse*, 17c–18c; gdns laid
out by William Kent.

ROUS LENCH Worcs
144 SP 0153 6m NNW of Evesham.
CP, 262. Eveshm RD. P Eveshm. Ch e.
S Worcs CC. Ch: Rous monmts. Rous Ct,
17c, black and white; topiary gdn.

ROUTH Yorks (E)
99 TA 0942 4m NE of Beverley. CP, 123.
Bvrly RD. P Bvrly. Ch e. Haltemprice CC.

ROW Cornwall
185, 186 SX 0976 5m S of Camelford. Loc,
St Breward CP.

ROW Westm
89 SD 4589 5m WSW of Kendal. Loc,
Crosthwaite and Lyth CP. S Westm RD.
Westm CC.

ROWBERROW Som
165 ST 4558 3m N of Cheddar. Loc,
Shipham CP. Ch e.

ROWDE Wilts
157 ST 9762 2m NW of Devizes. CP, 782.
Dvzs RD. P Dvzs. Ch e, m. Sch pe. Dvzs CC.

ROWELTOWN Cumb
76 NY 4971 7m NNW of Brampton. Loc,
Stapleton CP. P Carlisle.

ROWFOOT Nthmb
76 NY 6860 2m SW of Haltwhistle. Loc,
Featherstone CP. Hltwhstle RD.
Hexham CC.

ROWHEDGE Essex
149, 162 TM 0321 3m SE of Colchester.
Loc, E Donyland CP. Lexden and
Winstree RD. P Clchstr. Ch e, m, v.
Clchstr CC. Quay; ferry to Wivenhoe. To W,
Army firing ranges.

ROWHOOK Sussex (W)
182 TQ 1234 4m NW of Horsham. Loc,
Hshm RD. Hshm and Crawley CC (Hshm).

ROWINGTON Warwicks
131 SP 2069 6m NW of Warwick. CP, 790.
Wrwck RD. P WRWCK. Ch e. Sch e. Wrwck
and Leamington CC. See also Lowsonford.

ROWLAND Derbys
111 SK 2172 3m N of Bakewell. CP, 43.
Bkwll RD. W Derbys CC.

ROWLAND'S CASTLE Hants
181 SU 7310 3m NNE of Havant.
CP, 1,730. Petersfield RD. P. Ch e, v.
Sch pe. Ptrsfld CC. See also Finchdean.
Mostly Vctrn. Brickworks.

ROWLAND'S GILL Co Durham
78 NZ 1658 7m WSW of Gateshead. Loc,
Blaydon UD. P. To E, Gibside Chpl (NT)*,
by James Paine in 1760s. Restored 1965.

ROWLEDGE Surrey
169 SU 8243 2m SSW of Farnham. Loc,
Fnhm UD. P Fnhm.

ROWLEY Shrops
118 SJ 3006 5m E of Welshpool. Loc,
Worthen CP.

ROWLEY Yorks (E)
98 SE 9732 6m SW of Beverley. CP, 780.
Bvrly RD. Ch e. Haltemprice CC. See also
Bentley, High Hunsley, Lit Weighton,
Riplingham. In 1638 entire pop. emigrated
to Massachusetts with vicar, who was

evicted for refusing to read in his ch the Book of Sports, which allowed for games-playing on Sundays.

ROWLEY REGIS Worcs
130, 131 SO 9687 2m SE of Dudley. Loc, Warley CB. P Wly. Wly W BC (Rly Rgs and Tipton).

ROWLSTONE Herefs
142 SO 3727 9m NNE of Abergavenny. CP, 83. Dore and Bredwardine RD. Ch e. Hereford CC. Ch: Nmn carved stonework; unique 15c ironwork light brackets.

ROWLY Surrey
170, 182 TQ 0440 1m NW of Cranleigh. Loc, Crnlgh CP. P Crnlgh.

ROWNEY GREEN Worcs
131 SP 0471 3m N of Redditch. Loc, Alvechurch CP. P BIRMINGHAM.

ROWNHAMS Hants
180 SU 3817 4m NNW of Southampton. CP(Nursling and Rnhms), 2,584. Romsey and Stockbridge RD. P STHMPTN. Ch e. Sch pe. Eastleigh CC.

ROWRAH Cumb
82 NY 0518 5m E of Whitehaven. Loc, Arlecdon and Frizington CP. Ch m.

ROWSHAM Bucks
146 SP 8518 3m NE of Aylesbury. CP(Wingrave w Rwshm), 832. Wing RD. Ch c. Buckingham CC.

ROWSLEY Derbys
111 SK 2565 3m SE of Bakewell. CP, 225. Bkwll RD. P Matlock. Ch e, m. Sch pe. W Derbys CC. At confluence of R Derwent and R Wye. 1½m W, the mdvl Haddon Hall*.

ROWSTON Lincs (K)
113 TF 0856 7m N of Sleaford. CP, 200. E Kesteven RD. Ch e. Grantham CC.

ROWTON Ches
109 SJ 4464 3m ESE of Chester. CP, 297. Chstr RD. Ch m. City of Chstr CC.

ROWTON Shrops
118, 119 SJ 6119 6m NNW of Wellington. Loc, Ercall Magna CP. Wllngtn RD. Ch e. The Wrekin CC.

ROXBY Lincs (L)
104 SE 9216 4m NNE of Scunthorpe. CP(Rxby cum Risby), 416. Glanford Brigg RD. P Scnthpe. Ch e, m. Sch pe. Brgg and Scnthpe CC (Brgg).

ROXBY Yorks (N)
86 NZ 7616 3m SE of Loftus. CP, 159. Whitby RD. Ch e. Cleveland and Whtby CC (Scarborough and Whtby).

ROXTON Beds
147 TL 1554 4m NNW of Sandy. CP, 598. Bedford RD. P BDFD. Ch e, v. Sch pe. Mid-Beds CC. See also Chawston, Colesden, Wyboston.

ROXWELL Essex
161 TL 6408 4m WNW of Chelmsford. CP, 1,296. Chlmsfd RD. P Chlmsfd. Ch e. Sch pe. Braintree CC (Chlmsfd). See also Cooksmill Grn.

ROYAL LEAMINGTON SPA Warwicks
132 SP 3165 9m S of Coventry. See Leamington.

ROYAL TUNBRIDGE WELLS Kent
171 TQ 5839 31m SSE of London. See Tunbridge Wells.

ROYDON Essex
148, 161 TL 4010 3m W of Harlow. CP, 2,828. Epping and Ongar RD. P Hlw. Ch e, c. Sch p. Hlw CC (Eppng). See also Broadley Cmmn, Rdn Hmlt.

ROYDON Norfolk
124 TF 7022 6m ENE of King's Lynn. CP, 209. Freebridge Lynn RD. Ch e. NW Nflk CC (K's Lnn).

ROYDON Norfolk
136 TM 0980 1m W of Diss. CP, 638. Depwade RD. P Dss. Ch e. S Nflk CC.

ROYDON HAMLET Essex
161 TL 4107 3m SW of Harlow. Loc, Rdn CP.

ROYSTON Herts
148 TL 3540 13m SSW of Cambridge. UD, 8,272. P. Hitchin CC. At crossing of Icknield Way and Ermine St.

ROYSTON Yorks (W)
102, 103 SE 3611 3m NNE of Barnsley. UD, 8,839. P Bnsly. Wakefield BC.

ROYTON Lancs
101 SD 9207 2m N of Oldham. UD, 20,319.
P Oldhm. Heywood and Rtn CC. See also
Summit. Textiles tn.

RUAN HIGH LANES Cornwall
190 SW 9039 6m NE of St Mawes. Loc,
Truro RD. P Truro. Truro CC.

RUAN LANIHORNE Cornwall
190 SW 8942 6m NNE of St Mawes.
CP, 242. Truro RD. Ch e, m. Truro CC.

RUAN MINOR Cornwall
190 SW 7215 9m SSE of Helston. Loc,
Grade-Ruan CP. Kerrier RD. P Hlstn.
Ch e, m2. Sch pe. St Ives CC.

RUARDEAN Glos
142, 143 SO 6117 3m NW of Cinderford.
CP, 1,199. E Dean RD. P. Ch e, m, v.
Sch pe. W Glos CC. High up in Forest of
Dean; ch is both viewpoint and landmark.

RUARDEAN HILL Glos
142, 143 SO 6317 2m NNW of Cinderford.
Loc, Drybrook CP. P Drbrk. Ch b, m.
Nearly 1,000ft up in Forest of Dean.

RUARDEAN WOODSIDE Glos
142, 143 SO 6216 3m NW of Cinderford.
Loc, Drybrook CP. P Rdn. Ch m. Sch p.

RUBERY Warwicks and Worcs
130, 131 SO 9877 4m NNE of Bromsgrove.
Loc, Birmingham CB, Brmsgrve UD.
P Rednal, BMNGHM. Bmnghm,
Northfield BC; Brmsgrve and Redditch CC.
(Bmnghm, Nthfld BC; Brmsgrve CC.)

RUCKINGE Kent
173, 184 TR 0233 6m S of Ashford.
CP, 594. E Ashfd RD. P Ashfd. Ch e, m.
Ashfd CC. See also Bromley Grn.

RUCKLAND Lincs (L)
105 TF 3378 6m S of Louth. Loc,
Maidenwell CP. Lth RD. Ch e. Lth CC.

RUCKLERS GREEN Herts
160 TL 0604 2m SSE of Hemel Hempstead.
Loc, Kings Langley CP.

RUDBY Yorks (N)
85 NZ 4706 8m S of Teesside (Stockton).
CP, 84. Stokesley RD. Ch e. Sch p.
Richmond CC.

RUDDINGTON Notts
112, 121, 122 SK 5733 5m S of
Nottingham. CP, 5,158. Basford RD.
P NTTNGHM. Ch e, b, m, v. Sch i, je, s.
Rushcliffe CC.

RUDFORD Glos
143 SO 7721 4m WNW of Gloucester.
CP, 241. Newent RD. Ch e. W Glos CC. See
also Highleadon.

RUDGE Som
166 ST 8251 3m W of Westbury. Loc,
Beckington CP. Ch b, m.

RUDGEWAY Glos
155, 156 ST 6286 4m ESE of Severn Rd Br.
Loc, Alveston CP. P BRISTOL. Ch m.

RUDGWICK Sussex (W)
182 TQ 0934 6m WNW of Horsham.
CP, 1,597. Hshm RD. P Hshm. Ch e, c.
Sch p. Hshm and Crawley CC (Hshm). See
also Bucks Grn.

RUDHALL Herefs
142, 143 SO 6225 2m ENE of Ross-on-Wye.
Loc, Rss and Whitchurch RD. Hereford CC.

RUDSTON Yorks (E)
93 TA 0967 5m W of Bridlington. CP, 401.
Brdlngtn RD. P Driffield. Ch e, m.
Brdlngtn CC. Roman vlla with fine
tessalated pavements discovered 1933. In
churchyard, monolith 25ft high, origin
unknown.

RUDYARD Staffs
110 SJ 9557 2m WNW of Leek. Loc,
Horton CP. P Lk. Ch m. At S end of
2m-long Rdyd Reservoir.

RUFFORD Lancs
100 SD 4615 5m NE of Ormskirk.
CP, 1,427. W Lancs RD. P Ormskk. Ch e, m.
Sch pe. Ormskk CC. See also Holmeswood.
Beside Leeds-Liverpool Canal. Rffd Hall
(NT)*, Tdr and later half-timbered hse.

RUFFORTH Yorks (W)
97 SE 5251 5m W of York. CP, 265.
Nidderdale RD. P YK. Ch e, m. Sch p.
Barkston Ash CC. Airfield.

RUGBY Warwicks
132 SP 5075 11m E of Coventry.
MB, 59,372. P. Rgby CC. See also Newbold
on Avon. Rly and engineering tn. Well

known boys' public sch. Radio transmitting stn (several tall masts) to E.

RUGELEY Staffs
120 SK 0418 8m ESE of Stafford. UD, 22,234. P. Cannock CC (Lichfield and Tamworth). See also Brereton, Etchinghill. Indstrl tn on R Trent to E of Cnnck Chase.

RUISHTON Som
177 ST 2625 2m E of Taunton. CP, 813. Tntn RD. Ch e. Sch pe. Tntn CC.

RUISLIP London
160 TQ 0987 3m NE of Uxbridge. Loc, Hillingdon LB. P Middx. Rslp-Northwood BC. Rsdntl distr. Wds and cmmn to N, with Rslp Lido (reservoir).

RUISLIP COMMON London
160 TQ 0888 4m NNE of Uxbridge. Loc, Hillingdon LB. Rslp-Northwood BC.

RUMBURGH Suffolk (E)
137 TM 3481 3m NW of Halesworth. CP, 251. Wainford RD. P Hlswth. Ch e, m. Lowestoft CC.

RUMFORD Cornwall
185 SW 8970 4m SSW of Padstow. Loc, St Ervan CP. P Wadebridge. Ch m.

RUNCORN Ches
100, 109 SJ 5182 2m S of Widnes. UD, 35,953. P. Rncn CC. See also Halton, Norton, Weston. New tn pop. 35,646 (Apr 1971). Large chemical works. The rd and rly brs over R Mersey are the furthest downstream.

RUNCTON Sussex (W)
181 SU 8802 2m SE of Chichester. Loc, N Mundham CP.

RUNCTON HOLME Norfolk
124 TF 6109 4m N of Downham Mkt. CP, 330. Dnhm RD. P King's Lynn. Ch e. Sch pe. SW Nflk CC. See also S Rnctn.

RUNFOLD Surrey
169 SU 8747 2m E of Farnham. Loc, Fnhm UD. P Fnhm.

RUNHALL Norfolk
125 TG 0507 5m NW of Wymondham. CP, 339. Forehoe and Henstead RD. P NORWICH, NOR 31X. Ch e. S Nflk CC (Central Nflk). See also Brandon Parva, Coston, Welborne.

RUNHAM Norfolk
126 TG 4610 4m NW of Yarmouth. Loc, Mautby CP. P Gt Ymth. Ch e, m. Sch p.

RUNNINGTON Som
164 ST 1121 2m NW of Wellington. Loc, Langford Budville CP. Ch e.

RUNSWICK Yorks (N)
86 NZ 8016 6m WNW of Whitby. Loc, Hinderwell CP. P Saltburn-on-the-Sea. Small resort.

RUNWELL Essex
162 TQ 7594 5m NNE of Basildon. CP, 3,873. Chelmsford RD. Ch e. Sch j, p. Chlmsfd CC.

RUSCOMBE Berks
159 SU 7976 6m ENE of Reading. CP, 815. Wokingham RD. Ch e. Wknghm CC.

RUSHALL Herefs
142, 143 SO 6435 5m WSW of Ledbury. Loc, Much Marcle CP. P Ldbry.

RUSHALL Norfolk
137 TM 1982 5m ENE of Diss. Loc, Dickleburgh CP. P Dss. Ch e.

RUSHALL Staffs
120 SK 0201 2m NNE of Walsall. Loc, Aldridge-Brownhills UD. P Wlsll. A-B BC (Wlsll S). To S, rems of 14c R. Hall (now within Wlsll CB).

RUSHALL Wilts
167 SU 1256 4m SW of Pewsey. CP, 137. Psy RD. P Psy. Ch e, b. Sch pe. Dvzs CC.

RUSHBROOKE Suffolk (W)
136 TL 8961 3m SE of Bury St Edmunds. CP, 58. Thingoe RD. Ch e. Bury St Eds CC. Ch contains royal arms of Henry VIII, only surviving example in a ch.

RUSHBURY Shrops
129 SO 5191 4m ESE of Ch Stretton. CP, 589. Ludlow RD. Ch e. Sch pe. Ldlw CC. See also Longville in the Dale, Wall Bank, Wall under Heywood. On slopes of Wenlock Edge. Packhorse br. Rshbry Mnr, timber-framed.

RUSHDEN Herts
147 TL 3031 4m ESE of Baldock. CP, 216. Hitchin RD. P Buntingford. Ch e. Htchn CC.

Rushden

RUSHDEN Northants
134 SP 9566 4m ESE of Wellingborough.
UD, 20,156. P. Wllngbrgh CC. Footwear
mnfg tn, largely late Vctrn. Fine
14c—15c ch.

RUSHFORD Devon
175, 187 SX 4476 2m NW of Tavistock.
Loc, Lamerton CP. Ch m.

RUSHFORD Norfolk
136 TL 9281 4m ESE of Thetford. Loc,
Brettenham CP. P Thtfd. Ch e.

RUSHLAKE GREEN Sussex (E)
183 TQ 6218 4m SE of Heathfield. Loc,
Warbleton CP. P Hthfld.

RUSHMERE Suffolk (E)
137 TM 4987 5m SW of Lowestoft.
CP, 114. Lothingland RD. Ch e. Lwstft CC.

RUSHMERE ST ANDREW Suffolk (E)
150 TM 1946 2m ENE of Ipswich.
CP, 2,024. Deben RD. P(Rshmre), Ipswch.
Ch e, b. Sch p. Sudbury and
Woodbridge CC.

RUSHMOOR Surrey
169 SU 8740 5m SSE of Farnham. Loc,
Frensham CP. P Fnhm. To SW, small hills
known as The Devil's Jumps (NT).

RUSHOCK Worcs
130, 131 SO 8871 5m SE of Kidderminster.
CP, 149. Kddrmnstr RD. P Droitwich. Ch e.
Kddrmnstr CC.

RUSHTON Ches
109 SJ 5864 5m WSW of Winsford. CP, 390.
Northwich RD. Ch m. Nthwch CC. See also
Eaton. On W edge of Oulton Pk Motor
Racing Circuit. (See also Lit Budworth).

RUSHTON Northants
133 SP 8482 3m NNW of Kettering. CP, 402.
Kttrng RD. P Kttrng. Ch e. Sch p. Kttrng CC.
R. Hall, Elizn hse now sch for blind children,
was seat of Treshams. Late 16c, Sir Thomas
Trshm blt many edifices to express religious
concepts, eg triangular lodge (A.M.) symbolis-
ing Trinity.

RUSHTON Shrops
118, 119 SJ 6008 4m SW of Wellington.
Loc, Wroxeter CP.

RUSHTON SPENCER Staffs
110 SJ 9362 5m NNW of Leek.. Loc,
Rshtn . Lk RD. P Macclesfield. Ch e. Sch pe.
Lk CC.

RUSHWICK Worcs
143 SO 8253 2m WSW of Worcester.
CP, 918. Martley RD. P WCSTR. Sch pe.
Kidderminster CC.

RUSKINGTON Lincs (K)
113 TF 0850 3m NNE of Sleaford.
CP, 2,462. E Kesteven RD. P Slfd.
Ch e, m, v2. Sch p, pe, s. Grantham CC. Ch:
William Morris stained glass. Stream flows
down centre of main st.

RUSLAND Lancs
88, 89 SD 3488 7m NNE of Ulverston. Loc,
Colton CP. Ch e.

RUSPER Sussex (W)
170, 182 TQ 2037 4m W of Crawley.
CP, 1,232. Horsham RD. P Hshm. Ch e.
Sch p. Hshm and Crly CC (Hshm). See also
Lambs Grn.

RUSPIDGE Glos
142, 143 SO 6511 S of Cinderford.
CP, 2,180. E Dean RD. P Cndrfd. Ch m2.
Sch p. W Glos CC. See also Upr Soudley.

RUSSELL'S WATER Oxon
159 SU 7089 6m NW of Henley. Loc,
Pishill w Stonor CP. Ch m.

RUSTINGTON Sussex (W)
182 TQ 0501 2m E of Littlehampton.
CP, 5,590. Worthing RD. P Lttlhmptn.
Ch e, m, r, v3. Sch p. Arundel CC (Arndl
and Shoreham).

RUSTON Yorks (N)
93 SE 9583 6m SW of Scarborough. Loc,
Wykeham CP. Ch m.

RUSTON PARVA Yorks (E)
99 TA 0661 4m NE of Driffield. Loc,
Harpham CP. Ch e.

RUSWARP Yorks (N)
86, 93 NZ 8809 1m SSW of Whitby. Loc,
Whtby UD. P Whtby.

RUTHERNBRIDGE Cornwall
185, 186 SX 0166 4m W of Bodmin. Loc,
Lanivet CP.

RUTHVOES Cornwall
185 SW 9260 7m E of Newquay. Loc,
St Columb Major CP. Ch m.

RUYTON-ELEVEN-TOWNS Shrops
118 SJ 3922 9m NW of Shrewsbury.
CP, 826. Oswestry RD. P Shrsbry.
Ch e, m, v. Sch pe. Oswstry CC. See also
Eardiston, Wykey. In 12c the mnr
comprised eleven townships.

RYAL Nthmb
77 NZ 0174 6m NNE of Corbridge. Loc,
Matfen CP. Ch e.

RYAL FOLD Lancs
94, 95 SD 6621 4m SSW of Blackburn. Loc,
Tockholes CP.

RYALL Dorset
177 SY 4094 4m W of Bridport. Loc,
Whitechurch Canonicorum CP.

RYARSH Kent
171 TQ 6659 WNW of Maidstone. CP, 763.
Malling RD. P Mdstne. Ch e, b. Sch p.
Tonbridge and Mllng CC (Sevenoaks).

RYBURGH, GREAT Norfolk
125 TF 9527 3m SE of Fakenham. See Gt
Rbgh.

RYDAL Westm
83 NY 3606 1m NW of Ambleside. Loc,
Lakes UD. Westm CC. Home of Wordsworth
1817–50. Dora's Field (NT), full of
daffodils, by ch.

RYDE IOW
180 SZ 5992 6m ENE of Newport, 5m SSW
of Portsmouth (by sea). MB, 23,171. P Isle
of Wight CC. See also Binstead, Fishbourne,
Havenstreet, Nettlestone, St Helens,
Seaview. Resort.

RYE Sussex (E)
184 TQ 9220 9m NE of Hastings.
MB, 4,434. P. Rye CC. Picturesque tn;
formerly a port but now 2m from sea. 14c
Landgate. Ch has well known clock. Lamb
Hse (NT)*, 18c, former home of Henry
James. Mermaid Inn is 15c.

RYE FOREIGN Sussex (E)
184 TQ 8922 2m NW of Rye. CP, 419.
Battle RD. Rye CC.

RYE HARBOUR Sussex (E)
184 TQ 9319 1m SE of Rye. Loc,
Icklesham CP. P Rye. Ch e.

RYHALL Rutland
123 TF 0310 2m N of Stamford. CP, 1,052.
Ketton RD. P Stmfd, Lincs. Ch e, m. Rtlnd
and Stmfd CC. See also Belmesthorpe.
Green Dragon Inn on site of mdvl mnr hse.
Ch has broach spire.

RYHILL Yorks (E)
99 TA 2225 8m ESE of Hull. Loc, Thorngumbald CP. Ch m.

RYHILL Yorks (W)
102, 103 SE 3814 5m NNE of Barnsley.
CP, 2,446. Hemsworth RD. P Wakefield.
Ch e, m. Sch j. Hmswth CC.

RYHOPE Co Durham
78 NZ 4152 S distr of Sunderland. Loc,
Sndrlnd CB. P Sndrlnd. Sndrlnd S BC
(Houghton-le-Spring CC). Colliery closed.

RYLE, GREAT Nthmb
71 NU 0212 7m NNW of Rothbury. Loc,
Alnham CP.

RYLSTONE Yorks (W)
95 SD 9758 5m N of Skipton. CP, 111.
Skptn RD. Ch e. Skptn CC.

RYME INTRINSECA Dorset
177, 178 ST 5810 4m SSE of Yeovil.
CP, 129. Sherborne RD. Ch e. W Dst CC.

RYTHER Yorks (W)
97 SE 5539 5m ESE of Tadcaster. CP(Rthr
cum Ossendyke), 325. Tdcstr RD. P Tdcstr.
Ch e, m. Sch pe. Barkston Ash CC.

RYTON Co Durham
78 NZ 1564 6m W of Newcastle.
UD, 14,831. P. Blaydon BC (CC). See also
Clara Vale, Crawcrook, Greenside, Rtn
Woodside. Mdvl ch with 120ft spire above
bank of R Tyne.

RYTON Glos
143 SO 7332 4m SSE of Ledbury. Loc,
Dymock CP.

RYTON Shrops
118 SJ 4803 6m S of Shrewsbury. Loc,
Condover CP. P Shrsbry.

Ryton

RYTON Shrops
119 SJ 7602 3m SSE of Shifnal. CP, 264.
Shfnl RD. Ch e. The Wrekin CC.

RYTON Yorks (N)
92 SE 7975 3m NNE of Malton. CP, 124.
Mltn RD. Ch m. Thirsk and Mltn CC.

S

SABDEN Lancs
95 SD 7737 4m SE of Clitheroe. CP, 1,172.
Burnley RD. P Blackburn. Ch e, b, m, r.
Sch p, pr. Clthroe CC.

SACOMBE Hants
147 TL 3319 4m NNW of Ware. CP, 198.
Hertford RD. Ch e. Htfd and Stevenage CC
(Htfd).

SACRISTON Co Durham
85 NZ 2447 4m NW of Durham. CP, 4,871.
Chester-le-Street RD. P DRHM.
Ch e, m, r, s. Sch i, j, pr, s. Chstr-le-Strt CC.

SADBERGE Co Durham
85 NZ 3416 4m ENE of Darlington.
CP, 557. Dlngtn RD. P Dlngtn. Ch e, m.
Sch pe. Bishop Auckland CC (Sedgefield).

SADDINGTON Leics
132, 133 SP 6591 6m NW of Mkt
Harborough. CP, 193. Mkt Hbrgh RD.
P LCSTR. Ch e. Sch pe. Hbrgh CC.

SADDLE BOW Norfolk
124 TF 6015 3m SSW of King's Lynn. Loc,
Wiggenhall St Mary the Virgin CP. Ch m.

SADDLEWORTH Yorks (W)
101 SD 9905 5m E of Oldham. UD, 20,525.
Colne Valley CC. See also Delph, Denshaw,
Diggle, Dobcross, Grasscroft, Greenfield,
Grotton, Scouthead, Uppermill.

SAFFRON WALDEN Essex
148 TL 5338 11m NNE of Bishop's
Stortford. MB, 9,945. P. Sffrn Wldn CC. See
also Sewards End. Old tn with many
pargetted hses. Large 14c–15c ch, rems of
Nmn cstle, museum. 1m W, Audley End
(A.M.), large 17c mansion; pk laid out by
Capability Brown.

RYTON-ON-DUNSMORE Warwicks
132 SP 3874 4m SE of Coventry. CP, 1,243.
Rugby RD. P Cvntry. Ch e, m. Sch pe.
Rgby CC. Car factory. Police training college.

RYTON WOODSIDE Co Durham
78 NZ 1463 3m E of Prudhoe. Loc,
Rtn UD.

SAHAM HILLS Norfolk
125 TF 9003 2m NNW of Watton. Loc,
Saham Toney CP. P Thetford.

SAHAM TONEY Norfolk
125/136 TF 9001 1m NW of Watton.
CP, 902. Swaffham RD. P Thetford.
Ch e, m2. Sch pe. SW Nflk CC. See also Shm
Hills. Small mere, one of several in
E Breckland.

SAIGHTON Ches
109 SJ 4462 4m SE of Chester. CP, 308.
Chstr RD. P CHSTR. Sch pe. City
of Chstr CC.

ST AGNES Cornwall
185, 190 SW 7250 6m NNE of Redruth.
CP, 4,221. Truro RD. P. Ch e, m6, r. Sch p.
Truro CC. See also Goonbell, Mawla,
Mithian, Mt Hawke, Porthtowan, Trevellas.
Former tin-mining tn, now a resort with
beach at Trevaunance Cove.

ST AGNES Isles of Scilly
189 SV 8808. CP, 85. Is of S RD. P. Ch e.
Sch pe. St Ives CC. The island of Gugh is
joined by sand and rock bar to main island
at low tide.

ST ALBANS Herts
160 TL 1407 7m NNE of Watford.
MB, 52,057. P. St Albns CC. On W side of
tn, site of Roman *Verulamium*; rems of walls
(A.M.). Nmn and later cathedral with very
long nave. Many old hses but also much
modern development. 2½m W,
Gorhambury*, 18c hse; approach from
either ch on A414 (TL 1307) or The Pré on
A5 (TL 1308).

ST ALLEN Cornwall
185, 190 SW 8250 4m N of Truro. CP, 347.
Truro RD. Ch e, m. Truro CC. See also
Zelah.

ST ANNE'S Lancs
94 SD 3228 5m S of Blackpool. Loc,
Lytham St Anne's MB.

ST ANN'S CHAPEL Cornwall
175, 187 SX 4170 4m ENE of Callington.
Loc, Calstock CP. P Gunnislake. Ch m.

ST ANTHONY Cornwall
190 SW 7825 8m E of Helston.
CP(St Anthony-in-Meneage), 260.
Kerrier RD. Ch e, m. St Ives CC.

ST AUSTELL Cornwall
185, 186, 190 SX 0152 10m SSW of
Bodmin. MB(St Astll w Fowey), 32,252. P.
Truro CC. See also Boscoppa, Bugle,
Carlyon Bay, Carthew, Charlestown,
Holmbush, London Apprentice, Mevagissey,
Par, Penpillick, Pentewan, Penwithick
Stents, Polkerris, Porthpean, St Blazey,
St Blzy Gate, Stenalees, Tregeham Mills,
Trenarren, Trethurgy, Tywardreath, Twdrth
Highway. Centre of china clay industry.

ST BEES Cumb
82 NX 9711 4m S of Whitehaven.
CP, 1,198. Ennerdale RD. P. Ch e, m. Sch p.
Whthvn CC. Small resort. Large ch with
richly carved Nmn W door. St B. School,
founded 1583.

ST BLAZEY Cornwall
185, 186, 190 SX 0654 4m ENE of St
Austell. Loc, St Astll w Fowey MB. P Par.
Truro CC.

ST BLAZEY GATE Cornwall
185, 186, 190 SX 0553 3m E of St Austell.
Loc, St Astll w Fowey MB. Truro CC.

ST BREOCK Cornwall
185 SW 9771 just W of Wadebridge.
CP, 637. Wdbrdge and Padstow RD. Ch e.
N Cnwll CC. See also Burlawn, Trevanson,
Whitecross. Burial place of Jan Tregeagle (d
1655), subject of many legends.

ST BREWARD Cornwall
185, 186 SX 0977 4m S of Camelford.
CP, 762. Cmlfd RD. P Bodmin. Ch e, m2.
Sch p. N Cnwll CC. See also Row.

ST BRIAVELS Glos
155, 156 SO 5504 7m N of Chepstow.
CP, 1,087. Lydney RD. P Ldny. Ch e, v2.
Sch pe. W Glos CC. Restored 12c cstle; part
of it a Youth Hostel.

ST BRIDGET BECKERMET Cumb
82 NY 0206 8m SSE of Whitehaven.
CP, 620. Ennerdale RD. P(Bckrmt). Ch e.
Sch pe. Whthvn CC. See also Calder Br.

SAINTBURY Glos
144 SP 1139 2m W of Chipping Campden.
CP, 107. N Cotswold RD. Ch e. Cirencester
and Tewkesbury CC. Vllge runs down N
edge of Ctswlds.

ST BURYAN Cornwall
189 SW 4025 5m SW of Penzance. CP, 977.
W Penrith RD. P Pnznce. Ch e, m3. Sch p.
St Ives CC. 1m N, Nine Maidens, stone
circle· at Boleigh, 2m ESE, The Pipers, two
stones 14ft tall, and Merry Maidens, circle
of 19 stones.

ST CATHERINE Som
156 ST 7770 4m NE of Bath. CP, 90.
Bathavon RD. Ch e. N Som CC. St C's Ct,
17c hse mostly rebuilt 19c, set in terraced
gdns*.

ST CLEER Cornwall
186 SX 2468 2m N of Liskeard. CP, 1,524.
Lskd RD. P Lskd. Ch e, m2. Sch p.
Bodmin CC. See also Commonmoor, Darite,
Tremar, To N of ch, holy well with 15c
chpl. 1m NE, Trethevy Quoit (A.M.), a
cromlech.

ST CLEMENT Cornwall
190 SW 8543 2m ESE of Truro. CP, 584.
Truro RD. P Truro. Ch e. Truro CC.

ST CLETHER Cornwall
186 SX 2084 6m E of Camelford. CP, 129.
Cmlfd RD. P Launceston. Ch e, m2.
N Cnwll CC. Downstream from ch is
St C's Well with 15c chpl.

ST COLUMB MAJOR Cornwall
185 SW 9163 6m E of Newquay. CP, 3,441.
St Austell RD. P(St Clmb). Ch e, m2.
Sch p. N Cnwll CC. See also Ruthvoes,
Talskiddy, Trebudannon, Trevarren.

ST COLUMB MINOR Cornwall
185 SW 8362 2m E of Newquay. Loc,
Nquay UD. P Nquay. Ch has very tall twr.

ST COLUMB ROAD Cornwall
185 SW 9159 6m ESE of Newquay. Loc,
St Austell RD. P St Clmb. N Cnwll CC.

ST CROSS SOUTH ELMHAM Suffolk (E)
137 TM 2984 4m SW of Bungay. CP, 136.
Wainford RD. P Harleston, Norfolk. Ch e.
Lowestoft CC. Orig called Sancroft
St George, 'St Cross' being corruption of
'Sancroft'.

ST DAY Cornwall
190 SW 7342 2m E of Redruth. Loc,
Camborne-Rdrth UD. P Rdrth.

ST DENNIS Cornwall
185 SW 9557 5m NW of St Austell.
CP, 2,370. St Astll RD. P St Astll. Ch e, m4.
Sch ie, p. Truro CC.

ST DEVEREUX Herefs
142 SO 4431 7m SW of Hereford. CP, 151.
Dore and Bredwardine RD. Ch e. Hrfd CC.
See also Didley.

ST DOMINICK Cornwall
186/187 SX 4067 3m ESE of Callington.
CP, 588. St Germans RD. P Saltash.
Ch e, m. Sch pe. Bodmin CC. See also
Burraton.

ST EDITH'S MARSH Wilts
167 ST 9764 3m NW of Devizes. Loc,
Bromham CP.

ST ENDELLION Cornwall
185 SW 9978 4m N of Wadebridge.
CP, 1,129. Wdbrdge and Padstow RD. Ch e.
N Cnwll CC. See also Portgaverne, Port
Isaac, Trelights.

ST ENODER Cornwall
185 SW 8956 6m ESE of Newquay.
CP, 1,414. St Austell RD. Ch e. Sch pe.
N Cnwll CC. See also Fraddon, Summercourt.

ST ERME Cornwall
190 SW 8449 4m NNE of Truro. CP, 378.
Truro RD. Ch e, m. Sch p. Truro CC. See
also Trispen.

ST ERNEY Cornwall
186 SX 3759 4m W of Saltash. CP(Landrake
w St Erney), 611. St Germans RD. Ch e.
Bodmin CC.

ST ERTH Cornwall
189 SW 5535 4m SE of St Ives. CP, 884.
W Penwith RD. P Hayle. Ch e, m. Sch p.
St Ives CC. Rly junction for St Ives.

ST ERTH PRAZE Cornwall
189 SW 5735 5m WSW of Camborne. Loc,
St Erth CP.

ST ERVAN Cornwall
185 SW 8970 4m SSW of Padstow. CP, 298.
Wadebridge and Pdstw RD. Ch e. Sch p.
N Cnwll CC. See also Penrose, Rumford.

ST EVAL Cornwall
185 SW 8769 5m SW of Padstow.
CP, 1,408. Wadebridge and Pdstw RD.
P(St Evl RAF Stn), Wdbrdge. Ch e, m.
Sch p. N Cnwll CC. See also Porthcothan
Bay. 1½m W, Bedruthan Steps (NT): sand,
rocks, and caves.

ST EWE Cornwall
190 SW 9746 5m SW of St Austell. CP, 634.
St Astll RD. P Mevagissey, St Astll. Ch e, m.
Sch p. Truro CC. See also Polmassick.

ST GENNYS Cornwall
174 SX 1497 7m SSW of Bude. CP, 554.
Stratton RD. P Bde. Ch e, m2. Sch p.
N Cnwll CC. See also Crackington Haven.

ST GERMANS Cornwall
186 SX 3657 4m W of Saltash. CP, 1,877.
St Gmns RD. P Sltsh. Ch e, m3. Sch pe.
Bodmin CC. See also Downderry, Hessenford,
Tideford, Trerule Foot. Present Nmn and
later ch on site of Saxon cathedral of the
South West.

ST GILES IN THE WOOD Devon
163 SS 5318 2m E of Torrington. CP, 414.
Trrngtn RD. P Trrngtn. Ch e. W Dvn CC
(Trrngtn). See also Kingscott.

ST GILES ON THE HEATH Devon
174 SX 3590 4m NNE of Launceston.
CP, 252. Holsworthy RD.
P Lncstn, Cornwall. Ch e, m. Sch p.
W Dvn CC (Tavistock). See also E Panson,
W Pnsn.

ST HELENA Norfolk
126 TG 1916 6m NNW of Norwich. Loc,
Horsford CP.

ST HELEN AUCKLAND Co Durham
85 NZ 1826 2m SW of Bishop Auckland.
Loc, Bshp Aucklnd UD. P Bshp Aucklnd.
Vllge with mdvl ch and several old bldngs in
indstrl setting. Trading estate.

ST HELENS IOW
180 SZ 6289 3m SE of Ryde. Loc, Rde MB.
P Rde.

ST HELENS Lancs
100 SJ 5195 11m ENE of Liverpool.
CB, 104,173. P. St Hlns BC. Glass-mnfg tn
in S Lancs coalfield. Pilkington Glass
Museum.

ST HILARY Cornwall
189 SW 5531 5m E of Penzance. CP, 552.
W Penwith RD. Ch e, m. Sch p. St Ives CC.
See also Relubbus.

ST ISSEY Cornwall
185 SW 9271 4m W of Wadebridge.
CP, 601. Wdbrdge and Padstow RD.
P Wdbrdge. Ch e, c. Sch pe. N Cnwll CC. See
also Lit Petherick, Tredinnick, Trenance.

ST IVE Cornwall
186 SX 3067 4m ENE of Liskeard.
CP, 1,201. Lskd RD. P Lskd. Ch e, m.
Bodmin CC. See also Pensilva. Ch is good
example of Dec style.

ST IVES Cornwall
189 SW 5140 7m NNE of Penzance.
MB, 9,710. P. St Ives CC. See also Carbis
Bay, Halse Town, Lelant. Former fishing tn,
now resort and artists' haunt.

ST IVES Hants
179 SU 1203 2m WSW of Ringwood.
CP(St Leonards and St Ives), 3,374. Rngwd
and Fordingbridge RD. P Rngwd. Ch e. New
Forest CC.

ST IVES Hunts
134 TL 3171 5m E of Huntingdon.
MB, 7,130. P HNTNGDN. Hunts CC. On
R Ouse, spanned by 15c br with br chpl.
Boating. Statue on Market Hill of Oliver
Cromwell, who once lived here.

ST JAMES SOUTH ELMHAM Suffolk (E)
137 TM 3281 5m WNW of Halesworth.
CP, 165. Wainford RD. P Hlswth. Ch e.
Lowestoft CC.

ST JOHN Cornwall
187 SX 4053 2m SW of Torpoint. CP, 207.
St Germans RD. P Tpnt. Ch e. Bodmin CC.
See also Freathy.

ST JOHN BECKERMET Cumb
82 NY 0106 8m SSE of Whitehaven.
CP, 1,696. Ennerdale RD. Ch e. Sch pe.
Whthvn CC. See also Thornhill.

ST JOHN'S CHAPEL Co Durham
84 NY 8838 7m W of Stanhope. Loc,
Stnhpe CP. P Bishop Auckland. Ch e, m.

ST JOHN'S FEN END Norfolk
124 TF 5311 5m E of Wisbech. Loc,
Terrington St John CP. P Wsbch, Cambs.

ST JOHN'S HIGHWAY Norfolk
124 TF 5314 6m NE of Wisbech. Loc,
Terrington St John CP.

ST JOHN'S WOOD London
160 TQ 2683 3m NW of Charing Cross. Loc,
City of Westminster LB. St Marylebone BC.
Rsdntl distr W of Regent's Pk. Lord's
Cricket Grnd, HQ of MCC (Marylebone
Crckt Club) and of Middlesex County Club.

ST JUST Cornwall
189 SW 3731 6m W of Penzance.
UD, 3,573. P Pnznce. St Ives CC. See also
Bojewyan, Botallack, Carnyorth, Kelynack,
Pendeen, Trewellard. Former mining tn,
most westerly tn in England.

ST JUST Cornwall
190 SW 8435 2m N of St Mawes. CP(St Jst-
in-Roseland), 1,438. Truro RD. Ch e.
Truro CC. See also St Mawes. Creekside ch
with famous flower-strewn churchyard.

ST JUST LANE Cornwall
190 SW 8535 2m N of St Mawes. Loc,
St Just-in-Roseland CP. P Truro. Ch m.

ST KEVERNE Cornwall
190 SW 7921 9m ESE of Helston.
CP, 1,718. Kerrier RD. P Hlstn. Ch e, m4.
Sch p. St Ives CC. See also Coverack,
Porthallow, Porthoustock, Traboe. Offshore
to E, the notorious Manacle rocks. 2m SW,
Three Brothers of Grugwith, Bronze Age
burial chamber. Beyond on Goonhilly
Downs, Post Office Satellite-Tracking
Station.

ST KEW Cornwall
185, 186 SX 0276 4m NNE of Wadebridge.
CP, 866. Wdbrdge and Padstow RD.
Ch e, m. Sch p. N Cnwll CC. See also Chapel
Amble, Pendoggett, Trelill.

ST KEW HIGHWAY Cornwall
185, 186 SX 0375 4m NE of Wadebridge.
Loc, St Kew CP. P Bodmin. Ch m.

ST KEYNE Cornwall
186 SX 2460 2m S of Liskeard. CP, 173.
Lskd RD. P Lskd. Ch e. Bodmin CC. Holy
well, subject of poem by Southey.

ST LAWRENCE Cornwall
185, 186 SX 0466 1m WSW of Bodmin.
Loc, Bdmn MB. Wadebridge and
Padstow RD. Bdmn CC.

ST LAWRENCE Essex
162 TL 9604 7m E of Maldon. CP, 248.
Mldn RD. Ch e. Sch pe. Mldn CC. See also
Ramsey Island.

ST LAWRENCE IOW
180 SZ 5376 2m WSW of Ventnor. Loc,
Vntnr UD. P Vntnr.

ST LEONARDS Bucks
159 SP 9107 3m S of Tring.
CP(Cholesbury-cum-St Lnrds), 925.
Amersham RD. P Trng, Herts. Ch e. Sch pe.
Chesham and Amrshm CC (Aylesbury).

ST LEONARDS Hants
179 SU 1103 3m WSW of Ringwood.
CP(St Lnrds and St Ives), 3,374. Rngwd and
Fordingbridge RD. P Rngwd. Ch e. New
Forest CC. See also Ashley Hth.

ST LEONARDS Sussex (E)
184 TQ 8009 W distr of Hastings. Loc,
Hstngs CB. P(St Lnrds-on-Sea).

ST LEVAN Cornwall
189 SW 3822 8m SW of Penzance. CP, 615.
W Penwith RD. Ch e, m. Sch p. St Ives CC.
See also Porthcurno, Treen.

ST MABYN Cornwall
185, 186 SX 0473 3m E of Wadebridge.
CP, 488. Wdbrdge and Padstow RD.
P Bodmin. Ch e, m2. Sch pe. N Cnwll CC.

ST MARGARETS Hereford
142 SO 3533 10m WSW of Hereford.
CP, 160. Dore and Bredwardine RD. Ch e.
Hrfd CC. See also Upr Maes-Coed. Ch:
carved scrn.

ST MARGARET'S AT CLIFFE Kent
173 TR 3644 4m NE of Dover. CP, 1,513.
Dvr RD. P Dvr. Ch e, b. Sch pe. Dvr and
Deal CC (Dvr). See also W Clffe. Small
resort. To SE is S Foreland, two
lighthouses* and smock mill. On cliffs to N,
monmt to the Dover Patrol.

**ST MARGARET SOUTH ELMHAM Suffolk
(E)**
137 TM 3183 4m SSW of Bungay. CP, 122.
Wainford RD. P Harleston, Norfolk. Ch e.
Lowestoft CC.

ST MARTIN Cornwall
186 SX 2655 1m N of Looe. Loc, Looe UD.

ST MARTIN'S Isles of Scilly
189 SV 9215. CP, 118. Is of S RD. P.
Ch e, m. Sch pe. St Ives CC. See also Hr Tn,
Lr Tn, Middle Tn.

ST MARTIN'S Shrops
118 SJ 3236 5m W of Ellesmere. CP, 1,970.
Oswestry RD. P Oswstry. Ch e, c. Sch s.
Oswstry CC. See also Ifton Hth.

ST MARTIN'S GREEN Cornwall
190 SW 7323 5m ESE of Helston. Loc,
St Mtn-in-Meneage CP. Kerrier RD.
P (St Mtn), Hlstn. Ch e, m. Sch p.
St Ives CC.

ST MARY BOURNE Hants
168 SU 4250 5m NE of Andover.
CP, 1,271. Kingsclere and Whitchurch RD.
P Andvr. Ch e, m, s. Sch p. Basingstoke CC.
See also Binley, Stoke. Ch: rare black
marble font.

ST MARY CRAY London
171 TQ 4767 1m NE of Orpington. Loc,
Bromley LB. P Orpngtn, Kent.
Orpngtn BC (CC). Indstrl distr.

ST MARY IN THE MARSH Kent
184 TR 0627 10m ENE of Rye. CP, 1,085.
Romney Marsh RD. P Rmny Msh. Ch e.
Folkestone and Hythe CC. See also
St Mary's Bay. Remote among sheep
pastures and rhines.

ST MARYLEBONE London
160 TQ 2881 2m NW of Charing Cross. Loc,
City of Westminster LB. St Mrlbne BC. Distr
of central London. Incl Regent's Pk to N;
famous sts incl Baker St, Harley St,
Wimpole St.

ST MARY'S Isles of Scilly
189 SV 9111. CP, 1,736. Is of S RD. P.
Ch e, m, r. Sch p, s. St Ives CC. See also
Hugh Tn. The largest of the islands.
Terminus of air and sea services from
mainland. There is a 9-hole golf course.

ST MARY'S BAY Kent
184 TR 0927 6m SW of Hythe. Loc, St Mry
in the Marsh CP. P Romney Marsh. Resort.

ST MARY'S GROVE Som
155, 165 ST 4669 8m W of Bristol. Loc,
Nailsea CP.

ST MARY'S HOO Kent
172 TQ 8076 6m NE of Rochester. CP(St
Mary Hoo), 206. Strood RD. Ch e.
Gravesend CC.

ST MAWES Cornwall
190 SW 8433 3m E of Falmouth across
river. Loc, St Just-in-Roseland CP. P Truro.
Ch e, c, m, r. Sch p. Cstle (A.M.) blt by
Henry VIII, completed 1543.

ST MAWGAN Cornwall
185 SW 8765 5m NE of Newquay. Loc,
Mgn-in-Pydar CP. St Austell RD. P Nquay.
Ch e, m. Sch p. N Cnwll CC. Lanherne, next
to ch, was home of the Arundells from 13c
to 1794; thereafter, a nunnery.

ST MELLION Cornwall
186 SX 3865 3m SSE of Callington.
CP, 195. St Germans RD. P Saltash.
Ch e, m. Sch pe. Bodmin CC.

ST MERRYN Cornwall
185 SW 8874 2m WSW of Padstow.
CP, 1,107. Wadebridge and Pdstw RD.
P Pdstw. Ch e, m. Sch p. N Cnwll CC. See
also Shop, Treyarnon Bay. 1m NW, Harlyn
Bay Prehistoric Burial Ground and Museum.

ST MEWAN Cornwall
185, 190 SW 9951 1m WSW of St Austell.
CP, 1,507. St Astll RD. Ch e, m. Sch p.
Truro CC. See also Trewoon.

ST MICHAEL CAERHAYS Cornwall
190 SW 9642 7m SSW of St Austell.
CP, 124. St Astll RD. Ch e. Truro CC. To
SE, Caerhays Cstle, by Nash (1808). Gdns
of rhododendrons etc. Private.

ST MICHAEL PENKEVIL Cornwall
190 SW 8542 3m SE of Truro across river.
CP, 251. Truro RD. P Truro. Ch e. Sch pe.

Truro CC. See also Lamorran, Merther. To
S, Tregothnan, home of the Boscawens, blt
by William Wilkins, architect of National
Gallery, London.

ST MICHAELS Kent
172, 184 TQ 8835 1m N of Tenterden. Loc,
Tntdn MB. P Tntdn.

ST MICHAELS Worcs
129 SO 5865 2m SSW of Tenbury Wells.
Loc, Tnbry CP. Ch e. Large 19c Gothic
choir sch and music library.

ST MICHAEL'S MOUNT Cornwall
189 SW 5130 just S of Marazion. CP, 47.
W Penwith RD. St Ives CC. Once a
monastery, now home of St Aubyn family
but owned by NT*. Access on foot by
causeway at low tide.

ST MICHAEL'S ON WYRE Lancs
94 SD 4641 9m NNW of Preston. Loc, Upr
Rawcliffe-w-Tarnacre CP. Garstang RD. P(St
Mchl's), Prstn. Ch e. Sch pe. N Fylde CC.
Mdvl ch with low, massive twr.

ST MICHAEL SOUTH ELMHAM Suffolk
(E)
137 TM 3483 4m S of Bungay. CP, 58.
Wainford RD. Ch e. Lowestoft CC.

ST MINVER Cornwall
185 SW 9677 3m NNW of Wadebridge. Loc,
St Mnvr Highlands CP. Wdbrdge and
Padstow RD. P Wdbrdge. Ch e, m. Sch p.
N Cnwll CC.

ST NEOT Cornwall
186 SX 1867 5m WNW of Liskeard.
CP, 799. Lskd RD. P Lskd. Ch e, m4. Sch p.
Bodmin CC. See also Ley. The bones of the
saint, reputedly King Alfred's brother, were
carried off to Hunts (see below) in mdvl
times; returned to Cnwll; finally filched by
vandals in 19c.

ST NEOTS Hunts
134 TL 1860 8m SSW of Huntingdon.
UD, 15,137. P HNTNGDN. Hunts CC
(Hunts CC, Mid-Beds CC). See also Eaton
Socon, Eynesbury. Tn on R Ouse. 15c
ch: twr.

ST NICHOLAS AT WADE Kent
173 TR 2666 6m E of Herne Bay. CP, 640.
Eastry RD. P Birchington. Ch e, m. Sch pe.
Thanet W BC (Isle of Thnt CC). Nmn ch.

ST NICHOLAS SOUTH ELMHAM Suffolk (E)
137 TM 3282 4m S of Bungay. CP(All Saints and St Nchls, S Elmhm), 154. Wainford RD. Ch e. Lowestoft CC. Ch of St Nchls has almost disappeared.

ST OSYTH Essex
150 TM 1215 3m W of Clacton. CP, 1,857. Tendring RD. P Clcton-on-Sea. Ch e, m, v. Sch pe. Harwich CC. Tide mill on creek of R Colne. Ch 15c—16c; monmts. St O's Priory*, rems of 12c abbey with massive late 15c flint gatehouse joined to Tdr and later hse; gdns.

ST OWEN'S CROSS Herefs
142 SO 5324 4m W of Ross-on-Wye. Loc, Hentland CP. Rss and Whitchurch RD. P HEREFORD. Hrfd CC.

ST PANCRAS London
160 TQ 2983 2m N of Charing Cross. Loc, Camden LB. St Pncrs N BC, Holborn and St Pncrs S BC. Distr N of well known rly stn beloved of admirers of Vctrn architecture.

ST PAUL'S CRAY London
171 TQ 4768 2m NNE of Orpington. Loc, Bromley LB. P Orpngtn, Kent. Chislehurst BC (CC). Indstrl distr.

ST PAUL'S WALDEN Herts
147 TL 1922 3m WSW of Stevenage. CP, 1,039. Hitchin RD. Ch e, m. Sch p. Htchn CC. See also Whitwell. 14c and later ch: 18c scrn.

ST PETERS Kent
173 TR 3868 2m N of Ramsgate. UD(Broadstairs and St Ptr's), 19,996. P Brdstrs. Thanet E BC (Isle of Thnt CC).

ST PINNOCK Cornwall
186 SX 1963 3m WSW of Liskeard. CP, 342. Lskd RD. Ch e, v. Bodmin CC. See also E Taphouse.

ST STEPHEN Cornwall
185, 190 SX 9453 4m W of St Austell. CP(St Stphn-in-Brannel), 4,533. St Astll RD. P St Astll. Ch e, m4. Sch p. Truro CC. See also St Stephen's Coombe.

ST STEPHENS Cornwall
174, 186 SX 3285 just NW of Launceston. Loc, Lncstn MB. P Lncstn. The mother ch of Lncstn, with a fine view thereof.

ST STEPHENS Cornwall
187 SX 4158 1m WSW of Saltash. Loc, Sltsh MB.

ST STEPHEN'S COOMBE Cornwall
185, 190 SW 9551 4m W of St Austell. Loc, St Stephen-in-Brannel CP. P St Astll.

ST TEATH Cornwall
185, 186 SX 0680 3m SW of Camelford. CP, 1,691. Cmlfd RD. P Bodmin. Ch e, m. Sch p. N Cnwll CC. See also Delabole, Treligga.

ST TUDY Cornwall
185, 186 SX 0676 5m NE of Wadebridge. CP, 413. Wdbrdge and Padstow RD. P Bodmin. Ch e, m. Sch pe. N Cnwll CC. To W, Tremeer, hse prob of 14c, where Charles II's doctor was born and died. Gdns open.

ST VEEP Cornwall
186 SX 1455 4m SE of Lostwithiel. CP, 331. Liskeard RD. Ch e. Bodmin CC. See also Penpoll.

ST WENN Cornwall
185 SW 9664 5m SSW of Wadebridge. CP, 318. St Austell RD. Ch e, m2. Sch p. N Cnwll CC. See also Rosenannon, Tregonetha. S wall of ch has punning sundial of 1855.

ST WEONARDS Herefs
142 SO 4924 7m N of Monmouth. CP, 421. Ross and Whitchurch RD. P HEREFORD. Ch e. Sch p. Hrfd CC. To SW, Treago, fortified stone hse owned by Mynors family since early 14c.

SALCOMBE Devon
187, 188 SX 7439 3m S of Kingsbridge. UD, 2,471. P. Totnes CC. Small resort in Kngsbrdge estuary, near its mouth. Boating. Cliffs (NT) from Bolt Head to Blt Tail.

SALCOMBE REGIS Devon
176 SY 1488 2m ENE of Sidmouth. Loc, Sdmth UD. P Sdmth. At top of combe leading steeply to cliffs and sea, 1m.

SALCOTT Essex
149, 162 TL 9513 4m ESE of Tiptree. CP, 186. Lexden and Winstree RD. P Maldon. Ch e. Colchester CC.

SALE Ches
101 SJ 7991 5m SW of Manchester.

MB, 55,623. P. Altrincham and Sle CC. See also Ashton upon Mersey.

SALEBY Lincs (L)
105 TF 4578 2m N of Alford. CP(Slby w Thoresthorpe), 123. Louth RD. P Alfd. Ch e, m. Lth CC.

SALE GREEN Worcs
130, 131 SO 9358 4m SSE of Droitwich. Loc, Drtwch RD. Ch m. Worcester BC.

SALEHURST Sussex (E)
183, 184 TQ 7424 5m N of Battle. CP, 1,777. Bttle RD. Ch e. Sch pe. Rye CC. See also Robertsbridge.

SALESBURY Lancs
94, 95 SD 6732 3m N of Blackburn. CP, 283. Blckbn RD. P Blckbn. Ch e. Sch pe. Darwen CC. See also Copster Grn.

SALFORD Beds
146 SP 9339 5m NE of Bletchley. CP(Hulcote and Salford), 207. Ampthill RD. P Bltchly, Bucks. Ch e. Mid-Beds CC.

SALFORD Lancs
101 SJ 8298 just W of Manchester. CB, 130,641. P. BCs: Slfd E, Slfd W. Extensive docks beside Mnchstr Ship Canal. RC cathedral.

SALFORD Oxon
145 SP 2828 2m WNW of Chipping Norton. CP, 222. Chppng Ntn RD. P Chppng Ntn. Ch e, m. Sch p. Banbury CC.

SALFORD PRIORS Warwicks
144 SP 0751 5m NNE of Evesham. CP, 1,073. Alcester RD. P Eveshm, Worcs. Ch e. Sch pe. Stratford-on-Avon CC (Strtfd). See also Abbot's Slfd, Dunnington, Iron Cross.

SALFORDS Surrey
170 TQ 2846 3m SSE of Reigate. Loc, Horley CP. P Redhill. Ch e. Sch p.

SALHOUSE Norfolk
126 TG 3014 2m SSE of Wroxham. CP, 737. St Faith's and Aylsham RD. P NORWICH, NOR 53Z. Ch e, b, m. Sch pe. N Nflk CC (Central Nflk).

SALING, GREAT Essex
148, 149 TL 7025 4m WNW of Braintree. See Gt Slng.

SALISBURY Wilts
167 SU 1430 21m NW of Southampton. MB(New Sarum), 35,271. P. Slsbry CC. Tn planned by Bishop Poore, who founded it and cathedral (EE) in 1220. Cthdrl spire highest in England, 404ft. Handsome close; also other chs, public bldngs. To N, Old Sarum (A.M.), large earthworks which mark orig site of tn, cstle, and first cthdrl.

SALKELD, GREAT Cumb
83 NY 5536 5m NNE of Penrith. See Gt Slkld.

SALL Norfolk
125 TG 1124 6m WSW of Aylsham. CP, 137. St Faith's and Aylshm RD. Ch e. N Nflk CC (Central Nflk). Outstanding 15c ch.

SALMONBY Lincs (L)
114 TF 3273 5m ENE of Horncastle. CP, 43. Hncstle RD. Ch e. Hncstle CC.

SALPERTON Glos
144 SP 0720 8m E of Cheltenham. Loc, Hazleton CP. P Chltnhm. Ch e.

SALPH END Beds
147 TL 0752 3m NE of Bedford. Loc, Renhold CP.

SALT Staffs
119 SJ 9527 4m NE of Stafford. CP(Slt and Enson), 357. Stffd RD. P STFFD. Ch e. Sch pe. Stffd and Stone CC.

SALTASH Cornwall
187 SX 4358 4m NW of Plymouth. MB, 9,923. P. Bodmin CC. See also St Stephens, Trematon. Ancient borough on R Tamar, here spanned by Brunel's famous rly br and by the rd br opened in 1961.

SALTBURN-BY-THE-SEA Yorks (N)
86 NZ 6621 11m E of Teesside (Middlesbrough). UD(Sltbn and Marske-by-the-Sea), 19,562. P. Cleveland and Whitby CC (Scarborough and Whtby). See also New Mske. Resort with long firm sands.

SALTBY Leics
122 SK 8526 8m ENE of Melton Mowbray. Loc, Sproxton CP. P Mltn Mbry. Ch e, m. Sch pe.

SALTER Lancs
89, 94 SD 6063 8m E of Lancaster. Loc, Roeburndale CP. Lunesdale RD. Lncstr CC.

SALTERFORTH Yorks (W)
95 SD 8845 3m N of Colne. CP, 482.
Skipton RD. P Clne, Lancs. Ch b, f. Sch p.
Skptn CC.

SALTERSWALL Ches
110 SJ 6267 2m WNW of Winsford. Loc,
Wnsfd UD.

SALTFLEET Lincs (L)
105 TF 4593 6m NNW of Mablethorpe.
CP(Skidbrooke w Sltflt Haven), 415.
Louth RD. P Lth. Ch m. Lth CC.

SALTFLEETBY ALL SAINTS Lincs (L)
105 TF 4590 5m NW of Mablethorpe.
CP, 90. Louth RD. P(Sltfltby), Lth.
Ch e, m. Sch pe. Lth CC.

SALTFLEETBY ST CLEMENTS Lincs (L)
105 TF 4591 5m NNW of Mablethorpe.
CP, 69. Louth RD. P(Sltfltby), Lth. Ch e.
Lth CC.

SALTFLEETBY ST PETER Lincs (L)
105 TF 4389 5m NW of Mablethorpe.
CP, 262. Louth RD. P(Sltfltby), Lth.
Ch e, m. Lth CC. Two twrs: one is sole rems
of old ch, the other is Rgncy folly.

SALTFORD Som
156 ST 6867 5m WNW of Bath. Loc,
Keynsham UD. P BRISTOL.

SALTHOUSE Norfolk
125 TG 0743 3m N of Holt. CP, 233.
Erpingham RD. P Hlt. Ch e, m. N Nflk CC.

SALTMARSHE Yorks (E)
97, 98 SE 7824 3m E of Goole. Loc,
Laxton CP.

SALTON Yorks (N)
92 SE 7180 6m WSW of Pickering. CP, 91.
Kirkbymoorside RD. P YORK. Ch e, m.
Thirsk and Malton CC. Nmn ch.

SALTRENS Devon
163 SS 4521 3m S of Bideford. Loc,
Monkleigh CP.

SALTWICK Nthmb
78 NZ 1780 4m SSW of Morpeth. Loc,
Stannington CP.

SALTWOOD Kent
173 TR 1535 just N of Hythe. CP, 849.
Elham RD. P Hythe. Ch e. Sch pe.

Folkestone and Hthe CC. 12c–14c cstle
much restored.

SALWARPE Worcs
130 SO 8762 2m WSW of Droitwich. CP.
Drtwch RD. Ch e. Worcester BC.

SALWAYASH Devon
177 SY 4596 3m N of Bridport. Loc,
Netherbury CP. P Brdpt. Ch m. Sch pe.

SAMBOURNE Warwicks
131 SP 0661 3m NNW of Alcester. CP.
Alcstr RD. P Redditch, Worcs. Ch e.
Stratford-on-Avon CC (Strtfd).

SAMBROOK Shrops
119 SJ 7124 4m NW of Newport. Loc,
Chetwynd CP. Wellington RD. P Npt. Ch e.
Sch p. The Wrekin CC.

SAMLESBURY Lancs
94 SD 5930 3m E of Preston. CP, 1,180.
Prstn RD. P Prstn. Ch e, r. Sch pe, pr.
S Fylde CC. See also Smlsbry Bottoms.

SAMLESBURY BOTTOMS Lancs
94, 95 SD 6129 4m W of Blackburn. Loc,
Smlsbry CP. 1m N, Smlsbry Hr Hall,
restored 15c half-timbered hse.

SAMPFORD ARUNDEL Som
164 ST 1018 2m WSW of Wellington.
CP, 320. Wllngton RD. P Wllngton. Ch e.
Sch p. Taunton CC. See also Smpfd Moor.

SAMPFORD BRETT Som
164 ST 0840 2m SSE of Watchet. CP, 255.
Williton RD. P Taunton. Ch e.
Bridgwater CC.

SAMPFORD COURTENAY Devon
175 SS 6301 5m NE of Okehampton.
CP, 707. Okhmptn RD. P Okhmptn.
Ch e, m2. W Dvn CC (Torrington). See also
Honeychurch, Sticklepath. Colourwash and
thatch; granite Perp ch. Prayer Book
Rebellion began here, 1549.

SAMPFORD, GREAT Essex
148 TL 6435 3m NE of Thaxted. See Gt
Smpfd.

SAMPFORD MOOR Som
164 ST 1117 3m SW of Wellington. Loc,
Smpfd Arundel CP.

SAMPFORD PEVERELL Devon
164, 176 ST 0314 5m E of Tiverton.
CP, 711. Tvtn RD. P Tvttn. Ch e, m. Sch pe.
Tvtn CC.

SAMPFORD SPINEY Devon
175, 187 SX 5372 4m ESE of Tavistock.
CP, 124. Tvstck RD. Ch e. W Dvn CC
(Tvstck).

SANCREED Cornwall
189 SW 4129 3m W of, Penzance. CP, 568.
W Penwith RD. Ch e, m2. Sch pe.
St Ives CC. See also Brane, Drift. Various
old crosses and standing stones. Hill fort at
Caer Bran and fogou at Carn Uny (A.M.).

SANCTON Yorks (E)
98 SE 9039 2m SE of Mkt Weighton.
CP, 363. Pocklington RD. P YORK.
Ch e, m. Sch pe. Howden CC.

SANDBACH Ches
110 SJ 7560 5m NE of Crewe. UD, 13,303.
P. Crwe CC. See also Elworth, Wheelock.
Salt-mining tn and home of Fodens motor
works of brass band fame. Two large Saxon
crosses (A.M.) in mkt place.

SANDBANKS Dorset
179 SZ 0387 4m SW of Bournemouth. Loc,
Poole MB. P Ple. Almost encloses Ple
Harbour. Car ferry to Isle of Purbeck.

SANDERSTEAD London
170 TQ 3461 3m SSE of Croydon. Loc,
Crdn LB. P South Crdn, Surrey. Crdn S BC
(E Srry CC). Rsdntl distr in hilly area rising
to c 500ft.

SANDFORD Devon
176 SS 8202 2m NNW of Crediton.
CP, 982. Crdtn RD. P Crdtn. Ch e, c. Sch p.
Tiverton CC (Torrington). See also E Vllge,
Newbuildings.

SANDFORD Dorset
178, 179 SY 9289 1m N of Wareham. Loc,
Wrhm St Martin CP. Wrhm and Purbeck RD.
P Wrhm. S Dst CC.

SANDFORD Som
165 ST 4259 5m NNW of Cheddar. Loc,
Winscombe CP. P BRISTOL. Ch e, m. Sch p.

SANDFORD Westm
83/84 NY 7216 4m SE of Appleby. Loc,
Warcop CP. Ch m.

SANDFORD-ON-THAMES Oxon
158 SP 5301 3m SSE of Oxford. CP, 813.
Bullingdon RD. P OXFD. Ch e. Henley CC.

SANDFORD ORCAS Dorset
166 SY 6220 3m NNW of Sherborne.
CP, 170. Shbne RD. P Shbne. Ch e. W Dst CC.
Tdr mnr hse* and mainly Perp ch in Ham
stone.

SANDFORD ST MARTIN Oxon
145 SP 4226 7m E of Chipping Norton.
CP, 254. Chppng Ntn RD. P OXFORD.
Ch e. Banbury CC. See also Ledwell.

SANDGATE Kent
173 TR 2035 2m W of Folkestone. Loc,
Flkstne MB. P Flkstne. Resort. Military and
police barracks. Rems of Tdr cstle. Spade
Hse*, home of H.G. Wells.

SANDHILLS Oxon
158 SU 5607 3m ENE of Oxford.
CP(Risinghurst and Sndhlls), 3,271.
Bullingdon RD. Sch p. Mid-Oxon CC
(Henley).

SANDHILLS Surrey
169 SU 9337 4m SW of Godalming. Loc,
Witley CP.

SANDHOE Nthmb
77 NY 9766 2m NW of Corbridge. CP, 398.
Hexham RD. Hxhm CC.

SANDHOLME Lincs (H)
114, 123 TF 3337 4m S of Boston. Loc,
Frampton CP.

SANDHOLME Yorks (E)
98 SE 8230 7m NE of Goole. Loc,
Gilberdyke CP.

SANDHURST Berks
169 SU 8361 2m NW of Camberley.
CP, 6,445. Easthampstead RD.
P Cmbrly, Surrey. Ch e, b, m, r. Sch p2, pe.
Wokingham CC. See also Lit Sndhst. 1½m
E, Royal Military Academy; in grdns,
National Army Museum.

SANDHURST Glos
143 SO 8223 3m N of Gloucester. CP, 420.
Glcstr RD. P GLCSTR. Ch e, m. Sch p
W Glos CC.

SANDHURST

SANDHURST Kent
184 TQ 7928 9m NW of Rye. CP, 928.
Cranbrook RD. P Hawkhurst. Ch e, b, m.
Sch p. Royal Tunbridge Wells CC (Ashfd).
See also Sndhst Cross.

SANDHURST CROSS Kent
184 TQ 7827 1m SW of Sandhurst. Loc,
Sndhst CP.

SANDHUTTON Yorks (N)
91 SE 3882 3m W of Thirsk. CP, 182.
Thsk RD. P Thsk. Ch e, m. Thsk and
Malton CC.

SAND HUTTON Yorks (N)
97, 98 SE 6958 7m NE of York. CP, 151.
Flaxton RD. P YK. Ch e. Sch pe. Thirsk and
Malton CC.

SANDIACRE Derbys
112, 121 SK 4736 3m S of Ilkeston.
CP, 6,794. SE Derbys RD.
P NOTTINGHAM. Ch e, m2. Sch i, j, s.
SE Derbys CC.

SANDILANDS Lincs (L)
105 TF 5280 3m SSE of Mablethorpe. Loc,
Mblthpe and Sutton UD.

SANDIWAY Ches
110 SJ 6070 4m WSW of Northwich. Loc,
Cuddington CP. P Nthwch. Ch e, m. Sch p.

SANDLEHEATH Hants
179 SU 1214 2m W of Fordingbridge. Loc,
Fdngbrdge CP. P Fdngbrdge. Ch m.

SANDLEIGH Berks
158 SP 4701 3m NNW of Abingdon. Loc,
Wootton CP. P Abngdn.

SANDLING Kent
172 TQ 7558 2m N of Maidstone. Loc,
Boxley CP. P Mdstne. Sndlng Pk has fine
gdns*.

SANDON Essex
161, 162 TL 7404 3m ESE of Chelmsford.
CP, 966. Chlmsfd RD. P Chlmsfd. Ch e, v.
Sch s. Chlmsfd CC. See also Howe Grn. Ch
blt partly of Roman bricks.

SANDON Herts
147 TL 3234 4m SSW of Royston. CP, 539.
Hitchin RD. P Buntingford. Ch e, v2. Sch p.
Htchn CC. See also Mill End.

SANDON Staffs
119 SJ 9429 4m SE of Stone. CP, 494.
Stne RD. P STAFFORD. Ch e. Sch pe.
Stffd and Stne CC. See also Burston. To
SE along A51 rd, Sndn Hall, 19c hse in large
pk; 50-acre gdns*. Excavations have
uncovered part of lost vllge of Gt Sndn.

SANDOWN IOW
180 SZ 5984 5m S of Ryde.
UD (Sndn-Shanklin), 15,807. P. Isle of
Wight CC. See also Luccombe Vllge,
Yaverland. Resort. Geological museum.

SANDPLACE Cornwall
186 SX 2556 2m N of Looe. Loc,
Morval CP. P Looe.

SANDRIDGE Hants
147, 160 TL 1710 3m NE of St Albans. CP.
St Albns RD. P St Albns. Ch e, b. Sch p.
St Albns CC. Ch: chancel arch of Roman
bricks; 14c stone scrn.

SANDRIDGE Wilts
157 ST 9465 5m SW of Calne. Loc,
Melksham Without CP. Bradford and
Mlkshm RD. Sch pe. Westbury CC.

SANDRINGHAM Norfolk
124 TF 6928 7m NE of King's Lynn.
CP, 557. Freebridge Lynn RD. P(Sndrnghm
Hse). Ch e. NW Nflk CC (K's Lnn). See also
W Newton, Wolferton. Royal estate vllge.
Hse mid-19c in fine grnds*.

SANDSEND Yorks (N)
86 NZ 8612 3m WNW of Whitby. Loc,
Lythe CP. P Whtby. Ch e, m. Small resort.

SAND SIDE Lancs
88 SD 2282 5m NW of Ulverston. Loc,
Kirkby Ireleth CP. N Lonsdale RD. Morecambe and Lnsdle CC.

SANDTOFT Lincs (L)
103 SE 7408 4m NW of Epworth. Loc, Isle
of Axholme RD. Gainsborough CC.

SANDWAY Kent
172 TQ 8851 4m WNW of Charing. Loc,
Lenham CP. P Maidstone.

SANDWICH Kent
173 TR 3358 11m E of Canterbury.
MB, 4,467. P. Dover and Deal CC (Dvr). See
also Gt Stonar. First Cinque port; formerly
important naval base. Now resort. Famous
golf courses. 1m NE, Richborough Cstle

(A.M.). Power stns and factories on N side of tn.

SANDWITH Cumb
82 NX 9614 2m SSW of Whitehaven. Loc, Whthvn MB. P Whthvn.

SANDY Beds
147 TL 1749 8m E of Bedford. UD, 5,274. P. Mid—Beds CC. See also Beeston. Soil is indeed sandy here. Pine woods to E on low hills.

SANDY LANE Wilts
157 ST 9668 3m SW of Calne. Loc, Clne Without CP. Clne and Chippenham RD. Ch b. Chppnhm CC.

SANKEY, GREAT Lancs
100, 109 SJ 5688 2m W of Warrington. See Gt Snky.

SANTON Cumb
88 NY 1001 4m E of Seascale. CP(Irton w Sntn), 766. Millom RD. Ch m. Sch pe. Whitehaven CC.

SANTON BRIDGE Cumb
88 NY 1101 5m E of Seascale. Loc, Irton w Sntn CP. Millom RD. P Holmrook. Whitehaven CC.

SANTON DOWNHAM Suffolk (W)
136 TL 8187 2m ENE of Brandon. CP, 269. Mildenhall RD. P Brndn. Ch e. Bury St Edmunds CC. Surrounded by trees of Forestry Commission.

SAPCOTE Leics
132 SP 4993 4m E of Hinckley. CP, 851. Blaby RD. P LEICESTER. Ch e, m. Sch pe. Blby CC (Harborough).

SAPEY COMMON Herefs
130 SO 7063 7m NNE of Bromyard. Loc, Upr Sapey CP.

SAPISTON Suffolk (W)
136 TL 9175 6m SSE of Thetford. CP, 129. Thingoe RD. Ch e. Bury St Edmunds CC.

SAPPERTON Glos
157 SO 9403 5m W of Cirencester. CP, 377. Crncstr RD. P Crncstr. Ch e. Sch pe. Crncstr and Tewkesbury CC. See also Frampton Mansell. At head of wooded Golden Valley. Disused Thames-Severn Canal passes through 2m long tunnel.

SAPPERTON Lincs (K)
113, 123 TF 0133 7m E of Grantham. CP(Braceby and Spptn), 91. W Kesteven RD. Ch e. Rutland and Stamford CC.

SARACEN'S HEAD Lincs (H)
123 TF 3427 2m NW of Holbeach. Loc, Whaplode CP. P Spldng. Sch p.

SAREDON, GREAT Staffs
119 SJ 9508 2m WSW of Cannock.

SARISBURY Hants
180 SU 5008 5m WNW of Fareham. Loc, Frhm UD. P(Srsbry Grn), SOUTHAMPTON.

SARNESFIELD Herefs
142 SO 3750 9m SW of Leominster. CP, 74. Weobley RD. Ch e. Lmnstr CC.

SARRATT Herts
160 TQ 0499 4m WNW of Watford. CP, 2,870. Wtfd RD. P Rickmansworth. Ch e, b, v. Sch pe. SW Herts CC. See also Bucks Hill, Chandler's Cross. Vllge with a grn. Mdvl ch has saddleback twr.

SARRE Kent
173 TR 2565 8m W of Ramsgate. CP, 89. Eastry RD. P Birchington. Ch m. Thanet W BC (Isle of Thnt CC).

SARSDEN Oxon
145 SP 2823 3m SW of Chipping Norton. CP, 97. Chppng Ntn RD. Ch e. Banbury CC.

SATLEY Co Durham
84 NZ 1143 3m N of Tow Law. CP, 226. Lanchester RD. P Bishop Auckland. Ch e, m. Sch je. NW Drhm CC.

SATTERLEIGH Devon
163 SS 6622 4m SW of S Molton. CP(Sttlgh and Warkleigh), 175. S Mltn RD. Ch e, m. N Dvn CC.

SATTERTHWAITE Lancs
88, 89 SD 3392 4m SE of Coniston. CP, 297. N Lonsdale RD. P Ulverston. Ch e. Morecambe and Lnsdle CC. See also Grizedale.

SAUGHALL, GREAT Ches
109 SJ 3670 4m NW of Chester. See Gt Sghll.

SAUL Glos
156 SO 7409 7m WNW of Stroud.
CP(Fretherne w Sl), 718. Gloucester RD.
P GLCSTR. Ch e. Sch pe. Strd CC.

SAUNDBY Notts
104 SK 7888 2m SW of Gainsborough.
CP, 105. E Retford RD. Ch e. Bassetlaw CC.

SAUNDERTON Bucks
159 SP 7901 1m SW of Princes Risborough.
CP(Bledlow-cum-Sndrtn), 1,871.
Wycombe RD. Ch e. Aylesbury CC
(Wcmbe).

SAUNTON Devon
163 SS 4537 2m WNW of Braunton. Loc,
Brntn CP. P Brntn. Ch e. At N end of Brntn
Burrows and the extensive Sntn Sands.

SAUSTHORPE Lincs (L)
114 TF 3869 8m E of Horncastle. CP, 96.
Spilsby RD. Ch e. Sch pe. Hncstle CC.

SAVERLEY GREEN Staffs
110, 119 SJ 9638 5m NE of Stone. Loc,
Fulford CP.

SAWBRIDGEWORTH Herts
148 TL 4815 4m S of Bishop's Stortford.
UD, 7,083. P. E Herts CC. See also
Spellbrook. Ch: monmts, brasses.

SAWDON Yorks (N)
93 SE 9485 7m WSW of Scarborough. Loc,
Brompton CP. P Scbrgh. Ch m.

SAWLEY Derbys
112, 121 SK 4731 8m ESE of Derby. Loc,
Long Eaton UD. P Lng
Eatn, NOTTINGHAM.

SAWLEY Yorks (W)
91 SE 2467 5m WSW of Ripon. CP, 251.
Rpn and Pateley Br RD. P Rpn. Ch e, m.
Sch pe. Rpn CC.

SAWLEY Yorks (W)
95 SD 7746 4m NE of Clitheroe. CP, 108.
Bowland RD. P Clthroe, Lancs. Sch p.
Skipton CC. Rems of 12c abbey.

SAWSTON Cambs
148 TL 4849 6m SSE of Cambridge.
CP, 3,377. S Cambs RD. P CMBRDGE.
Ch e, c, m, r, s. Sch i, j, s. Cambs CC. Sstn
Hall, 16c mnr hse. First vllge college opened
here, 1930.

SAWTRY Hunts
134 TL 1683 9m NNW of Huntingdon.
CP, 986. Hntngdn RD. P HNTNGDN.
Ch e, m. Sch p, s. Hunts CC. Fenside vllge.
Ch: early 15c brass.

SAXBY Leics
122 SK 8220 4m E of Melton Mowbray.
Loc, Freeby CP. Ch e.

SAXBY Lincs (L)
104 TF 0086 7m WSW of Mkt Rasen.
CP, 66. Welton RD. Ch e. Gainsborough CC.
Monmts to Scarborough family in tiny
Ggn ch.

SAXBY ALL SAINTS Lincs (L)
104 SE 9916 4m SW of
Barton-upon-Humber. CP, 192. Glanford
Brigg RD. P Brgg. Ch e. Brgg and Scunthorpe
CC (Brgg).

SAXELBY Leics
122 SK 7021 3m WNW of Melton Mowbray.
Loc, Grimston CP. Ch e.

SAXHAM, GREAT Suffolk (W)
136 TL 7862 4m W of Bury
St Edmunds. See Gt Sxhm.

SAXILBY Lincs (L)
104/113 SK 8975 6m WNW of Lincoln.
CP(Sxlby w Ingleby), 1,636. Welton RD.
P LNCLN. Ch e, m. Sch pe.
Gainsborough CC.

SAXLINGHAM Norfolk
125 TG 0239 3m W of Holt. Loc, Field
Dalling CP. Ch e.

SAXLINGHAM NETHERGATE Norfolk
137 TM 2297 7m S of Norwich. CP, 562.
Forehoe and Henstead RD. P Nrwch.
Ch e, v. Sch pe. S Nflk CC (Central Nflk).

SAXMUNDHAM Suffolk (E)
137 TM 3863 11m NE of Woodbridge.
UD, 1,700. P. Eye CC.

SAXONDALE Notts
112, 122 SK 6839 7m E of Nottingham.
CP, 43. Bingham RD. Rushcliffe CC
(Carlton).

SAXON STREET Cambs
135 TL 6859 3m SE of Newmarket. Loc,
Woodditton CP. P Nmkt, Suffolk. Ch e.

SAXTEAD Suffolk (E)
137 TM 2665 2m NW of Framlingham.
CP, 279. Blyth RD. P Woodbridge. Ch e.
Eye CC. See also Sxtd Grn.

SAXTEAD GREEN Suffolk (E)
137 TM 2564 2m WNW of Framlingham.
Loc, Sxtd CP. Enormous green, with
restored 18c post-mill (A.M.).

SAXTHORPE Norfolk
125 TG 1130 6m SSE of Holt. Loc,
Corpusty CP. P NORWICH, NOR 15Y.
Ch e.

SAXTON Yorks (W)
97 SE 4736 4m S of Tadcaster. CP(Sxtn
w Scarthingwell), 294. Tdcstr RD. P Tdcstr.
Ch e. Sch pe. Barkston Ash CC.

SAYERS COMMON Sussex (E)
182 TQ 2618 3m W of Burgess Hill. Loc,
Hurstpierpoint CP. P Hassocks. Ch e.
Sch pe.

SCACKLETON Yorks (N)
92 SE 6472 7m SSE of Helmsley. CP, 92.
Malton RD. Thirsk and Malton CC.

SCAFTWORTH Notts
103 SK 6691 7m NNW of Retford. CP, 30.
E Rtfd RD. Bassetlaw CC.

SCAGGLETHORPE Yorks (E)
92 SE 8372 3m E of Malton. CP, 211.
Norton RD. P Mltn. Ch m. Howden CC.

SCALBY Yorks (E)
98 SE 8429 7m ENE of Goole. Loc,
Gilberdyke CP.

SCALBY Yorks (N)
93 TA 0090 2 m NW of Scarborough.
UD, 8,672. P Scbrgh. Scbrgh CC (Scbrgh
and Whitby).

SCALDWELL Northants
133 SP 7672 7m N of Northampton. CP, 251.
Brixworth RD. P NTHMPTN. Ch e. Sch pe.
Daventry CC (Kettering).

SCALEBY Cumb
76 NY 4563 5m NE of Carlisle. CP, 308.
Border RD. P Clsle. Ch e. Penrith and the
Bdr CC. See also Scalebyhill.

SCALEBYHILL Cumb
76 NY 4463 5m NNE of Carlisle. Loc,
Scaleby CP. Ch m.

SCALES Cumb
83 NY 3426 5m ENE of Keswick. Loc,
Threlkeld CP.

SCALES Lancs
88 SD 2772 5m ENE of Barrow. Loc,
Aldingham CP.

SCALES Lancs
94 SD 4530 6m W of Preston. Loc,
Newton-w-Clifton CP.

SCALFORD Leics
122 SK 7624 3m NNE of Melton Mowbray.
CP, 546. Mltn and Belvoir RD. P Mltn Mbry.
Ch e, m. Sch pe. Mltn CC. See also
Chadwell.

SCALING Yorks (N)
86 NZ 7413 3m SSE of Loftus. Loc,
Lfts UD, Whitby RD. Ch m. Cleveland and
Whtby CC (Scarborough and Whtby).

SCAMBLESBY Lincs (L)
105 TF 2778 6m N of Horncastle. CP, 165.
Hncstle RD. P Louth. Ch e. Sch pe.
Hncstle CC.

SCAMPSTON Yorks (E)
92 SE 8675 5m ENE of Malton. CP, 410.
Norton RD. P Mltn. Ch e. Howden CC. See
also E Knapton, W Knptn.

SCAMPTON Lincs (L)
104 SK 9579 6m NNW of Lincoln.
CP, 2,113. Welton RD. P LNCLN. Ch e, m.
Sch p, pe. Gainsborough CC. RAF stn,
famous in World War II. Many British and
German airmen's graves in churchyard.

SCARBOROUGH Yorks (N)
93 TA 0488 35m NE of York. MB, 44,370.
P. Scbrgh CC (Scbrgh and Whitby). See also
Eastfield, Osgodby. Old fishing port blt on
steep cliffside, now large resort and
conference tn. 12c cstle (A.M.). Woodend*,
formerly seaside hse of Sitwell family, now
museum.

SCARCLIFFE Derbys
112 SK 4968 6m NNW of Mansfield.
CP, 6,787. Blackwell RD. P Chesterfield.
Ch e, m. Sch p. Bolsover CC. See also
Palterton, Whaley Thorns.

SCARCROFT Yorks (W)
96 SE 3641 6m NE of Leeds. CP, 523.
Wetherby RD. P LDS. Barkston Ash CC.

Scargill

SCARGILL Yorks (N)
84 NZ 0510 4m S of Barnard Cstle. CP, 55.
Startforth RD. Richmond CC.

SCARISBRICK Lancs
100 SD 3713 4m SE of Southport.
CP, 2,895. W Lancs RD. P Ormskk. Ch e, m.
Sch p, pe, pr. Ormskk CC. See also Bescar,
Bscr Lane, Carr Cross, Heaton's Br, Pinfold,
Pool Hey, Snape Grn. To SE, Scrsbrck Hall,
by E.W. and A.W.N. Pugin. Now a sch.

SCARNING Norfolk
125 TF 9512 2m WSW of E Dereham.
CP, 666. Mitford and Launditch RD.
Ch e, c. Sch p. SW Nflk CC.

SCARRINGTON Notts
112, 122 SK 7341 9m SSW of Newark.
CP, 142. Bingham RD. Ch e, m.
Rushcliffe CC (Carlton). A cone of 60,000
used horseshoes stands in the vllge.

SCARTH HILL Lancs
100 SD 4206 1m SE of Ormskirk. Loc,
Ormskk UD. W Lancs RD. Ormskk CC.

SCARTHINGWELL Yorks (W)
97 SE 4937 4m S of Tadcaster. CP(Saxton
w Scthngwll), 294. Tdcstr RD. Ch r.
Barkston Ash CC.

SCAWBY Lincs (L)
104 SE 9605 2m WSW of Brigg. CP, 1,640.
Glanford Brgg RD. P Brgg. Ch e, m2. Sch p.
Brgg and Scunthorpe CC (Brgg). See also
Sturton.

SCAWTON Yorks (N)
92 SE 5483 4m W of Helmsley. CP, 84.
Hlmsly RD. Ch e. Thirsk and Malton CC.

SCAYNES HILL Sussex (E)
183 TQ 3623 2m E of Haywards Hth. Loc,
Lindfield Rural CP. Cuckfield RD. P Hwds
Hth. Ch e, b. Sch pe. Mid-Sx CC
(E Grinstead).

SCHOLAR GREEN Ches
110 SJ 8356 4m SSW of Congleton. Loc,
Odd Rode CP. Cngltn RD. P Stoke-on-Trent,
Staffs. Ch m. Knutsford CC. 1¼m N, Lit
Moreton Hall (NT)*, black and white moated
Elizn hse.

SCHOLES Yorks (W)
96, 102 SE 1625 4m S of Bradford. Loc,
Spenborough MB. P LEEDS. Brighouse and
Spnbrgh BC.

SCHOLES Yorks (W)
102 SE 1607 6m S of Huddersfield. Loc,
Holmfirth UD. P Rotherham.

SCILLY ISLES
See Isles of Scilly.

SCISSETT Yorks (W)
102 SE 2410 4m N of Penistone. Loc,
Denby Dale UD. P Huddersfield.

SCOLE Norfolk
136/137 TM 1578 2m ESE of Diss. CP, 927.
Depwade RD. P Dss. Ch e, b. Sch pe.
S Nflk CC. See also Billingford.

SCOLES Yorks (W)
96 SE 3736 5m ENE of Leeds. Loc,
Barwick in Elmet CP.

SCOPWICK Lincs (K)
113 TF 0758 8m N of Sleaford. CP, 783.
E Kesteven RD. P LINCOLN. Ch e, m.
Sch pe. Grantham CC. See also Kirkby Grn.
Stream flows through vllge.

SCORBOROUGH Yorks (E)
99 TA 0145 4m NNW of Beverley. Loc,
Leconfield CP. Ch e.

SCORRIER Cornwall
190 SW 7244 2m NE of Redruth. Loc,
Camborne-Rdrth UD. P Rdrth.

SCORRITON Devon
187, 188 SX 7068 3m NW of Buckfastleigh.
Loc, W Bckfstlgh CP. Totnes RD. Ch m.
Ttns CC.

SCORTON Lancs
94 SD 5048 8m S of Lancaster. Loc, Nether
Wyersdale CP. Garstang RD. P Preston.
Ch e, m, r. Sch pe.

SCORTON Yorks (N)
91 NZ 2500 5m E of Richmond. CP, 871.
Rchmnd RD. P Rchmnd. Ch m, r.
Rchmnd CC. Archery contests held here.

SCO RUSTON Norfolk
126 TG 2822 3m NNW of Wroxham. Loc,
Tunstead CP. Ch e. Coltishall airfield to W.

SCOTBY Cumb
76 NY 4455 3m E of Carlisle. Loc,
Wetheral CP. P Clsle. Ch e. Sch pe.

SCOTFORTH Lancs
94 SD 4859 1m S of Lancaster. Loc,

Lncstr MB; CP, Lncstr RD. P LNCSTR. Lncstr CC. See also Bailrigg.

SCOTHERN Lincs (L)
104 TF 0377 5m NE of Lincoln. CP, 537. Welton RD. P LNCLN. Ch e, m. Sch pe. Gainsborough CC.

SCOTLAND GATE Nthmb
78 NZ 2584 4m ESE of Morpeth. Loc, Bedlingtonshire UD. P Choppington. Blyth BC.

SCOT LANE END Lancs
101 SD 6209 4m NE of Wigan. Loc, Blackrod UD.

SCOTS' GAP Nthmb
77, 78 NZ 0386 10m W of Morpeth. Loc, Wallington Demesne CP. Mpth RD. Ch m. Mpth CC.

SCOTSWOOD Nthmb
78 NZ 2064 W distr of Newcastle. Loc, Ncstle upon Tyne CB. P NCSTLE UPON TYNE 5. Ncstle upon Tne W BC.

SCOTTER Lincs (L)
104 SE 8800 6m S of Scunthorpe. CP, 1,120. Gainsborough RD. P Gnsbrgh. Ch e, m3. Sch p. Gnsbrgh CC. See also Scotterthorpe, Susworth. Little old mkt tn blt round small grn. Scotton Forest to W.

SCOTTERTHORPE Lincs (L)
104 TE 8701 6m S of Scunthorpe. Loc, Scotter CP.

SCOTTON Lincs (L)
104 SK 8899 7m S of Scunthorpe. CP, 283. Gainsborough RD. P Gnsbrgh. Ch e, m2. Gnsbrgh CC. Large forestry area to W.

SCOTTON Yorks (N)
91 SE 1995 3m SSE of Richmond. CP, 4,370. Rchmnd RD. Rchmnd CC.

SCOTTON Yorks (W)
96 SE 3259 3m NE of Harrogate. CP, 389. Nidderdale RD. P Knaresborough. Ch e, m. Sch p. Hrrgte CC.

SCOTTOW Norfolk
126 TG 2623 4m SSW of N Walsham. CP, 1,388. Smallburgh RD. P NORWICH, NOR 58Y. Ch e. N Nflk CC. See also Fairstead.

SCOULTON Norfolk
136 TF 9800 4m E of Watton. CP, 213. Wayland RD. P NORWICH, NOR 21X. Ch e, m. Sch pe. S Nflk CC. Island in Scltn Mere is breeding place for many interesting birds.

SCOUTHEAD Yorks (W)
101 SD 9605 3m E of Oldham. Loc, Saddleworth UD. P Oldhm, Lancs.

SCRANE END Lincs (H)
114, 124 TF 3841 4m ESE of Boston. Loc, Freiston CP. Ch m.

SCRAINWOOD Nthmb
71 NT 9909 6m NW of Rothbury. Loc, Alnham CP.

SCRAPTOFT Leics
121, 122 SK 6405 4m E of Leicester. CP. Billesdon RD. Ch e. Harborough CC (Melton).

SCRATBY Norfolk
126 TG 5115 5m N of Yarmouth. CP(Ormesby St Margaret w Scrtby), 1,357. Blofield and Flegg RD. P Gt Ymth. Ch m. Ymth CC.

SCRAYINGHAM Yorks (E)
92, 97, 98 SE 7360 8m SSW of Malton. CP, 135. Norton RD. P YORK. Ch e. Howden CC. See also Leppington.

SCREDINGTON Lincs (K)
113, 123 TF 0940 4m SSE of Sleaford. CP, 230. E Kesteven RD. P Slfd. Ch e, m. Sch p. Rutland and Stamford CC.

SCREMBY Lincs (L)
114 TF 4467 5m SSW of Alford. CP, 85. Spilsby RD. P Splsby. Ch e, m. Horncastle CC.

SCREMERSTON Nthmb
64 NU 0049 3m SSE of Berwick-upon-Tweed. Loc, Ancroft CP. P BERWICK-UPN-TWD. Ch e, m. Sch p.

SCREVETON Notts
112, 122 SK 7343 8m SW of Newark. CP, 121. Bingham RD. Ch e. Rushcliffe CC (Carlton).

SCRIVEN Yorks
96 SE 3458 1m N of Knaresborough. CP, 130. Nidderdale RD. P Knsbrgh. Harrogate CC.

SCROOBY Notts
103 SK 6590 7m NNW of Retford. CP, 333.
E Rtfd RD. P Doncaster, Yorkshire.
Ch e, m. Bassetlaw CC. Home of William
Brewster, first of the Pilgrim Fathers. 1½m
SW, Serby Hall, 18c; six acres of gdns*.

SCROPTON Derbys
120 SK 1930 7m ESE of Uttoxeter.
CP(Foston and Scrptn), 668. Repton RD.
P DERBY. Ch e, m. Belper CC.

SCRUB HILL Lincs (L)
114 TF 2355 6m SSE of Woodhall Spa.
Loc, Horncastle RD. Hncstle CC.

SCRUTON Yorks (N)
91 SE 3092 4m W of Northallerton.
CP, 251. Bedale RD. P Nthlltn. Ch e, m.
Thirsk and Malton CC.

SCULTHORPE Norfolk
125 TF 8930 2m NW of Fakenham.
CP, 3,238. Walsingham RD. P Fknhm.
Ch e, m. Sch p, pe. NW Nflk CC (N Nflk).

SCUNTHORPE Lincs (L)
104 SE 8910 21m ENE of Doncaster.
MB, 70,880. P. Brigg and Scnthpe CC
(Brgg). Important iron and steel mnfg tn.

SEABOROUGH Dorset
177 ST 4206 3m SSW of Crewkerne.
CP, 52. Beaminster RD. Ch e. W Dst CC.

SEACROFT Lincs (L)
114 TF 5660 2m S of Skegness. Loc,
Croft CP.

SEAFORD Sussex (E)
183 TV 4899 8m W of Eastbourne.
UD, 16,196. P. Lewes CC. See also
Bishopstone, E Blatchington. Resort. Sea
encroachment.

SEAFORTH Lancs
100 SJ 3297 4m N of Liverpool. Loc,
Crosby MB. P LVPL 21. Extension to Lvpl
Docks incorporating container facilities.

SEAGRAVE Leics
121, 122 SK 6117 6m ESE of
Loughborough. CP, 330. Barrow
upon Soar RD. P Lghbrgh. Ch e, b, m.
Sch p. Melton CC.

SEAHAM Co Durham
85 NZ 4249 5m SSE of Sunderland.
UD, 23,410. P. Houghton-le-Spring CC.
Important coal etc port formerly called
Seaham Harbour. 1m N, ancient ch, hall and
former vicarage.

SEAHOUSES Nthmb
71 NU 2132 3m SE of Bamburgh. Loc,
N Sunderland CP. P. Ch m, r. Sch s. Old
fishing vllge with modern accretions. Sands
to N (NT).

SEAL Kent
171 TQ 5556 2m NE of Sevenoaks.
CP, 2,687. Svnks RD. P Svnks. Ch e.
Sch pe2. Svnks CC. Se See also Stone St,
Under River.

SEALE Surrey
169 SU 8947 4m E of Farnham. CP(Sle and
Tongham), 2,490. Guildford RD. P Fnhm.
Ch e. Sch pe. Fnhm CC.

SEAMER Yorks (N)
85 NZ 4910 6m S of Teesside
(Middlesborough). CP, 333. Stokesley RD.
P MDDLSBRGH, Tssde. Ch e, m.
Richmond CC.

SEAMER Yorks (N)
93 TA 0183 4m SSW of Scarborough.
CP, 1,205. Scbrgh RD. P Scbrgh. Ch e, m.
Sch p. Scbrgh CC (Scbrgh and Whitby). 2m
SE, site of mesolithic settlement; important
finds of tools, bones, ornaments.

SEA PALLING Norfolk
126 TG 4226 9m ESE of N Walsham.
CP, 426. Smallburgh RD.
P NORWICH, NOR 29Z. Ch e, b, m. Sch p.
N Nflk CC. See also Waxham. Has been
often inundated, esp in 1953. Holiday
shacks and caravans.

SEARBY Lincs (L)
104 TA 0705 4m NW of Caistor. CP(Sby
cum Owmby), 166. Cstr RD. Ch e, m.
Gainsborough CC.

SEASALTER Kent
172, 173 TR 0965 2m SW of Whitstable.
Loc, Whtstble UD. P Whtstble. Caravan
resort.

SEASCALE Cumb
88 NY 0301 11m SSE of Whitehaven.
CP, 1,990. Millom RD. P. Ch e, m, r. Sch p.
Whthvn CC. Small resort with much recent

bldng in connection with Calder Hall Power Stn to N.

SEATHORNE Lincs (L)
114 TF 5766 2m N of Skegness. Loc, Skgnss UD. P Skgnss.

SEATHWAITE Cumb
82 NY 2312 7m SSW of Keswick. Loc, Borrowdale CP. Mountain rescue post, at foot of Sty Head Pass. Sthwte Farm (NT) reputedly wettest inhabited place in England.

SEATHWAITE Lancs
88 SD 2296 5m WSW of Coniston. CP(Dunnerdale-w-Sthwte), 186. N Lonsdale RD. P Broughton-in-Furness. Ch e. Sch pe. Morecambe and Lnsdle CC. Remote Lake District vllge.

SEATOLLER Cumb
82 NY 2413 6m S of Keswick. Loc, Borrowdale CP.

SEATON Co Durham
85 NZ 3949 2m W of Seaham. CP(Stn w Slingley) 527. Easington RD. Houghton-le-Spring CC (Easngtn).

SEATON Cornwall
186 SX 3054 3m E of Looe. Loc, Liskeard RD, St Germans RD. P Torpoint. Bodmin CC. Modern holiday settlement.

SEATON Cumb
81, 82 NY 0130 2m NE of Workington. CP, 3,417. Cockermouth RD. P Wkngtn. Ch e, m. Sch i, pe. Wkngtn CC.

SEATON Devon
177 SY 2490 8m SE of Honiton. UD, 4,134. P. Hntn CC. Small resort at mouth of R Axe. To E, Dowlands Landslip, where cliffs partially collapsed, 1839.

SEATON Rutland
133 SP 9098 3m ESE of Uppingham. CP, 148. Uppnghm RD. P Uppnghm. Ch e. Rtlnd and Stamford CC. To E, 82-arched rly viaduct over Welland valley dominates landscape.

SEATON Yorks (E)
99 TA 1646 3m WSW of Hornsea. CP, 418. Holderness RD. P Hull. Bridlington CC.

SEATON BURN Nthmb
78 NZ 2373 6m N of Newcastle. Loc, Longbenton UD. P NCSTLE UPON TYNE.

SEATON CAREW Co Durham
85 NZ 5229 S distr of Hartlepool. Loc, Htlpl CB. P Htlpl. Resort with extensive sands on which scavengers may find coal and from which the intrepid may bathe.

SEATON DELAVAL Nthmb
78 NZ 3075 4m NW of Whitley Bay. Loc, Stn Valley UD. P Whtly Bay. Blyth BC. Mining vllge. 1½m ENE, S.D. Hall*, considered Vanbrugh's masterpiece.

SEATON ROSS Yorks (E)
97, 98 SE 7841 5m SSW of Pocklington. CP, 351. Pcklngtn RD. P YORK. Ch e, m. Howden CC.

SEATON SLUICE Nthmb
78 NZ 3376 3m SSE of Blyth. Loc, Whitley Bay MB. P Whtly Bay. Old vllge has disappeared under modern bldngs. Harbour orig constructed 17c–18c by Delavals of Stn Dlvl Hall.

SEAVE GREEN Yorks (N)
86, 92 NZ 5600 6m SSE of Stokesley. Loc, Bilsdale Midcable CP. Stksly RD. Richmond CC.

SEAVIEW IOW
180 SZ 6291 2m ESE of Ryde. Loc, Rde MB. P.

SEAVINGTON ST MARY Som
177 ST 3914 3m E of Ilminster. CP, 213. Chard RD. P Ilmnstr. Ch e, m. Yeovil CC.

SEAVINGTON ST MICHAEL Som
177 ST 4015 3m E of Ilminster. CP, 113. Chard RD. Ch e. Yeovil CC.

SEBERGHAM Cumb
83 NY 3641 8m SE of Wigton. CP, 356. Wgtn RD. P Carlisle. Ch e. Penrith and the Border CC. See also Welton.

SECKINGTON Warwicks
120 SK 2607 4m ENE of Tamworth. CP, 70. Atherstone RD. Ch e. Meriden CC.

SEDBERGH Yorks (W)
89 SD 6592 9m E of Kendal. CP, 2,219. Sdbgh RD. P. Ch e, f, m3, v. Sch p, s.

Skipton CC. See also Millthrop. Small stone-blt tn in wild moorland country. Boys' public sch.

SEDBURY Glos
155, 156 ST 5494 just E of Chepstow. Loc, Tidenham CP. Ch r, v.

SEDBUSK Yorks (N)
90 SD 8891 1m NE of Hawes. Loc, High Abbotside CP.   Aysgarth RD.   Ch m. Richmond CC.

SEDGEBERROW Worcs
144 SP 0238 3m S of Evesham. CP, 541. Eveshm RD.   P Eveshm.   Ch e.   Sch pe. S Worcs CC.

SEDGEBROOK Lincs (K)
113, 122 SK 8537 4m WNW of Grantham. CP, 175. W Kesteven RD. P Grnthm. Ch e. Sch pe. Grantham CC.

SEDGEFIELD Co Durham
85 NZ 3528 8m NW of Teesside (Stockton). CP, 4,605. Sdgfld RD. P STCKTN-ON-TEES, Tssde. Ch e, m, r. Sch p, s. Drhm CC (Sdgfld). Fine ch with Perp twr. Racecourse to SW.

SEDGEFORD Norfolk
124 TF 7036 4m SE of Hunstanton. CP, 4,605. Docking RD.   P King's Lynn. Ch e, m. Sch p. NW Nflk CC (K's Lnn).

SEDGEHILL Wilts
166 ST 8628 3m N of Shaftesbury. CP, 130. Mere and Tisbury RD. Ch e. Westbury CC.

SEDGLEY Staffs
130, 131 SO 9193 3m NNW of Dudley. Loc, Ddly CB. P Ddly, Worcs. Ddly W BC (Bilston).

SEDGWICK Westm
89 SD 5187 4m S of Kendal. CP, 215. S Westm RD. P Kndl. Westm CC. 1m NW, Sizergh Cstle (NT)*, 15c–18c hse incorporating 14c pele twr; home of Strickland family for 700 years.

SEDLESCOMBE Sussex (E)
184 TQ 7718 3m NE of Battle. CP, 991. Bttle RD. P Bttle. Ch e, c. Sch pe. Rye CC.

SEEND Wilts
167 ST 9461 4m W of Devizes. CP, 1,005. Dvzs RD.. P Melksham. Ch e, m. Sch pe. Dvzs CC. See also Sells Grn.

SEEND CLEEVE Wilts
167 ST 9361 5m W of Devizes. Loc, Snd CP. Ch m.

SEER GREEN Bucks
159, 160 SU 9691 2m NE of Beaconsfield. CP, 1,701. Amersham RD. P Bcnsfld. Ch e, b. Sch pe. Chesham and Amrshm CC (S Bucks).

SEETHING Norfolk
137 TM 3197 5m N of Bungay. CP, 281. Loddon RD. P NORWICH, NOR 35W. Ch e. Sch p. S Nflk CC.

SEFTON Lancs
100 SD 3501 4m NNE of Bootle. CP. W Lancs RD. Ch e. Sch p. Crosby BC (Ormskirk CC); detached part Ormskk CC. See also Lunt. Large Perp ch with spire, containing notable monmts; brasses, scrns.

SEGHILL Nthmb
78 NZ 2874 5m WNW of Whitley Bay. Loc, Seaton Valley UD. P Dudley. Blyth CC.

SEIGHFORD Staffs
119 SJ 8825 3m NW of Stafford. CP, 1,320. Stffd RD. P STFFD. Ch e. Sch p. Stffd and Stone CC. See also Coton Clanford, Derrington, Gt Bridgeford, Lit Brdgfd. To W, Sghfd Airfield.

SEISDON Staffs
130 SO 8394 5m WSW of Wolverhampton. CP (Trysull and Ssdn), 866. Ssdn RD. P Wlvrhmptn. SW Staffs CC (Brierley Hill).

SELATTYN Shrops
117 SJ 2633 3m NNW of Oswestry. CP (Slttn and Gobowen), 1,830. Oswstry RD. P Oswstry. Ch e. Sch pe. Oswstry CC. See also Hengoed. On edge of Welsh hills. Ch: roof with carved bosses.

SELBORNE Hants
169, 181 SU 7433 4m SSE of Alton. CP, 1,034. Altn RD. P Altn. Ch e, c, v. Sch pe. Petersfield CC. See also Blackmoor, Oakhanger. Home of Gilbert White, 18c naturalist. His hse now museum, with memorial room to Captain Oates, explorer.

SELBY Yorks (W)
97, 98 SE 6132 12m S of York. UD, 11,610. P. Barkston Ash CC. Abbey ch. 18c toll br. Flour mills.

SELHAM Sussex (W)
181 SU 9320 3m E of Midhurst. Loc,
Mdhst RD. Ch e. Chichester CC (Horsham).

SELLACK Herefs
142 SO 5627 3m NW of Ross-on-Wye.
CP, 226. Rss and Whitchurch RD. Ch e.
Sch pe. Hereford CC. See also Upr Grove
Cmmn.

SELLINDGE Kent
172, 173, 184 TR 0938 WNW of Hythe.
CP, 790. Elham RD. P Ashford. Ch e, b, m.
Sch p. Folkestone and Hthe CC.

SELLING Kent
172, 173 TR 0456 3m SSE of Faversham.
CP, 595. Swale RD. P Fvrshm. Ch e. Sch pe.
Fvrshm CC.

SELLS GREEN Wilts
167 ST 9561 4m W of Devizes. Loc,
Seend CP.

SELMESTON Sussex (E)
183 TQ 5107 5m NNE of Seaford. CP, 196.
Hailsham RD. Ch e. Lewes CC (Eastbourne).

SELSEY Sussex (W)
181 SZ 8592 8m S of Chichester. CP, 4,007.
Chchstr RD. P Chchstr. Ch e, m, r, v.
Sch p, s. Chchstr CC. See also Ch Norton.
Resort running down to Slsy Bill.

SELSFIELD COMMON Sussex (E)
182 TQ 3434 4m SW of E Grinstead. Loc,
W Hoathly CP.

SELSIDE Westm
89 SD 5399 4m NNE of Kendal.
CP(Whitwell and Slsde), 177. S Westm RD.
Ch e. Sch pe. Westm CC.

SELSIDE Yorks (W)
90 SD 7875 8m NNW of Settle. Loc,
Horton in Ribblesdale CP.

SELSLEY Glos
156 SO 8303 1m SW of Stroud. Loc, King's
Stanley CP. P Strd. Ch e. Ch by G.F. Bodley,
with windows by Morris & Co.

SELSTEAD Kent
173 TR 2144 6m N of Folkestone. Loc,
Swingfield CP. Elham RD. P Dvr. Sch pe.
Flkstne and Hythe CC.

SELSTON Notts
112 SK 4553 3m SE of Alfreton. CP, 9,904.
Basford RD. P NOTTINGHAM.
Ch e, c2, m5, v2. Sch ie, p3, s. Ashfield CC.
See also Bagthorpe, Underwood.

SELWORTHY Som
164 SS 9146 3m W of Minehead. CP, 556.
Williton RD. Ch e. Sch pe. Bridgwater CC.
See also Allerford, Bossington, Lynch.
Picture vllge on NT Holnicote estate.

SEMER Suffolk (W)
149 TM 0046 3m NNW of Hadleigh. CP, 154.
Cosford RD. P Ipswich. Ch e. Sudbury and
Woodbridge CC.

SEMINGTON Wilts
166, 167 ST 8960 3m NE of Trowbridge.
CP, 692. Bradford and Melksham RD.
P Trwbrdge. Ch e, m. Sch pe. Westbury CC.

SEMLEY Wilts
166, 167 ST 8926 3m NE of Shaftesbury.
CP, 477. Mere and Tisbury RD. P Shftsbry.
Ch e, b. Sch pe. Westbury CC.

SEND Surrey
169, 170 TQ 0255 2m SE of Woking.
CP, 3,680. Guildford RD. P Wkng.
Ch e, c, r. Sch pe, s. Dorking CC.

SENNEN Cornwall
189 SW 3525 8m WSW of Penzance.
CP, 691. W Penwith RD. P Pnznce. Ch e, m2.
Sch p. St Ives CC.

SENNEN COVE Cornwall
189 SW 3526 8m WSW of Penzance. Loc,
Sennen CP. Extensive sands to E on
Whitesand Bay. Transatlantic cables surface
in cove.

SESSAY Yorks (N)
91 SE 4575 5m SSE of Thirsk. CP, 213.
Thsk RD. P Thsk. Ch e, m. Sch pe. Thsk and
Malton CC.

SETCHEY Norfolk
124 TF 6313 4m S of King's Lynn. Loc,
W Winch CP. P(Setch), K's Lnn. Ch e.

SETLEY Hants
180 SU 3000 1m S of Brockenhurst. Loc,
Brcknhst CP.

SETTLE Yorks (W)
90 SD 8163 13m NW of Skipton. CP, 2,307.
Sttle RD. P. Ch e, f, m2, r, v. Sch pe, s.

Skptn CC. See also Mearbeck. Mkt tn, in limestone country.

SETTRINGTON Yorks (E)
92 SE 8370 3m ESE of Malton. CP, 325. Norton RD. P Mltn. Ch e, m. Sch pe. Howden CC.

SEVENHAMPTON Glos
144 SP 0321 5m E of Cheltenham. CP, 311. Northleach RD. Ch e. Sch pe. Cirencester and Tewkesbury CC. See also Brockhampton. Cotswold stone vllge.

SEVENHAMPTON Wilts
157 SU 2090 5m NE of Swindon. Loc, Highworth CP. P Swndn. Ch e.

SEVEN KINGS London
161 TQ 4587 4m WSW of Romford. Loc, Redbridge LB. P Ilford, Essex. Ilfd N BC.

SEVENOAKS Kent
171 TQ 5355 21m SE of London. UD, 18,240. P. Svnks CC. Hilltop tn, largely rsdntl. Knole Pk (NT)*, 15c–17c mansion in large deer pk; ancestral seat of Sackville family.

SEVENOAKS WEALD Kent
171 TQ 5250 3m S of Sevenoaks. CP, 1,279. Svnks RD. P(Wld), Svnks. Ch m, r, v. Sch p. Svnks CC.

SEVERN BEACH Glos
155, 156 ST 5485 8m NNW of Bristol. CP(Pilning and Svn Bch). Thornbury RD. P BRSTL. Ch m, v2. Sch p. S Glos CC.

SEVERN STOKE Worcs
143 SO 8544 7m S of Worcester. CP, 593. Upton upon Severn RD. P WCSTR. Ch e. Sch p. S Worcs CC. See also Clifton, Kinnersley.

SEVINGTON Kent
172, 173, 184 TR 0340 2m SE of Ashford. CP, 226. E Ashfd RD. Ch e. Ashfd CC.

SEWARDS END Essex
148 TL 5738 2m E of Saffron Walden. Loc, Sffrn Wldn MB. P Sffrn Wldn.

SEWERBY Yorks (E)
93 TA 2068 2m NE of Bridlington. Loc, Brdlngtn MB. P Brdlngtn.

SEWORGAN Cornwall
189, 190 SW 7030 4m NE of Helston. Loc, Constantine CP. Ch m.

SEWSTERN Leics
122 SK 8921 8m N of Oakham. Loc, Buckminster CP. P Grantham, Lincs. Ch e, m. Iron stone wks in area.

SHABBINGTON Bucks
158, 159 SP 6607 3m W of Thame. CP, 304. Aylesbury RD. P Aylesbury. Ch e. Aylesbury CC.

SHACKERSTONE Leics
120, 121 SK 3706 6m SW of Coalville. CP, 712. Mkt Bosworth RD. P Nuneaton, Warwickshire. Ch e, m. Bswth CC. See also Barton in the Beans, Bilstone, Congerstone, Odstone.

SHACKLEFORD Surrey
169 SU 9345 2m NW of Godalming. CP, 894. Guildford RD. P Gdlmng. Ch e. Sch pe. Gldfd CC. See also Eashing, Norney.

SHADFORTH Co Durham
85 NZ 3441 4m ESE of Durham. CP, 2,010. Drhm RD. P DRHM. Ch e. Drhm CC. See also Ludworth.

SHADINGFIELD Suffolk (E)
137 TM 4384 4m S of Beccles. CP, 122. Wainford RD. P Bccls. Ch e. Lowestoft CC.

SHADOXHURST Kent
172, 184 TQ 9737 4m SW of Ashford. CP, 582. W Ashfd RD. P Ashfd. Ch e, m. Ashfd CC.

SHADWELL London
161 TQ 3580 3m E of Charing Cross. Loc, Twr Hmlts LB. Stepney and Poplar BC (Stpny). Dockland on N bank of Thames.

SHAFTESBURY Dorset
166 ST 8622 18m WSW of Salisbury. MB, 3,976. P. N Dst CC. Small tn on hillside overlooking Blackmoor Vale. Slight rems of abbey (A.M.).

SHAFTON Yorks (W)
102, 103 SE 3910 4m NE of Barnsley. CP, 2,272. Hemsworth RD. P Bnsly. Ch m. Sch p. Hmswth CC.

SHALBOURNE Wilts
168 SU 3162 4m SSW of Hungerford. CP, 547. Marlborough and Ramsbury RD. P Mlbrgh. Ch e, m. Sch pe. Devizes CC. See also Bagshot, Oxenwood, Rivar.

SHALCOMBE IOW
180 SZ 3985 4m SE of Yarmouth. Loc, Shalfleet CP.

SHALDEN Hants
169 SU 6941 2m NNW of Alton. CP, 447. Altn RD. P Altn. Ch e. Petersfield CC. See also Golden Pot.

SHALDON Devon
176, 188 SX 9372 5m E of Newton Abbot. Loc, Teignmouth UD. P Tgnmth. Resort. Br across Teign estuary to Tgnmth.

SHALFLEET IOW
180 SZ 4189 4m E of Yarmouth. CP, 1,136. Isle of Wight RD and CC. P Newport. Ch e, m. Sch pe. See also Cranmore, Hamstead, Newbridge, Ningwood, Shalcombe, Wellow. Ch has massive Nmn twr.

SHALFORD Essex
148, 149 TL 7229 4m NW of Braintree. CP, 583. Brntree RD. P Brntree. Ch e. Sch p. Brntree CC (Maldon). See also Shlfd Grn.

SHALFORD Surrey
169, 170 TQ 0047 1m S of Guildford. CP, 3,939. Gldfd RD. P Gldfd. Ch e, m. Sch p. Gldfd CC. 18c water mill (NT)* on R Tillingbourne.

SHALFORD GREEN Essex
148, 149 TL 7127 4m NW of Braintree. Loc, Shlfd CP. Ch c.

SHALMSFORD STREET Kent
172, 173 TR 0954 4m SW of Canterbury. Loc, Chartham CP. P Cntrbry. Ch m, s2. Rly, indstrl.

SHALSTONE Bucks
145, 146 SP 6436 4m WNW of Buckingham. CP, 161. Bcknghm RD. P BCKNGHM. Ch e. Bcknghm CC.

SHAMLEY GREEN Surrey
170, 182 TQ 0343 4m NNW of Cranleigh. Loc, Wonersh CP. P Guildford. Ch e, c. Sch pe. Half-timbered hses.

SHANGTON Leics
133 SP 7196 6m N of Mkt Harborough. CP, 47. Mkt Hbrgh RD. Ch e. Hbrgh CC.

SHANKHOUSE Nthmb
78 NZ 2778 3m SW of Blyth. Loc, Seaton Valley UD. P(Shnkhse Colliery), Cramlington. Blth BC.

SHANKLIN IOW
180 SZ 5881 7m S of Ryde. UD(Sandown-Shnkln), 15,807. P. Isle of Wight CC. Resort.

SHAP Westm
83 NY 5615 8m WSW of Appleby. CP, 1,149. N Westm RD. P Penrith, Cumberland. Ch e, m. Sch pe. Westm CC. See also Keld. High moorland vllge. Main rd (M6) and rly (summit of Euston-Carlisle line). 1m W, Shp Abbey (A.M.), rems of 13c–16c monastery.

SHAPWICK Dorset
179 ST 9301 5m SE of Blandford. CP, 214. Wimborne and Cranborne RD. P Blndfd Forum. Ch e, m. N Dst CC. On Roman rd from Sarum to Durnovaria (Dorchester). 1¾m ENE, Badbury Rings, Iron Age fort which later became Roman rd junction.

SHAPWICK Som
165 ST 4138 5m W of Glastonbury. CP, 341. Bridgwater RD. P Brdgwtr. Ch e. Sch p. Brdgwtr CC. Shpwck Hth is part of county's great turbary (peat-producing area).

SHARDLOW Derbys
112, 121 SK 4330 6m SE of Derby. CP(Shdlw and Gt Wilne), 922. SE Derbys RD. P DBY. Ch e. Sch p. SE Derbys CC.

SHARESHILL Staffs
119 SJ 9406 3m SW of Cannock. CP, 354. Cnnck RD. P Wolverhampton. Ch e. Sch pe. SW Staffs CC (Cnnck).

SHARLSTON Yorks (W)
96, 102, 103 SE 3918 4m ESE of Wakefield. CP, 2,967. Wkfld RD. P Wkfld. Ch e, m. Normanton CC. See also Shlstn Cmmn.

SHARLSTON COMMON Yorks (W)
96, 102, 103 SE 3819 4m ESE of Wakefield. Loc, Shlstn CP. P Wkfld. Ch e, m.

SHARNBROOK Beds
134 SP 9959 5m SSE of Rushden.
CP, 1,053. Bedford RD. P BDFD.
Ch e, b, m. Sch p. Bdfd CC.

SHARNFORD Leics
132 SP 4891 4m ESE of Hinckley. CP, 5u9.
Blaby RD. P Hnckly. Ch e, m. Sch pe.
Blby CC (Harborough).

SHAROE GREEN Lancs
94 SD 5333 3m N of Preston. Loc,
Fulwood UD.

SHAROW Yorks (W)
91 SE 3271 1m ENE of Ripon. CP, 269.
Rpn and Pateley Br RD. P Rpn. Ch e.
Sch pe. Rpn CC.

SHARPENHOE Beds
147 TL 0630 5m SSE of Ampthill. Loc,
Streatley CP. Ch b. 500ft hill to S partly
NT; views.

SHARPERTON Nthmb
71 NT 9503 6m WNW of Rothbury. Loc,
Harbottle CP. P Morpeth.

SHARPNESS Glos
155, 156 SO 6702 6m WNW of Dursley.
Loc, Hinton CP. P Berkeley. Ch e, bc. Sch p.
Gloucester Canal joins Severn
estuary; docks.

SHARPTHORNE Sussex (E)
183 TQ 3732 4m SSE of E Grinstead. Loc,
W Hoathly CP. P: E Grnstd.

SHARRINGTON Norfolk
125 TG 0336 3m WSW of Holt. Loc,
Brinton CP. P Melton Constable. Ch e, m.

SHATTERFORD Worcs
130 SO 7981 4m NW of Kidderminster.
Loc, Upr Arley CP. P Bewdley.

SHATTON Derbys
111 SK 2082 9m E of Chapel-en-le-Frith.
CP(Brough and Shttn), 150. Chpl en le
Frth RD. High Peak CC.

SHAUGH PRIOR Devon
187 SX 5463 7m NE of Plymouth. CP, 959.
Plympton St Mary RD. P Plmth. Ch e.
Sch p. W Dvn CC (Tavistock). See also Lee
Moor, Wotter. Ch: font cover. To SE, china
clay workings.

SHAVINGTON Ches
110 SJ 7051 2m S of Crewe. CP(Shvngtn
cum Gresty), 2,027. Nantwich RD. P Crwe.
Ch m3. Sch p, s. Nntwch CC.

SHAW Berks
158 SU 4768 1m NE of Newbury. CP(Shw
cum Donnington), 2,091. Nbry RD. P Nbry.
Ch e. Sch pe. Nbry CC.

SHAW Lancs
101 SD 9308 3m NNE of Oldham. Loc,
Crompton UD. P Oldhm. Heywood and
Royton CC. Textiles.

SHAW Wilts
156, 157 ST 8865 6m SSW of Chippenham.
Loc, Melksham Without CP. Bradford and
Mlkshm RD. P Mlkshm. Ch e. Sch pe.
Westbury CC.

SHAWBURY Shrops
118 SJ 5521 7m NE of Shrewsbury.
CP, 2,366. N Shrops RD. P Shrsbry. Ch e.
Sch p2, pe. Oswestry CC. See also
Edgebolton, Gt Wytheford, Lit Wthfd,
Muckleton. Airfield to N.

SHAWELL Leics
132 SP 5480 3m S of Lutterworth. CP, 150.
Lttrwth RD. P Rugby, Warwickshire.
Ch e, m. Sch pe. Blaby CC (Harborough).

SHAWFORD Hants
168 SU 4624 3m S of Winchester. Loc,
Compton CP. P Wnchstr. Ch v.

SHAWFORTH Lancs
95 SD 8920 2m SE of Bacup. Loc,
Whitworth UD. P Rochdale.

SHAW GREEN Lancs
100 SD 5218 4m W of Chorley. Loc,
Euxton CP.

SHAW MILLS Yorks (W)
91 SE 2562 6m NNW of Harrogate. Loc,
Bishop Thornton CP. P Hrrgte. Ch m.

SHEAR CROSS Wilts
166 ST 8642 2m S of Warminster. Loc,
Longbridge Deverill CP.

SHEARSBY Leics
132, 133 SP 6290 7m WNW of Mkt
Harborough. CP, 156. Lutterworth RD.
Ch e. Blaby CC (Hbrgh).

SHEBBEAR Devon
175 SS 4309 7m NE of Holsworthy.
CP, 589. Torrington RD. P Beaworthy.
Ch e, b, m3. Sch p. W Dvn CC (Torrington).

SHEBDON Staffs
119 SJ 7625 5m NNE of Newport. Loc,
High Offley CP. P STAFFORD. On Shrops
Union Canal.

SHEDFIELD Hants
180 SU 5513 3m S of Bishop's Waltham.
CP, 2,142. Droxford RD.
P SOUTHAMPTON. Ch e. Sch pe.
Petersfield CC. See also Shirrell Hth,
Wltham Chase.

SHEEN Staffs
111 SK 1161 8m SW of Bakewell. CP, 260.
Leek RD. P Buxton, Derbyshire. Ch e, m.
Sch pe. Lk CC.

SHEEP HILL Co Durham
78 NZ 1757 6m SW of Gateshead. Loc,
Stanley UD.

SHEEPSCOMBE Glos
143, 144 SO 8910 5m NE of Stroud. Loc,
Painswick CP. P Strd. Ch e, m. Sch p. Amid
steep wooded hills.

SHEEPSTOR Devon
187 SX 5567 6m SE of Tavistock. CP, 53.
Tvstck RD. Ch e. W Dvn CC (Tvstck).

SHEEPWASH Devon
175 SS 4806 9m ENE of Holsworthy.
CP, 240. Trrngtn RD. P Beaworthy.
Ch e, b, m. W Dvn CC (Trrngtn).

SHEEPY MAGNA Leics
120, 121 SK 3201 2m NNE of Atherstone.
Loc, Shpy CP. Mkt Bosworth RD.
P(Shpy), Athrstne, Warwickshire. Ch e.
Sch pe. Bswth CC. Ch: stained glass
windows by Burne-Jones and Kempe.

SHEEPY PARVA Leics
120, 121 SK 3301 2m NE of Atherstone.
Loc, Shpy CP. Mkt Bosworth RD.
Bswth CC.

SHEERING Essex
148, 161 TL 5013 4m NE of Harlow.
CP, 1,457. Epping and Ongar RD. P Bishop's
Stortford, Herts. Ch e. Sch pe. Hlw CC
(Eppng).

SHEERNESS Kent
172 TQ 9175 11m ENE of Chatham. Loc,
Queenborough-in-Sheppey MB. P. Naval
dockyards and barracks, now converted to
industrial use.

SHEET Hants
181 SU 7524 1m NE of Petersfield. Loc,
Ptrsfld UD. P Ptrsfld. Bedales co-educational
boarding sch, founded 1893.

SHEFFIELD Yorks (W)
102, 103, 111 SK 3587 34m ESE of
Manchester. CB, 519,703. P(SHFFLD). BCs:
Attercliffe, Brightside, Hallam, Heeley,
Hillsborough, Park. (Same, plus parts of
NE Derbys CC, Penistone CC.) Largest city
in Yorkshire and centre of steel industry.
Impressive modern architectural development.

SHEFFORD Beds
147 TL 1439 5m SW of Biggleswade.
CP, 2,216. Bgglswde RD. P. Ch e, b, m, r.
Sch p, s. Mid-Beds CC.

SHEFFORD, GREAT Berks
158 SU 3875 5m NE of Hungerford. See Gt
Shffd.

SHEFFORD WOODLANDS Berks
158 SU 3673 4m NNE of Hungerford. Loc,
W Shffd CP. Hngrfd RD. P Newbury.
Nbry CC.

SHEINTON Shrops
118, 119 SJ 6103 3m NNW of Much
Wenlock. CP, 100. Atcham RD. Ch e.
Shrewsbury CC.

SHELDON Derbys
111 SK 1768 3m W of Bakewell. CP, 96.
Bkwll RD. Ch e. W Derbys CC.

SHELDON Devon
176 ST 1108 6m NNW of Honiton. CP, 109.
Hntn RD. Ch e, v. Hntn CC.

SHELDWICH Kent
172 TR 0156 3m S of Faversham. CP, 448.
Swale RD. P(Shldwch Lees), Fvrshm. Ch e.
Sch p. Fvrshm CC.

SHELF Yorks (W)
96, 102 SE 1228 3m NE of Halifax.
UD(Queensbury and Shlf), 10,603. P Hlfx.
Bradford S BC.

SHELFANGER Norfolk
136 TM 1083 2m N of Diss. CP, 261.
Depwade RD. P Dss. Ch e, b, m. Sch pe.
S Nflk CC. Ch: 13c wall-paintings.

SHELFIELD Staffs
120 SK 0302 3m NE of Walsall. Loc,
Aldridge-Brownhills UD. P Wlsll. A-B BC
(Wlsll N).

SHELFORD Notts
112, 121, 122 SK 6642 6m E of
Nottingham. CP, 1,249. Bingham RD.
P NTTNGHM. Ch e, m. Rushcliffe CC
(Carlton). See also Newton. Ch: Saxon relief
of Virgin and Child.

SHELFORD, GREAT Cambs
148 TL 4652 4m S of Cambridge. See Gt
Shlfd.

SHELLEY Essex
161 TL 5505 1m N of Ongar. Loc, Ongr CP.
Ch e. Sch p.

SHELLEY Suffolk (E)
149 TM 0338 3m S of Hadleigh. CP, 41.
Samford RD. P Ipswich. Ch e. Sudbury and
Woodbridge CC.

SHELLEY Yorks
102 SE 2011 5m SE of Huddersfield. Loc,
Kirkburton UD. P Hddsfld.

SHELLINGFORD Berks
158 SU 3193 2m ESE of Faringdon.
CP, 168. Frngdn RD. P Frngdn. Ch e, v.
Sch pe. Abingdon CC.

SHELLOW BOWELLS Essex
161 TL 6108 5m NE of Ongar. Loc,
Willingale CP. Ch e.

SHELSLEY BEAUCHAMP Worcs
130 SO 7363 7m SW of Stourport. CP, 176.
Martley RD. P WORCESTER. Ch e. Sch pe.
Kidderminster CC.

SHELSLEY WALSH Worcs
130 SO 7263 8m SW of Stourport. CP, 50.
Martley RD. Ch e. Kidderminster CC. Well
known hill-climb for cars. Ch Nmn and
later; carved scrn and pews.

SHELSWELL Oxon
145, 146 SP 6030 4m SSE of Brackley.
CP(Newton Purcell w Shlswll), 91.
Ploughley RD. Ch e. Banbury CC (Henley).

SHELTON Beds
134 TL 0368 5m ENE of Rushden.
CP(Dean and Shltn), 309. Bedford RD.
Ch e. Bdfd CC. See also Lr Dn, Upr Dn.

SHELTON Norfolk
137 TM 2290 7m W of Bungay. CP, 232.
Depwade RD. Ch e. Sch p. S Nflk CC. See
also Hardwick. Outstanding 15c brick ch.

SHELTON Notts
112, 122 SK 7844 6m S of Newark.
CP, 105. Bingham RD. P Nwk. Ch e.
Rushcliffe CC (Carlton).

SHELVE Shrops
129 SO 3399 6m N of Bishop's Cstle.
CP, 102. Clun and Bp's Cstle RD. Ch e.
Ludlow CC. See also Black Marsh. Among
hills and disused lead mines.

SHELWICK Herefs
142 SO 5243 2m NNE of Hereford. Loc,
Holmer CP.

SHENFIELD Essex
161 TQ 6094 1m NE of Brentwood. Loc,
Brntwd UD. P Brntwd.

SHENINGTON Oxon
145 SP 3742 5m WNW of Banbury.
CP, 232. Bnbry RD. P Bnbry. Ch e. Sch pe.
Bnbry CC.

SHENLEY Herts
160 TL 1900 5m SSE of St Albans.
CP, 4,243. Elstree RD. P St Albns.
Ch e, m, v. Sch p. S Herts CC (Barnet). See
also Shenleybury. 18c lock-up. Large mental
hsptl to NW. 1m N, Salisbury Hall*, moated
17c hse.

SHENLEY BROOK END Bucks
146 SP 8335 3m WNW of Bletchley.
CP, 171. Winslow RD. Buckingham CC.

SHENLEYBURY Herts
160 TL 1801 4m SSE of St Albans. Loc,
Shenley CP. Location of Shnly ch.

SHENLEY CHURCH END Bucks
146 SP 8336 3m NW of Bletchley. CP, 242.
Newport Pagnell RD. P Bltchly. Ch e. Sch p.
Buckingham CC.

SHENMORE Herefs
142 SO 3938 7m W of Hereford. Loc,
Madley CP.

SHENSTONE Staffs
120 SK 1104 3m S of Lichfield. CP, 5,174.
Lchfld RD. P Lchfld. Ch e, m. Sch p. Lchfld
and Tamworth CC. See also Lit Aston,
Lit Hay, Shnstne Wd End, Stonnall. To N,
site of Roman bldng; finds at museum at
Wall (Staffs), qv.

SHENSTONE Worcs
130 SO 8673 3m SE of Kidderminster. Loc,
Stone CP.

SHENSTONE WOOD END Staffs
120 SK 1101 5m S of Lichfield. Loc,
Shnstne CP. P Lchfld.

SHENTON Leics
120, 121 SK 3800 5m NW of Hinckley.
L o c, S u t t o n C h e n e y C P.
P Nuneaton, Warwickshire. Ch e.

SHEPERDINE Glos
155, 156 ST 6295 5m NE of Severn Rd Br.
Loc, Oldbury-upon-Svn CP.

SHEPHALL Herts
147 TL 2522 2m SE of Stevenage. Loc,
Stvnge UD.

SHEPHERD'S BUSH London
160 TR 2380 4m W of Charing Cross. Loc,
Hammersmith LB. Hmmrsmth N BC. White
City Stadium.

SHEPHERD'S GREEN Oxon
159 SU 7183 3m W of Henley. Loc,
Hnly RD. Hnly CC.

SHEPHERDSWELL Kent
173 TR 2548 6m NW of Dover.
CP(Shphdswll w Coldred), 1,238. Dvr RD.
P Dvr. Ch e, m. Sch pe. Dvr and Deal CC
(Dvr).

SHEPLEY Yorks (W)
102 SE 1909 5m SE of Huddersfield. Loc,
Kirkburton UD. P Hddsfld.

SHEPPERTON Surrey
170 TQ 0767 1m W of Walton-on-Thames.
Loc, Sunbury-on-Thames UD. P(Shpprtn,
Middx).

SHEPRETH Cambs
148 TL 3947 5m NNE of Royston. CP, 530.
S Cambs RD. P Rstn, Herts. Ch e, c. Sch p.
Cambs CC.

SHEPSHED Leics
121 SK 4719 3m W of Loughborough.
UD, 8,456. P Lghbrgh. Lghbrgh CC.

SHEPTON Som
166 ST 6731 2m S of Bruton. CP(Shptn
Montagu), 192. Wincanton RD. P(Shptn
Mntgu), Wncntn. Ch e. Wells CC.

SHEPTON BEAUCHAMP Som
177 ST 4017 3m ENE of Ilminster. CP, 533.
Chard RD. P Ilmnstr. Ch e. Sch pe.
Yeovil CC.

SHEPTON MALLET Som
166 ST 6143 10m WSW of Frome.
UD, 5,910. P. Wells CC. See also Downside.
Grey stone tn; ch has richly carved wagon
roof. Industries incl glove-making, dairy
produce, and 'champagne perry'. Site of
Bath and West Agricultural Show.

SHEPWAY Kent
172 TQ 7753 2m SSE of Maidstone. Loc,
Mdstne MB P Mdstne.

SHERATON Co Durham
85 NZ 4435 5m WNW of Hartlepool.
CP(Shrtn w Hulam), 118. Easington RD.
Easngtn CC.

SHERBORNE Dorset
178 ST 6316 5m E of Yeovil. UD, 7,265. P.
W Dst CC. Centre of agricultural distr. Mdvl
abbey, Nmn to Perp; fan-vaulting. Adjacent
sch incl some former abbey bldngs. To E,
Shbne Old Cstle (A.M.). Also present cstle*
blt by Raleigh, in grnds by Capability
Brown.

SHERBORNE Glos
144 SP 1714 4m E of Northleach. CP, 392.
Nthlch RD. P Cheltenham. Ch e. Sch pe.
Cirencester and Tewkesbury CC.

SHERBORNE ST JOHN Hants
168 SU 6255 2m N of Basingstoke.
CP, 2,855. Bsngstke RD. P Bsngstke.
Ch e, v. Sch pe. Bsngstke CC. Ch: brasses,
monmts. 1m NE, The Vyne (NT)*, Tdr and
later hse visited by Henry VIII, Elizabeth I.

SHERBOURNE Warwicks
131 SP 2661 3m SW of Warwick. CP, 143.
Wrwck RD. P WRWCK. Ch e. Wrwck and
Leamington CC.

SHERBURN Co Durham
85 NZ 3142 3m E of Durham. CP, 3,127.
Drhm RD. P DRHM. Ch e2, m, s. Sch p, s.
Drhm CC.

SHERBURN Yorks (E)
93 SE 9577 10m WSW of Filey. CP, 671.
Norton RD. P Malton. Ch e, m. Sch pe.
Howden CC.

SHERBURN HILL Co Durham
85 NZ 3342 4m E of Durham. Loc,
Drhm RD. P DRHM. Ch m2, s. Sch p.
Drhm CC.

SHERBURN IN ELMET Yorks (W)
97 SE 4933 6m S of Tadcaster. CP, 2,776.
Tdcstr RD. P LEEDS. Ch e, m. Sch jb, jgi, s.
Barkston Ash CC.

SHERE Surrey
170 TQ 0747 5m ESE of Guildford.
CP, 3,876. Gldfd RD. P Gldfd. Ch e. Sch pe.
Dorking CC. See also Gomshall, Peaslake.
Ch with Nmn twr, shingled spire.
Half-timbered hses. Has bypass, much
needed.

SHEREFORD Norfolk
125 TF 8829 2m W of Fakenham. Loc,
Dunton CP. Ch e.

SHERFIELD ENGLISH Hants
168 SU 2922 4m W of Romsey. CP, 1,194.
Rmsy and Stockbridge RD. P Rmsy. Ch e, r.
Sch pe. Eastleigh CC (Winchester). See also
Awbridge, Kent's Oak, Ratley.

SHERFIELD ON LODDON Hants
168, 169 SU 6757 5m NE of Basingstoke.
CP(Shfld on Lodden), 988. Bsngstke RD.
P Bsngstke. Ch e, b. Bsngstke CC. See also
Ch End.

SHERFORD Devon
187, 188 SX 7744 3m E of Kingsbridge.
CP, 258. Kngsbrdge RD. Ch e. Ttns CC.

SHERIFFHALES Shrops
119 SJ 7512 4m S of Newport. CP, 678.
Shifnal RD. P Shfnl. Ch e, m. Sch p. The
Wrekin CC. See also Hth Hill, Weston Hth.

SHERIFF HUTTON Yorks (N)
92 SE 6566 10m NNE of York. CP(Shrff
Httn w Cornbrough), 615. Malton RD.
P YK. Ch e, m. Thirsk and Mltn CC. Rems
of 14c cstle. S.H. Hall, Jcbn and later hse.

SHERINGHAM Norfolk
126 TG 1543 22m NNW of Norwich.
UD, 4,666. P. N Nflk CC. Seaside resort
mostly developed late 19c - early 20c. 1m
W, Shrnghm Hall, Rgncy hse in fine grnds*.
Hse and grnds by Repton.

SHERINGTON Bucks
146 SP 8846 2m NNE of Newport Pagnell.
CP, 549. Npt Pgnll RD. P Npt Pgnll.
Ch e, c, m. Sch pe. Buckingham CC.

SHERMANBURY Sussex (W)
182 TQ 2118 2m N of Henfield. CP, 415.
Chanctonbury RD. P Horsham. Ch e.
Shoreham CC (Arundel and Shrhm).

SHERNBORNE Norfolk
124 TF 7132 6m SSE of Hunstanton.
CP, 124. Docking RD. P King's Lynn. Ch e.
NW Nflk CC (K's Lnn). Estate vllge. Ch has
15c brasses.

SHERRINGTON Wilts
167 ST 9639 7m SE of Warminster. CP, 104.
Wmnstr and Westbury RD. Ch e. Wstbry CC.
Watercress beds.

SHERSTON Wilts
156 ST 8585 5m W of Malmesbury. CP,
1,184. Mlmsbry RD. P Mlmsbry. Ch e, c, m.
Sch pe. Chippenham CC. See also Shstn
Parva. Wilts Cotswold-style; stone and
colourwashed hses. Nmn-EE ch.

SHERSTON PARVA Wilts
156 ST 8686 4m W of Malmesbury. Loc,
Shstn CP. Ch e.

SHEVINGTON Lancs
100 SD 5408 3m NW of Wigan. CP, 4,887.
Wgn RD. P Wgn. Ch e, m4, r. Sch i, j, p, s.
Westhoughton CC. See also Shvngtn Moor,
Shvngtn Vale.

SHEVINGTON MOOR Lancs
100 SD 5410 4m NNW of Wigan. Loc,
Shvngtn CP. P Standish, Wgn.

SHEVINGTON VALE Lancs
100 SD 5209 4m NW of Wigan. Loc,
Shvngtn CP.

SHEVIOCK Cornwall
186 SX 3755 4m W of Torpoint. CP, 465.
St Germans RD. Ch e. Bodmin CC. See also
Crafthole, Portwrinkle.

SHIBDEN HEAD Yorks (W)
96, 102 SE 0929 2m N of Halifax. Loc,
Queensbury and Shelf UD.

SHIFFORD Oxon
158 SP 3702 5m SSE of Witney. CP(Aston Bampton and Shffd), 646. Wtny RD. Ch e. Mid-Oxon CC (Banbury).

SHIFNAL Shrops
119 SJ 7407 3m ESE of Oakengates. CP, 3,896. Shfnl RD. P. Ch e, m2, r. Sch pe, s. The Wrekin CC. Large red sandstone ch. Rly viaduct. Some half-timbered hses.

SHILBOTTLE Nthmb
71 NU 1908 3m S of Alnwick. CP, 1,862. Alnwck RD. P Alnwck. Ch e, m. Sch p, pe. Berwick-upon-Tweed CC. Mining vllge.

SHILDON Co Durham
85 NZ 2226 2m SSE of Bishop Auckland. UD, 14,499. P. Bshp Aucklnd CC. See also Eldon, Middridge, Old Eldn. Mnfg tn, esp rly wagons.

SHILLINGFORD Devon
164 SS 9823 2m NE of Bampton. Loc, Bmptn CP. P Tiverton. Ch b. Sch p.

SHILLINGFORD Oxon
158 SU 5992 2m N of Wallingford. Loc, Warborough CP. P OXFORD.

SHILLINGFORD ST GEORGE Devon
176 SX 9087 3m SSW of Exeter. CP, 212. St Thomas RD. Ch e. Tiverton CC.

SHILLINGSTONE Dorset
178 ST 8210 5m NW of Blandford. CP, 724. Sturminster RD. P Blndfd Forum. Ch e, m, v. Sch pe. N Dst CC.

SHILLINGTON Beds
147 TL 1234 5m NW of Hitchin. CP, 2,787. Ampthill RD. P Htchn, Herts. Ch e, c, m2. Sch p. Mid-Beds CC. See also Apsley End, Lr Stondon, Pegsdon. Ch of c 1300 on hill.

SHILTON Oxon
157 SP 2608 6m WSW of Witney. CP, 666. Wtny RD. P OXFORD.   Ch e, b. Sch p. Mid-Oxon CC (Banbury).

SHILTON Warwicks
132 SP 4084 6m NE of Coventry. CP, 695. Rugby RD. P Cvntry. Ch e, b. Sch pe. Rgby CC. See also Barnacle.

SHIMPLING Norfolk
137 TM 1583 3m NE of Diss. Loc, Burston CP. Ch e.

SHIMPLING Suffolk (W)
149 TL 8651 4m WNW of Lavenham. CP, 329. Melford RD. P Bury St Edmunds. Ch e. Sch pe. Sudbury and Woodbridge CC. See also Shmplng St. Agricultural college at Chadacre Pk, Ggn hse 1m NNW.

SHIMPLING STREET Suffolk (W)
149 TL 8752 4m NW of Lavenham. Loc, Shmplng CP.

SHINCLIFFE Co Durham
85 NZ 2940 2m SE of Durham. CP, 673. Drhm RD. P DRHM. Ch e, m. Sch pe. Drhm CC.

SHINEY ROW Co Durham
78 NZ 3252 2m NNW of Houghton-le-Spring. Loc, Htn-le-Sprng UD. P Htn-le-Sprng.

SHINFIELD Berks
169 SU 7368 4m S of Reading. CP, 5,187. Wokingham RD. P Rdng. Ch e, v. Sch pe2, s. Rdng S CC (Wknghm). See also Spencers Wd, Threemile Cross.

SHINNER'S BRIDGE Devon
187, 188 SX 7862 1m NW of Totnes. Loc, Dartington CP.

SHIPBOURNE Kent
171 TQ 5952 4m N of Tonbridge. CP, 460. Malling RD. P Tnbrdge. Ch e. Sch p. Tnbrdge and Mllng CC (Sevenoaks).

SHIPDHAM Norfolk
125 TF 9507 4m SW of E Dereham. CP, 1,237. Mitford and Launditch RD. P Thetford. Ch e, c, m2. Sch pe. SW Nflk CC.

SHIPHAM Som
165 ST 4457 3m NNW of Cheddar. CP, 735. Axbridge RD. P Winscombe. Ch e, m. Sch pe. Weston-super-Mare CC. See also Rowberrow. Once a lead-mining vllge.

SHIPHAY Devon
188 SX 8965 2m NW of Torquay. Loc, Torbay CB. P(Shiphay Collaton), Tquay.

SHIPLAKE Oxon
159 SU 7678 3m S of Henley. CP, 1,365. Hnly RD. P(Shplke Cross), Hnly-on-Thames. Ch e. Sch pe. Hnly CC. See also Binfield Hth, Lr Shplke.

SHIPLEY Shrops
130 SO 8095 6m ENE of Bridgnorth. Loc,
Claverley CP.

SHIPLEY Sussex (W)
182 TQ 1421 4m SE of Billingshurst.
CP, 1,244. Horsham RD. P Hshm. Ch e.
Sch pe. Hshm and Crawley CC (Hshm). See
also Broomer's Corner, Coolham. Nmn ch
added to in 19c; reliquary in chancel.
Belloc's Mill*, smock-mill in working order.

SHIPLEY Yorks (W)
96 SE 1437 3m NNW of Bradford.
UD, 28,444. P. Shply CC. Worsted mnfg,
engineering. Includes Saltaire, model vllge
blt by Sir Titus Salt for workpeople of his
worsted and alpaca mills.

SHIPMEADOW Suffolk (E)
137 TM 3890 3m W of Beccles. CP, 89.
Wainford RD. Ch e. Lowestoft CC. Name
means 'meadow for sheep'. Setting above
Waveney marshes.

SHIPPON Berks
158 SU 4898 1m NW of Abingdon. Loc,
St Helen Without CP. Abngdn RD. Ch e.
Abngdn CC.

SHIPSTON ON STOUR Warwicks
144 SP 2540 10m SSE of Stratford.
CP, 1,900. Shpstn on Str RD. P.
Ch e, b, f, m, r. Sch p, s. Strtfd-on-Avon CC
(Strtfd).

SHIPTON Glos
144 SP 0318 6m ESE of Cheltenham.
CP, 254. Northleach RD. P(Shptn
Oliffe), Chltnhm. Ch e2, m. Cirencester and
Tewkesbury CC. The vllge consists of Shptn
Oliffe and Shptn Solers (or Sollars).

SHIPTON Shrops
129 SO 5691 6m SW of Much Wenlock.
CP, 138. Bridgnorth RD. Ch e. Ludlow CC.
In Corvedale below Wnlck Edge. Shptn
Hall*, Elizn mnr hse; 18c stabling, walled
gdn. To N, Larden Hall, 17c.

SHIPTON Yorks (N)
97 SE 5558 5m NNW of York. CP, 502.
Easingwold RD. P(Shptn-
by-Beningbrough), YK. Ch e, m. Sch pe.
Thirsk and Malton CC.

SHIPTON BELLINGER Hants
167 SU 2345 8m W of Andover. CP, 1,003.
Andvr RD. P Tidworth. Ch e, v. Sch p.
Winchester CC (Basingstoke).

SHIPTON GORGE Dorset
177 SY 4991 2m ESE of Bridport. CP, 210.
Brdpt RD. P Brdpt. Ch e, m. W Dst CC.

SHIPTON GREEN Sussex (W)
181 SZ 8099 5m SW of Chichester. Loc,
Chchstr RD. Chchstr CC.

SHIPTON MOYNE Glos
156, 157 ST 8989 2m S of Tetbury.
CP, 337. Ttbry RD. P Ttbry. Ch e. Sch pe.
Stroud CC.

SHIPTON-ON-CHERWELL Oxon
145 SP 4716 2m E of Woodstock.
CP(Shptn-on-Chrwll and Thrupp), 493.
Ploughley RD. Ch e. Mid-Oxon CC
(Banbury).

SHIPTONTHORPE Yorks (E)
98 SE 8543 2m WNW of Mkt Weighton.
CP, 380. Pocklington RD. P YORK.
Ch e, m. Sch p. Howden CC.

SHIPTON-UNDER-WYCHWOOD Oxon
144 SP 2717 4m NNE of Burford. CP, 775.
Chipping Norton RD. P OXFORD. Ch e, b.
Sch pe. Banbury CC. Cotswold vllge. The
Shaven Crown Inn has Tdr doorway. Large
EE to Perp ch.

SHIRBURN Oxon
159 SU 6995 6m S of Thame. CP, 182.
Bullingdon RD. Ch e. Henley CC. Shbn
Cstle, 14c and later.

SHIRDLEY HILL Lancs
100 SD 3612 3m SSE of Southport. Loc,
Halsall CP. P Ormskirk. Ch m.

SHIREBROOK Derbys
112 SK 5267 4m N of Mansfield.
CP, 11,635. Blackwell RD. P Mnsfld, Notts.
Ch e, c, r, s, v. Sch i, j2, p, pr, s, sb, sg.
Bolsover CC.

SHIREHAMPTON Glos
155 ST 5376 NW distr of Bristol. Loc,
Brstl CB. P Avonmouthh, BRSTL.
Brstl NW BC.

SHIREMOOR Nthmb
78 NZ 3171 3m NW of Tynemouth. Loc,
Seaton Valley UD. P. Blyth BC.

SHIRE OAK Staffs
120 SK 0504 5m NE of Walsall. Loc, Aldridge-Brownhills UD. A—B BC (Wlsll N).

SHIRLAND Derbys
111 SK 3958 2m NNW of Alfreton. CP(Shlnd and Higham), 5,196. Chesterfield RD. P DERBY. Ch e, f, m2. Sch i, p, pe. NE Derbys CC. See also Stonebroom.

SHIRLEY Derbys
120 SK 2141 4m SE of Ashbourne. CP, 208. Ashbne RD. P DERBY. Ch e, m. W Derbys CC.

SHIRL HEATH Herefs
129 SO 4359 4m W of Leominster. Loc, Kingsland CP.

SHIRRELL HEATH Hants
180 SU 5714 3m SSE of Bishop's Waltham. Loc, Shedfield CP. P SOUTHAMPTON. Ch m.

SHIRWELL Devon
163 SS 5937 4m NE of Barnstaple. CP, 359. Bnstple RD. P Bnstple. Ch e. Sch p: N Dvn CC. See also Shwll Cross.

SHIRWELL CROSS Devon
163 SS 5836 3m NE of Barnstaple. Loc, Shwll CP. P Bnstple. Ch m.

SHOBDON Herefs
129 SO 4062 6m WNW of Leominster. CP, 403. Lmnstr and Wigmore RD. P Lmnstr. Ch e, m. Sch p. Lmnstr CC. See also Ledicot, Uphampton. 12c ch pulled down and re-erected as a folly on hilltop. Present ch 18c rococo 'Gothic'; large fireplace in family pew.

SHOBROOKE Devon
176 ST 8601 2m ENE of Crediton. CP, 375. Crdtn RD. P Crdtn. Ch e. Tiverton CC (Torrington). See also Efford.

SHOCKLACH Ches
109 SJ 4349 7m E of Wrexham. Loc, Church Shcklch CP. Tarvin RD. P Malpas. Ch e, m. Sch pe. Nantwich CC.

SHOEBURYNESS Essex
162 TQ 9384 3m E of Southend. Loc, Sthnd-on-Sea CB. P Sthnd-on-Sea. Sthnd E BC. Army barracks and ranges.

SHOLDEN Kent
173 TR 3552 1m W of Deal. CP, 511. Eastry RD. Ch e. Sch pe. Dover and Dl CC (Dvr).

SHOOTERS HILL London
161, 171 TQ 4376 7m ESE of Lndn Br. Loc, Greenwich LB. Wlwch W BC. On the Dover Rd (A2) at over 400ft; a stretch once infested with highwaymen.

SHOP Cornwall
174 SS 2214 6m N of Bude. Loc, Morwenstow CP. Ch m.

SHOP Cornwall
185 SW 8873 3m WSW of Padstow. Loc, St Merryn CP. Ch m.

SHOREDITCH London
160 TQ 3382 3m NE of Charing Cross. Loc, Hackney LB. Hckny S and Shdtch BC (Shdtch and Finsbury). In Lndn's East End.

SHOREHAM Kent
171 TQ 5161 4m N of Sevenoaks. CP, 1,863. Svnks RD. P Svnks. Ch e. Sch p. Svnks CC. See also Badgers Mt, Well Hill. Among wooded hills, beside R Darent. Painter Samuel Palmer lived here.

SHOREHAM-BY-SEA Sussex (W)
182 TQ 2105 6m W of Brighton. UD, 18,804. P. Shrhm CC (Arundel and Shrhm). See also Kingston-by-Sea. Port at mouth of R Adur. Vast Nmn ch.

SHORESDEAN Nthmb
64 NT 9546 5m SSW of Berwick-upon-Tweed. Loc, Shoreswood CP. P BRWCK-UPN-TWD.

SHORESWOOD Nthmb
64 NT 9446 5m SW of Berwick-upon-Tweed. CP, 155. Norham and Islandshires RD. Ch m. Brwck-upn-Twd CC. See also Shoresdean.

SHORNCOTE Glos
157 SU 0296 3m S of Cirencester. Loc, Somerford Keynes CP. Ch e.

SHORNE Kent
161, 171 TQ 6971 4m ESE of Gravesend. CP. Strood RD. P Grvsnd. Ch e, m2, r, v. Sch pe. Grvsnd CC. See also Shne Ridgeway.

SHORNE RIDGEWAY Kent
161, 171 TQ 6970 4m SE of Gravesend.
Loc, Shne CP.

SHORTGATE Sussex (E)
183 TQ 4915 6m ENE of Lewes. Loc,
Laughton CP.

SHORT HEATH Leics
120, 121 SK 3115 3m W of Ashby de la
Zouch. Loc, Ashby Woulds UD.
Loughborough CC.

SHORTLANDS London
171 TQ 3968 just SW of Bromley. Loc,
Brmly BL. P Brmly, Kent. Beckenham BC.

SHORTLANESEND Cornwall
190 SW 8047 2m NW of Truro. Loc,
Kenwyn CP. Truro RD. P Truro. Ch m.
Sch p.

SHORWELL IOW
180 SZ 4583 5m SW of Newport. CP, 497.
Isle of Wight RD and CC P Npt. Ch e, m.
Sch p. See also Kingston, Lit Atherfield,
Yafford. Ch has 15c wall-painting of
St Christopher.

SHOSCOMBE Som
166 ST 7156 2m ENE of Radstock.
CP, 442. Bathavon RD. P Bath.
Ch e(Foxcote). Sch pe. N Som CC.

SHOTESHAM Norfolk
137 TM 2499 6m S of Norwich. CP, 487.
Forehoe and Henstead RD. P Nrwch.
Ch e2, m. Sch p. S Nflk CC (Central Nflk).
Two chs in use; ruins of two others.

SHOTGATE Essex
162 TQ 7693 4m NE of Basildon. Loc,
Bsldn UD. P Wickford.

SHOTLEY Suffolk (E)
150 TM 2336 7m SE of Ipswich. CP, 1,512.
Samford RD. P Ipswch. Ch e, m. Sch p.
Sudbury and Woodbridge CC. See also Shtly
Gate, Shtly St.

SHOTLEY BRIDGE Co Durham
77, 78 NZ 0952 2m NW of Consett. Loc,
Cnstt UD. P Cnstt. Br over R Derwent is
of 1838.

SHOTLEY GATE Suffolk (E)
150 TM 2433 1m NW of Harwich (fy F).

Loc, Shtly CP. P Ipswich. Naval training
establishment. Ferry (for predestrians) plies
to Harwich.

SHOTLEY STREET Suffolk (E)
150 TM 2335 7m SE of Ipswich. Loc,
Shtly CP.

SHOTTENDEN Kent
172, 173 TR 0454 5m SSE of Faversham.
Loc, Chilham CP. P Canterbury. Ch m.

SHOTTERMILL Surrey
169 SU 8832 1m W of Haslemere. Loc,
Hslmre UD. P Hslmre.

SHOTTERY Warwicks
131/144 SP 1854 1m W of Stratford. Loc,
Strtfd-upon-Avon MB. P Strtfd-upn-Avn.
Anne Hathaway's Cottage*, bthplce of
Shakespeare's wife.

SHOTTESWELL Warwicks
145 SP 4245 4m NNW of Banbury. CP, 217.
Southam RD. P Bnbry, Oxon. Ch e, m.
Sch pe. Stratford-on-Avon CC (Strtfd).

SHOTTISHAM Suffolk (E)
150 TM 3244 4m SE of Woodbridge.
CP, 176. Deben RD. Wdbrdge. Ch e.
Sudbury and Wdbrdge CC.

SHOTTLE Derbys
111 SK 3149 3m NW of Belper. CP(Shttle
and Postern), 277. Blpr RD. Blpr CC. See
also Cowers Lane.

SHOTTON Co Durham
85 NZ 4139 1m SW of Peterlee. Loc,
Ptrlee CP. Ch e, m, r, v. Sch p, pr, s.

SHOTTON Nthmb
64, 70 NT 8430 6m S of Coldstream. Loc,
Kilham CP.

SHOTTON COLLIERY Co Durham
85 NZ 3940 2m W of Peterlee. Loc,
Shttn CP. Easington RD. P DRHM.
Ch e, m2, s2, v. Easngtn CC.

SHOTWICK Ches
109 SJ 3371 5m NW of Chester. CP, 72.
Chstr RD. Ch e. City of Chstr CC. Ch has
Nmn doorway, and three-decker plpt.

SHOULDHAM Norfolk
124 TF 6708 6m NE of Downham Mkt.
CP, 465. Dnhm RD. P King's Lynn. Ch e, m.
Sch pe. SW Nflk CC.

SHOULDHAM THORPE Norfolk
124 TF 6607 4m NE of Downham Mkt.
CP, 205. Dnhm RD. P King's Lynn. Ch e.
SW Nflk CC.

SHOULTON Worcs
130 SO 8158 3m NW of Worcester. Loc,
Hallow CP.

SHRAWARDINE Shrops
118 SJ 3915 6m WNW of Shrewsbury. Loc,
Montford CP. P Shrsbry. Ch e. Scanty rems
of castle beside small lake.

SHRAWLEY Worcs
130 SO 8064 4m S of Stourport. CP, 396.
Martley RD. P WORCESTER. Ch e. Sch pe.
Kidderminster CC. See also Noutard's Grn.

SHREWLEY Warwicks
131 SP 2167 5m WNW of Warwick.
CP, 653. Wrwck RD. P WRWCK. Ch v.
Wrwck and Leamington CC.

SHREWSBURY Shrops
118 SJ 4912 39m WNW of Birmingham.
MB, 56,140. P. Shrsbry CC. See also Battlefield, Meole Brace. County, mkt, and
garrison tn in loop of R Severn. Cstle*.
Many old half-timbered bldngs. Boys' public
sch.

SHREWTON Wilts
167 SU 0643 6m WNW of Amesbury.
CP, 1,283. Amesbury RD. P Salisbury.
Ch e, b. Sch pe. Slsbry CC.

SHRIPNEY Sussex (W)
181 SU 9302 2m N of Bognor. Loc,
Bersted CP.

SHRIVENHAM Berks
157 SU 2489 6m ENE of Swindon.
CP, 2,016. Faringdon RD. P Swndn, Wilts.
Ch e, m, r. Sch pe. Abngdn CC. Royal
Military College of Science moved here from
Woolwich in 1947.

SHROPHAM Norfolk
136 TL 9893 4m WSW of Attleborough.
CP, 261. Wayland RD. P Attlbrgh. Ch e, m.
S Nfllk CC.

SHROTON Dorset
178 ST 8512 4m NNW of Blandford.
Alternative name for Iwerne Courtney, qv.

SHRUB END Essex
149, 162 TL 9723 2m SW of Colchester.
Loc, Clchstr MB.

SHUCKNALL Herefs
142 SO 5842 5m ENE of Hereford. Loc,
Weston Beggard CP.

SHUDY CAMPS Cambs
148 TL 6144 3m W of Haverhill. CP, 258.
S Cambs RD. P CAMBRIDGE. Ch e.
Cambs CC.

SHURDINGTON Glos
143, 144 SO 9218 3m SW of Cheltenham.
CP, 1,648. Chltnhm RD. P Chltnhm. Ch e, v.
Sch pe. Cirencester and Tewkesbury CC.

SHURLOCK ROW Berks
159 SU 8374 5m SW of Maidenhead. Loc,
Waltham St Lawrence CP. P Reading.

SHURTON Som
165 ST 2044 8m NW of Bridgwater. Loc,
Stogursey CP.

SHUSTOKE Warwick
131 SP 2290 2m ENE of Coleshill. CP, 574.
Meriden RD. P (Shstke Grn), BIRMINGHAM.
Ch e. Sch pe. Mrdn CC. See also Ch End.

SHUTE Devon
177 SY 2597 3m W of Axminster. CP, 590.
Axmnstr RD. P Axmnstr. Ch e. Sch p.
Honiton CC. See also Whitford. Shte Barton
(NT), rems of mdvl mnr hse.

SHUTFORD Oxon
145 SP 3840 4m W of Banbury. CP, 268.
Bnbry RD. P Bnbry. Ch e, m. Bnbry CC.

SHUTHONGER Glos
143, 144 SO 8835 2m N of Tewkesbury.
Loc, Twyning CP. P Tksbry.

SHUTLANGER Northants
146 SP 7249 2m ENE of Towcester.
CP, 215. Tcstr RD. P Tcstr. Ch m.
Daventry CC (S Nthnts).

SHUTTINGTON Warwicks
120 SK 2505 3m E of Tamworth. CP.
Atherstone RD. P Tmwth, Staffs. Ch e.
Sch pe. Meriden CC. See also Alvecote.

SHUTTLEWOOD Derbys
112 SK 4672 5m E of Chesterfield. Loc,
Bolsover UD. P Chstrfld.

SIBBERTOFT Northants
133 SP 6882 4m SW of Mkt Harborough.
CP, 238. Brixworth RD. P Mkt
Hbrgh, Leics. Ch e. Sch pe. Daventry CC
(Kettering).

SIBDON CARWOOD Shrops
129 SO 4183 1m W of Craven Arms. CP, 78.
Ludlow RD. Ch e. Ldlw CC.

SIBERTSWOLD Kent
173 TR 2548 6m NW of Dover. Alternative
name for Shepherdswell, qv.

SIBFORD FERRIS Oxon
145 SP 3537 7m WSW of Banbury. CP, 293.
Bnbry RD. P Bnbry. Ch e. Bnbry CC.

SIBFORD GOWER Oxon
145 SP 3537 7m WSW of Banbury. CP, 378.
Bnbry RD. P Bnbry. Ch e, f, m. Sch pe.
Bnbry CC.

SIBLE HEDINGHAM Essex
149 TL 7834 3m NW of Halstead.
CP, 2,377. Hlstd RD. P Hlstd. Ch e, b2.
Sch pe, s. Saffron Walden CC.

SIBSEY Lincs (L)
114 TF 3550 5m NNE of Boston.
CP, 1,023. Spilsby RD. P Bstn. Ch e, m2.
Sch pe. Horncastle CC. See also Northlands.
To N, twr windmill, intact.

SIBSON Hunts
134 TL 0997 6m W of Peterborough.
CP(Sbsn cum Stibbington), 447. Norman
Cross RD. Ch e. Hunts CC.

SIBSON Leics
120, 121 SK 3500 3m ENE of Atherstone.
Loc, Sheepy CP. Mkt Bosworth RD.
P Nuneaton, Warwickshire. Ch e. Sch p.
Bswth CC.

SIBTHORPE Notts
112 SK 7645 6m SSW of Newark. CP, 71.
Bingham RD. Ch e. Rushcliffe CC (Carlton).
Large circular 13c or 14c dovecote in a
field.

SIBTON Suffolk (E)
137 TM 3669 4m NNW of Saxmundham.
CP, 277. Blyth RD. Ch e. Sch pe. Eye CC.
See also Poys St. Rems of 12c abbey.

SICKLESMERE Suffolk (W)
136 TL 8760 3m SSE of Bury St Edmunds.
Loc, Thingoe RD. Bury St Eds CC.

SICKLINGHALL Yorks (W)
96 SE 3648 3m W of Wetherby. CP, 287.
Wthrby RD. P Wthrby. Ch m, r. Sch p.
Barkston Ash CC.

SIDBURY Devon
176 SY 1391 3m NNE of Sidmouth. Loc,
Sdmth UD. P Sdmth.

SIDBURY Shrops
130 SO 6885 5m SSW of Bridgnorth. CP, 48.
Brdgnth RD. Ch e. Ludlow CC.

SIDCUP London
161, 171 TQ 4671 6m ESE of Lewisham.
Loc, Bexley LB. P Kent. Sdcp BC
(Chislehurst CC).

SIDDICK Cumb
81, 82 NY 0031 1m N of Workington. Loc,
Wkngtn MB. P Wkngtn.

SIDDINGTON Ches
110 SJ 8470 5m WSW of Macclesfield.
CP, 504. Mcclsfld RD. P Mcclsfld. Ch e, m.
Sch pe. Mcclsfld CC. To N is large lake,
Redes Mere; also Capesthorne Hall*, 19c in
Jcbn style, with pk.

SIDDINGTON Glos
157 SU 0399 1m SSE of Cirencester.
CP, 659. Crncstr RD. P Crncstr. Ch e.
Sch pe. Crncstr and Tewkesbury CC.

SIDESTRAND Norfolk
126 TG 2639 3m SE of Cromer. CP, 169.
Erpingham RD. P Crmr. Ch e. N Nflk CC.

SIDFORD Devon
176 SY 1390 2m NNE of Sidmouth. Loc,
Sdmth UD. P Sdmth.

SIDLESHAM Sussex (W)
181 SZ 8598 4m S of Chichester. CP, 1,302.
Chchstr RD. P Chchstr. Ch e, m. Sch p.
Chchstr CC. See also Highleigh.

SIDLEY Sussex (E)
183, 184 TQ 7309 N distr of Bexhill. Loc,
Bxhll MB. P Bxhll-on-Sea.

SIDLOW BRIDGE Surrey
170 TQ 2546 2m S of Reigate. Loc,
Horley CP. Ch e. Sch pe.

SIDMOUTH Devon
176 SY 1287 13m ESE of Exeter.
UD, 12,039. P. Honiton CC. See also Bowd,
Harcombe, Salcombe Regis, Sidbury,
Sidford. Dignified resort. Many Rgncy and
cottage orné hses.

SIGFORD Devon
175, 187, 188 SX 7773 3m NNE of
Ashburton. Loc, Ilsington CP.

SIGGLESTHORNE Yorks (E)
99 TA 1545 3m WSW of Hornsea. CP, 274.
Holderness RD. P Hull. Ch e. Sch pe.
Bridlington CC.

SIGNET Oxon
144 SP 2410 1m S of Burford. CP(Bfd and
Upton and Sgnt), 1,453. Witney RD.
Mid-Oxon CC (Banbury).

SILCHESTER Hants
168 SU 6262 6m N of Basingstoke. CP, 511.
Bsngstke RD. P Reading, Berks. Ch e, m.
Sch pe. Bsngstke CC. Site of Roman *Calleva
Atrebatum*; parts of outer wall remain.
Many 'finds' in Calleva Museum; others in
Rdng.

SILEBY Leics
121, 122 SK 6015 7m N of Leicester.
CP, 4,421. Barrow upon Soar RD.
P Loughborough. Ch e, b, m2, r. Sch ie, p.
Melton CC.

SILECROFT Cumb
88 SD 1381 3m WNW of Millom. Loc,
Whicham CP. P Mllm.

SILKSTONE Yorks (W)
102 SE 2905 4m W of Barnsley. CP, 1,614.
Penistone RD. P Bnsly. Ch e, m, v. Sch p.
Pnstne CC. See also Slkstne Cmmn.

SILKSTONE COMMON Yorks (W)
102 SE 2904 4m WSW of Barnsley. Loc,
Slkstne CP. P Bnsly. Ch m. Sch p.

SILK WILLOUGHBY Lincs (K)
113, 123 TF 0542 2m SSW of Sleaford.
CP, 173. E Kesteven RD. P Slfd. Ch e.
Sch pe. Grantham CC.

SILLOTH Cumb
75 NY 1153 12m NNE of Maryport.
CP, 2,726. Wigton RD. P Carlisle.
Ch e2, m, r, v3. Sch i, j, s. Penrith and the
Border CC. See also E Cote, Skinburness.
Laid out mid-19c as port and resort. Views
across Solway Firth to Scottish hills.

SILPHO Yorks (N)
93 SE 9692 5m WNW of Scarborough.

CP, 40. Scbrgh RD. Ch m. Scbrgh CC
(Scbrgh and Whitby).

SILSDEN Yorks (W)
96 SE 0446 4m NNW of Keighley.
UD, 5,588. P Kghly. Kghly BC.

SILSOE Beds
147 TL 0835 3m ESE of Ampthill. CP, 672.
Ampthll RD. P BEDFORD. Ch e. Sch pe.
Mid-Beds CC. Wrest Pk, 1m E, has 18c
gdns*.

SILTON Dorset
166 ST 7829 5m E of Wincanton. CP, 131.
Shaftesbury RD. Ch e. N Dst CC. 15c ch:
painted barrel-vault; 17c life-size monmt;
chantry chpl with fan-vaulting.

SILVERDALE Lancs
89 SD 4675 4m NW of Carnforth.
CP, 1,213. Lancaster RD. P Cnfth. Ch e, m.
Sch pe. Morecambe and Lonsdale CC. Small
resort on Mcmbe Bay.

SILVERDALE Staffs
110 SJ 8146 2m W of
Newcastle-under-Lyme. Loc,
Ncstle-undr-Lme MB. P Ncstle.

SILVER END Beds
147 TL 0942 6m SSE of Bedford. Loc,
Haynes CP.

SILVER END Essex
149, 162 TL 8019 3m NNW of Witham.
Loc, Wthm UD. P Wthm. 20c vllge begun in
1920s. Factory for disabled workers.

SILVERSTONE Northants
145, 146 SP 6644 3m SSW of Towcester.
CP, 1,067. Tcstr RD. P Tcstr. Ch e, m.
Sch i, je. Daventry CC (S Nthnts). Motor
racing circuit to S.

SILVERTON Devon
176 SS 9502 6m S of Tiverton. CP, 1,248.
Tvtn RD. P Exeter. Ch e, m, v. Sch pe.
Tvtn CC.

SILVINGTON Shrops
129, 130 SO 6279 4m NW of Cleobury
Mortimer. Loc, Wheathill CP. Ch e. Vllge in
deep country; hills. Ch largely Nmn.

SIMONBURN Nthmb
77 NY 8773 7m NW of Hexham. CP, 230.
Hxhm RD. P Hxhm. Ch e. Hxhm CC.
Compact vllge blt around square. Ch has
sloping floor. Ruined cstle to W.

SIMONSBATH Som
163 SS 7739 7m SSE of Lynton. Loc,
Exmoor CP. Dulverton RD. P Minehead.
Ch e. Taunton CC. In the heart of Exmoor.

SIMONSTONE Lancs
95 SD 7734 4m WNW of Burnley. CP, 660.
Bnly RD. Sch pe. Clitheroe CC. Radio
equipment factory.

SIMPSON Bucks
146 SP 8836 2m NNE of Bletchley. Loc,
Bltchly UD. P Bltchly.

SINDERBY Yorks (N)
91 SE 3481 5m W of Thirsk. CP, 80.
Thsk RD. P Thsk. Ch m. Thsk and
Malton CC.

SINDERHOPE Nthmb
77 NY 8452 8m S of Haydon Br. Loc,
Allendale CP. Hexham RD. P Hxhm. Ch m.
Hxhm CC.

SINDLESHAM Berks
169 SU 7769 2m WNW of Wokingham. Loc,
Winnersh CP. Ch b, r. Royal Merchant Navy
College is ½m S at Bearwood, Vctrn hse blt
for the then proprietor of *The Times.*

SINGLETON Lancs
94 SD 3838 5m ENE of Blackpool. CP, 872.
Fylde RD. Ch e. Sch pe. S Flde CC. See also
Lit Sngltn.

SINGLETON Sussex (W)
181 SU 8713 6m N of Chichester. CP, 552.
Chchstr RD. P Chchstr. Ch e. Sch pe.
Chchstr CC. See also Charlton.

SINNINGTON Yorks (N)
86, 92 SE 7485 4m WNW of Pickering.
CP, 319. Pckrng RD. P YORK. Ch e, m.
Sch p. Scarborough CC (Thirsk and Malton).
Snnngtn Grange water mill still in use.

SINTON GREEN Worcs
130 SO 8160 4m NNW of Worcester. Loc,
Grimley CP. P WCSTR.

SIPSON London
160, 170 TQ 0777 4m SSE of Uxbridge.
Loc, Hillingdon LB. Hayes and
Harlington BC (Uxbrdge CC).

SISLAND Norfolk
137 TM 3498 5m N of Bungay. CP, 53.
Loddon RD. Ch e. S Nflk CC.

SISSINGHURST Kent
172, 184 TQ 7937 2m NE of Cranbrook.
Loc, Crnbrk CP. P Crnbrk. Ch e, m. Sch pe.
Sssnghst Ct and Sssnghst Place have fine
gdns*. To E, Sssnghst Cstle (NT)*, Tdr hse
whose famous garden was created by V.
Sackville-West.

SISTON Glos
156 ST 6875 7m ENE of Bristol. CP, 1,821.
Warmley RD. Ch e. Kingswood CC (S Glos).
See also Bridgeyate.

SITHNEY Cornwall
189 SW 6328 2m NW of Helston. CP, 772.
Kerrier RD. Ch m3, v. Sch p. St Ives CC.

SITTINGBOURNE Kent
172 TQ 9063 8m ESE of Gillingham.
UD(Sttngbne and Milton), 30,861. P.
Faversham CC. See also Highsted. Indstrl.
Rly and maritime museums.

SIX ASHES Shrops and Staffs
130 SO 7988 5m ESE of Bridgnorth. Loc,
Brdgnth RD, Seisdon RD. P Brdgnth, Salop.
Ludlow CC, SW Staffs CC. (Ldlw CC,
Brierley Hill CC.)

SIXHILLS Lincs (L)
105 TF 1787 4m ESE of Mkt Rasen.
CP, 86. Caistor RD. Ch e, m.
Gainsborough CC.

SIX MILE BOTTOM Cambs
135 TL 5756 6m SW of Newmarket. Loc,
Lit Wilbraham CP. P Nmkt, Suffolk.

SIXPENNY HANDLEY Dorset
179 ST 9917 9m ESE of Shaftesbury.
CP, 732. Wimborne and Cranborne RD.
Ch e, m3. Sch p. N Dst CC. See also
Cashmoor, Deanland, Gussage St Andrew,
Woodcutts.

SIZEWELL Suffolk (E)
137 TM 4762 5m E of Saxmundham.
UD(Leiston-cum-Szwll), 4,864. P. Eye CC.
'Sizewell B' nuclear power stn.

SKEEBY Yorks (N)
91 NZ 2002 2m ENE of Richmond. CP, 253.
Rchmnd RD. P Rchmnd. Ch m. Rchmnd CC.

SKEFFINGTON Leics
122 SK 7402 8m WNW of Uppingham.

CP, 178. Billesdon RD. P LEICESTER. Ch e. Harborough CC (Melton).

SKEFFLING Yorks (E)
105 TA 3719 6m SSE of Withernsea. CP, 152. Holderness RD. P Hull. Ch e, m. Bridlington CC.

SKEGBY Notts
112 SK 5060 2m W of Mansfield. Loc, Sutton in Ashfield UD. P Sttn-in-Ashfld.

SKEGNESS Lincs (L)
114 TF 5663 19m NE of Boston. UD, 13,557. P. Horncastle CC. See also Seathorne, Winthorpe. Resort. Good sands; amusements, holiday camp, airfield. To S, Gibraltar Point nature reserve.

SKELBROOKE Yorks (W)
103 SE 5112 7m NW of Doncaster. Loc, Hampole CP. P Dncstr. Ch e. Robin Hood's Well, possibly designed by Vanbrugh.

SKELDYKE Lincs (H)
114, 123 TF 3337 4m S of Boston. Loc, Kirton CP.

SKELLINGTHORPE Lincs (K)
113 SK 9272 3m W of Lincoln. CP, 1,328. N Kesteven RD. P LNCLN. Ch e, m. Sch pe. Grantham CC.

SKELLOW Yorks (W)
103 SE 5210 6m NW of Doncaster. Loc, Adwick le Street UD. P Carcroft, Dncstr.

SKELMANTHORPE Yorks (W)
102 SE 2310 6m SE of Huddersfield. Loc, Denby Dale UD. P Hddsfld.

SKELMERSDALE Lancs
100 SD 4606 4m ESE of Ormskirk. UD(Sklmsdle and Holland), 30,522. P. Ince BC. See also Crawford, Digmoor, Roby Mill, Stormy Corner. New tn development around former mining vllge. Industries incl rubber, glass, textiles. Sklmrsdale New Tn pop. 26,681.

SKELTON Cumb
83 NY 4335 6m NW of Penrith. CP, 953. Pnrth RD. P Pnrth. Ch e, m. Sch p. Pnrth and the Border CC. See also Low Braithwaite.

SKELTON Yorks (E)
97, 98 SE 7625 2m NE of Goole. Loc, Kilpin CP.

SKELTON Yorks (N)
86 NZ 6518 2m SSW of Saltburn. UD(Skltn and Brotton), 15,083. P(Skltn-in-Cleveland), Sltbn-by-the-Sea. Cleveland and Whitby CC (Clvdn). See also Boosbeck, Carlin How, Charlton, Kilton, Kltn Thorpe, Lingdale, Moorsholm, N Skltn, Stanghow. Iron-mining distr. Skltn Cstle 18c Gothic.

SKELTON Yorks (N)
97 SE 5756 3m NNW of York. CP, 944. Flaxton RD. P YK. Ch e. Sch p. Thirsk and Malton CC. Perfect complete EE ch.

SKELTON Yorks (W)
91 SE 3668 2m NW of Boroughbridge. CP, 230. Ripon and Pateley Br RD. P(Skltn-on-Ure), Rpn. Ch e. Sch pe. Rpn CC. Newby Hall*, 18c hse partly by Adam in beautiful gdn bordering R Ure.

SKELWITH BRIDGE Lancs and Westm
88, 89 NY 3403 2m WSW of Ambleside. Loc, N Lonsdale RD; Lakes UD. Sch pe. Morecambe and Lnsdle CC; Westm CC. Much NT property in area. Sklwth Force is well known waterfall.

SKENDLEBY Lincs (L)
114 TF 4369 4m SSW of Alford. CP, 164. Spilsby RD. P Splsby. Ch e, m, r. Horncastle CC.

SKERNE Yorks (E)
99 TA 0455 2m SE of Driffield. CP, 332. Drffld RD. P Drffld. Ch e. Howden CC. See also Wansford.

SKEWSBY Yorks (N)
92 SE 6271 6m E of Easingwold. CP(Dalby-cum-Sksby), 78. Easngwld RD. P YORK. Thirsk and Malton CC.

SKEYTON Norfolk
126 TG 2425 3m ESE of Aylsham. CP, 237. Smallburgh RD. Ch e, m. Sch pe. N Nflk CC.

SKIDBROOKE Lincs (L)
105 TF 4492 6m NW of Mablethorpe. CP(Skdbrke w Saltfleet Haven), 415. Louth RD. Ch e, m. Lth CC.

SKIDBY Yorks (E)
99 TA 0133 4m SSW of Beverley. CP, 839. Bvrly RD. P Cottingham. Ch e, m. Sch pe. Haltemprice CC. Windmill on hill to S; only one intact N of Humber.

SKILGATE Som
164 SS 9827 5m E of Dulverton. CP, 109.
Dlvtn RD. P Taunton. Ch e. Tntn CC.

SKILLINGTON Lincs (K)
122 SK 8925 6m S of Grantham. CP, 251.
W Kesteven RD. P Grnthm. Ch e, m. Sch pe.
Rutland and Stamford CC.

SKINBURNESS Cumb
75 NY 1255 2m NE of Silloth. Loc,
Sllth CP. P Carlisle.

SKINNINGROVE Yorks (N)
86 NZ 7119 1m N of Loftus. Loc, Lfts UD.
P Saltburn-by-the-Sea.

SKIPSEA Yorks (E)
99 TA 1655 5m NNW of Hornsea. CP, 454.
Bridlington RD. P Driffield. Ch e, m. Sch p.
Brdlngtn CC. Extensive earthworks, rems of
Skpsea Cstle (A.M.), prob Nmn.

SKIPTON Yorks (W)
95 SD 9851 8m NW of Keighley.
UD, 12,422. P. Skptn CC. Mkt and indstrl
tn; important centre for surrounding
agricultural area, and for explorers of Dales.
Skptn Cstle* dates from 11c, but mainly
14c–15c.

SKIPTON-ON-SWALE Yorks (N)
91 SE 3679 4m WSW of Thirsk. CP, 76.
Thsk RD. Ch e, m. Thsk and Malton CC. Br
designed by Carr of York.

SKIPWITH Yorks (E)
97, 98 SE 6638 5m NE of Selby. CP, 161.
Derwent RD. P Slby. Ch e, m. Howden CC.

SKIRMETT Bucks
159 SU 7790 5m N of Henley. Loc,
Hambleden CP. Ch e.

SKIRPENBECK Yorks (E)
97, 98 SE 7457 6m NW of Pocklington.
CP, 124. Pcklngtn RD. P YORK. Ch e.
Howden CC.

SKIRWITH Cumb
83 NY 6132 7m ENE of Penrith. Loc,
Culgaith CP. P Pnrth. Ch e, m. Sch pe.

SLACK Yorks (W)
95 SD 9328 1m NW of Hebden Br. Loc,
Heptonstall CP. Ch b.

SLAD Glos
156 SO 8707 2m NE of Stroud. Loc,
Painswick CP. Ch e. Subject of childhood
memories of Laurie Lee recorded in *Cider
with Rosie*.

SLADE Devon
163 SS 5146 1m SSW of Ilfracombe. Loc,
Ilfrcmbe UD. P Ilfrcmbe.

SLAGGYFORD Nthmb
76 NY 6752 5m NW of Alston. Loc,
Knaresdale and Kirkhaugh CP.
Haltwhistle RD. P Carlisle, Cumberland.
Ch m. Hexham CC.

SLAIDBURN Yorks (W)
95 SD 7152 7m NNW of Clitheroe. CP, 319.
Bowland RD. P Clthroe, Lancs. Ch e, m.
Sch pe. Skipton CC. Orig seat of courts of
Forest of Bowland.

SLAITHWAITE Yorks (W)
102 SE 0814 4m WSW of Huddersfield.
Loc, Colne Valley UD. P Hddsfld. Clne
Vlly CC.

SLALEY Nthmb
77 NY 9757 5m SE of Hexham. CP, 668.
Hxhm RD. P Hxhm. Ch e, m. Sch p.
Hxhm CC.

SLAPTON Bucks
146 SP 9320 3m S of Leighton Buzzard.
CP, 245. Wing RD. P Lghtn Bzzd, Beds.
Ch e, m. Sch p. Buckingham CC.

SLAPTON Devon
188 SX 8244 5m E of Kingsbridge. CP, 460.
Kngsbrdge RD. P Kngsbrdge. Ch e, v.
Totnes CC. To S, long sand bar (Slptn Sands)
has formed freshwater lake behind.

SLAPTON Northants
145, 146 SP 6446 3m WSW of Towcester.
CP, 79. Tcstr RD. Ch e, m. Daventry CC
(S Nthnts). Ch has 14c–16c wall-paintings.

SLATTOCKS Lancs
101 SD 8808 3m SSW of Rochdale. Loc,
Middleton MB. P Mddltn, MANCHESTER.

SLAUGHAM Sussex (E)
182 TQ 2528 5m S of Crawley. CP, 2,047.
Cuckfield RD. P Haywards Hth. Ch e, b.
Mid-Sx CC (E Grinstead). See also
Handcross, Warninglid.

SLAUGHTERFORD Wilts
156 ST 8374 5m W of Chippenham. Loc,
Biddestone CP. Ch e. Paper mills.

SLAWSTON Leics
133 SP 7794 5m NE of Mkt Harborough.
CP, 105. Mkt Hbrgh RD. P Mkt Hbrgh.
Ch e. Hbrgh CC.

SLEAFORD Hants
169 SU 8038 6m SSW of Farnham. Loc,
Alton RD. Petersfield CC.

SLEAFORD Lincs (K)
113 TF 0645 11m ENE of Grantham.
UD, 7,975. P. Grnthm CC. See also
Holdingham, Quarrington. 12c—15c ch with
144ft spire. Large maltings blt 1905.

SLEAGILL Westm
83 NY 5919 6m W of Appleby. CP, 103.
N Westm RD. Ch m. Sch pe. Westm CC.

SLEAPFORD Shrops
118, 119 SJ 6315 3m NNW of Wellington.
Loc, Wllngtn RD. The Wrekin CC.

SLEDGE GREEN Worcs
143 SO 8134 5m W of Tewkesbury. Loc,
Pendock CP.

SLEDMERE Yorks (E)
98 SE 9364 7m NW of Driffield. CP, 359.
Drffld RD. P Drffld. Ch e, m. Sch pe.
Howden CC. High on Wolds. Sldmre Hse*,
Ggn mansion in grnds by Capability Brown,
seat of Sykes family, who in 18c and 19c
revolutionised agriculture and forestry in
Wolds and blt or reblt many chs in area (see
also Garton-on-the-Wolds).

SLEIGHTS Yorks (N)
86 NY 8607 3m SW of Whitby. Loc,
Eskdaleside cum Ugglebarnby CP.
Whtby RD. P Whtby. Ch e, r. Sch pe.
Cleveland and Whtby CC (Scarborough and
Whtby).

SLEPE Dorset
179 SY 9293 4m N of Wareham. Loc,
Lytchett Minster CP.

SLIMBRIDGE Glos
156 SO 7403 4m NNW of Dursley. CP, 862.
Dsly RD. P GLOUCESTER. Ch b. Sch p.
Stroud CC. To SW, Severn Wildfowl Trust
grnds.

SLINDON Staffs
110, 119 SJ 8232 5m WSW of Stone. Loc,
Eccleshall CP. P STAFFORD. Ch e.

SLINDON Sussex (W)
181, 182 SU 9608 7m ENE of Chichester.
CP, 601. Chchstr RD. P Arundel. Ch e, r.
Sch pe. Arndl CC (Chchstr). Attractive
downland vllge. Ch has only wooden effigy
in Sussex.

SLINFOLD Sussex (W)
182 TQ 1131 4m W of Horsham. CP, 1,464.
Hshm RD. P Hshm. Ch e, c. Sch pe. Hshm
and Crawley CC (Hshm).

SLINGSBY Yorks (N)
92 SE 6974 6m WNW of Malton. CP, 449.
Mltn RD. P YORK. Ch e, m. Sch p. Thirsk
and Mltn CC.

SLIP END Beds
147 TL 0718 2m SSW of Luton. Loc,
Caddington CP. P Ltn. Ch m. Sch p.

SLIPPER'S BOTTOM Norfolk
126 TG 2812 4m NE of Norwich. Loc,
Rackheath CP.

SLIPTON Northants
134 SP 9579 3m W of Thrapston. Loc,
Lowick CP. Ch e.

SLOLEY Norfolk
126 TG 2924 4m S of N Walsham. CP, 195.
Smallburgh RD. Ch e, m. Sch pe.
N Nflk CC.

SLOOTHBY Lincs (L)
114 TF 4970 4m SE of Atford.
CP(Willoughby w Slthby), 541. Spilsby RD.
P Alfd. Ch m. Horncastle CC.

SLOUGH Bucks
159, 160, 170 SU 9779 20m W of London.
MB, 86,757. P. Eton and Slgh BC. See also
Langley, Upton. Indstrl tn of rapid growth.

SLOUGH GREEN Som
177 ST 2720 4m SE of Taunton. Loc,
W Hatch CP. P Tntn.

SLYNE Lancs
89 SD 4765 3m N of Lancaster.
CP(Slne-w-Hest). Lncstr RD. P LNCSTR.
Ch e, v. Sch pe. Morecambe and
Lonsdale CC.

SMALLBRIDGE Lancs
95, 101 SD 9115 2m NE of Rochdale. Loc,

Smallburgh

Rchdle CB, Wardle UD. P Rchdle. Rchdle BC, Heywood and Royton CC.

SMALLBURGH Norfolk
126 TG 3324 5m NNE of Wroxham. C P , 4 0 5 . S m l l b r g h R D . P NORWICH, NOR 15Z. Ch e, m. Sch pe. N Nflk CC. See also Low St.

SMALL DOLE Sussex (W)
182 TQ 2112 2m S of Henfield. Loc, Chanctonbury RD. P Hnfld. Shoreham CC (Arundel and Shoreham).

SMALLEY Derbys
112, 121 SK 4044 4m WNW of Ilkeston. CP, 1,768. Belper RD. P DERBY. Ch e, b. Sch pe. Blpr CC.

SMALLFIELD Surrey
170, 182 TQ 3143 2m E of Horley. Loc, Burstow CP. P Hly. Ch b, v. Sch p.

SMALL HYTHE Kent
184 TQ 8930 2m S of Tenterden. Loc, Tntdn MB. Smll Hthe Place (NT)*, 15c hse, home of actress Ellen Terry. Museum and barn theatre.

SMALLRIDGE Devon
177 ST 3001 2m N of Axminster. Loc, Chardstock CP. P Axmnstr.

SMALLWOOD Ches
110 SJ 8060 4m WSW of Congleton. CP, 502. Cngltn RD. Ch e, m. Sch pe. Knutsford CC. See also Brookhouse Grn, Overton Grn.

SMANNELL Hants
168 SU 3849 3m NNE of Andover. CP, 292. Andvr RD. Ch e, b. Sch pe. Winchester CC (Basingstoke). See also Lit London.

SMARDEN Kent
172, 184 TQ 8842 8m W of Ashford. CP, 989. W Ashfd RD. P Ashfd. Ch e, b3. Sch p. Ashfd CC. See also Haffenden Quarter. Timbered and weatherboarded cottages; flowers.

SMEATHARPE Devon
164, 176 ST 1910 7m NNE of Honiton. Loc, Hntn RD. Hntn CC.

SMEATON, GREAT Yorks (N)
91 NZ 3404 7m NNW of Northallerton. See Gt Smtn.

SMEETH Kent
172, 173, 184 TR 0739 4m SE of Ashford. CP, 673. E Ashfd RD. Ch e. Sch p. Ashfd CC.

SMEETH, THE Norfolk
124 TF 5209 4m E of Wisbech. Loc, Marshland St James CP. Mshlnd RD. P(Mshlnd Smth), Wsbch, Cambs. Ch m. Sch pe. NW Nflk CC (King's Lynn).

SMEETON WESTERBY Leics
132, 133 SP 6792 5m NW of Mkt Harborough. CP, 275. Mkt Hbrgh RD. P LEICESTER. Ch e. Hbrgh CC.

SMETHWICK Worcs
131 SP 0288 3m WNW of Birmingham. Loc, Warley CB. P Wly. Wly E BC (Smthwck). Engineering and other wks.

SMISBY Derbys
120, 121 SK 3519 2m N of Ashby de la Zouch. CP, 303. Repton RD. P Ashby de la Zch, Leics. Ch e, m. Sch p. Belper CC. S end of vllge: octagonal brick lock-up.

SMITHFIELD Cumb
76 NY 4465 6m NNE of Carlisle. Loc, Kirklinton Middle CP. Border RD. Penrith and the Bdr CC.

SMITHINCOTT Devon
164, 176 ST 0611 7m E of Tiverton. Loc, Uffculme CP.

SNAILBEACH Shrops
118 SJ 3702 10m SW of Shrewsbury. Loc, Worthen CP. P Shrsbry. Ch b, m.

SNAILWELL Cambs
135 TL 6467 3m N of Newmarket. CP, 216. Nmkt RD. P Nmkt, Suffolk. Ch e. Cambs CC. Thatched cottages.

SNAINTON Yorks (N)
93 SE 9282 8m E of Pickering. CP, 648. Scarborough RD. P Scbrgh. Ch e, m. Sch pe. Scbrgh CC (Scbrgh and Whitby).

SNAITH Yorks (W)
97, 98 SE 6422 6m W of Goole. CP(Snth and Cowick), 1,787. Gle RD. P Gle. Ch e, m. Sch p, s. Gle CC. See also E Cwck, W Cwck.

SNAPE Suffolk (E)
137 TM 3959 2m S of Saxmundham.

CP, 572. Blyth RD. P Sxmndhm. Ch e, m. Sch p. Eye CC. See also Snpe St. Danish burial ship of 7c unearthed here, 1862.

SNAPE Yorks (N)
91 SE 2684 2m S of Bedale. CP(Snpe w Thorp), 395. Bdle RD. P Bdle. Ch e, m. Sch p. Thirsk and Malton CC. Snpe Cstle, partly ruined Tdr and earlier, once home of Henry VIII's wife, Catherine Parr; 15c chpl*.

SNAPE GREEN Lancs
100 SD 3814 3m SE of Southport. Loc, Scarisbrick CP.

SNAPE STREET Suffolk (E)
137 TM 3958 3m S of Saxmundham. Loc, Snpe CP. On R Alde. Over br at The Maltings, concert hall of Aldeburgh Festival, burnt out 1969, rebuilt 1970.

SNARESTONE Leics
120, 121 SK 3409 5m S of Ashby de la Zouch. CP, 329. Ashby de la Zouch RD. P Burton-on-Trent, Staffs. Ch e, m. Sch pe. Loughborough CC.

SNARFORD Lincs (L)
104 TF 0582 5m SW of Mkt Rasen. CP, 70. Welton RD. Ch e, m. Gainsborough CC. Lonely little ch has vast Elizn monmts to Wray family, who once had a great hse here.

SNARGATE Kent
184 TQ 9928 7m NE of Rye. CP, 140. Romney Marsh RD. Ch e. Folkestone and Hythe CC.

SNAVE Kent
184 TR 0129 8m S of Ashford. Loc, Brenzett CP. Ch e.

SNEATON Yorks (N)
86, 93 NZ 8907 2m S of Whitby. CP, 163. Whtby RD. P Whtby. Ch e. Cleveland and Whtby CC (Scarborough and Whtby).

SNELLAND Lincs (L)
104 TF 0780 6m SSW of Mkt Rasen. CP, 98. Welton RD. Ch e. Gainsborough CC. Surrounded by disused airfields with accompanying ruins.

SNELSTON Derbys
120 SK 1543 3m SW of Ashbourne. CP, 177. Ashbne RD. P Ashbne. Ch e. W Derbys CC.

SNETTERTON Norfolk
136 TL 9991 4m SW of Attleborough. CP, 144. Wayland RD. Ch e. S Nflk CC. Motor racing circuit on disused airfield to SE.

SNETTISHAM Norfolk
124 TF 6834 4m S of Hunstanton. CP, 1,671. Docking RD. P King's Lynn. Ch e, m2, s. Sch p. NW Nflk CC (K's Lnn). See also Southgate. 14c ch: tall spire; monmts; brasses.

SNITTER Nthmb
71 NU 0203 2m WNW of Rothbury. CP, 143. Rthbry RD. Berwick-upon-Tweed CC.

SNITTERBY Lincs (L)
104 SK 9894 8m S of Brigg. CP, 220. Caistor RD. P Gainsborough. Ch e, m2. Gnsbrgh CC.

SNITTERFIELD Warwicks
131 SP 2159 3m NNE of Stratford. CP, 1,021. Strtfd-on-Avon RD. P Strtfd-on-Avn. Ch e, m. Sch p. Strtfd-on-Avn CC (Strtfd). Bthplce of Shakespeare's father.

SNODHILL Herefs
142 SO 3240 6m ESE of Hay-on-Wye. Loc, Peterchurch CP.

SNODLAND Kent
171, 172 TQ 7061 5m SSW of Rochester. CP, 3,834. Malling RD. P. Ch e, c, m, s, v. Sch p, pe, s. Tonbridge aand Mllng CC (Sevenoaks). Indstrl; cement wks.

SNORING, GREAT Norfolk
125 TF 9434 4m NNE of Fakenham. See Gt Snrng.

SNOWS HILL Glos
144 SP 0933 2m S of Broadway. CP, 224. Cheltenham RD. P Brdwy, Worcs. Ch e. Cirencester and Tewkesbury CC. Cotswold vllge. Mnr Hse (NT)*, 16c–17c.

SNYDALE Yorks (W)
97 SE 4020 4m SSW of Castleford. Loc, Featherstone UD.

SOBERTON Hants
180 SU 6116 4m E of Bishop's Waltham. CP, 1,425. Droxford RD.

Soberton Heath

P SOUTHAMPTON. Ch e. Petersfield CC. See also Hoe Gate, Hundred Acres, Newtown. Ch: wall-paintings; rare 17c altar cloth.

SOBERTON HEATH Hants
180 SU 6014 4m SE of Bishop's Waltham. Loc, Sbtn CP. Ch m.

SOCKBRIDGE Westm
83 NY 5026 2m SSW of Penrith. CP(Sckbrdge and Tirril), 196. N Westm RD. Westm CC.

SOCKBURN Co Durham
85 NZ 3407 6m SE of Darlington. CP, 32. Dlngtn RD. Ch e. Bishop Auckland CC (Sedgefield).

SOHAM Cambs
135 TL 5973 5m SE of Ely. CP, 5,077. Newmarket RD. P Ely. Ch e, b2, m2, r, s, v. Sch i, j, je, s2. Cambs CC. See also Barway, Broad Hill. Vllge has rare weighing machine, and remains of four windmills.

SOLDON Devon
174 SS 3210 4m N of Holsworthy. Loc, Hlswthy Hmlts CP. Hlswthy RD. Ch m. W Dvn CC (Tavistock).

SOLDRIDGE Hants
168, 169 SU 6535 5m SW of Alton. Loc, Medstead CP.

SOLE STREET Kent
171 TQ 6567 4m S of Gravesend. Loc, Cobham CP. P Grvsnd.

SOLESTREET Kent
172, 173, 184 TR 0949 7m NE of Ashford. Loc, Crundale CP.

SOLIHULL Warwicks
131 SP 1579 7m SE of Birmingham. CB, 106,968. P. Slhll BC (CC). See also Dorridge, Elmdon, Knowle. Tn centre development.

SOLLERS DILWYN Herefs
129 SO 4255 5m WSW of Leominster. Loc, Dlwn CP.

SOLLERS HOPE Herefs
142, 143 SO 6133 7m SW of Ledbury. CP, 83. Ross and Whitchurch RD. Ch e. Hereford CC.

SOLLOM Lancs
100 SD 4518 7m E of Southport. Loc, Tarleton CP.

SOMERBY Leics
122 SK 7710 5m WNW of Oakham. CP, 903. Melton and Belvoir RD. P Mltn Mowbray. Ch e, m. Sch p. Mltn CC. See also Burrough on the Hill, Pickwell.

SOMERBY Lincs (L)
104 TA 0606 4m E of Brigg. CP, 77. Caistor RD. Ch e. Gainsborough CC. Obelisk blt 1770 by a Mr and Mrs Weston to celebrate 29 years of happy marriage.

SOMERCOTES Derbys
112 SK 4253 1m SE of Alfreton. Loc, Alfrtn UD. P DERBY.

SOMERFORD, GREAT Wilts
157 ST 9682 3m SE of Malmesbury. See Gt Smrfd.

SOMERFORD KEYNES Glos
157 SU 0195 4m S of Cirencester. CP, 272. Crncstr RD. P Crncstr. Ch e. Crncstr and Tewkesbury CC. See also Shorncote. Tdr mnr hse.

SOMERLEY Sussex (W)
181 SZ 8198 5m SSW of Chichester. Loc, Chchstr RD. Chchstr CC. Windmill.

SOMERLEYTON Suffolk (E)
137 TM 4897 5m NW of Lowestoft. CP, 377. Lothingland RD. P Lwstft. Ch e. Sch p. Lwstft CC. 16c and 19c Smrltn Hall*; maze in gdns.

SOMERSAL HERBERT Derbys
120 SK 1335 3m ENE of Uttoxeter. CP, 70. Ashbourne RD. P DERBY. Ch e, m. W Derbys CC. Smsl Hall, Elizn, half-timbered.

SOMERSBY Lincs (L)
114 TF 3472 6m ENE of Horncastle. CP, 118. Hncstle RD. Ch e. Hncstle CC. See also Ashby Puerorum, Bag Enderby. Bthplce of Tennyson, whose father was rector here. Ch a Tennyson shrine.

SOMERSHAM Hunts
135 TL 3677 5m NNE of St Ives. CP, 1,401. St Ives RD. P HUNTINGDON. Ch e, b, m. Sch p. Hunts CC. Ch: 16c brass.

SOMERSHAM Suffolk (E)
149 TM 0848 5m NW of Ipswich. CP, 299.
Gipping RD. Ch e, b. Sch p. Eye CC.

SOMERTON Oxon
145 SP 4928 7m NW of Bicester. CP, 244.
Ploughley RD. P OXFORD. Ch e.
Banbury CC (Henley). Ch: reredos, scrn,
Fermor tombs. To SE, Upr Heyford Airfield
beyond ancient Port Way. To E, rly, canal,
R Cherwell.

SOMERTON Som
177 ST 4828 4m NNW of Ilchester.
CP, 2,182. Langport RD. P.
Ch e, f, m2 , r, s, v3. Sch je, p. Yeovil CC.
Small mkt tn with fine ch, early 18c tn hall,
and mkt cross.

SOMERTON Suffolk (W)
149 TL 8153 5m NNE of Clare. CP, 85.
Melford RD. Ch e. Sudbury and
Woodbridge CC.

SOMPTING Sussex (W)
182 TQ 1605 2m NE of Worthing.
CP, 5,830. Wthng RD. P Lancing. Ch e, c, r.
Sch p. Shoreham CC (Arundel and Shrhm).
See also Upr Cokeham. Ch has famous
Saxon twr capped by 'Rhenish helm' unique
in England.

SONNING Berks
159 SU 7575 3m ENE of Reading.
CP, 1,027. Wokingham RD. P Rdng. Ch e, v.
Sch p. Rdng S CC (Wknghm). Rsdntl distr
of R Thames, crossed by late 18c br. To S,
famous rly cutting, long and deep.

SONNING COMMON Berks
159 SU 7080 4m WSW of Henley.
CP, 1,998. Hnly RD. P Reading, Berks.
Ch c, r, v. Sch p, s. Hnly CC.

SOPLEY Hants
179 SZ 1597 3m N of Christchurch.
CP, 1,063. Ringwood and
Fordingbridge RD. P Chrstchch. Ch e.
Sch p. New Forest CC. See also Avon,
Ripley.

SOPWORTH Wilts
156 ST 8286 6m SW of Tetbury. CP, 109.
Malmesbury RD. P Chippenham. Ch e.
Chppnhm CC.

SOTBY Lincs (L)
105 TF 2078 7m NW of Horncastle. CP, 49.
Hncstle RD. Ch e. Hncstle CC.

SOTS HOLE Lincs (K)
113 TF 1264 4m W of Woodhall Spa. Loc,
Metheringham CP.

SOTTERLEY Suffolk (E)
137 TM 4584 4m SE of Beccles. CP, 142.
Wainford RD. Ch e. Sch pe. Lowestoft CC.
S. Hall, 18c, in large pk containing ch with
notable brasses.

SOUDLEY, GREAT Shrops
119 SJ 7228 5m SE of Mkt Drayton. See Gt
Sdly.

SOULBURY Bucks
146 SP 8827 2m NW of Linslade. CP, 486.
Wing RD. P Leighton Buzzard, Beds.
Ch e, m. Buckingham CC.

SOULBY Westm
84 NY 7411 2m NW of Kirkby Stephen.
CP, 186. N Westm RD. P Kby Stphn.
Ch e, m. Sch p. Westm CC.

SOULDERN Oxon
145 SP 5231 5m SW of Brackley. CP, 347.
Ploughley RD. P Bicester. Ch e, r, v.
Banbury CC (Henley).

SOULDROP Beds
134 SP 9861 4m SSE of Rushden.
CP (Knotting and Souldrop), 258.
Bedford RD. P BDFD. Ch e, m. Bdfd CC.

SOUND HEATH Ches
110 SJ 6148 3m SW of Nantwich. Loc,
Snd CP. Nntwch RD. Ch m. Nntwch CC.

SOUNDWELL Glos
155, 156 ST 6575 5m ENE of Bristol. Loc,
Kingswood UD. P Fishponds, BRSTL.

SOURTON Devon
175 SX 5390 5m SW of Okehampton.
CP, 408. Okhmpton RD. P Okhmptn.
Ch e, b, m. W Dvn CC (Torrington).

SOUTERGATE Lancs
88 SD 2281 4m WNW of Ulverston. Loc,
Kirkby Ireleth CP. N Lonsdale RD.
Morecambe and Lnsdle CC.

SOUTH ACRE Norfolk
125 TF 8114 3m N of Swaffham. CP, 74.
Swffhm RD. SW Nflk CC. Ch: brasses, esp
one of 1384.

SOUTHALL London
160 TQ 1280 3m W of Ealing. Loc,
Ealng LB. P Middx. Sthall BC.

SOUTHAM Glos
143, 144 SO 9725 2m NE of Cheltenham.
CP, 409. Chltnhm RD. Ch e. Cirencester and
Tewkesbury CC.

SOUTHAM Warwicks
132 SP 4161 7m ESE of Leamington.
CP, 2,212. Sthm RD. P Lmngtn Spa.
Ch e, r, v. Sch i, j, pr, s. Stratford-on-
Avon CC (Strtfd).

SOUTH AMBERSHAM Sussex (W)
181 SU 9120 2m E of Midhurst. CP, 117.
Mdhst RD. Chichester CC (Horsham).

SOUTHAMPTON Hants
180 SU 4112 70m SW of London.
C B, 214,826. P(STHMPTN).
BCs: Sthmptn, Itchen; Sthmptn, Test.
Transatlantic and container port. Boat and
hovercraft ferries to IOW. University,
industry. Extensive rebuilding since World
War II damage; also many historic bldngs.
Rems of mdvl walls.

SOUTH ASCOT Berks
169 SU 9267 6m SSW of Windsor. Loc,
Sunninghill CP. P Asct. Ch e, r.

SOUTH BADDESLEY Hants
180 SZ 3596 2m ENE of Lymington. Loc,
Boldre CP. Ch e. Sch pe.

SOUTH BARROW Som
166 ST 6027 7m W of Wincanton. CP, 130.
Wncntn RD. Ch e, m. Wells CC.

SOUTH BENFLEET Essex
162 TQ 7786 4m ESE of Basildon. Loc,
Bnflt UD. P Bnflt. SE Essx CC. Views to
Kent across Canvey Island and Thames
estuary.

SOUTHBOROUGH Kent
171 TQ 5842 2m N of Tunbridge Wells.
UD, 9,750. P Tnbrdge Wells. Royal Tnbrdge
Wlls CC (Tnbrdge). Joined to Tnbrdge Wlls,
but old vllge grn remains.

SOUTHBOURNE Sussex (W)
181 SU 7705 4m E of Havant. CP.
Chichester RD. P Emsworth, Hants. Ch e, v.

Sch p, s. Chchstr CC. See also Hermitage,
Nutbourne, Prinsted.

SOUTH BRENT Devon
187, 188 SX 6960 4m SW of Buckfastleigh.
CP, 1,803. Totnes RD. P. Ch e, c, m, r.
Sch p. Ttns CC. See also Aish, Didworthy.

SOUTH BREWHAM Som
166 ST 7236 3m ENE of Bruton. Loc,
Brhm CP. Wincanton RD. P Brtn. Ch e.
Wells CC. 2m SE on Kingsettle Hill, Alfred's
Twr, blt 1776 to commemorate one of King
Alfred's victories of 879.

SOUTH BROOMHILL Nthmb
71 NU 2500 3m SSW of Amble. Loc,
E Chevington CP. Sch s.

SOUTHBURGH Norfolk
125 TG 0004 5m S of E Dereham. Loc,
Cranworth CP. P Thetford. Ch e.

SOUTH BURLINGHAM Norfolk
126 TG 3807 9m W of Yarmouth. Loc,
Blnghm CP. Blofield and Flegg RD. Ch e.
Ymth CC.

SOUTHBURN Yorks (E)
98 SE 9954 3m SW of Driffield. Loc,
Kirkburn CP.

SOUTH CADBURY Som
166 ST 6325 5m WSW of Wincanton.
CP, 273. Wncntn RD. P Yeovil. Ch e.
Wells CC. See also Sutton Montis. Extensive
Iron Age camp excavated in 1960s. Possible
site of King Arthur's legendary Camelot.

SOUTH CARLTON Lincs (L)
104 SK 9576 4m NNW of Lincoln. CP, 138.
Welton RD. Ch e. Sch pe. Gainsborough CC.

SOUTH CAVE Yorks (E)
98 SE 9231 7m SSE of Mkt Weighton.
CP, 1,521. Beverley RD. P Brough.
Ch e, c, m2. Sch pe. Haltemprice CC.

SOUTH CERNEY Glos
157 SU 0497 4m SSE of Cirencester.
CP, 1,772. Crncstr RD. P Crncstr.
Ch e, c, m, v. Sch pe. ncstrr and
Tewkesbury CC. See also Cny Wick.

SOUTH CHARD Som
177 ST 3205 2m S of Chard. Loc, Chd CP.
Chd RD. P Chd. Ch b, v. Yeovil CC.

SOUTH CHARLTON Nthmb
71 NU 1620 5m NNW of Alnwick. Loc,
Eglingham CP. Ch e. Sch p.

SOUTH CHERITON Som
166 ST 6924 3m SSW of Wincanton. Loc,
Horsington CP. Ch c, m.

SOUTH CHURCH Co Durham
85 NZ 2128 just SE of Bishop Auckland.
Loc, Bshp Aucklnd UD. P Bshp Aucklnd.
The late 13c ch is the ancient parish ch of
Bshp Aucklnd.

SOUTH CLIFFE Yorks (E)
98 SE 8736 4m S of Mkt Weighton.
CP, 147. Pocklington RD. Howden CC. See
also N Clffe.

SOUTH CLIFTON Notts
113 SK 8270 10m W of Lincoln. CP, 219.
Newark RD. P Nwk. Ch m. Nwk CC.

SOUTH COCKERINGTON Lincs (L)
105 TF 3889 4m ENE of Louth. CP, 184.
Lth RD. Ch e, m. Lth CC.

SOUTH COLLINGHAM Notts
113 SK 8261 5m NNE of Newark. CP, 598.
Nwk RD. Ch e, m. Sch p, s. Nwk CC. See
also Brough.

SOUTH COVE Suffolk (E)
137 TM 4980 3m N of Southwold. CP, 74.
Lothingland RD. Ch e. Lowestoft CC.

SOUTH CREAKE Norfolk
125 TF 8536 6m NW of Fakenham.
CP, 703. Docking RD. P Fknhm. Ch e, m, v.
Sch pe. NW Nflk CC (King's Lynn).
Outstanding mdvl ch, colourfully decorated.

SOUTH CROXTON Leics
122 SK 6910 7m NE of Leicester. CP, 188.
Barrow upon Soar RD. P LCSTR. Ch e, m.
Melton CC.

SOUTH DALTON Yorks (E)
98 SE 9645 6m NW of Beverley. Loc, Dltn
Holme CP. Bvrly RD. P(Dltn Hlme), Bvrly.
Ch m. Haltemprice CC.

SOUTH DARENTH Kent
171 TQ 5669 4m SE of Dartford. Loc,
Horton Kirby CP. P Dtfd. Ch f, v.

SOUTH DUFFIELD Yorks (E)
97, 98 SE 6833 4m E of Selby. Loc,
Cliffe CP. P Slby. Ch m.

SOUTHEASE Sussex (E)
183 TQ 4205 3m NNW of Newhaven.
CP, 42. Chailey RD. Ch e. Lewes CC. Ch has
round Nmn twr.

SOUTH ELKINGTON Lincs (L)
105 TF 2988 2m WNW of Louth. CP, 282.
Louth RD. P(Elkngtn), Lth. Ch e, m.
Sch pe. Lth CC.

SOUTH ELMSALL Yorks (W)
103 SE 4711 7m S of Pontefract. CP, 7,385.
Hemsworth RD. P Pntfrct. Ch e, m2, s, v.
Sch i2, s2. Hmswth CC.

SOUTH END Berks
158 SU 5970 4m SW of Pangbourne. Loc,
Bradfield CP. P Reading.

SOUTH END Lancs
88 SD 2063 4m S of Barrow, on Walney
Island. Loc, Brrw-in-Furness CB.

SOUTHEND-ON-SEA Essex
162 TQ 8885 35m E of London.
CB, 162,326. P. BCs: Sthnd E, Sthnd W. See
also Leigh on Sea, Shoeburyness, Thorpe
Bay, Westcliff on Sea. Resort, esp for
day-trippers from Lndn. Mile-long pier with
electric rly. Much new office bldng. Airpt.

SOUTHERY Norfolk
135 TL 6294 5m S of Downham Mkt.
CP, 1,209. Dnhm RD. P Dnhm Mkt.
Ch e, b, m. Sch p. SW Nflk CC. See also
Brandon Creek.

SOUTH FAMBRIDGE Essex
162 TQ 8595 7m N of Southend. Loc,
Ashingdon CP. Ch e.

SOUTH FAWLEY Berks
158 SU 3980 5m S of Wantage. Loc,
Fwly CP.

SOUTH FERRIBY Lincs (L)
98 SE 9821 3m WSW of
Barton-upon-Humber. CP, 663. Glanford
Brigg RD. P Btn-on-Hmbr. Ch e, m. Sch p.
Brgg and Scunthorpe CC (Brgg). Cement
wks; cable rly passes over vllge. Boats,
fishing. Views to Yorks Wolds across
Humber.

SOUTHFLEET Kent
161, 171 TQ 6171 3m SW of Gravesend.
CP, 1,813. Dartford RD. P Grvsnd. Ch e, c.
Sch pe. Dtfd CC. See also Betsham. Largely
indstrl.

SOUTHGATE London
160 TQ 3093 2m SW of Enfield. Loc,

Southgate

Enfld LB. Sthgte BC. Broomfield Hse*, 17c hse incorporating a museum. Grovelands, late 18c Nash hse now a hsptl.

SOUTHGATE Norfolk
124 TF 6833 4m S of Hunstanton. Loc, Snettisham CP.

SOUTH GORLEY Hants
179 SU 1610 3m SSE of Fordingbridge. Loc, Harbridge and Ibsley CP. P Fdngbrdge.

SOUTH GREEN Essex
161 TQ 6893 1m SE of Billericay. Loc, Basildon UD.

SOUTH GREEN Kent
172 TQ 8560 4m SW of Sittingbourne. Loc, Stockbury CP. P Sttngbne.

SOUTH HANNINGFIELD Essex
161, 162 TQ 7497 6m SSE of Chelmsford. CP, 1,757. Chlmsfd RD. P Chlmsfd. Ch e. Chlmsfd CC. See also Downham, Ramsden Hth. On shore of H. Water, reservoir.

SOUTH HARTING Sussex (W)
181 SU 7819 3m SE of Petersfield. Loc, Htng CP. Midhurst RD. P(Htng), Ptrsfld, Hants. Ch e, c. Sch pe. Chichester CC (Horsham). Under S Downs close to Hants border. 1¼m SSW, Uppark (NT)*, 17c—18c hse.

SOUTH HAYLING Hants
181 SZ 7299 4m S of Havant. Loc, Hvnt and Waterloo UD. P(Hlng Island). Resort. Amusements, holiday camps. Yachting.

SOUTH HAZELRIGG Nthmb
64, 71 NU 0532 4m WSW of Belford. Loc, Chatton CP.

SOUTH HEATH Bucks
159 SP 9001 3m W of Chesham. Loc, Gt Missenden CP. P Gt Mssndn.

SOUTH HEIGHTON Sussex (E)
183 TQ 4502 1m N of Newhaven. CP, 341. Chailey RD. P Nhvn. Lewes CC.

SOUTH HETTON Co Durham
85 NZ 3745 4m NW of Peterlee. Loc, Haswell CP. P DRHM. Ch e, m2, s, v. Sch p.

SOUTH HIENDLEY Yorks (W)
102, 103 SE 3912 5m NE of Barnsley. CP, 1,425. Hemsworth RD. P Bnsly. Ch m. Sch p. Hmswth CC.

SOUTH HILL Cornwall
186 SX 3372 3m NW of Callington. CP, 374. Liskeard RD. Ch e, m. Bodmin CC. See also Golberdon.

SOUTH HINKSEY Berks
158 SP 5004 1m S of Oxford. CP, 360. Abingdon RD. Ch e. Abngdn CC.

SOUTH HOLE Devon
174 SS 2220 9m N of Bude. Loc, Hartland CP.

SOUTH HOLME Yorks (N)
92 SE 7077 6m NW of Pickering. CP, 44. Malton RD. Thirsk and Mltn CC.

SOUTH HOLMWOOD Surrey
170 TQ 1745 3m S of Dorking. Loc, Holmwood CP. Dkng and Horley RD. P(Hlmwd), Dkng. Ch e. Sch pe. Dkng CC.

SOUTH HORNCHURCH London
161 TQ 5283 2m E of Dagenham. Loc, Havering LB. P Hnchch, Essex. Hnchch BC.

SOUTH HUISH Devon
187, 188 SX 6941 3m SW of Kingsbridge. CP, 472. Kngsbrdge RD. Ch e. Totnes CC. See also Galmpton.

SOUTH HYKEHAM Lincs (K)
113 SK 9364 5m SSW of Lincoln. CP(Aubourn Haddington and S Hkhm), 755. N Kesteven RD. Ch e. Sch p. Grantham CC.

SOUTHILL Beds
147 TL 1542 3m WSW of Biggleswade. CP, 991. Bgglswde RD. P Bgglswde. Ch e, b. Sch p. Mid-Beds CC. See also Broom, Stanford. Sthll Pk, to W, once home of Admiral Byng, shot in 1757 for neglect of duty.

SOUTH KELSEY Lincs (L)
104 TF 0498 5m WSW of Caistor. CP, 435. Cstr RD. P LINCOLN. Ch e, m2. Sch p. Gainsborough CC. See also Moortown.

SOUTH KILLINGHOLME Lincs (L)
105 TA 1516 2m NW of Immingham. CP, 966. Glanford Brigg RD. P Grimsby. Ch m2. Sch p. Brgg and Scunthorpe CC (Brgg). At foot of Lindsey Oil Refinery.

SOUTH KILVINGTON Yorks (N)
91 SE 4284 1m N of Thirsk. CP, 170.
Thsk RD. Ch e. Sch pe. Thsk and
Malton CC.

SOUTH KILWORTH Leics
132, 133 SP 6081 4m ESE of Lutterworth.
CP, 369. Lttrwth RD. P Rugby, Warwickshire. Ch e, c. Sch pe. Blaby CC (Harborough).

SOUTH KIRKBY Yorks (W)
103 SE 4511 7m S of Pontefract.
CP, 12,222. Hemsworth RD. P Pntfrct.
Ch e, m, r, v3. Sch i2, j, p, pr, s4.
Hmswth CC.

SOUTH KNIGHTON Devon
176, 188 SX 8172 3m WNW of Newton
Abbot. Loc, Ilsington CP.

SOUTH KYME Lincs (K)
113 TF 1749 7m ENE of Sleaford. CP, 420.
E Kesteven RD. P LINCOLN. Ch e, m.
Sch p. Grantham CC. Rems of 14c twr
hse, 77ft.

SOUTH LANCING Sussex (W)
182 TQ 1804 3m ENE of Worthing. See
Lancing.

SOUTHLEIGH Devon
177 SY 2093 3m NW of Seaton. CP, 167.
Honiton RD. P Colyton. Ch e. Hntn CC.

SOUTH LEIGH Oxon
158 SP 3908 2m ESE of Witney. CP.
Wtny RD. P Wtny. Ch e, m. Mid-Oxon CC
(Banbury). See also High Cogges. Ch:
remarkable 14c wall-paintings. From the
18c plpt John Wesley first preached, 1725.

SOUTH LEVERTON Notts
104 SK 7881 6m SSW of Gainsborough.
CP, 341. E Retford RD. P Rtfd. Ch e, m.
Sch pe. Bassetlaw CC.

SOUTH LITTLETON Worcs
144 SP 0746 3m ENE of Evesham. CP, 556.
Eveshm RD. P Eveshm. Ch e, f. Sch pe.
S Worcs CC.

SOUTH LOPHAM Norfolk
136 TM 0481 5m W of Diss. CP, 360.
Wayland RD. P Dss. Ch e, v. Sch pe.
S Nflk CC.

SOUTH LUFFENHAM Rutland
122 SK 9401 5m ENE of Uppingham.
CP, 295. Uppnghm RD. P Oakham. Ch e.
Rtlnd and Stamford CC.

SOUTH MALLING Sussex (E)
183 TQ 4111 just NE of Lewes. Loc,
Lws MB; CP(S Mllng Without), 159,
Chailey RD. Lws CC.

SOUTH MARSTON Wilts
157 SU 1988 4m NE of Swindon. CP, 540.
Highworth RD. P Swndn. Ch e, m. Sch pe.
Devizes CC.

SOUTH MIDDLETON Nthmb
71 NT 9923 3m S of Wooler. Loc,
Ilderton CP.

SOUTH MILFORD Yorks (W)
97 SE 4931 6m NE of Pontefract.
CP, 1,042. Tadcaster RD. P LEEDS.
Ch e, m. Sch p. Barkston Ash CC. See also
Lumby. To W, Steeton Hall Gatehouse
(A.M.), 14c, with interesting carved corbels.

SOUTH MILTON Devon
187, 188 SX 7042 3m WSW of Kingsbridge.
CP, 324. Kngsbrdge RD. P Kngsbrdge.
Ch e, m. Sch pe. Totnes CC.

SOUTH MIMMS Herts
160 TL 2201 2m W of Potters Bar. Loc,
Pttrs Bar UD. P Pttrs Bar. Ch: Frowyk
tombs.

SOUTHMINSTER Essex
162 TQ 9599 2m N of Burnham-on-Crouch.
CP, 1,897. Maldon RD. P. Ch e, b, c.
Sch i, je. Mldn CC.

SOUTH MOLTON Devon
163 SS 7125 11m ESE of Barnstaple.
CP, 2,993. S Mltn RD. P. Ch e, b, c, r, s.
Sch je, p, s. N Dvn CC. See also Stag's Head.
Small mkt tn. Ch: Perp, with tall twr.
18c guildhall.

SOUTH MOOR Co Durham
78 NZ 1951 5m E of Consett. Loc,
Stanley UD. P Stnly.

SOUTH MORETON Berks
158 SU 5688 3m W of Wallingford. CP, 397.
Wllngfd RD. P Didcot. Ch e, b. Sch p.
Abingdon CC.

South Mundham

SOUTH MUNDHAM Sussex (W)
181 SU 8700 3m SSE of Chichester. Loc,
N Mundham CP. View of Chchstr Cathedral
backed by S Downs.

SOUTH MUSKHAM Notts
112 SK 7957 2m NNW of Newark. CP, 292.
Southam RD. P Nwk. Ch e. Nwk CC.

SOUTH NEWINGTON Oxon
145 SP 4033 5m SW of Banbury. CP, 219.
Bnbry RD. P Bnbry. Ch e. Bnbry CC. Ch:
S porch, glass, wall-paintings.

SOUTH NEWTON Wilts
167 SU 0834 5m NW of Salisbury. CP, 763.
Slsbry and Wilton RD. P Slsbry. Ch e, m.
Slsbry CC. See also Stoford.

SOUTH NORMANTON Derbys
112 SK 4456 2m ENE of Alfreton.
CP, 6,946. Blackwell RD. P DERBY.
Ch e, m3, v. Sch i2, j, s. Bolsover CC.

SOUTH NUTFIELD Surrey
170 TQ 3049 3m ESE of Reigate. Loc,
Ntfld CP. P Redhill. Ch e. Sch ie.

SOUTH OCKENDON Essex
161 TQ 5881 3m NE of Purfleet. Loc,
Thurrock UD. P. Thrrck BC (CC). Gravel
wks and quarries abound. To E, S Ockndn
Hall, 19c on mdvl moated site, and
smock-mill. To W, Belhus Pk, grnds (by
Capability Brown) of now vanished B. Hse.

SOUTHOE Hunts
134 TL 1864 3m N of St Neots. CP(Sthoe
and Midloe), 225. St Nts RD.
P HUNTINGDON. Ch e, v. Hunts CC.

SOUTHOLT Suffolk (E)
137 TM 1968 5m SE of Eye. CP, 65.
Hartismere RD. Ch e. Eye CC. Cottages
scattered round a grn.

SOUTH ORMSBY Lincs (L)
105 TF 3775 5m W of Alford. CP(S Ormsby
cum Ketsby), 141. Spilsby RD. P Louth.
Ch e. Sch pe. Horncastle CC.

SOUTHORPE Hunts
123 TF 0803 4m SE of Stamford. CP, 138.
Barnock RD. Peterborough BC (CC).

SOUTH OTTERINGTON Yorks (N)
91 SE 3787 4m S of Northallerton. CP, 312.

Thirsk RD. P Nthlltn. Ch e. Thsk and
Malton CC.

SOUTH OWERSBY Lincs (L)
104 TF 0693 4m NW of Mkt Rasen. Loc,
Owrsby CP. Caistor RD. Sch pe.
Gainsborough CC.

SOUTHOWRAM Yorks (W)
96, 102 SE 1123 2m SE of Halifax. Loc,
Brighouse MB. P Hlfx.

SOUTH OXHEY Herts
160 TQ 1192 3m S of Watford. Loc, Wtfd
Rural CP. Wtfd RD. P(Oxhey), Wtfd.
Ch e3, b, m, r, s, v. Sch p6, pr, s.
SW Herts CC.

SOUTH PERROTT Dorset
177 ST 4706 3m SE of Crewkerne. CP, 155.
Beaminster RD. P Bmnstr. Ch e.
W Dst CC.

SOUTH PETHERTON Som
177 ST 4316 5m ENE of Ilminster.
CP, 2,169. Yeovil RD. P. Ch e, m, r, v.
Sch j, pe. Yvl CC. See also Over Stratton.

SOUTH PETHERWIN Cornwall
186 SX 3081 2m SW of Launceston.
CP, 578. Lnstn RD. P Lncstn. Ch e, m3.
Sch pe. N Cnwll CC. Ch has only Nmn stoup
in Cornwall.

SOUTH PICKENHAM Norfolk
125 TF 8504 4m SE of Swaffham. CP, 169.
Swffhm RD. P Swffhm. Ch e. SW Nflk CC.

SOUTH POOL Devon
187, 188 SX 7740 4m SE of Kingsbridge.
CP, 237. Kngsbrdge RD. P Kngsbrdge. Ch e.
Totnes CC. At head of tidal creek. Ch: scrn.

SOUTH POORTON Dorset
177 SY 5297 5m NE of Bridport. Loc,
Powerstock CP.

SOUTHPORT Lancs
100 SD 3317 17m N of Liverpool.
CB, 84,349. P. Sthpt BC. See also Ainsdale,
Birkdale. Largely 19c resort.

SOUTH RADWORTHY Devon
163 SS 7432 5m NNE of S Molton. Loc,
N Mltn CP.

SOUTH RAUCEBY Lincs (K)
113 TF 0245 3m W of Sleaford. CP, 261.

E Kesteven RD. P Slfd. Ch e. Grantham CC. 19c estate vllge.

SOUTH RAYNHAM Norfolk
125 TF 8723 5m SSW of Fakenham. Loc, Rnhm CP. Walsingham RD. P Fknhm. Ch e. NW Nflk CC (N Nflk). To N, Rnhm Hall, 17c hse, seat of Townshend family.

SOUTHREPPS Norfolk
126 TG 2536 4m SE of Cromer. CP, 650. Erpingham RD. P Norwich. Ch e, m2. Sch p. N Nflk CC. See also Lr St.

SOUTH RESTON Lincs (L)
105 TF 4083 5m ESE of Louth. CP, 169. Lth RD. P Lth. Ch e, m. Sch pe. Lth CC.

SOUTHREY Lincs (L)
113 TF 1366 4m NW of Woodhall Spa. Loc, Bardney CP. P LINCOLN. Ch e, m.

SOUTHROP Glos
157 SP 2003 3m N of Lechlade. CP, 214. Northleach RD. P Lchlde. Ch e. Sch pe. Cirencester and Tewkesbury CC.

SOUTHROPE Hants
168, 169 SU 6744 5m SSE of Basingstoke. Loc, Herriard CP.

SOUTH RUNCTON Norfolk
124 TF 6308 4m NNE of Downham Mkt. Loc, Rnctn Holme CP. Ch e.

SOUTH SCARLE Notts
113 SK 8464 7m NNE of Newark. CP, 111. Nwk RD. P Nwk. Ch e, m. Nwk CC. Ch: Nmn N arcade.

SOUTHSEA Hants
180, 181 SZ 6498 S distr of Portsmouth. Loc, Ptsmth CB. P. Ptsmth S BC. Resort with large cmmn and pier. Naval war memorial. Sthsea Cstle is military museum. 19c lighthouse*.

SOUTH SHIELDS Co Durham
78 NZ 3666 6m NNW of Sunderland. CB, 100,513. P. S Shields BC. Important Tyneside port with large docks on S bank of river. Long sands on seaward side. Considerable rems of Roman fort.

SOUTH SKIRLAUGH Yorks (E)
99 TA 1439 7m NNE of Hull. Loc, Skrlgh CP. Holderness RD. P(Skrlgh), Hll. Ch e, m. Sch pe. Bridlington CC.

SOUTH SOMERCOTES Lincs (L)
105 TF 4193 7m NE of Louth. CP, 257. Lth RD. P Lth. Ch e, m. Lth CC.

SOUTH STAINLEY Yorks (W)
91 SE 3063 5m N of Harrogate. CP(S Stnly w Cayton), 172. Nidderdale RD. Ch e. Hrrgte CC.

SOUTH STOKE Oxon
158 SU 5983 4m S of Wallingford. CP, 406. Henley RD. P Reading, Berks. Ch e, v. Sch p. Hnly CC.

SOUTH STOKE Som
166 ST 7461 2m S of Bath. CP(Southstoke), 464. Bathavon RD. Ch e, v. Sch pe. N Som CC. See also Midford.

SOUTH STOKE Sussex (W)
181, 182 TQ 0210 2m NNE of Arundel. CP, 65. Worthing RD. Ch e. Arndl CC (Arndl and Shoreham). See also Offham. In bend of R Arun NE of Arndl Pk.

SOUTHSTREET Kent
172, 173 TR 0557 3m SE of Faversham. Loc, Boughton under Blean CP. Swale RD. P Fvrshm. Fvrshm CC.

SOUTH STREET Sussex (E)
183 TQ 3918 5m N of Lewes. Loc, Chailey CP.

SOUTH TAWTON Devon
175 SS 6594 4m E of Okehampton. CP, 1,260. Okhmptn RD. Ch e. Sch p. W Dvn CC (Torrington). See also S Zeal, Taw Grn. Thatched ch hse, 16c.

SOUTH THORESBY Lincs (L)
105 TF 4076 3m WNW of Alford. CP, 78. Louth RD. P Alfd. Ch e, m. Lth CC.

SOUTH TIDWORTH Hants
167 SU 2347 8m WNW of Andover. CP(S Tedworth), 3,370. Andvr RD. P(Tdwth). Ch e, r. Sch p, pe. Winchester CC (Basingstoke). Garrison tn.

SOUTH TOWN Hants
168, 169 SU 6536 4m WSW of Alton. Loc, Medstead CP. Ch c.

SOUTHWAITE Cumb
83 NY 4445 8m SSE of Carlisle. Loc, Hesket CP. Penrith RD. P Clsle. Pnrth and the Border CC.

SOUTH WALSHAM Norfolk
126 TG 3613 5m SE of Wroxham. CP, 504.
B l o f i e l d a n d F l e g g R D .
P NORWICH, NOR 57Z. Ch e, m. Sch pe.
Yarmouth CC.

SOUTHWARK London
160, 170 TQ 3278 1m S of Lndn Br.
LB, 259,982. BCs: Bermondsey, Dulwich,
Peckham (Bmndsy, Dlwch, Pckhm, Sthwk).
See also Bmndsy, Camberwell, Dlwch,
Nunhead, Pckhm, Rotherhithe, Walworth.
Brs over Thames: Blackfriars, Sthwk, Lndn,
Twr; also two rly brs. Sthwck Cathedral at S
end of Lndn Br.

SOUTH WARNBOROUGH Hants
169 SU 7247 5m N of Alton. CP, 410.
Hartley Wintney RD. P Basingstoke. Ch e.
Bsngstke CC (Aldershot). Ch: monmts.

SOUTHWATER Sussex (W)
182 TQ 1526 3m SSW of Horsham. Loc,
Hshm Rural CP. Hshm RD. P Hshm. Ch e, v.
Sch p. Hshm and Crawley CC (Hshm).

SOUTH WEALD Essex
161 TQ 5793 2m W of Brentwood. Loc,
Brntwd UD. P Brntwd.

SOUTHWELL Dorset
178 SY 6870 on Isle of Portland, S of
Weymouth. Loc, Portland UD. P Ptlnd.

SOUTHWELL Notts
112 SK 6953 6m W of Newark. CP, 4,301.
Sthwll RD. Ch e2, b, m, r. Sch pe, pem, s.
Nwk CC. See also Normanton. Small
unpretentious country tn. Nmn to Perp
cathedral.

SOUTH WESTON Oxon
159 SU 7098 5m S of Thame. Loc,
Lewknor CP. Ch e.

SOUTH WHEATLEY Cornwall
174 SX 2492 7m NW of Launceston. Loc,
N Petherwin CP.

SOUTH WHEATLEY Notts
104 SK 7685 4m SW of Gainsborough.
CP, 58. E Retford RD. Bassetlaw CC.

SOUTHWICK Hants
180 SU 6208 3m ENE of Fareham.
CP(Sthwck and Widley), 1,088.
Droxford RD. P Frhm. Ch e. Sch i.

Petersfield CC. Naval establishments.
Palmerston fort (see Portsmouth).

SOUTHWICK Northants
134 TL 0292 3m NNW of Oundle. CP, 226.
Oundle and Thrapston RD. Ch e.
Wellingborough CC (Peterborough).

SOUTHWICK Sussex (W)
182 TQ 2405 2m E of Shoreham-by-Sea.
UD, 11,850. P Brighton. Shrhm CC
(Arundel and Shrhm).

SOUTHWICK Wilts
166 ST 8355 2m SW of Trowbridge.
CP, 737. Warminster and Westbury RD.
P Trwbrdge. Ch e, b2. Sch pe. Wstbry CC.

SOUTH WIDCOMBE Som
165, 166 ST 5856 7m NNE of Wells. Loc,
Hinton Blewett CP.

SOUTH WIGSTON Leics
132, 133 SP 5998 4m S of Leicester. Loc,
Wgstn UD. P LCSTR.

SOUTH WILLINGHAM Lincs (L)
105 TF 1983 7m SE of Mkt Rasen. CP, 153.
Louth RD. P LINCOLN. Ch e, m. Lth CC.

SOUTH WINGFIELD Derbys
111 SK 3755 2m W of Alfreton. CP, 1,644.
Belper RD. P DERBY. Ch e, b, m3, v. Sch p.
Blpr CC. To S, extensive rems of Wngfld
Mnr Hse (A.M.), 15c.

SOUTH WITHAM Lincs (K)
122 SK 9219 8m NE of Oakham. CP, 660.
W Kesteven RD. P Grantham. Ch e. Sch p.
Rutland and Stamford CC.

SOUTHWOLD Suffolk (E)
137 TM 5076 8m E of Halesworth.
MB, 1,992. P. Lowestoft CC. Small resort.
Splendid Perp ch. Lighthouse stands among
hses near cliff top. Marshes to landward.
Sthwld Museum contains relics of Sthwld
Rly etc.

SOUTH WONSTON Hants
168 SU 4635 4m N of Winchester. Loc,
Wnstn CP. P Wnchstr.

SOUTHWOOD Norfolk
126 TG 3905 8m W of Yarmouth. Loc,
Cantley CP.

SOUTHWOOD Som
165, 166 ST 5533 5m SE of Glastonbury.
Loc, Baltonsborough CP.

SOUTH WOODHAM FERRERS Essex
162 TQ 8097 7m SSW of Maldon. Loc,
Wdhm Frrs CP. P Chelmsford. Ch b. Sch p.

SOUTH WOOTTON Norfolk
124 TF 6422 2m NE of King's Lynn.
CP, 1,090. Freebridge Lynn RD. P K's Lnn.
Ch e. Sch i. NW Nflk CC (K's Lnn). To SE
in Reffley Wd, small 18c temple and obelisk
blt by a Friendly Society called Rffly
Brethren. Still used for social functions.

SOUTH WRAXALL Wilts
166 ST 8364 4m N of Trowbridge. CP, 418.
Bradford and Melksham RD.
P Brdfd-on-Avon. Ch e. Sch pe.
Westbury CC. See also Brdfd Leigh. Ch:
monmts to Long family, owners from 1430
of mnr hse blt round three sides of
courtyard, retaining mdvl great hall and
gatehouse.

SOUTH ZEAL Devon
175 SX 6593 4m ESE of Okehampton. Loc,
S Tawton CP. P Okhmpton. Ch e, m.
Oxenham Arms, early 16c, has menhir or
standing stone blt into an inside wall.

SOWERBY Yorks (N)
91 SE 4381 just S of Thirsk. CP, 2,471.
Thsk RD. P Thsk. Ch e, m. Sch pe. Thsk and
Malton CC.

SOWERBY Yorks (W)
96, 102 SE 0423 4m WSW of Halifax. Loc,
Sby Br UD. P(Sby Tn), Sby Br.

SOWERBY BRIDGE Yorks (W)
96, 102 SE 0623 2m SW of Halifax.
UD, 16,260. P. Sby CC. See also
Luddenden, Lddndnfoot, Lumb, Midgley,
Mill Bank, Norland Tn, Sowerby, Triangle.

SOWERBY ROW Cumb
83 NY 3940 10m S of Carlisle. Loc, Castle
Sby CP. Penrith RD. P Clsle. Pnrth and the
Border CC.

SOWOOD GREEN Yorks (W)
96, 102 SE 0718 4m WNW of Huddersfield.
Loc, Elland UD.

SOWTON Devon
176 SX 9792 4m E of Exeter. CP, 425.
St Thomas RD. Ch e. Honiton CC.

SPA COMMON Norfolk
126 TG 2930 just E of N Walsham. Loc,
N Wlshm UD. P: N Wlshm.

SPALDING Lincs (H)
123 TF 2422 15m NNE of Peterborough.
UD, 16,950. P. Holland w Boston CC. See
also Lit London, Pode Hole. Old mkt tn
now centre of bulb-growing industry; annual
festival of flowers in spring.

SPALDINGTON Yorks (E)
97, 98 SE 7633 6m NNE of Goole. CP, 163.
Howden RD. P Gle. Ch m. Sch p. Hdn CC.

SPALDWICK Hunts
134 TL 1272 7m W of Huntingdon.
CP, 275. Hntngdn RD. P HNTNGDN.
Ch e, bc, v. Sch p. Hunts CC.

SPALFORD Notts
113 SK 8369 9m W of Lincoln. CP, 80.
Newark RD. Ch m. Nwk CC.

SPANBY Lincs (K)
113, 123 TF 0938 5m SSE of Sleaford. Loc,
Threekingham CP. Ch e.

SPARHAM Norfolk
125 TG 0719 6m NE of E Dereham.
CP, 216. Mitford and Launditch RD.
P NORWICH, NOR 64X. Ch e, m.
SW Nflk CC. Ch has interesting paintings of
Dance of Death.

SPARK BRIDGE Lancs
88, 89 SD 3084 4m NNE of Ulverston. Loc,
N Lonsdale RD. P Ulvstn. Ch m. Morecambe
and Lnsdle CC.

SPARKFORD Som
166 ST 6026 7m W of Wincanton. CP, 385.
Wncntn RD. P Yeovil. Ch e. Wells CC. See
also Weston Bampfylde.

SPARKWELL Devon
187 SX 5857 4m WNW of Ivybridge. CP.
Plympton St Mary RD. P Plymouth. Ch e.
Sch pe. W Dvn CC (Tavistock).

SPARROWPIT Derbys
111 SK 0980 5m NNE of Buxton. Loc,
Chapel en le Frith RD. Ch m. High Peak CC.

SPARSHOLT Berks
158 SU 3487 3m W of Wantage. CP, 265.
Wntge RD. P Wntge. Ch e. Abingdon CC.
Thatched cottages.

SPARSHOLT Hants
168 SU 4331 3m WNW of Winchester.
CP, 715. Wnchstr RD. P Wnchstr. Ch e, m.
Sch pe. Wnchstr CC.

SPARTYLEA Nthmb
84 NY 8548 10m SSW of Hexham. Loc,
Allendale CP. Hxhm RD. P Hxhm. Ch m.
Hxhm CC.

SPAUNTON Yorks (N)
86, 92 SE 7289 6m NW of Pickering.
CP, 63. Kirkbymoorside RD. Thirsk and
Malton CC.

SPAXTON Som
165 ST 2236 5m W of Bridgwater. CP, 891.
Brdgwtr RD. P Brdgwtr. Ch e, m. Sch pe.
Brdgwtr CC. See. also Courtway,
Four Forks.

SPEEN Berks
158 SU 4568 1m NW of Newbury.
CP, 1,247. Nbry RD. P Nbry. Ch e.
Nbry CC. See also Stockcross.

SPEEN Bucks
159 SU 8499 5m NNW of High Wycombe.
Loc, Lacey Grn CP. P Aylesbury. Ch e, b.
Sch pe.

SPEETON Yorks (E)
93 TA 1574 4m SSE of Filey. Loc,
Reighton CP. P Filey. Ch e, m. Very ancient
small ch.

SPEKE Lancs
100, 109 SJ 4283 SE distr of Liverpool.
Loc, Lvpl CB. P LVPL 24.
Lvpl, Garston BC. Large indstrl estate. Car
mnfg. Airpt for Livpl. Spke Hall (NT)*, 16c
half-timbered hse.

SPELDHURST Kent
171 TQ 5541 2m NW of Tunbridge Wells.
CP, 2,887. Tonbridge RD. P Tnbrdge Wlls.
Ch e, v. Sch pe. Royal Tnbrdge Wlls CC
(Tnbrdge). See also Ashurst, Langton Grn.

SPELLBROOK Herts
148 TL 4817 2m S of Bishop's Stortford.
Loc, Sawbridgeworth UD.

SPELSBURY Oxon
145 SP 3521 4m SE of Chipping Norton.
CP, 293. Chppng Ntn RD. P OXFORD.
Ch e. Banbury CC. See also Taston.
Ch: tombs.

SPENCERS WOOD Berks
169 SU 7166 4m S of Reading. Loc,
Shinfield CP. P Rdng. Ch e, c.

SPENNITHORNE Yorks (N)
91 SE 1389 2m ESE of Leyburn. CP, 183.
Lbn RD. P Lbn. Ch e. Sch pe.
Richmond CC.

SPENNYMOOR Co Durham
85 NZ 2533 4m NE of Bishop Auckland.
UD, 19,063. P. NW Durham CC (Drhm). See
also Byers Grn, Kirk Merrington,
Middlestone Moor, Tudhoe. Mining,
electrical equipment, textiles. Indstrl estate.

SPETCHLEY Worcs
143, 144 SO 8954 3m ESE of Worcester.
CP, 116. Pershore RD. P WCSTR. Ch e.
Sch pr. S Worcs CC. Sptchly Pk, classical
hse; deer pk with lake and gdns*.

SPETISBURY Dorset
178, 179 ST 9102 3m SE of Blandford.
CP, 416. Blndfd RD. P Blndfd Forum.
Ch e, m. Sch pe. N Dst CC. Sometimes
spelt Spettisbury. Crawford Br, mdvl, over
R Stour. Sptsbry Rings, Iron Age fort.

SPEXHALL Suffolk (E)
137 TM 3780 2m NNW of Halesworth.
CP, 202. Wainford RD. Ch e. Lowestoft CC.

SPILSBY Lincs (L)
114 TF 4066 7m SW of Alford. CP, 1,665.
Splsby RD. P. Ch e, m, r, v. Sch p, s2.
Horncastle CC. Ch: monmts to Willoughbys.
Bthplce of Sir John Franklin, explorer,
1768; tn has monmt to him.

SPINDLESTONE Nthmb
71 NU 1533 3m E of Belford. Loc,
Easington CP.

SPINKHILL Derbys
103 SK 4578 8m SE of Sheffield. Loc,
Eckington CP. P SHFFLD. Ch r.

SPIRTHILL Wilts
157 ST 9975 3m N of Calne. Loc,
Bremhill CP. Ch m.

SPITHURST Sussex (E)
183 TQ 4217 5m N of Lewes. Loc,
Barcombe CP. Ch e.

SPITTAL Nthmb
64 NU 0051 1m SSE of

Berwick-upon-Tweed. Loc,
Brwck-upn-Twd MB. P BRWCK-UPN-TWD.

SPIXWORTH Norfolk
126 TG 2415 4m N of Norwich. CP.
St Faith's and Aylsham RD.
P NRWCH, NOR 01Y. Ch e, m. Sch p.
N Nflk CC (Central Nflk).

SPLATT Devon
175 SS 6005 6m N of Okehampton. Loc,
Broadwoodkelly CP. Ch m.

SPOFFORTH Yorks (W)
96 SE 3651 3m NW of Wetherby. CP(Spffth
w Stockeld), 786. Wthrby RD. P Harrogate.
Ch e, m. Sch pe. Barkston Ash CC. Spffth
Cstle (A.M.), rems of 14c fortified mnr hse.

SPOONER ROW Norfolk
136 TM 0997 3m SSW of Wymondham.
Loc, Wndhm UD. P Wndhm.

SPORLE Norfolk
125 TF 8411 2m NE of Swaffham. CP(Sple
w Palgrave), 680. Swffhm RD. P King's
Lynn. Ch e, m. Sch p. SW Nflk CC.

SPRATTON Northants
133 SP 7170 6m NNW of Northampton.
CP, 795. Brixworth RD. P NTHMPTN.
Ch e, b. Sch pe. Daventry CC (Kettering).

SPREAKLEY Surrey
169 SU 8441 3m S of Farnham. Loc,
Frensham CP.

SPREYTON Devon
175 SX 6996 7m E of Okehampton.
CP, 267. Okhmptn RD. P Crediton. Ch e, m.
Sch p. W Dvn CC (Torrington).

SPRIDLINGTON Lincs (L)
104 TF 0084 7m WSW of Mkt Rasen.
CP, 166. Welton RD. P LINCOLN. Ch e, m.
Gainsborough CC.

SPRINGFIELD Essex
161, 162 TL 7207 1m E of Chelmsford.
Loc, Chlmsfd MB; CP, 534, Chlmsfd RD.
P Chlmsfd. Ch e2. Chlmsfd CC,
Braintree CC (Chlmsfd CC.) County goal.

SPRINGTHORPE Lincs (L)
104 SK 8789 4m E of Gainsborough.
CP, 123. Gnsbrgh RD. Ch e, m. Gnsbrgh CC.

SPRINGWELL Co Durham
78 NZ 2858 3m SE of Gateshead. Loc,
Washington UD. P Gtshd 9.

SPROATLEY Yorks (E)
99 TA 1934 7m ENE of Hull. CP, 307.
Holderness RD. P Hll. Ch e, m. Sch pe.
Bridlington CC.

SPROSTON GREEN Ches
110 SJ 7366 2m E of Middlewich. Loc,
Sprstn CP. Northwich RD. P Crewe. Ch m.
Nthwch CC.

SPROTBROUGH Yorks (W)
103 SE 5302 3m WSW of Doncaster.
CP, 7,469. Dncstr RD. P Dncstr. Ch e, m2.
Sch i3, j, s. Don Valley CC.

SPROUGHTON Suffolk (E)
150 TM 1244 3m W of Ipswich. CP, 787.
Samford RD. P Ipswch. Ch e. Sch pe.
Sudbury and Woodbridge CC. Sugar beet
factory.

SPROWSTON Norfolk
126 TG 2411 2m NNE of Norwich.
CP, 9,609. St Faith's and Aylsham RD.
Ch e. Sch i2, j2, s. N Nflk CC (Central Nflk).

SPROXTON Leics
122 SK 8524 7m ENE of Melton Mowbray.
CP, 505. Mltn and Belvoir RD. P Mltn
Mbray. Ch e, m. Mltn CC. See also Saltby,
Stonesby. 10c churchyard cross.

SPROXTON Yorks (N)
92 SE 6181 1m S of Helmsley. CP, 115.
Hmlsly RD. Ch e, m. Thirsk and Malton CC.

SPURSTOW Ches
109 SJ 5557 7m WNW of Nantwich.
CP, 352. Nntwch RD. P Tarporley. Ch m2.
Sch p. Nntwch CC.

STACKHOUSE Yorks (W)
90 SD 8165 1m N of Settle. Loc,
Giggleswick CP.

STACKSTEADS Lancs
95 SD 8521 1m WSW of Bacup. Loc,
Bcp MB. P Bcp.

STADDISCOMBE Devon
187 SX 5151 3m SE of Plymouth. Loc,
Plmth CB. P Plmth. Plmth, Sutton BC
(Tavistock).

STADDLETHORPE Yorks (E)
98 SE 8328 7m ENE of Goole. Loc,
Gilberdyke CP.

STADHAMPTON Oxon
158 SU 6098 6m N of Wallingford. CP, 668.
Bullingdon RD. P OXFORD. Ch e. Sch p.
Henley CC. See also Chislehampton.

STAFFORD Staffs
119 SJ 9223 14m S of Stoke-on-Trent.
MB, 54,890. P(STFFD). Stffd and
Stone CC. See also Baswich, Weeping Cross.
Mainly indstrl tn - footwear, electrical plant,
etc. Some old hses; William Salt Library in
18c hse*. 1½m WSW, Stffd Cstle, 19c
unfinished structure beside M6 motorway,
on site of earlier cstle.

STAGSDEN Beds
147 SP 9849 4m W of Bedford. CP, 400.
Bdfd RD. P BDFD. Ch e, bc. Sch ie.
Mid-Beds CC. Stgsdn Bird Gdns contain
collection of game birds.

STAG'S HEAD Devon
163 SS 6727 3m WNW of S Molton. Loc,
S Mltn CP. Ch m, v.

STAIN Lincs (L)
105 TF 4684 2m W of Mablethorpe.
CP(Withern w Stn), 269. Louth RD.
Lth CC.

STAINBURN Cumb
82 NY 0229 1m E of Workington. Loc,
Wkngtn MB. P Wkngtn.

STAINBURN Yorks (W)
96 SE 2448 4m ENE of Otley. CP, 122.
Wharfedale RD. Ch e, m. Ripon CC.

STAINBY Lincs (K)
122 SK 9022 8m S of Grantham. CP(Gunby
and Stnby) 162. W Kesteven RD. Ch e.
Sch p. Rutland and Stamford CC.

STAINCROSS Yorks (W)
102 SE 3310 3m NNW of Barnsley. Loc,
Darton UD.

STAINDROP Co Durham
84/85 NZ 1220 5m ENE of Barnard Cstle.
CP, 1,252. Bnd Cstle RD. P Darlington.
Ch e, f, m. Sch pe, s. Bishop Auckland CC.
Interesting ch at end of long grn. To N,
Raby Cstle*, mainly 14c with later
additions. Pictures, gdns.

STAINES Surrey
160, 170 TQ 0371 6m SE of Slough.
UD, 56,386. P(Stns, Middx). Spelthorne BC
(CC). See also Ashford, Laleham, Poyle,
Stanwell, Stnwll Moor. Busy tn on
R Thames.

STAINFIELD Lincs (K)
123 TF 0725 3m NW of Bourne. Loc,
Haconby CP. (See Hacconby.)

STAINFIELD Lincs (L)
113 TF 1173 9m E of Lincoln. CP, 118.
Welton RD. P LNCLN. Ch e. Sch pe.
Gainsborough CC.

STAINFORTH Yorks (W)
90 SD 8267 2m N of Settle. CP, 220.
Sttle RD. P Sttle. Ch e. Sch pe. Skipton CC.

STAINFORTH Yorks (W)
103 SE 6411 3m WSW of Thorne. CP, 7,361.
Thne RD. P Doncaster. Ch e, m3, r, v2.
Sch i, p, pr, s. Goole CC.

STAINING Lancs
94 SD 3436 3m E of Blackpool. CP.
Fylde RD. Sch pe. S Flde CC. See also
Newton.

STAINLAND Yorks (W)
96, 102 SE 0719 4m SSW of Halifax. Loc,
Elland UD. P Hlfx.

STAINSACRE Yorks (N)
86, 93 NZ 9108 2m SE of Whitby.
CP(Hawsker-cum-Stnscre), 494. Whtby RD.
Ch e. Cleveland and Whtby CC
(Scarborough and Whtby).

STAINTON Co Durham
84 NZ 0718 2m NE of Barnard Cstle.
CP(Streatlam and Stntn), 575. Bnd
Cstle RD. Ch m. Bishop Auckland CC.

STAINTON Cumbs
83 NY 4828 2m SW of Penrith. Loc,
Dacre CP. P Pnrth. Ch m. Sch pe.

STAINTON Westm
89 SD 5285 4m S of Kendal. CP, 297.
S Westm RD. P Kndl. Ch v. Sch pe.
Westm CC.

STAINTON Yorks (N)
91 SE 1096 5m WSW of Richmond. CP, 18.
Rchmnd RD. Rchmnd CC.

STAINTON Yorks (W)
103 SK 5593 6m S of Doncaster. CP, 216. Dncstr RD. P Rotherham. Ch e. Sch p. Don Valley CC.

STAINTON BY LANGWORTH Lincs (L)
104 TF 0677 7m NE of Lincoln. CP, 67. Welton RD. Ch e. Gainsborough CC.

STAINTONDALE Yorks (N)
93 SE 9998 7m NNW of Scarborough. CP, 286. Scbrgh RD. P Scbrgh. Ch m. Sch p. Scbrgh CC (Scbrgh and Whitby). See also Ravenscar.

STAINTON, GREAT Co Durham
85 NZ 3322 6m NE of Darlington. See Gt Stntn.

STAINTON LE VALE Lincs (L)
105 TF 1794 5m NE of Mkt Rasen. CP, 964. Caistor RD. Ch e. Gainsborough CC.

STAINTON WITH ADGARLEY Lancs
88 SD 2472 4m NE of Barrow. Loc, Urswick CP. N Lonsdale RD. Morecambe and Lnsdle CC.

STAIR Cumb
82 NY 2321 2m SW of Keswick. Loc, Above Derwent CP. Cockermouth RD. Workington CC.

STAITHES Yorks (N)
86 NZ 7818 4m E of Loftus. Loc, Hinderwell CP. P Saltburn-by-the-Sea. Ch c, m2, r. Sch p. Fishing vllge surrounded by high cliffs.

STAKEFORD Nthmb
78 NZ 2685 5m E of Morpeth. Loc, Bedlingtonshire UD. P Choppington. Blyth BC.

STAKEPOOL Lancs
94 SD 4147 5m E across river from Fleetwood. Loc, Pilling CP. P Preston.

STALBRIDGE Dorset
178 ST 7317 6m E of Sherborne. CP, 1,520. Sturminster RD. P Stmnstr Newton. Ch e, c, m. Sch pe. N Dst CC. 14c mkt cross.

STALBRIDGE WESTON Dorset
178 ST 7216 5m E of Sherborne. Loc, Stlbrdge CP.

STALHAM Norfolk
126 TG 3725 6m SE of N Walsham. CP, 1,190. Smallburgh RD. P NORWICH, NOR 34Z. Ch e, b. Sch p, s. N Nflk CC. See also Stlhm Grn.

STALHAM GREEN Norfolk
126 TG 3824 7m SE of N Walsham. Loc, Stlhm CP. Ch m.

STALISFIELD GREEN Kent
172 TQ 9552 2m N of Charing. Loc, Stlsfld CP. Swale RD. P Faversham. Ch e. Sch p. Fvrshhm CC.

STALLINGBOROUGH Lincs (L)
105 TA 2011 5m WNW of Grimsby. CP, 653. Grmsby RD. P Grmsby. Ch e, m. Sch pe. Louth CC.

STALLING BUSK Yorks (N)
90 SD 9185 4m SE of Hawes. Loc, Bainbridge CP.

STALMINE Lancs
94 SD 3745 3m SE across river from Fleetwood. CP(Stlmne-w-Staynall), 851. Garstang RD. P Blackpool. Ch e. Sch p. N Fylde CC.

STALYBRIDGE Ches
101 SJ 9698 8m E of Manchester. MB, 22,782. P. Stlbrdge and Hyde CC. Cotton mills and engineering works.

STAMBOURNE Essex
148, 149 TL 7238 5m SW of Clare. CP, 266. Halstead RD. P Hlstd. Ch e, v. Saffron Walden CC. See also Chapelend Way. Ch has large square Nmn twr.

STAMBRIDGE, GREAT Essex
162 TQ 8991 4m N of Southend. See Gt Stmbrdge.

STAMFORD Lincs (K)
123 TF 0307 11m WNW of Peterborough. MB, 14,485. P. Rutland and Stamford CC. Ancient tn blt mainly of local stone. Bldngs of all periods. To S (just in Hunts), Burghley Hse*, blt by William Cecil, Lord High Treasurer to Elizabeth I.

STAMFORD Nthmb
71 NU 2219 4m NE of Alnwick. Loc, Rennington CP.

STAMFORD BRIDGE Yorks (E)
97, 98 SE 7155 7m ENE of York. CP, 674.
Pocklington RD. P YK. Ch e, m. Sch p.
Howden CC. Site of battle, 1066, in which
King Harold defeated Norwegian invaders.

STAMFORDHAM Nthmb
77, 78 NZ 0772 6m N of Prudhoe.
CP, 1,186. Cstle Ward RD.
P NEWCASTLE UPON TYNE. Ch e, v.
Sch p. Hexham CC. See also Dalton, Harlow
Hill, Heugh. Grn with lock-up and small 18c
mkt bldng. 13c ch heavily restored 1848.

STANBOROUGH Herts
147, 160 TL 2211 1m SW of Welwyn
Garden City. Loc, Hatfield CP. P Wlwn Gdn
Cty.

STANBRIDGE Beds
147 SP 9624 4m WNW of Dunstable.
CP, 625. Luton RD. P Leighton Buzzard.
Ch e, m. Sch p. S Beds CC.

STANDALONE Co Durham
85 NZ 3035 4m ENE of Spennymoor. Loc,
Cassop-cum-Quarrington CP. Drhm RD.
Drhhm CC.

STANDEFORD Staffs
119 SJ 9107 5m WSW of Cannock. Loc,
Brewood CP.

STANDEN Kent
172, 184 TQ 8540 6m ENE of Cranbrook.
Loc, Biddenden CP.

STANDFORD Hants
169, 181 SU 8134 6m W of Haslemere. Loc,
Headley CP. Ch v.

STANDISH Glos
156 SO 8008 4m WNW of Stroud. CP, 646.
Gloucester RD. Ch e. Strd CC.

STANDISH Lancs
100 SD 5610 3m NNW of Wigan. UD(Stndsh-
w-Langtree), 11,159. P Wgn. Westhoughton CC. See also Boar's Head. Mainly
a textile tn. Fine ch rebuilt late 16c.

STANDLAKE Oxon
158 SP 3903 5m SE of Witney. CP, 666.
Wtny RD. P Wtny. Ch e, b, m. Sch pe.
Mid-Oxon CC (Banbury). See also
Brighthampton.

STANDON Hants
168 SU 4226 4m WSW of Winchester. Loc,
Hursley CP.

STANDON Herts
148 TL 3922 6m W of Bishop's Stortford.
CP, 2,763. Ware RD. P Ware. Ch e, r.
Sch pe. E Herts CC. See also Collier's End,
High Cross, Puckeridge. 13c and later ch has
detached twr; monmts.

STANDON Staffs
110, 119 SJ 8135 5m W of Stone. CP, 530.
Stne RD. P STAFFORD. Ch e. Sch pe.
Stffd and Stne CC. See also Bowers.

STANFIELD Norfolk
125 TF 9320 6m NW of E Dereham.
CP, 136. Mitford and Launditch RD.
P Drhm. Ch e. SW Nflk CC.

STANFORD Beds
147 TL 1641 3m SW of Biggleswade. Loc,
Southill CP. Ch m.

STANFORD Kent
173 TR 1237 3m NW of Hythe. CP, 505.
Elham RD. P Ashfd. Ch e. Folkestone and
Hythe CC.

STANFORD Norfolk
136 TL 8594 7m NE of Brandon. CP, 73.
Swaffham RD. Ch e. SW Nflk CC. In Battle
Sch area.

STANFORD BISHOP Herefs
143 SO 6851 3m SE of Bromyard. CP, 136.
Brmyd RD. Ch e. Leominster CC. In ch a
chair reputedly used by St Augustine at
conference here in 603.

STANFORD BRIDGE Worcs
130 SO 7165 7m WSW of Stourport. Loc,
Martley RD, Tenbury RD. P WORCESTER.
Kidderminster CC.

STANFORD DINGLEY Berks
158 SU 5771 7m ENE of Newbury.
CP, 136. Bradfield RD. P Reading. Ch e.
Nbry CC.

STANFORD IN THE VALE Berks
158 SU 3493 5m NW of Wantage. CP, 909.
Faringdon RD. P Frngdn. Ch e, m, v.
Sch pe. Abingdon CC. Long, winding vllge
in Vale of White Horse.

STANFORD LE HOPE Essex
161 TQ 6882 5m NE of Tilbury. Loc,
Thurrock UD. P. Thrrck BC (CC).

STANFORD ON AVON Northants
132, 133 SP 5878 6m ENE of Rugby.
CP(Stnfd), 36. Daventry RD. Ch e.
Dvntry CC (S Nthnts). Fine mainly 15c ch.
Stnfd Hall*, William and Mary hse blt 1690.
Motor museum. Annual steam engine rally.
In pk, monmt to pioneer airman Percy
Pilcher, killed here 1899.

STANFORD ON SOAR Notts
121 SK 5422 1m NNE of Loughborough.
CP, 267. Basford RD. P Lghbrgh, Leics. Ch e.
Rushcliffe CC.

STANFORD ON TEME Worcs
130 SO 7065 7m E of Tenbury Wells.
CP(Stnfd w Orleton), 169. Tnbry RD. Ch e.
Kidderminster CC.

STANFORD RIVERS Essex
161 TL 5300 2m SW of Ongar. CP, 836.
Epping and Ongr RD. P Ongr. Ch e.
Brentwood and Ongr CC (Chigwell). See
also Lit End, Toot Hill.

STANFREE Derbys
112 SK 4774 6m ENE of Chesterfield. Loc,
Bolsover UD. P Chstrfld.

STANGHOW Yorks (N)
86 NZ 6715 3m WSW of Loftus. Loc,
Skelton and Brotton UD.

STANGROUND Hunts
134 TL 2097 1m SSE of Peterborough. Loc,
Old Fletton UD. P PTRBRGH.

STANHOE Norfolk
125 TF 8037 8m ESE of Hunstanton.
CP, 338. Docking RD. P King's Lynn.
Ch e, m. Sch pe. NW Nflk CC (K's Lnn).

STANHOPE Co Durham
84 NY 9939 8m W of Tow Law. CP, 5,121.
Weardale RD. P Bishop Auckland. Ch e, m4.
Sch pe. NW Drhm CC. See also Cowshill,
Crawley Side, Daddry Shield, Eastgate,
Frosterley, Hill End, Ireshopeburn,
Rookhope, St John's Chpl, Wearhead,
Westgate. Wearside tn. 18c cstle.

STANION Northants
133 SP 9186 2m SE of Corby. CP, 508.
Kettering RD. P Kttrng. Ch e, m. Sch pe.
Kttrng CC.

STANLEY Co Durham
78 NZ 1953 7m SSW of Gateshead.
UD, 41,940. P. Consett CC. See also
Annfield Plain, Burnopfield, Catchgate,
Craghead, Dipton, Hobson, Leazes, Middles,
Sheep Hill, S Moor, Tanfield, Tnfld Lea,
Tantobie. Mining tn.

STANLEY Co Durham
85 NZ 1637 1m N of Crook. Loc, Crk and
Willington UD.

STANLEY Derbys
112, 121 SK 4140 3m WSW of Ilkeston.
CP, 2,359. SE Derbys RD. P DERBY.
Ch e, m2. Sch pe. SE Derbys CC. See also
Stnly Cmmn.

STANLEY Staffs
110 SJ 9352 6m NE of Stoke-on-Trent.
CP(Endon and Stnly), 2,697. Leek RD.
P Stke-on-Trent. Lk CC. Stnly Pool, small
reservoir, to S.

STANLEY Yorks (W)
96, 102 SE 3423 2m NNE of Wakefield.
UD, 20,776. P Wkfld. Normanton CC. See
also Kirkhamgate, Outwood, Wrenthorpe.

STANLEY COMMON Derbys
112, 121 SK 4142 3m W of Ilkeston. Loc,
Stnly CP. P DERBY. Ch m. Sch p, pe.

STANMER Sussex (E)
182 TQ 3309 4m NNE of Brighton. Loc,
Brghtn CB. P Brghtn. Brghtn, Pavilion BC.

STANMORE Berks
158 SU 4779 7m N of Newbury. Loc,
Beedon CP.

STANMORE London
160 TQ 1692 4m NW of Hendon. Loc,
Harrow LB. P Middx. Hrrw E BC. Heriots*,
Stnmre Cmmn; woodland, deer pk.

STANNINGFIELD Suffolk (W)
149 TL 8756 5m NNW of Lavenham.
CP, 211. Thingoe RD. P Bury St Edmunds.
Ch e. Bury St Eds CC. See also Hoggard's
Grn.

STANNINGTON Nthmb
78 NZ 2179 4m SSE of Morpeth. CP. Cstle
Ward RD. P Mpth. Ch e. Sch p. Hexham CC.
See also Clifton, Saltwick. 1m S along
Gt N Rd, lodges by James Wyatt of Blagdon
Hall (also by Wyatt, late 18c, but much
altered since).

STANNINGTON Yorks (W)
102, 111 SK 3088 3m W of Sheffield. Loc,
Bradfield CP. P SHFFLD. Ch e, m, r, v.
Sch p.

STANSBATCH Herefs
129 SO 3461 3m SE of Presteigne. Loc,
Staunton on Arrow CP. Ch b.

STANSFIELD Suffolk (W)
149 TL 7852 4m NNE of Clare. CP, 186.
Clre RD. P Sudbury. Ch e, c. Bury
St Edmunds CC.

STANSTEAD Suffolk (W)
149 TL 8449 3m NNW of Long Melford.
CP, 276. Mlfd RD. P Sudbury. Ch e, m.
Sdbry and Woodbridge CC.

STANSTEAD ABBOTS Herts
148, 161 TL 3811 2m SE of Ware. CP, 1,466.
Ware RD. P Ware. Ch e2, r, v. Sch pe.
E Herts CC. Ch (St James): wooden S porch,
15c. 18c interior; monmts, plpt. Parish ch
(St Andrew) is of 1880.

STANSTED Kent
171 TQ 6062 7m NE of Sevenoaks.
CP, 562. Malling RD. P Svnks. Ch e. Sch pe.
Tonbridge and Mllng CC (Svnks). See also
Fairseat.

STANSTED MOUNTFITCHET Essex
148 TL 5124 3m NNE of Bishop's
Stortford. CP, 3,376. Saffron Walden RD.
P(Stnstd). Ch e3, c, f, r. Sch pe, s. Sffrn
Wldn CC. To SE, Stnstd Airpt. To N,
Norman Hse Wildlife Pk*. Twr windmill*,
with machinery intact.

STANTON Derbys
120 SK 2719 3m SSE of Burton-on-Trent.
Loc, Swadlincote UD.

STANTON Glos
144 SP 0634 3m SW of Broadway. CP, 262.
Cheltenham RD. P Brdwy, Worcs. Ch e, b.
Cirencester and Tewkesbury CC.
Outstanding Cotswold vllge.

STANTON Nthmb
78 NZ 1390 5m NW of Morpeth. Loc,
Netherwitton CP.

STANTON Staffs
111 SK 1246 3m W of Ashbourne. CP, 202.
Uttoxeter RD. P Ashbne, Derbyshire. Ch m.
Sch pe. Burton CC.

STANTON Suffolk (W)
136 TL 9673 9m NE of Bury St Edmunds.
CP, 1,252. Thingoe RD. P Bury St Eds.
Ch e, m2. Sch p. Bury St Eds CC.
St John's ch a picturesque ruin beyond
bypass.

STANTON BY BRIDGE Derbys
120, 121 SK 3727 6m SSE of Derby.
CP, 159. SE Derbys RD. P DBY. Ch e.
SE Derbys CC.˙ The br is Swarkestone Br,
which with causeway is some ¾m long; see
Swkstne.

STANTON BY DALE Derbys
112, 121 SK 4638 3m S of Ilkeston.
CP, 461. SE Derbys RD. P Ilkestn. Ch e, m.
Sch pe. SE Derbys CC.

STANTON DREW Som
165, 166 ST 5963 6m S of Bristol. CP, 536.
Clutton RD. P BRSTL. Ch e, m. Sch p.
N Som CC. See also Stntn Wick. To E, three
Bronze Age stone circles; N of these,
Hautville's Quoit.

STANTON FITZWARREN Wilts
157 SU 1790 4m NNE of Swindon.
CP, 204. Highworth RD. P Swndn. Ch e.
Devizes CC. Nearly part of Swndn.
Engineering wks.

STANTON HARCOURT Oxon
158 SP 4105 3m SSW of Eynsham. CP, 699.
Witney RD. P OXFORD. Ch e. Sch pe.
Mid-Oxon CC (Banbury). See also Sutton.
Parsonage Hse, 16c–17c. 16c gatehouse
survives from earlier mnr hse. Pope's twr
and mdvl kitchen. Ch: 13c scrn; Harcourt
monmts.

STANTON HILL Notts
112 SK 4860 3m W of Mansfield. Loc,
Sutton in Ashfield UD. P Sttn-in-Ashfld.

STANTON IN PEAK Derbys
111 SK 2464 3m SSE of Bakewell.
CP(Stntn), 387. Bkwll RD. P Matlock.
Ch e, v2. Sch pe. W Derbys CC.

STANTON LACY Shrops
129 SO 4978 3m NNW of Ludlow. CP, 462.
Ldlw RD. P Ldlw. Ch e. Sch pe. Ldlw CC.
See also Hayton's Bent, Lr Htn, Upr Htn.
Ch partly Saxon. Half-timbered hses.

STANTON LONG Shrops
129 SO 5790 7m SW of Much Wenlock.
CP, 148. Bridgnorth RD. P Mch Wnlck.
Ch e. Ludlow CC. In Corvedale between
Wnlck Edge and Brown Clee Hill.

STANTON ON THE WOLDS Notts
112, 121, 122 SK 6330 7m SE of
Nottingham. CP, 339. Bingham RD. Ch e.
Rushcliffe CC (Carlton).

STANTON PRIOR Som
166 ST 6762 5m W of Bath. Loc,
Marksbury CP. Ch e, m. To NE and NW,
large stretches of Wansdyke, ancient
earthwork over 50m long, prob for defence,
running roughly E-W from near Hungerford,
Berks, to Portishead; much of it now
obliterated.

STANTON ST BERNARD Wilts
167 SU 0962 5m WNW of Pewsey. CP, 196.
Devizes RD. P Marlborough. Ch e. Dvzs CC.

STANTON ST JOHN Oxon
158 SP 5709 4m ENE of Oxford. CP, 438.
Bullingdon RD. P OXFD. Ch e. Sch pe.
Mid-Oxon CC (Henley). Bthplce of John
White, 1575, 'chief founder of the colony of
Massachusetts'.

STANTON ST QUINTON Wilts
156, 157 ST 9079 4m N of Chippenham.
CP, 877. Calne and Chppnhm RD.
P Chppnhm. Ch e. Sch p. Chppnhm CC. See
also Lr S St Q. On edge of disused airfield.

STANTON STREET Suffolk (W)
136 TL 9566 6m ENE of Bury St Edmunds.
Loc, Norton CP.

STANTON UNDER BARDON Leics
121 SK 4610 4m SE of Coalville. Loc,
Markfield CP. P LEICESTER. Ch e, c.
Sch p.

STANTON UPON HINE HEATH Shrops
118 SJ 5624 5m SE of Wem. CP, 563.
N Shrops RD. P(Stntn), Shrewsbury. Ch e.
Oswestry CC. See also Booley, High Hatton.
Hatton.

STANTON WICK Som
166 ST 6161 7m NW of Radstock. Loc,
Stanton Drew CP.

STANWAY Essex
149, 162 TL 9324 4m W of Colchester.
CP, 2,426. Lexden and Winstree RD.
P Clchstr. Ch e, v. Sch p, s. Clchstr CC. See
also Beacon End.

STANWAY Glos
144 SP 0632 3m NE of Winchcombe.
CP, 415. Cheltenham RD. P Chltnhm. Ch e.
Sch p. Cirencester and Tewkesbury CC. See
also Didbrook, Hailes. Cotswold vllge with
14c tithe barn nowadays used as a hall.

STANWELL Surrey
160, 170 TQ 0574 2m NE of Staines. Loc,
Stns UD. P Stns, Middx.

STANWELL MOOR Surrey
160, 170 TQ 0474 2m N of Staines. Loc,
Stns UD.

STANWICK Northants
134 SP 9771 3m NNE of Rushden. Loc,
Raunds UD. P Wellingborough. Ch spire
considered one of finest in Nthnts.

STAPE Yorks (N)
86, 92 SE 7993 6m N of Pickering. Loc,
Pckrng UD.

STAPEHILL Dorset
179 SU 0500 3m E of Wimborne. Loc,
Hampreston CP. P Wmbne. Ch m, r.

STAPELEY Ches
110 SJ 6849 2m SE of Nantwich. CP, 484.
Nntwch RD. Ch m. Nntwch CC. See also
Butt Grn.

STAPLE Kent
173 TR 2756 4m W of Sandwich. CP, 382.
Eastry RD. P Canterbury. Ch e, b. Sch pe.
Dover and Deal CC (Dvr).

STAPLE CROSS Sussex (E)
184 TQ 7822 5m NNE of Battle. Loc,
Ewhurst CP. P Robertsbridge. Ch m.
Sch pm.

STAPLEFIELD Sussex (E)
182 TQ 2728 5m S of Crawley. Loc,
Cuckfield Rural CP. Cckfld RD.
P Haywards Hth. Ch e. Sch pe. Mid-Sx CC
(E Grinstead).

STAPLE FITZPAINE Som
177 ST 2618 5m SSE of Taunton. CP, 183.
Tntn RD. Ch e. Sch pe. Tntn CC. Ch has
ornate twr.

Stapleford

STAPLEFORD Cambs
148 TL 4751 4m SSE of Cambridge. CP, 1,548. Chesterton RD. P CMBRDGE. Ch e, b. Sch p. Cambs CC.

STAPLEFORD Herts
147 TL 3117 3m NNW of Hertford. CP, 497. Htfd RD. P HTFD. Ch e. Sch pe. Htfd and Stevenage CC (Htfd). See also Waterford.

STAPLEFORD Leics
122 SK 8118 4m E of Melton Mowbray. Loc, Freeby CP. Ch e. Stplfd Pk*, seat of Earls of Harborough, 17c and later. In grnds: lion reserve; lake with miniature liner and rly.

STAPLEFORD Lincs (K)
113 SK 8857 6m ENE of Newark. CP, 117. N Kesteven RD. Ch e. Sch pe. Grantham CC.

STAPLEFORD Notts
112, 121 SK 4837 3m SSE of Ilkeston. UD(Beeston and Stplfd), 63,498. P NOTTINGHAM. Bstn CC (Rushcliffe).

STAPLEFORD Wilts
167 SU 0737 7m NW of Salisbury. CP, 212. Slsbry and Wilton RD. P Slsbry. Ch e, m. Slsbry CC. Thatched hses. Partly Nmn ch.

STAPLEFORD ABBOTTS Essex
161 TQ 5095 5m SSE of Epping. CP, 894. Eppng and Ongar RD. P Romford. Ch e. Sch p. Brentwood and Ongr CC (Chigwell). See also Bournbridge.

STAPLEFORD TAWNEY Essex
161 TQ 5099 3m ESE of Epping. CP, 129. Eppng and Ongar RD. P Romford. Ch e. Brentwood and Ongr CC (Chigwell).

STAPLEGROVE Som
177 ST 2126 2m NW of Taunton. CP, 449. Tntn RD. P Tntn. Ch e. Sch pe. Tntn CC.

STAPLEHURST Kent
172, 184 TQ 7843 5m N of Cranbrook. CP, 2,103. Maidstone RD. P Tonbridge. Ch e, b, v. Sch p. Mdstne CC.

STAPLERS IOW
180 SZ 5189 1m E of Newport. Loc, Npt MB.

STAPLETON Cumb
76 NY 5071 7m NNW of Brampton. CP, 256. Border RD. Ch e. Sch pe. Penrith and the Bdr CC. See also Roweltown.

STAPLETON Herefs
129 SO 3265 1m NE of Presteigne. CP, 91. Kington RD. Leominster CC.

STAPLETON Leics
132 SP 4398 3m N of Hinckley. Loc, Peckleton CP. P LEICESTER. Ch e, m.

STAPLETON Shrops
118 SJ 4704 5m SSW of Shrewsbury. Loc, Condover CP. Ch e.

STAPLETON Som
177 ST 4620 4m WSW of Ilchester. Loc, Martock CP.

STAPLETON Yorks (N)
85 NZ 2612 2m SW of Darlington. CP, 170. Croft RD. P Dlngtn, Co Durham. Richmond CC.

STAPLEY Som
164, 176 ST 1813 5m SSE of Wellington. Loc, Churchstanton CP. Ch v.

STAPLOE Beds
134 TL 1460 2m W of St Neots. CP. Bedford RD. Ch m, v. Mid-Beds CC. See also Duloe.

STARBOTTON Yorks (W)
90 SD 9574 11m SSE of Hawes. CP(Kettlewell w Stbttn), 290. Skptn RD. P Skptn. Skptn CC.

STARCROSS Devon
176 SX 9781 8m SSE of Exeter. Loc, Kenton CP. P Extr. Ch e, m. Sch p. Bldng at rly stn once housed pumping wks for Brunel's atmospheric rly. Foot-passenger ferry plies to Exmouth.

STARSTON Norfolk
137 TM 2384 7m WSW of Bungay. CP, 340. Depwade RD. P Harleston. Ch e. S Nflk CC.

STARTFORTH Yorks (N)
84 NZ 0416 just W of Barnard Cstle. CP, 1,162. Sttfth RD. Ch e. Sch pe. Richmond CC.

STARTLEY Wilts
157 ST 9482 3m S of Malmesbury. Loc, Gt Somerford CP. Ch m.

STATHE Som
177 ST 3729 9m N of Ilminster. Loc, Stoke St Gregory CP. Ch b.

STATHERN Leics
112, 122 SK 7731 7m N of Melton
Mowbray. CP, 487. Mltn and Belvoir RD.
P Mltn Mbry. Ch e, m. Sch p. Mltn CC.

STATION TOWN Co Durham
85 NZ 4036 3m SW of Peterlee. Loc,
Hutton Henry CP. P Wingate.

STAUGHTON, GREAT Hunts
134 TL 1264 5m NW of St Neots. See Gt
Stghtn.

STAUGHTON HIGHWAY Hunts
134 TL 1364 4m NW of St Neots. Loc,
Gt Stghtn CP.

STAUNTON Glos
142 SO 5412 3m E of Monmouth. CP, 206.
W Dean RD. P Coleford. Ch e. W Glos CC.
Ch has two fonts.

STAUNTON Glos
143 SO 7929 7m WSW of Tewkesbury.
CP, 362. Newent RD. P GLOUCESTER.
Ch e, m. W Glos CC.

STAUNTON HAROLD Leics
120, 121 SK 3720 3m NNE of Ashby de la
Zouch. CP, 162. Ashby de la Zch RD. Ch e.
Loughborough CC. See also Lount. Ch
(NT)*, blt 1653 during Commonwealth,
which is very rare. S.H. Hall, mainly Palladian
hse, now NT and Cheshire Home for
Incurables. To N, S.H. Reservoir (in
Derbys).

STAUNTON IN THE VALE Notts
113, 122 SK 8043 6m S of Newark.
CP(Stntn), 81. Nwk RD. P NOTTINGHAM.
Ch e. Nwk CC.

STAUNTON ON ARROW Herefs
129 SO 3760 4m SE of Presteigne. CP, 203.
Kington RD. P Leominster. Ch e. Sch pe.
Lmnstr CC. See also Stansbatch.

STAUNTON ON WYE Herefs
142 SO 3645 9m WNW of Hereford.
CP, 325. Weobley RD. P HRFD. Ch e, m.
Sch pe. Leominster CC.

STAVELEY Derbys
112 SK 4374 4m NE of Chesterfield.
UD, 17,644. P Chstrfld. Chstrfld BC. See
also Far Duckmanton, Mastin Moor,
Poolsbrook, Woodthorpe. Ironworks, coal
mines.

STAVELEY Lancs
88, 89 SD 3786 6m NNW of
Grange-over-Sands. CP, 380.
N Lonsdale RD. Ch e. Sch pe. Morecambe
and Lnsdle CC. See also Ayside, Newby Br.

STAVELEY Westm
89 SD 4798 4m E of Windermere. Loc,
S Westm RD. P Kendal. Ch e, m. Sch pe.
Westm CC.

STAVELEY Yorks (W)
91 SE 3662 3m SW of Boroughbridge.
CP, 273. Nidderdale RD. P Knaresborough.
Ch e, m. Sch p. Harrogate CC.

STAVERTON Devon
187, 188 SX 7964 2m N of Totnes.
CP, 612. Ttnes RD. Ch e, m. Ttns CC. See
also Landscove. Br over R Dart next to
former rly stn was blt in 1413.

STAVERTON Glos
143, 144 SO 8923 4m W of Cheltenham.
CP, 703. Chltnhm RD. Ch e. Sch p.
Cirencester and Tewkesbury CC. See also
Golden Valley. There is an aircraft museum.

STAVERTON Northants
132 SP 5461 2m WSW of Daventry.
CP, 365. Dvntry RD. P Dvntry. Ch e.
Sch pe. Dvntry CC (S Nthnts).

STAVERTON Wilts
166 ST 8560 2m N of Trowbridge. CP, 243.
Bradford and Melksham RD. Ch e, m.
Sch pe. Westbury CC. Large red-brick
factory (Nestlés).

STAWELL Som
165 ST 3638 4m E of Bridgwater. CP, 296.
Brdgwtr RD. P Brdgwtr. Ch e, v. Sch p.
Brdgwtr CC. See also Sutton Mallet.

STAWLEY Som
164 ST 0622 5m WNW of Wellington.
CP, 245. Wllngtn RD. Ch e, bc. Sch p.
Taunton CC. Se See also Appley, Greenham,
Kittisford.

STAXTON Yorks (N)
93 TA 0179 6m SSW of Scarborough. Loc,
Willerby CP. P Scbrgh. Ch m.

STAYNALL Lancs
94 SD 3643 3m SSE across river from
Fleetwood. CP(Stalmine-w-Stnll), 851.
Garstang RD. N Fylde CC.

STAYTHORPE Notts
112 SK 7554 3m W of Newark. CP, 69.
Southwell RD. Nwk CC.

STEAN Yorks (W)
90 SE 0873 7m NW of Pateley Br. Loc,
Stonebeck Down CP. Ripon and Ptly
Br RD. Rpn CC.

STEARSBY Yorks (N)
92 SE 6171 5m ENE of Easingwold.
CP(Brandsby-cum-Stsby), 270.
Easngwld RD. Thirsk and Malton CC.

STEART Som
165 ST 2745 6m NNW of Bridgwater. Loc,
Otterhampton CP.

STEBBING Essex
148 TL 6624 3m NE of Dunmow.
CP, 1,035. Dnmw RD. P Dnmw. Ch e, v.
Sch p. Saffron Walden CC. See also Bran
End. Water mill still in use. 14c ch has great
stone rood scrn.

STEDHAM Sussex (W)
181 SU 8622 2m WNW of Midhurst.
CP, 649. Mdhst RD. P Mdhst. Ch e. Sch p.
Chichester CC (Horsham).

STEEN'S BRIDGE Herefs
129 SO 5457 3m ESE of Leominster. Loc,
Lmnstr and Wigmore RD. P Lmnstr. Ch m.
Lmnstr CC.

STEEP Hants
181 SU 7425 1m N of Petersfield. CP, 906.
Ptrsfld RD. P Ptrsfld. Ch e, m. Sch pe.
Ptrsfld CC.

STEEPING, GREAT Lincs (L)
114 TF 4364 8m W of Skegness. See Gt
Stpng.

STEEPLE Dorset
178, 179 SY 9181 4m S of Wareham.
CP, 115. Wrhm and Purbeck RD. Ch e.
S Dst CC.

STEEPLE Essex
162 TL 9303 6m ESE of Maldon. CP, 338.
Mldn RD. P Southminster. Ch e, v.
Mldn CC.

STEEPLE ASHTON Wilts
166, 167 ST 9056 3m E of Trowbridge.
CP, 777. Warminster and Westbury RD.
P Trwbrdge. Ch e, m. Sch pe. Wstbry CC.
See also Ashtn Cmmn. Perp ch.

STEEPLE ASTON Oxon.
145 SP 4725 6m NNE of Woodstock.
CP, 628. Banbury RD. P OXFORD. Ch e, m.
Sch pe, se. Bnbry CC.

STEEPLE BARTON Oxon
145 SP 4425 5m N of Woodstock. CP, 777.
Chipping Norton RD. Ch e. Banbury CC.
See also Middle Btn. To E, Btn
Abbey; gdns*.

STEEPLE BUMPSTEAD Essex
148 TL 6841 3m S of Haverhill. CP, 729.
Halstead RD. P Hvrhll, Suffolk. Ch e, v.
Sch p. Saffron Walden CC.

STEEPLE CLAYDON Bucks
146 SP 6926 4m S of Buckingham.
CP, 1,079. Bcknghm RD. P Bletchley.
Ch e, m. Sch p. Bcknghm CC.

STEEPLE GIDDING Hunts
134 TL 1381 7m SE of Oundle. CP, 56.
Huntingdon RD. Ch e. Hunts CC.

STEEPLE LANGFORD Wilts
167 SU 0337 8m NW of Salisbury. CP, 465.
Slsbry and Wilton RD. P Slsbry. Ch e.
Sch pe. Slsbry CC. See also Hanging Lngfd,
Lit Lngfd.

STEEPLE MORDEN Cambs
147 TL 2842 6m ESE of Biggleswade.
CP, 630. S Cambs RD. P Royston, Herts.
Ch e, m. Sch p, pe. Cambs CC. Steeple fell
in storm, 1633. Present one tile-hung,
topped by shingle spire.

STEETON Yorks (W)
96 SE 0344 3m NW of Keighley. CP(Sttn
w Eastburn), 44. Skipton RD. P Kghly.
Ch e, m. Sch p. Kghly BC.

STELLING MINNIS Kent
173 TR 1446 7m S of Canterbury. CP, 185.
Elham RD. Ch e, m2. Sch pe. Folkestone
and Hythe CC. 19c smock-mill, in working
order.

STENALEES Cornwall
185, 186 SX 0157 3m N of St Austell. Loc,
St Astll w Fowey MB. P St Astll. Truro CC.

STENSON Derbys
120, 121 SK 3230 4m SSW of Derby.
CP(Twyford and Stnsn), 231. Repton RD.
Ch m. Belper CC.

STEPNEY London
161 TQ 3681 4m E of Charing Cross. Loc,
Twr Hmlts LB. Stpny and Poplar BC
(Stpny). Dockland on N bank of Thames.

STEPPINGLEY Beds
147 TL 0135 2m SW of Ampthill. CP, 243.
Ampthll RD. P BEDFORD. Ch e, m. Sch p.
Mid-Beds CC.

STERNFIELD Suffolk (E)
137 TM 3961 1m SSE of Saxmundham.
CP, 152. Blyth RD. Ch e. Eye CC.

STERT Wilts
167 SU 0359 2m SE of Devizes. CP, 89.
Dvzs RD. Ch e. Dvzs CC.

STETCHWORTH Cambs
135 TL 6458 3m S of Newmarket. CP, 514.
Nmkt RD. P Nmkt, Suffolk. Ch e, c. Sch p.
Cambs CC. Racehorse training. Ch is
approached through 'cathedral' of beeches.

STEVENAGE Herts
147 TL 2325 28m N of London.
UD, 66,918. P. Hertford and Stvnge CC
(Hitchin). See also Broadwater, Shephall.
New tn development to S: indstrl, rsdntl.
New tn pop. 66,975.

STEVENTON Berks
158 SU 4791 3m WNW of Didcot.
CP, 1,109. Abingdon RD. P Abngdn.
Ch e, m. Sch pe. Abngdn CC. Priory
Cottages (NT), part of monastic bldngs
converted into two hses. South Hse open.

STEVENTON Hants
168 SU 5448 6m WSW of Basingstoke.
CP, 223. Bsngstke RD. P Bsngstke. Ch e, m.
Bsngstke CC. Bthplce of Jane Austen, whose
father was rector here for over forty years.

STEVINGTON Beds
147 SP 9853 4m NW of Bedford. CP, 386.
Bdfd RD. P BDFD. Ch e. Sch p. Bdfd CC.
See also W End. Ch: pre-Nmn twr. Post-mill
at SE end of vllge still in working order.

STEWARTBY Beds
147 TL 0142 3m NNW of Ampthill.
CP, 1,235. Bedford RD. P BDFD. Ch v.
Sch p, s. Mid-Beds CC. Large brickworks.

STEWKLEY Bucks
146 SP 8526 4m W of Linslade. CP. 1.016.
Winslow RD. P Leighton Buzzard, Beds.

Ch e, m2. Sch pe. Buckingham CC. Ch
famous for Nmn carving. Situated on edge
of Wing airfield.

STEWPONEY Staffs
130 SO 8684 3m W of Stourbridge. Loc,
Kinver CP.

STEWTON Lincs (L)
105 TF 3686 2m E of Louth. CP, 83.
Lth RD. Ch e. Lth CC.

STEYNING Sussex (W)
182 TQ 1711 4m NW of Shoreham-by-Sea.
CP, 2,695. Chanctonbury RD. P. Ch e, m, r, v.
Sch pe, s2. Shrhm CC (Arundel and Shrhm).
Under S Downs. Splendid Nmn ch.

STIBB Cornwall
174 SS 2210 3m NNE of Bude. Loc,
Kilkhampton CP.

STIBBARD Norfolk
125 TF 9828 4m ESE of Fakenham.
CP, 295. Walsingham RD. P Fknhm.
Ch e, m. Sch pe. NW Nflk CC (N Nflk).

STIBB CROSS Devon
163, 175 SS 4214 5m SW of Torrington.
Loc, Langtree CP. Ch m.

STIBB GREEN Wilts
167 SU 2262 5m SSE of Marlborough. Loc,
Burbage CP.

STIBBINGTON Hunts
134 TL 0898 6m W of Peterborough.
CP(Sibson cum Stbbngtn), 447. Norman
Cross RD. Ch e, m. Sch p. Hunts CC.

STICKER Cornwall
185, 190 SW 9750 3m SW of St Austell.
Loc, St Astll RD. Ch m. Truro CC.

STICKFORD Lincs (L)
114 TF 3560 8m SE of Horncastle. CP, 363.
Spilsby RD. P Boston. Ch e, m. Sch p.
Hncstle CC.

STICKLEPATH Devon
175 SX 6394 3m E of Okehampton. Loc,
Sampford Courtenay CP. P Okhmptn.
Ch e, m. Sch p.

STICKNEY Lincs (L)
114 TF 3456 8m N of Boston. CP, 692.
Spilsby RD. P Bstn. Ch e, m2, v. Sch pe, s.
Horncastle CC.

STIFFKEY Norfolk
125 TF 9743 4m E of Wells. CP, 338. Walsingham RD. P Wlls-next-the-Sea. Ch e, m. NW Nflk CC (N Nflk). Pronounced 'Stewky'. Famous for cockles (and for a past vicar). Elizn hall blt by Francis Bacon's father, c 1570.

STIFFORD Essex
161 TQ 6080 4m NW of Tilbury. Loc, Thurrock UD. P Grays. Thrrck BC (CC). Ch: 14c brasses.

STIFFORD'S BRIDGE Herefs
143 SO 7348 3m NW of Malvern. Loc, Cradley CP.

STILLINGFLEET Yorks (E)
97 SE 5940 7m S of York. CP, 309. Derwent RD. P YK. Ch e, m. Howden CC. Ch has fine Nmn doorway and 12c ironwork.

STILLINGTON Co Durham
85 NZ 3723 5m NW of Teesside (Stockton). CP, 162. Sedgefield RD. P STCKTN-ON-TEES, Tssde. Ch e. Sch p. Drhm CC (Sdgfld).

STILLINGTON Yorks (N)
92 SE 5867 10m N of York. CP, 494. Easingwold RD. P YK. Ch e, m. Sch p. Thirsk and Malton CC.

STILTON Hunts
134 TL 1689 6m SSW of Peterborough. CP, 633. Norman Cross RD. P PTRBRGH. Ch e, m. Sch pe. Hunts CC. The Bell Inn was formerly collecting-point for Stltn cheese, made in Leics.

STINCHCOMBE Glos
156 ST 7398 8m WSW of Stroud. CP, 423. Dursley RD. Ch e. Strd CC. On edge of Cotswold ridge. Views to W over Severn estuary.

STINSFORD Dorset
178 SY 7191 1m ENE of Dorchester. CP, 329. Dchstr RD. Ch e. W Dst CC. See also Hr Bockhampton, Kingston Maurward, Lr Bckhmptn. Place beloved of Thomas Hardy, whose heart is buried in ch.

STIPERSTONES, THE Shrops
118 SJ 3600 11m SW of Shrewsbury. Loc, Worthen CP. Sch pe. Takes name from rock-strewn upland to S; rock outcrops incl Devil's Chair.

STIRCHLEY Shrops
119 SJ 6906 3m S of Oakengates. Loc, Dawley UD. P Telford. The Wrekin CC.

STIRTON Yorks (W)
95 SD 9752 1m NW of Skipton. CP(Strtn w Thorlby), 183. Skptn RD. Skptn CC.

STISTED Essex
149, 162 TL 8024 3m ENE of Braintree. CP, 531. Brntree RD. P Brntree. Ch e, c. Sch pe. Brntree CC (Maldon).

STITHIANS Cornwall
190 SW 7336 4m SE of Redruth. CP, 1,290. Kerrier RD. P Truro. Ch e, m2. Sch p. Falmouth and Camborne CC. See also Penhalvean.

STIXWOULD Lincs (L)
113 TF 1765 2m NNW of Woodhall Spa. CP, 150. Horncastle RD. P LINCOLN. Ch e. Hncstle CC.

STOAK Ches
109 SJ 4273 4m NNE of Chester. CP(Stoke). Chstr RD. Ch e. City of Chstr CC.

STOBOROUGH Dorset
178, 179 SY 9286 just S of Wareham. Loc, Arne CP. P Wrhm. Sch pe.

STOBOROUGH GREEN Dorset
179 SY 9285 1m S of Wareham. Loc, Arne CP.

STOCK Essex
161 TQ 6898 3m NNE of Billericay. CP, 1,527. Chelmsford RD. P Ingatestone. Ch e, c, r. Sch pe. Chlmsfd CC. Ch has timbered twr and shingled spire. Twr windmill, with machinery intact.

STOCKBRIDGE Hants
168 SU 3535 8m WNW of Winchester. CP, 679. Romsey and Stckbrdge RD. P Stckbrdge. Ch e, b. Sch p, s. Wnchstr CC. On stretch of R Test famous for trout-fishing.

STOCKBURY Kent
172 TQ 8461 4m WSW of Sittingbourne. CP, 528. Hollingbourn RD. P Sttngbne. Ch e, m2. Sch pe. Maidstone CC. See also S Grn.

STOCKCROSS Berks
158 SU 4368 3m WNW of Newbury. Loc,
Speen CP. P Nbry. Ch e, m. Sch pe. Model
vllge of early 20c.

STOCKDALEWATH Cumb
83 NY 3845 7m S of Carlisle. Loc,
Dalston CP. Ch m.

STOCKERSTON Leics
133 SP 8397 2m SW of Uppingham. CP, 24.
Mkt Harborough RD. Ch e. Hbrgh CC.

STOCK GREEN Worcs
130, 131 SO 9858 6m ESE of Droitwich.
Loc, Drtwch RD, Evesham RD.
Worcester BC, S Worcs CC.

STOCKING PELHAM Herts
148 TL 4529 5m NNW of Bishop's
Stortford. CP, 134. Braughing RD. Ch e.
E Herts CC.

STOCKLAND Devon
177 ST 2404 5m NW of Axminster.
CP, 625. Axmnstr RD. P Honiton. Ch e.
Sch pe. Honiton CC.

STOCKLAND BRISTOL Som
165 ST 2443 6m NW of Bridgwater.
CP, 135. Brdgwtr RD. P(Stcklnd), Brdgwtr.
Ch e. Brdgwtr CC.

STOCKLEIGH ENGLISH Devon
176 SS 8506 4m N of Crediton. CP, 44.
Crdtn RD. Ch e. Tiverton CC (Torrington).

STOCKLEIGH POMEROY Devon
176 SS 8703 3m NE of Crediton. CP, 105.
Crdtn RD. P Crdtn. Ch e. Tiverton CC
(Torrington).

STOCKLEY Wilts
157 SU 0067 2m S of Calne. Loc, Clne
Without CP. Clne and Chippenham RD.
Chppnhm CC.

STOCKLINCH Som
177 ST 3817 2m NE of Ilminster. CP, 114.
Chard RD. P Ilmnstr. Ch e2. Yeovil CC.

STOCKPORT Ches
101 SJ 8989 6m SE of Manchester. CB,
139,633. P. Stckpt N BC, Stckpt S BC.
Mnfg tn on R Mersey.

STOCKSBRIDGE Yorks (W)
102 SK 2698 3m SSE of Penistone.
UD, 13,400. P SHEFFIELD. Pnstne CC. See
also Bolsterstone, Deepcar, Ewden Vllge.

STOCKSFIELD Nthmb
77, 78 NZ 0561 3m WSW of Prudhoe.
CP(Broomley and Stcksfld), 2,035.
Hexham RD. P. Ch m. Hxhm CC.

STOCKTON Herefs
129 SO 5161 2m NE of Leominster. Loc,
Kimbolton CP. Ch m. At Stcktn Bury, mdvl
dovecote with revolving ladder.

STOCKTON Norfolk
137 TM 3894 3m NW of Beccles. CP, 78.
Loddon RD. Ch e. S Nflk CC.

STOCKTON Shrops
130 SO 7299 4m N of Bridgnorth. CP, 396.
Brdgnth RD. Ch e. Ludlow CC (The
Wrekin). See also Norton.

STOCKTON Warwicks
132 SP 4363 2m NE of Southam. CP, 862.
Sthm RD. P Rugby. Ch e, m. Sch p.
Stratford-on-Avon (Strtfd).

STOCKTON Wilts
167 ST 9838 8m SE of Warminster.
CP, 244. Wmnstr and Westbury RD.
P Wmnstr. Ch e. Sch pe. Wstbry CC. Stone
and timbered thatched cottages; Elizn mnr;
almshouses. Nmn - EE ch: monmts.

STOCKTON BROOK Staffs
110 SJ 9152 5m NNE of Stoke-on-Trent.
Loc, Leek RD. P Stke-on-Trnt. Ch m.
Lk CC.

STOCKTON HEATH Ches
101 SJ 6186 1m SSE of Warrington.
CP, 6,684. Runcorn RD. P WRRNGTN.
Ch e, m3, v. Sch p2, pe, s2. Rncn CC.

STOCKTON-ON-TEES Yorks (N)
85 NZ 4419 10m ENE of Darlington. Loc,
Teesside CB. P(STCKTN-ON-TS, Tssde).
Tssde, Stcktn BC. Large indstrl tn. Rly
between here and Dlngtn opened 1825.
Racecourse. Tn centre development.

STOCKTON ON TEME Worcs
130 SO 7167 7m WSW of Stourport.
CP, 69. Tenbury RD. Ch e.
Kidderminster CC.

STOCKTON-ON-THE-FOREST Yorks (N)
97, 98 SE 6556 4m NE of York. CP, 859.
Flaxton RD. P YK. Ch e, m. Sch pe. Thirsk
and Malton CC.

STOCKWELL London
160, 170 TQ 3075 3m S of Charing Cross.
Loc, Lambeth LB. Lmbth Central BC
(Brixton).

STOCKWOOD Dorset
177, 178 ST 5906 6m SSE of Yeovil.
CP, 44. Sherborne RD. Ch e. W Dst CC.

STOCK WOOD Worcs
131 SP 0058 5m W of Alcester. Loc,
Inkberrow CP.

STODMARSH Kent
173 TR 2160 5m ENE of Canterbury. Loc,
Wickhambreaux CP. P Cntrbry. Ch e. On
edge of Gt Stour marshes. Ch has 13c glass.

STODY Norfolk
125 TG 0535 3m SSW of Holt. CP, 247.
Erpingham RD. Ch e. N Nflk CC. See also
Hunworth.

STOFORD Som
177, 178 ST 5613 2m S of Yeovil. Loc,
Barwick'CP. P Yvl. Ch m.

STOFORD Wilts
167 SU 0835 5m NW of Salisbury. Loc,
S Newton CP.

STOGUMBER Som
164 ST 0937 4m SSE of Watchet. CP, 568.
Williton RD. P Taunton. Ch e, b. Sch pe.
Bridgwater CC.

STOGURSEY Som
165 ST 2042 7m WNW of Bridgwater.
CP, 1,391. Williton RD. P Brdgwtr. Ch e, c.
Sch pe. Brdgwtr CC. See also Burton,
Shurton. Par ch and dovecote sole rems of
Benedictine priory. 2m N, Hinkley Point
Atomic Power Stns.

STOKE Devon
174 SS 2324 12m N of Bude. Loc,
Hartland CP. Ch e. Ch is that of Htlnd, qv.

STOKE Hants
168 SU 4051 5m NNE of Andover. Loc,
St Mary Bourne CP. P Andvr. Ch m.

STOKE Kent
172 TQ 8275 6m NE of Rochester. CP, 541.
Strood RD. Ch e. Sch p. Gravesend CC. See
also Lr Stke.

STOKE ABBOTT Devon
177 ST 4500 5m N of Bridport. CP, 355.
Beaminster RD. P Bmnstr. Ch e. W Dst CC.

STOKE ALBANY Northants
133 SP 8087 5m E of Mkt Harborough.
CP, 292. Kettering RD. P Mkt Hbrgh, Leics.
Ch e, m. Kttrng CC.

STOKE ASH Suffolk (E)
136 TM 1170 3m SW of Eye. CP, 235.
Hartismere RD. P Eye. Ch e, b. Sch p.
Eye CC.

STOKE BARDOLPH Notts
112, 121, 122 SK 6441 5m E of
Nottingham. CP, 179. Basford RD. Sch pe.
Carlton CC.

STOKE BLISS Worcs
129, 130 SO 6562 5m SE of Tenbury Wells.
CP, 203. Tnbry RD. P Tnbry Wlls. Ch e.
Kidderminster CC. See also Bank St.

STOKE BRUERNE Northants
146 SP 7449 3m ENE of Towcester.
CP, 270. Tcstr RD. P Tcstr. Ch e, m. Sch pe.
Daventry CC (S Nthnts). On Grand Union
Canal at S end of Blisworth Tunnel (1¾m
long). Waterways museum in old corn mill.
Staircase locks. To SW, Stke Pk Pavilions,
prob by Inigo Jones, are sole rems of 17c
mansion.

STOKE-BY-CLARE Suffolk (W)
148, 149 TL 7443 2m WSW of Clare.
CP, 393. Clre RD. P Sudbury. Ch e, b2, v.
Sch ie. Bury St Edmunds CC. Pink cottages.
Thatch. Stke College incorporates rems of
mdvl priory.

STOKE-BY-NAYLAND Suffolk (W)
149 TL 9836 5m SW of Hadleigh. CP, 706.
Melford RD. P Colchester, Essex. Ch e, r.
Sch pe, s. Sudbury and Woodbridge CC. See
also Thorington St. Perp ch, often painted
by Constable: monmts, brasses.
Half-timbered hses nearby.

STOKE CANON Devon
176 SX 9397 4m NNE of Exeter. CP, 336.
St Thomas RD. P Extr. Ch e, v. Sch pe.
Tiverton CC. Ch: carved Nmn font.

STOKE CHARITY Hants
168 SU 4839 6m N of Winchester. Loc,
Wonston CP. P Wnchstr. Ch e. Ch: 13c
wall-paintings; monmts.

STOKE CLIMSLAND Cornwall
186 SX 3674 3m N of Callington.
CP(Stkclmslnd). 1,147. Launceston RD.

P Cllngtn. Ch e, m3 , v. Sch p. N Cnwll CC. See also Downgate, Luckett.

STOKE D'ABERNON Surrey
170 TQ 1259 3m NW of Leatherhead. Loc, Esher UD. P Cobham. Ch, beside R Mole, has oldest brass in England (Sir John d'Abernon, 1277).

STOKE DOYLE Northants
134 TL 0286 1m SW of Oundle. CP, 95. Oundle and Thrapston RD. Ch e. Wellington CC (Peterborough).

STOKE DRY Rutland
133 SP 8596 2m SSW of Uppingham. CP, 29. Uppnghm RD. Ch e. Rtlnd and Stamford CC. Small 13c–15c ch; large 20c reservoir (Eye Brook).

STOKE EDITH Herefs
142, 143 SO 6040 6m E of Hereford. CP, 114. Hrfd RD. Ch e. Hrfd CC. Stke Edth Pk, 17c mansion, burnt down 1927 and rebuilding never completed. Grnds by Repton.

STOKE FERRY Norfolk
124 TF 7000 6m ESE of Downham Mkt. CP, 723. Dn m RD. P King's Lynn. Ch e, m. Sch pe. S.V Nflk CC.

STOKE FLEMING Devon
188 SX 8648 2m SSW of Dartmouth. CP, 683. Kingsbridge RD. P Dtmth. Ch e, v. Sch p. Totnes CC. See also Bowden.

STOKE GABRIEL Devon
188 SX 8457 4m SW of Paignton. CP, 967. Totnes RD. P Ttns. Ch e, b. Sch p. Ttns CC.

STOKE GIFFORD Glos
155, 156 ST 6279 5m NNE of Bristol. CP, 3,949. Sodbury RD. P BRSTL. Ch e, b. Sch p, pe. S Glos CC.

STOKE GOLDING Leics
132 SP 3997 3m NW of Hinckley. Loc, Hnckly UD. P Nuneaton, Warwickshire. Pure unaltered 13c–14c ch, much admired.

STOKE GOLDINGTON Bucks
146 SP 8348 4m NNW of Newport Pagnell. CP, 385. Npt Pgnll RD. P Npt Pgnll. Ch e, v. Sch pe. Buckingham CC.

STOKEHAM Notts
104 SK 7876 5m ESE of Retford. CP, 66. E Rtfd RD. Ch e. Bassetlaw CC.

STOKE HAMMOND Bucks
146 SP 8829 2m S of Bletchley. CP, 422. Wing RD. P Bltchly. Ch e, m. Sch pe. Buckingham CC.

STOKE HOLY CROSS Norfolk
137 TG 2301 5m S of Norwich. CP, 984. Forehoe and Henstead RD. P NRWCH, NOR 55W. Ch e. Sch j, p. S Nflk (Central Nflk). See also Dunston.

STOKEINTEIGNHEAD Devon
176, 188 SX 9170 4m E of Newton Abbot. CP. Ntn Abbt RD. P Ntn Abbt. Ch e. Sch p. Totnes CC.

STOKE LACY Herefs
142, 143 SO 6249 4m SSW of Bromyard. CP, 319. Brmyd RD. P Brmyd. Ch e. Leominster CC.

STOKE LYNE Oxon
145, 146 SP 5628 4m NNW of Bicester. CP, 241. Ploughley RD. P Bcstr. Ch e. Sch pe. Banbury CC (Henley).

STOKE MANDEVILLE Bucks
146, 159 SP 8310 2m SSE of Aylesbury. CP, 1,217. Aylesbury RD. P Aylesbury. Ch e, m. Sch p. Aylesbury CC. At S end, Stke Hse, early 18c.

STOKENCHURCH Bucks
159 SU 7696 7m WNW of High Wycombe. CP, 2,794. Wcmbe RD. P Hgh Wcmbe. Ch e, m2, v2. Sch p, s. Aylesbury CC (Wcmbe). See also Beacon's Bottom. Vllge known for chair-making.

STOKE NEWINGTON London
160 TQ 3286 4m NNE of Charing Cross. Loc, Hackney LB. Hckny N and Stke Nwngtn BC (Stke Nwngtn and Hckny N).

STOKENHAM Devon
188 SX 8042 5m E of Kingsbridge. CP, 1,314. Kngsbrdge RD. P Kngsbrdge. Sch p. Totnes CC. See also Beesands, Beeson, Chillington, Hallsands, Kellaton, Torcross. Ch: scrn. 1m E, Slapton Sands - see Slptn.

STOKE-ON-TRENT Staffs
110 SJ 8745 33m S of Manchester. CB, 265,153. P. BCs: S-o-T Central, N, S. See also Burslem, Fenton, Hanley, Longton, Trentham, Tunstall. 'Capital' of Potteries and N Staffs coalfield; an amalgam of once separate tns. Spode-Copeland Museum.

STOKE ORCHARD Glos
143, 144 SO 9128 4m NNW of Cheltenham. CP, 279. Chltnhm RD. P Chltnhm. Ch e. Sch p. Cirencester and Tewkesbury CC. See also Tredington.

STOKE PERO Som
164 SS 8743 6m WSW of Minehead. Loc, Luccombe CP. Ch e.

STOKE POGES Bucks
159, 160 SU 9884 3m N of Slough. CP, 2,886. Eton RD. P Slgh. Ch e. Sch j, p. Beaconsfield CC (S Bucks). Gray wrote elegy in churchyard. Monmt to him by James Wyatt in field nearby.

STOKE PRIOR Herefs
129 SO 5256 2m SE of Leominster. CP, 249. Lmnstr and Wigmore RD. P Lmnstr. Ch e, m. Sch p. Lmnstr CC.

STOKE PRIOR Worcs
130, 131 SO 9567 2m S of Bromsgrove. CP, 2,460. Brmsgrve RD. Ch e. Sch p. Brmsgrve and Redditch CC (Brmsgrve). See also Finstall, Woodgate. Many locks on Worcester and Birmingham Canal to S. Salt wks.

STOKE RIVERS Devon
163 SS 6335 5m ENE of Barnstaple. CP, 128. Bnstple RD. P Bnstple. Ch e, b. N Dvn CC.

STOKE ROCHFORD Lincs (K)
122 SK 9227 5m S of Grantham. CP, 379. W Kesteven RD. P Grnthm. Ch e. Sch pe. Rutland and Stamford CC. Vctrn Tdr vllge just off A1 rd. Large hall now training college.

STOKE ROW Oxon
159 SU 6883 5m W of Henley. CP, 580. Hnly RD. P Hnly-on-Thames. Ch e, c. Sch pe. Hnly CC. Maharajah's Well, 350ft deep, ornate gift of the Maharajah of Benares in 1864.

STOKE ST GREGORY Som
177 ST 3427 8m N of Ilminster. CP, 1,118. Taunton RD. P Tntn. Ch e, b. Sch pe. Tntn CC. See also Burrow Br, Mare Grn, Stathe.

STOKE ST MARY Som
177 ST 2622 3m SE of Taunton. CP, 542. Tntn RD. P Tntn. Ch e, v. Tntn CC.

STOKE ST MICHAEL Som
166 ST 6646 4m NE of Shepton Mallet. CP, 705. Shptn Mllt RD. P Bath. Ch e, m2. Sch p. Wells CC.

STOKE ST MILBOROUGH Shrops
129 SO 5682 6m NE of Ludlow. CP, 254. Ldlw RD. P Ldlw. Ch e, m. Ldlw CC. See also Cleedownton.

STOKESAY Shrops
129 SO 4381 just S of Craven Arms. CP, 1,217. Ludlow RD. Ch e. Sch p. Ldlw CC. See also Crvn Arms. Stksy Cstle*, 13c fortified mnr hse.

STOKESBY Norfolk
126 TG 4310 6m WNW of Yarmouth. CP(Stksby w Herringby), 333. Blofield and Flegg RD. P Gt Ymth. Ch e, m. Sch p. Ymth CC.

STOKESLEY Yorks (N)
85 NZ 5208 8m SSE of Teesside (Middlesborough). CP, 2,529. Stksly RD. P MDDLSBRGH, Tssde. Ch e, m, r, v. Sch p, s. Richmond CC. Small tn with grn and trees.

STOKE SUB HAMDON Som
177 ST 4717 5m W of Yeovil. CP, 1,782. Yvl RD. P. Ch e, m, v. Sch p, s. Yvl CC. Quarries on hill produce famous golden-yellow stone. The Priory (NT)*, 15c hse incorporating rems of old chantry.

STOKE TALMAGE Oxon
158, 159 SU 6799 5m SSW of Thame. CP, 88. Bullingdon RD. Henley CC.

STOKE TRISTER Som
166 ST 7328 2m E of Wincanton. CP, 274. Wncntn RD. Ch e. Wells CC. See also Bayford.

STOKE UPON TERN Shrops
118, 119 SJ 6428 4m SSW of Mkt Drayton. CP, 1,225. Mkt Drtn RD. P Mkt Drtn. Ch e, m. Sch p. Oswestry CC. See also Eaton upn Tn, Ollerton, Wistanswick.

STOKE WAKE Dorset
178 ST 7606 8m W of Blandford. CP, 64. Sturminster RD. Ch e. N Dst CC.

STONAR, GREAT Kent
173 TR 3359 1m N of Sandwich. Loc, Sndwch MB.

STONDON MASSEY Essex
161 TL 5800 2m SE of Ongar. CP, 486.
Epping and Ongr RD. P(Stndn), Brntwd.
Ch e. Brntwd and Ongr CC (Chigwell).
Home of William Byrd, composer
(1543–1623).

STONE Bucks
146, 159 SP 7812 2m WSW of Aylesbury.
CP, 2,106. Aylesbury RD. P Aylesbury.
Ch e, m. Sch pe. Aylesbury CC. See also
Bishopstone. Ch has famous carved Nmn
font.

STONE Glos
156 ST 6895 8m NE of Severn Rd Br.
CP(Ham and Stne), 1,103. Thornbury RD.
P Berkeley. Ch e. Sch pe. S Glos CC.

STONE Kent
161, 171 TQ 5774 2m E of Dartford.
CP, 7,721. Dtfd RD. P Dtfd. Ch e, b, c.
Sch p, pe. Dtfd CC. See also Bean. Indstrl.
13c ch; inside remarkably similar to
Westminster Abbey.

STONE Kent
184 TQ 9327 5m NNE of Rye.
CP(Stne-cum-Ebony), 434. Tenterden RD.
P Tntdn. Ch e, b. Ashfd CC.

STONE Staffs
110, 119 SJ 9034 7m NNW of Stafford.
UD, 10,985. P. Stffd and Stne CC. Trent
Valley tn.

STONE Worcs
130 SO 8575 2m SE of Kidderminster.
CP, 706. Kddrmnstr RD. P Kddrmnstr.
Ch e. Sch pe. Kddrmnstr CC. See also
Shenstone.

STONE ALLERTON Som
165 ST 4051 4m WSW of Cheddar. Loc,
Chpl Allerton CP. Ch b, m.

STON EASTON Som
166 ST 6253 4m W of Radstock. CP, 489.
Clutton RD. P Bath. Ch e, m. N Som CC.
See also Clapton. Stn Eastn Pk, stone hse in
style of William Kent.

STONEBROOM Derbys
112 SK 4159 3m N of Alfreton. Loc,
Shirland and Higham CP. P DERBY.
Ch e, b, m2. Sch p, s.

STONE CHAIR Yorks (W)
96, 102 SE 1127 2m NE of Halifax. Loc,
Queensbury and Shelf UD.

STONE CROSS Sussex (E)
183 TQ 6104 4m N of Eastbourne. Loc,
Westham CP. Ch e.

STONEGATE Sussex (E)
183 TQ 6628 3m SE of Wadhurst. Loc,
Ticehurst CP. P Wdhst. Ch e. Sch pe.

STONEGRAVE Yorks (N)
92 SE 6577 5m SE of Helmsley. CP, 76.
Hlmsly RD. P YORK. Ch e. Thirsk and
Malton CC.

STONEHAUGH Nthmb
77 NY 7976 5m SSW of Bellingham. Loc,
Wark CP. P Hexham. Unfinished Forestry
Commission vllge.

STONEHOUSE Glos
156 SO 8005 3m W of Stroud. CP, 5,311.
Strd RD. P. Ch e, b, m, r, v. Sch p, s.
Strd CC.

STONEHOUSE Nthmb
76 NY 6958 3m S of Haltwhistle. Loc,
Coanwood CP.

STONE HOUSE Yorks (W)
90 SD 7785 7m WSW of Hawes. Loc,
Dent CP.

STONELEIGH Warwicks
132 SP 3372 4m S of Coventry. CP.
Warwick RD. P Cvntry. Ch e. Sch pe. Wrwck
and Leamington CC. Red sandstone ch,
mainly Nmn. Stnlgh Abbey, Ggn hse with
rems of mdvl monastic bldngs. Hse badly
damaged by fire, 1960.

STONELY Hunts
134 TL 1067 6m NW of St Neots. Loc,
Kimbolton CP.

STONESBY Leics
122 SK 8224 6m NE of Melton Mowbray.
Loc, Sproxton CP. P Mltn Mbry. Ch e, m.

STONESFIELD Oxon
145 SP 3917 3m SE of Charlbury. CP, 752.
Chipping Norton RD. P OXFORD. Ch e, m.
Sch p. Banbury CC.

STONE'S GREEN Essex
150 TM 1626 5m SE of Manningtree. Loc,
Gt Oakley CP. P Harwich. Ch m.

STONE STREET Kent
171 TQ 5754 3m E of Sevenoaks. Loc,
Seal CP.

Stoney Cross

STONEY CROSS Hants
179 SU 2611 9m SW of Romsey. Loc, Minstead CP. 1m NE, Rufus Stone commemorates death of William II.

STONEYHILLS Essex
162 TQ 9497 1m N of Burnham-on-Crouch. Loc, Bnhm-on-Crch UD.

STONEY MIDDLETON Derbys
111 SK 2375 4m N of Bakewell. CP, 531. Bkwll RD. P SHEFFIELD. Ch e, v. Sch pe. W Derbys CC. Octagonal ch.

STONEY STANTON Leics
132 SP 4994 4m E of Hinckley. CP, 1,341. Blaby RD. P LEICESTER. Ch e, m, v. Sch pe. Blby CC (Harborough). Large stone quarries.

STONEY STRATTON Som
166 ST 6539 3m NNW of Bruton. Loc, Evercreech CP.

STONEY STRETTON Shrops
118 SJ 3809 7m WSW of Shrewsbury. Loc, Westbury CP.

STONHAM ASPAL Suffolk (E)
136 TM 1359 5m E of Stowmarket. CP, 418. Gipping RD. P Stmkt. Ch e, m. Sch pe. Eye CC.

STONNALL Staffs
120 SK 0703 5m NE of Walsall. Loc, Shenstone CP. P Wlsll Wood, Wlsll. Ch e. Sch pe.

STONOR Oxon·
159 SU 7388 4m NNW of Henley. CP(Pishill w Stnr), 306. Hnly RD. P Hnly-on-Thames. Ch r. Hnly CC. RC chpl attached to Tdr and later Stnr Pk.

STONTON WYVILLE Leics
133 SP 7395 5m N of Mkt Harborough. CP, 40. Mkt Hbrgh RD. Ch e. Hbrgh CC. Ch has Brudenell monmts.

STONY STRATFORD Bucks
146 SP 7840 2m W of Wolverton. Loc, Wlvtn UD. P Wlvtn.

STOODLEIGH Devon
164 SS 9218 4m NNW of Tiverton. CP, 278. Tvtn RD. P Tvtn. Ch e. Sch p. Tvtn CC.

STOPHAM Sussex (W)
181, 182 TQ 0218 2m W of Pulborough. CP, 140. Petworth RD. Ch e. Chichester CC (Horsham). 15c br of seven arches span R Arun.

STOPSLEY Beds
147 TL 1023 2m NNE of Luton. Loc, Ltn CB. P Ltn. Ltn E BC (Ltn).

STOPTIDE Cornwall
185 SW 9475 4m NW of Wadebridge. Loc, St Minver Lowlands CP. Wdbrdge and Padstow RD. N Cnwll CC.

STORETON Ches
100, 109 SJ 3084 3m SSW of Birkenhead. Loc, Bebington MB.

STORMY CORNER Lancs
100 SD 4707 ESE of Ormskirk. Loc, Skelmersdale and Holland UD.

STORRIDGE Herefs
143 SO 7548 3m NW of Malvern. Loc, Cradley CP. P Mlvn, Worcs. Ch e.

STORRINGTON Sussex (W)
182 TQ 0184 4m SE of Pulborough. CP, 2,784. Chanctonbury RD. P Plbrgh. Ch e, m, r, v. Sch p. Shoreham CC (Arundel and Shrhm).

STORTH Westm
89 SD 4780 6m NNW of Carnforth. Loc, Beetham CP. P Milnthorpe. Ch m. Sch pe.

STOTFOLD Beds
147 TL 2136 3m NNW of Baldock. CP, 5,334. Biggleswade RD. P Hitchin, Herts. Ch e, b3, m2, s. Sch jb, jgie. Mid-Beds CC. Mental hsptl.

STOTTESDON Shrops
129, 130 SO 6782 7m SSW of Bridgnorth. CP, 811. Brdgnth RD. P Kidderminster, Worcs. Ch e. Sch pe. Ludlow CC. See also Chorley. Vllge in remote hilly country. Ch has Saxon doorway, elaborate Nmn font, Dec windows etc.

STOUGHTON Leics
121, 122 SK 6402 4m ESE of Leicester. CP, 236. Billesdon RD. Ch e. Harborough CC (Melton).

STOUGHTON Surrey
169, 170 SU 9851 1m NNW of Guildford. Loc, Gldfd MB. P Gldfd.

STOUGHTON Sussex (W)
181 SU 8011 6m NW of Chichester.
CP, 691. Chchstr RD. Ch e. Chchstr CC. See
also Forestside, Walderton. Downland vllge
with Nmn ch.

STOULTON Worcs
143, 144 SO 9049 4m NW of Pershore.
CP, 423. Pshre RD. P WORCESTER. Ch e.
S Worcs CC.

STOURBRIDGE Worcs
130, 131 SO 9084 6m NE of Kidderminster.
MB, 54,331. P. Halesowen and Stbrdge BC.
See also Amblecote, Lye, Pedmore. Indstrl
tn mnfg iron and glass.

STOURPAINE Dorset
178 ST 8609 3m NNW of Blandford.
CP, 388. Blndfd RD. P Blndfd Forum.
Ch e, m. Sch pe. N Dst CC.

STOURPORT-ON-SEVERN Worcs
130 SO 8171 3m SSW of Kidderminster.
UD, 17,913. P. Kddrmnstr CC. See also
Areley Kings, Astley Cross, Wilden. R Svn,
R Stour, and Staffs and Worcs Canal meet
here. Locks; Ggn canal basin full of boats.
Iron wks, carpet factories.

STOUR PROVOST Dorset
166 ST 7921 4m W of Shaftesbury.
CP, 453. Shftsbry RD. P Gillingham. Ch e.
Sch p. N Dst CC. See also Stour Row.

STOUR ROW Dorset
166 ST 8221 3m WSW of Shaftesbury. Loc,
Stour Provost CP. Ch e.

STOURTON Staffs
130 SO 8585 3m W of Stourbridge. Loc,
Kinver CP. P Stbrdge, Worcs.

STOURTON Warwicks
145 SP 2936 3m SE of Shipston on Stour.
CP, 118. Shpstn on Str RD. Ch m. Sch pe.
Stratford-on-Avon CC (Strtfd).

STOURTON Wilts
166 ST 7834 6m E of Bruton. CP(Sttn
w Gasper), 302. Mere and Tisbury RD.
P Warminster. Ch e. Westbury CC. See also
Gspr. Partly in grnds of Stourhead (NT)*,
18c Palladian hse. Pk with lake, temples etc.
On hill to W, King Alfred's Twr (see
S Brewham). On hill to E, White Sheet
Cstle, Iron Age fort, Neolithic earthworks.

STOURTON CAUNDLE Dorset
178 ST 7115 5m ESE of Sherborne.
CP, 371. Sturminster RD. P Stmnstr
Newton. Ch e, c. Sch p. N Dst CC.

STOVEN Suffolk (E)
137 TM 4481 5m NE of Halesworth.
CP, 110. Wainford RD. Ch e.
Lowestoft CC.

STOW Lincs (L)
104 SK 8881 7m SE of Gainsborough.
CP, 358. Gnsbrgh RD. P LINCOLN.
Ch e, m. Gnsbrgh CC. Great Saxon/Nmn ch,
landmark for miles. Traditionally site of
Saxon cathedral city of Sidnacester.

STOW BARDOLPH Norfolk
124 TF 6205 2m NE of Downham Mkt.
CP, 1,054. Dnhm RD. P King's Lynn.
Ch e, m2. SW Nflk CC. See also Barroway
Drove, Stowbridge. Ch: monmts to Hare
family, esp life-size wax effigy in real
clothes, 1744.

STOW BEDON Norfolk
136 TL 9596 6m W of Attleborough.
CP, 309. Wayland RD. P Attlbrgh. Ch e.
S Nflk CC. See also Breckles. Small mere,
one of several in E Breckland.

STOWBRIDGE Norfolk
124 TF 6007 3m NNW of Downham Mkt.
Loc, Stow Bardolph CP. P King's Lynn.
Sch p.

STOW CUM QUY Cambs
135 TL 5260 5m ENE of Cambridge.
CP, 447. Chesterton RD.
P(Quy), CMBRDGE. Ch e, m. Sch p.
Cambs CC.

STOWE Shrops
129 SO 3173 2m ENE of Knighton.
CP, 167. Clun and Bishop's Cstle RD. Ch e.
Ludlow CC.

STOWE Staffs
120 SK 0027 6m NE of Stafford. CP, 1,071.
Stffd RD. P(Stwe-by-Chartley), STFFD.
Ch e. Sch p. Stffd and Stone CC. See also
Drointon, Hixon.

STOWELL Som
166 ST 6822 4m SSW of Wincanton. Loc,
Charlton Horethorne CP. Ch e.

Stowey

STOWEY Som
165, 166 ST 5959 8m S of Bristol. Loc,
Stowey-Sutton CP. Clutton RD. Ch e.
N Som CC.

STOWFORD Devon
163 SS 6540 7m SW of Lynton. Loc,
Bratton Fleming CP.

STOWFORD Devon
175 SX 4386 7m ENE of Launceston.
CP, 266. Tavistock RD. Ch e. W Dvn CC
(Tvstck). See also Portgate.

STOWLANGTOFT Suffolk (W)
136 TL 9568 7m ENE of Bury St Edmunds.
CP, 266. Thedwastre RD. P Bury St Eds.
Ch e. Bury St Eds CC. Ch: wood-carving.

STOW LONGA Hunts
134 TL 1070 8m W of Huntingdon. CP, 89.
St Neots RD. Ch e. Hunts CC.

STOW MARIES Essex
162 TQ 8399 5m SSW of Maldon. CP, 182.
Mldn RD. P Chelmsford. Ch e. Mldn CC.

STOWMARKET Suffolk (E)
136 TM 0558 11m NW of Ipswich.
UD, 8,670. P. Eye CC. See also Combs
Ford. Mkt and indstrl tn. Abbots Hall
museum of rural E Anglian life.

STOW-ON-THE-WOLD Glos
144 SP 1925 8m W of Chipping Norton.
CP, 1,780. N Cotswold RD. P Cheltenham.
Ch e, b, m, r. Sch p. Cirencester and
Tewkesbury CC. Hilltop Cotswold tn on a
main rd. Wide mkt square. Old ch restored
19c. New housing in local stone on S outskirts.

STOWTING Kent
173 TR 1241 5m NNW of Hythe. CP, 166.
Elham RD. P Ashfd. Ch e, v. Sch pe.
Folkestone and Hthe CC. See also
Lymbridge Grn.

STOWUPLAND Suffolk (E)
136 TM 0659 1m ENE of Stowmarket.
CP, 1,070. Gipping RD. P Stmkt. Ch e, c.
Sch p. Eye CC. To N, Columbine Hall,
moated mnr hse, now a farmhouse.

STRADBROKE Suffolk (E)
137 TM 2373 5m E of Eye. CP, 835.
Hartismere RD. P Diss, Norfolk. Ch e, b.
Sch pe, s. Eye CC. See also Ashfield Grn.

STRADISHALL Suffolk (W)
148, 149 TL 7452 5m NNW of Clare.
CP, 483. Clre RD. P Newmarket. Ch e.
Bury St Edmunds CC. Airfield.

STRADSETT Norfolk
124 TF 6605 4m ENE of Downham Mkt.
CP, 99. Dnhm RD. Ch e. SW Nflk CC.

STRAGGLETHORPE Lincs (K)
113 SK 9152 7m E of Newark. CP(Brant
Broughton and Strgglthpe), 618.
N Kesteven RD. Ch e. Grantham CC.

STRAMSHALL Staffs
120 SK 0835 2m NNW of Uttoxeter. Loc,
Uttxtr Rural CP. Uttxtr RD. Ch e, m.
Burton CC.

STRANDS Cumb
88 NY 1204 6m ENE of Seascale. Loc,
Nether Wasdale CP. Ennerdale RD. Ch e.
Whitehaven CC.

STRATFIELD MORTIMER Berks
168, 169 SU 6664 7m SSW of Reading.
CP, 2,267. Bradfield RD. P(Mtmr), Rdng.
Ch e, m2. Sch ie, pe. Newbury CC. See also
Mtmr Cmmn.

STRATFIELD SAYE Hants
169 SU 6861 7m NNE of Basingstoke.
CP, 296. Bsngstke RD. P Reading, Berks.
Ch e. Bsngstke CC. See also W End Grn. To
E, S.S. Pk, given by nation to Duke of
Wellington. 1m E of hse, Wllngtn monmt.

STRATFIELD TURGIS Hants
169 SU 6960 6m NE of Basingstoke.
CP, 125. Bsngstke RD. Ch e. Bsngstke CC.

STRATFORD London
161 TQ 3884 6m ENE of Charing Cross.
Loc, Newham LB. Nwhm NW BC
(W Ham N). To E of Lee valley. Large rly
wks.

STRATFORD ST ANDREW Suffolk (E)
137 TM 3560 3m SW of Saxmundham.
CP, 158. Blyth RD. Ch e. Eye CC. Beside
the Alde and the A12 rd, opposite
Farnham, qv. Bernard Shaw made his wife's
'acquaintance seriously' at former rectory,
now The Grange.

STRATFORD ST MARY Suffolk (E)
149 TM 0434 4m WNW of Manningtree.

CP, 480. Samford RD. P Colchester, Essex. Ch e, v. Sch p. Sudbury and Woodbridge CC. Bypass between vllge and its ch.

STRATFORD TONY Wilts
167 SU 0926 4m SW of Salisbury. CP(Strtfd Toney), 82. Slsbry and Wilton RD. Ch e. Slsbry CC.

STRATFORD-UPON-AVON Warwicks
131/144 SP 2055 10m, SW of Leamington. MB, 19,449. P. Strtfd-on-Avn CC (Strtfd). See also Alveston, Shottery. Bthplce and home of Shakespeare; three hses* with Shkspre associations. Shkspre Memorial Theatre. Harvard Hse*. Tn has half-timbered and Ggn hses. Brewery.

STRATTON Cornwall
174 SS 2306 1m E of Bude. UD(Bde-Strttn), 5,629. P Bde. N Cnwll CC. Being inland, has kept its old character, unlike Bude.

STRATTON Dorset
178 SY 6593 3m NW of Dorchester. CP, 273. Dchstr RD. P Dchstr. Ch e, m. W Dst CC. See also Grimstone.

STRATTON Glos
157 SP 0103 1m NNW of Cirencester. Loc, Crncstr UD. P Crncstr.

STRATTON AUDLEY Oxon
145, 146 SP 6026 3m NNE of Bicester. CP, 339. Ploughley RD. P Bcstr. Ch e. Sch ie. Banbury CC (Henley).

STRATTON ON THE FOSSE Som
166 ST 6550 3m SSW of Radstock. CP, 1,025. Shepton Mallet RD. P Bath. Ch e, m, r2. Sch pe, pr. Wells CC. Downside Abbey, Benedictine monastery and RC boys' public sch. Abbey bldngs late 19c and early 20c.

STRATTON ST MARGARET Wilts
157 SU 1787 2m NE of Swindon. CP, 11,191. Highworth RD. P Swndn. Ch e, b2, m3, v. Sch i, j, p2, s. Devizes CC.

STRATTON ST MICHAEL Norfolk
137 TM 2093 8m SE of Wymondham. Loc, Long Strttn CP. Ch e.

STRATTON STRAWLESS Norfolk
126 TG 2220 4m SSE of Aylsham. CP, 229.

St Faith's and Aylshm RD. P NORWICH, NOR 03Y. Ch e. N Nflk CC (Central Nflk).

STREAT Sussex (E)
183 TQ 3515 5m NW of Lewes. CP, 193. Chailey RD. Ch e. Lws CC.

STREATHAM London
160, 171 TQ 3072 5m S of Charing Cross. Loc, Lambeth LB. Strthm BC.

STREATLEY Beds
147 TL 0728 4m N of Luton. CP, 2,452. Ltn RD. P Ltn. Ch e, b. Sch p. S Beds CC. See also Sharpenhoe.

STREATLEY Berks
158 SU 5980 4m NW of Pangbourne. CP, 829. Bradfield RD. Ch e. Sch pe. Newbury CC. On Thames, with br across to Goring. To NW are Lardon Chase and Lough Down (NT): views over Thames valley.

STREET Lancs
94 SD 5252 6m SSE of Lancaster. Loc, Nether Wyersdale CP. Garstang RD. N Fylde CC.

STREET Som
165 ST 4836 2m SW of Glastonbury. UD, 8,161. P. Wells CC. Shoe factory. Tanneries.

STREET END Sussex (W)
181 SZ 8599 3m S of Chichester. Loc, Chchstr RD. Chchstr CC.

STREET GATE Co Durham
78 NZ 2159 4m SW of Gateshead. Loc, Whickham UD.

STREETHAY Staffs
120 SK 1410 2m ENE of Lichfield. CP, 301. Lchfld RD. Lchfld and Tamworth CC.

STREETHOUSE Yorks (W)
96, 102 SE 3920 4m WSW of Pontefract. Loc, Featherstone UD. P Pntfrct.

STREET ON THE FOSSE Som
166 ST 6138 3m S of Shepton Mallet. Loc, Pylle CP.

STREFFORD Shrops
129 SO 4485 2m NNE of Craven Arms. Loc, Wistanstow CP.

STRELLEY Notts
112, 121 SK 5141 4m WNW of Nottingham.
CP, 97. Basford RD. Ch e. Beeston CC
(Rushcliffe). Ch. 14c chancel; monmts;
scrn. Close to M1 motorway just N of
Trowell Service Area.

STRENSALL Yorks (N)
92, 97, 98 SE 6360 6m NNE of York.
CP, 1,138. Flaxton RD. P YK. Ch e, m.
Sch pe. Thirsk and Malton CC. Garrison tn.

STRETCHOLT Som
165 ST 2944 5m N of Bridgwater. Loc,
Pawlett CP.

STRETE Devon
188 SX 8446 4m SW of Dartmouth.
CP, 346. Kingsbridge RD. P Dtmth. Ch e, m.
Totnes CC.

STRETFORD Lancs
101 SJ 7994 4m SW of Manchester.
MB, 54,011. P MNCHSTR. Strtfd BC.
Engineering, chemicals.

STRETHALL Essex
148 TL 4839 3m WNW of Saffron Walden.
CP, 23. Sffrn Wldn RD. Ch e. Sffrn
Wldn CC. Ch partly Saxon; palimpsest
brasses.

STRETHAM Cambs
135 TL 5174 4m SSW of Ely. CP, 1,009.
Ely RD. P Ely. Ch e, b, m. Sch p. Isle of
Ely CC. Reputedly driest place in England.
There is a rare preserved example of
steam-driven beam engine* once used for
fen drainage.

STRETTINGTON Sussex (W)
181 SU 8807 2m NE of Chichester. Loc,
Westhampnett CP. To N in large pk,
Goodwood Hse*, late 18c hse; art
collection.

STRETTON Ches
101 SJ 6182 4m S of Warrington. CP, 579.
Runcorn RD. P WRRNGTN. Ch e. Sch pe.
Rncn CC.

STRETTON Ches
109 SJ 4452 7m ENE of Wrexham. CP, 43.
Tarvin RD. Nantwich CC.

STRETTON Derbys
111 SK 3961 6m E of Matlock. CP, 601.
Chesterfield RD. P DERBY. Ch m. Sch pe.
NE Derbys CC.

STRETTON Rutland
122/123 SK 9415 7m NE of Oakham.
CP, 97. Oakhm RD. P Oakhm. Ch e. Rtlnd
and Stamford CC.

STRETTON Staffs
119 SJ 8811 6m W of Cannock. CP, 176.
Cnnck RD. P STAFFORD. Ch e. Sch pe.
SW Staffs CC (Cnnck). On line of Roman rd
near its junction with Watling St; Roman
sites in area.

STRETTON Staffs
120 SK 2526 2m N of Burton-on-Trent.
CP, 2,222. Tutbury RD. P Btn-on-Trnt.
Ch e, m. Sch p. Btn CC.

STRETTON GRANDISON Herefs
142, 143 SO 6344 7m S of Bromyard.
CP, 127. Ledbury RD. Ch e. Leominster CC.

STRETTON-ON-DUNSMORE Warwicks
132 SP 4072 6m SE of Coventry. CP, 919.
Rugby RD. P Rgby. Ch e. Sch pe.
Rgby CC.

STRETTON ON FOSSE Warwicks
144 SP 2238 4m NNE of Moreton-in-Marsh.
CP, 311. Shipston on Stour RD.
P Mtn-in-Msh, Glos. Ch e, m. Sch pe.
Stratford-on-Avon CC (Strtfd).

STRETTON SUGWAS Herefs
142 SO 4642 3m NW of Hereford. CP, 501.
Hrfd RD. Ch e. Sch pe. Leominster CC. Ch,
19c reconstruction from old materials, has
richly carved Nmn typmpanum and black
and white timbered twr.

STRETTON UNDER FOSSE Warwicks
132 SP 4581 5m NW of Rugby. CP, 378.
Rgby RD. P Rgby. Ch m. Rgby CC.

STRICKLAND, GREAT Westm
83 NY 5522 5m SSE of Penrith. See
Gt Strcklnd.

STRINGSTON Som
164 ST 1742 7m E of Watchet. CP, 145.
Williton RD. Ch e. Bridgwater CC. See also
Kilton, Lilstock.

STRIXTON Northants
133 SP 9061 4m S of Wellingborough.
CP, 46. Wllngbrgh RD. Ch e. Wllngbrgh CC.

STROOD Kent
171, 172 TQ 7369 just NW of Rochester.
Loc, Rchstr MB. P Rchstr. Indstrl. Temple
Mnr (A.M.), 13c commandery of Knights
Templar.

STROOD GREEN Surrey
170 TQ 1948 2m SE of Dorking. Loc,
Betchworth CP. P Btchwth.

STROUD Glos
156 SO 8505 8m S of Gloucester.
UD, 19,125. P. Strd CC. See also
Rodborough. Hilly. Indstrl tn since mdvl
times. A centre of wool cloth manufacture,
but industry now much diversified. 16c tn
hall, restored in 19c.

STROUD Hants
181 SU 7223 2m W of Petersfield. Loc,
Ptrsfld UD. P Ptrsfld.

STROXTON Lincs (K)
113, 122 SK 9031 3m S of Grantham.
CP(Lit Ponton and Strxtn), 255.
W Kesteven RD. Ch e. Rutland and
Stamford CC.

STRUBBY Lincs (L)
105 TF 4582 4m WSW of Mablethorpe.
CP(Strbby w Woodthorpe), 222. Louth RD.
P Alford. Ch e, m. Lth CC. RAF stn.

STRUMPSHAW Norfolk
126 TG 3507 8m E of Norwich. CP, 486.
Blofieldd and Flegg RD.
P NRWCH, NOR 77Z. Ch e. Sch p.
Yarmouth CC. See also Buckenham,
Hassingham.

STUBBINGTON Hants
180 SU 5503 3m SW of Fareham. Loc,
Frhm UD. P Frhm.

STUBBINS Lancs
95, 101 SD 7918 5m N of Bury. Loc,
Ramsbottom UD. P Rmsbttm, Bury.

STUBB'S CROSS Kent
172, 184 TQ 9838 3m SW of Ashford. Loc,
Kingsnorth CP. P Ashfd.

STUBHAMPTON Dorset
178, 179 ST 9113 5m NNE of Blandford.
Loc, Tarrant Gunville CP.

STUBTON Lincs (K)
113 SK 8748 6m ESE of Newark. CP, 226.
W Kesteven RD. Ch e. Sch pe. Grantham CC.

STUCKTON Hants
179 SU 1613 1m SE of Fordingbridge. Loc,
Fdngbrdge CP. P Fdngbrdge. Ch v.

STUDHAM Beds
147, 159 TL 0215 4m S of Dunstable.
CP, 760. Luton RD. P Dnstble. Ch e, m.
Sch pe. S Beds CC.

STUDLAND Dorset
179 SZ 0382 2m N of Swanage. CP, 635.
Wareham and Purbeck RD. P Swnge.
Ch e, m. S Dst CC. Overlooks sweep of
Stdlnd Bay. Nmn ch. 1m SW, Ballard Point.
To N, nature reserve round Little Sea.

STUDLEY Oxon
145, 146 SP 5912 6m NE of Oxford.
CP(Horton-cum-Stdly), 284. Ploughley RD.
P(Htn-cum-Stdly), OXFD. Ch e.
Mid-Oxon CC (Henley). Thatched cottages.
17c almshouses. Stdly Prior, Jcbn, now a
hotel.

STUDLEY Warwicks
131 SP 0763 3m SSE of Redditch. CP.
Alcester RD. P. Ch e, b, m, r. Sch i, j, pr, s.
Stratford-on-Avon CC (Strtfd). See also
Mappleborough Grn. Stdly Cstle, 19c bldng
on site of Nmn cstle, now agricultural
college.

STUDLEY Wilts
157 ST 9671 2m W of Calne. Loc, Clne
Without CP. Clne and Chippenham RD.
Ch e, b, m. Chppnhm CC.

STUDLEY ROGER Yorks (W)
91 SE 2970 1m WSW of Ripon. CP, 119.
Rpn and Pateley Br RD. Rpn CC. To W,
Stdly Royal*, 18c pk with lakes, temples,
statues (orig hse burned down 1945).
Beyond pk, Fountains Abbey*, impressive
rems of Cistercian abbey, and 17c hse*
largely blt with materials from its ruins.

STUKELEY, GREAT Hunts
134 TL 2174 2m NNW of Huntingdon. See
Gt Stkly.

STUNTNEY Cambs
135 TL 5578 2m SE of Ely. Loc, Ely UD.
P Ely.

STURBRIDGE Staffs
110, 119 SJ 8330 5m WSW of Stone. Loc,
Eccleshall CP. Drake Hall Prison.

STURMER Essex
148 TL 6943 2m SE of Haverhill. CP, 321.
Halstead RD. P Hvrhll, Suffolk. Ch e.
Saffron Walden CC.

Sturminster Common

STURMINSTER COMMON Dorset
178 ST 7812 7m NW of Blandford. Loc,
Stmnstr Newton CP.

STURMINSTER MARSHALL Dorset
179 SY 9499 4m W of Wimborne. CP, 1,189.
Wmbne and Cranborne RD. P Wmbne.
Ch e, c, m. Sch p. N Dst CC. See also Almer.

STURMINSTER NEWTON Dorset
178 ST 7814 8m NW of Blandford.
CP, 1,958. Stmnstr RD. P. Ch e, m2.
Sch p, s. N Dst CC. See also Broad Oak,
Stmnstr Cmmn. Mdvl br over R Stour has
transportation tablet; cf Durweston.

STURRY Kent
173 TR 1760 2m NE of Canterbury.
CP, 3,305. Bridge-Blean RD. P Cntrbry.
Ch e, v. Sch pe, s. Cntrbry CC. See also
Broadoak.

STURTON Lincs (L)
104 SE 9704 3m SW of Brigg. Loc,
Scawby CP.

STURTON BY STOW Lincs (L)
104 SK 8980 8m SE of Gainsborough.
CP, 662. Gnsbrgh RD. P LINCOLN.
Ch e, m3. Sch p, s. Gnsbrgh CC.

STURTON, GREAT Lincs (L)
105 TF 2176 5m NW of Horncastle. See
Gt Sttn.

STURTON LE STEEPLE Notts
104 SK 7884 4m SSW of Gainsborough.
CP, 399. E Retford RD. P Rtfd. Ch e, m.
Sch pe. Bassetlaw CC. See also
Littleborough. The 'steeple' is tall and a
notable landmark.

STUSTON Suffolk (E)
136 TM 1378 2m SE of Diss. CP, 179.
Hartismere RD. Ch e. Eye CC. Hses
scattered round gorse-sprinkled commons
running down to Dss golf course. Ch aloof
behind trees.

STUTTON Suffolk (E)
150 TM 1534 6m S of Ipswich. CP, 780.
Samford RD. P Ipswich. Ch e, m. Sch pe.
Sudbury and Woodbridge CC.

STUTTON Yorks (W)
97 SE 4841 1m S of Tadcaster. CP(Stttn
w Hazlewood), 359. Tdcstr RD. P Tdcstr.
Barkston Ash CC.

STYAL Ches
101 SJ 8383 2m NNW of Wilmslow. Loc,
Wlmslw UD. P Wlmslw. 18c vllge owned by
NT, together with Quarry Bank Cotton Mill
(1784) and a stretch of Bollin valley; early
example of complete indstrl community.

STYRRUP Notts
103 SK 6090 7m NNE of Worksop.
CP(Strrp w Oldcotes), 430. Wksp RD. Ch m.
Bassetlaw CC.

SUCKLEY Worcs
143 SO 7251 5m NW of Malvern. CP, 566.
Martley RD. P WORCESTER. Ch e. Sch p.
Kidderminster CC. See also Longley Grn.

SUDBOROUGH Northants
134 SP 9682 3m NW of Thrapston. CP, 154.
Oundle and Thrpstn RD. P Kettering. Ch e.
Wellingborough CC (Peterborough).

SUDBOURNE Suffolk (E)
150 TM 4153 2m N of Orford. CP, 345.
Deben RD. P Woodbridge. Ch e, b.
**Eye CC. On edge of Forestry Commission
forest. Ch isolated.**

SUDBROOKE Lincs (L)
104 TF 0375 5m NE of Lincoln. CP, 257.
Welton RD. Ch e. Gainsborough CC.

SUDBURY Derbys
120 SK 1632 4m ESE of Uttoxeter.
CP, 997. Ashbourne RD. P DERBY. Ch e.
Sch p. W Derbys CC. SdbryHall (NT)*, 17c.
Sdbry open prison, formerly hsptl.

SUDBURY Suffolk (W)
149 TL 8741 12m NW of Colchester.
MB, 8,183. P. Sdbry and Woodbridge CC.
Stour valley tn with many old hses and
many new. Gainsborough's Hse*, bthplce of
the painter, 1727.

SUDGROVE Glos
157 SO 9307 7m WNW of Cirencester. Loc,
Miserden CP.

SUFFIELD Norfolk
126 TG 2232 4m WNW of N Walsham.
C P , 1 4 2 . Erpingham R D .
P NORWICH, NOR 48Y. Ch e. N Nflk CC.

SUFFIELD Yorks (N)
93 SE 9890 4m WNW of Scarborough.
CP(Sffld-cum-Everley), 50. Scbrgh RD.
Scbrgh CC (Scbrgh and Whitby).

SUGNALL Staffs
110, 119 SJ 7930 7m WSW of Stone. Loc,
Eccleshall CP. P STAFFORD.

SULGRAVE Northants
145, 146 SP 5545 5m NNW of Brackley.
CP, 335. Brckly RD. P Bnbry, Oxon.
Ch e, b. Sch pe. Daventry CC (S Nthnts).
Slgrve Mnr*, home of George Washington's
great-grandfather, who emigrated to
America 1657. Wshngtn arms - stars and
stripes - carved over doorway (cf Garsdon,
Wickhamford).

SULHAM Berks
158, 159 SU 6474 2m SSE of Pangbourne.
CP, 98. Bradfield RD. Ch e. Sch pe.
Newbury CC.

SULHAMSTEAD Berks
158, 169 SU 6368 6m WSW of Reading.
CP, 1,522. Bradfield RD. P Rdng. Ch e.
Sch pe. Newbury CC. The ch belongs to the
eccl par of Slhmstd Bannister.

SULHAMSTEAD ABBOTS Berks
158, 169 SU 6467 6m SW of Reading. Loc,
Slhmstd CP. Ch e, c.

SUMMERBRIDGE Yorks (W)
91 SE 2062 3m ESE of Pateley Br. Loc,
Hartwith cum Winsley CP. Ripon and Ptly
Br RD. P Harrogate. Ch m. Sch p. Rpn CC.

SUMMERCOURT Cornwall
185 SW 8856 6m SE of Newquay. Loc,
St Enoder CP. P Nquay. Ch m3.

SUMMERHOUSE Co Durham
85 NZ 2019 6m WNW of Darlington.
CP, 86. Dlngtn RD. P Dlngtn. Ch m. Bishop
Auckland CC (Sedgefield).

SUMMERSEAT Lancs
101 SD 7914 3m N of Bury. Loc, Bury CB,
Ramsbottom UD. P Bury. Bury and
Radcliffe BC, Rossendale BC.

SUMMIT Lancs
95, 101 SD 9418 4m S of Todmorden. Loc,
Littleborough UD. P Lttlbrgh.

SUMMIT Lancs
101 SD 9109 3m SSE of Rochdale. Loc,
Royton UD. P Heywood.

SUNBURY Surrey
170 TQ 0969 4m ESE of Staines.
UD (Snbry-on-Thames), 40,035.

P (Snbry-on-Thms, Middx)
Spelthorne BC (CC). See also Littleton,
Shepperton. Among reservoirs S of London
(Heathrow) Airpt. Kempton Pk Racecourse
to E.

SUNDERLAND Co Durham
78 NZ 3956 10m ESE of Newcastle.
CB, 216,892. P. BCs: Sndrlnd N, Sndrlnd S.
See also Monkwearmouth, Roker, Ryhope.
Important port and shipbuilding tn. Other
industries incl engineering, iron and steel,
glass.

SUNDERLAND Cumb
82 NY 1735 5m NE of Cockermouth. Loc,
Blindcrake CP.

SUNDERLAND Lancs
94 SD 4256 5m S of Morecambe. Loc,
Overton CP. P (Sndlnd Point), Mcmbe.
Formerly port for Lancaster.

SUNDERLAND BRIDGE Co Durham
85 NZ 2637 3m S of Durham. CP, 907.
Drhm RD. P DRHM. Ch e. Drhm CC. See
also Croxdale.

SUNDON Beds
147 TL 0427 4m NE of Dunstable.
CP, 6,392. Luton RD. P Ltn. Ch e, m.
Sch p. S Beds CC. See also Upr Sndn.

SUNDON PARK Beds
147 TL 0525 3m NW of Luton. Loc,
Ltn CB. Ltn W BC (S Beds CC).

SUNDRIDGE Kent
171 TQ 4855 3m W of Sevenoaks.
CP, 2,248. Svnks RD. P Svnks. Ch e. Sch pe.
Svnks CC. See also Ide Hill. Sndrdge Old
Hall (NT), restored 15c timbered hse. To
NW, Combe Bank*, 18c mansion with
Adam and Walter Crane rooms.

SUNK ISLAND Yorks (E)
105 TA 2619 7m SW of Withernsea.
CP, 409. Holderness RD. Ch e.
Bridlington CC.

SULLINGTON Sussex (W)
182 TQ 0913 1m SE of Storrington.
CP, 1,354. Chanctonbury RD. Ch e.
Shoreham CC (Arundel and Shrhm). Ch and
farm under S Downs.

SUNNINGDALE Berks
169, 170 SU 9567 6m WSW of Staines.

CP, 2,522. Windsor RD. P Ascot. Ch e, b, c, m. Sch pe, s. Wndsr and Maidenhead CC (Wndsr). Rsdntl.

SUNNINGHILL Berks
169 SU 9367 6m NE of Camberley. CP, 7,799. Windsor RD. P Ascot. Ch e, m2. Sch pe2, pr, s. Wndsr and Maidenhead CC (Wndsr). See also Asct, S Asct. Merges into Sunningdale, qv.

SUNNINGWELL Berks
158 SP 4900 2m N of Abingdon. CP, 954. Abngdn RD. P Abngdn. Ch e, b. Sch pe. Abngdn CC. Ch has 16c hexagonal porch.

SUNNISIDE Co Durham
78 NZ 2058 4m SW of Gateshead. Loc, Whickham UD. P NEWCASTLE UPON TYNE.

SUNNISIDE Co Durham
85 NZ 1438 1m ESE of Tow Law. Loc, Crook and Willington UD.

SUNNY BROW Co Durham
85 NZ 1934 just S of Willington. Loc, Crook and Wllngtn UD. P Crk.

SUNNYSIDE Sussex (E)
171, 183 TQ 3936 just S of E Grinstead. Loc, E Grnstd UD.

SURBITON London
170 TQ 1867 1m S of Kingston. Loc, Kngstn upon Thames LB. P Surrey. Sbtn BC. Rsdntl distr.

SURFLEET Lincs (H)
123 TF 2528 4m NNE of Spalding. CP, 931. Spldng RD. P Spldng. Ch e, m. Holland w Boston CC.

SURFLEET SEAS END Lincs (H)
123 TF 2728 4m NNE of Spalding. Loc, Spldng RD. Sch p. Holland w Boston CC.

SURLINGHAM Norfolk
126 TG 3106 6m ESE of Norwich. CP, 515. Forehoe and Henstead RD. P NRWCH, NOR 07W. Ch e, m. Sch p. S Nflk CC (Central Nflk).

SUSTEAD Norfolk
126 TG 1837 4m SSW of Cromer. CP, 208. Erpingham RD. Ch e, m. N Nflk CC. See also Bessingham, Metton.

SUSWORTH Lincs (L)
104 SE 8302 6m SSW of Scunthorpe. Loc, Scotter CP. Ch m.

SUTCOMBE Devon
174 SS 3411 5m N of Holsworthy. CP, 245. Hlswthy RD. P Hlswthy. Ch e, m2. Sch p. W Dvn CC (Tavistock).

SUTTERBY Lincs (L)
114 TF 3872 5m WSW of Alford. Loc, Langton by Spilsby CP.

SUTTERTON Lincs (H)
114, 123 TF 2835 6m SSW of Boston. CP, 1,019. Bstn RD. P Bstn. Ch e, b, m. Sch pe. Holland w Bstn CC.

SUTTON Beds
147 TL 2247 3m NE of Biggleswade. CP, 292. Bgglswde RD. P Sandy. Ch e, m. Sch pe. Mid-Beds CC.

SUTTON Cambs
135 TL 4478 6m W of Ely. CP, 1,650. Ely RD. P Ely. Ch e, b, m. Sch pe. Isle of Ely CC. Ch has 'double octagon' twr.

SUTTON Hunts
134 TL 0998 6m W of Peterborough. CCP, 5 Ptrbrgh RD. Ch e. Ptrbrgh BC (CC).

SUTTON Kent
173 TR 3349 3m SW of Deal. CP, 756. Eastry RD. Ch e, b. Dover and Dl CC (Dvr). See also E Studdal.

SUTTON London
170 TQ 2463 5m WSW of Croydon. LB, 168,775. P Surrey. BCs: Carshalton, Cheam. (Cshltn CC, Mitcham BC, Sttn and Chm BC.) See also Beddington, Cshltn, Chm, Wallington.

SUTTON Norfolk
126 TG 3823 7m NE of Wroxham. CP, 451. Smallburgh RD. P NORWICH, NOR 32Z. Ch e, m. Sch pe. N Nflk CC.

SUTTON Notts
103 SK 6884 3m NNW of Retford. CP, 423. E Rtfd RD. P Rtfd. Ch e, m2. Bassetlaw CC.

SUTTON Notts
112, 122 SK 7637 10m W of Grantham. Loc, Granby CP. Ch v.

SUTTON Oxon
158 SP 4106 2m SSW of Eynsham. Loc, Stanton Harcourt CP. Ch m.

SUTTON Shrops
118 SJ 3527 5m ESE of Oswestry. Loc, W Felton CP.

SUTTON Shrops
130 SO 7286 4m S of Bridgnorth. Loc, Chelmarsh CP.

SUTTON Staffs
119 SJ 7622 2m NNE of Newport. Loc, Forton CP. To W of series of locks on Shrops Union Canal - see Norbury.

SUTTON Suffolk (E)
150 TM 3046 3m SE of Woodbridge. CP, 1,691. Deben RD. P Wdbrdge. Ch e, b. Sch p. Sudbury and Wdbrdge CC. Heathland. Sttn Hoo, site of burial-ship discoveries, to NW near Melton. Large airfield to NE.

SUTTON Surrey
170 TQ 1046 5m WSW of Dorking. Loc, Dkng and Horley RD, Guildford RD. Dkng CC.

SUTTON Sussex (W)
181, 182 SU 9715 4m S of Petworth. CP, 190. Ptwth RD. P Pulborough. Ch e. Chichester CC (Horsham).

SUTTON Yorks (E)
103 SE 5512 6m NNW of Doncaster. Loc, Norton CP.

SUTTON Yorks (W)
97 SE 4925 just N of Knottingley. CP(Byram cum Sttn), 940. Osgoldcross RD. Goole CC.

SUTTON-AT-HONE Kent
161, 171 TQ 5570 3m S of Dartford. CP, 3,371. Dtfd RD. P Dtfd. Ch e, b, m, v. Sch pe. Dtfd CC. See also Hawley. Indstrl. Near R Darent, St John's Jerusalem (NT)*, moated 16c–18c hse with rems of Knights Hospitallers chpl.

SUTTON BASSETT Northants
133 SP 7790 3m NE of Mkt Harborough. CP, 59. Kettering RD. Ch e. Kttrng CC.

SUTTON BENGER Wilts
157 ST 9478 4m NNE of Chippenham.

CP, 756. Calne and Chppnhm RD. P Chppnhm. Ch e. Sch pe. Chppnhm CC. See also Lr Seagry, Upr Sgry.

SUTTON BINGHAM Som
177, 178 ST 5411 3m S of Yeovil. Loc, Closworth CP. Ch e. On edge of reservoir. Ch has mdvl wall-paintings.

SUTTON BONINGTON Notts
121 SK 5025 4m NNW of Loughborough. CP, 1,154. Basford RD. P Lghbrgh, Leics. Ch e2, b, m. Sch p. Rushcliffe CC. Sch of Agriculture.

SUTTON BRIDGE Lincs (H)
124 TF 4721 7m N of Wisbech. CP, 3,309. E Elloe RD. P Spalding. Ch e, m, r. Sch i, j. Holland w Boston CC. Swing br over R Nene. Late 19c docks collapsed month after opening and were never rebuilt.

SUTTON CHENEY Leics
121 SK 4100 4m NNW of Hinckley. CP, 481. Mkt Bosworth RD. P Nuneaton, Warwickshire. Ch e. Bswth CC. See also Dadlington, Shenton. To W, site of Battle of Bswth Field, 1485.

SUTTON COLDFIELD Warwicks
131 SP 1296 7m NNE of Birmingham. MB, 83,130. P. Sttn Cldfld BC. See also Walmley. Sttn Pk, over 2,000 acres with lakes and woods to W.

SUTTON COURTENAY Berks
158 SU 5093 2m S of Abingdon. CP, 2,490. Abngdn RD. P Abngdn. Ch e, c. Sch pe. Abngdn CC. Burial place of Ld Asquith, sometime prime minister, and of George Orwell, writer. Old hses incl Nmn Hall (12c), Abbey (14c), and Mnr Hse (15c–17c).

SUTTON CROSSES Lincs (H)
124 TF 4321 1m S of Long Sutton. Loc, Long Sttn CP.

SUTTON GRANGE Yorks (W)
91 SE 2874 2m NW of Ripon. CP, 40. Rpn and Pateley Br RD. Rpn CC.

SUTTON, GREAT Ches
100, 109 SJ 3775 1m WSW of Ellesmere Port. Loc, Ellesmere Pt MB. P Lit Sttn, Wirral.

SUTTON, GREAT Shrops
129 SO 5183 5m N of Ludlow. Loc, Diddlebury CP.

SUTTON HOWGRAVE Yorks (N)
91 SE 3179 5m N of Ripon. CP(Sttn
w Hgrve), 64. Bedale RD. Ch m2. Thirsk
and Malton CC.

SUTTON IN ASHFIELD Notts
112 SK 5059 3m WSW of Mansfield.
UD, 40,725. P. Ashfld CC. See also
Fulwood, Huthwaite, Skegby, Stanton Hill,
Teversal. Colliery tn.

SUTTON-IN-CRAVEN Yorks (W)
96 SE 0044 4m WNW of Keighley.
CP(Sttn), 2,550. Skipton RD. P Kghly.
Ch e, b, m. Sch p, pe. Kghly BC.

SUTTON LANE ENDS Ches
110 SJ 9271 2m SSE of Macclesfield. Loc,
Sttn CP. Mcclsfld RD. P(Sttn), Mcclsfld.
Sch pe. Mcclsfld CC.

SUTTON MADDOCK Shrops
119 SJ 7201 4m SSW of Shifnal. CP, 372.
Bridgnorth RD. Ch e. Ludlow CC (The
Wrekin). See also Brockton.

SUTTON MALLET Som
165 ST 3736 5m E of Bridgwater. Loc,
Stawell CP. P Brdgwtr. Ch e.

SUTTON MANDEVILLE Wilts
167 ST 9828 9m ENE of Shaftesbury.
CP, 164. Mere and Tisbury RD. Ch e.
Westbury CC. To S, regimental badges cut in
hillside (see Fovant).

SUTTON MONTIS Som
166 ST 6224 5m NNW of Sherbourne. Loc,
S Cadbury CP. P Yeovil. Ch e. To E, Cdbry
Camp (see S Cdbry).

SUTTON ON SEA Lincs (L)
105 TF 5282 2m SSE of Mablethorpe.
UD(Mblthpe and Sttn), 6,156. P Mblthpe.
Horncastle CC.

SUTTON-ON-THE-FOREST Yorks (N)
92, 97 SE 5864 8m N of York. CP, 645.
Easingwold RD. P YK. Ch e, m. Sch pe.
Thirsk and Malton CC. Sttn Pk*, 18c hse in
beautiful gdn.

SUTTON ON THE HILL Derbys
120 SK 2333 6m N of Burton-on-Trent.
CP, 95. Repton RD. P DERBY. Ch e.
Sch pe. Belper CC.

SUTTON ON TRENT Notts
112/113 SK 7965 7m N of Newark.
CP, 986. Southwell RD. P Nwk. Ch e, m.
Sch p. Nwk CC.

SUTTON ST EDMUND Lincs (H)
124 TF 3613 6m WNW of Wisbech.
CP, 527. E Elloe RD. P Spalding. Ch e, m2.
Sch p. Holland w Boston CC.

SUTTON ST JAMES Lincs (H)
124 TF 3918 4m SW of Long Sutton.
CP, 613. E Elloe RD. P Spalding. Ch e, b, m.
Sch p. Holland w Boston CC.

SUTTON ST NICHOLAS Herefs
142 SO 5345 4m NNE of Hereford. Loc,
Sttn CP. Hrfd RD. P HRFD. Ch e. Sch p.
Leominster CC. 1m NW, Sttn Walls, large
Iron Age hill fort. At foot of ramparts, Sttn
St Michael ch.

SUTTON SCARSDALE Derbys
112 SK 4468 4m ESE of Chesterfield. Loc,
Sttn cum Duckmanton CP. Chstrfld RD.
P Chstrfld. Ch e. NE Derbys CC. Ruins of
Sttn Hall, 18c mansion.

SUTTON SCOTNEY Hants
168 SU 4639 6m N of Winchester. Loc,
Wonston CP. P Wnchstr. Ch e, m.

SUTTON-UNDER-BRAILES Warwicks
145 SP 3037 4m SE of Shipston on Stour.
CP, 95. Shpston on Stour RD. Ch e.
Stratford-on-Avon CC (Strtfd).

**SUTTON-UNDER-WHITESTONECLIFFE
Yorks (N)**
91 SE 4882 3m E of Thirsk. CP, 244.
Thsk RD. P(Sttn), Thsk. Ch m. Sch pe. Thsk
and Malton CC. 1m E, Sttn Bank, very steep
rd with hairpin bends. Gliding stn at top.

SUTTON UPON DERWENT Yorks (E)
97, 98 SE 7047 6m WSW of Pocklington.
CP, 319. Pcklngtn RD. P YORK. Ch e.
Sch pe. Howden CC.

SUTTON VALENCE Kent
172, 184 TQ 8149 5m SE of Maidstone.
CP, 1,610. Hollingbourn RD. P Mdstne.
Ch e, v. Sch p. Mdstne CC. Hilltop tn. Boys'
public sch.

SUTTON VENY Wilts
166, 167 ST 8942 3m SE of Warminster.

CP, 497. Wmnstr and Westbury RD.
P Wmnstr. Ch e, v. Sch pe. Wstbry CC.

SUTTON WALDRON Dorset
178 ST 8615 5m S of Shaftesbury. CP, 172.
Shftsbry RD. Ch e. N Dst CC.

SUTTON WEAVER Ches
100, 109 SJ 5479 3m SE of Runcorn. Loc,
Sttn CP. Rncn RD. P WARRINGTON.
Ch m. Rncn CC.

SWABY Lincs (L)
105 TF 3877 4m WNW of Alford. CP, 162.
Louth RD. P Alfd. Ch e. Sch pe. Lth CC.

SWADLINCOTE Derbys
120, 121 SK 3019 4m SE of
Burton-on-Trent. UD, 20,235.
P Btn-on-Trnt, Staffs. Belper CC. See also
Ch Gresley, Newhall, Stanton.

SWAFFHAM Norfolk
125 TF 8209 11m W of E Dereham.
UD, 4,270. P. SW Nflk CC. Old mkt tn.
Many fine 18c hses. Palladian mkt cross.
Outstanding 15c ch.

SWAFFHAM BULBECK Cambs
135 TL 5562 5m W of Newmarket. CP, 633.
Nmkt RD. P CAMBRIDGE. Ch e, v. Sch pe.
Cambs CC.

SWAFFHAM PRIOR Cambs
135 TL 5764 5m W of Newmarket. CP, 634.
Nmkt RD. P CAMBRIDGE. Ch e, bv, m.
Sch pe. Cambs CC. See also River Bank.
Two chs in one churchyard (cf Alvingham
and N Cockerington, Lincs). One ch now
used as mortuary chpl.

SWAFIELD Norfolk
126 TG 2832 1m N of N Walsham. CP, 267.
Smallburgh RD. Ch e. N Nflk CC. See also
Bradfield.

SWAINBY Yorks (N)
91 NZ 4702 9m NE of Northallerton. Loc,
Whorlton CP. P Nthlltn. Ch e, m.

SWAINSHILL Herefs
142 SO 4641 3m WNW of Hereford. Loc,
Hrfd RD. P HRFD. Leominster CC. 2m NW,
The Weir (NT), 18c hse; riverside gdn*.

SWAINSTHORPE Norfolk
137 TG 2101 5m S of Norwich. CP, 424.
Forehoe and Henstead RD.
P NRWCH, NOR 56W. Ch e. S Nflk CC
(Central Nflk).

SWAINSWICK Som
156 ST 7568 2m N of Bath. CP, 1,000.
Bathavon RD. P Bth. Ch e. Sch pe.
N Som CC. See also Tadwick.

SWALCLIFFE Oxon
145 SP 3737 5m WSW of Banbury. CP, 248.
Bnbry RD. P Bnbry. Ch e. Bnbry CC. Ch
Saxon to Perp. Old tithe barn.

SWALECLIFFE Kent
173 TR 1367 1m E of Whitstable. Loc,
Whtstble UD. P Whtstble.

SWALLOW Lincs (L)
105 TA 1703 4m ENE of Caistor. CP, 201.
Cstr RD. P LINCOLN. Ch e, m.
Gainsborough CC. See also Cuxwold. Name
possibly derived from 'wallow' or hole in
grnd into which stream vanishes.

SWALLOWCLIFFE Wilts
167 ST 9627 7m ENE of Shaftesbury.
CP, 192. Mere and Tisbury RD. P Slsbry.
Ch e. Sch p. Westbury CC.

SWALLOWFIELD Berks
169 SU 7264 6m S of Reading. CP, 1,663.
Wokingham RD. P Rdng. Ch e, b, m. Sch p.
Rdng S CC (Wknghm). See also Farley Hill,
Riseley. Burial place of Mary Mitford,
author of *Our Village*. Swllwfld Pk*,
17c–19c hse in large grnds with river and
decoy pond.

SWALLOWNEST Yorks (W)
103 SK 4585 5m SSE of Rotherham. Loc,
Aston cum Aughton CP. P SHEFFIELD.
Ch b, m, s, v. Sch p.

SWANAGE Dorset
179 SZ 0378 9m SE of Wareham.
UD, 8,550. P. S Dst CC. Vctrn resort with
20c accretions.

SWANBOURNE Bucks
146 SP 8027 6m WSW of Bletchley.
CP, 394. Winslow RD. P Bltchly. Ch e, b, m.
Sch pe. Buckingham CC.

SWANLAND Yorks (E)
98 SE 9927 7m W of Hull. CP, 1,330.
Beverley RD. P: N Ferriby. Ch m, v. Sch p.
Bridlington CC.

SWANLEY Kent
171 TQ 5168 4m S of Dartford. CP, 12,707.
Dtfd RD. P. Ch e, c, m, r. Sch i, p, pe2, s.
Sevenoaks CC (Dtfd). See also Hextable.

SWANMORE Hants
180 SU 5716 2m ESE of Bishop's Waltham.
CP, 1,678. Droxford RD.
P SOUTHAMPTON. Ch e, m. Sch pe, s.
Petersfield CC.

SWANNINGTON Leics
121 SK 4116 1m N of Coalville. CP, 1,279.
Ashby de la Zouch RD. P LEICESTER.
Ch m, v. Sch pe. Loughborough CC.
Coal-mining vllge.

SWANNINGTON Norfolk
125 TG 1319 6m SW of Aylsham. CP, 285.
St Faith's and Aylshm RD.
P NORWICH, NOR 82X. Ch e, m. Sch pe.
N Nflk CC (Central Nflk).

SWANSCOMBE Kent
161, 171 TQ 6074 3m W of Gravesend.
UD, 9,184. P. Dartford CC. Indstrl tn.

SWANTON ABBOTT Norfolk
126 TG 2625 3m SSW of N Walsham.
CP, 332. Smallburgh RD.
P NORWICH, NOR 55Y. Ch e, v. Sch p.
N Nflk CC.

SWANTON MORLEY Norfolk
125 TG 0116 3m NNE of E Dereham.
CP, 1,775. Mitford and Launditch RD.
P Drhm. Ch e, m. Sch pe. SW Nflk CC. See
also Mill St, Woodgate.

SWANTON NOVERS Norfolk
125 TG 0232 5m SW of Holt. CP, 209.
Walsingham RD. P Melton Constable.
Ch e, m. NW Nflk CC (N Nflk).

SWANWICK Derbys
112 SK 4053 2m S of Alfreton. Loc,
Alfrtn UD. P DERBY.

SWANWICK Hants
180 SU 5109 5m NW of Fareham. Loc,
Frhm UD. P SOUTHAMPTON. Strawberry
fields.

SWARBY Lincs (K)
113, 123 TF 0440 4m SSW of Sleaford.
CP (Aswarby and Swby), 163.
E Kesteven RD. Ch e. Sch pe. Rutland and
Stamford CC.

SWARDESTON Norfolk
126 TG 2002 4m SSW of Norwich. CP, 447.
Forehoe and Henstead RD.
P NORWCH, NOR 95W. Ch e. Sch p.
S Nflk CC (Central Nflk).

SWARKESTONE Derbys
120, 121 SK 3628 5m SSE of Derby. CP.
SE Derbys RD. P DBY. Ch e. SE Derbys CC.
Swkstne Br and causeway over R Trent, ¾m
long; mdvl, restored.

SWARLAND Nthmb
71 NU 1601 7m SSW of Alnwick. Loc,
Newton-on-the-Moor CP. P Morpeth.

SWARLAND ESTATE Nthmb
71 NU 1603 6m SSW of Alnwick. Loc,
Newton-on-the-Moor CP.

SWATON Lincs (K)
113, 123 TF 1337 7m SE of Sleaford.
CP, 242. E Kesteven RD. P Slfd. Ch e.
Sch pe. Rutland and Stamford CC.

SWAVESEY Cambs
135 TL 3668 8m NW of Cambridge.
CP, 964. Chesterton RD. P CMBRDGE.
Ch e, b2. Sch p, s. Cambs CC. Vllge college.

SWAY Hants
179 SZ 2798 4m NW of Lymington.
CP, 2,289. New Forest RD. P Lmngtn.
Ch e, b, m. Sch pe. Nw Frst CC. See also
Marley Mt. To S, Peterson's Twr, 218ft, blt
1879 by retired Indian judge.

SWAYFIELD Lincs (K)
123 SK 9922 7m WNW of Bourne. CP, 180.
S Kesteven RD. P Grantham. Ch e. Sch pe.
Rutland and Stamford CC.

SWEETHAM Devon
176 SX 8899 3m E of Crediton. Loc,
Newton St Cyres CP. Ch m.

SWEETSHOUSE Cornwall
185, 186 SX 0861 2m NW of Lostwithiel.
Loc, Lanlivery CP.

SWEFLING Suffolk (E)
137 TM 3463 2m W of Saxmundham.
CP, 228. Blyth RD. P Sxmndhm. Ch e.
Eye CC.

SWELL Som
177 ST 3623 6m N of Ilminster. Loc,
Fivehead CP. Ch e.

SWEPSTONE Leics
120, 121 SK 3610 4m S of Ashby de la
Zouch. CP, 505. Ashby de la Zch RD. Ch e.
Loughborough CC. See also Newton
Burgoland.

SWERFORD Oxon
145 SP 3731 5m NE of Chipping Norton.
CP, 163. Chppng Ntn RD. P OXFORD.
Ch e, m. Banbury CC.

SWETTENHAM Ches
110 SJ 8067 4m WNW of Congleton.
CP, 314. Cngltn RD. P Cngltn. Ch e. Sch pe.
Knutsford CC.

SWILLAND Suffolk (E)
150 TM 1852 5m NNE of Ipswich. CP, 130.
Deben RD. P Ipswch. Ch e. Eye CC.
Extraordinary late 19c belfry on top of ch
twr, visible from afar.

SWILLINGTON Yorks (W)
96 SE 3830 6m ESE of Leeds. CP, 2,438.
Tadcaster RD. P LDS. Ch e, m. Sch p.
Normanton CC.

SWIMBRIDGE Devon
163 SS 6230 4m ESE of Barnstaple.
CP, 910. Bnstple RD. P Bnstple. Ch e, b, m.
Sch pe. N Dvn CC. See also Cobbaton,
Gunn. Ch: scrn, font.

SWINBROOK Oxon
144/145 SP 2812 2m E of Burford.
CP(Swnbrk and Widford), 175. Witney RD.
Ch e, m. Mid-Oxon CC (Banbury). Ch:
monmts.

SWINBURNE, GREAT Nthmb
77 NY 9375 7m N of Hexham. Loc,
Chollerton CP.

SWINDERBY Lincs (K)
113 SK 8663 8m SW of Lincoln. CP, 1,522.
N Kesteven RD. P LNCLN. Ch e, m. Sch pe.
Grantham CC. RAF stn to SE.

SWINDON Glos
143, 144 SO 9325 2m N of Cheltenham.
CP, 448. Chltnhm RD. P Chltnhm. Ch e.
Cirencester and Tewkesbury CC. Suburb of
Chltnhm. Ch has hexagonal Nmn twr (cf
Ozleworth).

SWINDON Staffs
130 SO 8690 5m W of Dudley. CP, 578.
Seisdon RD. P Ddly, Worcs. Ch e, c, m.
Sch pe. SW Staffs CC (Brierley Hill).

SWINDON Wilts
157 SU 1584 70m W of London.
MB, 90,830. P. Swndn BC. Large indstrl tn
with rly locomotive wks and many modern
factories on perimeter. Tn centre development. Further expansion. Large modern
hsptl. Rly museum.

SWINE Yorks (E)
99 TA 1335 5m NNE of Hull. CP, 222.
Holderness RD. P Hll. Ch e. Bridlington CC.
Ch incorporates rems of 12c priory.

SWINEFLEET Yorks (W)
97, 98 SE 7722 2m SE of Goole. CP, 1,031.
Gle RD. P Gle. Ch e, m. Sch p. Gle CC.

SWINESHEAD Beds
134 TL 0565 6m E of Rushden. CP, 109.
Bedford RD. P BDFD. Ch e, m. Bdfd CC.

SWINESHEAD Lincs (H)
114, 123 TF 2340 6m WSW of Boston.
CP, 1,824. Bstn RD. P Bstn. Ch e, m3.
Sch pe. Holland w Bstn CC. See also Swnshd
Br.

SWINESHEAD BRIDGE Lincs (H)
114, 123 TF 2142 7m W of Boston. Loc,
Swnshd CP.

SWINETHORPE Lincs (K)
113 SK 8769 6m WSW of Lincoln. CP(Eagle
and Swnthpe), 463. N Kesteven RD. Ch e.
Grantham CC.

SWINFORD Berks
158 SP 4408 1m SE of Eynsham. Loc,
Cumnor CP.

SWINFORD Leics
132, 133 SP 5679 5m ENE of Rugby.
CP, 340. Lutterworth RD. P Rgby, Warwickshire. Ch e, v. Sch pe. Blaby CC (Harborough).

SWINGFIELD MINNIS Kent
173 TR 2143 5m N of Folkestone. Loc,
Swngfld CP. Elham RD. Ch m. Flkstne and
Hythe CC.

SWINGFIELD STREET Kent
173 TR 2343 5m N of Folkestone. Loc,
Swngfld CP. Elham RD. Ch e. Flkstne and
Hythe CC.

SWINHOE Nthmb
71 NU 2128 4m SSE of Bamburgh. Loc,
Beadnell CP. P Chathill.

SWINHOPE Lincs (L)
105 TL 2196 8m NE of Mkt Rasen. CP, 90.
Caistor RD. Ch e. Gainsborough CC.

SWINITHWAITE Yorks (N)
90 SE 0489 5m WSW of Leyburn. Loc,
W Witton CP.

SWINSCOE Staffs
111 SK 1348 3m WSW of Ashbourne.
CP(Blore w Swnscoe), 131. Cheadle RD.
P Ashbne, Derbyshire. Ch m. Leek CC.

SWINSTEAD Lincs (K)
123 TF 0122 5m WNW of Bourne. CP, 222.
S Kesteven RD. P Grantham. Ch e. Sch pe.
Rutland and Stamford CC.

SWINTON Lancs
101 SD 7701 5m WNW of Manchester.
MB(Swntn and Pendlebury), 40,124.
P MNCHSTR. Eccles BC.

SWINTON Yorks (N)
91 SE 2179 1m SW of Masham. CP(Swntn
w Warthermarske), 101. Mshm RD.
P Ripon. Richmond CC. Swntn Pk, mansion
by Wyatt with later additions. In grnds,
Druids' Temple, early 19c copy of
Stonehenge.

SWINTON Yorks (N)
92 SE 7573 2m WNW of Malton. CP, 398.
Mltn RD. P Mltn. Ch m. Thirsk and
Mltn CC.

SWINTON Yorks (W)
103 SK 4599 4m NNE of Rotherham.
UD, 14,897. P Mexborough. Dearne
Valley CC. See also Kilnhurst.

SWITHLAND Leics
121 SK 5413 4m S of Loughborough. CP.
Barrow upon Soar RD. P Lghbrgh. Ch e.
Sch pe. Melton CC. Formerly famous for
quarries of slate widely used in area for
roofs, headstones, monmts.

SWORTON HEATH Ches
101 SJ 6984 6m ESE of Warrington. Loc,
High Legh CP.

SWYNNERTON Staffs
110, 119 SJ 8535 3m WNW of Stone.
CP, 3,022. Stne RD. P Stne. Ch e, m, r.
Sch pr. Stafford and Stne CC. See also
Beech, Hanchurch, Tittensor, Yarnfield. To
S, Defence Department chemical unit.

SWYRE Dorset
177 SY 5288 5m SE of Bridport. CP, 91.

Brdpt RD. Ch e. W Dst CC. Original home
of the Russells who became Dukes of
Bedford from late 17c.

SYDE Glos
143, 144 SO 9410 7m S of Cheltenham.
CP, 37. Cirencester RD. Ch e. Crncstr and
Tewkesbury CC.

SYDENHAM London
161, 171 TQ 3571 6m SSE of Lndn Br.
Loc, Lewisham LB. Lwshm W BC.

SYDENHAM Oxon
159 SP 7301 3m SSE of Thame. CP, 237.
Bullingdon RD. P OXFORD. Ch e, m.
Henley CC.

SYDENHAM DAMEREL Devon
175, 187 SX 4076 5m WNW of Tavistock.
CP, 168. Tvstck RD. P Tvstck. Ch e, m.
W Dvn CC (Tvstck).

SYDERSTONE Norfolk
125 TF 8332 6m WNW of Fakenham.
CP, 489. Docking RD. P King's Lynn.
Ch e, m. Sch pe. NW Nflk CC (K's Lnn).

SYDLING ST NICHOLAS Dorset
178 SY 6399 7m NNW of Dorchester.
CP, 338. Dchstr RD. P(Sdlng), Dchstr.
Ch e, c. W Dst CC. See also Up Sdlng. Perp
ch: gargoyles, monmts. Thatched tithe barn.

SYDMONTON Hants
168 SU 4857 6m S of Newbury.
CP(Ecchinswell and Sdmntn), 1,072.
Kingsclere and Whitchurch RD. Ch e.
Basingstoke CC.

SYERSTON Notts
112 SK 7447 5m SW of Newark. CP, 94.
Nwk RD. P Nwk. Ch e. Nwk CC.

SYKEHOUSE Yorks (W)
103 SE 6216 4m NW of Thorne. CP, 443.
Thne RD. P Goole. Ch e. Sch p. Gle CC.

SYLEHAM Suffolk (E)
137 TM 2178 5m NE of Eye. CP, 185.
Hartismere RD. P Diss, Norfolk. Ch e.
Eye CC.

SYMONDSBURY Dorset
177 SY 4493 1m W of Bridport. CP, 918.
Brdpt RD. P Brdpt. Ch e. Sch pe. W Dst CC.
See also Broad Oak, Eype.

SYMONDS YAT Herefs
142 SO 5516 4m NE of Monmouth. Loc,
Ross and Whitchurch RD. P Rss-on-Wye.
Ch b. Hereford CC. Rocky wooded gorge in
Wye valley - famous beauty spot.

SYREFORD Glos
144 SP 0220 5m E of Cheltenham. Loc,
Whittington CP.

SYRESHAM Northants
145, 146 SP 6341 4m NE of Brackley.
CP, 665. Brckly RD. P Brckly. Ch e, v.
Sch pe. Daventry CC (S Nthnts). See also
Crowfield.

SYSTON Leics
121, 122 SK 6211 5m NNE of Leicester.
CP, 6,455. Barrow upon Soar RD. P LCSTR.
Ch e, b, m, r, v. Sch ie, je. Melton CC.

SYSTON Lincs (K)
113, 122 SK 9240 4m NNE of Grantham.
CP, 144. W Kesteven RD. Ch e. Sch pe.
Grnthm CC. Only landscaped grnds and lake
remain of 18c hse of Thorold family. See
also Marston.

SYTCHAMPTON Worcs
130 SO 8466 4m WNW of Droitwich. Loc,
Ombersley CP. Sch pe.

SYWELL Northants
133 SP 8267 4m W of Wellingborough.
C P , 5 5 6 . W l l n g b r g h R D .
P NORTHAMPTON. Ch e. Sch pe.
Wllngbrgh CC.

T

TACKLEY Oxon
145 SP 4720 3m NE of Woodstock.
CP, 561. Chipping Norton RD. P OXFORD.
Ch e, m. Sch pe. Banbury CC.

TACOLNESTON Norfolk
136 TM 1495 4m SSE of Wymondham.
C P , 2 9 2 . D e p w a d e R D .
P NORWICH, NOR 87W. Ch e. Sch pe.
S Nflk CC.

TADCASTER Yorks (W)
9 7 SE 4843 9m SW of York.
CP(Tdcstr E), 2,068, CP(Tdcstr W), 2,135;
Tdcstr RD. P. Ch e, m, r, s, v. Sch i, j, pr, s.
Barkston Ash CC. Breweries. Timbered hse,
The Ark, now museum.

TADDINGTON Derbys
111 SK 1471 5m WNW of Bakewell.
CP, 472. Bkwll RD. P Buxton. Ch e, m.
Sch pe. W Derbys CC. 1,100ft above sea
level.

TADDIPORT Devon
163 SS 4818 just SW of Torrington. Loc,
Lit Trrngtn CP.

TADLEY Hants
168 SU 6060 6m NNW of Basingstoke.
CP, 4,443. Kingsclere and Whitchurch RD.
P Bsngstke. Ch e2, m2, r, s, v. Sch i, j, p.
Bsngstke CC. See also Hth End, New Tn.

TADLOW Cambs
147 TL 2847 6m ENE of Biggleswade.
CP, 89. S Cambs RD. P Royston, Herts.
Ch e. Cambs CC.

TADMARTON Oxon
145 SP 3937 4m WSW of Banbury. CP, 386.
Bnbry RD. Ch e. Sch pe. Bnbry CC.

TADWICK Som
156 ST 7470 4m N of Bath. Loc,
Swainswick CP.

TADWORTH Surrey
170 TQ 2356 3m SSE of Epsom. Loc,
Banstead UD. P.

TAKELEY Essex
148 TL 5621 5m E of Bishop's Stortford.
CP, 1,647. Dunmow RD. P Bshp's Sttfd.
Ch e, c. Sch p. Saffron Walden CC. See also
Molehill Grn.

TALATON Devon
176 SY 0699 6m W of Honiton. CP, 369.
Hntn RD. P Exeter. Ch e. Sch pe. Hntn CC.

TALKE Staffs
110 SJ 8253 6m NW of Stoke-on-Trent.
Loc, Kidsgrove UD. P Stke-on-Trnt.

TALKIN Cumb
76 NY 5457 3m SSE of Brampton. Loc,
Hayton CP. P Brmptn. Ch e. Sch pe.

TALLENTIRE Cumb
82 NY 1035 3m NNW of Cockermouth.
Loc, Bridekirk CP.

TALLINGTON Lincs (K)
123 TF 0908 4m E of Stamford. CP, 213.
S Kesteven RD. P Stmfd. Ch e. Sch p.
Rutland and Stmfd CC. To NE, stretch of
rly much used for speed trials.

TALSKIDDY Cornwall
185 SW 9165 7m ENE of Newquay. Loc,
St Columb Major CP. Ch m.

TAMERTON FOLIOT Devon
187 SX 4760 4m N of Plymouth. Loc,
Plmth CB. P Plmth. Plmth, Drake BC
(Plmth, Sutton).

TAMWORTH Staffs
120 SK 2004 14m NE of Birmingham.
MB, 40,245. P. Lichfield and Tmwth CC
(Lchfld and Tmwth CC, Meriden CC). See
also Amington, Dosthill, Glascote, Hockley,
Kettlebrook, Two Gates, Wilncote. Cstle*,
Nmn and later. Dominant ch. Tn largely
Ggn. Tn hall early 18c. High and low level
rly stns.

TANDRIDGE Surrey
171 TQ 3750 1m SW of Oxted. CP, 713.
Godstone RD. P Oxtd. Ch e. Sch pe.
E Srry CC (Reigate). See also Crowhurst
Lane End.

TANFIELD Co Durham
78 NZ 1855 6m SW of Gateshead. Loc,
Stanley UD.

TANFIELD LEA Co Durham
78 NZ 1854 7m SW of Gateshead. Loc,
Stanley UD. P NEWCASTLE UPON TYNE.

TANGLEY Hants
168 SU 3252 5m NNW of Andover.
CP, 557. Andvr RD. Ch e. Winchester CC
(Basingstoke). See also Hatherden,
Wildhern.

TANGMERE Sussex (W)
181 SU 9006 3m ENE of Chichester.
CP, 1,025. Chchstr RD. Ch e. Sch p.
Chchstr CC. RAF stn and airfield.

TANKERSLEY Yorks (W)
102 SK 3399 4m S of Barnsley. CP, 2,031.
Wortley RD. P Bnsly. Ch e, m. Sch pe.
Penistone CC. See also Pilley.

TANNINGTON Suffolk (E)
137 TM 2467 3m NW of Framlingham.
CP, 119. Hartismere RD. Ch e. Eye CC.

TANSLEY Derbys
111 SK 3259 2m E of Matlock. Loc,
Mtlck UD. P Mtlck.

TANSOR Northants
134 TL 0590 2m NNE of Oundle. CP, 171.
Oundle and Thrapston RD. Ch e. Sch pe.
Wellingborough CC (Peterborough).

TANTOBIE Co Durham
78 NZ 1754 7m SW of Gateshead. Loc,
Stanley UD. P NEWCASTLE UPON TYNE.

TANWORTH IN ARDEN Warwicks
131 SP 1170 5m ENE of Redditch.
CP(Tnwth), 3,061. Stratford-on-Avon RD.
P Solihull. Ch e. Sch pe. Strtfd-on-Avn CC
(Strtfd). See also Earlswood, Nuthurst,
Portway, Wd End.

TAPLOW Bucks
159 SU 9182 2m ENE of Maidenhead.
CP, 2,183. Eton RD. P Mdnhd, Berks. Ch e.
Sch pe. Beaconsfield CC (S Bucks).
Thames-side rsdntl distr.

TARBOCK GREEN Lancs
100, 109 SJ 4687 3m WNW of Widnes. Loc,
Tbck CP. Whiston RD. P Prescot. Ch v.
Wdns CC.

TARDEBRIGGE Worcs
130, 131 SO 9969 3m ESE of Bromsgrove.
Loc, Tutnall and Cobley CP. P Brmsgrve.
Ch e. Sch pe. Locks on Worcester and
Birmingham Canal. Hewell Grange, in large
pk with lake laid out by Repton, now a
Borstal Institute.

TARLETON Lancs
94 SD 4520 8m ENE of Southport.
CP, 3,001. W Lancs RD. P Preston.
Ch e, m3, r. Sch p, pe. Ormskirk CC. See
also Mere Brow, Sollom.

TARLSCOUGH Lancs
100 SD 4314 4m NNE of Ormskirk. Loc,
Ormskk UD.

TARLTON Glos
157 ST 9599 4m WSW of Cirencester. Loc,
Rodmarton CP. P Crncstr. Ch e, m.

TARNBROOK Lancs
94 SD 5855 8m ESE of Lancaster. Loc,
Over Wyresdale CP. Lncstr RD. Lncstr CC.

TARPORLEY Ches
109 SJ 5562 7m WSW of Winsford.
CP, 1,552. Northwick RD. P. Ch e, b, m, r.
Sch p, pe, s. Nthwch CC.

TARR Som
164 ST 1030 8m WNW of Taunton. Loc,
Lydeard St Lawrence CP.

TARRANT CRAWFORD Dorset
178, 179 ST 9203 3m SE of Blandford.
CP, 34. Blndfd RD. Ch e. N Dst CC. Ch: 14c
wall-paintings.

TARRANT GUNVILLE Dorset
178, 179 ST 9212 5m NNE of Blandford.
CP, 257. Blndfd RD. P Blndfd Forum. Ch e.
Sch pe. N Dst CC. See also Stubhampton.
Rems of Eastbury Hse, by Vanbrugh.

TARRANT HINTON Dorset
179 ST 9311 4m NE of Blandford. CP, 211.
Blndfd RD. P Blndfd Forum. Ch e.
N Dst CC.

TARRANT KEYNESTON Dorset
178, 179 ST 9204 3m ESE of Blandford.
CP, 192. Blndfd RD. P Blndfd Forum. Ch e.
Sch pe. N Dst CC.

TARRANT LAUNCESTON Dorset
179 ST 9409 4m NE of Blandford. CP, 768.
Blndfd RD. N Dst CC.

TARRANT MONKTON Dorset
179 ST 9408 4m ENE of Blandford.
CP, 891. Blndfd RD. P Blndfd Forum.
Ch e, m. N Dst CC.

TARRANT RAWSTON Dorset
179 ST 9306 3m E of Blandford. CP, 67.
Blndfd RD. Ch e. N Dst CC.

TARRANT RUSHTON Dorset
179 ST 9305 3m E of Blandford. CP, 128.
Blndfd RD. Ch e. N Dst CC.

TARRING NEVILLE Sussex (E)
183 TQ 4403 2m N of Newhaven. CP, 36.
Chailey RD. Ch e. Lewes CC.

TARRINGTON Herefs
142, 143 SO 6140 7m E of Hereford.
CP, 390. Ledbury RD. P HRFD. Ch e, v.
Sch pe. Leominster CC.

TARVIN Ches
109 SJ 4967 5m E of Chester. CP. Tvn RD.
P CHSTR. Ch e, m3. Sch pe. Northwich CC.

TASBURGH Norfolk
137 TM 1996 6m SE of Wymondham.
C P , 3 4 3 . D e p w a d e R D .
P NORWICH, NOR 66W. Ch e, m. Sch pe.
S Nflk CC. See also Upr Tsbrgh.

TASLEY Shrops
130 SO 6994 2m NW of Bridgnorth.
CP, 195. Brdgnth RD. Ch e. Ludlow CC.

TASTON Oxon
145 SP 3621 4m SE of Chipping Norton.
Loc, Spelsbury CP.

TATENHILL Staffs
120 SK 2022 2m WSW of Burton-on-Trent.
CP, 681. Tutbury RD. P Btn-on-Trnt. Ch e.
Btn CC. See also Rangemore.

TATHAM Lancs
89 SD 6069 6m S of Kirkby Lonsdale.
CP, 365. Lunesdale RD. Ch e. Sch pe.
Lancaster CC. See also Lowgill.

TATHWELL Lincs (L)
105 TF 3283 3m S of Louth. CP, 216.
Lth RD. P Lth. Ch e, m. Sch pe. Lth CC. Blt
round small lake.

TATSFIELD Surrey
171 TQ 4157 1m S of Biggin Hill.
C P , 1 , 4 6 2 . G o d s t o n e R D .
P Westerham, Kent. Ch e, c. Sch p.
E Srry CC (Reigate).

TATTENHALL Ches
109 SJ 4858 7m SE of Chester. CP, 1,167.
Tarvin RD. P CHSTR. Ch e, m. Sch pe, s.
Nantwich CC.

TATTERFORD Norfolk
125 TF 8628 3m WSW of Fakenham. Loc,
Tattersett CP. Ch e.

TATTERSETT Norfolk
125 TF 8430 5m W of Fakenham. CP, 373.
Walsingham RD. P King's Lynn. Ch e.
NW Nflk CC (N Nflk). See also Coxford,
Tatterford.

TATTERSHALL Lincs (L)
114 TF 2157 4m SSE of Woodhall Spa.
CP, 828. Horncastle RD. P Lincoln. Ch e.
Sch pe, s. Hncstle CC. Rems of cstle (NT)*,
blt 1434 by Ld Cromwell, treasurer to
Henry VI.

TATTERSHALL BRIDGE Lincs (K)
113 TF 1956 4m S of Woodhall Spa. Loc,
E Kesteven RD. P LINCOLN. Ch m.
Grantham CC.

TATTERSHALL THORPE Lincs (L)
114 TF 2159 3m SE of Woodhall Spa.
CP, 178. Horncastle RD. Hncstle CC.

TATTINGSTONE Suffolk (E)
150 TM 1337 5m SSW of Ipswich. CP, 600.
Samford RD. P Ipswch. Ch e, m. Sch pe.
Sudbury and Woodbridge CC.

TAUNTON Som
177 ST 2224 37m SW of Bristol.
MB, 37,373. P. Tntn CC. County tn, in
fertile Vale of T. Deane. Two fine Perp chs,
both rebuilt; rems of cstle, county museum,
civic centre. Industries incl bacon, pies,
cider, agricultural machinery, shirts.

TAVERHAM Norfolk
126 TG 1613 5m NW of Norwich.
CP, 1,219. St Faith's and Aylsham RD.
P NRWCH, NOR 53X. Ch e. Sch pe.
N Nflk CC (Central Nflk).

TAVISTOCK Devon
175, 187 SX 4874 12m N of Plymouth.
CP, 6,088. Tvstck RD. P. Ch e, c, m2, r, s, v.
Sch p, pe, s. W Dvn CC (Tvstck). Mkt tn;
former prosperity based, in turn, on tin,
wool, copper.

TAW GREEN Devon
175 SX 6597 4m ENE of Okehampton.
Loc, S Tawton CP. Ch b.

TAWSTOCK Devon
163 SS 5529 2m S of Barnstaple. CP, 1,285.
Bnstple RD. P Bnstple. Ch e. Sch pe.
N Dvn CC. See also Chapelton, Eastacombe,
Ensis, Hiscott. Ch: monmts; twr over
crossing.

TAXAL Derbys
111 SK 0079 5m NW of Buxton. Loc,
Whaley Br UD.

TAYNTON Glos
143 SO 7321 7m WNW of Gloucester.
CP, 394. Newent RD. Ch e, m. W Glos CC.
See also Glasshouse Hill.

TAYNTON Oxon
144 SP 2313 2m NW of Burford. CP, 124.
Witney RD. P OXFORD. Ch e. Mid-Oxon CC
(Banbury).

TEALBY Lincs (L)
105 TF 1590 3m ENE of Mkt Rasen.
CP, 462. Caistor RD. P LINCOLN. Ch e, m.
Sch p. Gainsborough CC. Vllge sch blt by
Tennyson's uncle, who also blt nearby
Bayons Mnr 1836—40, now in ruins.

TEBAY Westm
89 NY 6104 8m NNW of Sedbergh.
CP, 683. N Westm RD. P Penrith,
Cumberland. Ch e, m2. Sch p. Westm CC.
Rly vllge. M6 motorway passes to W.

TEBWORTH Beds
147 SP 9926 4m NNW of Dunstable. Loc,
Chalgrave CP. P Leighton Buzzard. Ch m.

TEDBURN ST MARY Devon
176 SX 8194 4m SSW of Crediton. CP, 559.
St Thomas RD. P Exeter. Ch e, m. Sch p.
Tiverton CC.

TEDDINGTON Glos
143, 144 SO 9633 5m E of Tewkesbury.
CP, 187. Cheltenham RD. P Tksbry. Ch e.
Cirencester and Tksbry CC. See also
Alstone, Lit Washbourne.

TEDDINGTON London
160, 170 TQ 1671 3m SSE of Hounslow.
Loc, Richmond upon Thames LB. P Middx.
Twickenham BC. Thames-side rsdntl distr.
T. Lock is largest on river; marks upper
limit of tides.

TEDSTONE DELAMERE Herefs
130 SO 6958 4m NE of Bromyard. CP, 127.
Brmyd RD. Ch e. Leominster CC.

TEDSTONE WAFER Herefs
129, 130 SO 6759 3m NNE of Bromyard.
CP, 35. Brmyd RD. P Brmyd. Ch e.
Leominster CC.

TEESSIDE Yorks (N)
85 NZ 4620 12m ENE of Darlington.
CB, 395,477. BCs: Tssde, Middlesbrough;
Redcar; Stockton; Thornaby. (Mddlsbrgh E;
Mddlsbrgh W; Stcktn-on-Tees. Also parts of
Cleveland CC, Richmond CC, Sedgefield CC.)
See also Billingham, Eston, Kirkleatham,
Mddlsbrgh, Nunthorpe, Ormesby, Rdcr,
Stcktn-on-Ts, Thnby-on-Ts. Large indstrl
complex with shipbuilding, engineering, iron
and steel wks, chemicals, etc.

TEETON Northants
133 SP 6970 7m NNW of Northampton.
Loc, Hollowell CP.

TEFFONT EVIAS Wilts
167 ST 9931 10m W of Salisbury. Loc,
Tffnt CP. Mere and Tisbury RD.
P(Tffnt), Slsbry. Ch e. Westbury CC. Stream
runs beside vllge st.

TEFFONT MAGNA Wilts
167 ST 9832 10m W of Salisbury. Loc,
Tffnt CP. Mere and Tisbury RD.
P(Tffnt), Salisbury. Ch e. Westbury CC. EE
ch has fragments of Saxon carving.

TEIGH Rutland
122 SK 8616 4m N of Oakham. CP, 89.
Oakhm RD. P Oakhm. Ch e. Rtlnd and
Stamford CC. Ch with 18c Gothic interior;
unusual arrangement of pews and plpt.

TEIGNGRACE Devon
176, 188 SX 8473 2m NNW of Newton
Abbot. CP, 201. Ntn Abbt RD. Ch e.
Totnes CC.

TEIGNMOUTH Devon
176, 188 SX 9473 5m ENE of Newton
Abbot. UD, 12,554. P. Tiverton CC. See
also Shaldon. Small resort, with pier. Boat
building.

TELLISFORD Som
166 ST 8055 5m NNE of Frome. CP, 168.
Frme RD. Ch e. Wells CC. See also
Woolverton.

TELSCOMBE Sussex (E)
183 TQ 4003 3m WNW of Newhaven.
CP, 3,501. Chailey RD. Ch e, v. Lewes CC.
See also Tlscmbe Cliffs. S Downs vllge
accessible by car from NE only.

TELSCOMBE CLIFFS Sussex (E)
183 TQ 3901 3m W of Newhaven. Loc,
Tlscmbe CP. P Nhvn. Sch p. Access to
Tlscmbe on foot only.

TEMPLE Cornwall
186 SX 1473 6m NE of Bodmin. Loc,
Blisland CP. Ch e.

TEMPLE BALSALL Warwicks
131 SP 2076 4m SE of Solihull. Loc,
Blsll CP. Meriden RD. Ch e. Sch pe.
Mrdn CC.

TEMPLE BRUER Lincs (K)
113 TF 0053 6m NW of Sleaford. CP(Tmple
Bruer w Tmple High Grange), 144.
E Kesteven RD. Ch e. Grantham CC. Site of

Knights Templar's preceptory of which only
twr remains.

TEMPLE CLOUD Som
166 ST 6257 5m WNW of Radstock. Loc,
Cameley CP. P BRISTOL. Ch e.

TEMPLE COMBE Som
166 ST 7022 4m S of Wincanton. CP(Abbas
and Tmplcmbe), 910. Wncntn RD.
P(Tmplcmbe). Ch e, v. Sch pe. Wells CC.

TEMPLE EWELL Kent
173 TR 2844 3m NW of Dover. CP(Tmple
Ewell w River), 1,154. Dvr RD. P Dvr.
Ch e, b, v. Sch pe. Dvr and Deal CC (Dvr).

TEMPLE GRAFTON Warwicks
144 SP 1254 5m W of Stratford. CP, 415.
Strtfd-on-Avon RD. Ch e. Sch pe.
Strtfd-on-Avn CC (Strtfd).

TEMPLE GUITING Glos
144 SP 0928 4m E of Winchcombe.
CP, 391. N Cotswold RD. P Cheltenham.
Ch e. Sch pe. Cirencester and
Tewkesbury CC. See also Barton, Farmcote,
Ford, Kineton. Fine Ctswld setting.

TEMPLE HIRST Yorks (W)
97, 98 SE 6025 5m SSW of Selby. CP, 129.
Slby RD. Ch m. Sch p. Barkston Ash CC.

TEMPLE NORMANTON Derbys
112 SK 4167 3m SE of Chesterfield.
CP, 550. Chstrfld RD. P Chstrfld. Ch e.
Sch p. NE Derbys CC.

TEMPLES, Inner and Middle, London
160 TQ 3180 just ENE of Charing Cross.
Loc, City of Lndn. Pop. 281. The City of
Lndn and Westminster S BC (The Cities of
Lndn and Wstmnstr). Two of the Inns of
Court; lawyers' chambers. Several old bldngs
damaged in World War II, now restored, incl
Tmple Ch, round ch orig blt by Knights
Templar.

TEMPLE SOWERBY Westm
83 NY 6127 6m ESE of Penrith. CP, 316.
N Westm RD. P Pnrth, Cumberland.
Ch e, m. Sch pe. Westm CC. Vllge of red
stone. Acorn Bank (NT), mnr hse; gdns*.

TEMPLETON Devon
164, 176 SS 8813 4m WNW of Tiverton.
CP, 128. Tvtn RD. P Tvtn. Ch e. Tvtn CC.
See also Tmpltn Br.

TEMPLETON BRIDGE Devon
164, 176 SS 8714 5m WNW of Tiverton.
Loc, Templeton CP. Ch m.

TEMPLETOWN Co Durham
84 NZ 1049 just S of Consett. Loc,
Cnstt UD.

TEMPSFORD Beds
147 TL 1652 2m NNW of Sandy. CP, 494.
Biggleswade RD. P Sndy. Ch e, m. Sch p.
Mid-Beds CC. See also Langford End.

TENBURY WELLS Worcs
129 SO 5967 7m SE of Ludlow.
CP(Tnbry), 2,015. Tnbry RD. P. Ch e, m, r.
Sch pe, s. Kidderminster CC. See also
Berrington, Callows Grave, Kyrewood,
St Michaels. Small mkt tn on R Teme,
developed as spa in 19c.

TENDRING Essex
150 TM 1424 6m NNW of Clacton. CP, 815.
Tndrng RD. P Clctn-on-Sea. Ch e. Sch p.
Harwich CC.

TEN MILE BANK Norfolk
135 TL 6096 4m S of Downham Mkt. Loc,
Hilgay CP. P Dnhm Mkt.

TENTERDEN Kent
184 TQ 8833 10m WSW of Ashford.
MB, 5,922. P. Ashfd CC. See also Leigh Grn,
Reading St, St Michaels, Small Hythe. Mkt
and rsdntl tn; tree-lined main street has wide
verges. Ch twr landmark for miles.

TERLING Essex
149, 162 TL 7715 3m W of Witham.
CP, 813. Braintree RD. P Chelmsford. Ch e.
Sch pe. Brntree CC (Maldon). T. Place, late
Ggn, partly farm research laboratories.

TERNHILL Shrops
110, 118, 119 SJ 6332 3m WSW of Mkt
Drayton. Loc, Moreton Say CP. P Mkt Drtn.

TERRINGTON Yorks (N)
92 SE 6770 7m W of Malton. CP(Trrngtn
w Wiganthorpe), 350. Mltn RD. P YORK.
Ch e, m. Sch pe. Thirsk and Mltn CC.

TERRINGTON ST CLEMENT Norfolk
124 TF 5520 4m W of King's Lynn.
CP, 3,038. Marshland RD. P K's Lnn.
Ch e, m. Sch i, j, s. NW Nflk CC (K's Lnn).
See also Ongar Hill. In mkt gdn area. 14c ch
known as 'Cathedral of the Marshes'.

TERRINGTON ST JOHN Norfolk
124 TF 5315 6m NE of Wisbech. CP, 586.
Marshland RD. P Wsbch, Cambs. Ch e, m.
Sch p. NW Nflk CC (King's Lynn). See also
St John's Fen End, St John's Highway.

TESTON Kent
171, 172 TQ 7053 4m WSW of Maidstone.
CP, 648. Mdstne RD. P Mdstne. Ch e.
Mdstne CC.

TESTWOOD Hants
180 SU 3514 5m WNW of Southampton.
Loc, Eling CP. Ch e, b.

TETBURY Glos
156, 157 ST 8993 5m NNW of Malmesbury.
CP, 3,117. Ttbry RD. P. Ch e, b, c, m, r, v2.
Sch pe, s2. Stroud CC. Characteristic
Cotswold tn. Mkt hall, 17c; stands on thick
pillars. One end filled in, early 19c.

TETBURY UPTON Glos
156, 157 ST 8895 1m NNW of Tetbury.
CP, 466. Ttbry RD. Stroud CC. See also
Doughton.

TETCHILL Shrops
118 SJ 3932 1m SSW of Ellesmere. Loc,
Ellesmre Rural CP. N Shrops RD. P Ellesmre.
Oswestry CC.

TETCOTT Devon
174 SX 3396 5m S of Holsworthy. CP, 141.
Hlswthy RD. P Hlswthy. Ch e, m. W Dvn CC
(Tavistock).

TETFORD Lincs (L)
114 TF 3374 6m NE of Horncastle.
CP, 358. Hncstle RD. P Hncstle. Ch e.
Sch p. Hncstle CC.

TETNEY Lincs (L)
105 TA 3100 6m SSE of Grimsby. CP, 987.
Louth RD. P Grmsby. Ch e, m. Sch p.
Lth CC. See also Ttny Lock.

TETNEY LOCK Lincs (L)
105 TA 3402 6m SE of Grimsby. Loc,
Ttny CP.

TETSWORTH Oxon
159 SP 6801 3m SSW of Thame. CP, 463.
Bullingdon RD. P OXFORD. Ch e, c. Sch p.
Henley CC.

TETTENHALL Staffs
119 SJ 8700 2m WNW of Wolverhampton.
Loc, Wlvrhmptn CB. P Wlvhmptn.
Wlvrhmptn SW BC (Brierley Hill CC). 1m
SW, Wightwick Mnr (NT)*, late 19c hse
displaying William Morris fabrics and
wallpapers, and pre-Raphaelite wks of art.

TETWORTH Hunts
147 TL 2153 5m SSE of St Neots. CP, 118.
St Nts RD. Ch e. Hunts CC.

TEVERSAL Notts
112 SK 4761 4m W of Mansfield. Loc,
Sutton in Ashfield UD. P Sttn-in-Ashfld.
Large ch with many features of interest incl
doorway, arcades, monmts, squire's pew.

TEVERSHAM Cambs
135 TL 4958 3m E of Cambridge. CP, 808.
Chesterton RD. P CMBRDGE. Ch e, b.
Sch pe. Cambs CC.

TEW, GREAT Oxon
145 SP 3929 5m ENE of Chipping Norton.
See Gt Tew.

TEWIN Herts
147, 160 TL 2714 3m ENE of Welwyn Gdn
City. CP. Hertford RD. P Wlwn. Ch e.
Sch pe. Htfd and Stevenage CC (Htfd).

TEWITFIELD Lancs
89 SD 5273 2m NE of Carnforth. Loc,
Priest Hutton CP. Ch m.

TEWKESBURY Glos
143, 144 SO 8932 7m NNW of Cheltenham.
MB, 8,742. P. Cirencester and Tksbry CC.
Famous abbey ch; fine Nmn central twr. To
S, site of Wars of the Roses battle, 1471.

TEY, GREAT Essex
149 TL 8925 6m W of Colchester. See Gt
Tey.

TEYNHAM Kent
172 TQ 9562 3m ESE of Sittingbourne.
CP, 2,370. Swale RD. P Sttngbne. Ch e.
Sch pe. Faversham CC. See also Conyer.
Cherry-growing place since Tdr times.

THAKEHAM Sussex (W)
182 TQ 1017 2m NNE of Storrington.
CP, 1,117. Chanctonbury RD.
P Pulborough. Ch e, f. Sch p, s.
Shoreham CC (Arundel and Shrhm).

THAME Oxon
159 SP 7005 9m SW of Aylesbury.
UD, 5,940. P. Henley CC. See also Moreton.
Mkt tn with wide main st. Many old bldngs
15c and later.

THAMES DITTON Surrey
170 TQ 1667 2m SW of Kingston. Loc,
Esher UD. P. Thames-side rsdntl distr
opposite Hampton Ct Pk.

THANINGTON Kent
173 TR 1356 SW distr of Canterbury. Loc,
Cntrbry CB. P Cntrbry.

THARSTON Norfolk
137 TM 1894 7m SE of Wymondham.
CP, 364. Depwade RD. Ch e. S Nflk CC. See
also Hapton.

THATCHAM Berks
158 SU 5167 3m E of Newbury. CP, 7,483.
Nbry RD. P Nbry. Ch e, c, m, r, v.
Sch i, je, p, s. Nbry CC. See also Crookham.
Much recent expansion.

THAXTED Essex
148 TL 6130 6m N of Dunmow. CP, 1,905.
Dnmw RD. P Dnmw. Ch e b, r, v. Sch p.
Saffron Walden CC. Outstanding 15c ch; tall
spire of 1822. Many timbered, plastered,
and pargetted hses. 16c guildhall. Twr
windmill.

THEAKSTON Yorks (N)
91 SE 3085 3m SE of Bedale. CP, 56.
Bdle RD. Thirsk and Malton CC.

THEALBY Lincs (L)
104 SE 8918 5m N of Scunthorpe. Loc,
Burton upon Stather CP. Ch m.

THEALE Berks
158, 159 SU 6471 5m WSW of Reading.
CP, 1,638. Bradfield RD. P Rdng.
Ch e, c, m. Sch pe, s. Newbury CC.

THEALE Som
165 ST 4646 5m W of Wells. Loc,
Wedmore CP. P Wdmre. Ch e.

THEARNE Yorks (E)
99 TA 0736 3m SE of Beverley. Loc,
Woodmansey CP.

THEBERTON Suffolk (E)
137 TM 4365 4m ENE of Saxmundham.
CP, 445. Blyth RD. P Leiston. Ch e. Sch p.
Eye CC. See also E Br.

THEDDINGWORTH Leics
132, 133 SP 6685 4m W of Mkt
Harborough. CP, 213. Mkt Hbrgh RD.
P Rugby, Warwickshire. Ch e, v. Hbrgh CC.

THEDDLETHORPE ALL SAINTS Lincs
(L)
105 TF 4688 3m NW of Mablethorpe.
CP, 157. Louth RD. P Mblthpe. Ch e. Sch p.
Lth CC. Grand mainly 14c ch known as
'Cathedral of the Marshes'.

THEDDLETHORPE ST HELEN Lincs (L)
105 TF 4788 3m NW of Mablethorpe.
CP, 308. Louth RD. P Mblthpe. Ch e, m.
Lth CC.

THELBRIDGE Devon
163 SS 7812 8m NNW of Crediton.
CP, 260. Crdtn RD. Ch e. Tiverton CC
(Torrington). See also Nomansland.

THELNETHAM Suffolk (W)
136 TM 0178 6m W of Diss. CP, 233.
Thingoe RD. Ch e. Bury St Edmunds CC.

THELWALL Ches
101 SJ 6587 3m E of Warrington. Loc,
Grappenhall CP. P Wrrngtn, Lancs. Ch e.
Sch p. Between Manchester Ship Canal and
Bridgwater Canal. On the black and white
Pickering Arms is the inscription 'Edward
the Elder founded a city here in 923'.

THEMELTHORPE Norfolk
125 TG 0524 8m NE of E Dereham. CP, 77.
St Faith's and Aylsham RD. Ch e, m.
N Nflk CC (Central Nflk).

THENFORD Northants
145 SP 5141 4m E of Banbury. CP, 84.
Brackley RD. P Bnbry, Oxon. Ch e.
Daventry CC (S Nthnts).

THERFIELD Herts
147 TL 3337 3m SSW of Royston. CP, 403.
Hitchin RD. P Rstn. Ch e, v2. Sch p.
Htchn CC.

THETFORD Norfolk
136 TL 8683 12m N of Bury St Edmunds.
MB, 13,706. P. S Nflk CC. Important eccl
centre in mdvl times with many chs and
monastic hses; from this period cstle,
Cluniac priory, hunting lodge (all A.M.), and
several chs, are extant. Ggn and Rgncy hses.
Forestry development to N and W. Planned
New Tn.

THEYDON BOIS Essex
161 TQ 4499 2m SSW of Epping.
CP, 3,925. Eppng and Ongar RD. P Eppng.
Ch e, b, v. Sch p. Eppng Forest CC (Eppng).
Birch Hall gdns*.

THICKWOOD Wilts
156 ST 8272 6m W of Chippenham. Loc,
Colerne CP.

THIMBLEBY Lincs (L)
114 TF 2369 1m W of Horncastle. CP, 206.
Hncstle RD. P Hncstle. Ch e. Hncstle CC.
Thatch and whitewash; reminiscent of
Devon.

THIMBLEBY Yorks (N)
91 SE 4595 5m E of Northallerton. CP, 85.
Nthlltn RD. Richmond CC. See also
Foxton.

THIRKLEBY Yorks (N)
91 SE 4778 4m SE of Thirsk. CP(Thklby
High and Low w Osgodby), 219. Thsk RD.
P Thsk. Ch e. Thsk and Malton CC.

THIRLBY Yorks (N)
91 SE 4884 4m ENE of Thirsk. CP, 74.
Thsk RD. Ch m. Thsk and Malton CC.

THIRN Yorks (N)
91 SE 2185 3m N of Masham. CP, 56.
Bedale RD. Ch m. Thirsk and Malton CC.

THIRSK Yorks (N)
91 SE 4282 8m SSE of Northallerton.
CP, 2,856. Thsk RD. P. Ch e, f, m, r.
Sch i, j, pr, s. Thsk and Malton CC. Old
mkt tn with very fine mainly 15c ch. Large
main square. Racecourse.

THIRTLEBY Yorks (E)
99 TA 1734 6m NE of Hull. Loc,
Coniston CP.

THISTLETON Lancs
94 SD 4037 6m E of Blackpool.
CP(Greenhalgh-w-Thstltn), 466. Fylde RD.
P Preston. S Flde CC.

THISTLETON Rutland
122 SK 9117 7m NNE of Oakham. CP, 94.
Oakhm RD. P Oakhm. Ch e. Rtlnd and
Stamford CC.

THISTLEY GREEN Suffolk (W)
135 TL 6776 8m NNE of Newmarket. Loc,
Mildenhall CP.

THIXENDALE Yorks (E)
92, 98 SE 8461 7m SSE of Malton. CP, 178.
Norton RD. P Mltn. Ch e, m. Howden CC.

THOCKRINGTON Nthmb
77 NY 9579 9m N of Hexham. Loc,
Bavington CP. Bellingham RD. Ch e.
Hxhm CC.

THOLOMAS DROVE Cambs
124 TF 4006 4m SW of Wisbech. Loc,
Wsbch St Mary CP.

THOLTHORPE Yorks (N)
91 SE 4766 6m E of Boroughbridge.
CP, 158. Easingwold RD. P YORK. Ch m.
Thirsk and Malton CC.

THOMPSON Norfolk
136 TL 9296 8m W of Attleborough. CP.
Wayland RD. P Thetford. Ch e, m. Sch p.
S Nflk CC. Large mere. (Several meres exist
in E Breckland.)

THONGSBRIDGE Yorks (W)
102 SE 1409 4m S of Huddersfield. Loc,
Holmfirth UD. P Hlmfth, Hddsfld.

THORALBY Yorks (N)
90 SE 0086 7m WSW of Leyburn. CP, 132.
Aysgth RD. P Lbn. Ch m. Richmond CC.

THORESTHORPE Lincs (L)
105 TF 4677 1m NNE of Alford. CP(Saleby
w Thsthpe), 123. Louth RD. Lth CC.

THORESWAY Lincs (L)
105 TF 1696 4m SE of Caistor. CP, 152.
Cstr RD. P Mkt Rasen. Ch e.
Gainsborough CC.

THORGANBY Lincs (L)
105 TF 2097 8m SSW of Grimsby. CP, 67.
Caistor RD. Ch e. Gainsborough CC.

THORGANBY Yorks (E)
97, 98 SE 6941 8m NE of Selby. CP, 278.
Derwent RD. P YORK. Ch e, m. Sch pe.
Howden CC.

THORGILL Yorks (N)
86, 92 SE 7096 10m NW of Pickering. Loc,
Rosedale West Side CP. Pckrng RD.
Scarborough CC (Thirsk and Malton).

THORINGTON Suffolk (E)
137 TM 4174 3m SE of Halesworth. CP, 86.
Blyth RD. Ch e. Eye CC.

THORINGTON STREET Suffolk (W)
149 TM 0135 5m SSW of Hadleigh. Loc,
Stoke-by-Nayland CP. T. Hall (NT), 17c hse.

THORLBY Yorks (W)
95 SD 9652 2m WNW of Skipton.
CP(Stirton w Thlby), 183. Skptn RD. Ch m.
Skptn CC.

THORLEY Herts
148 TL 4719 2m SSW of Bishop's
Stortford. CP, 269. Braughing RD. P Bshp's
Sttfd. Ch e. E Herts CC.

THORLEY STREET IOW
180 SZ 3788 1m ESE of Yarmouth. Loc,
Ymth CP. Ch e.

THORMANBY Yorks (N)
91 SE 4974 6m SE of Thirsk. CP, 87.
Easingwold RD. P YORK. Ch e. Thsk and
Malton CC.

THORNABY-ON-TEES Yorks (N)
85 NZ 4517 S distr of Teesside. Loc,
Tssde CB. P STOCKTON-ON-TEES, Tssde.
Tssde, Thnby BC.

THORNAGE Norfolk
125 TG 0536 2m SW of Holt. CP, 236.
Erpingham RD. P Hlt. Ch e, v. N Nflk CC.

THORNBOROUGH Bucks
146 SP 7433 3m E of Buckingham. CP, 472.
Bcknghm RD. P BCKNGHM. Ch e, m.
Sch p. Bcknghm CC.

THORNBOROUGH Yorks (N)
91 SE 2979 4m E of Masham. Loc,
W Tanfield CP. T. Circles, Bronze Age
monmts.

THORNBURY Devon
175 SS 4008 5m NE of Holsworthy.
CP, 223. Hlswthy RD. P Hlswthy. Ch e.
W Dvn CC (Tavistock). See also Woodacott.

THORNBURY Glos
155, 156 ST 6389 4m E of Severn Rd Br.
CP, 3,473. Thnbry RD. P BRISTOL.
Ch b, c, m, r. Sch p2, pe, s2. S Glos CC. See
also Morton. Fine Dec to Perp ch; 130ft
twr. Unfinished Tdr cstle.

THORNBURY Herefs
129, 130 SO 6259 4m NW of Bromyard.
CP, 141. Brmyd RD. Ch e. Leominster CC.

THORNBY Northants
132, 133 SP 6775 8m SSW of Mkt
Harborough. CP, 106. Brixworth RD.
P NORTHAMPTON. Ch e. Daventry CC
(Kettering).

THORNCLIFF Staffs
111 SK 0158 2m NE of Leek. Loc,
Tittesworth CP. Lk RD. Ch m. Lk CC.

THORNCOMBE Dorset
177 ST 3703 5m SE of Chard. CP, 743.
Beaminster RD. P Chd. Ch e, v. Sch pe.
W Dst CC. 1½m NW, Forde Abbey*, 12c
monastery converted to a hse in 17c.

THORNCOMBE Dorset
178 ST 8703 2m SSW of Blandford. Loc,
Blndfd RD. N Dst CC.

THORNCOMBE STREET Surrey
169, 170, 182 TQ 0042 5m S of Guildford.
Loc. Bramley CP.

THORNDON Suffolk (E)
136 TM 1469 3m S of Eye. CP, 462.
Hartismere RD. P Eye. Ch e, b. Sch pe.
Eye CC.

THORNE Som
177 ST 5217 2m WNW of Yeovil. Loc,
Brympton CP. Ch e.

THORNE Yorks (W)
103 SE 6813 8m SSW of Goole. CP, 15,280.
Thne RD. P Doncaster. Ch e, c, m3, s, v.
Sch i, j, p, pe, s, sb, sg. Gle CC. See also
Moorends.

THORNER Yorks (W)
96 SE 3740 6m NE of Leeds. CP, 1,165.
Wetherby RD. P LDS. Ch e, m. Sch pe.
Barkston Ash CC.

THORNE ST MARGARET Som
164 ST 0921 3m W of Wellington. CP, 82.
Wllngtn RD. Ch e. Taunton CC.

THORNEY Hunts
123 TF 2804 7m ENE of Peterborough.
CP, 2,142. Thny RD. P PTRBRGH. Ch e, m.
Sch p. Ptrbrgh BC (Isle of Ely CC). See also
N Side. Once an island, stronghold of
Hereward the Wake. Rems of 12c abbey.
18c windmill.

THORNEY Notts
113 SK 8572 7m W of Lincoln. CP, 215.
Newark RD. P Nwk. Ch e. Nwk CC.

THORNEY HILL Hants
179 SZ 1999 5m NE of Christchurch. Loc,
Chrstchch E CP. Ringwood and
Fordingbridge RD. P Bransgore, Chrstchch.
Ch e, m. Sch pe. New Forest CC.

THORNEY TOLL Cambs
123 TF 3403 7m NW of March. Loc,
Wisbech St Mary CP. P Wsbch. Ch r.

THORNFALCON Som
177 ST 2823 4m ESE of Taunton. CP, 170.
Tntn RD. Ch e. Tntn CC.

THORNFORD Dorset
178 ST 6013 3m SW of Sherborne. CP, 359.
Shbne RD. P Shbne. Ch e, m. Sch pe.
W Dst CC.

THORNGUMBALD Yorks (E)
99 TA 2026 7m ESE of Hull. CP, 774.
Holderness RD. P Hll. Ch e, m. Sch p.
Bridlington CC. See also Ryhill.

THORNHAM Norfolk
124 TF 7343 4m ENE of Hunstanton.
CP, 507. Docking RD. P King's Lynn.
Ch e, m. Sch p. NW Nflk CC (K's Lnn).

THORNHAM MAGNA Suffolk (E)
136 TM 1070 3m SW of Eye. CP, 144.
Hartismere RD. P Eye. Ch e. Eye CC.

THORNHAM PARVA Suffolk (E)
136 TM 1072 2m WSW of Eye. CP, 66.
Hartismere RD. Ch e. Eye CC.

THORNHAUGH Hunts
123 TF 0600 5m SSE of Stamford. CP, 205.
Barnack RD. P PETERBOROUGH. Sch p.
Ptrbrgh BC (CC). Ch contains tomb of
William Russell, 1st Duke of Bedford.

THORNHILL Cumb
82 NY 0108 6m SSE of Whitehaven. Loc,
St John Beckermet CP. P Egremont. Ch m.
Sch p.

THORNHILL Derbys
111 SK 1983 9m N of Bakewell. CP, 169.
Chapel en le Frith RD. Ch m2. High
Peak CC.

THORNHOLME Yorks (E)
99 TA 1163 4m WSW of Bridlington. Loc,
Burton Agnes CP. Ch m.

THORNLEY Co Durham
84 NZ 1137 1m S of Tow Law. Loc,
Wolsingham CP. Ch e.

THORNLEY Co Durham
85 NZ 3639 4m WSW of Peterlee.
CP, 4,535. Easington RD. P DRHM.
Ch e, m, r, s. Sch p̂, pr. Easngtn CC.

THORNS Suffolk (W)
135, 149 TL 7455 8m SE of Newmarket.
Loc, Wickhambrook CP.

THORNTHWAITE Cumb
82 NY 2225 3m WNW of Keswick. Loc,
Above Derwent CP. Cockermouth RD.
P Kswck. Ch e. Workington CC.

THORNTHWAITE Yorks (W)
96 SE 1758 5m SSE of Pateley Br.
CP(Thnthwte w Padside), 136. Ripon and
Ptly Br RD. Ch e. Rpn CC.

THORNTON Bucks
146 SP 7536 3m SW of Stony Stratford.
CP, 233. Buckingham RD. Ch e.
Bcknghm CC. Ch has outstanding brass of
1472.

THORNTON Lancs
94 SD 3442 4m S of Fleetwood. UD(Thntn
Cleveleys), 26,869. P(Thntn
Clvlys), Blackpool. N Fylde CC. See also Lit
Thntn.

THORNTON Lancs
100 SD 3301 5m SSE of Formby.
CP, 1,876. W Lancs RD. P LIVERPOOL 23.
Ch r. Sch j. Crosby BC (Ormskirk CC).

THORNTON Leics
121 SK 4607 5m SE of Coalville. Loc,
Bagworth CP. P LEICESTER. Ch e, b, m.
Sch p. In coal-mining area, beside reservoir.

THORNTON Lincs (L)
114 TF 2467 2m SW of Horncastle. CP, 86.
Hncstle RD. Ch e. Hncstle CC.

THORNTON Yorks (E)
97, 98 SE 7645 4m SW of Pocklington.
CP, 157. Pcklngtn RD. Ch e, m.
Howden CC.

THORNTON CURTIS Lincs (L)
104 TA 0817 4m SE of Barton-upon-Humber.
CP, 403. Glanford Brigg RD. P Ulceby.
Ch e, m. Sch pe. Brgg and Scunthorpe CC
(Brgg). See also Burnham. Ch has rare black
Tournai marble font. 1½m NE, Thntn Abbey
(A.M.), rems of Augustinian hse with
impressive gatehouse.

THORNTON DALE Yorks (N)
92 SE 8383 2m ESE of Pickering.
CP, 1,199. Pckrng RD. Ch e, m2. Sch pe.
Scarborough CC (Scbrgh and Whitby).
Pleasant vllge with stream running alongside
main street. 17c almshouses.

THORNTON HOUGH Ches
100, 109 SJ 3080 5m SSW of Birkenhead.
Loc, Bebington MB. P Wirral.

THORNTON-IN-CRAVEN Yorks (W)
95 SD 9048 6m SWS of Skipton. CP, 290.
Skptn RD. P Skptn. Ch e. Sch p. Skptn CC.

THORNTON IN LONSDALE Yorks (W)
89 SD 6873 6m SE of Kirkby Lonsdale.
CP, 288. Settle RD. Ch e, m. Skipton CC.
See also Masongill, Westhouse.

THORNTON-LE-BEANS Yorks (N)
91 SE 3990 3m SE of Northallerton.
CP, 157. Nthlltn RD. P Nthlltn. Ch e,, m.
Richmond CC.

THORNTON-LE-CLAY Yorks (N)
92 SE 6865 8m SW of Malton. CP, 167.
Mltn RD. P YORK. Ch f, m. Thirsk and
Mltn CC.

THORNTON LE MOOR Lincs (L)
104 TF 0596 6m NW of Mkt Rasen. Loc,
Owersby CP. Caistor RD. Ch e.
Gainsborough CC.

THORNTON-LE-MOOR Yorks (N)
91 SE 3988 4m SSE of Northallerton.
CP, 297. Thirsk RD. P Nthlltn. Ch e, m.
Sch pe. Thsk and Malton CC.

THORNTON-LE-MOORS Ches
109 SJ 4474 6m NNE of Chester. CP.
Chstr RD. P CHSTR. Ch e. City of
Chstr CC.

THORNTON-LE-STREET Yorks (N)
91 SE 4186 3m NNW of Thirsk. CP, 95.
Thsk RD. P Thsk. Ch e. Thsk and
Malton CC.

THORNTON RUST Yorks (N)
90 SD 9788 2m W of Aysgarth. CP, 142.
Aysgth RD. P Leyburn. Richmond CC.

THORNTON STEWARD Yorks (N)
91 SE 1787 3m E of Middleham. CP, 163.
Leyburn RD. P Ripon. Ch e, r.
Richmond CC.

THORNTON WATLASS Yorks (N)
91 SE 2385 3m SW of Bedale. CP, 146.
Bdle RD. P Ripon. Ch e. Sch pe. Thirsk and
Malton CC.

THORNWOOD COMMON Essex
161 TL 4704 2m NNE of Epping. Loc,
N Weald Bassett CP. P Eppng.

THOROTON Notts
112, 122 SK 7642 7m SSW of Newark.
CP, 105. Bingham RD. Ch e. Rushcliffe CC
(Carlton).

THORP ARCH Yorks (W)
97 SE 4346 2m ESE of Wetherby. CP, 658.
Wthrby RD. Ch e. Sch pe. Barkston CC.

THORPE Derbys
111 SK 1550 3m NNW of Ashbourne.
CP, 173. Ashbne RD. P Ashbne. Ch e.
W Derbys CC. S entrance to Dovedale.

THORPE Lincs (L)
105 TF 4982 2m SSW of Mablethorpe. Loc,
Mblthpe and Sutton UD.

THORPE Norfolk
137 TM 4398 5m NNE of Beccles. Loc,
Haddiscoe CP. Ch e.

THORPE Notts
112 SK 7650 3m SW of Newark. CP, 60.
Nwk RD. Ch e. Nwk CC.

THORPE Surrey
169, 170 TQ 0268 2m SSW of Staines. Loc,
Egham UD. P Eghm. Sailing on gravel
workings to E of vllge.

THORPE Yorks (E)
98 SE 9946 5m NNW of Beverley. Loc,
Lockington CP. Ch e.

THORPE Yorks (W)
90 SE 0161 7m NNE of Skipton. CP, 41.
Skptn RD.

THORPE ABBOTTS Norfolk
137 TM 1979 5m E of Diss. Loc,
Brockdish CP. P Dss. Ch e.

THORPE ACRE Leics
121 SK 5120 1m W of Loughborough. Loc,
Lghbrgh MB.

THORPE ARNOLD Leics
122 SK 7720 1m ENE of Melton Mowbray.
Loc, Waltham CP. Ch e.

THORPE AUDLIN Yorks (W)
103 SE 4715 4m SSE of Pontefract.
CP, 313. Hemsworth RD. Ch m.
Hmswth CC.

THORPE BASSETT Yorks (E)
92 SE 8673 5m E of Malton. CP, 131.
Norton RD. P Mltn. Ch e. Howden CC.

THORPE BAY Essex
162 TQ 9184 2m E of Southend. Loc,
Sthnd-on-Sea CB. P Sthnd-on-Sea.
Sthnd E BC.

THORPE BY WATER Rutland
133 SP 8996 3m SE of Uppingham. CP, 35.
Uppnghm RD. Rtlnd and Stamford CC.

THORPE CONSTANTINE Staffs
120 SK 2508 4m NE of Tamworth.
CP, 144. Lichfield RD. Ch e. Lchfld and
Tmwth CC.

THORPE END GARDEN VILLAGE
Norfolk
126 TG 2811 4m ENE of Norwich. Loc, Gt
and Lit Plumstead CP. Blofield and
Flegg RD. P NRWCH, NOR 50Z.
Yarmouth CC (Central Nflk).

THORPE GREEN Suffolk (W)
149 TL 9354 4m NNE of Lavenham. Loc,
Thpe Morieux CP.

THORPE HESLEY Yorks (W)
102, 103 SK 3796 4m NW of Rotherham.
Loc, Rthrhm CB. P Rthrhm. Keppel's
Column, with viewing platform, blt as
decoration in grnds of Wentworth
Woodhouse (see Wntwth).

THORPE IN BALNE Yorks (W)
103 SE 5910 5m NNE of Doncaster.
CP, 123. Dncstr RD. Ch m. Don Valley CC.

THORPE LANGTON Leics
133 SP 7492 3m N of Mkt Harborough.
CP, 94. Mkt Hbrgh RD. Ch e. Hbrgh CC.

THORPE LARCHES Co Durham
85 NZ 3826 6m NW of Teesside (Stockton).
Loc, Sedgefield RD, Stcktn RD. Drhm CC,
Easington CC (Sdgfld.)

THORPE-LE-SOKEN Essex
150 TM 1822 5m N of Clacton. CP, 1,606.
Tendring RD. P Clctn-on-Sea.
Ch e, b, m, v2. Sch pe, s. Harwich CC.

THORPE MALSOR Northants
133 SP 8379 2m W of Kettering. CP, 147.
Kttrng RD. P Kttrng. Ch e. Kttrng CC.

THORPE MANDEVILLE Northants
145 SP 5344 5m ENE of Banbury. CP, 136.
Brackley RD. Ch e. Daventry CC (S Nthnts).

THORPE MARKET Norfolk
126 TG 2436 4m SSE of Cromer. CP, 227.
Erpingham RD. P NORWICH, NOR 36Y.
Ch e, m. N Nflk CC.

THORPE MORIEUX Suffolk (W)
149 TL 9453 3m NE of Lavenham. CP, 281.
Cosford RD. P Bury St Edmunds. Ch e.
Sudbury and Woodbridge CC. See also Thpe
Grn.

THORPENESS Suffolk (E)
137 TM 4759 2m NNE of Aldeburgh. Loc,
Aldringham cum Thorpe CP. P Leiston.
Seaside holiday settlement. Boating on
mere.

THORPE ON THE HILL Lincs (K)
113 SK 9065 6m SW of Lincoln. CP, 749.
N Kesteven RD. P LNCLN. Ch e, m. Sch pe.
Grantham CC.

THORPE ST ANDREW Norfolk
126 TG 2609 3m E of Norwich. CP, 10,788.
Blofield and Flegg RD. P Nrwch. Ch e2, m.
Sch p2, s2. Yarmouth CC (Central Nflk).

THORPE ST PETER Lincs (L)
114 TF 4860 6m WSW of Skegness. CP, 392.
Spilsby RD. Ch e, m2. Sch p. Horncastle CC.
See also Fendike Corner.

THORPE SALVIN Yorks (W)
103 SK 5281 4m WNW of Worksop.
CP, 349. Kiveton Pk RD. P Wksp, Notts.
Ch e, m. Sch p. Rother Valley CC. Small
Nmn ch and rems of Elizn mnr hse.

THORPE SATCHVILLE Leics
122 SK 7311 5m SSW of Melton Mowbray.
CP(Twyford and Thpe), 487. Mltn and
Belvoir RD. P Mltn Mbry. Ch e. Mltn CC. To
NW, Thorpe Trussels, well known fox-cover.

THORPE THEWLES Co Durham
85 NZ 4023 4m NW of Teesside (Stockton).
Loc, Grindon CP. Stcktn RD.
P STCKTN-ON-TEES, Tssde. Easington CC
(Sedgefield).

THORPE UNDERWOOD Yorks (W)
97 SE 4659 8m NNE of Wetherby. CP(Thpe
Undrwds), 82. Nidderdale RD.
Harrogate CC.

THORPE WATERVILLE Northants
134 TL 0281 2m NE of Thrapston. Loc,
Thpe Achurch CP. Oundle and Thrpstn RD.
Wellingborough CC (Peterborough).

THORPE WILLOUGHBY Yorks (W)
97 SE 5731 3m WSW of Selby. CP, 292.
Slby RD. P Slby. Ch m. Barkston Ash CC.

THORRINGTON Essex
149, 162 TM 0920 7m ESE of Colchester.
CP, 689. Tendring RD. P Clchstr. Ch e, m.
Harwich CC.

THORVERTON Devon
176 SS 9202 6m N of Exeter. CP, 674.
Tiverton RD. P Extr. Ch e, b. Sch pe.
Tvtn CC.

THRANDESTON Suffolk (E)
136 TM 1176 2m S of Diss. CP, 158.
Hartismere RD. Ch e, m. Eye CC.

THRAPSTON Northants
134 SO 9978 8m E of Kettering. CP, 1,994.
Oundle and Thrpstn RD. P Kttrng.
Ch e, b, m, r. Sch p, s. Wellingborough CC
(Peterborough).

THREAPLAND Cumb
82 NY 1539 8m E of Maryport. CP(Bothel
and Thrplnd), 297. Cockermouth RD.
Workington CC.

THREAPLAND Yorks (W)
90 SD 9860 6m N of Skipton. Loc,
Cracoe CP.

THREAPWOOD Ches
109 SJ 4445 7m WNW of Whitchurch.
CP, 239. Tarvin RD. Ch e, c. Nantwich CC.

THREE BRIDGES Sussex (W)
170, 182 TQ 2837 1m E of Crawley. Loc,
Crly UD. P Crly.

THREE HOLES Norfolk
124 TF 5000 6m SSE of Wisbech. Loc,
Upwell CP. P(Three Hls Br), Wsbch, Cambs.

THREEKINGHAM Lincs (K)
113, 123 TF 0936 6m SSE of Sleaford.

CP, 186. E Kesteven RD. P Slfd. Ch e. Rutland and Stamford CC. See also Spanby. Arched gateway of whalebone.

THREELEG CROSS Sussex (E)
183 TQ 6831 3m E of Wadhurst. Loc, Ticehurst CP.

THREE LEGGED CROSS Dorset
179 SU 0805 4m W of Ringwood. Loc, Verwood CP. P Wimborne. Ch c, m, v. Sch p.

THREEMILE CROSS Berks
169 SU 7167 4m S of Reading. Loc, Shinfield CP. P Rdng. Ch m, v. Mary Mitford's Cottage*, former home of author of Our Village etc.

THREE MILE STONE Cornwall
190 SW 7845 3m W of Truro. Loc, Kenwyn CP. Truro RD. P Truro. Sch p.

THRELKELD Cumb
82 NY 3225 4m ENE of Keswick. CP, 539. Penrith RD. P Kswck. Ch e, m. Sch pe. Pnrth and the Border CC. See also Scales.

THRESHFIELD Yorks (W)
90 SD 9963 8m N of Skipton. CP, 366. Skptn RD. P Skptn. Ch m. Sch pe. Skptn CC.

THRIGBY Norfolk
126 TG 4612 5m NW of Yarmouth. Loc, Mautby CP. Ch e.

THRINGARTH Yorks (N)
84 NY 9322 2m SW of Middleton in Teesdale. Loc, Lunesdale CP. Startforth RD. Richmond CC.

THRINGSTONE Leics
121 SK 4217 2m N of Coalville. Loc, Clvlle UD. P Clvlle, LEICESTER.

THRINTOFT Yorks (N)
91 SE 3293 3m W of Northallerton. CP, 109. Nthlltn RD. Richmond CC.

THRIPLOW Cambs
148 TL 4446 6m NE of Royston. CP, 836. S Cambs RD. P Rstn, Herts. Ch e, c. Sch pe. Cambs CC.

THROCKING Herts
147 TL 3330 6m ESE of Baldock. Loc, Cottered CP. Ch e.

THROCKLEY Nthmb
78 NZ 1566 6m WNW of Newcastle. Loc, Newburn UD. P NCSTLE UPON TYNE 5.

THROCKLEY BANK TOP Nthmb
78 NZ 1566 6m WNW of Newcastle. Loc, Newburn UD.

THROCKMORTON Worcs
143, 144 SO 9849 3m NE of Pershore. CP, 152. Pshre RD. Ch e. S Worcs CC. On edge of Pshre Airfield.

THROPHILL Nthmb
78 NZ 1385 4m W of Morpeth. Loc, Meldon CP.

THROPTON Nthmb
71 NU 0202 2m W of Rothbury. CP, 251. Rthbry RD. P Morpeth. Ch r, v. Sch p. Berwick-upon-Tweed CC.

THROWLEIGH Devon
175 SX 6690 6m ESE of Okehampton. CP, 272. Okhmptn RD. P Okhmptn. Ch e, m. Sch p. W Dvn CC (Torrington).

THROWLEY Kent
172 TQ 9955 4m SSW of Faversham. CP, 289. Swale RD. Ch e. Sch pe. Fvrshm CC. See also Thrly Forstal.

THROWLEY FORSTAL Kent
172 TQ 9854 5m SSW of Faversham. Loc, Thrly CP. P Fvshm.

THRUMPTON Notts
112, 121 SK 5131 7m SW of Nottingham. CP, 127. Basford RD. P NTTNGHM. Ch e. Rushcliffe CC. Jcbn hall.

THRUNTON Nthmb
71 NU 0810 6m WSW of Alnwick. Loc, Whittingham CP.

THRUPP Glos
156 SO 8603 1m SSE of Stroud. CP, 1,650. Strd RD. Sch p. Strd CC. See also Brimscombe.

THRUPP Oxon
145 SP 4815 2m ESE of Woodstock. CP(Shipton-on-Cherwell and Thrpp), 493. Ploughley RD. Mid-Oxon CC (Banbury).

THRUSCROSS Yorks (W)
96 SE 1558 4m S of Pateley Br. CP, 65. Ripon and Ptly Br RD. Ch e, m. Rpn CC. See also W End. Reservoir.

THRUSHELTON Devon
175 SX 4487 8m ENE of Launceston.
CP, 257. Tavistock RD. Ch e, m. W Dvn CC
(Tvstck).

THRUSSINGTON Leics
121, 122 SK 6415 7m WSW of Melton
Mowbray. CP, 392. Barrow upon Soar RD.
P LEICESTER. Ch e. Sch pe. Mltn CC.

THRUXTON Hants
168 SU 2945 4m W of Andover. CP, 417.
Andvr RD. P Andvr. Ch e. Winchester CC
(Basingstoke). Ch: brass of 1407; monmts.

THRUXTON Herefs
142 SO 4334 6m SW of Hereford. CP, 42.
Dore and Bredwardine RD. P HRFD. Ch e.
Hrfd CC.

THRYBERGH Yorks (W)
103 SK 4695 3m NE of Rotherham.
CP, 5,611. Rthrhm RD. P Rthrhm. Ch e, r.
Sch p, pe, pr, s. Rother Valley CC.

THULSTON Derbys
112, 121 SK 4031 4m SE of Derby. Loc,
Elvaston CP. P DBY.

THUNDERSLEY Essex
162 TQ 7888 4m E of Basildon. Loc,
Benfleet UD. P Bnflt. SE Essx CC.

THURCASTON Leics
121, 122 SK 5610 4m N of Leicester. CP.
Barrow upon Soar RD. P LCSTR. Ch e, m.
Sch pe. Melton CC. See also Cropston.

THURCROFT Yorks (W)
103 SK 4988 5m ESE of Rotherham.
CP, 7,941. Rthrhm RD. P Rthrhm.
Ch e, m, r, s. Sch i, j, s. Rother Valley CC.
See also Brampton en le Morthen,
Brookhouse, Laughton en le Mthn.

THURGARTON Norfolk
126 TG 1834 5m SSW of Cromer. Loc,
Aldborough CP. Ch e, m.

THURGARTON Notts
112 SK 6949 7m WSW of Newark. CP, 348.
Southwell RD. P NOTTINGHAM. Ch e, m.
Sch pe. Nwk CC. Ch incorporates parts of
13c priory.

THURGOLAND Yorks (W)
102 SE 2901 3m ESE of Penistone.
CP, 1,551. Pnstne RD. P SHEFFIELD.
Ch e, m. Sch pe. Pnstne CC. See also Crane
Moor.

THURLASTON Leics
132 SP 5099 6m SW of Leicester. CP, 378.
Blaby RD. P LCSTR. Ch e, b. Sch pe.
Blby CC (Harborough).

THURLASTON Warwicks
132 SP 4671 3m SW of Rugby. CP, 262.
Rgby RD. P Rgby. Ch e. Rgby CC.

THURLBEAR Som
177 ST 2621 3m SE of Taunton. Loc,
Orchard Portman CP. Ch e. Sch pe.

THURLBY Lincs (K)
113 SK 9061 8m SW of Lincoln. CP, 125.
N Kesteven RD. Ch e. Grantham CC.

THURLBY Lincs (K)
123 TF 0916 2m S of Bourne. CP, 738.
S Kesteven RD. P Bne. Ch e, m2. Sch p.
Rutland and Stamford CC. See also
Northorpe.

THURLBY Lincs (L)
105 TF 4975 2m E of Alford. Loc,
Bilsby CP.

THURLEIGH Beds
134 TL 0558 6m N of Bedford. CP, 531.
Bdfd RD. P BDFD. Ch e, b. Sch p. Bdfd CC.

THURLESTONE Devon
187, 188 SX 6742 4m W of Kingsbridge.
CP, 685. Kngsbrdge RD. P Kngsbrdge. Ch e.
Sch pe. Totnes CC. See also Bantham, Buckland. Cliff-top vllge resort with many new
hses. Golf course.

THURLOW, GREAT Suffolk (W)
148 TL 6750 3m N of Haverhill. See Gt
Thlw.

THURLOXTON Som
165 ST 2730 5m SSW of Bridgwater.
CP, 139. Brdgwtr RD. P Taunton. Ch e.
Brdgwtr CC.

THURLSTONE Yorks (W)
102 SE 2303 1m W of Penistone. Loc,
Pnstne UD. P SHEFFIELD.

THURLTON Norfolk
137 TM 4198 5m N of Beccles. CP, 341.

Lodden RD. P NORWICH, NOR 27W. Ch e, m. Sch p. S Nflk CC. See also Low Thltn.

THURMASTON Leics
121, 122 SK 6109 3m NNE of Leicester. CP, 7,160. Barrow upon Soar RD. P LCSTR. Ch e, m. Sch i, je, p, pr, s. Harborough CC (Melton).

THURNBY Leics
121, 122 SK 6403 4m E of Leicester. CP. Billesdon RD. P LCSTR. Ch e. Sch p, pe. Harborough CC (Melton).

THURNE Norfolk
126 TG 4015 7m E of Wroxham. CP, 172. Blofield and Flegg RD. P Gt Yarmouth. Ch e, m. Ymth CC. To W, two drainage mills of twr type with cap and sails.

THURNHAM Kent
172 TQ 8057 3m ENE of Maidstone. CP, 990. Hollingbourn RD. Ch e, m. Sch pe. Mdstne CC.

THURNING Norfolk
125 TG 0829 6m S of Holt. CP, 69. Walsingham RD. Ch e. NW Nflk CC (N Nflk).

THURNING Northants
134 TL 0883 4m SE of Oundle. CP, 102. Oundle and Thrapston RD. Ch e. Wellingborough CC (Peterborough).

THURNSCOE Yorks (W)
103 SE 4505 7m E of Barnsley. Loc, Dearne UD. P Rotherham. Hemsworth CC.

THURSBY Cumb
75 NY 3250 6m SW of Carlisle. CP, 882. Wigton RD. P Clsle. Ch e, m. Sch p. Penrith and the Border CC.

THURSFORD Norfolk
125 TF 9933 5m ENE of Fakenham. CP, 201. Walsingham RD. P Fknhm. Ch e, m. NW Nflk CC (N Nflk).

THURSLEY Surrey
169 SU 9039 5m WSW of Godalming. CP, 615. Hambledon RD. P Gdlmng. Ch e. Guildford CC. See also Bowlhead Grn. Ch: 15c wooden belfry. Sad epitaph on tombstone to unknown sailor in churchyard.

THURSTASTON Ches
100, 108, 109 SJ 2484 5m SW of Birkenhead. Loc, Wirral UD. Wrrl CC.

THURSTON Suffolk (W)
136 TL 9265 5m E of Bury St Edmunds. CP, 1,002. Thedwastre RD. P Bury St Eds. Ch e, m. Sch pe. Bury St Eds CC.

THURSTONFIELD Cumb
75 NY 3156 5m W of Carlisle. Loc, Burgh by Sands CP. Ch m.

THURSTONLAND Yorks (W)
102 SE 1610 4m SSE of Huddersfield. Loc, Kirkburton UD. P Hddsfld.

THURTON Norfolk
137 TG 3200 7m N of Bungay. CP, 287. Loddon RD. P NORWICH, NOR 15W. Ch e. Sch pe. S Nflk CC.

THURVASTON Derbys
120 SK 2437 7m W of Derby. CP(Osleston and Thvstn), 218. Repton RD. Ch m. Sch pe. Belper CC.

THUXTON Norfolk
125 TG 0307 5m SE of E Dereham. Loc, Garvestone CP. Ch e.

THWAITE Suffolk (E)
136 TM 1168 4m SSW of Eye. CP, 76. Hartismere RD. P Eye. Ch e. Eye CC.

THWAITE Yorks (N)
90 SD 8998 5m NNE of Hawes. Loc, Muker CP. Ch v.

THWAITE ST MARY Norfolk
137 TM 3395 3m N of Bungay. CP(Thwte), 83. Loddon RD. Ch e. S Nflk CC.

THWING Yorks (E)
93 TA 0470 8m WNW of Bridlington. CP, 244. Brdlngtn RD. P Driffield. Ch e, m. Brdlngtn CC.

TIBBERTON Glos
143 SO 7621 5m WNW of Gloucester. CP, 279. Newent RD. P GLCSTR. Ch e, m. Sch p. W Glos CC.

TIBBERTON Shrops
119 SJ 6820 4m W of Newport. CP, 319. Wellington RD. P Npt. Ch e, m. Sch pe. The Wrekin CC.

TIBBERTON Worcs
130, 131 SO 9057 4m ENE of Worcester.
CP, 321. Droitwich RD. P Drtwch. Ch e, m.
Sch pe. Wcstr BC.

TIBENHAM Norfolk
136 TM 1389 6m N of Diss. CP, 424.
Depwade RD.   NORWICH, NOR 82W.
Ch e, m. Sch p. S Nflk CC.

TIBSHELF Derbys
112 SK 4360 4m NNE of Alfreton.
CP, 3,620. Blackwell RD. P DERBY.
Ch e, m2. Sch i, j, s. Bolsover CC.

TIBTHORPE Yorks (E)
98 SE 9655 4m WSW of Driffield. CP, 213.
Drffld RD. P Drffld. Ch m. Howden CC.

TICEHURST Sussex (E)
183 TQ 6830 4m ESE of Wadhurst.
CP, 2,840. Battle RD. P Wdhst. Ch e, m.
Sch pe. Rye CC. See also Flimwell,
Stonegate, Threeleg Cross, Wallcrouch.
Wealden vllge on ridge; views.

TICHBORNE Hants
168 SU 5730 6m E of Winchester. CP, 192.
Wnchstr RD. P Alresford. Ch e, r.
Wnchstr CC. Ch has many monmts to
Tchbne family, whose succession was
subject of famous lawsuit, 1871. Annual
spring dole-giving ceremony.

TICKENCOTE Rutland
123 SK 9909 3m NW of Stamford. CP, 77.
Oakham RD. Ch e. Rtlnd and Stmfd CC. Ch
has famous Nmn chancel arch of astounding
proportions.

TWICKENHAM Som
155, 165 ST 4571 8m W of Bristol. CP, 838.
Long Ashton RD. P Clevedon. Ch e. Sch pe.
N Som CC.

TICKHILL Yorks (W)
103 SK 5993 6m S of Doncaster.
UD, 3,257. P Dncstr. Don Valley CC. Fine
13c–14c ch. Rems of cstle. Restored
timber-frame hse St Leonard's Hsptl blt
1470.

TICKLERTON Shrops
129 SO 4890 3m SE of Ch Stretton. Loc,
Eaton-under-Heywood CP.

TICKNALL Derbys
120, 121 SK 3523 5m N of Ashby de la
Zouch. CP, 535. Repton RD. P DERBY.
Ch e, b, m. Sch pe. Belper CC. Circular
lock-up with spire roof and studded floor.
To E, Staunton Harold Reservoir.

TICKTON Yorks (E)
99 TA 0641 3m NE of Beverley. CP, 540.
Bvrly RD. P Bvrly. Ch e, m. Sch pe.
Haltemprice CC.

TIDCOMBE Wilts
168 SU 2958 7m SSW of Hungerford.
CP (Tdcmbe and Fosbury), 112.
Marlborough and Ramsbury RD. Ch e.
Devizes CC.

TIDDINGTON Oxon
158, 159 SP 6504 4m W of Thame. CP
(Tddngtn-w-Albury), 382. Bullingdon RD.
P OXFORD. Ch e. Mid-Oxon CC (Henley).

TIDDINGTON Warwicks
131 SP 2255 1m E of Stratford. Loc,
Strtfd-upon-Avon MB. P Strtfd-upn-Avn.

TIDEBROOK Sussex (E)
183 TQ 6129 2m SW of Wadhurst. Loc,
Wdhst CP. Ch e.

TIDEFORD Cornwall
186 SX 3459 5m W of Saltash. Loc,
St Germans CP. P Sltsh. Ch e, m.

TIDENHAM Glos
155, 156 ST 5595 2m NE of Chepstow.
CP, 4,195. Lydney RD. P Chpstw, Mon.
Ch e, v2. Sch pe. W Glos CC. See also
Beachley, Boughspring, Sedbury, Wibdon.

TIDESWELL Derbys
111 SK 1575 6m ENE of Buxton.
CP, 1,829. Bakewell RD. P Bxtn.
Ch e, c, m3, r. Sch pe, s. W Derbys CC. See
also Miller's Dale. Impressive ch known as
'Cathedral of the Peak'. Well-dressing.

TIDMARSH Berks
158, 159 SU 6374 1m S of Pangbourne.
CP, 257. Bradfield RD. Ch e. Newbury CC.

TIDMINGTON Warwicks
144 SP 2638 1m S of Shipston on Stour.
CP, 33. Shpstn on Str RD. Ch e.
Stratford-on-Avon CC (Strtfd).

TIFFIELD Northants
146 SP 6951 2m N of Towcester. CP, 255.
Tcstr RD. P Tcstr. Ch e. Sch pe.
Daventry CC (S Nthnts).

TIGLEY Devon
187, 188 SX 7560 3m W of Totnes. Loc,
Dartington CP.

TILBROOK Hunts
134 TL 0769 9m NW of St Neots. CP, 234.
St Nts RD. P HUNTINGDON. Ch e, m.
Hunts CC. Ch: broach spire, Perp scrn.

TILBURY Essex
161, 171 TQ 6475 9m SSW of Basildon.
Loc, Thurrock UD. Thrrck BC (CC). Docks,
factories, power stn; modern container port.
To E on waterside, T. Fort (A.M.), blt by
Henry VIII. Elizabeth I reviewed troops
here 1588.

TILEHURST Berks
158, 159 SU 6673 W distr of Reading. Loc,
Rdng CB; CP, 5,215, Bradfield RD. Ch e.
Sch p2, s. Rdng N BC, Newbury CC.
(Nbry CC.) See also Calcot Row.

TILFORD Surrey
169 SU 8743 2m SE of Farnham. CP, 714.
Hambledon RD. P Fnhm. Ch e. Sch pe, s.
Fnhm CC. On edge of large cmmns to S.

TILLINGHAM Essex
162 TL 9903 9m ESE of Maldon. CP, 764.
Mldn RD. P Southminster. Ch e, c, v.
Sch pe. Mldn CC.

TILLINGTON Herefs
142 SO 4645 4m NNW of Hereford. Loc,
Burghill CP. P HRFD. Ch m.

TILLINGTON Sussex (W)
181, 182 SU 9621 1m W of Petworth.
CP, 582. Midhurst RD. P Ptwth. Ch e.
Chichester CC (Horsham). See also Upperton.
Estate vllge W of Ptwth Pk. Ch has unusual
'crown' on twr.

TILLINGTON COMMON Herefs
142 SO 4546 5m NNW of Hereford. Loc,
Burghill CP.

TILMANSTONE Kent
173 TR 3051 5m W of Deal. CP, 279.
Eastry RD. P Dl. Ch e, m. Dover and Dl CC
(Dvr). In mining area.

TILNEY ALL SAINTS Norfolk
124 TF 5618 4m WSW of King's Lynn.
CP, 475. Marshland RD. P K's Lnn. Ch e, m.
Sch pe. NW Nflk CC (K's Lnn). See also
Tlny High End.

TILNEY HIGH END Norfolk
124 TF 5616 4m WSW of King's Lynn. Loc,
Tlny All Saints CP.

TILNEY ST LAWRENCE Norfolk
124 TF 5414 6m ENE of Wisbech.
CP, 1,265. Marshland RD. P King's Lynn.
Ch e, m2. Sch p. NW Nflk CC (K's Lnn).

TILSHEAD Wilts
167 SU 0347 9m WNW of Amesbury.
CP, 314. Amesbury RD. P Salisbury.
Ch e, b. Sch pe. Slsbry CC. Thatched
cottages of stone and flint chequerwork.

TILSTOCK Shrops
118 SJ 5437 2m S of Whitchurch. Loc,
Whtchch Rural CP. N Shrops RD. P Whtchch.
Ch e. Sch pe. Oswestry CC.

TILSTON Ches
109 SJ 4551 8m E of Wrexham. CP, 426.
Tarvin RD. P Malpas. Ch e, m. Sch pe.
Nantwich CC.

TILSTONE FEARNALL Ches
109 SJ 5660 7m SW of Winsford. CP, 99.
Tarvin RD. Ch e. Sch p. Northwich CC.

TILSWORTH Beds
147 SP 9724 3m NW of Dunstable. CP, 250.
Luton RD. P Leighton Buzzard. Ch e, m.
S Beds CC.

TILTON ON THE HILL Leics
122 SK 7405 8m WSW of Oakham.
CP(Tltn), 375. Billesdon RD.
P LEICESTER. Ch e. Sch pe.
Harborough CC (Melton). See also Halstead.
Highest vllge in Leics (700ft).

TILTY Essex
148 TL 5926 3m NNW of Dunmow. CP, 73.
Dnmw RD. Ch e. Saffron Walden CC. Ch is
all that remains of 12c abbey bldngs;
brasses.

TIMBERLAND Lincs (K)
113 TF 1258 5m SW of Woodhall Spa.
CP, 514. E Kesteven RD. P LINCOLN.
Ch e, m2. Sch pe. Grantham CC.

TIMBERSBROOK Ches
110 SJ 8962 2m E of Congleton. Loc,
Cngltn MB. P Cngltn.

TIMBERSCOMBE Som
164 SS 9542 3m SSW of Minehead. CP, 359.
Williton RD. P Mnhd. Ch e, m. Sch pe.
Bridgwater CC.

TIMBLE YORKS (W)
96 SE 1852 5m NNW of Otley. CP(Gt
Tmble), 66. Wharfedale RD. Ripon CC.

TIMPERLEY Ches
101 SJ 7988 2m ENE of Altrincham. Loc,
Altrnchm MB. P Altrnchm. Ch e.

TIMSBURY Hants
168 SU 3424 2m N of Romsey. Loc,
Michelmersh CP.Ch e, m.

TIMSBURY Som
166 ST 6658 3m NNW of Radstock.
CP, 1,587. Clutton RD. P Bath. Ch e, c, m2.
Sch pe, s. N Som CC.

TIMWORTH Suffolk (W)
136 TL 8669 3m N of Bury St Edmunds.
CP, 69. Thingoe RD. Ch e. Bury St Eds CC.

TINCLETON Dorset
178 SY 7791 5m E of Dorchester. CP, 176.
Dchstr RD. P Dchstr. Ch e. Sch pe.
W Dst CC.

TINDALE Cumb
76 NY 6159 6m ESE of Brampton. Loc,
Farlam CP. P(Tndle Fell), Brmptn.

TINDALE CRESCENT Co Durham
85 NZ 2027 1m SSW of Bishop Auckland.
Loc, Bshp Aucklnd UD. P Bshp Aucklnd.

TINGEWICK Bucks
145, 146 SP 6532 3m W of Buckingham.
CP, 755. Bcknghm RD. P BCKNGHM.
Ch e, c. Sch p. Bcknghm CC.

TINGLEY Yorks (W)
96, 102 SE 2826 5m SSW of Leeds. Loc,
Morley MB. P Wakefield.

TINGRITH Beds
147 TL 0032 4m SSW of Ampthill. CP, 114.
Ampthll RD.P Bletchley, Bucks. Ch e.
Mid-Beds CC.

TINHAY Devon
174, 186 SX 3985 4m E of Launceston.
Loc, Lifton CP. Ch m.

TINTAGEL Cornwall
175, 185, 186 SX 0588 4m NW of
Camelford. CP, 1,300. Cmlfd RD. P.
Ch e, m, r. Sch p. N Cnwll CC. See also
Bossiney, Trebarwith, Treknow,
Trewarmett. In village, the 14c Old Post
Office (NT)*. On headland, T. Cstle,
legendary stronghold of King Arthur (A.M.).

TINTINHULL Som
177 ST 4919 2m SW of Ilchester. CP, 694.
Yeovil RD. P Yvl. Ch e. Sch pe. Yvl CC. To
E, T. Hse (NT)*, c 1700, in formal gdns.

TINTWISTLE Ches
102 SK 0297 2m NNW of Glossop.
CP, 1,436. Tntwstle RD. P Hadfield, Hyde.
Ch e, m, v. Sch pe. Stalybridge and Hde CC.
See also Crowden. Formerly Tingetwissel.
At lower end of chain of reservoirs supply-
ing Manchester.

TINWELL Rutland
123 TF 0006 2m W of Stamford. CP, 238.
Ketton RD. P Stmfd, Lincs. Ch e. Rtlnd and
Stmfd CC.

TIPTON Staffs
130, 131 SO 9592 1m NNE of Dudley. Loc,
W Bromwich CB. P. W Brmwch W BC
(Rowley Regis and Tptn).

TIPTON ST JOHN Devon
176 SY 0991 3m NNW of Sidmouth. Loc,
Ottery St Mary UD. P Sdmth.

TIPTREE Essex
149, 162 TL 8916 5m E of Witham.
CP, 3,018. Lexden and Winstree RD.
P Colchester. Ch e, s, v. Sch p2, pe, s.
Clchstr CC. Jam factory surrounded by fruit
fields. Printing wks.

TIRLEY Glos
143 SO 8328 4m SW of Tewkesbury.
CP, 316. Gloucester RD. P GLCSTR.
Ch e, m. W Glos CC.

TIRRIL Westm
83 NY 5026 2m SSW of Penrith.
CP(Sockbridge and Trrl), 196. N Westm RD.
P Pnrth, Cumberland. Ch m. Westm CC.

TISBURY Wilts
167 ST 9429 7m NE of Shaftesbury.
CP, 1,656. Mere and Tsbry RD. P Salisbury.
Ch e, m, r2, v. Sch pe, s. Westbury CC. Nmn
and later ch: angel wagon roof. At Place
Farm mdvl bldngs incl thatched tithe barn,

perhaps largest in England. 1½m SW, Old Wardour Cstle (A.M.) and New Wdr Cstle*, 18c hse now sch.

TISSINGTON Derbys
111 SK 1752 4m N of Ashbourne. CP, 173. Ashbne RD. P Ashbne. Ch e, m. Sch pe. W Derbys CC. Ch: font, monmts. Jcbn Hall. Well-dressing on Ascension Day.

TITCHBERRY Devon
174 SS 2427 13m N of Bude. Loc, Hartland CP. E Ttchbrry Farm (NT); ancient farmhouse with land incl cliffs. Public access on foot to bay.

TITCHFIELD Hants
180 SU 5405 2m W of Fareham. Loc, Frhm UD. P Frhm. To N, T. Abbey (A.M.), rems of 13c abbey converted in 16c into hse called Place Hse.

TITCHMARSH Northants
134 TL 0279 2m ENE of Thrapston. CP, 486. Oundle and Thrpstn RD. P Kettering. Ch e, m. Sch pe. Wellingborough CC (Peterborough). Ch: Perp twr of Weldon stone.

TITCHWELL Norfolk
125 TF 7643 6m ENE of Hunstanton. CP, 161. Docking RD. Ch e. NW Nflk CC (King's Lynn).

TITHBY Notts
112, 122 SK 6936 8m ESE of Nottingham. CP, 71. Bingham RD. Ch e. Rushcliffe CC (Carlton).

TITLEY Herefs
129 SO 3359 3m NE of Kington. CP, 203. Kngtn RD. P Kngtn. Ch e. Leominster CC.

TITSEY Surrey
171 TQ 4055 2m NE of Oxted. CP, 155. Godstone RD. Ch e. E Srry CC (Reigate). On Pilgrims' Way below steep escarpment of N Downs.

TITTENSOR Staffs
110, 119 SJ 8738 4m S of Stoke-on-Trent. Loc, Swynnerton CP. P Stke-on-Trnt. Ch e. Sch pe.

TITTLESHALL Norfolk
125 TF 8921 6m SSW of Fakenham. CP, 282. Mitford and Launditch RD.

P King's Lynn. Ch e, b, m. Sch pe. SW Nflk CC. Ch has many monmts to Coke family, who lived here before they blt Holkham Hall (see Holkham).

TIVERTON Ches
109 SJ 5560 7m SW of Winsford. CP, 477. Tarvin RD. P Tarporley. Ch m. Northwich CC. See also Brassey Grn.

TIVERTON Devon
164, 176 SS 9512 12m N of Exeter. MB, 15,548. P. Tvtn CC. See also Bolham, Chevithorne, Cove, Withleigh. Mkt and mnfg tn. Old Blundell's Sch (NT); Blndll's Sch itself moved 1m E, 1882. Almshouses. Rems of cstle. Ch with Greenaway Chpl.

TIVETSHALL ST MARGARET Norfolk
137 TM 1687 5m NNE of Diss. CP, 277. Depwade RD. P NORWICH, NOR 79W. Ch e, f. S Nflk CC.

TIVETSHALL ST MARY Norfolk
137 TM 1686 5m NE of Diss. CP, 207. Depwade RD. P NORWICH, NOR 80W. Sch p. S Nflk CC.

TIXALL Staffs
119 SJ 9722 4m E of Stafford. CP, 190. Stffd RD. P STFFD. Ch e. Stffd and Stone CC. Elizn gatehouse survives from former T. Hall.

TIXOVER Rutland
123/134 SK 9700 5m SW of Stamford. CP, 61. Ketton RD. Ch e. Rtlnd and Stmfd CC. Lonely ch with massive Nmn twr.

TOCKENHAM Wilts
157 SU 0379 6m NNE of Calne. CP, 119. Cricklade and Wootton Bassett RD. P Swindon. Ch e. Chippenham CC.

TOCKHOLES Lancs
94, 95 SD 6623 4m SSW of Blackburn. CP, 341. Blckbn RD. P Darwen. Ch e, c. Sch pe. Dwn CC. See also Ryal Fold.

TOCKINGTON Glos
155, 156 ST 6086 3m SE of Severn Rd Br. Loc, Olveston CP. P BRISTOL. Ch m.

TOCKWITH Yorks (W)
97 SE 4652 5m NE of Wetherby. CP, 493. Wthrby RD. P YORK. Ch e, m. Sch pe. Barkston Ash CC. See also Cowthorpe.

TODBER Dorset
166 ST 7920 4m WSW of Shaftesbury.
CP, 108. Shftsbry RD. P Sturminster
Newton. Ch e. N Dst CC.

TODDINGTON Beds
147 TL 0028 4m N of Dunstable. CP,
3,227. Luton RD. P Dnstble. Ch e, b, m.
Sch pe, s. S Beds CC. See also Chalton.
Monmouth hid in mnr hse after Rye House
plot, 1683. T. Service Area on M1 motorway 1m E.

TODDINGTON Glos
144 SP 0333 3m N of Winchcombe.
CP, 381. Cheltenham RD. P Chltnhm. Ch e.
Sch p. Cirencester and Tewkesbury CC.

TODENHAM Glos
144 SP 2436 3m NE of Moreton-in-Marsh.
CP, 202. N Cotswold RD. P Mtn-in-Msh.
Ch e. Cirencester and Tewkesbury CC.

TODHILLS Cumb
76 NY 3663 5m NNW of Carlisle. Loc,
Rockcliffe CP.

TODMORDEN Yorks (W)
95 SD 9324 8m SE of Burnley. MB, 15,150.
P(TDMDN, Lancs). Sowerby CC. See also
Bottoms, Clough Foot, Cornholme,
Eastwood, Lydgate, Mankinholes,
Portsmouth, Walsden.

TODWICK Yorks (W)
103 SK 4984 7m SE of Rotherham.
CP, 398. Kiveton Pk RD. P SHEFFIELD.
Ch e. Sch p. Rother Valley CC.

TOFT Cambs
135 TL 3556 6m WSW of Cambridge.
CP, 332. Chesterton RD. P CMBRDGE.
Ch e, m. Cambs CC.

TOFT Lincs (K)
123 TF 0617 3m SW of Bourne. CP(Tft
w Lound and Manthorpe), 153.
S Kesteven RD. Rutland and Stamford CC.

TOFT HILL Co Durham
85 NZ 1528 3m WSW of Bishop Auckland.
Loc, Etherley CP. Barnard Castle RD. P Bshp
Aucklnd. Ch m. Bshp Aucklnd CC.

TOFT MONKS Norfolk
137 TM 4394 3m NNE of Beccles. CP, 328.
Lodden RD. Ch e. Sch p. S Nflk CC. See
also Maypole Grn.

TOFT NEXT NEWTON Lincs (L)
104 TF 0488 4m W of Mkt Rasen. Loc, Tft
Ntn CP. Caistor RD. Ch e.
Gainsborough CC.

TOFTREES Norfolk
125 TF 8927 2m SSW of Fakenham. Loc,
Dunton CP. Ch e.

TOFTWOOD COMMON Norfolk
125 TF 9811 1m S of E Dereham. Loc,
E Drhm UD. P(Tftwd), Drhm.

TOGSTON Nthmb
71 NU 2401 2m SW of Amble. CP, 412.
Alnwick RD. Berwick-upon-Tweed CC. See
also N Tgstn.

TOKERS GREEN Oxon
159 SU 7077 3m NNW of Reading. Loc,
Kidmore End CP. Ch v.

TOLLAND Som
164 ST 1032 7m SSE of Watchet. CP, 72.
Taunton RD. Ch e. Tntn CC.

TOLLARD ROYAL Wilts
179 ST 9417 6m SE of Shaftesbury.
CP, 104. Mere and Tisbury RD.
P Salisbury. Ch e,v. Westbury CC. King
John's Hse, traditionally a royal hunting
lodge, well restored 13c–14c hse of stone
and wood. Larmer Grnds*, laid out by
General Pitt-Rivers of Rushmore (see also
Farnham, Dorset).

TOLL BAR Yorks (W)
103 SE 5607 3m NNW of Doncaster. Loc,
Bentley w Arksey UD. P Dncstr.

TOLLER FRATRUM Dorset
177, 178 SY 5797 8m ENE of Bridport.
CP, 27. Dorchester RD. Ch e. W Dst CC.

TOLLER PORCORUM Dorset
177, 178 SY 5698 7m NE of Bridport.
CP, 225. Dorchester RD. P Dchstr. Ch e.
Sch pe. W Dst CC.

TOLLERTON Notts
112, 121, 122 SK 6134 4m SE of
Nottingham. CP, 1,207. Bingham RD.
P NTTNGHM. Ch e. Sch p. Rushcliffe CC
(Carlton). To N, Nttnghm Airpt.

TOLLERTON Yorks (N)
92, 97 SE 5164 9m NW of York. CP, 513.

Easingwold RD. P YK. Ch m. Sch pm. Thirsk and Malton CC.

TOLLER WHELME Dorset
177 ST 5101 6m NE of Bridport. Loc, Corscombe CP. Ch e.

TOLLESBURY Essex
162 TL 9510 5m SE of Tiptree. CP, 1,577. Maldon RD. P Mldn. Ch e, v2. Sch p. Mldn CC. Oyster fisheries.

TOLLESHUNT D'ARCY Essex
162 TL 9211 3m SE of Tiptree. CP, 864. Maldon RD. P Mldn. Ch e, c. Mldn CC. Ch: brasses. To S, beside R Blackwater, a 'Red Hill', rems of prehistoric salt wks.

TOLLESHUNT KNIGHTS Essex
149, 162 TL 9114 1m SE of Tiptree. CP, 326. Maldon RD. P Mldn. Ch e. Mldn CC. Old rectory and ch are lent to Greek Orthodox Church.

TOLLESHUNT MAJOR Essex
162 TL 9011 3m S of Tiptree. CP, 341. Maldon RD. Ch e, v. Sch pe. Mldn CC.

TOLPUDDLE Dorset
178 SY 7994 7m ENE of Dorchester. CP, 203. Dchstr RD. P Dchstr. Ch e. W Dst CC. Famous for T. Martyrs, agricultural labourers transported to Australia for opposing drop in wages, 1834.

TONBRIDGE Kent
171 TQ 5946 28m SE of London. UD, 31,006. P. Tnbrdge and Mllng CC (Tnbrdge). Indstrl and rsdntl tn at busy crossing of R Medway. Boys' public sch. 12c cstle, grnds*.

TONG Shrops
119 SJ 7907 3m E of Shifnal. CP, 299. Shfnl RD. P Shfnl. Ch e. The Wrekin CC. Outstanding Perp ch; fan-vaulting, monmts. To E, rems of Whiteladies Priory (A.M.), 12c; Boscobel Hse (A.M.), early 17c, preserving hiding place of Charles II.

TONGE Leics
121 SK 4123 6m NE of Ashby de la Zouch. Loc, Breedon on the Hill CP.

TONGHAM Surrey
169 SU 8848 2m SE of Aldershot. CP (Seale and Tnghm), 2,490. Guildford RD. P Farnham. Ch e, v. Sch pe. Fnhm CC.

TONGUE END Lincs (H)
123 TF 1518 4m ESE of Bourne. Loc, Deeping St Nicholas CP. P Spalding. Sch p.

TONWELL Herts
147 TL 3317 3m NW of Ware. Loc, Bengeo Rural. Hertford RD. Ch e. Sch pe. Htfd and Stevenage CC (Htfd).

TOOT BALDON Oxon
158 SP 5600 5m SE of Oxford. CP, 146. Bullingdon RD. Ch e. Henley CC.

TOOT HILL Essex
161 TL 5102 2m W of Ongar. Loc, Stanford Rivers CP. P Ongr.

TOOT HILL Hants
180 SU 3818 5m NNW of Southampton. Loc, Nursling and Rownhams CP.

TOOTING London
160, 170 TQ 2872 5m SSW of Charing Cross. Loc, Wandsworth LB. Ttng BC (Wndswth Central).

TOPCLIFFE Yorks (N)
91 SE 4076 4m SSW of Thirsk. CP, 1,393. Thsk RD. P Thsk. Ch e, m. Sch p, pe. Thsk and Malton CC. On banks of R Swale. Ch has 14c brass.

TOPCROFT Norfolk
137 TM 2693 5m WNW of Bungay. CP, 264. Loddon RD. P Bngy, Suffolk. Ch e, c. Sch p. S Nflk CC. See also Tpcrft St.

TOPCROFT STREET Norfolk
137 TM 2691 5m WNW of Bungay. Loc, Tpcrft CP.

TOP OF HEBERS Lancs
101 SD 8607 4m SSW of Rochdale. Loc, Middleton MB.

TOPPESFIELD Essex
148, 149 TL 7337 5m SSW of Clare. CP, 417. Halstead RD. P Hlstd. Ch e, c. Sch pe. Saffron Walden CC. See also Gainsford End.

TOPPINGS Lancs
101 SD 7213 3m N of Bolton. Loc, Turton UD. Darwen CC.

TOPSHAM Devon
176 SX 9688 SE distr of Exeter. Loc, Extr CB. P Extr. Extr BC (Honiton CC).

Ancient tn and former port for Extr. The Strand has several 17c and 18c hses.

TORBAY Devon
188 SX 9163 18m S of Exeter. CB, 108,880. Tby BC (Torquay). See also Brixham, Churston Ferrers, Cockington, Collaton St Mary, Galmpton, Goodrington, Maidencombe, Paignton, Shiphay, Torquay. CB formed in 1968; large seaside resort noted for mild climate.

TORBRYAN Devon
188 SX 8266 4m SW of Newton Abbot. CP, 500. Ntn Abbt RD. Ch e. Totnes CC. See also Denbury. In valley with limestone caves. Outstanding 15c ch.

TORCROSS Devon
188 SX 8241 6m ESE of Kingsbridge. Loc, Stokenham CP. P Kngsbrdge. Ch c.

TORKSEY Lincs (L)
104 SK 8378 7m S of Gainsborough. CP, 187. Gnsbrgh RD. P LINCOLN. Ch e, m. Sch p. Gnsbrgh CC. Important port in Roman times. Canal (Fossedyke Navigation) said to be oldest in England. Large petroleum installations.

TORMARTON Glos
156 ST 7678 9m N of Bath. CP, 352. Sodbury RD. P Badminton. Ch e. S Glos CC. See also W Littleton.

TORONTO Co Durham
85 NZ 1930 1m NNW of Bishop Auckland. Loc, Bshp Aucklnd UD. P Bshp Aucklnd.

TORPENHOW Cumb
82 NY 2039 7m SW of Wigton. CP(Blennerhasset and Tpnhw), 509. Wgtn RD. P Carlisle. Ch e. Penrith and the Border CC.

TORPOINT Cornwall
187 SX 4355 3m W of Plymouth. UD, 4,782. P. Bodmin CC.

TORQUAY Devon
188 SX 9163 18m S of Exeter. Loc, Torbay CB. P. Large resort with harbour and several beaches. Architecture mainly 19c in centre, 20c at edges. Formerly a borough, pop. over 50,000, until absorbed into new CB of Tby, 1968.

TORRINGTON Devon
163 SS 4919 5m SSE of Bideford. See Gt Trrngtn.

TORTINGTON Sussex (W)
181, 182 TQ 0005 1m S of Arundel. CP, 617. Chichester RD. Ch e. Arndl CC (Chchstr).

TORTWORTH Glos
156 ST 7093 9m ENE of Severn Rd Br. CP, 590. Thornbury RD. Ch e. Sch pe. S Glos CC. Famous chestnut tree near ch thought to be c 1,000 yrs old.

TORVER Lancs
88 SD 2894 2m SSW of Coniston. CP, 198. N Lonsdale RD. P Cnstn. Ch e, b. Morecambe and Lnsdle CC.

TORWORTH Notts
103 SK 6586 5m NW of Retford. CP, 259. E Rtfd RD. Ch m. Bassetlaw CC.

TOSELAND Hunts
134 TL 2462 4m ENE of St Neots. CP, 100. St Nts RD. Ch e, m. Hunts CC.

TOSSIDE Yorks (W)
95 SD 7656 6m SW of Settle. Loc, Gisburn Forest CP. Bowland RD. P Skipton. Ch e, v. Sch pe. Skptn CC.

TOSSON, GREAT Nthmb
71 NU 0200 2m WSW of Rothbury. See Gt Tssn.

TOSTOCK Suffolk (W)
136 TL 9563 6m E of Bury St Edmunds. CP, 381. Thedwastre RD. P Bury St Eds. Ch e, m. Bury St Eds CC.

TOTHAM, GREAT Essex
149, 162 TL 8613 3m ESE of Witham. See Gt Tthm.

TOTHILL Lincs (L)
105 TF 4181 4m NNW of Alford. CP, 39. Louth RD. Ch e. Lth CC.

TOTLAND IOW
180 SZ 3287 3m SW of Yarmouth. CP, 1,724. Isle of Wight RD and CC. P(Ttlnd Bay). Ch e, m, r. Sch p, pr. Resort. 1½m SW, Alum Bay, famous for variegated sand. Beyond, The Needles, jagged cliffs; lighthouse.

TOTNES Devon
188 SX 8060 8m SSW of Newton Abbot.
MB, 5,771. P. Ttns CC. Ancient tn on
hillside at head of tidal Dart estuary. Several
old hses. Butterwalk in High St: hses
overhanging colonnade. Rems of cstle
(A.M.).

TOTTENHAM London
160 TQ 3490 7m NNE of Charing Cross.
Loc, Haringey LB. Tttnhm BC. Lee Valley
reservoirs to E. Bruce Cstle Museum
(Lordship Lane) contains record of Hrngey
LB; housed in 16c–18c bldng in small
pk.

TOTTENHILL Norfolk
124 TF 6311 6m S of King's Lynn. CP, 232.
Downham RD. P K's Lnn. Ch e.
SW Nflk CC.

TOTTERIDGE London
160 TQ 2494 1m S of Barnet. Loc, Bnt LB.
Chipping Bnt BC (Bnt CC).

TOTTERNHOE Beds
147 SP 9821 2m W of Dunstable. CP, 1,566.
Luton RD. P Dnstble. Ch e, m2. Sch p.
S Beds CC. See also Ch End. Bronze Age
fort NW end of vllge. T. Quarries supplied
stone for Windsor Cstle.

TOTTINGTON Lancs
101 SD 7712 2m NW of Bury. UD, 9,740.
P Bury. Bury and Radcliffe BC. See also
Greenmount, Walshaw.

TOTTINGTON Norfolk
136 TL 8995 8m NNE of Thetford. CP, nil.
Wayland RD. Ch e. S Nflk CC. In Battle Sch
area.

TOTTON Hants
180 SU 3613 4m W of Southampton. Loc,
Eling CP. P STHMPTN. Ch e, c, m, r2, v3.
Sch i, j, p2, s2.

TOULSTON Yorks (W)
97 SE 4544 2m WNW of Tadcaster.
CP(Newton Kyme cum Tlstn), 236. Tdcstr
RD. Barkston Ash CC.

TOWCESTER Northants
146 SP 6948 9m N of Buckingham.
CP, 2,743. Tcstr RD. P. Ch e, b, m, r, v.
Sch i, p, s2. Daventry CC (S Nthnts). See
also Caldecote. To NE, Easton Neston Hse,

early 18c, by Nicholas Hawksmoor; seat of
Fermors, whose monmts fill ch. Tcstr
Racecourse in pk.

TOWEDNACK Cornwall
189 SW 4838 2m SW of St Ives. CP, 292.
W Penwith RD. Ch e, m. St Ives CC.

TOWERSEY Oxon
159 SP 7305 2m E of Thame. CP, 346.
Bullingdon RD. P Thme. Ch e. Henley CC.

TOW LAW Co Durham
84 NZ 1238 4m NW of Crook. UD, 2,547.
P Bishop Auckland. NW Drhm CC. Grey tn
standing 1,000ft above sea level. Ch has
remarkable scrn.

TOWN END Westm
89 SD 4483 4m NNE of Grange-over-Sands.
Loc, Witherslack CP.

TOWN GREEN Lancs
100 SD 4005 2m SSW of Ormskirk. Loc,
Aughton CP.

TOWNSHEND Cornwall
189 SW 5932 5m NW of Helston. Loc,
Crowan CP. P Hayle. Ch m.

TOWN STREET Suffolk (W)
136 TL 7785 just SW of Brandon. Loc,
Brndn CP.

TOWTHORPE Yorks (N)
97, 98 SE 6258 5m NNE of York.
CP, 1,056. Flaxton RD. Ch e. Thirsk and
Malton CC. Virtually part of Strensall army
camp.

TOWTON Yorks (W)
97 SE 4839 2m S of Tadcaster. CP, 132.
Tdcstr RD. Barkston Ash CC.

TOYNTON ALL SAINTS Lincs (L)
114 TF 3963 9m ESE of Horncastle.
CP, 279. Spilsby RD. P Splsby. Ch e, m.
Sch p. Hncstle CC.

TOYNTON FEN SIDE Lincs (L)
114 TF 3962 10m SE of Horncastle. Loc,
Spilsby RD. Ch m. Hncstle CC.

TOYNTON ST PETER Lincs (L)
114 TF 4063 9m SW of Alford. CP, 259.
Spilsby RD. P Splsby. Ch e, m2.
Horncastle CC.

TOY'S HILL Kent
171 TQ 4651 4m SW of Sevenoaks. Loc, Brasted CP. P Westerham. Much NT land with fine views.

TRABOE Cornwall
190 SW 7421 7m SE of Helston. Loc, St Keverne CP.

TRANWELL Nthmb
78 NZ 1883 2m SSW of Morpeth. Loc. Mitford CP.

TRAWDEN Lancs
95 SD 9138 2m SE of Colne. UD, 1,854. P(Trdn Forest), Clne. Nelson and Clne BC.

TREALES Lancs
94 SD 4432 7m WNW of Preston. CP(Trls, Roseacre and Wharles), 348. Fylde RD. Ch e. Sch pe. S Flde CC.

TREBARTHA Cornwall
186 SX 2677 6m SW of Launceston. Loc, North Hill CP.

TREBARWITH Cornwall
174, 185, 186 SX 0586 3m WNW of Camelford. Loc, Tintagel CP. N of narrow combe is long sandy beach backed by cliffs (NT).

TREBETHERICK Cornwall
185 SW 9378 5m NW of Wadebridge. Loc, St Minver Lowlands CP. Wdbrdge and Padstow RD. P Wdbrdge. N Cnwll CC.

TREBOROUGH Som
164 ST 0136 6m SW of Watchet. CP, 44. Williton RD. Ch e. Bridgwater CC.

TREBUDANNON Cornwall
185 SW 8961 5m E of Newquay. Loc, St Columb Major CP. Ch m.

TREBULLETT Cornwall
186 SX 3278 4m S of Launceston. Loc, Lezant CP. P Lncstn. Ch m. Along lane to W, Trecarrel, 16c hall of mnr hse, with chpl alongside.

TREBURLEY Cornwall
186 SX 3477 5m SSE of Launceston. Loc, Lezant CP. Ch m.

TREDAVOE Cornwall
189 SW 4528 2m SW of Penzance. Loc, Pnznce MB.

TREDINGTON Glos
143, 144 SO 9029 2m SSE of Tewkesbury. Loc, Stoke Orchard CP. P Tksbry. Ch e. Ch: fossilized ichthyosaurus on floor of S porch.

TREDINGTON Warwicks
144 SP 2543 2m N of Shipston on Stour. CP, 1,033. Shpstn on Str RD. P Shpstn on Str. Ch e. Sch pe. Stratford-on-Avon CC (Strtfd). See also Armscote, Blackwell, Darlingscott, Newbold on Stour.

TREDINNICK Cornwall
185 SW 9270 3m S of Padstow. Loc, St Issey CP.

TREEN Cornwall
189 SW 3923 7m SW of Penzance. Loc, St Levan CP. P Pnznce. Ch m. On coast (NT) to S, Logan Rock.

TREETON Yorks (W)
103 SK 4387 3m S of Rotherham. CP, 2,289. Rthrhm RD. P Rthrhm. Ch e b, m. Sch p. Rother Valley CC.

TREFONEN Shrops
117 SJ 2526 3m SW of Oswestry. Loc, Oswstry Rural CP. Oswstry RD. P Oswstry. Ch e. Sch pe.

TREGADILLETT Cornwall
186 SX 2983 2m W of Launceston. Loc, Lncstn RD. Ch m. Sch pe. N Cnwll CC.

TREGEARE Cornwall
174, 186 SX 2486 6m WNW of Launceston. Loc, Egloskerry CP. Ch m.

TREGONETHA Cornwall
185 SW 9563 6m SSW of Wadebridge. Loc, St Wenn CP. Ch m.

TREGONY Cornwall
190 SW 9245 6m E of Truro. CP(Tregoney), 513. Truro RD. P Truro. Ch e, m, v. Sch p, s. Truro CC. A busy port until the R Fal was silted.

TREGREHAN MILLS Cornwall
185, 186, 190 SX 0453 2m ENE of St Austell. Loc, St Astll w Fowey MB. P St Astll. Truro CC.

TREKENNER Cornwall
186 SX 3478 4m SSE of Launceston. Loc, Lezant CP. P Lncstn. Sch p.

TREKNOW Cornwall
174, 185, 186 SX 0586 4m NW of
Camelford. Loc, Tintagel CP.

TRELIGGA Cornwall
185, 186 SX 0584 4m W of Camelford. Loc,
St Teath CP. Ch m.

TRELIGHTS Cornwall
185 SW 9979 4m N of Wadebridge. Loc,
St Endellion CP. P Port Isaac. Ch m.

TRELILL Cornwall
185, 186 SX 0478 5m NE of Wadebridge.
Loc, St Kew CP. P Bodmin. Ch m.

TREMAIL Cornwall
174, 186 SX 1686 4m ENE of Camelford.
Loc, Davidstow CP. Ch m.

TREMAINE Cornwall
174, 186 SX 2388 6m WNW of Launceston.
CP, 67. Lncstn RD. Ch e, m. N Cnwll CC.

TREMAR Cornwall
186 SX 2568 2m N of Liskeard. Loc,
St Cleer CP. Ch m.

TREMATON Cornwall
186 SX 3959 2m WNW of Saltash. Loc,
Sltsh MB.

TRENANCE Cornwall
185 SW 8567 5m NNE of Newquay. Loc,
Mawgan-in-Pydar CP. St Austell RD.
P Nquay. N Cnwll CC.

TRENANCE Cornwall
185 SW 9270 3m S of Padstow. Loc,
St Issey CP. Ch m.

TRENARREN Cornwall
186, 190 SX 0348 3m SSE of St Austell.
Loc, St Astll w Fowey MB. Truro CC.

TRENCH Shrops
119 SJ 6913 2m NW of Oakengates. Loc,
Oakngts UD. P Telford.

TRENEAR Cornwall
189 SW 6831 3m NNE of Helston. Loc,
Wendron CP. P Hlstn.

TRENEGLOS Cornwall
174, 186 SX 2088 7m ENE of Camelford.
CP, 101. Launceston RD. Ch e, m.
N Cnwll CC.

TRENEWAN Cornwall
186 SX 1753 5m W of Looe. Loc,
Lansallos CP.

TRENT Dorset
177, 178 ST 5918 3m NE of Yeovil.
CP, 293. Sherborne RD. P Shbne. Ch e.
Sch pe. W Dst CC. See also Adber.
Transferred from Somerset in 1896.

TRENTHAM Staffs
110, 119 SJ 8641 3m SSW of
Stoke-on-Trent. Loc, Stke-on-Trnt CB,
Stone RD. P Stke-on-Trnt. S-o-T S BC,
Stafford and Stne CC. Large public pk; two
golf courses.

TRENTISHOE Devon
163 SS 6448 5m W of Lynton. CP, 47.
Barnstaple RD. Ch e. N Dvn CC. Ch and a
farm. To E, Heddon's Mouth Cleave, deep
gorge running down to sea.

TRERULE FOOT Cornwall
186 SX 3258 6m W of Saltash. Loc,
St Germans CP.

TRESCO Isles of Scilly
189 SV 8915. CP, 283. Is of S RD. P. Ch e.
Sch pe. St Ives CC. See also New Grimsby.
Large freshwater lake nearly divides it.
Abbey Gdns, on site of 12c abbey, with
sub-tropical plants. On W coast, Cromwell's
Cstle and ruins of King Charles's Cstle. On N
tip, Piper's Hole, underground cavern.

TRESCOWE Cornwall
189 SW 5730 5m WNW of Helston. Loc,
Breage CP. Ch m.

TRESHAM Glos
156 ST 7991 6m W of Tetbury. Loc,
Hawkesbury CP. P Wotton-under-Edge.
Ch e.

TRESILLIAN Cornwall
190 SW 8746 3m ENE of Truro. Loc,
Truro RD. P Truro. Ch m. Sch i. Truro CC.

TRESMEER Cornwall
174, 186 SX 2387 6m WNW of Launceston.
CP, 150. Lncstn RD. P Lncstn. Ch e, m.
N Cnwll CC.

TRESPARRETT Cornwall
174 SX 1491 6m NNE of Camelford. Loc,
St Juliot CP. Cmlfd RD. Ch m. N Cnwll CC.

TRESWELL Notts
104 SK 7879 5m ESE of Retford. CP, 203.
E Rtfd RD. Ch e, m2. Bassetlaw CC.

TRETHURGY Cornwall
185, 186 SX 0355 3m NE of St Austell.
Loc, St Astll w Fowey MB. P St Astll.
Truro CC.

TRETIRE Herefs
142 SO 5223 5m W of Ross-on-Wye.
CP,(Trtre w Michaelchurch), 79. Rss and
Whitchurch RD. Ch e. Hereford CC.

TREVALGA Cornwall
174, 185 SX 0889 4m NNW of Camelford.
CP, 79. Cmlfd RD. Ch e. N Cnwll CC.

TREVANSON Cornwall
185 SW 9772 just NW of Wadebridge. Loc,
St Breock CP.

TREVARRACK Cornwall
189 SW 4731 1m NE of Penzance. Loc,
Pnznce MB.

TREVARREN Cornwall
185 SW 9160 6m E of Newquay. Loc,
St Columb Major CP.

TREVEIGHAN Cornwall
185, 186 SX 0779 3m SSW of Camelford.
Loc, Michaelstow CP. P St Teath, Bodmin.

TREVELLAS Cornwall
185, 190 SW 7451 7m NNE of Redruth.
Loc, St Agnes CP. P St Agnes.

TREVELMOND Cornwall
186 SX 2063 3m W of Liskeard. Loc,
Lskd CP. Lskd RD. P Lskd. Ch m.
Bodmin CC.

TREVERVA Cornwall
190 SW 7531 3m W of Falmouth. Loc,
Budock CP. Kerrier RD. P Penryn. Ch m.

TREVISCOE Cornwall
185 SW 9455 5m WNW of St Austell. Loc,
St Stephen-in-Brannel CP. St Astll RD.
P St Stphn, St Astll. Ch m. Truro CC.

TREVONE Cornwall
185 SW 8975 2m W of Padstow. Loc,
Pdstw CP. P Pdstw. Ch m.

TREWARMETT Cornwall
174, 185, 186 SX 0686 3m NW of
Camelford. Loc, Tintagel CP. Ch m.

TREWASSA Cornwall
174, 186 SX 1486 3m NE of Camelford.
Loc, Davidstow CP. Ch m.

TREWELLARD Cornwall
189 SW 3733 6m WNW of Penzance. Loc,
St Just UD.

TREWEN Cornwall
186 SX 2583 5m W of Launceston. CP, 80.
Lncstn RD. Ch e. N Cnwll CC. See also
Pipers Pool.

TREWIDLAND Cornwall
186 SX 2559 3m S of Liskeard. Loc,
Lskd CP. Lskd RD. P St Keyne, Lskd.
Ch m, v. Sch p. Bodmin CC.

TREWITHIAN Cornwall
190 SW 8737 3m NE of St Mawes. Loc,
Gerrans CP. P Porthscatho, Truro.

TREWOON Cornwall
185, 190 SW 9952 1m W of St Austell. Loc,
St Mewan CP. P St Astll. Ch m.

TREYARNON BAY Cornwall
185 SW 8673 4m WSW of Padstow. Loc,
St Merryn CP.

TREYFORD Sussex (W)
181 SU 8218 4m SW of Midhurst. CP, 104.
Mdhst RD. Chichester CC (Horsham). 13c
ch replaced by 19c ch blown up in 20c.

TRIANGLE Yorks (W)
96, 102 SE 0422 4m SW of Halifax. Loc,
Sowerby Br UD. P Hlfx.

TRICKETT'S CROSS Dorset
179 SU 0801 5m E of Wimborne. Loc,
Hampreston CP.

TRIMDON Co Durham
85 NZ 3634 4m NNE of Sedgefield.
CP, 6,052. Sdgfld RD. P Trmdn Stn.
Ch e, m, r. Sch i, p, pe, pr, s. Drhm CC
(Sdgfld). See also Trmdn Colliery, Trmdn
Grange.

TRIMDON COLLIERY Co Durham
85 3835 5m NNE of Sedgefield. Loc,
Trmdn CP. P Trmdn Stn. Ch m, s.

TRIMDON GRANGE Co Durham
85 NZ 3735 5m NNE of Sedgefield. Loc,
Trmdn CP. P Trmdn Stn. Ch e, m, v.

TRIMINGHAM Norfolk
126 TG 2838 5m SE of Cromer. CP, 231.
Erpingham RD. P NORWICH, NOR 31Y.
Ch e. N Nflk CC.

TRIMLEY Suffolk (E)
150 TM 2836 2m NW of Felixtowe.
CP(Trmly St Mary), 1,039. Deben RD.
P Ipswich. Ch e2, r, v. Sch p. Sudbury and
Woodbridge CC. The two chs are side by
side.

TRIMLEY HEATH Suffolk (E)
150 TM 2737 3m NW of Felixtowe. Loc,
Trmly St Martin CP. Deben RD. Ch m.
Sch p. Sudbury and Woodbridge CC.

TRIMPLEY Worcs
130 SO 7978 3m WNW of Kidderminster.
Loc, Kddrmnstr Foreign CP.
Kddrmnstr RD. P Bewdley. Sch pe.
Kddrmnstr CC.

TRIMSTONE Devon
163 SS 5043 3m SSW of Ilfracombe. Loc,
W Down CP.

TRING Herts
146, 159 SP 9211 5m WNW of
Berkhamsted. UD, 9,155. P. Hemel
Hempstead CC. See also Hastoe, New Mill.
In NW corner of county near Bucks border
at N edge of Chilterns. Zoological museum.
Reservoirs to N are a nature reserve.

TRISPEN Cornwall
185, 190 SW 8450 4m NNE of Truro. Loc,
St Erme CP. P Truro.

TRITLINGTON Nthmb
78 NZ 2092 4m N of Morpeth. CP, 216.
Mpth RD. Sch pe. Mpth CC. See also
Fenrother.

TROON Cornwall
189 SW 6638 2m SSE of Camborne. Loc,
Cmbne-Redruth UD. P Cmbne.

TROSTON Suffolk (W)
136 TL 8972 6m NNE of Bury St Edmunds.
CP, 1,071. Thingoe RD. P Bury St Eds.
Ch e, m. Bury St Eds CC.

TROTTISCLIFFE Kent
171 TQ 6460 8m ENE of Sevenoaks. CP.
Malling RD. P Maidstone. Ch e. Sch pe.
Tonbridge and Mllng CC (Svnks).

Pronounced 'trozly'. 1m E, Coldrum Long
Barrow (NT), neolithic burial chamber.

TROTTON Sussex (W)
181 SU 8322 3m W of Midhurst. CP, 475.
Mdhst RD. P Rogate, Petersfield, Hants.
Ch e. Chichester CC (Horsham). See also
Milland. 15c br over R Rother. Ch has gaunt
Saxon-looking twr actually EE.

TROUTBECK Cumb
83 NY 3826 8m WSW of Penrith. Loc,
Hutton CP. P Pnrth.

TROUTBECK Westm
89 NY 4103 3m N of Windermere. Loc,
Lakes UD. P Wndrmre. Westm CC.

TROUTBECK BRIDGE Westm
89 NY 4000 1m NNW of Windermere. Loc,
Lakes UD. P Wndrmre. Westm CC.
Brockhole Pk, National Pk Information
Centre.

TROWBRIDGE Wilts
166 ST 8557 8m SE of Bath.
UD, 19,245. P. Westbury CC. See also
Trowle Cmmn. Cloth-mnfg tn since 14c.
Perp ch; many Ggn hses. Other industries
incl brewing, light engineering, dairies.
Administrative capital of county.

TROWELL Notts
112, 121 SK 4839 5m W of Nottingham.
CP, 1,877. Basford RD. P NTTNGHM. Ch e.
Sch pe. Beeston CC (Rushcliffe). In
coal-mining area, beside M1 motorway
(T. Service Area).

TROWLE COMMON Wilts
166 ST 8358 1m NW of Trowbridge. Loc,
Trwbrdge UD.

TROWSE NEWTON Norfolk
126 TG 2406 2m SE of Norwich. CP(Trse
w Ntn), 569. Forehoe and Henstead RD.
P(Trse), Nrwch. Ch e. Sch p. S Nflk CC
(Central Nflk).

TRUDOXHILL Som
166 ST 7443 3m SW of Frome. CP, 335.
Frme RD. P Frme. Ch c. Wells CC. See also
Marston Bigot.

TRULL Som
177 ST 2122 2m SSW of Taunton.
CP, 1,668. Tntn RD. P Tntn. Ch e, b.
Sch pe. Tntn CC. Ch has richly carved scrn,
plpt, bench-ends.

TRUMPET Herefs
142, 143 SO 6539 4m WNW of Ledbury.
Loc, Pixley CP. P Ldbry.

TRUMPINGTON Cambs
135/148 TL 4455 2m S of Cambridge. Loc,
Cmbrdge MB. P CMBRDGE. Ch has second
oldest brass in England (1289) - oldest is at
Stoke D'Abernon, qv.

TRUNCH Norfolk
126 TG 2834 3m N of N Walsham. CP, 340.
Smallburgh RD. P: N Wlshm. Ch e, m.
N Nflk CC. Outstanding 14c–15c ch.

TRURO Cornwall
190 SW 8244 13m WSW of St Austell.
MB, 14,830. P. Truro CC. See also Kenwyn,
Malpas. Administrative capital of county,
with cathedral by J.L. Pearson completed
1910. Quays in city centre.

TRUSHAM Devon
176 SX 8582 7m N of Newton Abbot.
CP, 138. Ntn Abbt RD. P Ntn Abbt. Ch e.
Totnes CC.

TRUSLEY Derbys
120 SK 2535 6m W of Derby. CP, 103.
Repton RD. Ch e. Belper CC.

TRUSTHORPE Lincs (L)
105 TL 5183 1m SSE of Mablethorpe. Loc,
Mblthpe and Sutton UD. P Mblthpe.

TRYSULL Staffs
130 SO 8594 5m SW of Wolverhampton.
CP(Trsll and Seisdon), 866. Ssdn RD.
P Wlvrhmptn. Ch e. Sch pe. SW Staffs CC
(Brierley Hill).

TUBNEY Berks
158 SU 4398 4m W of Abingdon.
CP(Fyfield and Tbny), 514. Abngdn RD.
Ch e. Abngdn CC.

TUCKENHAY Devon
188 SX 8155 3m SSE of Totnes. Loc,
Ashprington CP. P Ttns. Quay on Bow
Creek. Paper mill.

TUCKHILL Shrops and Staffs
130 SO 7888 5m SE of Bridgnorth. Loc,
Brdnth RD, Seisdon RD. Ch e. Sch pe.
Ludlow CC, SW Staffs CC. (Ldlw CC,
Brierley Hill CC.)

TUDDENHAM Suffolk (E)
150 TM 1948 3m NE of Ipswich.
CP(Tddnhm St Martin), 356. Deben RD.
P Ipswch. Ch e, v. Sch p. Sudbury and
Woodbridge CC. Vllge climbs hill. Hall,
Jcbn, ¾m N.

TUDDENHAM Suffolk (W)
135 TL 7371 8m NE of Newmarket.
CP, 335. Mildenhall RD. P Bury
St Edmunds. Ch e, m. Sch pe. Bury
St Eds CC.

TUDELEY Kent
171 TQ 6245 2m E of Tonbridge. Loc,
Capel CP. P Tnbrdge. Ch e

TUDHOE Co Durham
85 NZ 2635 2m NNE of Spennymoor. Loc,
Spnnmr UD. P(Tdhoe Colliery), Spnnmr.

TUGBY Leics
122 SK 7600 7m W of Uppingham.
CP(Tgby and Keythorpe), 220.
Billesdon RD. P LEICESTER. Ch e. Sch pe.
Harborough CC (Melton).

TUGFORD Shrops
129 SO 5587 8m NNE of Ludlow. CP, 86.
Ldlw RD. Ch e. Ldlw CC. See also Holdgate.
Vllge of pleasing aspect in a side valley off
Corvedale.

TUGHALL Nthmb
71 NU 2126 6m SSE of Bamburgh. Loc,
Beadnall CP.

TULSE HILL London
160, 170 TQ 3173 5m SSE of Charing
Cross. Loc, Lambeth LB. Norwood BC.

TUMBY Lincs (L)
114 TF 2359 3m SE of Woodhall Spa.
CP, 299. Horncastle RD. Hncstle CC. See
also Tmby Woodside.

TUMBY WOODSIDE Lincs (L)
114 TF 2657 6m SE of Woodhall Spa. Loc,
Tmby CP. Sch pe.

TUNBRIDGE WELLS Kent
171 TQ 5839 31m SSE of London.
MB, 44,506. P. Royal Tnbrdge Wlls CC
(Tonbridge). Rsdntl and shopping tn,
formerly spa (Chalybete springs); many
Rgncy bldngs, large cmmn. Paved 18c street,
The Pantiles.

TUNLEY Som
166 ST 6959 3m N of Radstock. Loc,
Dunkerton CP. P Bath. Ch m.

TUNSTALL Kent
172 TQ 8961 1m S of Sittingbourne.
CP, 638. Swale RD. Ch e. Sch pe.
Faversham CC.

TUNSTALL Lancs
89 SD 6073 3m S of Kirkby Lonsdale.
CP, 94. Lunesdale RD. P Carnforth. Ch e.
Lancaster CC. Ch: glass; Roman altar.

TUNSTALL Norfolk
126 TG 4108 7m W of Yarmouth. Loc,
Halvergate CP. Ch e.

TUNSTALL Staffs
110 SJ 8651 4m N distr of Stoke-on-Trent.
Loc, Stke-on-Trnt CB. P Stke-on-Trnt.
S-o-T N BC. Pottery distr. One of Arnold
Bennett's *Five Towns* ('Turnhill').

TUNSTALL Suffolk (E)
150 TM 3555 5m SSW of Saxmundham.
CP, 466. Deben RD. P Woodbridge. Ch e, b.
Sch pe. Eye CC.

TUNSTALL Yorks (E)
99 TA 3031 3m NW of Withernsea. Loc,
Roos CP. Ch e. Sea encroaching.

TUNSTALL Yorks (N)
91 SE 2195 4m SE of Richmond. CP, 250.
Rchmnd RD. P Rchmnd. Ch e, m.
Rchmnd CC.

TUNSTEAD Norfolk
126 TG 3022 3m N of Wroxham. CP, 536.
Smallburgh RD. P NORWICH, NOR 11Z.
Ch e. Sch p. N Nflk CC. See also Mkt St,
Sco Ruston.

TUNWORTH Hants
168, 169 SU 6748 3m SE of Basingstoke.
CP, 79. Bsngstke RD. P Bsngstke. Ch e.
Bsngstke CC.

TUPSLEY Herefs
142 SO 5340 1m E of Hereford. Loc,
Hrfd MB and Hampton Bishop CP. Hrfd CC.

TURGIS GREEN Hants
169 SU 6958 6m NE of Basingstoke. Loc,
Bsngstke RD. Bsngstke CC.

TURKDEAN Glos
144 SP 1017 2m N of Northleach. CP, 106.

Nthlch RD. Ch e. Cirencester and
Tewkesbury CC.

TUR LANGTON Leics
133 SP 7194 5m N of Mkt Harborough.
CP, 190. Mkt Hbrgh RD. P LEICESTER.
Ch e, v. Hbrgh CC.

TURLEIGH Wilts
166 ST 8060 4m NW of Trowbridge. Loc,
Winsley CP. P Bradford-on-Avon.

TURNASTONE Herefs
142 SO 3536 10m W of Hereford. CP, 47.
Dore and Bredwardine RD. Ch e. Hrfd CC.

TURNDITCH Derbys
111 SK 2946 3m W of Belper. CP, 242.
Blpr RD. Ch e, v. Sch pe. Blpr CC.

TURNER'S HILL Sussex (E)
170, 182 TQ 3435 4m WSW of E Grinstead.
Loc, Worth CP. P Crawley. Ch e, v. Sch pe.

TURNERS PUDDLE Dorset
178 SY 8393 7m NW of Wareham. CP, 59.
Wrhm and Purbeck RD. Ch e. S Dst CC. One
hse and the ch.

TURNWORTH Dorset
178 ST 8207 4m W of Blandford. CP, 48.
Blndfd RD. Ch e. N Dst CC.

TURTON BOTTOMS Lancs
95, 102 SD 7315 4m NNE of Bolton. Loc,
Ttn UD. P(Ttn), Bltn. Darwen CC.

TURVEY Beds
146 SP 9452 4m E of Olney. CP, 745.
Bedford RD. P BDFD. Ch e, m, v. Sch i.
Bdfd CC. Pre-Nmn ch, altered in 14c, 15c,
19c. Inn of 17c. T. Hse, 18c, in large pk
between vllge and R Ouse.

TURVILLE Bucks
159 SU 7691 5m N of Henley. CP, 300.
Wycombe RD. Ch e. Sch pe. Wcmbe CC. See
also Northend. Ch of interest. T. Hill to N
has restored windmill; views.

TURVILLE HEATH Bucks
159 SU 7491 6m NNW of Henley. Loc,
Tvlle CP.

TURWESTON Bucks
145, 146 SP 6037 1m NE of Brackley.
CP, 226. Buckingham RD.
P Brckly, Northants. Ch e. Bcknghm CC.

TUTBURY Staffs
120 SK 2128 4m NNW of Burton-on-Trent.
CP, 2,566. Ttbry RD. P Btn-on-Trnt.
Ch e, m, r, v. Sch pe. Btn CC. On R Dove.
Ruins of 14c cstle*; Mary Queen of Scots
imprisoned here. Nmn ch nearby.
Half-timbered inn.

TUTNALL Worcs
130, 131 SO 9870 2m E of Bromsgrove.
CP(Ttnll and Cobley), 1,010. Brmsgrve RD.
Brmsgrve and Redditch CC (Brmsgrve).

TUTTINGTON Norfolk
126 TG 2227 2m E of Aylsham. CP, 253.
St Faith's and Aylshm RD.
P NORWICH, NOR 51Y. Ch e, v. N Nflk CC
(Central Nflk). See also Burgh next Aylshm.

TUTTS CLUMP Berks
158 SU 5871 5m SW of Pangbourne. Loc,
Bradfield CP. P Reading.

TUXFORD Notts
112 SK 7371 6m ENE of Ollerton.
CP, 1,510. E Retford RD. P Newark.
Ch e, m. Sch p, s. Bassetlaw CC.

TWEEDMOUTH Nthmb
64 NT 9952 just S of Berwick-upon-Tweed.
Loc, Brwck-upn-Twd MB. P BRWCK-UPN-
TWD. Across river from Brwck.

TWELVE HEADS Cornwall
190 SW 7642 4m E of Redruth. Loc,
Truro RD. P Truro. Ch m2. Truro CC.
Old tin workings.

TWENTY Lincs (K)
123 TF 1520 4m E of Bourne. Loc,
Bne UD.

TWERTON Som
166 ST 7264 W distr of Bath. Loc, Bth CB.
P(Twtn-on-Avon), Bth.

TWICKENHAM London
160, 170 TQ 1473 2m S of Hounslow. Loc,
Richmond upon Thames LB. P Middx.
Twcknhm BC. Thames-side rsdntl distr.
T. Br. Marble Hill Hse*, 18c, in public pk
beside river ½m above Rchmnd Br.

TWIGWORTH Glos
143 SO 8422 3m NNE of Gloucester.
CP, 409. Glcstr RD. P GLCSTR. Ch e.
Sch pe. W Glos CC.

TWINEHAM Sussex (E)
182 TQ 2519 4m W of Burgess Hill.
CP, 283. Cuckfield RD. Ch e. Sch pe.
Midd-Sx CC (Lewes).

TWINHOE Som
166 ST 7459 3m S of Bath. Loc,
Wellow CP.

TWINSTEAD Essex
149 TL 8636 3m S of Sudbury. CP, 195.
Halstead RD. P Sdbry, Suffolk. Ch e.
Saffron Walden CC.

TWISS GREEN Lancs
101 SJ 6595 6m NNE of Warrington. Loc,
Golborne UD.

TWISTON Lancs
95 SD 8143 5m ENE of Clitheroe. CP, 72.
Clthroe RD. Clthroe CC.

TWITCHEN Devon
163 SS 7830 6m ENE of S Molton. CP, 81.
S Mltn RD. Ch e, m. N Dvn CC.

TWITCHEN Shrops
129 SO 3779 5m WSW of Craven Arms.
Loc, Clunbury CP. Ch m.

TWO BRIDGES Devon
175, 187, 188 SX 6075 8m E of Tavistock.
Loc, Lydford CP. 2m N, Wistman's Wd of
stunted oaks.

TWO DALES Derbys
111 SK 2762 2m NNW of Matlock. Loc,
Mtlck UD. P Mtlck.

TWO GATES Staffs
120 SK 2101 2m SSE of Tamworth. Loc,
Tmwth MB. P Tmwth. Lichfield and
Tmwth CC (Meriden).

TWYCROSS Leics
120, 121 SK 3304 5m NNE of Atherstone.
CP, 745. Mkt Bosworth RD. P Athrstne,
Warwickshire. Ch e. Bswth CC. See also
Norton juxta Twcrss, Orton on the Hill. Ch
has notable French stained glass. To N, zoo
pk*.

TWYFORD Berks
159 SU 7876 5m ENE of Reading.
CP, 2,206. Wokingham RD. P Rdng.
Ch e, c, v. Sch ie, j. Wknghm CC.

Twyford

TWYFORD Bucks
145, 146 SP 6626 5m SSW of Buckingham.
CP, 430. Bcknghm RD. P BCKNGHM.
Ch e, c. Sch pe. Bcknghm CC. Ch of
interest, esp porch.

TWYFORD Derbys
120, 121 SK 3228 5m SSW of Derby.
CP(Twfd and Stenson). Repton RD. Ch e.
Belper CC.

TWYFORD Hants
168 SU 4825 3m S of Winchester.
CP, 1,411. Wnchstr RD. P Wnchstr. Ch e, m.
Sch pe. Wnchstr CC.

TWYFORD Leics
122 SK 7310 6m SSW of Melton Mowbray.
CP(Twfd and Thorpe), 487. Mltn and
Belvoir RD. P Mltn Mbry. Ch e, m. Mltn CC.

TWYFORD Norfolk
125 TG 0124 7m ESE of Fakenham.
CP, 35. Mitford and Launditch RD. Ch e.
SW Nflk CC.

TWYFORD COMMON Herefs
142 SO 5135 3m S of Hereford. Loc,
Hrfd RD. Hrfd CC.

TWYNING Glos
143, 144 SO 8936 2m N of Tewkesbury.
CP, 819. Cheltenham RD. P Tksbry. Ch e.
Sch p. Cirencester and Tksbry CC. See also
Shuthonger.

TWYNING GREEN Glos
143, 144 SO 9036 3m N of Tewkesbury.
Loc, Twnng CP.

TWYWELL Northants
134 SP 9578 3m W of Thrapston. CP, 274.
Oundle and Thrpstn RD. P Kettering. Ch e.
Sch pe. Wellingborough CC (Peterborough).

TYBERTON Herefs
142 SO 3839 8m W of Hereford. CP, 84.
Dore and Bredwardine RD. Ch e. Hrfd CC.

TYDD GOTE Lincs (H)
124 TF 4517 3m SSE of Long Sutton. Loc,
Tdd St Mary CP. Ch m.

TYDD ST GILES Cambs
124 TF 4216 5m NNW of Wisbech. CP, 876.
Wsbch RD. P Wsbch. Ch e, m2. Sch p. Isle
of Ely CC. See also Four Gotes. Ch has 13c
detached twr.

TYDD ST MARY Lincs (H)
124 TF 4418 3m SSE of Long Sutton.
CP, 772. E Elloe RD. Ch e. Sch pe. Holland
w Boston CC. See also Tdd Gote.

TYLDESLEY Lancs
101 SD 6802 2m ENE of Leigh.
UD, 21,163. P MANCHESTER. Lgh BC. See
also Astley Grn.

TYLER HILL Kent
173 TR 1460 2m N of Canterbury. Loc,
Hackington CP. Bridge-Blean RD.
P Cntrbry. Cntrbry CC.

TYLERS GREEN Bucks
159 SU 9093 3m E of High Wycombe. Loc,
Chepping Wcmbe CP. Wcmbe RD. P Hgh
Wcmbe. Ch e, m. Sch j, p. Wcmbe CC.

TYNEHAM Dorset
178, 179 SY 8880 5m SSW of Wareham.
CP, nil. Wrhm and Purbeck RD. Ch e.
S Dst CC. Derelict; taken over by War Office
in World War II. Cf Imber.

TYNEMOUTH Nthmb
78 NZ 3568 7m ENE of Newcastle.
CB, 68,861. P: N Shields. Tnmth BC. See
also Cullercoats, New York, N Shlds. Resort
and rsdntl tn. Port (Tyne Commission
Quay). Rems of mdvl priory and
cstle (A.M.).

TYRINGHAM Bucks
146 SP 8547 2m NNW of Newport Pagnell.
CP(Tyrnghm w Filgrave), 181. Npt Pgnll RD.
Ch e. Buckingham CC.

TYTHERINGTON Ches
101 SJ 9175 1m N of Macclesfield. Loc,
Mcclesfld MB.

TYTHERINGTON Glos
155, 156 ST 6688 6m E of Severn Rd Br.
CP, 595. Thornbury RD. Ch e, b. Sch p.
S Glos CC. See also Itchington.

TYTHERINGTON Wilts
166, 167 ST 9141 4m SE of Warminster.
Loc, Heytesbury CP. Ch e.

TYTHERLEIGH Devon
177 ST 3103 3m S of Chard. Loc,
Chardstock CP.

TYWARDREATH Cornwall
185, 186, 190 SX 0854 5m E of St Austell.
Loc, St Astll w Fowey MB. P Par. Ch e.
Truro CC.

TYWARDREATH HIGHWAY Cornwall
185, 186 SX 0755 3m SW of Lostwithiel.
Loc, St Austell w Fowey MB. Truro CC.

U

UBBESTON GREEN Suffolk (E)
137 TM 3271 5m SW of Halesworth. Loc,
Ubbestn CP. Blyth RD. Ch e. Eye CC.

UBLEY Som
165 ST 5258 6m NE of Cheddar. CP, 294.
Clutton RD. P BRISTOL. Ch e, m. Sch pe.
N Som CC.

UCKERBY Yorks (N)
91 NZ 2402 5m E of Richmond. CP, 43.
Rchmnd RD. Rchmnd CC.

UCKFIELD Sussex (E)
183 TQ 4721 8m NNE of Lewes. CP, 4,412.
Uckfld RD. P. Ch e, b2, c, m2, r, s, v.
Sch p, pe, pr, s. E Grinstead CC. See also
Ridgewood. Considerable recent
development. High St is main A22 rd with
level-crossing at foot.

UCKINGTON Glos
143, 144 SO 9124 3m NW of Cheltenham.
CP, 367. Chltnhm RD. Ch e. Cirencester and
Tewkesbury CC. See also Elmstone
Hardwicke.

UDIMORE Sussex (E)
184 TQ 8718 3m W of Rye. CP, 393.
Battle RD. P Rye. Ch e. Sch p. Rye CC.

UFFCULME Devon
164, 176 ST 0612 7m E of Tiverton.
CP, 1,663. Tvtn RD. P Cullompton.
Ch e, b, v. Sch p, s. Tvtn CC. See also Ashill,
Smithincott. Ch: scrn, longest in county.

UFFORD Hunts
123 TF 0904 4m ESE of Stamford. CP, 190.
Barnack RD. P Stmfd, Lincs. Ch e. Peterborough BC (CC). Mainly limestone vllge.

UFFORD Suffolk (E)
150 TM 2952 3m NE of Woodbridge.
CP, 745. Deben RD. P Wdbrdge. Ch e, m.
Sch p. Eye CC. Ch: famous font cover;
bench-ends. Stocks and whipping post
outside.

UFFINGTON Berks
158 SU 3089 6m W of Wantage. CP, 581.
Faringdon RD. P Frngdn. Ch e, b, c. Sch pe.
Abingdon CC. Bthplce, 1822, of Thomas
Hughes, author of *Tom Brown's
Schooldays*; many scenes therein set here.
To S, U. White Horse, prob cut c 100 BC.

UFFINGTON Lincs (K)
123 TF 0607 2m E of Stamford. CP, 341.
S Kesteven RD. Ch e. Sch pe. Rutland and
Stmfd CC. Ch: monmts. U. Hall seat of
Earls of Lindsey.

UFFINGTON Shrops
118 SJ 5213 2m ENE of Shrewsbury. CP.
Atcham RD. P Shrsbry. Ch e. Shrsbry CC.
Squashed between R Severn and Shrops
Union Canal. To N, Sundorne Cstle, hse of
1800 with large lake. To NE, rems of
Haumond Abbey.

UFTON Warwicks
132 SP 3762 4m ESE of Leamington.
CP, 224. Southam RD. P Lmngtn Spa. Ch e.
Sch pe. Stratford-on-Avon CC (Strtfd).

UFTON NERVET Berks
158, 169 SU 6367 6m SW of Reading.
CP, 181. Bradfield RD. Ch e. Sch pe.
Newbury CC.

UGBOROUGH Devon
187, 188 SX 6755 3m E of Ivybridge.
CP, 2,051. Totnes RD. P Ivybridge. Ch e, v.
Sch p. Ttns CC. See also Bittaford,
Wrangaton.

UGGESHALL Suffolk (E)
137 TM 4480 4m ENE of Halesworth.
CP, 148. Lothingland RD. P Beccles. Ch e.
Lowestoft CC.

UGGLEBARNBY Yorks (N)
86, 93 NZ 8807 3m SSW of Whitby.
CP(Eskdaleside cum Ugglebarnby), 1,539.
Whtby RD. Ch e. Cleveland and Whtby CC
(Scarborough and Whtby).

UGLEY Essex
148 TL 5228 5m NNE of Bishop's Stortford. CP, 423. Saffron Walden RD. P Bshp's Sttfd, Herts. Ch e. Sch p. Sffrn Wldn CC.

UGLEY GREEN Essex
148 TL 5227 4m NNE of Bishop's Stortford. Loc, Ugley CP.

UGTHORPE Yorks (N)
86 NZ 7911 6m W of Whitby. CP, 218. Whtby RD. P Whtby. Ch e, r. Sch pr. Cleveland and Whtby CC (Scarborough and Whtby).

ULCEBY Lincs (L)
104 TA 1014 5m W of Immingham. CP, 775. Glanford Brigg RD. P. Ch e, m, v. Sch pe. Brgg and Scunthorpe CC (Brgg).

ULCEBY Lincs (L)
114 TF 4272 3m SW of Alford. CP(Ulceby w Fordington), 155. Spilsby RD. P Alfd. Ch e, m. Horncastle CC.

ULCEBY SKITTER Lincs (L)
104 TA 1214 4m W of Immingham. Loc, Glanford Brigg RD. Ch m. Brgg and Scunthorpe CC (Brgg).

ULCOMBE Kent
172, 184 TQ 8448 7m SE of Maidstone. CP, 696. Hollingbourn RD. P Mdstne. Ch e, m. Sch pe. Mdstne CC.

ULDALE Cumb
82 NY 2537 7m S of Wigton. Loc, Ireby CP. P Carlisle. Sch pe. Ch e at U. Mill, 1m NW.

ULEY Glos
156 ST 7898 6m SW of Stroud. CP, 1,083. Dursley RD. Ch e, v. Sch pe. Strd CC. To N, Hetty Peglar's Tump (A.M.), long barrow.

ULGHAM Nthmb
78 NZ 2392 5m NNE of Morpeth. CP, 2,288. Mpth RD. P Mpth. Ch e, m. Mpth CC.

ULLENHALL Warwicks
131 SP 1267 5m E of Redditch. CP, 570. Stratford-on-Avon RD. P Solihull. Ch e. Sch pe. Strtfd-on-Avn CC (Strtfd).

ULLESKELF Yorks (W)
97 SE 5140 3m SE of Tadcaster. CP, 1,166. Tdcstr RD. P Tdcstr. Ch e, m. Sch pe. Barkston Ash CC.

ULLESTHORPE Leics
132 SP 5087 3m NW of Lutterworth. CP, 612. Lttrwth RD. P Rugby, Warwickshire. Ch v. Sch ie. Blaby CC (Harborough).

ULLEY Yorks (W)
103 SK 4687 4m SE of Rotherham. CP, 184. Rthrhm RD. P SHEFFIELD. Ch e. Rother Valley CC.

ULLINGSWICK Herefs
142 SO 5949 8m NE of Hereford. CP, 240. Bromyard RD. P HRFD. Ch e. Leominster CC.

ULLOCK Cumb
82 NY 0724 5m SSW of Cockermouth. Loc, Dean CP. P Workington.

ULPHA Cumb
88 SD 1993 8m NNE of Millom. CP, 123. Mllm RD. P Broughton-in-Furness, Lancs. Ch e. Whitehaven CC.

ULROME Yorks (E)
99 TA 1656 7m SSW of Bridlington. CP, 383. Brdlngtn RD. Ch e, m. Brdlngtn CC. See also Lissett. Rems of prehistoric lake vllge discovered 1880, cf Godney, Meare.

ULTING WICK Essex
162 TL 8008 3m WNW of Maldon. Loc, Ultng CP. Mldn RD. Ch e. Mldn CC.

ULVERSTON Lancs
88 SD 2878 8m NE of Barrow. UD, 11,888. P. Morecambe and Lonsdale CC. Engineering, chemicals. Formerly port connected to sea by canal now long disused. 1m SW, Swarthmoor Hall*, once home of George Fox, founder of Quakers.

UMBERLEIGH Devon
163 SS 6023 7m SSE of Barnstaple. Loc, Chittlehampton CP. P. Sch p.

UNCLEBY Yorks (E)
98 SE 8159 6m N of Pocklington. Loc, Kirby Underdale CP. Ch m.

UNDERBARROW Westm
89 SD 4692 3m W of Kendal. CP(Undrbrrw and Bradleyfield), 322. S Westm RD. Ch e. Sch pe. Westm CC. See also Grigghall.

UNDER RIVER Kent
171 TQ 5552 3m SE of Sevenoaks. Loc,
Seal CP. Ch e. Sch pe.

UNDERWOOD Notts
112 SK 4750 4m E of Ripley. Loc,
Selston CP. P NOTTINGHAM. Ch e, v.
Sch pe.

UNSTONE Derbys
103, 111 SK 3777 4m N of Chesterfield.
CP, 2,376. Chstrfld RD. P SHEFFIELD.
Ch e, m. Sch i, j. NE Derbys CC. See also
Apperknowle, Middle Handley, W Hndly.

UPAVON Wilts
167 SU 1355 4m SW of Pewsey. CP, 1,521.
Psy RD. P Psy. Ch e, b, m. Sch p.
Devizes CC. Thatched cottages decorated
with birds. Caravans.

UP CERNE Dorset
178 ST 6502 8m NNW of Dorchester.
CP, 50. Dchstr RD. Ch e. W Dst CC.

UPCHURCH Kent
172 TQ 8467 5m NW of Sittingbourne.
CP, 1,465. Swale RD. P Sttngbne. Ch e, m.
Sch p, pe. Faversham CC. Ch has 13c
wall-paintings. Sir Francis Drake lived here
as a boy.

UPDOWN HILL Surrey
169 SU 9363 5m ENE of Camberley. Loc,
Windlesham CP.

UPEND Cambs
135 TL 7058 5m SE of Newmarket. Loc,
Kirtling CP.

UP EXE Devon
176 SS 9402 6m N of Exeter. Loc,
Rewe CP.

UPHAM Devon
176 SS 8808 5m WSW of Tiverton. Loc,
Cheriton Fitzpaine CP.

UPHAM Hants
168 SU 5320 7m SSE of Winchester.
CP, 681. Droxford RD. Ch e. Sch pe.
Petersfield CC. See also Lr Uphm.

UPHAMPTON Herefs
129 SO 3963 5m E of Presteigne. Loc,
Shobdon CP.

UP HATHERLEY Glos
143, 144 SO 9120 2m WSW of Cheltenham.

CP, 305. Chltnhm RD. Ch e. Cirencester
and Tewkesbury CC.

UP HILL Kent
173 TR 2140 3m N of Folkestone. Loc,
Hawkinge CP. Ch bv.

UPHILL Som
165 ST 3158 2m S of Weston. Loc,
Wstn-super-Mare MB. P Wstn-spr-Mre.

UP HOLLAND Lancs
100 SD 5205 4m W of Wigan.
UD(Skelmersdale and Hllnd), 30,522.
P Wgn. Ince BC. Mining tn. Ch is part of
former priory.

UPLEADON Glos
143 SO 7527 7m NW of Gloucester.
CP, 196. Newent RD. P Nwnt. Ch e, m.
W Glos CC. Ch has 16c timber-framed twr.

UPLEATHAM Yorks (N)
86 NZ 6319 2m SW of Saltburn. Loc,
Guisborough UD. P REDCAR, Teesside.

UPLEES Kent
172 TQ 9964 2m NNW of Faversham. Loc,
Oare CP.

UPLOWMAN Devon
164 ST 0115 4m ENE of Tiverton. CP, 272.
Tvtn RD. P(Uplmn Cross) Tvtn. Ch e.
Sch pe. Tvtn CC. See also Whitnage.

UPLYME Devon
177 SY 3293 1m NW of Lyme Regis.
CP, 1,243. Axminster RD. P Lme Rgs. Ch e.
Sch pe. Honiton CC.

UPMINSTER London
161 TQ 5586 5m SSW of Brentwood. Loc,
Havering LB. P Essex. Upmnstr BC
(Hornchurch). Rsdntl distr. Windmill.

UP NATELY Hants
169 SU 6951 4m E of Basingstoke.
CP(Mapledurwell and Up Ntly), 322.
Bsngstke RD. Ch e. Bsngstke CC.

UPOTTERY Devon
177 ST 2007 5m NNE of Honiton. CP, 450.
Hntn RD. P Hntn. Ch e, b. Sch p. Hntn CC.

UPPER ARLEY Worcs
130 SO 7680 5m WNW of Kidderminster.
CP, 712. Kddrmnstr RD. P(Arley), Bewdley.
Ch e. Sch pe. Kddrmnstr CC. See also

Shatterford. Manually operated passenger ferry over R Severn.

UPPER ARNCOTT Oxon
145, 146 SP 6117 4m SSE of Bicester. Loc, Arnctt CP. Ploughley RD. Mid-Oxon CC (Henley).

UPPER ASTROP Northants
145 SP 5137 4m ESE of Banbury. Loc, King's Sutton CP.

UPPER BASILDON Berks
158 SU 5976 3m W of Pangbourne. Loc, Bsldn CP. P Reading. Ch e, c. Sch pe.

UPPER BEEDING Sussex (W)
182 TQ 1910 4m NNW of Shoreham-by-Sea. CP, 2,396. Chanctonbury RD. Ch e, b2. Sch p. Shrhm CC (Arundel and Shrhm). See also Edburton.

UPPER BENEFIELD Northants
134 SP 9889 4m W of Oundle. Loc, Bnfld CP. P PETERBOROUGH.

UPPER BENTLEY Worcs
130, 131 SO 9966 4m SSE of Bromsgrove. Loc, Bntly Pauncefoot CP. Brmsgrve RD. Brmsgrve and Redditch CC (Brmsgrve).

UPPER BODDINGTON Northants
145 SP 4853 8m NNE of Banbury. Loc, Bddngtn CP. Brackley RD. P Rugby, Warwickshire. Ch e, m. Sch pe. Daventry CC (S Nthnts). To SE, lake with sailing boats.

UPPER BRAILES Warwicks
145 SP 3039 3m ESE of Shipston on Stour. Loc, Brls CP. Shpstn on Str RD. Ch m. Stratford-on-Avon CC (Strtfd). Joined to Lr Brls, qv.

UPPER BREINTON Herefs
142 SO 4640 3m W of Hereford. Loc, Brntn CP.

UPPER BROADHEATH Worcs
130 SO 8058 3m W of Worcester. Loc, Brdhth CP. Martley RD. Kidderminster CC.

UPPER BROUGHTON Notts
122 SK 6826 6m NW of Melton Mowbray. CP, 216. Bingham RD. P Mltn Mbry, Leics. Ch e, b. Sch p. Rushcliffe CC (Carlton).

UPPER BUCKLEBURY Berks
158 SU 5468 5m E of Newbury. Loc, Bcklbry CP. P Reading.

UPPER CALDECOTE Beds
147 TL 1645 2m NW of Biggleswade. Loc, Northill CP. P Bgglswde. Ch e, m. Sch pe.

UPPER CATESBY Northants
132 SP 5259 3m WSW of Daventry. Loc, Ctsby CP. Dvntry RD. Dvntry CC (S Nthnts).

UPPER CHEDDON Som
177 ST 2328 3m N of Taunton. Loc, Cheddon Fitzpaine CP.

UPPER CHUTE Wilts
168 SU 2953 7m NNW of Andover. Loc, Chte CP. Pewsey RD. Ch e. Devizes CC.

UPPER CLATFORD Hants
168 SU 3543 1m S of Andover. CP, 740. Andvr RD. P Andvr. Ch e, m. Winchester CC (Basingstoke).

UPPER COKEHAM Sussex (W)
182 TQ 1705 3m NE of Worthing. Loc, Sompting CP.

UPPER CUMBERWORTH Yorks (W)
102 SE 2108 4m NNW of Penistone. Loc, Denby Dale UD. P Huddersfield.

UPPER DEAN Beds
134 TL 0467 6m E of Rushden. Loc, Dn and Shelton CP. Bedford RD. P HUNTINGDON. Ch e, c. Sch p. Bdfd CC. 15c ch with 14c spire.

UPPER DENBY Yorks (W)
102 SE 2207 3m NNW of Penistone. Loc, Dnby Dale UD. P Huddersfield.

UPPER DENTON Cumb
76 NY 6165 6m ENE of Brampton. CP, 130. Border RD. Ch e, m. Sch p. Penrith and the Border CC.

UPPER DICKER Sussex (E)
183 TQ 5510 2m WNW of Hailsham. Loc, Hellingly CP. P Hlshm. Ch e. To S, Michelham Priory*; Tdr hse, 14c gatehouse. Exhibits of Sussex ironwork etc.

UPPER DUNSFORTH Yorks (W)
91, 97 SE 4463 4m SE of Boroughbridge. Loc, Dnsfths CP. Nidderdale RD. Harrogate CC.

UPPER EGLETON Herefs
142, 143 SO 6345 6m NW of Ledbury. Loc,
Eggltn CP. Ldbry RD. Leominster CC.

UPPER ELKSTONE Staffs
111 SK 0559 5m ENE of Leek. Loc,
Warslow and Elkstones CP. Sch p.

UPPER END Derbys
111 SK 0876 3m NE of Buxton. Loc,
Wormhill CP.

UPPER FRAMILODE Glos
143 SO 7510 7m SW of Gloucester. Loc,
Fretherne w Saul CP.

UPPER GRAVENHURST Beds
147 TL 1136 5m ESE of Ampthill. Loc,
Grvnhst CP. Ampthll RD. Ch e, m. Sch p.
Mid-Beds CC.

UPPER GREEN Berks
168 SU 3763 4m SE of Hungerford. Loc,
Inkpen CP.

UPPER GROVE COMMON Herefs
142 SO 5526 3m WNW of Ross-on-Wye.
Loc, Sellack CP.

UPPER HACKNEY Derbys
111 SK 2961 1m NNW of Matlock. Loc,
Mtlck UD. P(Hckny), Mtlck.

UPPER HALE Surrey
169 SU 8348 2m SW of Aldershot. Loc,
Farnham UD. P Fnhm.

UPPER HALLING Kent
171 TQ 6964 4m SW of Rochester. Loc,
Hllng CP. P Rchstr.

UPPER HARTFIELD Sussex (E)
183 TQ 4634 5m ESE of E Grinstead. Loc,
Htfld CP. P Htfld. Hmlt on edge of
Ashdown Forest.

UPPER HARTSHAY Derbys
111 SK 3850 1m W of Ripley. Loc,
Rply UD.

UPPER HAYTON Shrops
129 SO 5181 4m N of Ludlow. Loc,
Stanton Lacy CP.

UPPER HEATH Shrops
129 SO 5685 7m NNE of Ludlow. Loc,
Hth CP. Ldlw RD. Ch e. Ldlw CC.

UPPER HELMSLEY Yorks (N)
97, 98 SE 6956 7m ENE of York. CP, 30.
Flaxton RD. Ch e. Thirsk and Malton CC.

UPPER HERGEST Herefs
141 SO 2654 2m SW of Kington. Loc,
Kngtn Rural CP. Kngtn RD. Leominster CC.

UPPER HEYFORD Northants
132, 133 SP 6659 6m W of Northampton.
CP, 68. Nthmptn RD. Daventry CC
(S Nthnts).

UPPER HEYFORD Oxon
145 SP 4926 6m WNW of Bicester.
CP, 2,190. Ploughley RD. P OXFORD.
Ch e, m. Sch pe. Banbury CC (Henley).

UPPER HILL Herefs
142 SO 4753 4m SSW of Leominster. Loc,
Hope under Dinmore CP. Ch m.

UPPER HOPTON Yorks (W)
96, 102 SE 1918 4m ENE of Huddersfield.
Loc, Mirfield UD.

UPPER HULME Staffs
111 SK 0160 3m NNE of Leek. Loc,
Heathylee CP. Lk RD. P Lk. Lk CC. On
edge of Peak Distr National Pk. To N, The
Roaches and Hen Cloud, hills well known to
climbers.

UPPER INGLESHAM Wilts
157 SU 2096 8m NNE of Swindon. Loc,
Inglshm CP.

UPPER LAMBOURN Berks
158 SU 3180 7m SW of Wantage. Loc,
Lmbn CP. Ch e.

UPPER LANGWITH Derbys
112 SK 5169 5m NNW of Mansfield. Loc,
Blackwell RD. Ch e.

UPPER LONGDON Staffs
120 SK 0614 3m SSE of Rugeley. Loc,
Lngdn CP.

UPPER LYDBROOK Glos
142 143 SO 6015 3m W of Cinderford.
Loc, Ldbrk CP. W Dean RD. Ch e, b, c, m.
Sch p2. W Glos CC.

UPPER MAES-COED Herefs
142 SO 3334 12m WSW of Hereford. Loc,
St Margaret CP. Ch m.

UPPERMILL Yorks (W)
101 SD 9905 5m E of Oldham. Loc, Saddleworth UD. P Oldhm, Lancs.

UPPER MINETY Wilts
157 SU 0091 5m NE of Malmesbury. Loc, Mnty CP. P Mlmsbry. Ch e.

UPPER OUTWOODS Staffs
120 SK 2225 2m NW of Burton-on-Trent. Loc, Outwds CP. Tutbury RD. Ch m. Btn CC.

UPPER POPPLETON Yorks (W)
97 SE 5554 3m WNW of York. CP, 1,365. Nidderdale RD. P YK. Ch e, m. Sch p. Barkston Ash CC.

UPPER QUINTON Warwicks
144 SP 1746 6m SSW of Stratford. Loc, Quntn CP. Strtfd-on-Avon RD. Ch m. Strtfd-on-Avn CC (Strtfd).

UPPER ROCHFORD Worcs
129, 130 SO 6267 2m ESE of Tenbury Wells. Loc, Rchfd CP. Tnbry RD. P(Rchfd), Tnbry Wlls. Kidderminster CC.

UPPER SAPEY Herefs
130 SO 6863 6m NNE of Bromyard. CP, 231. Brmyd RD. P WORCESTER. Ch e, m. Sch pe. Leominster CC. See also Sapey Cmmn.

UPPER SEAGRY Wilts
157 ST 9480 4m S of Malmesbury. Loc, Sutton Benger CP. P(Sgry), Chippenham. Ch e, m. Sch pe.

UPPER SHELTON Beds
147 SP 9943 5m SW of Bedford. Loc, Marston Moretaine CP.

UPPER SHERINGHAM Norfolk
125 TG 1441 1m SW of Sheringham. CP, 280. Erpingham RD. P Shrnghm. Ch e. N Nflk CC. Shrnghm Hall (see Shrnghm).

UPPER SHUCKBURGH Warwicks
132 SP 4961 5m E of Southam. CP, 21. Sthm RD. Ch e. Stratford-on-Avon CC (Strtfd).

UPPER SLAUGHTER Glos
144 SP 1523 3m WSW of Stow-on-the-Wold. CP, 224. N Cotswold RD. P Cheltenham. Ch e. Sch pe. Cirencester and Tewkesbury CC. Ctswld vllge famous for beauty.

UPPER SOMBORNE Hants
168 SU 3932 6m WNW of Winchester. Loc, Kings Smbne CP. P (Up Smbne), Stockbridge. Ch m.

UPPER SOUDLEY Glos
142, 143 SO 6510 2m S of Cinderford. Loc, Ruspidge CP. P(Sdly), Cndrfd. Ch m. Sch p.

UPPER STONDON Beds
147 TL 1535 4m NNW of Hitchin. CP, 79. Biggleswade RD. Ch e. Mid-Beds CC.

UPPER STOWE Northants
132, 133 SP 6456 6m SE of Daventry. Loc, Stwe Nine Churches CP. Dvntry RD. Dvntry CC (S Nthnts).

UPPER STREET Hants
179 SU 1418 3m N of Fordingbridge. Loc, Breamore CP.

UPPER STREET Norfolk
126 TG 3517 4m E of Wroxham. Loc, Horning CP.

UPPER STRENSHAM Worcs
143, 144 SO 9039 4m N of Tewkesbury. Loc, Strnshm CP. Pershore RD. P(Strnshm), WORCESTER. S Worcs CC.

UPPER SUNDON Beds
147 TL 0427 4m NNE of Dunstable. Loc, Sndn CP.

UPPER SWELL Glos
144 SP 1726 1m NW of Stow-on-the-Wold. Loc, Swll CP. N Cotswold RD. Ch e. Cirencester and Tewkesbury CC. Tiny Cotswold vllge at bottom of hill.

UPPER TASBURGH Norfolk
137 TM 2095 7m SE of Wymondham. Loc, Tsbrgh CP.

UPPER TEAN Staffs
120 SK 0139 2m S of Cheadle. Loc, Checkley CP. Ch e, c, m, r. Sch p, pr.

UPPERTHONG Yorks (W)
102 SE 1208 5m S of Huddersfield. Loc, Holmfirth UD.

UPPER THURNHAM Lancs
94 SD 4654 5m SSW of Lancaster. Loc,
Thnhm CP. Lncstr RD. Ch r. Lncstr CC.

UPPERTON Sussex (W)
181, 182 SU 9522 1m NW of Petworth.
Loc, Tillington CP. Well grouped hmlt on W
edge of Ptwth Pk with views to S. To N just
inside pk wall, tall Gothic folly of c 1800.

UPPER TOWN Som
155, 165 ST 5265 6m SW of Bristol. Loc,
Winford CP.

UPPER TYSOE Warwicks
145 SP 3343 8m WNW of Banbury. Loc,
Tysoe CP. Shipston on Stour RD.
P(Tysoe),WARWICK. Stratford-on-Avon CC
(Strtfd). Mnr hse of three periods.

UPPER UPHAM Wilts
157 SU 2277 6m NNE of Marlborough.
Loc, Aldbourne CP.

UPPER UPNOR Kent
172 TQ 7570 1m NNE of Rochester. Loc,
Frindsbury Extra CP. Strood RD. Ch e, c.
Gravesend CC. To N, U. Cstle (A.M.),
where Elizabeth I reviewed fleet 1581.

UPPER WARDINGTON Oxon
145 SP 4946 4m NE of Banbury. Loc,
Wdngtn CP.

UPPER WEALD Bucks
146 SP 8037 2m SSW of Wolverton. Loc,
Wlvtn UD.

UPPER WEEDON Northants
132, 133 SP 6258 4m ESE of Daventry.
Loc, Wdn Bec CP.

UPPER WELLAND Worcs
143 SO 7740 3m S of Malvern. Loc,
Mlvn UD. P Mlvn.

UPPER WINCHENDON Bucks
146, 159 SP 7414 5m W of Aylesbury.
CP, 105. Aylesbury RD. Ch e.
Aylesbury CC.

UPPER WOODFORD Wilts
167 SU 1237 5m N of Salisbury. Loc,
Wdfd CP. Amesbury RD. Slsbry CC.

UPPER WRAXALL Wilts
156 ST 8074 7m W of Chippenham. Loc,
N Wrxll CP.

UPPINGHAM Rutland
122, 133 SP 8699 6m S of Oakham.
CP, 1,940. Uppnghm RD. P. Ch e, b, m, v.
Sch p, pe, s. Rtlnd and Stamford CC. Small
mkt tn. Boys' public sch.

UPPINGTON Shrops
118 SJ 6009 4m WSW of Wellington.
CP, 86. Atcham RD. Ch e. Shrewsbury CC.

UPSALL Yorks (N)
91 SE 4587 4m NNE of Thirsk. CP, 91.
Thsk RD. P Thsk. Ch m. Thsk and
Malton CC.

UPSHIRE Essex
161 TL 4101 2m E of Waltham Abbey. Loc,
Wltham Holy Cross UD. P Wlthm Abbey.
Epping Forest CC (Eppng). NE and NW,
obelisks improbably associated with Queen
Boadicea.

UPSTREET Kent
173 TR 2263 4m SE of Herne Bay. Loc,
Chislet CP. P Canterbury.

UP SYDLING Dorset
178 ST 6201 8m NNW of Dorchester. Loc,
Sdlng St Nicholas CP.

UPTON Berks
158 SU 5186 2m S of Didcot. CP, 279.
Wantage RD. P Ddct. Ch e, m. Sch pe.
Abingdon CC.

UPTON Bucks
146, 159 SP 7711 3m WSW of Aylesbury.
CP(Dinton-w-Ford and Upton), 651.
Aylesbury RD. Aylesbury CC.

UPTON Bucks
159, 160, 170 SU 9879 just SE of Slough.
Loc, Slgh MB.

UPTON Ches
109 SJ 4069 2m N of Chester.
CP(Uptn-by-Chstr), 7,708. Chstr RD.
Ch e, c. Sch ie, p3, s. City of Chstr CC.

UPTON Dorset
179 SY 9893 3m NW of Poole. Loc,
Lytchett Minster CP. P Ple. Sch p.

UPTON Hants
168 SU 3655 6m N of Andover. Loc,
Andvr RD. P Andvr. Ch m. Winchester CC (Basingstoke).

UPTON Hants
180 SU 3716 4m NW of Southampton.
Loc, Nursling and Rownhams CP.

UPTON Hunts
123 TF 1000 5m W of Peterborough.
CP, 100. Ptrbrgh RD. Ch e. Ptrbrgh BC
(CC).

UPTON Hunts
134 TL 1778 6m NW of Huntingdon.
CP(Uptn and Coppingford), 262.
Hntngdn RD. P HNTNGDN. Ch e.
Hunts CC.

UPTON Leics
132 SP 3699 4m ENE of Atherstone. Loc,
Sheepy CP. Mkt Bosworth RD. Bswth CC.

UPTON Lincs (L)
104 SK 8686 4m SE of Gainsborough.
CP, 570. Gnsbrgh RD. P Gnsbrgh. Ch e, m.
Gnsbrgh CC.

UPTON Norfolk
126   TG 3912 7m ESE of Wroxham.
CP(Uptn w Fishley), 429. Blofield and
Flegg RD. P NORWICH, NOR 58Z. Ch e, m.
Sch pe. Yarmouth CC.

UPTON Northants
133 SP 7160 2m W of Northampton. CP.
Nthmptn RD. Ch e. Daventry CC
(S Nthnts). County mental hsptl.

UPTON Notts
103 SK 7476 4m SE of Retford. CP(Headon
cum Uptn), 177. E Rtfd RD. Bassetlaw CC.

UPTON Notts
112 SK 7354 4m W of Newark. CP, 522.
Southwell RD. P Nwk. Ch e, m. Sch pe.
Nwk CC. Ch twr has nine pinnacles.

UPTON Oxon
144 SP 2412 just W of Burford. CP(Bfd and
Uptn and Signet), 1,453. Witney RD.
Mid-Oxon CC (Banbury).

UPTON Som
164 SS 9929 5m E of Dulverton. CP, 133.
Dlvtn RD. P Wiveliscombe, Taunton. Ch m.
Sch p. Tntn CC.

UPTON Yorks (W)
103 SE 4713 6m S of Pontefract. CP, 2,358.
Hemsworth RD. P Pntfrct. Ch m, r. Sch s.
Hmswth CC.

UPTON BISHOP Herefs
142, 143 SO 6527 4m ENE of Ross-on-Wye.
CP, 455. Rss and Whitchurch RD.
P Rss-on-Wye. Ch e. Sch pe. Hereford CC.
See also Crow Hill, Phocle Grn, Uptn Crews.

UPTON CHEYNEY Glos
156 ST 6969 5m NW of Bath. Loc,
Bitton CP. Ch v. Sch p.

UPTON CRESSETT Shrops
129, 130 SO 6592 4m W of Bridgnorth.
CP, 39. Brdgnth RD. Ch e. Ludlow CC.
Remote vllge. Ch has Nmn S doorway and
chancel arch.

UPTON CREWS Herefs
142, 143 SO 6427 4m NE of Ross-on-Wye.
Loc, Uptn Bishop CP.

UPTON CROSS Cornwall
186 SX 2872 5m WNW of Callington. Loc,
Linkinhorne CP. P Liskeard. Ch m. Sch p.

UPTON GREY Hants
169 SU 6948 5m SE of Basingstoke.
CP, 453. Bsngstke RD. P Bsngstke. Ch e, m.
Sch pe. Bsngstke CC.

UPTON HELLIONS Devon
176 SS 8403 2m N of Crediton. CP, 76.
Crdtn RD. Ch e. Tiverton CC (Torrington).

UPTON LOVELL Wilts
167 ST 9440 5m ESE of Warminster.
CP, 144. Wmnstr and Westbury RD.
P Wmnstr. Ch e. Wstbry CC.

UPTON MAGNA Shrops
118 SJ 5512 4m E of Shrewsbury. CP, 379.
Atcham RD. P Shrsbry. Ch e. Sch pe.
Shrsbry CC. See also Haughton. View of
Wrekin.

UPTON NOBLE Som
166 ST 7139 4m NNE of Bruton. CP, 112.
Frome RD. P Shepton Mallet. Ch e, m.
Sch pe. Wells CC.

UPTON PYNE Devon
176 SX 9197 3m N of Exeter. CP, 417.
St Thomas RD. P Extr. Ch e. Tiverton CC.
See also Cowley.

UPTON ST LEONARDS Glos
143 SO 8614 3m SE of Gloucester. CP.
Glcstr RD. Ch e, r. Sch pe. Strd CC.

UPTON SCUDAMORE Wilts
166 ST 8647 2m N of Warminster. CP, 250. Wmnstr and Westbury RD. P Wmnstr. Ch e. Wstbry CC.

UPTON SNODSBURY Worcs
143, 144 SO 9454 6m E of Worcester. CP, 281. Pershore RD. P WCSTR. Ch e. Sch pe. S Worcs CC.

UPTON UPON SEVERN Worcs
143 SO 8540 5m NNW of Tewkesbury. CP, 2,075. Uptn upn Svn RD. P WORCESTER. Ch e, b, r. Sch pe, s. S Worcs CC. Old mkt tn. Boats.

UPTON WARREN Worcs
130, 131 SO 9267 3m SW of Bromsgrove. CP, 321. Droitwich RD. Ch e. Sch pe. Worcester BC.

UPWALTHAM Sussex (W)
181 SU 9413 8m NE of Chichester. CP, 25. Chchstr RD. Ch e. Chchstr CC.

UPWARE Cambs
135 TL 5370 6m S of Ely. Loc, Wicken CP.

UPWELL Cambs and Norfolk
124 TF 5002 5m SSE of Wisbech. CP, 1,401. Wsbch RD; CP, 1,883, Marshland RD. P Wsbch, Cambs. Ch e 2, b, m3. Sch p2, s. Isle of Ely CC, King's Lynn CC. See also Christchurch, Lakes End, Three Holes.

UPWEY Dorset
178 SY 6685 4m N of Weymouth. Loc, Wmth and Melcombe Regis MB. P Wmth.

UPWOOD Hunts
134 TL 2582 2m SW of Ramsey. CP(Upwd and the Raveleys), 550. Huntingdon RD. P HNTNGDN. Ch e, m. Sch p. Hunts CC. See also Gt Raveley, Lit Rvly.

URCHFONT Wilts
167 SU 0457 4m SE of Devizes. CP, 706. Dvzs RD. P Dvzs. Ch e, v. Sch pe. Dvzs CC. See also Wedhampton. Ch mainly EE: monmts. Ggn hses and thatched cottages; mnr hse now college.

URDIMARSH Herefs
142 SO 5249 6m N of Hereford. Loc, Marden CP.

URE BANK Yorks (W)
91 SE 3172 just N of Ripon. Loc, Rpn MB.

URMSTON Lancs
101 SJ 7794 5m WSW of Manchester. UD, 44,523. P MNCHSTR. Stretford BC. See also Flixton. Modern shopping centre development.

URRA Yorks (N)
86, 92 NZ 5701 5m SE of Stokesley. Loc, Bilsdale Midcable CP. Stksly RD. Richmond CC.

URSWICK, GREAT Lancs
88 SD 2774 3m SSW of Ulverston. See Gt Urswck.

USHAW MOOR Co Durham
85 NZ 2242 3m W of Durham. Loc, Brandon and Byshottles UD. P DRHM.

USSELBY Lincs (L)
104 TF 0993 3m NNW of Mkt Rasen. Loc, Osgodby CP. Ch e.

UTLEY Yorks (W)
96 SE 0542 1m NNW of Keighley. Loc, Kghly MB. P Kghly.

UTON Devon
176 SX 8298 1m SSW of Crediton. Loc, Crdtn Hmlts CP. Crdtn RD. Tiverton CC (Torrington).

UTTERBY Lincs (L)
105 TF 3093 4m NNW of Louth. CP, 201. Lth RD. P Lth. Ch e, m. Sch p. Lth CC.

UTTOXETER Staffs
120 SK 0933 11m NW of Burton-on-Trent. UD, 9,034. P. Btn CC. See also Bramshall. Mkt tn. Racecourse. Sculpture in mkt place recalls penance of Dr Johnson.

UXBRIDGE London
160 TQ 0584 6m ENE of Slough. Loc, Hillingdon LB. P Middx. Uxbrdge BC (CC).

V

VANGE Essex
161. 162 TQ 7287 just S of Basildon. Loc, Bsldn UD. P Bsldn.

VAULD, THE Herefs
142 SO 5349 6m NNE of Hereford. Loc Marden CP.

VAUXHALL London
160, 170 TQ 3078 1m SSE of Charing Cross. Loc, Lambeth LB. Vxhll BC. Former gdns were resort of fashion from late 17c to early 19c; now warehouses etc.

VENNINGTON Shrops
118 SJ 3309 7m ENE of Welshpool. Loc, Westbury CP.

VENN OTTERY Devon
176 SY 0791 4m NW of Sidmouth. Loc, Harpford CP. Ch e.

VENTNOR IOW
180 SZ 5677 3m SSW of Shanklin. UD, 6,910. P. Isle of Wight CC. See also St Lawrence, Wroxall. Resort and rsdntl tn.

VERNHAM DEAN Hants
168 SU 3456 7m N of Andover. CP(Vernhams Dean), 361. Andvr RD. P Andvr. Ch e, m2, v. Sch pe. Winchester CC (Basingstoke). See also Vnhm St.

VERNHAM STREET Hants
168 SU 3457 8m N of Andover. Loc, Vernhams Dean CP.

VERNOLDS COMMON Shrops
129 SO 4780 3m ESE of Craven Arms. Loc, Ludlow RD. Ch m. Ldlw CC.

VERWOOD Dorset
179 SU 0808 5m NW of Ringwood. CP, 2,820. Wimborne and Cranborne RD. P Wmbne. Ch e, c, m, v. Sch ie, j. N Dst CC. See also Three Legged Cross.

VERYAN Cornwall
190 SW 9139 6m NE of St Mawes. CP, 895. Truro RD. P Truro. Ch e, m2. Sch pe.

Truro CC. See also Portloe. Has several round hses, supposedly to ward off the devil.

VICARAGE Devon
177 SY 2088 3m WSW of Seaton. Loc, Branscombe CP.

VICKERSTOWN Lancs
88 SD 1868 on Walney Island just W of Barrow. Loc, Brrw-in-Furness CB. Estate blt early 20c to house shipbuilding workers.

VICTORIA Cornwall
185 SW 9861 6m NNW of St Austell. Loc, Roche CP.

VILLAVIN Devon
163 SS 5816 6m ESE of Torrington. Loc, Roborough CP.

VINEHALL STREET Sussex (E)
184 TQ 7520 3m N of Battle. Loc, Bttle RD. Rye CC.

VINE'S CROSS Sussex (E)
183 TQ 5917 2m SSE of Heathfield. Loc, Horam CP. P Hthfld.

VIRGINIA WATER Surrey
169, 170 SU 9968 3m SW of Staines. Loc, Egham UD. P. Named after large lake on S edge of Windsor Gt Pk. Wentworth GC to W (S of lake). Affluent rsdntl distr.

VIRGINSTOW Devon
174 SX 3792 6m NNE of Launceston. CP, 96. Holsworthy RD. Ch e, m. W Dvn CC (Tavistock).

VOBSTER Som
166 ST 7049 5m W of Frome. Loc, Mells CP. P Bath. Ch e m.

VOWCHURCH Herefs
142 SO 3636 10m W of Hereford. CP, 191. Dore and Bredwardine RD. P HRFD. Ch e. Hfrd CC. 1m NW, Iron Age hill fort where many finds of pottery excavated.

WACKERFIELD Co Durham
85 NZ 1522 6m SW of Bishop Auckland.
CP, 88. Barnard Cstle RD. Bshp
Aucklnd CC.

WACTON Norfolk
137 TM 1791 7m SSE of Wymondham.
CP, 172. Depwade RD. Ch e, m. S Nflk CC.

WACTON, GREAT Herefs
129, 130 SO 6256 3m NW of Bromyard.
See Gt Wctn.

WADBOROUGH Worcs
143, 144 SO 9047 3m WNW of Pershore.
CP(Drakes Broughton and Wdbrgh), 625.
Pshre RD. P WORCESTER. S Worcs CC.

WADDESDON Bucks
146, 159 SP 7416 5m WNW of Aylesbury.
CP, 1,583. Aylesbury RD. P Aylesbury.
Ch e, b, m. Sch p, pe. Aylesbury CC.
Wddsdn Mnr (NT)*, 1880s hse in French
Renaissance style.

WADDINGHAM Lincs (L)
104 SK 9896 7m S of Brigg. CP, 531.
Caistor RD. P Gainsborough. Ch e, m.
Sch p. Gnsbrgh CC.

WADDINGTON Lincs (K)
113 SK 9764 5m S of Lincoln. CP, 4,193.
N Kesteven RD. P LNCLN. Ch e, m.
Sch i, j, p. Grantham CC. RAF stn.

WADDINGTON Yorks (W)
95 SD 7243 2m NW of Clitheroe. CP, 687.
Bowland RD. P Clthroe, Lancs. Ch e, m.
Sch pe. Skipton CC. Hsptl founded 1700.
Wddngtn Hall refuge for Henry VI after
Battle of Hexham, 1464.

WADEBRIDGE Cornwall
185 SW 9872 6m NW of Bodmin.
CP, 2,998. Wdbrdge and Padstow RD. P.
Ch m3, r, v. Sch p, s. N Cnwll CC. See also
Bodieve. Mkt tn on Camel estuary. 15c br,
since widened, has 13 arches.

WADEFORD Som
177 ST 3110 2m NW of Chard. Loc, Combe
St Nicholas CP. P Chd. Ch b.

WADENHOE Northants
134 TL 0183 3m SSW of Oundle. CP, 140.
Oundle and Thrapston RD.
P PETERBOROUGH. Ch e.
Wellingborough CC (Ptrbrgh).

WADESMILL Herts
148 TL 3517 2m N of Ware. Loc,
Thundridge CP. Ware RD. P Ware. Sch pe.
E Herts CC.

WADHURST Sussex (E)
183 TQ 6431 6m SSE of Tunbridge Wells.
CP, 4,008. Uckfield RD. P.
Ch e, b2, m, r2, s, v. Sch pe, s.
E Grinstead CC. See also Cousley Wd,
Tidebrook. Wealden place once a centre of
iron industry. Ch has iron tomb-slabs and
shingled spire.

WADSHELF Derbys
111 SK 3170 4m W of Chesterfield. Loc,
Brampton CP. Chstrfld RD. P Chstrfld.
Ch m. NE Derbys CC.

WADSWICK Wilts
156 ST 8467 6m ENE of Bath. Loc,
Box CP.

WADWORTH Yorks (W)
103 SK 5697 4m S of Doncaster. CP, 622.
Dncstr RD. P Dncstr. Ch e m. Sch p. Don
Valley CC. Fine mainly 13c ch. Wdwth
Hall, grand 18c mansion by James Paine.

WAINFLEET ALL SAINTS Lincs (L)
114 TF 4958 5m SW of Skegness.
CP, 1,184. Spilsby RD. P(Wnflt), Skgnss.
Ch e, m, s. Sch pe. Horncastle CC. Wnflt Sch
founded 1484 by Bishop Waynflete of
Winchester, who also founded Magdalen
College, Oxford.

WAINFLEET BANK Lincs (L)
114 TF 4759 7m WSW of Skegness. Loc,
Spilsby RD. Ch e, m. Horncastle CC.

WAINHOUSE CORNER Cornwall
174 SX 1895 7m SSW of Bude. Loc,
Stratton RD. N Cnwll CC.

WAINSCOTT Kent
161, 171, 172 TQ 7471 2m N of Rochester.
Loc, Frindsbury Extra CP. Strood RD.
P Rchstr. Ch v. Sch p. Gravesend CC.

WAITBY Westm
84 NY 7508 1m W of Kirkby Stephen.
CP, 60. N Westm RD. Westm CC. .

WAKEFIELD Yorks (W)
96, 102 SE 3320 8m SSE of Leeds.
CB, 59,650. P. Administrative capital of
W Riding. Centre for cloth trade since 15c.
Coal-mining area. Orig parish ch now
cathedral. 14c toll chpl on br; cf
R o t h e r h a m , St Ives (Hunts),
Bradford-on-Avon.

WAKERING, GREAT Essex
162 TQ 9487 4m ENE of Southend. See Gt
Wkrng.

WAKERLEY Northants
134 SP 9599 6m E of Uppingham. CP, 111.
O u n d l e and Thrapston RD. Ch e.
Wellingborough CC (Peterborough).

WAKES COLNE Essex
149 TL 8928 5m ESE of Halstead. CP, 435.
Lexden and Winstree RD. P Colchester.
Ch e, v. Clchstr CC. Water mill.

WALBERSWICK Suffolk (E)
137 TM 4974 1m SW of Southwold.
CP, 491. Blyth RD. P Sthwld. Ch e, m.
Sch p. Eye CC. Former port. Resort of
artists. Shingle and sand beach. Hths to
landward. Ch partly ruined.

WALBERTON Sussex (W)
181, 182 SU 9606 3m W of Arundel.
CP, 1,614. Chichester RD. P Arndl. Ch e, b.
Sch pe. Arndl CC (Chchstr).

WALBOTTLE Nthmb
78 NZ 1766 5m WNW of Newcastle. Loc,
Newburn UD. P NCSTLE UPON TYNE 5.

WALCOT Lincs (K)
113 TF 1356 6m SW of Woodhall Spa.
CP(Wlct near Billinghay), 470.
E Kesteven RD. P LINCOLN. Ch e, m.
Sch p. Grantham CC.

WALCOT Lincs (K)
113, 123 TF 0635 7m S of Sleaford.
CP(Wlct near Folkingham), 84.

E Kesteven RD. Ch e. Rutland and
Stamford CC.

WALCOT Shrops
118 SJ 5912 4m W of Wellington. Loc,
Wrockwardine CP. P Telford.

WALCOT Warwicks
131 SP 1258 5m WNW of Stratford. Loc,
Haselor CP.

WALCOTE Leics
132, 133 SP 5683 2m ESE of Lutterworth.
Loc, Misterton CP. P Rugby, Warwickshire.
Ch c. Sch pe.

WALCOTT Norfolk
126 TG 3632 5m ENE of N Walsham. Loc,
Happisburgh CP. P NORWICH, NOR 23Z.
Ch e.

WALDEN STUBBS Yorks (W)
103 SE 5516 7m ESE of Pontefract. CP, 71.
Hemsworth RD. Hmswth CC.

WALDERSLADE Kent
172 TQ 7663 3m S of Chatham. Loc,
Chthm MB. P Chthm. Modern rsdntl.

WALDERTON Sussex (W)
181 SU 7910 5m NE of Havant. Loc,
Stoughton CP. P Chichester. Ch m.

WALDINGFIELD, GREAT Suffolk (W)
149 TL 9143 3m NE of Sudbury. See Gt
Wldngfld.

WALDITCH Dorset
177 SY 4892 1m E of Bridport. Loc,
Bothenhampton CP. Ch e.

WALDRIDGE Co Durham
78/85 NZ 2550 2m SW of Chester-le-Street.
CP, 552. Chstr-le-Strt RD. Ch m. Sch p.
Chstr-le-Strt CC.

WALDRINGFIELD Suffolk (E)
150 TM 2844 3m S of Woodbridge.
CP, 341. Deben RD. P Wdbrdge. Ch e, b.
Sch p. Sudbury and Wdbrdge CC. Small
vllge with quay and pub by Deben estuary.
Populous in summer.

WALDRON Sussex (E)
183 TQ 5419 2m SW of Heathfield.
CP, 2,634. Hailsham RD. P Hthfld. Ch e.
Rye CC. See also Cross-in-Hand,
Lit London.

WALES Yorks (W)
103 SK 4782 7m SSE of Rotherham.
CP, 5,601. Kiveton Pk RD. P SHEFFIELD.
Ch e, m2. Sch p. Rother Valley CC. See also
Kvtn Pk. Nmn ch.

WALESBY Lincs (L)
104 TF 1392 3m NE of Mkt Rasen.
CP, 188. Caistor RD. P Mkt Rsn. Ch e2, m.
Gainsborough CC. Old ch on hilltop used
annually for local ramblers' service. Newer
ch (1914) in vllge.

WALESBY Notts
112 SK 6870 3m NE of Ollerton. CP, 524.
Southwell RD. P Newark. Ch e, m. Sch pe.
Nwk CC.

WALFORD Herefs
129 SO 3972 7m E of Knighton. CP(Wlfd,
Letton and Newton), 86. Leominster and
Wigmore RD. Ch m. Lmnstr CC.

WALFORD Herefs
142 SO 5820 2m SSW of Ross-on-Wye.
CP, 1,153. Rss and Whitchurch RD.
P Rss-on-Wye. Ch e, m. Sch p. Hereford CC.
See also Hom Grn, Howle Hill, Kerne Br.

WALFORD Shrops
118 SJ 4320 6m NW of Shrewsbury. Loc,
Baschurch CP.

WALFORD HEATH Shrops
118 SJ 4519 5m NNW of Shrewsbury. Loc,
Pimhill CP. Atcham RD. P Shrsbry. Ch m.
Shrsbry CC.

WALGHERTON Ches
110 SJ 6948 3m ESE of Nantwich. CP, 153.
Nntwch RD. Nntwch CC.

WALGRAVE Northants
133 SP 8072 6m WNW of Wellingborough.
C P , 6 4 8 . B r i x w o r t h R D .
P NORTHAMPTON. Ch e, b2. Sch p.
Daventry CC (Kettering). Pitsford Reservoir
to W.

WALKDEN Lancs
101 SD 7303 4m SSE of Bolton. Loc,
Worsley UD.

WALKER Nthmb
78 NZ 2964 E distr of Newcastle. Loc,
N c s t l e u p o n T y n e CB. P NCSTLE
UPON TYNE 6. Ncstle upn Tne E BC.
Shipbuilding. Ironworks.

WALKERINGHAM Notts
104 SK 7792 3m WNW of Gainsborough.
CP, 810. E Retford RD. P Doncaster,
Yorkshire. Ch e, m. Sch p. Bassetlaw CC.

WALKERITH Lincs (L)
104 SK 7893 3m NW of Gainsborough.
CP, 65. Gnsbrgh RD. Ch m. Gnsbrgh CC.

WALKERN Herts
147 TL 2826 3m E of Stevenage. CP, 816.
Hertford RD. P Stvnge. Ch e, c, m. Sch p.
Htfd and Stvnge CC (Htfd). Ch Nmn and
later: effigy of knight, brasses.

WALKER'S GREEN Herefs
142 SO 5247 5m N of Hereford. Loc,
Marden CP.

WALKHAMPTON Devon
187 SX 5369 4m SE of Tavistock. CP, 577.
Tvstck RD. P Yelverton. Ch e, m. Sch pe.
W Dvn CC (Tvstck).

WALKINGTON Yorks (E)
98 SE 9937 3m WSW of Beverley.
CP, 1,336. Bvrly RD. P Bvrly. Ch e, m.
Sch p. Haltemprice CC.

WALK MILL Lancs
95 SD 8629 3m SE of Burnley. Loc,
Cliviger CP. Bnly RD. P Bnly. Ch v.
Clitheroe CC.

WALL Nthmb
77 NY 9169 3m NNW of Hexham. CP, 444.
Hxhm RD. P Hxhm. Ch e, m. Sch pe.
Hxhm CC. See also Low Brunton. Near
Roman Wall.

WALL Staffs
120 SK 1006 2m SSW of Lichfield. CP, 397.
Lchfld RD. P Lchfld. Ch e. Sch pe. Lchfld
and Tamworth CC. See also Chesterfield.
Bath hse (NT and A.M.) of Roman stn,
Letocetum; museum of finds, with those
from Shenstone, qv.

WALLASEY Ches
100 SJ 2992 3m NNW of Birkenhead.
CB, 97,061. P. Wllsy BC. Playground of
Liverpool and Bknhd. Good for watching
ships go by.

WALL BANK Shrops
120 SO 5092 3m E of Ch Stretton. Loc,
Rushbury CP.

WALLCROUCH Sussex (E)
183 TQ 6630 2m ESE of Wadhurst. Loc, Ticehurst CP. P Wdhst.

WALLEND Kent
172 TQ 8775 9m ENE of Rochester. Loc, Isle of Grain CP. Strood RD. Gravesend CC.

WALLINGFORD Berks
158 SU 6089 12m NNW of Reading. MB, 6,184. P. Abingdon CC. Old Thames-side tn, with ancient 14-arch br. Annual regatta.

WALLINGTON Hants
180 SU 5806 just E of Fareham. Loc, Frhm UD.

WALLINGTON Herts
147 TL 2933 3m E of Baldock. CP, 156. Hitchin RD. P Bldck. Ch e. Htchn CC.

WALLINGTON London
170 TQ 2863 2m WSW of Croydon. Loc, Sutton LB. P Surrey. Carshalton BC (Mitcham). Rsdntl distr.

WALLISWOOD Surrey
170, 182 TQ 1138 4m E of Cranleigh. Loc, Abinger CP. Sch pe.

WALLSEND Nthmb
78 NZ 2966 3m ENE of Newcastle. MB, 45,793. P. Wllsnd BC. See also Willington. At E end of Roman Wall. Shipbuilding. Engineering. At boundary with Tynemouth, N entrance to Tyne rd tunnel, opened 1967.

WALL UNDER HEYWOOD Shrops
129 SO 5092 4m E of Ch Stretton. Loc, Rushbury CP. P Ch Strttn.

WALMER Kent
173 TR 3750 1m S of Deal. Loc, Dl MB. P Dl. Wlmr Cstle (A.M.), official residence of Ld Warden of the Cinque Ports.

WALMER BRIDGE Lancs
94 SD 4724 5m SW of Preston. Loc, Prstn RD. P Prstn. Ch m, v. Sch p. S Fylde CC.

WALMLEY Warwicks
131 SP 1393 2m SSE of Sutton Coldfield. Loc, Sttn Cldfd MB. P Sttn Cldfld.

WALPOLE Suffolk (E)
137 TM 3674 2m SW of Halesworth. CP, 254. Blyth RD. P Hlswth. Ch e, v. Eye CC.

WALPOLE CROSS KEYS Norfolk
124 TF 5119 2m ESE of Sutton Br. Loc, Wlple St Andrew CP. P King's Lynn. Ch m. Sch p.

WALPOLE HIGHWAY Norfolk
124 TF 5113 4m NE of Wisbech. Loc, Wlple St Peter CP. P Wsbch, Cambs. Ch e, m. Sch p.

WALPOLE ISLAND Norfolk
124 TF 4817 2m S of Sutton Br. Loc, Wlple St Peter CP.

WALPOLE ST ANDREW Norfolk
124 TF 5017 6m NNE of Wisbech. CP, 625. Marshland RD. P Wsbch, Cambs. Ch e. Sch p. NW Nflk CC (King's Lynn). See also Wlple Cross Keys.

WALPOLE ST PETER Norfolk
124 TF 5016 5m NNE of Wisbech. CP, 1,581. Marshland RD. Ch e, m2. Sch pe. NW Nflk CC (King's Lynn). See also Wlple Highway, Wlple Island. Outstanding 15c ch.

WALSALL Staffs
131 SP 0198 8m NNW of Birmingham. CB, 184,606. P. BCs: Wlsll N, Wlsll S. See also Darlaston, Willenhall. Coal-mining and general industry.

WALSALL WOOD Staffs
120 SK 0403 4m NE of Walsall. Loc, Aldridge-Brownhills UD. P Wlsll. A-B BC (Wlsll N).

WALSDEN Yorks (W)
95 SD 9322 2m S of Todmorden. Loc. Tdmdn MB. P Tdmdn, Lancs.

WALSHAM LE WILLOWS Suffolk (W)
136 TM 0071 8m NNW of Stowmarket. CP, 791. Thedwastre RD. P Bury St Edmunds. Ch e, c. Sch pe. Bury St Eds CC. See also Four Ashes.

WALSHAW Lancs
101 SD 7711 2m WNW of Bury. Loc, Bury CB, Tottington UD. P Bury. Bury and Radcliffe BC.

WALSHFORD Yorks (W)
97 SE 4153 3m N of Wetherby. CP(Gt
Ribston w Wlshfd), 132. Nidderdale RD.
Harrogate CC.

WALSINGHAM, GREAT Norfolk
125 TF 9437 4m SSE of Wells. See Gt
Wlsnghm.

WALSOKEN Norfolk
124 TF 4710 1m NE of Wisbech. CP, 705.
Marshland RD. Ch e. NW Nflk CC (King's
Lynn).

WALTERSTONE Herefs
142 SO 3425 7m NNE of Abergavenny.
CP, 86. Dore and Bredwardine RD.
P HEREFORD. Ch e, m. Hrfd CC.

WALTHAM Kent
173 TR 1048 6m SSW of Canterbury.
CP, 354. Bridge-Blean RD. P Cntrbry.
Ch e, m, v. Sch p. Cntrbry CC.

WALTHAM Lincs (L)
105 TA 2603 3m S of Grimsby. CP.
Grmsby RD. P Grmsby. Ch e, m. Sch p, s.
Louth CC. Twr windmill still in use.

WALTHAM ABBEY Essex
161 TL 3800 2m SE of Cheshunt. Loc,
Wlthm Holy Cross UD. P. Epping Forest CC
(Eppng). Large mkt gdns in surrounding
areas. Gt ch dates from Saxon times. King
Harold buried here after battle of Hastings.
Abbey blt by Henry II; gatehouse and
br A.M.

WALTHAM CHASE Hants
180 SU 5615 2m SSE of Bishop's Waltham.
Loc, Shedfield CP. P SOUTHAMPTON.
Ch m.

WALTHAM CROSS Herts
161 TL 3600 1m S of Cheshunt. Loc,
Chsnt UD. P. The cross, much restored,
erected by Edward I to mark a resting place
of his dead queen Eleanor on the way to
burial in Westminster Abbey. (See
Geddington, Hardingstone.)

WALTHAM, GREAT Essex
148, 161 TL 6913 4m N of Chelmsford. See
Gt Wlthm.

WALTHAM ON THE WOLDS Leics
122 SK 8025 5m NE of Melton Mowbray.

CP(Wlthm), 697. Mltn and Belvoir RD.
P Mltn Mbry. Ch e, m. Sch pe. Mltn CC. See
also Thorpe Arnold.

WALTHAM ST LAWRENCE Berks
159 SU 8376 5m WSW of Maidenhead.
CP, 1,276. Cookham RD. P Reading. Ch e2.
Sch p. Windsor and Mdnhd CC (Wndsr). See
also Shurlock Row. Several timber-framed
bldngs, notably Bell Inn. Cattle pound
consisting of railings connecting four elm
trees.

WALTHAMSTOW London
161 TQ 3789 7m NE of Charing Cross. Loc,
Waltham Forest LB. Wlthmstw BC
(Wlthmstw E, Wlthmstw W). On E side of
Lee valley. William Morris Gallery* housed
in former home of Morris. Vestry Hse
Museum (local history).

WALTON Bucks
146 SP 8936 2m NE of Bletchley. CP, 116.
Newport Pagnell RD. Ch e. Buckingham CC.

WALTON Cumb
76 NY 5264 2m N of Brampton. CP, 262.
Border RD. P Brmptn. Ch e, m. Sch pe.
Penrith and the Bdr CC. Hadrian's Wall
passes immediately to S; many Roman
antiquities in area.

WALTON Derbys
111 SK 3569 2m SW of Chesterfield.
CP, 1,849. Chstrfld RD. NE Derbys CC. See
also Holymoorside.

WALTON Leics
132, 133 SP 5987 4m ENE of Lutterworth.
CP(Kimcote and Wltn), 389. Lttrwth RD.
P Rugby, Warwickshire. Ch e. Blaby CC
(Harborough).

WALTON Shrops
118 SJ 5918 6m NW of Wellington. Loc,
Ercall Magna CP. Wllngtn RD. The
Wrekin CC.

WALTON Som
165 ST 4636 3m WSW of Glastonbury.
CP, 544. Wells RD. P Street. Ch e, m.
Sch pe. Wells CC.

WALTON Suffolk (E)
150 TM 2935 just N of Felixtowe. Loc,
Flxtwe UD.

Walton

WALTON Warwicks
145 SP 2853 5m ESE of Stratford. Loc,
Wellesbourne CP. Strtfd-on-Avon RD.
P WARWICK. Ch e. Strtfd-on-Avn CC
(Strtfd).

WALTON Yorks (W)
96, 102, 103 SE 3517 3m SSE of Wakefield.
CP, 1,724. Wkfld RD. P Wkfld. Ch m. Sch p.
Wkfld BC.

WALTON Yorks (W)
97 SE 4447 2m E of Wetherby. CP, 172.
Wthrby RD. P Boston Spa. Ch e. Barkston
Ash CC.

WALTON CARDIFF Glos
143, 144 SO 9032 1m E of Tewkesbury.
CP, 57. Cheltenham RD. Ch e. Cirencester
and Tksbry CC.

WALTON-IN-GORDANO Som
155, 165 ST 4273 10m W of Bristol.
CP, 178. Long Ashton RD. P Clevedon.
Ch e2. N Som CC. Rems of cstle blt early
17c largely for ornament.

WALTON-LE-DALE Lancs
94 SD 5528 1m SE of Preston. UD, 26,841.
P Prstn. Prstn S BC. See also Bamber Br,
Hr Wltn.

WALTON-ON-THAMES Surrey
170 TQ 1066 5m WSW of Kingston.
UD(Wltn and Weybridge), 51,004. P.
Chertsey and Wltn BC (Esher CC). See also
Hersham, Whiteley Vllge.

WALTON-ON-THE-HILL Staffs
119 SJ 9521 3m SE of Stafford. Loc,
Baswich CP. Ch e, m.

WALTON-ON-THE-HILL Surrey
170 TQ 2255 3m NNW of Reigate. Loc,
Banstead UD. P Tadworth. Ch: Nmn lead
font. Wltn Hth GC to SE.

WALTON ON THE NAZE Essex
150 TM 2521 6m NE of Clacton.
UD(Frinton and Wltn), 12,431. P.
Harwich CC. Resort, esp for day trips.
Lighthouse. Martello twr. Cliffs rich in
fossils.

WALTON ON THE WOLDS Leics
121, 122 SK 5919 4m E of Loughborough.
CP, 221. Barrow upon Soar RD.
P(Wltn-le-Wlds), Lghbrgh. Ch e. Melton CC.

WALTON UPON TRENT Derbys
120 SK 2118 4m SSW of Burton-on-Trent.
CP, 787. Repton RD. P Btn-on-Trnt, Staffs.
Ch e. Sch pe. Belper CC.

WALWORTH Co Durham
85 NZ 2318 5m NW of Darlington. CP, 182.
Dlngtn RD. Bishop Auckland CC
(Sedgefield). See also Low Wlwth. W. Cstle,
large mansion of c 1600.

WALWORTH London
160, 170 TQ 3278 2m SE of Charing Cross.
Loc, Southwark LB. Bermondsey BC,
Dulwich BC (Sthwk). Cuming Museum,
Sthwk Central Library, shows history and
antiquities of Sthwk.

WAMBROOK Som
177 ST 2907 2m W of Chard. CP, 142.
Chd RD. P Chd. Ch e, m. Yeovil CC.

WANBOROUGH Surrey
169 SU 9348 4m W of Guildford. CP, 334.
Gldfd RD. P Gldfd. Ch e. Gldfd CC. Under
N side of Hog's Back, chalk ridge
commanding long views. Large tithe barn.

WANBOROUGH Wilts
157 SU 2082 4m ESE of Swindon. CP, 972.
Highworth RD. P Swndn. Ch e, m. Sch p.
Devizes CC.

WANDSWORTH London
160, 170 TQ 2574 5m SW of Charing Cross.
LB, 298,931. BCs: Battersea N, Bttrsea S,
Putney, Tooting (Bttrsea N, Bttrsea S,
Clapham, Ptny, Streatham, Wndswth
Central). See also Balham, Bttrsea, Nine
Elms, Ptny, Roehampton, Ttng. S of
Thames; Ptny, Wndswth, Bttrsea, Albert,
Chelsea Brs, and three rly brs. Indstrl
waterfront. R Wandle joins Thames above
Wndswth Br.

WANGFORD Suffolk (E)
137 TM 4679 3m NW of Southwold.
CP, 427. Lothingland RD. P Beccles.
Ch e, m. Lowestoft CC.

WANGFORD Suffolk (W)
136 TL 7583 3m SW of Brandon. CP, 36.
Mildenhall RD. Ch e. Bury St Edmunds CC.
At E edge of Lakenheath Airfield.

WANLIP Leics
121, 122 SK 6010 4m N of Leicester. CP, 113. Barrow upon Soar RD. Ch e. Melton CC. Ch 13c. Inscription in English on brass of 1393 is earliest in country.

WANSFORD Hunts
134 TL 0799 7m W of Peterborough. CP, 283. Barnack RD. P PTRBRGH. Ch e. Ptrbrgh BC (CC). Attractive stone vllge; formerly half, now wholly, in Hunts. Mdvl ten-arch br spans R Nene.

WANSFORD Yorks (E)
99 TA 0656 3m ESE of Driffield. Loc, Skerne CP. P Drffld. Ch e.

WANSTEAD London
161 TQ 4087 8m NE of Charing Cross. Loc, Redbridge LB. Wnstd and Woodford BC. Partly marshland beside R Lee valley. City of Lndn Cemetery.

WANSTROW Som
166 ST 7141 5m SW of Frome. CP, 366. Frme RD. P Shepton Mallet. Ch e, m. Wells CC. See also Cloford, Leighton.

WANSWELL GREEN Glos
156 SO 6801 5m WNW of Dursley. Loc, Hamfallow CP. Thornbury RD. S Glos CC.

WANTAGE Berks
158 SU 3987 15m E of Swindon. UD, 8,007. P. Abingdon CC. Red-brick mkt tn, bthplce of King Alfred in 849; statue in mkt place. England's first steam tramway ran hence to Wntge Rd on main line, 1873; closed 1948.

WANTISDEN Suffolk (E)
150 TM 3653 6m ENE of Woodbridge. CP, 33. Deben RD. Ch e. Eye CC. Hths; Bentwaters Airfield.

WAPLEY Glos
156 ST 7179 9m NE of Bristol. Loc, Dodington CP. Ch e.

WAPPENBURY Warwicks
132 SP 3769 4m NE of Leamington. CP, 72. Warwick RD. Ch e, r. Wrwck and Lmngtn CC. Partly enclosed in Iron Age camp.

WAPPENHAM Northants
145, 146 SP 6245 5m WSW of Towcester. CP, 245. Tcstr RD. P Tcstr. Ch e, m. Daventry CC (S Nthnts).

WAPPING London
160 TQ 3480 3m E of Charing Cross. Loc, Twr Hmlts LB. Stepney and Poplar BC (Stpny). Dockland on N bank of Thames below Twr Br. Just above br, Twr of Lndn*, orig blt by William I.

WARBLETON Sussex (E)
183 TQ 6018 3m SE of Heathfield. CP, 1,213. Hailsham RD. Ch e, b, v. Rye CC. See also Bodle St Grn, Rushlake Grn.

WARBOROUGH Oxon
158 SU 5993 3m N of Wallingford. CP, 799. Bullingdon RD. P OXFORD. Ch e. Sch pe. Henley CC. See also Shillingford.

WARBOYS Hunts
134 TL 3080 3m SSE of Ramsey. CP, 1,950. St Ives RD. P HUNTINGDON. Ch e, b, m. Sch ie, j. Hunts CC. Ch:13c twr, broach spire.

WARBSTOW Cornwall
174 SX 2090 9m WNW of Launceston. CP, 259. Lncstn RD. Ch e, m, v. Sch p. N Cnwll CC. To NW, W. Bury, large Iron Age fort with barrow called Giant's Grave.

WARBURTON Ches
101 SJ 6989 6m E of Warrington. CP, 328. Bucklow RD. P Lymm. Ch e. Knutsford CC. Iron rd br over Manchester Ship Canal. Ch has brick twr at E end, oak nave pillars.

WARCOP Westm
84 NY 7415 5m NNW of Kirkby Stephen. CP, 484. N Westm RD. P Appleby. Ch e, m2. Sch pe. Westm CC. See also Sandford.

WARDEN Kent
172, 173 TR 0271 7m ESE of Sheerness. Loc, Queenborough-in-Sheppey MB.

WARDEN Nthmb
77 NY 9166 2m NW of Hexham. CP, 551. Hxhm RD. Ch e, m2. Hxhm CC. See also Fourstones. At junction of N and S Tyne.

WARDGATE Derbys
111 SK 2547 5m E of Ashbourne. Loc, Hulland Ward CP. Ashbne RD. P(Hllnd Wd), DERBY. W Derbys CC.

WARD GREEN Suffolk (E)
136 TM 0463 3m N of Stowmarket. Loc, Old Newton w Dagworth CP.

WARDINGTON Oxon
145 SP 4946 4m NE of Banbury. CP, 546.
Bnbry RD. P Bnbry. Ch e, m. Sch pe.
Bnbry CC. See also Upr Wdngtn.

WARDLE Ches
110 SJ 6157 4m NW of Nantwich. CP, 239.
Nntwch RD. P Nntwch. Nntwch CC.

WARDLE Lancs
95, 101 SD 9117 3m NNE of Rochdale.
UD, 5,334. P Rchdle. Heywood and
Royton CC. See also Smallbridge.

WARDLEY Rutland
122 SK 8300 2m W of Uppingham. CP, 22.
Uppnghm RD. Ch e. Rutland and
Stamford CC. Mdvl ch with Ggn interior.

WARDLOW Derbys
111 SK 1874 5m NNW of Bakewell. CP, 80.
Bkwll RD. W Derbys CC.

WARDY HILL Cambs
135 TL 4782 4m WNW of Ely. Loc,
Coveney CP. Ch m.

WARE Herts
148, 161 TL 3514 8m E of Welwyn Gdn
City. UD, 14,666. P. Hertford and
Stevenage CC (E Herts). Old tn on R Lee;
maltings, canal.

WAREHAM Dorset
178, 179 SY 9287 6m WSW of Poole.
MB, 4,379. P. S Dst CC. Four-square tn
founded by Saxons, developed by Romans,
rebuilt by Georgians.

WAREHORNE Kent
184 TQ 9932 6m E of Tenterden. CP, 301.
E Ashford RD. Ch e, m. Sch p. Ashfd CC.

WARENFORD Nthmb
71 NU 1328 4m SSE of Belford. Loc,
Adderstone w Lucker CP. Ch v.

WAREN MILL Nthmb
64, 71 NU 1434 2m E of Belford. Loc,
Easington CP.

WARENTON Nthmb
64, 71 NU 1030 2m S of Belford. Loc,
Blfd CP.

WARESIDE Herts
148 TL 3915 2m ENE of Ware. Loc, Ware
Rural CP. Ware RD. P Ware. Ch e, m, r.
Sch pe. E Herts CC.

WARESLEY Hunts
147 TL 2554 7m NE of Biggleswade.
CP, 183. St Neots RD. P Sandy, Beds. Ch e.
Hunts CC.

WARFIELD Berks
169 SU 8872 2m NNE of Bracknell.
CP, 1,497. Easthampstead RD. Ch e, v.
Sch pe. Wokingham CC. See also Hawthorn
Hill, Newell Grn.

WARGRAVE Berks
159 SU 7878 3m SSE of Henley. CP, 2,895.
Wokingham RD. P Reading. Ch e, r, v.
Sch ie, je, pe, se. Wknghm CC. See also Hare
Hatch.

WARHAM ALL SAINTS Norfolk
125 TF 9441 2m SE of Wells. Loc,
Wrhm CP. Walsingham RD.
P Wlls-next-the-Sea. Ch e. NW Nflk CC
(N Nflk).

WARHAM ST MARY Norfolk
125 TF 9441 2m SE of Wells. Loc,
Wrhm CP. Walsingham RD. Ch e.
NW Nflk CC (N Nflk). To S, large Iron Age
fort.

WARK Nthmb
64, 70 NT 8238 1m SW of Coldstream. Loc,
Carham CP. P Cornhill-on-Tweed. Once a
great Border bastion. The cstle has vanished,
though its mound remains.

WARK Nthmb
77 NY 8677 4m SSE of Bellingham.
CP, 683. Bllnghm RD. P Hexham.
Ch e, m, v. Sch pe. Hxhm CC. See also
Stonehaugh. On the N Tyne. 1½m SE
downstream, Chipchase Cstle, 14c pele twr
and Jcbn hse of 1621.

WARKLEIGH Devon
163 SS 6422 5m WSW of S Molton.
CP(Satterleigh and Wklgh), 175. S Mltn RD.
Ch e. N Dvn CC.

WARKTON Northants
133 SP 8979 2m ENE of Kettering.
CP, 141. Kttrng RD. P Kttrng. Ch e.
Kttrng CC. Ch crammed with monmts to
Dukes of Montagu and Buccleuch of
Boughton Pk (see Weekley).

WARKWORTH Northants
145 SP 4840 2m E of Banbury. CP, 40.
Brackley RD. Ch e. Daventry CC (S Nthnts).

WARKWORTH Nthmb
71 NU 2406 1m NW of Amble. CP, 1,246. Alnwick RD. P Morpeth. Ch e, v. Sch pe. Berwick-upon-Tweed CC. See also Old Barns. In loop of R Coquet, 1m from mouth. Nmn and later cstle (A.M.) dominates the scene. Mdvl fortified br (A.M.). Fine ch with longest nave in county.

WARLABY Yorks (N)
91 SE 3591 2m SW of Northallerton. CP, 35. Nthllvn RD. Richmond CC.

WARLEGGAN Cornwall
186 SX 1569 6m ENE of Bodmin. CP, 154. Liskeard RD. Ch e, m2. Bodmin CC. See also Mount.

WARLEY Worcs
131 SP 0086 4m W of Birmingham. CB, 163,388. P. BCs: Wly E, Wly W. (Oldbury and Halesowen, Rowley Regis and Tipton, Smethwick.) See also Oldbury, Rly Rgs, Smthwck. Coalmines; brick, glass, chemical, iron and steel wks; quarries.

WARLEY, GREAT Essex
161 TQ 5890 2m SSW of Brentwood. See Gt Wly.

WARLINGHAM Surrey
171 TQ 3558 5m SSE of Croydon. UD(Caterham and Wlnghm), 35,781. P. E Srry CC.

WARMFIELD Yorks (W)
96, 102 SE 3720 3m E of Wakefield. CP(Wmfld cum Heath), 983. Wkfld RD. P Wkfld. Ch e. Sch pe. Normanton CC.

WARMINGHAM Ches
110 SJ 7061 3m W of Sandbach. CP, 215. Nantwich RD. P Sndbch. Ch e. Sch pe. Nntwch CC.

WARMINGTON Northants
134 TL 0791 3m NE of Oundle. CP, 560. Oundle and Thrapston RD. P PETERBOROUGH. Ch e, m. Sch p. Wellingborough CC (Ptrbrgh).

WARMINGTON Warwicks
145 SP 4147 5m NNW of Banbury. CP, 296. Southam RD. P Bnbry. Ch e, m. Sch p. Stratford-on-Avon CC (Strtfd). Show vllge; grn, pond. 17c mnr hse. Old ch up the hill beside main A41 rd.

WARMINSTER Wilts
166 ST 8745 14m SSE of Bath. UD, 13,593. P. Westbury CC. See also Boreham. Largely Ggn stone tn. Much Army bldng on outskirts.

WARMLEY Glos
155, 156 ST 6773 5m E of Bristol. Loc, Siston CP. P Kingswood, BRSTL. Ch e, c. Sch pe. Kngswd CC (S Glos).

WARMSWORTH Yorks (W)
103 SE 5400 3m SW of Doncaster. CP, 2,959. Dncstr RD. P Dncstr. Ch e, v. Sch p, pe. Don Valley CC.

WARMWELL Dorset
178 SY 7585 5m SE of Dorchester. CP, 210. Dchstr RD. P Dchstr. Ch e. W Dst CC.

WARNDON Worcs
130, 131 SO 8856 3m ENE of Worcester. CP, 98. Droitwich RD. Ch e. Worcester BC. Ch has some 14c stained glass.

WARNFORD Hants
168 SU 6223 8m W of Peterfield. CP, 195. Droxford RD. P SOUTHAMPTON. Ch e. Ptrsfld CC. Ch partly Saxon.

WARNHAM Sussex (W)
182 TQ 1533 2m NNW of Horsham. CP, 1,592. Hshm RD. P Hshm. Ch e, v. Hshm and Crawley CC (Hshm). See also Kingsfold.

WARNINGCAMP Sussex (W)
182 TQ 0307 1m E of Arundel. CP, 177. Worthing RD. Arndl CC (Arndl and Shoreham).

WARNINGLID Sussex (E)
182 TQ 2526 6m SE of Horsham. Loc, Slaugham CP. P Haywards Hth. Ch e. Sch p.

WARREN Ches
110 SJ 8870 3m SW of Macclesfield. Loc, Gawsworth CP.

WARREN ROW Berks
159 SU 8180 5m W of Maidenhead. Loc, Hurley CP. P Reading.

WARREN STREET Kent
172 TQ 9253 3m NW of Charing. Loc, Hollingbourn RD. P Lenham, Maidstone. Mdstne CC.

WARRINGTON Bucks
146 SP 8954 2m N of Olney. CP, 40.
Newport Pagnell RD. Ch e. Buckingham CC.

WARRINGTON Lancs
101 SJ 6088 16m WSW of Manchester.
CB, 68,262. P. Wrrngtn BC. Divers
manufactures incl wire, chemicals, paper,
beer. New tn designated, 1968.
(Pop. 119,534.)

WARSASH Hants
180 SU 4906 5m W of Fareham. Loc,
Frhm UD. P SOUTHAMPTON. Modern Sch
of Navigation, part of Sthmptn University.

WARSLOW Staffs
111 SK 0858 7m ENE of Leek. CP(Wslw
and Elkstones), 357. Lk RD. P Buxton,
Derbyshire. Ch e, m. Sch p, s. Lk CC. See
also Upr Elkstone.

WARSOP Notts
112 SK 5667 5m NNE of Mansfield.
UD, 13,036. P Mnsfld. Mnsfld CC. See also
Ch Wsp, Welbeck Colliery Vllge.

WARTER Yorks (E)
98 SE 8650 4m E of Pocklington. CP, 297.
Pcklngtn RD. P YORK. Ch e, m. Sch pe.
Howden CC. Thatched hses round grn and
stream. Wtr Priory, mansion in large pk, on
site of Augustinian monastic hse.

WARTHILL Yorks (N)
97, 98 SE 6755 5m ENE of York. CP, 164.
Flaxton RD. P YK. Ch e, m. Sch pe. Thirsk
and Malton CC.

WARTLING Sussex (E)
183 TQ 6509 5m WNW of Bexhill. CP, 445.
Hailsham RD. Ch e. Rye CC. See also
Boreham St. On edge of Pevensey Levels SE
of Royal Greenwich Observatory at
Herstmonceux Cstle.

WARTNABY Leics
122 SK 7123 4m NW of Melton Mowbray.
Loc, Ab Kettleby CP. P Mltn Mbry. Ch e.

WARTON Lancs
89 SD 5072 1m N of Carnforth. CP, 1,769.
Lancaster RD. P Cnfth. Ch e, m. Sch i, pe.
Morecambe and Lonsdale CC. See also
Millhead.

WARTON Lancs
94 SD 4128 8m W of Preston.
CP(Bryning-w-Wtn), 2,558. Fylde RD.
P Prstn. Ch e, r. Sch pe. S Flde CC.

WARTON Warwicks
120, 121 SK 2803 4m NNW of Atherstone.
Loc, Polesworth CP. P Tamworth, Staffs.
Ch e. Sch pe.

WARWICK Cumb
76 NY 4656 4m E of Carlisle. Loc,
Wetheral CP. Ch e.

WARWICK Warwicks
132 SP 2865 9m SSW of Coventry.
MB, 18,289. P(WRWCK). Wrwck and
Leamington CC. See also Longbridge. On
R Avon. Cstle*, 14c and 15c. Ld Leycester's
Hsptl*, Mkt Hall*, Ct Hse*. Other old
bldngs and chs.

WARWICK BRIDGE Cumb
76 NY 4756 5m E of Carlisle. Loc,
Wetheral CP. P Clsle. Ch e, m, r. Sch p.

WASDALE HEAD Cumb
82 NY 1808 11m ENE of Seascale. Loc,
Nether Wsdle CP. Ennerdale RD. Ch e.
Whitehaven CC. At SW end of path over Sty
Head Pass into Borrowdale.

WASHAWAY Cornwall
185, 186 SX 0369 3m NW of Bodmin. Loc,
Egloshayle CP. P Bdmn.

WASHBOURNE Devon
187, 188 SX 7954 4m S of Totnes. Loc,
Halwell CP.

WASHBOURNE, GREAT Glos
143, 144 SO 9834 6m E of Tewkesbury.
Loc, Dumbleton CP. Ch e.

WASHBROOK Suffolk (E)
150 TM 1142 3m WSW of Ipswich. CP, 368.
Samford RD. Ch e, b. Sudbury and
Woodbridge CC.

WASHERWALL Staffs
110 SJ 9347 ENE of Stoke-on-Trent. Loc,
Caverswall CP.

WASHFIELD Devon
164 SS 9315 2m NNW of Tiverton. CP, 323.
Tvtn RD. P Tvtn. Ch e. Tvtn CC. Ch: Jcbn
scrn, surmounted by royal arms.

WASHFOLD Yorks (N)
90 NZ 0502 8m WNW of Richmond. Loc,
Marrick CP.

WASHFORD Som
164 ST 0441 2m SW of Watchet. Loc, Old
Cleeve CP. P Wtcht. Ch m. Clve Abbey
(A.M.), rems of 13c Cistercian monastery;
gatehouse, dormitory, refectory. To SE,
Bardon Mnr*, old hse with cockpit. 1m E,
BBC radio stn.

WASHFORD PYNE Devon
164, 176 SS 8111 9m W of Tiverton.
CP, 79. Crediton RD. Ch e, v. Tvtn CC
(Torrington).

WASHINGBOROUGH Lincs (K)
113 TF 0170 3m E of Lincoln. CP, 1,141.
N Kesteven RD. P LNCLN. Ch e, m. Sch p.
Grantham CC.

WASHINGTON Co Durham
78 NZ 3156 5m W of Sunderland.
UD, 24,105. P. Chester-le-Strt CC. See also
Springwell. New tn. Wshngtn Old Hall
(NT)*, early 17c incorporating parts of
older hse, home of George Washington's
ancestors.

WASHINGTON Sussex (W)
182 TQ 1212 6m NNW of Worthing.
CP, 1,201. Chanctonbury RD.
P Pulborough. Ch e. Sch pe. Shoreham CC
(Arundel and Shrhm). See also Hth Cmmn.
1m ESE on S Downs, Chanctonbury Ring;
beech clump on site of Iron Age fort – see
also Buncton.

WASING Berks
168 SU 5764 7m ESE of Newbury. CP, 56.
Nbry RD. Ch e. Nbry CC.

WASKERLEY Co Durham
84 NZ 0545 5m SW of Consett. Loc,
Muggleswick CP. Ch m.

WASPERTON Warwicks
131 SP 2658 4m SSW of Warwick. CP, 141.
Wrwck RD. P WRWCK. Ch e. Wrwck and
Leamington CC.

WASS Yorks (N)
92 SE 5579 5m SW of Helmsley. CP(Byland
w Wss), 101. Hlmsly RD. P YORK. Thirsk
and Malton CC. To SW, Byland Abbey
(A.M.), rems of 12c monastery.

WATCHET Som
164 ST 0743 15m WNW of Bridgwater.
UD, 2,892. P. Brdgwtr CC. Small harbour

used by ships carrying esparto grass to large
paper mill on edge of tn. Mainly Perp ch:
Wyndham monmts.

WATCHFIELD Berks
157 SU 2490 7m NE of Swindon.
CP, 1,824. Faringdon RD. P Swndn, Wilts.
Ch e, m. Sch p. Abingdon CC.

WATCHGATE Westm
89 SD 5299 4m N of Kendal. Loc, Whitwell
and Selside CP. S Westm RD. P Kndl.
Westm CC.

WATER Lancs
95 SD 8425 4m S of Burnley. Loc,
Rawtenstall MB.

WATERBEACH Cambs
135 TL 4965 5m NE of Cambridge.
CP, 2,561. Chesterton RD. P CMBRDGE.
Ch e, b, m, s. Sch p. Cambs CC. See also
Chittering.

WATERCOMBE Dorset
178 SY 7584 6m SE of Dorchester. CP, 23.
Dchstr RD. W Dst CC.

WATER EATON Oxon
145 SP 5112 4m N of Oxford. CP(Gosford
and Wtr Eatn), 1,260. Ploughley RD.
Mid-Oxon CC (Banbury). Jcbn mnr hse
beside R Cherwell.

WATER END Herts
147, 160 TL 0310 2m NNW of Hemel
Hempstead. Loc, Gt Gaddesden CP. P Hml
Hmpstd. NT owns 4½ acres of vllge grn by
R Gade.

WATER END Herts
160 TL 2204 3m S of Hatfield. Loc,
N Mymms CP. Htfld RD. Welwyn and
Htfld CC (Hertford).

WATERFALL Staffs
111 SK 0851 7m SE of Leek. Loc, Waterhouses CP. Ch e. Sch pe.

WATERFOOT Lancs
95 SD 8322 1m ESE of Rawtenstall. Loc,
Rtnstll MB. P Rossendale.

WATERFORD Herts
147 TL 3114 2m NNW of Hertford. Loc,
Stapleford CP. P HTFD. Ch e.

WATERHEAD Westm
88, 89 NY 3703 just S of Ambleside. Loc, Lakes UD. Westm CC.

WATERHOUSES Co Durham
85 NZ 1841 6m W of Durham. Loc, Brandon and Byshottles UD. P DRHM.

WATERHOUSES Staffs
111 SK 0850 7m WNW of Ashbourne. CP, 1,085. Cheadle RD. P Stoke-on-Trent. Ch e, m. Sch pe, s. Leek CC. See also Calton, Cauldon, Waterfall, Winkhill. On boundary of Peak Distr National Pk.

WATERINGBURY Kent
171 TQ 6853 5m W of Maidstone. CP, 1,029. Malling RD. P Mdstne. Ch e. Sch pe. Tonbridge and Mllng CC (Sevenoaks).

WATERLIP Som
166 ST 6544 3m ENE of Shepton Mallet. Loc, Cranmore CP. Shptn Mllt RD. Ch m. Wells CC.

WATERLOO Norfolk
126 TG 2219 5m WNW of Wroxham. Loc, Hainford CP.

WATERLOOVILLE Hants
181 SU 6809 3m NW of Havant. Loc, Hvnt and Waterloo UD. P Portsmouth. Largely rsdntl for Ptsmth.

WATER NEWTON Hunts
134 TL 1097 5m W of Peterborough. CP, 69. Norman Cross RD. Ch e. Hunts CC. Stone vllge formerly on A1, now bypassed to S. On N side, R Nene. To E, traces of Roman tn, *Durobrivae.*

WATER ORTON Warwicks
131 SP 1791 2m NW of Coleshill. CP, 2,615. Meriden RD. P BIRMINGHAM. Ch e, m. Sch p. Mrdn CC.

WATERPERRY Oxon
158 SP 6206 7m E of Oxford. CP, 161. Bullingdon RD. P OXFD. Ch e. Mid-Oxon CC (Henley). Ggn mnr hse contains horticultural sch for girls: gdns*. Ch in mnr hse grnds has work of all periods Saxon to 18c.

WATERROW Som
164 ST 0525 6m ENE of Bampton. Loc, Chipstable CP. P Taunton. Ch v.

WATERSFIELD Sussex (W)
181, 182 TQ 0115 3m SW of Pulborough. Loc, Coldwaltham CP. P Plbrgh. Ch c.

WATERSTOCK Oxon
158, 159 SP 6305 4m W of Thame. CP, 73. Bullingdon RD. P OXFORD. Ch e. Mid-Oxon CC (Henley).

WATER STRATFORD Bucks
145, 146 SP 6534 3m W of Buckingham. CP, 99. Bcknghm RD. P BCKNGHM. Ch e. Bcknghm CC.

WATERS UPTON Shrops
118, 119 SJ 6319 5m NNW of Wellington. CP, 187. Wllngtn RD. P Telford. Ch e, m. The Wrekin CC.

WATER YEAT Lancs
88 SD 2889 7m N of Ulverston. Loc, Blawith CP.

WATFORD Herts
160 TQ 1096 20m NW of London. MB, 78,117. P. Wtfd BC. Indstrl and rsdntl. Largest tn in Herts.

WATFORD Northants
132, 133 SP 6068 4m NNE of Daventry. CP, 236. Dvntry RD. P Rugby, Warwickshire. Ch e, m. Dvntry CC (S Nthnts).

WATH Yorks (N)
91 SE 3277 4m N of Ripon. CP, 179. Wth RD. P Rpn. Ch e. Sch pe. Thirsk and Malton CC.

WATH Yorks (W)
91 SE 1467 1m NNW of Pateley Br. Loc, Ripon and Ptly Br RD. Ch m. Rpn CC.

WATH UPON DEARNE Yorks (W)
103 SE 4400 5m N of Rotherham. UD, 15,022. P Rthrhm. Dne Valley CC. Colliery tn. Nmn ch.

WATLINGTON Norfolk
124 TF 6110 6m S of King's Lynn. CP, 734. Downham RD. P K's Lnn. Ch e, v. Sch p. SW Nflk CC.

WATLINGTON Oxon
159 SU 6894 6m ENE of Wallingford. CP, 1,791. Bullingdon RD. P OXFORD. Ch e, m, r. Sch p, s. Henley CC. See also Christmas Cmmn. At N foot of Chilterns. 17c mkt hall. Ggn houses. 1½m SE, Wtlngtn Hill (NT); views.

WATNALL CHAWORTH Notts
112 SK 5046 6m NW of Nottingham. Loc,
Greasley CP. P(Wtnll), NTTNGHM. Wtnll
Hall, late 17c brick hse.

WATTISFIELD Suffolk (W)
136 TM 0074 8m WSW of Diss. CP, 414.
Thedwastre RD. P Dss, Norfolk. Ch e, c.
Sch pe. Bury St Edmunds CC.

WATTISHAM Suffolk (W)
149 TM 0151 5m SW of Stowmarket.
CP, 118. Cosford RD. P Ipswich. Ch e, b.
Sudbury and Woodbridge CC. Airfield.

WATTON Norfolk
136 TF 9100 9m SSW of E Dereham.
CP, 2,462. Wayland RD. P Thetford.
Ch e, c, m, v. Sch p, s. S Nflk CC.

WATTON Yorks (E)
99 TA 0150 5m S of Driffield. CP, 262.
Drffld RD. P Drffld. Ch e, m. Howden CC.
Scanty rems of largest Gilbertine priory in
England of which porter's lodge, largely
rebuilt in Tdr period, survives intact.

WATTON-AT-STONE Herts
147 TL 3019 4m NNW of Hertford.
CP, 869. Htfd RD. P HTFD. Ch e, m. Sch p.
Htfd and Stevenage CC (Htfd). 15c ch:
brasses.

WAULDBY Yorks (E)
98 SE 9629 8m W of Hull. Loc, Welton CP.

WAVENDON Bucks
146 SP 9137 3m NE of Bletchley. CP, 814.
Newport Pagnell RD. P Bltchly. Ch e, m.
Sch pe. Buckingham CC.

WAVERTON Ches
109 SJ 4663 4m ESE of Chester. CP, 523.
Tarvin RD. P CHSTR. Ch e, m. Sch p.
Northwich CC.

WAVERTON Cumb
82 NY 2247 2m WSW of Wigton. CP, 376.
Wgtn RD. P Wgtn. Ch e. Sch p. Penrith and
the Border CC. See also Lessonhall.

WAWNE Yorks (E)
99 TA 0936 5m N of Hull. CP.
Beverley RD. P Hll. Ch e, m. Sch p.
Haltemprice CC.

WAXHAM Norfolk
126 TG 4426 10m ESE of N Walsham. Loc,
Sea Palling CP. Ch e.

WAXHOLME Yorks (E)
99 TA 3229 1m NNW of Withernsea. Loc,
Rimswell CP.

WAYFIELD Kent
172 TQ 7665 2m S of Chatham. Loc,
Chthm MB.

WAYFORD Som
177 ST 4006 3m SW of Crewkerne. CP.
Chard RD. Ch e. Yeovil CC.

WAY VILLAGE Devon
164, 176 SS 8810 5m WSW of Tiverton.
Loc, Cruwys Morchard CP. Ch c.

WEALD Kent
171 TQ 5250 3m S of Sevenoaks. See
Sevenoaks Weald.

WEALDSTONE London
160 TQ 1689 1m NE of Harrow. Loc,
Hrrw LB. P Hrrw, Middx. Hrrw Central BC.

WEARDLEY Yorks (W)
96 SE 2944 7m N of Leeds. Loc,
Harewood CP. Ch m.

WEARE Som
165 ST 4152 3m W of Cheddar. CP, 419.
Axbridge RD. P Axbrdge. Ch e, m. Sch pe.
Weston-super-Mare CC. See also Lr Weare.

WEARE GIFFARD Devon
163 SS 4721 2m NW of Torrington.
CP, 275. Trrngtn RD. P Bideford. Ch e, m2.
W Dvn CC (Trrngtn).

WEARHEAD Co Durham
84 NY 8539 9m W of Stanhope. Loc,
Stnhpe CP. P Bishop Auckland. Ch m.

WEASENHAM ALL SAINTS Norfolk
125 TF 8521 7m SW of Fakenham. CP, 258.
Mitford and Launditch RD. Ch e, m. Sch pe.
SW Nflk CC.

WEASENHAM ST PETER Norfolk
125 TF 8522 6m SW of Fakenham.
CP, 171. Mitford and Launditch RD.
P King's Lynn. Ch e. SW Nflk CC.

WEAVERHAM Ches
110 SJ 6174 3m W of Northwich.
CP, 7,764. Nthwch RD. P Nthwch.
Ch e, m3, r, v. Sch p2, pr, s. Nthwch CC.
The Gate Inn has sign of hanging gate with
curious inscription; cf Whaley Br, Derbys.

WEAVERTHORPE Yorks (E)
93 SE 9670 9m NNW of Driffield. CP, 298.
Norton RD. P Malton. Ch e, m. Sch pe.
Howden CC. Stream alongside vllge st
spanned by many small brs.

WEBHEATH Worcs
131 SP 0166 2m W of Redditch. Loc,
Rddtch UD. P Rddtch.

WEDHAMPTON Wilts
167 SU 0657 4m SE of Devizes. Loc,
Urchfont CP.

WEDMORE Som
165 SY 4347 4m SSW of Cheddar.
CP, 2,191. Axbridge RD. P. Ch e, b2, m2, v.
Sch p. Weston-super-Mare CC. See also
Blackford, Clewer, Cocklade, Hth Hse,
Middle Stoughton, Mudgley, Theale,
Westham, W Stghtn. Overlooking great Som
turbary (peat-cutting area). Treaty of
Wdmre concluded 879 between Alfred and
Danes.

WEDNESBURY Staffs
130, 131 SO 9894 2m NNW of W
Bromwich. Loc, W Brmwch CB. P.
W Brmwch W BC (Wdnsbry). Iron and steel
wks, etc.

WEDNESFIELD Staffs
119 SJ 9400 2m ENE of Wolverhampton.
Loc, Wlvrhmptn CB. P Wlvrhmptn.
Wlvrhmptn NE BC (Cannock CC). Mnfg
distr, esp locks and keys.

WEEDON Bucks
146 SP 8118 3m N of Aylesbury. CP, 312.
Aylesbury RD. P Aylesbury. Ch m.
Aylesbury CC.

WEEDON BEC Northants
132, 133 SP 6359 4m ESE of Daventry.
CP, 1,489. Dvntry RD.
P(Wdn), NORTHAMPTON. Ch e, m, r, v.
Sch p. Dvntry CC (S Nthnts). See also Upr
Wdn.

WEEDON LOIS Northants
145, 146 SP 6047 6m N of Brackley. Loc,
Weston and Wdn CP. Ch e. Sch pe.

WEEFORD Staffs
120 SK 1403 4m SSE of Lichfield. CP, 233.
Lchfld RD. P Lchfld. Ch e. Sch pe. Lchfld
and Tamworth CC.

WEEK Devon
163 SS 7316 6m SSE of S Molton. Loc,
Chulmleigh CP.

WEEKLEY Northants
133 SP 8880 2m NE of Kettering. CP, 164.
Kttrng RD. P Kttrng. Ch e. Kttrng CC. On
edge of Boughton Pk, seat of Dukes of
Montagu and Buccleuch, a basically
15c–16c hse remodelled late 17c in
Versailles style (see also Warkton).

WEEK ST MARY Cornwall
174 SX 2397 6m SSE of Bude. CP, 410.
Stratton RD. P Holsworthy, Devon.
Ch e, m. Sch p. N Cnwll CC.

WEELEY Essex
150 TM 1422 5m NNW of Clacton. CP, 951.
Tendring RD. P Clctn-on-Sea. Ch e, m.
Sch pe. Harwich CC.

WEELEY HEATH Essex
150 TM 1520 4m NNW of Clacton. Loc,
Wly CP. P Clctn-on-Sea. Ch m.

WEEPING CROSS Staffs
119 SJ 9421 2m SE of Stafford. Loc,
Stffd MB. P STFFD.

WEETING Norfolk
136 TL 7788 1m NNW of Brandon.
CP (Wtng-w-Broomhill), 1,069.
Swaffham RD. P Brndn, Suffolk. Ch e, r.
Sch pe. SW Nflk CC. Rems of 11c fortified
mnr hse (A.M.). 2½m NE in forestry area,
Grimes Graves (A.M.), Neolithic flint mines.

WEETON Lancs
94 SD 3834 5m ESE of Blackpool.
CP(Wtn-w-Presse), 1,995. Fylde RD. Ch e.
Sch p, pe. S Flde CC.

WEETON Yorks (E)
99 TA 3520 5m S of Withernsea. Loc,
Welwick CP.

WEETON Yorks (W)
96 SE 2846 5m SSW of Harrogate. CP, 718.
Wetherby RD. P LEEDS. Ch e. Barkston
Ash CC. See also Huby.

WEIR Lancs
95 SD 8725 1m N of Bacup. Loc, Bcp MB.
P Bcp.

WELBECK COLLIERY VILLAGE Notts
112 SK 5869 5m WNW of Ollerton. Loc,
Warsop UD. P Mansfield.

WELBORNE Norfolk
125 TG 0609 5m ESE of E Dereham. Loc,
Runhall CP. Ch e.

WELBOURN Lincs (K)
113 SK 9654 8m NW of Sleaford. CP, 543.
N Kesteven RD. P LINCOLN. Ch e, m.
Sch pe, s. Grantham CC.

WELBURN Yorks (N)
92 SE 6884 2m SW of Kirkbymoorside.
CP, 108. Kbmsde RD. Ch m. Thirsk and
Malton CC. See also Kirkdale.

WELBURN Yorks (N)
92 SE 7268 5m WSW of Malton. CP, 397.
Mltn RD. P YORK. Ch e. Sch p. Thirsk and
Mltn CC. 1½m N, Cstle Howard (see
Coneysthorpe).

WELBURY Yorks (N)
91 NZ 3902 6m NNE of Northallerton.
CP, 170. Nthlltn RD. P Nthlltn. Ch e.
Richmond CC.

WELBY Lincs (K)
113, 123 SK 9738 4m ENE of Grantham.
CP, 200. W Kesteven RD. P Grnthm.
Ch e, m. Sch pe. Grnthm CC.

WELCHES DAM Cambs
135 TL 4786 5m E of Chatteris. Loc,
Manea CP.

WELCOMBE Devon
174 SS 2218 8m N of Bude. CP, 117.
Bideford RD. P Bdfd. Ch e. N Dvn CC
(Torrington). Ch: early 14c wooden scrn.
1m W, beach at Wlcmbe Mouth: jagged
rocks continuing folded strata of cliffs
above.

WELDON, GREAT Northants
133 SP 9289 2m E of Corby. See Gt Wldn.

WELFORD Berks
158 SU 4073 5m NW of Newbury. CP, 796.
Nbry RD. Ch e. Sch pe. Nbry CC. See also
Wickham.

WELFORD Northants
132, 133 SP 6480 7m SW of Mkt
Harborough. CP, 710. Brixworth RD.
P Rugby, Warwickshire. Ch e, v. Sch pe.
Daventry CC (Kettering).

WELFORD-ON-AVON Warwicks
144 SP 1452 4m WSW of Stratford.
CP, 818. Strtfd-on-Avon RD.

P Strtfd-upon-Avn. Ch e, m. Sch p.
Strtfd-on-Avn CC (Strtfd). Many thatched
hses. Maypole.

WELHAM Leics
133 SP 7692 4m NNE of Mkt Harborough.
CP, 45. Mkt Hbrgh RD. Ch e. Hbrgh CC.

WELHAMGREEN Herts
160 TL 2305 2m S of Hatfield. Loc,
N Mymms CP. Htfld RD. Ch r. Sch je.
Welwyn and Htfld CC (Hertford).

WELL Hants
169 SU 7646 5m NE of Alton. Loc, Long
Sutton CP.

WELL Lincs (L)
114 TF 4473 1m SSW of Alford. CP, 90.
Spilsby RD. Ch e. Horncastle CC. Wll Vale,
Ggn hse with ch alongside; extensive grnds*
with lakes and streams.

WELL Yorks (N)
91 SE 2681 3m ENE of Masham. CP, 224.
Bedale RD. P Bdle. Ch e, m. Thirsk and
Malton CC.

WELLAND Worcs
143 SO 7939 4m SSE of Malvern. CP, 622.
Upton upon Severn RD. P Mlvn. Ch e.
Sch p. S Worcs CC.

WELL END Bucks
159 SU 8988 3m ENE of Marlow. Loc,
Wycombe RD. Beaconsfield CC, Wcmbe CC.

WELLESBOURNE HASTINGS Warwicks
132 SP 2855 5m E of Stratford. Loc,
Wllsbne CP. Strtfd-on-Avon RD.
P(Wllsbne), WARWICK. Ch e, m2. Sch pe.
Strtfd-on-Avn CC (Strtfd).

WELLESBOURNE MOUNTFORD
Warwicks
131 SP 2755 5m E of Stratford. Loc,
Wllsbne CP. Strtfd-on-Avon RD. Ch e.
Strtfd-on-Avn CC (Strtfd).

WELL HILL Kent
171 TQ 4963 3m SE of Orpington. Loc,
Shoreham CP.

WELLINGBOROUGH Northants
133 SP 8967 10m ENE of Northampton.
UD, 37,589. P. Wllngbrgh CC. See also
Finedon. Footwear and clothing factories.
Ironworks. Ch by Sir Ninian Comper, 1908.

WELLINGHAM Norfolk
125 TF 8722 6m SSW of Fakenham.
CP, 47. Mitford and Launditch RD. Ch e, m.
SW Nflk CC.

WELLINGORE Lincs (K)
113 SK 9856 9m S of Lincoln. CP, 612.
N Kesteven RD. P LNCLN. Ch e, m, r.
Sch pe. Grantham CC.

WELLINGTON Herefs
142 SO 4948 5m N of Hereford. CP, 671.
Hrfd RD. P HRFD. Ch e, v. Sch p.
Leominster CC.

WELLINGTON Shrops
118, 119 SJ 6511 10m E of Shrewsbury.
UD, 17,154. P Telford. The Wrekin CC. See
also Arleston. Tn of varied industries;
scheduled to be included in Telford (new
tn). Close to The Wrekin, which dominates
landscape.

WELLINGTON Som
164 ST 1320 5m WSW of Taunton.
UD, 9,343. P. Tntn CC. Bldngs mostly Ggn.
Bedding mnftre has taken place of cloth
trade. 3m S on Blackdown Hills, Wllngtn
Monmt (NT), obelisk erected 1817.
Viewpoint, with direction table.

WELLINGTON HEATH Herefs
143 SO 7140 2m N of Ledbury. CP, 370.
Ldbry RD. P Ldbry. Ch e. Leominster CC.

WELLOW IOW
180 SZ 3888 2m ESE of Yarmouth. Loc,
Shalfleet CP. P Ymth. Ch b.

WELLOW Notts
112 SK 6766 1m SE of Ollerton. CP, 347.
Southwell RD. P Newark. Ch e, m. Nwk CC.
Picturesque vllge with maypole on grn.

WELLOW Som
166 ST 7458 4m S of Bath. CP, 408.
Bathavon RD. P Bth. Ch e, m3 r. Sch pe.
N Som CC. See also Twinhoe. 14c ch:
wall-paintings of c 1500. 1m SW, Stoney
Littleton Long Barrow (A.M.)—grave 107ft
long.

WELLS Som
165, 166 ST 5445 17m S of Bristol.
MB, 8,586. P. Wlls CC. Cathedral city.
Centre still largely mdvl. Moated Bishop's
Palace. Industries incl cheese-making, cider,
textiles, electrical instruments.

WELLSBOROUGH Leics
120, 121 SK 3602 4m NE of Atherstone.
Loc, Sheepy CP. Mkt Bosworth RD.
Bswth CC.

WELLS-NEXT-THE-SEA Norfolk
125 TF 9143 24m NE of King's Lynn.
UD, 2,342. P. NW Nflk CG (N Nflk). Small
commercial port and yachting centre.

WELNETHAM, GREAT Suffolk (W)
136 TL 8859 4m SSE of Bury St Edmunds.
See Gt Wlnthm.

WELNEY Norfolk
135 TL 5294 5m NNW of Littleport.
CP, 601. Downham RD. P Wisbech, Cambs.
Ch e, b, m, v. Sch pe. SW Nflk CC.

WELSHAMPTON Shrops
118 SJ 4335 2m E of Ellesmere. CP, 388.
N Shrops RD. P Ellesmre. Ch e, m. Sch pe.
Oswestry CC.

WELSH BICKNOR Herefs
142 SO 5917 4m S of Ross-on-Wye. CP, 53.
Rss and Whitchurch RD. Ch e, r.
Hereford CC.

WELSH FRANKTON Shrops
118 SJ 3632 3m WSW of Ellesmere. Loc,
Ellesmre Rural CP. N Shrops RD.
P Whittington, Oswestry. Ch e, c.
Oswstry CC.

WELSH NEWTON Herefs
142 SO 4918 3m N of Monmouth. CP, 175.
Ross and Whitchurch RD. P MNMTH.
Ch e, m. Sch pe. Herefs CC.

WELTON Cumb
83 NY 3544 8m SSW of Carlisle. Loc,
Sebergham CP. P Clsle. Ch e, m. Sch p.

WELTON Lincs (L)
104 TF 0179 6m NNE of Lincoln. CP, 939.
Wltn RD. P LNCLN. Ch e, m. Sch pe, se.
Gainsborough CC.

WELTON Northants
132, 133 SP 5866 2m NNE of Daventry.
CP, 364. Dvntry RD. P Dvntry. Ch e.
Sch pe. Dvntry CC (S Nthnts).

WELTON Yorks (E)
98 SE 9527 9m W of Hull. CP, 1,240.
Beverley RD. P Brough. Ch e. Sch p.
Haltemprice CC. See also Melton, Wauldby.

Dick Turpin, highwayman, arrested here 1739. Views across Humber to Lincs.

WELTON LE MARSH Lincs (L)
114 TF 4768 4m S of Alford. CP, 194. Spilsby RD. P Splsby. Ch e, m. Sch pe. Horncastle CC.

WELTON LE WOLD Lincs (L)
105 TF 2787 3m W of Louth. CP, 171. Lth RD. P Lth. Ch e. Sch pe. Lth CC. Gravel wks.

WELWICK Yorks (E)
99 TA 3421 4m S of Withernsea. CP, 307. Holderness RD. P Hull. Ch e, m. Sch p. Bridlington CC. See also Weeton.

WELWYN Herts
147 TL 2316 2m N of Welwyn Gdn City. CP. Wlwn RD. P. Ch e, b, m, r, v. Wlwn and Hatfield CC (Hertford). See also Harmer Grn, Woolmer Grn. Little old tn, still separate from the gdn city. To E of A1, Lockleys*, early 18c hse now a sch; rems of Roman villa found in grnds. To SE, B1000 rd passes under famous rly viaduct (see Digswell).

WELWYN GARDEN CITY Herts
147, 160 TL 2312 6m NE of St Albans. UD, 40,369. P. Wlwn and Hatfield CC (Hertford). See also Digswell. Extensive New Tn development worked out in conjunction with Hatfield (qv).

WEM Shrops
118 SJ 5128 8m SSW of Whitchurch. CP(Wm Urban), 2,606. N Shrops RD. P Shrewsbury. Ch e, b, m, v2. Sch pe, s2. Oswestry CC.

WEMBDON Som
165 ST 2837 1m W of Bridgwater. CP, 1,141. Brdgwtr RD. P Brdgwtr. Ch e. Sch pe. Brdgwtr CC.

WEMBLEY London
160 TQ 1885 8m WNW of Charing Cross. Loc, Brent LB. P Middx. Brnt N BC, Brnt S BC (Wmbly N, Wmbly S). Famous sports stadium.

WEMBURY Devon
187 SX 5248 5m SSE of Plymouth. CP. Plympton St Mary RD. P Plmth. Ch e, v. Sch p. W Dvn CC (Tavistock). See also Down Thomas, Heybrook Bay.

WEMBWORTHY Devon
175 SS 6609 10m NNE of Okehampton. CP, 210. Crediton RD. P Chulmleigh. Ch e, c. Sch p. Tiverton CC (Torrington).

WENDENS AMBO Essex
148 TL 5136 2m SW of Saffron Walden. CP, 319. Sffrn Wldn RD. P(Wndn), Sffrn Wldn. Ch e. Sffrn Wldn CC. Ch: mdvl wall-paintings.

WENDLEBURY Oxon
145, 146 SP 5619 2m SW of Bicester. CP, 165. Ploughley RD. P Bcstr. Ch e. Mid-Oxon CC (Henley).

WENDLING Norfolk
125 TF 9313 4m W of E Dereham. CP, 311. Mitford and Launditch RD. P Drhm. Ch e, m. Sch p. SW Nflk CC.

WENDOVER Bucks
159 SP 8607 5m SE of Aylesbury. CP, 6,151. Aylesbury RD. P Aylesbury. Ch e, b, c, r. Sch i, je, s. Aylesbury CC. See also World's End.

WENDRON Cornwall
189 SW 6731 3m NNE of Helston. CP, 2,490. Kerrier RD. Ch e, m8. Sch pe. Falmouth and Camborne CC. See also Carnkie, Porkellis, Rame, Trenear.

WENDY Cambs
147 TL 3247 5m NNW of Royston. CP(Shingay cum Wndy), 137. S Cambs RD. Ch e. Cambs CC.

WENHAM, GREAT Suffolk (E)
149 TM 0738 4m SE of Hadleigh. See Gt Wnhm.

WENHASTON Suffolk (E)
137 TM 4275 3m SE of Halesworth. CP (Wnhstn w Mells Hamlet), 688. Blyth RD. P Hlswth. Ch e, m. Sch p. Eye CC. Ch contains famous doom (portrayal of Last Judgement), showing sinners being eaten by devils etc. Wnhstn Cmmn a riot of gorse in season (May).

WENNINGTON Hunts
134 TL 2379 5m N of Huntingdon. Loc, Abbots Ripton CP. Ch v.

WENNINGTON Lancs
89 SD 6170 5m S of Kirkby Lonsdale. CP, 159. Lunesdale RD. P LANCASTER. Lncstr CC.

WENNINGTON London
161 TQ 5381 3m ESE of Dagenham. Loc, Havering LB. P Rainham, Essex. Hornchurch BC.

WENSLEY Derbys
111 SK 2661 2m WNW of Matlock. Loc, Mtlck UD. P Mtlck.

WENSLEY Yorks (N)
90 SE 0989 2m WSW of Leyburn. CP, 210. Lbn RD. P Lbn. Ch e. Richmond CC.

WENTBRIDGE Yorks (W)
103 SE 4817 4m SE of Pontefract. Loc, Hemsworth RD, Osgoldcross RD. P Pntfrct. Ch e. Hmswth CC, Goole CC. In steep-sided valley of R Went, crossed by A1 rd on impressive viaduct to E.

WENTNOR Shrops
129 SO 3892 4m W of Ch Stretton. CP, 308. Clun and Bishop's Cstle RD. P Bp's Cstle. Ch e. Ludlow CC.

WENTWORTH Cambs
135 TL 4878 4m W of Ely. CP, 165. Ely RD. Ch e. Isle of Ely CC.

WENTWORTH Yorks (W)
102, 103 SK 3898 7m NNE of Sheffield. CP, 1,471. Rotherham RD. P Rthrhm. Ch e, m. Sch pe. Rother Valley CC. See also Nether Haugh. Wntwth Woodhouse, vast 18c mansion in large pk with temples, statuary, and lakes. Stables by Carr of York, who also designed parts of hse.

WEOBLEY Herefs
142 SO 4051 8m SW of Leominster. CP, 747. Wbly RD. P HEREFORD. Ch e, m, r. Sch p, s. Lmnstr CC. Many black and white timbered hses, notably The Ley, 1589.

WEOBLEY MARSH Herefs
142 SO 4151 7m SW of Leominster. Loc, Wbly CP.

WEREHAM Norfolk
124 TF 6801 5m ESE of Downham Mkt. CP, 478. Dnhm RD. P King's Lynn. Ch e, v. Sch p. SW Nflk CC.

WERGS Staffs
119 SJ 8700 3m WNW of Wolverhampton. Loc, Wrottesley CP.

WERRINGTON Cornwall
174, 186 SX 3287 2m N of Launceston. CP, 533. Lncstn RD. Ch e, m. Sch p. N Cnwll CC (Tavistock). See also Bridgetown, Polapit Tamar, Yeolmbridge.

WERRINGTON Hunts
123 TF 1603 3m NNW of Peterborough. Loc, Ptrbrgh MB. P PTRBRGH.

WERRINGTON Staffs
110 SJ 9447 5m ENE of Stoke-on-Trent. Loc, Caverswall CP. P Stke-on-Trent. Ch e, m. Sch i, j.

WERVIN Ches
109 SJ 4271 4m NNE of Chester. CP. Chstr RD. City of Chstr CC.

WESHAM Lancs
94 SD 4132 7m ESE of Blackpool. CP (Medlar-w-Wshm), 2,422. Fylde RD. P Kirkham, Preston. Ch e, m, r. Sch pe, pr. S Flde CC.

WESSINGTON Derbys
111 SK 3757 3m NW of Alfreton. CP, 589. Chesterfield RD. P DERBY. Ch e, m. Sch p. NE Derbys CC.

WEST ACRE Norfolk
125 TF 7715 5m NNW of Swaffham. CP, 265. Freebridge Lynn RD. P King's Lynn. Ch e, m. NW Nflk CC (K's Lnn). Rems of 11c priory.

WEST ADDERBURY Oxon
145 SP 4635 3m S of Banbury. CP, 534. Bnbry RD. P(Addrbry), Bnbry. Bnbry CC. One vllge with E Addrbry but divided by A41 rd. Noble spired ch, Dec and Perp.

WEST ALLERDEAN Nthmb
64 NT 9646 5m SSW of Berwick-upon-Tweed. Loc, Norham and Islandshires RD. Brwck-upn-Twd CC.

WEST ALLOTMENT Nthmb
78 NZ 3070 4m WNW of Tynemouth. Loc, Longbenton UD. P Shiremoor.

WEST ALVINGTON Devon
187, 188 SX 7243 just W of Kingsbridge. CP, 476. Kngsbrdge RD. P Kngsbrdge. Ch e. Sch pe. Totnes CC.

WEST ANSTEY Devon
164 SS 8527 4m W of Dulverton. CP, 128.
S Molton RD. P: S Mltn. Ch e, m.
N Dvn CC.

WEST APPLETON Yorks (N)
91 SE 2294 5m SSE of Richmond.
CP(Appltn E and W), 73. Rchmnd RD.
Rchmnd CC.

WEST ASHBY Leics (L)
114 TF 2672 2m N of Horncastle. CP, 262.
Hncstle RD. P Hncstle. Ch e. Sch pe.
Hncstle CC.

WEST ASHLING Sussex (W)
181 SU 8107 4m WNW of Chichester. Loc,
Funtington CP. P Chchstr.

WEST ASHTON Wilts
166 ST 8755 2m SE of Trowbridge.
CP, 299. Warminster and Westbury RD.
P Trwbrdge. Ch e. Sch pe. Wstbry CC.

WEST AUCKLAND Co Durham
85 NZ 1826 3m SW of Bishop Auckland.
Loc, Bshp Aucklnd UD. P Bshp Aucklnd.

WEST AYTON Yorks (N)
93 SE 9884 4m SW of Scarborough.
CP, 412. Scbrgh RD. Scbrgh CC (Scbrgh and
Whitby).

WEST BAGBOROUGH Som
164 ST 1733 7m NW of Taunton. CP, 400.
Tntn RD. P(Bgbrgh), Tntn. Ch e, v. Sch pe.
Tntn CC.

WEST BARKWITH Lincs (L)
105 TF 1680 6m SSE of Mkt Rasen. CP, 68.
Horncastle RD. Ch e. Hncstle CC.

WEST BARNBY Yorks (N)
86 NZ 8212 5m WNW of Whitby. Loc,
Bnby CP. Whtby RD. Cleveland and Whitby
CC (Scarborough and Whtby).

WEST BARSHAM Norfolk
125 TF 9033 3m NNW of Fakenham. Loc,
Bshm CP. Walsingham RD. Ch e. Sch p.
NW Nflk CC (N Nflk).

WEST BAY Dorset
177 SY 4690 2m S of Bridport. Loc,
Brdpt MB, Brdpt RD. P Brdpt. W Dst CC.
Harbour enlarged in 19c but silting has
caused its decline.

WEST BECKHAM Norfolk
125 TG 1339 3m SSW of Sheringham.
CP, 227. Erpingham RD. Ch e, m.
N Nflk CC.

WESTBERE Kent
173 TR 1961 4m NE of Canterbury.
CP, 413. Bridge-Blean RD. Ch e, v.
Cntrbry CC.

WEST BERGHOLT Essex
149 TL 9627 3m NW of Colchester.
CP, 1,294. Lexden and Winstree RD.
P Clchstr. Ch e, m2. Sch pe. Clchstr CC.

WEST BEXINGTON Dorset
177, 178 SY 5386 6m SE of Bridport. Loc,
Puncknowle CP. P Dorchester. Holiday
vllge. Mnr hse mentioned in Domesday, now
hotel. Other bldngs modern.

WEST BILNEY Norfolk
124 TF 7115 7m ESE of King's Lynn. Loc,
E Winch CP. Ch e. Sch p.

WESTBOROUGH Lincs (K)
113, 122 SK 8544 7m NW of Grantham.
CP(Wstbrgh and Dry Doddington), 262.
W Kesteven RD. Ch e. Grnthm CC.

WESTBOURNE Sussex (W)
181 SU 7507 3m ENE of Havant. CP.
Chichester RD. P Emsworth, Hants.
Ch e, b, s. Sch p. Chchstr CC. See also
Woodmancote.

WEST BRADENHAM Norfolk
125 TF 9108 5m WSW of E Dereham. Loc,
Brdnhm CP. Swaffham RD. P Thetford.
Ch e. Sch pe. SW Nflk CC.

WEST BRADFORD Yorks (W)
95 SD 7444 2m N of Clitheroe. CP, 317.
Bowland RD. P Clthroe, Lancs. Ch m.
Sch pe. Skipton CC.

WEST BRADLEY Som
165, 166 ST 5536 4m ESE of Glastonbury.
CP, 259. Shepton Mallet RD. Ch e.
Wells CC. See also Hornblotton Grn,
Lottisham, Parbrook.

WEST BRETTON Yorks (W)
102 SE 2813 5m SW of Wakefield. CP, 299.
Wkfld RD. P(Brttn), Wkfld. Ch m. Sch p.
Wkfld BC. B. Hall, early 19c hse in large pk,
now training college.

WEST BRIDGFORD Notts
112, 121, 122 SK 5837 2m SSE of
Nottingham. UD, 28,496. P. Rushcliffe CC
(Nttnghm S BC.) See also Edwalton. This is
Nttnghm-S-of-the-river (Trent).

WEST BROMWICH Staffs
131 SP 0091 5m NW of Birmingham.
CB, 166,626. P. BCs: W Brmwch E,
W Brmwch W. (Bilston, Rowley Regis and
Tipton, Wednesbury, W Brmwch.) See also
Tptn, Wdnsbry. Mnfg tn. M5/M6
interchange to NE of borough.

WEST BUCKLAND Devon
163 SS 6531 5m NW of S Molton. CP, 251.
S Mltn RD. P Barnstaple. Ch e, m.
N Dvn CC.

WEST BUCKLAND Som
164 ST 1720 2m E of Wellington. CP, 793.
Wllngton RD. P Wllngtn. Ch e, v2. Sch p.
Taunton CC.

WEST BURTON Notts
104 SK 7985 3m SSW of Gainsborough.
CP, 29. E Retford RD. Bassetlaw CC. Power
stn.

WEST BURTON Sussex (W)
181, 182 TQ 0014 4m SW of Pulborough.
Loc, Bury CP. Cooke's Hse*, Elizn, with
gdn incl topiary.

WEST BURTON Yorks (N)
90 SE 0186 6m WSW of Leyburn. Loc,
Btn-cum-Walden CP. Aysgarth RD. P Lbn.
Ch m. Sch pe. Richmond CC. Pleasant vllge
blt round large grn.

WESTBURY Bucks
145, 146 SP 6235 3m ESE of Brackley.
CP, 287. Buckingham RD. P Brckly,
Northants. Ch e. Sch pe. Bcknghm CC.

WESTBURY Shrops
118 SJ 3509 8m ENE of Welshpool.
CP, 957. Atcham RD. P Shrewsbury. Ch e.
Sch pe. Shrsbry CC. See also Stoney
Stretton, Vennington, Westley, Yockleton.

WESTBURY Wilts
166 ST 8751 11m SE of Bath. UD, 6,456.
P. Wstbry CC. See also Dilton, Wstbry
Leigh. Largely Ggn. 1m W, Brokerswood Pk,
natural history centre. 1m E, White Horse
cut in hillside 1778 (A.M.).

WESTBURY LEIGH Wilts
166 ST 8650 just SW of Westbury. Loc,
Wstbry UD. P Wstbry.

WESTBURY-ON-SEVERN Glos
143 SO 7114 4m E of Cinderford.
CP, 1,795. Gloucester RD. P. Ch e, v.
Sch p, pe. W Glos CC. See also Boxbush,
Northwood Grn, Rodley. Ch has detached
13c twr topped by 14c shingled spire.
Wstbry Ct Gdn, formal 17c–18c water gdn;
canals restored 1969.

WESTBURY-SUB-MENDIP Som
165 ST 5048 4m NW of Wells.
CP(Westbury), 544. Wlls RD. P Wlls. Ch e.
Sch pe. Wlls CC.

WEST BUTTERWICK Lincs (L)
104 SE 8305 4m ENE of Epworth. CP, 663.
Isle of Axholme RD. P Scunthorpe. Ch e, m.
Sch pe. Gainsborough CC.

WESTBY Lancs
94 SD 3831 6m SE of Blackpool.
CP(Wstby-w-Plumptons), 990. Fylde RD.
Ch r. Sch pe, pr. S Flde CC. See also Gt
Plmptn, Hr Ballam, Lit Plmptn.

WEST BYFLEET Surrey
170 TQ 0460 3m ENE of Woking. Loc,
Wkng UD. P Weybridge.

WEST CAISTER Norfolk
126 TG 5011 3m NNW of Yarmouth.
CP, 202. Blofield and Clegg RD. Ymth CC.
See also W End.

WEST CAMEL Som
166, 177 ST 5724 4m ENE of Ilchester.
CP, 378. Yeovil RD. P Yvl. Ch e, m. Yvl CC.

WEST CHALDON Dorset
178 SY 7782 7m SE of Dorchester. Loc,
Chldn Herring CP.

WEST CHALLOW Berks
158 SU 3688 2m W of Wantage. CP, 183.
Wntge RD. Ch e. Abingdon CC. Ch: bell
inscribed 'Povel Le Poter me Fist 1283'.

WEST CHELBOROUGH Dorset
177, 178 ST 5405 7m S of Yeovil. CP, 29.
Beaminster RD. Ch e. W Dst CC.

WEST CHEVINGTON Nthmb
71 NZ 2297 5m SSW of Amble. CP, 118.
Morpeth RD. Mpth CC.

WEST CHILTINGTON Sussex (W)
182 TQ 0918 3m E of Pulborough.
CP, 1,267. Chanctonbury RD. P Plbrgh.
Ch e, c. Sch p. Shoreham CC (Arundel and
Shrhm). See also Coneyhurst Cmmn,
Gay St, W Chltngtn Cmmn.

WEST CHILTINGTON COMMON Sussex
(W)
182 TQ 0817 3m ESE of Pulborough. Loc,
W Chltngtn CP. P Plbrgh.

WEST CHINNOCK Som
177 ST 4613 3m NNE of Crewkerne.
CP, 444. Yeovil RD. P Crkne. Ch e, m.
Sch pe. Yvl CC. See also Middle Chinnock.

WEST CLANDON Surrey
170 TQ 0451 3m ENE of Guildford.
CP, 1,111. Gldfd RD. P Gldfd. Ch e. Sch pe.
Dorking CC. Clndn Pk (NT)*, 18c hse;
notable plasterwork etc.

WEST CLIFFE Kent
173 TR 3544 3m NE of Dover. Loc,
St Margaret's at Cliffe CP. Ch e.

WESTCLIFF ON SEA Essex
162 TQ 8685 W distr of Southend. Loc,
Sthnd-on-Sea CB. P. Sthnd W BC. Rsdntl.
Obelisk on beach marks limit of City of
London's authority over R Thames.

WEST COKER Som
177 ST 5113 3m WSW of Yeovil. CP, 936.
Yvl RD. P Yvl. Ch e, m. Sch pe. Yvl CC.

WESTCOMBE Som
166 ST 6739 3m N of Bruton. Loc,
Batcombe CP.

WEST COMPTON Dorset
177, 178 SY 5694 6m E of Bridport.
CP, 45. Dchstr RD. Ch e. W Dst CC.

WEST COMPTON Som
165, 166 ST 5942 4m SE of Wells. Loc,
Pilton CP.

WESTCOTE Glos
144 SP 2120 3m E of Bourton-on-
the-Water. CP, 190. N Cotswold RD.
P OXFORD. Ch e, m. Cirencester and
Tewkesbury CC. See also Nether Wstcte.

WESTCOTT Bucks
146, 159 SP 7117 7m WNW of Aylesbury.

CP, 429. Aylesbury RD. P Aylesbury. Ch r.
Sch pe. Aylesbury CC.

WESTCOTT Devon
176 ST 0204 7m SE of Tiverton. Loc,
Cullompton CP.

WESTCOTT Surrey
170 TQ 1448 2m WSW of Dorking. Loc,
Dkng UD. P Dkng.

WESTCOTT BARTON Oxon
145 SP 4225 6m N of Woodstock.
CP(Westcot Btn), 114. Chipping
Norton RD. Ch e, m. Banbury CC.

WEST COWICK Yorks (W)
97, 98 SE 6521 6m WSW of Goole. Loc,
Snaith and Cwck CP. Ch e, m.

WEST CRANMORE Som
166 ST 6643 3m E of Shepton Mallet. Loc,
Crnmre CP. Shptn Mllt RD. Ch e. Sch pe.
Wells CC.

WEST CREETING GREEN Suffolk (E)
136 TM 0758 2m ESE of Stowmarket. Loc,
Crtng St Peter or W Crtng CP. Gipping RD.
P(Crtng St Ptr), Ipswich. Ch e, c. Eye CC.

WEST CURTHWAITE Cumb
82 NY 3248 4m E of Wigton. Loc,
Westward CP.

WESTDEAN Sussex (E)
183 TV 5299 3m E of Seaford. CP, 64.
Hailsham RD. Ch e. Eastbourne CC. Well
situated in S Downs. To N, Charl(e)ston*,
mdvl and later mnr hse, with large gdns.

WEST DEAN Sussex (W)
181 SU 8512 5m N of Chichester. CP, 512.
Chchstr RD. P Chchstr. Ch e. Sch pe.
Chchstr CC. See also Chilgrove. W Dn Pk;
arboretum.

WEST DEAN Wilts
167 SU 2527 7m ESE of Salisbury. CP, 177.
Slsbry and Wilton RD. P Slsbry. Ch e, m.
Slsbry CC. Rems of mdvl ch: monmts. River
and thatched cottages.

WEST DEEPING Lincs (K)
123 TF 1108 5m ENE of Stamford.
CP, 235. S Kesteven RD.
P PETERBOROUGH. Ch e. Sch pe. Rutland
and Stmfd CC.

WEST DEREHAM Norfolk
124 TF 6500 3m SE of Downham Mkt.
CP, 448. Dnhm RD. P King's Lynn. Ch e, m.
Sch pe. SW Nflk CC.

WEST DITCHBURN Nthmb
71 NU 1220 6m NW of Alnwick. Loc,
Eglingham CP.

WEST DOWN Devon
163 SS 5142 3m S of Ilfracombe. CP, 514.
Barnstaple RD. P Ilfrcmbe. Ch e, v. Sch p.
N Dvn CC. See also Trimstone.

WEST DRAYTON London
160, 170 TQ 0679 3m S of Uxbridge. Loc,
Hillingdon LB. P Middx. Uxbrdge BC (CC).

WEST DRAYTON Notts
112 SK 7074 4m S of Retford. CP, 256.
E Rtfd RD. Ch e, m. Bassetlaw CC.

WEST END Beds
147 SP 9853 5m NW of Bedford. Loc,
Stevington CP. Ch b.

WEST END Hants
180 SU 4714 4m ENE of Southampton.
CP, 5,064. Winchester RD. P STHMPTN.
Ch b, m3, r. Sch pe. Eastleigh CC.

WEST END Herts
160 TL 3306 3m NNW of Cheshunt. Loc,
Brickendon Liberty CP. Hertford RD. Htfd
and Stevenage CC (Htfd).

WEST END Norfolk
126 TG 4911 3m NNW of Yarmouth. Loc,
W Caister CP.

WEST END Surrey
169, 170 SU 9561 4m WNW of Woking. CP.
Bagshot RD. P Wkng. Ch e. Sch pe.
NW Srry CC (Chertsey). See also Donkey
Tn.

WEST END Yorks (W)
96 SE 1457 5m SSW of Pateley Br. Loc,
Thruscross CP. Ch e. Large reservoirs.

WEST END GREEN Hants
168, 169 SU 6661 6m NNE of Basingstoke.
Loc, Stratfield Saye CP.

WESTERDALE Yorks (N)
86 NZ 6605 7m SSE of Gainsborough.
CP, 158. Whitby RD. P Whtby. Ch e, m.
Cleveland and Whtby CC (Scarborough and
Whtby).

WESTERFIELD Suffolk (E)
150 TM 1747 N distr of Ipswich. Loc,
Ipswch CB; CP, 44,   Deben RD. P Ipswch.
Ipswch BC, Sudbury and Woodbridge CC.
Ch has angel hammerbeam roof.

WESTERGATE Sussex (W)
181 SU 9305 5m E of Chichester. Loc,
Aldingbourne CP. Ch m, s. Sch s.

WESTERHAM Kent
171 TQ 4454 5m W of Sevenoaks.
CP, 4,228. Svnks RD. P. Ch e, c, r, v.
Sch pe, s. Svnks CC. See also Crockham Hill.
17c mkt tn. Ch has brasses. Quebec Hse
(NT)*, 16c–17c, home of General Wolfe.
To W, Squerryes Ct*, 17c mnr hse.

WSTERHOPE Nthmb
78 NZ 1967 4m WNW of Newcastle. Loc,
Newburn UD. P NCSTLE UPON TYNE 5.

WESTERLEIGH Glos
156 ST 6979 8m NE of Bristol. CP, 2,158.
Sodbury RD. P BRSTL. Ch e, c. Sch pe2.
S Glos CC. See also Nibley.

WESTERTON Co Durham
85 NZ 2431 2m SSW of Spennymoor. Loc,
Bishop Auckland UD.

WEST FARLEIGH Kent
171, 172 TQ 7152 4m SW of Maidstone.
CP, 442. Mdstne RD. P Mdstne. Ch e.
Sch pe. Mdstne CC. See also Frlgh Grn.

WEST FELTON Shrops
118 SJ 3425 4m SE of Oswestry. CP, 787.
Oswstry RD. P Oswstry. Ch e, m. Sch pe.
Oswstry CC. See also Grimpo, Haughton,
Sutton, Woolston.

WESTFIELD Herefs
143 SO 7247 3m WNW of Malvern. Loc,
Cradley CP.

WESTFIELD Norfolk
125 TF 9909 2m S of E Dereham. Loc,
Whinburgh CP. Ch e, m.

WESTFIELD Sussex (E)
184 TQ 8115 4m N of Hastings. CP, 1,779.
Battle RD. P Bttle. Ch e, m. Sch p. Rye CC.

WEST FIRLE Sussex (E)
183 TQ 4707 4m ESE of Lewes. CP, 374.
Chailey RD. Ch e. Sch pe. Lws CC. Under
ridge of S Downs; F. Beacon, 713ft, 1¼m

SE. F. Place*, mainly Ggn hse with Tdr core.

WESTGATE Co Durham
84 NY 9038 5m W of Stanhope. Loc, Stnhpe CP. P Bishop Auckland. Ch e, m.

WESTGATE Lincs (L)
104 SE 7707 2m N of Epworth. Loc, Belton CP. Ch m.

WESTGATE Norfolk
125 TF 9740 4m SE of Wells. Loc, Binham CP.

WESTGATE ON SEA Kent
173 TR 3270 2m W of Margate. Loc, Mgte MB. P.

WEST GINGE Berks
158 SU 4486 3m ESE of Wantage. Loc, Ardington CP.

WEST GRAFTON Wilts
167 SU 2460 5m E of Pewsey. Loc, Grftn CP. Marlborough and Ramsbury RD. Devizes CC.

WEST GREEN Hants
169 SU 7456 8m ENE of Basingstoke. Loc, Hartley Wintney CP. P Bsngstke. W Grn Hse (NT)*, early 18c.

WEST GRIMSTEAD Wilts
167 SU 2126 5m ESE of Salisbury. Loc, Grmstd CP. Slsbry and Wilton RD. P Slsbry. Ch e, m. Sch pe. Slsbry CC.

WEST GRINSTEAD Sussex (W)
182 TQ 1620 6m S of Horsham. CP, 1,751. Hshm RD. P Hshm. Ch e, r. Hshm and Crawley CC (Hshm). See also Dial Post, Partridge Grn.

WEST HADDLESEY Yorks (W)
97 SE 5626 5m SW of Selby. CP, 149. Slby RD. P Slby. Ch m. Barkston Ash CC.

WEST HADDON Northants
132, 133 SP 6371 7m NNE of Daventry. CP, 770. Dvntry RD. P Rugby, Warwickshire. Ch e, b. Sch pe. Dvntry CC (S Nthnts).

WEST HAGBOURNE Berks
158 SU 5187 2m SSW of Didcot. CP, 290. Wallingford RD. P Ddct. Ch e. Abingdon CC.

WEST HALL Cumb
76 NY 5667 5m NNE of Brampton. Loc, Kingwater CP. Border RD. P Brmptn. Ch m. Penrith and the Bdr CC.

WESTHALL Suffolk (E)
137 TM 4280 3m NE of Halesworth. CP, 278. Wainford RD. Ch e, m. Lowestoft CC. See also Cox Cmmn, Mill Cmmn. Ch: seven-sacrament font; scrn.

WEST HALLAM Derbys
112, 121 SK 4341 2m WSW of Ilkeston. CP, 1,952. SE Derbys RD. P DERBY. Ch e. Sch pe, se. SE Derbys CC.

WEST HALTON Lincs (L)
98 SE 9021 6m N of Scunthorpe. CP, 240. Glanford Brigg RD. P Scnthpe. Ch e, m. Brgg and Scnthpe CC (Brgg). See also Coleby.

WEST HAM London
161 TQ 4082 7m E of Charing Cross. Loc, Newham LB. Nwhm NW BC, Nwhm S BC (W Hm N, W Hm S).

WESTHAM Som
165 ST 4046 5m SW of Cheddar. Loc, Wedmore CP.

WESTHAM Sussex (E)
183 TQ 6304 4m NE of Eastbourne. CP, 1,932. Hailsham RD. P Pevensey. Ch e. Sch pe. Eastbne CC. See also Hankham, Stone Cross.

WESTHAMPNETT Sussex (W)
181 SU 8806 2m NE of Chichester. CP, 437. Chchstr RD. P Chchstr. Ch e. Sch pe. Chchstr CC. See also Strettington.

WEST HANDLEY Derbys
103, 111 SK 3977 4m N of Chesterfield. Loc, Unstone CP.

WEST HANNEY Berks
158 SU 4092 3m N of Wantage. CP, 342. Wntge RD. P Wntge. Ch e. Abingdon CC.

WEST HANNINGFIELD Essex
161, 162 TQ 7299 5m SSE of Chelmsford. CP, 786. Chlmsfd RD. P Chlmsfd. Ch e. Sch p, pe Chlmsfd CC. On N edge of H. Water, reservoir. Ch has 15c timber twr.

WEST HARDWICK Yorks (W)
103 SE 4118 3m SW of Pontefract. CP, 20. Hemsworth RD. Hmswth CC.

WEST HARPTREE Som
165, 166 ST 5656 7m N of Wells. CP, 440. Clutton RD. P BRISTOL. Ch e. Sch pe. N Som CC. See also N Widcombe. To N, Chew Valley Lake (Brstl reservoir). Old vllge water mill now at Blaise Cstle Folk Museum, Brstl.

WEST HATCH Som
177 ST 2821 4m SE of Taunton. CP, 256. Tntn RD. Ch e, m. Tntn CC. See also Meare Grn, Slough Grn.

WEST HATCH Wilts
166, 167 ST 9227 5m NE of Shaftesbury. Loc, W Tisbury CP. Mere and Tisbury RD. Westbury CC.

WESTHAY Som
165 ST 4342 5m WNW of Glastonbury. Loc, Meare CP. P Glstnbry. In Som turbary (peat-cutting area).

WESTHEAD Lancs
100 SD 4407 2m ESE of Ormskirk. Loc, Ormskk UD. P Ormskk.

WEST HEATH Hants
169 SU 8556 3m SW of Camberley. Loc, Farnborough UD.

WEST HENDRED Berks
158 SU 4488 3m E of Wantage. CP, 325. Wntge RD. P Wntge. Ch e, m. Sch pe. Abingdon CC. See also E Ginge. Thatched cottages.

WEST HESLERTON Yorks (E)
93 SE 9176 8m ENE of Malton. Loc, Hslrtn CP. P Mltn. Ch e. Sch pe.

WESTHIDE Herefs
142 SO 5844 5m ENE of Hereford. CP, 84. Hrfd RD. P HRFD. Ch e. Leominster CC.

WEST HILL Devon
176 SY 0794 5m NNW of Sidmouth. Loc, Ottery St Mary UD. P Ottery St M.

WEST HOATHLY Sussex (E)
183 TQ 3632 4m SSW of E Grinstead. CP, 1,665. Cuckfield RD. P: E Grnstd. Ch e, r, v2. Sch pe. Mid-Sx CC (E Grnstd). See also Highbrook, Selsfield Cmmn, Sharpthorne. On steep ridge; long views both N and S. 15c Priest's Hse now museum.

WEST HOLME Dorset
178, 179 SY 8885 3m WSW of Wareham. Loc, E Stoke CP.

WESTHOPE Herefs
142 SO 4651 5m SSW of Leominster. Loc, Canon Pyon CP. P HEREFORD.

WESTHOPE Shrops
129 SO 4786 3m NE of Craven Arms. Loc, Diddlebury CP.

WEST HORNDON Essex
161 TQ 6288 4m SSE of Brentwood. Loc, Brntwd UD. P Brntwd.

WESTHORPE Lincs (H)
114, 123 TF 2231 6m NNW of Spalding. Loc, Gosberton CP.

WESTHORPE Suffolk (E)
136 TM 0469 6m N of Stowmarket. CP, 138. Hartismere RD. P Stmkt. Ch e. Eye CC.

WEST HORRINGTON Som
165, 166 ST 5747 2m NE of Wells. Loc, St Cuthbert Out CP. Wlls RD. P Wlls. Wlls CC.

WEST HORSLEY Surrey
170 TQ 0752 6m ENE of Guildford. CP, 2,685. Gldfd RD. P Lthrhd. Ch e, m, r. Sch p, pe. Dorking CC. Ch may be burial place of Sir Walter Raleigh; has massive 12c twr and 14c shingled spire.

WEST HOUGHAM Kent
173 TR 2640 4m WSW of Dover. Loc, Hghm Without CP. Dvr RD. P Dvr. Ch m. Dvr and Deal CC (Dvr).

WESTHOUGHTON Lancs
101 SD 6506 4m WSW of Bolton. UD, 17,729. P Bltn. Wsthtn CC. See also Wingates. In mining distr.

WESTHOUSE Yorks (W)
89 SD 6774 5m SE of Kirkby Lonsdale. Loc, Thornton in Lnsdle CP.

WESTHOUSES Derby
112 SK 4358 2m NE of Alfreton. Loc, Blackwell CP. P DERBY. Sch p.

WEST HUMBLE Surrey
170 TQ 1651 1m N of Dorking. Loc, Dkng UD. In gap of N Downs opposite Box Hill. To W, rems of 12c chpl (NT)*, blt for those unable to cross R Mole to Mickleham Church.

WEST HYDE Herts
160 TQ 0391 3m SW of Rickmansworth.
Loc, Rckmnswth UD. P Rckmnswth.

WEST ILSLEY Berks
158 SU 4782 6m SW of Didcot. CP, 295.
Wantage RD. P Newbury. Ch e.
Abingdon CC.

WEST ITCHENOR Sussex (W)
181 SU 7901 4m SW of Chichester.
CP, 280. Chchstr RD.· Ch e. Chchstr CC.
Yachting vllge. Ferry (for foot passengers)
across Chchstr Channel.

WEST KEAL Lincs (L)
114 TF 3663 8m SE of Horncastle. CP, 291.
Spilsby RD. P Splsby. Ch e. Hncstle CC.

WEST KENNETT Wilts
157 SU 1168 5m W of Marlborough. Loc,
Avebury CP. W.K. Long Barrow on hill
to SW.

WEST KINGSDOWN Kent
171 TQ 5762 6m NE of Sevenoaks.
CP, 3,382. Dartford RD. P Svnks. Ch e.
Sch pe. Svnks CC (Dtfd). To N, Brand's
Hatch motor-racing circuit.

WEST KINGTON Wilts
156 ST 8177 7m WNW of Chippenham.
Loc, Nettleton CP. P Chppnhm. Ch e, b.

WEST KIRBY Ches
100, 109 SJ 2186 7m W of Birkenhead.
Loc, Hoylake UD. P Wirral. Mainly rsdntl.
To N, golf course of Royal Liverpool GC.

WEST KNAPTON Yorks (E)
92, 93 SE 8775 6m ENE of Malton. Loc,
Scampston CP. Ch e, m.

WEST KNIGHTON Dorset
178 SY 7387 3m SE of Dorchester.
CP, 423. Dchstr RD. Ch e. Sch p. W Dst CC.

WEST KNOYLE Wilts
166 ST 8532 6m N of Shaftesbury. CP, 131.
Mere and Tisbury RD. P Warminster. Ch e.
Westbury CC.

WEST KYLOE Nthmb
64 NU 0540 5m NW of Belford. Loc,
Kyloe CP. Norham and Islandshires RD.
Ch e. Berwick-upon-Tweed CC.

WEST LAMBROOK Som
117 ST 4118 4m NE of Ilminster. Loc,
Kingsbury Episcopi CP.

WEST LANGDON Kent
173 TR 3247 4m N of Dover. Loc,
Lngdn CP. Dvr RD. Ch e. Dvr and Deal CC
(Dvr).

WEST LAVINGTON Sussex (W)
181 SU 8920 just SE of Midhurst. CP, 488.
Mdhst RD. Ch e. Sch pe. Chichester CC
(Horsham). Richard Cobden, champion of
free trade, buried in yard of Butterfield's ch.

WEST LAVINGTON Wilts
167 SU 0053 5m S of Devizes. CP, 965.
Dvzs RD. P Dvzs. Ch e, b. Sch pe. Dvzs CC.
See also Littleton Pannell.

WEST LAYTON Yorks (N)
85 NZ 1410 6m NNW of Richmond. CP, 49.
Rchmnd RD. Rchmnd CC.

WEST LEAKE Notts
121 SK 5226 4m N of Loughborough.
CP, 114. Basford RD. P Lghbrgh, Leics.
Ch e. Rushcliffe CC.

WEST LEARMOUTH Nthmb
64, 70 NT 8537 1m SSE of Coldstream
Loc, Carham CP.

WESTLEIGH Devon
163 SS 4728 2m NNE of Bideford. CP, 380.
Barnstaple RD. P Bdfd. Ch e, m. Sch p.
N Dvn CC. See also Eastleigh.

WESTLEIGH Devon
164 ST 0617 5m WSW of Wellington. Loc,
Burlescombe CP. P Tiverton. Ch c.

WESTLETON Suffolk (E)
137 TM 4469 5m NE of Saxmundham.
CP, 577. Blyth RD. P Sxmndhm. Ch e, m.
Eye CC. Hths to E. Ch twr blown down late
18c.

WEST LEXHAM Norfolk
125 TF 8417 5m NNE of Swaffham. Loc,
Lxhm CP. Mitford and Launditch RD.
P King's Lynn. Ch e. SW Nflk CC.

WESTLEY Shrops
118 SJ 3607 9m WSW of Shrewsbury. Loc,
Westbury CP.

WESTLEY Suffolk (W)
136 TL 8264 2m W of Bury St Edmunds.
CP, 61. Thingoe RD. P Newmarket. Ch e.
Bury St Eds CC.

WESTLEY WATERLESS Cambs
135 TL 6256 5m SSW of Newmarket
CP, 165. Nmkt RD. P(Wstly), Nmkt,
Suffolk. Ch e. Cambs CC. Ch contains
famous brass of Sir John and Lady
Creke, 1325.

WEST LILLING Yorks (N)
92 SE 6465 9m NNE of York. Loc, Lllngs
Ambo CP. Flaxton RD. Thirsk and
Malton CC.

WESTLINGTON Bucks
146, 159 SP 7610 4m WSW of Aylesbury.
Loc, Dinton-w-Ford and Upton CP.

WESTLINTON Cumb
76 NY 3964 5m N of Carlisle. CP, 327.
Border RD. Penrith and the Bdr CC. See
also Blackford.

WEST LITTLETON Glos
156 ST 7675 7m N of Bath. Loc,
Tormarton CP. Ch e.

WEST LOOE Cornwall
186 SX 2553 7m S of Liskeard. See Looe.

WEST LULWORTH Dorset
178 SY 8280 7m SW of Wareham.
CP, 1,054. Wrhm and Purbeck RD. P Wrhm.
Ch e. Sch pe. S Dst CC. To S, L. Cove,
famous beauty spot.

WEST LUTTON Yorks (E)
93 SE 9469 9m ESE of Malton. Loc,
Lttns CP. Norton RD. P Mltn. Ch e, m.
Sch p. Howden CC.

WEST LYDFORD Som
165, 166 ST 5631 6m SE of Glastonbury.
Loc, Ldfd CP. Shepton Mallet RD. Ch e, m.
Sch pe. Wells CC.

WEST MALLING Kent
171 TQ 6757 5m WNW of Maidstone.
CP, 2,488. Mllng RD. P Mdstne.
Ch e, b, m, r. Sch pe. Tonbridge and
Mllng CC (Sevenoaks). To S, St Leonard's
Twr (A.M.); rems of Nmn keep.

WEST MALVERN Worcs
143 SO 7646 just W of Malvern. Loc,
Mlvn UD. P Mlvn.

WEST MARDEN Sussex (W)
181 SU 7713 6m NNE of Havant. Loc,
Compton CP. Ch v.

WEST MARKHAM Notts
112 SK 7272 5m S of Retford. CP, 112.
E Rtfd RD. Ch e. Bassetlaw CC. See also
Milton.

WEST MARTON Yorks (W)
95 SD 8950 6m W of Skipton. Loc, Mtns
Both CP. Skptn RD. P Skptn. Skptn CC.

WEST MEON Hants
168, 181 SU 6424 7m W of Petersfield.
CP, 726. Droxford RD. P Ptrsfld. Ch e, m.
Sch pe. Ptrsfld CC.

WEST MERSEA Essex
149, 162 TM 0112 8m S of Colchester.
UD, 4,131. P Clchstr. Clchstr CC. On M.
Island, linked to mainland by sometimes
flooded causeway, the 'Strood'. Holiday
caravans, chalets, amusements.

WESTMESTON Sussex (E)
182 TQ 3313 5m WNW of Lewes. CP, 277.
Chailey RD. Ch e. Lws CC.

WEST MIDDLETON Co Durham
85 NZ 3611 5m ESE of Darlington. Loc,
Mddltn St George CP.

WESTMILL Herts
148 TL 3627 8m N of Ware. CP, 246.
Braughing RD. P Buntingford. Ch e. Sch pe.
E Herts CC.

WEST MILTON Dorset
177 SY 5096 3m NE of Bridport. Loc,
Powerstock CP. P Brdpt. Ch e, m.

WESTMINSTER London
160, 170 TQ 2979. Central Lndn. LB(City
of Wstmnstr), 225,632. BCs: The City of
Lndn and Wstmnstr S, Paddington,
St Marylebone (The Cities of Lndn and
Wstmnstr, Pddngton N, Pddngtn S,
St Mrlbne). See also Bayswater, Belgravia,
Maida Vale, Pddngtn, Pimlico, St John's Wd,
St Mrlbne. At the heart of Wstmnstr are the
Abbey, Hses of Parliament, Whitehall
leading to Trafalgar Square.

WEST MOLESEY Surrey
170 TQ 1368 2m NE of Walton-on-Thames.
Loc, Esher UD. P: E Mlsy.

WEST MONKTON Som
177 ST 2628 3m NE of Taunton. CP, 1,697.
Tntn RD. P Tntn. Ch e, v2. Sch pe, s.
Tntn CC. See also Bathpool, Mnktn
Heathfield.

WEST MOORS Dorset
179 SU 0703 5m WSW of Ringwood.
CP, 2,947. Wimborne and Cranborne RD.
P Wmbne. Ch e, v. Sch pe. N Dst CC.

WEST NESS Yorks (N)
92 SE 6879 6m ESE of Helmsley. Loc,
Nss CP. Kirkbymoorside RD. Ch m. Thirsk
and Malton CC.

WESTNEWTON Cumb
82 NY 1344 8m NE of Maryport. CP, 223.
Wigton RD. P Carlisle. Ch e, m. Sch pe.
Penrith and the Border CC.

WEST NEWTON Norfolk
124 TF 6927 7m NE of King's Lynn. Loc,
Sandringham CP. P K's Lnn. Ch e. Sch pe.
Sndrnghm estate vllge.

WESTNEWTON Nthmb
64, 71 NT 9030 6m WNW of Wooler. Loc,
Kirknewton CP. Ch e.

WEST NEWTON Yorks (E)
99 TA 1937 6m S of Hornsea. Loc, Burton
Constable CP.

WEST OGWELL Devon
176, 188 SX 8270 3m WSW of Newton
Abbot. Loc, Ogwll CP. Ch e. Ch and mnr
hse.

WESTON Ches
100, 109 SJ 5080 1m S of Runcorn. Loc,
Rncn UD. P Rncn. To S, chemical wks at
Rocksavage.

WESTON Ches
110 SJ 7352 3m SE of Crewe. CP, 570.
Nantwich RD. P Crwe. Ch e, m3. Sch p.
Crwe CC.

WESTON Dorset
178 SV 6871 on Isle of Portland, S of
Weymouth. Loc, Portland UD. P Ptlnd.

WESTON Hants
181 SU 7321 1m SW of Petersfield. Loc,
Buriton CP.

WESTON Herts
147 TL 2530 2m SSE of Baldock. CP, 921.
Hitchin RD. P Htchn. Ch e, m. Sch pe.
Htchn CC. See also Hall's Grn. Ch has Nmn
crossing.

WESTON Lincs (H)
123 TF 2923 3m ENE of Spalding.
CP, 1,364. Spldng RD. P Spldng. Ch e, m.
Sch pe. Holland w Boston CC. See also Wstn
Hills.

WESTON Northants
145, 146 SP 5946 6m N of Brackley.
CP(Wstn and Weedon), 294. Towcester RD.
P Tcstr. Ch b. Daventry CC (S Nthnts). See
also Plumpton, Wdn Lois.

WESTON Notts
112 SK 7767 7m E of Ollerton. CP, 269.
Southwell RD. P Newark. Ch e, m. Nwk CC.

WESTON Shrops
118 SJ 5628 3m E of Wem.
CP(Wstn-under-Redcastle), 289.
N Shrops RD. P Shrewsbury. Ch e. Sch pe.
Oswestry CC.

WESTON Staffs
119 SJ 9727 4m ENE of Stafford. CP, 308.
Stffd RD. P STFFD. Ch e, m. Sch pe. Stffd
and Stone CC.

WESTON Yorks (W)
96 SE 1747 2m WNW of Otley. CP, 75.
Wharfedale RD. Ch e. Ripon CC.

WESTON BAMPFYLDE Som
166 ST 6124 6m NNW of Sherborne. Loc,
Sparkford CP. Ch e.

WESTON BEGGARD Herefs
142 SO 5841 5m E of Hereford. CP, 210.
Hrfd RD. Ch e. Leominster CC. See also
Shucknall.

WESTONBIRT Glos
156 ST 8589 3m SW of Tetbury. CP(Wstnbt
w Lasborough), 226. Ttbry RD. Ch e.
Stroud CC. Wstnbt Hse, now a girls' sch, was
blt in Elizn style in Vctrn times for R.S.
Holford. Arboretum*, also orig Holford's,
now in Forestry Commission estate.

WESTON BY WELLAND Northants
133 SP 7791 4m NE of Mkt Harborough.
CP, 91. Kettering RD. P Mkt Hbrgh, Leics.
Ch e. Kttrng CC.

WESTON COLVILLE Cambs
148 TL 6153 6m NW of Haverhill. CP, 348.
S Cambs RD. P CAMBRIDGE. Ch e, m.
Sch p. Cambs CC. See also Wstn Grn.

WESTON CORBETT Hants
169 SU 6846 4m SE of Basingstoke. CP, 32.
Bsngstke RD. Bsngstke CC.

WESTON FAVELL Northants
133 SP 7862 2m ENE of Northampton.
Loc, Nthmptn CB. P NTHMPTN.
Nthmptn S BC (S Nthnts CC).

WESTON GREEN Cambs
148 TL 6252 5m NW of Haverhill. Loc,
Wstn Colville CP.

WESTON HEATH Shrops
119 SJ 7713 4m SSE of Newport. Loc,
Sheriffhales CP.

WESTON HILLS Lincs (H)
123 TF 2821 2m E of Spalding. Loc,
Wstn CP. P Spldng. Ch e, m2. Sch pe.

WESTONING Beds
147 TL 0332 3m S of Ampthill. CP, 792.
Ampthll RD. P BEDFORD. Ch e, b, m.
Sch p. Mid-Beds CC.

WESTON-IN-GORDANO Som
155, 165 ST 4474 9m W of Bristol. CP, 165.
Long Ashton RD. P BRSTL. Ch e.
N Som CC.

WESTON JONES Staffs
119 SJ 7624 3m NNE of Newport. Loc,
Norbury CP.

WESTON LONGVILLE Norfolk
125 TG 1115 9m NW of Norwich. CP, 317.
St Faith's and Aylsham RD.
P NRWCH, NOR 59X. Ch e. Sch pe.
N Nflk CC (Central Nflk). Ch: 14c
wall-paintings. Home of Parson Woodforde,
the 18c diarist.

WESTON LULLINGFIELDS Shrops
118 SJ 4224 6m WSW of Wem. Loc,
Baschurch CP. P Shrewsbury. Ch e. Sch pe.

WESTON-ON-AVON Warwicks
144 SP 1551 3m WSW of Stratford.
CP, 107. Strtfd-on-Avon RD. Ch e.
Strtfd-on-Avn CC (Strtfd).

WESTON-ON-THE-GREEN Oxon
145 SP 5318 4m SW of Bicester. CP, 437.
Ploughley RD. Ch e, m. Sch i. Mid-Oxon CC
(Henley). Stocks on grn. Sundial on wall of
old inn.

WESTON PATRICK Hants
169 SU 6946 5m SE of Basingstoke. CP, 82.
Bsngstke RD. Ch e. Bsngstke CC.

WESTON RHYN Shrops
118 SJ 2835 4m N of Oswestry. CP, 1,934.
Oswstry RD. P Oswstry. Ch e, m4. Sch p.
Oswstry CC. See also Preesgweene. 1m N,
two viaducts side by side carry rly and
canal over R Dee into Wales. To E, Moreton
Hall, 17c brick hse, now part of girls'
boarding sch.

WESTON SUBEDGE Glos
144 SP 1240 2m NW of Chipping Campden.
CP, 572. N Cotswold RD. P Chppng Cmpdn.
Ch e. Sch pe. Cirencester and
Tewkesbury CC.

WESTON-SUPER-MARE Som
165 ST 3261 18m WSW of Bristol.
MB, 50,794. P. W-s-M CC. See also Uphill,
Worle. Resort. Many amenities; mild
climate. To N on headland, Worlebury
Camp, Iron Age fort.

WESTON TURVILLE Bucks
146, 159 SP 8510 3m SE of Aylesbury.
CP, 1,681. Aylesbury RD. P Aylesbury.
Ch e, bv. Sch pe. Aylesbury CC.

WESTON-UNDER-LIZARD Staffs
119 SJ 8010 4m ENE of Shifnal. CP, 294.
Cannock RD. P Shfnl, Salop. Ch e. Sch pe.
SW Staffs CC (Cnnck). On A5 rd. Wstn Pk*,
17c hse in large pk laid out by Capability
Brown.

WESTON UNDER PENYARD Herefs
142, 143 SO 6323 2m E of Ross-on-Wye.
CP, 714. Rss and Whitchurch RD.
P Rss-on-Wye. Ch e, b. Sch pe. Hereford CC.
See also Pontshill. Site of Roman tn. Partly
Nmn ch. To NE, Bollitree Cstle, 17c hse
with 18c 'Gothic' outbuildings.

WESTON UNDER WETHERLEY Warwicks
132 SP 3669 4m NE of Leamington.
CP, 429. Warwick RD. Ch e. Wrwck and
Lmngtn CC.

WESTON UNDERWOOD Bucks
146 SP 8650 2m WSW of Olney. CP, 218.
Newport Pagnell RD. P Olney. Ch e.
Buckingham CC. Home of the poet Cowper
from 1786 to 1795.

WESTON UNDERWOOD Derbys
120, 121 SK 2942 6m NW of Derby.
CP, 253. Belper RD. P DBY. Sch pe.
Blpr CC. See also Mugginton.

WESTON UPON TRENT Derbys
121 SK 4028 6m SSE of Derby. CP, 875.
SE Derbys RD. P DBY. Ch e, b, m. Sch pe.
SE Derbys CC.

WESTONZOYLAND Som
165 ST 3534 4m ESE of Bridgwater.
CP, 763. Brdgwtr RD. P Brdgwtr. Ch e, m.
Sch p. Brdgwtr CC. 14c–15c ch has
impressive twr of over 100ft and richly
carved nave roof. Monmouth's men
imprisoned here after Battle of
Sedgemoor, 1685. Battlefield just N of vllge.

WEST ORCHARD Dorset
178 ST 8216 5m SSW of Shaftesbury.
CP, 57. Shftsbry RD. Ch e. N Dst CC.

WEST OVERTON Wilts
157 SU 1368 4m W of Marlborough.
CP, 471. Mlbrgh and Ramsbury RD. Ch e.
Sch pe. Devizes CC. See also Lockeridge.

WESTOW Yorks (E)
92 SE 7565 4m SSW of Malton. CP, 257.
Norton RD. P YORK. Ch e, m. Sch pe.
Howden CC.

WEST PANSON Devon
174 SX 3491 4m N of Launceston. Loc,
St Giles on the Hth CP.

WEST PARLEY Dorset
179 SZ 0897 4m N of Bournemouth.
CP, 2,002. Wimborne and Cranborne RD.
Ch e, c. N Dst CC. See also Parley Cross.

WEST PECKHAM Kent
171 TQ 6452 5m NE of Tonbridge.
CP, 327. Malling RD. P Mdstne. Ch e.
Tnbrdge and Mllng CC (Sevenoaks).

WEST PELTON Co Durham
78 NZ 2353 3m WNW of Chester-le-Street.
Loc, Chstr-le-Strt RD. P Stanley. Ch m2.
Chstr-le-Strt CC.

WEST PENNARD Som
165, 166 ST 5438 3m E of Glastonbury.
CP, 562. Wells RD. P Glstnbry. Ch e.
Sch pe. Wlls CC. 1m SW, Ct Barn (NT)*,
15c barn with interesting roof.

WEST PENTIRE Cornwall
185 SW 7760 2m WSW of Newquay. Loc,
Nquay UD.

WESTPORT Som
177 ST 3819 4m NNE of Ilminster. Loc,
Langport RD. Ch v. Yeovil CC.

WEST PUTFORD Devon
174 SS 3515 8m N of Holsworthy. CP, 185.
Hlswthy RD. Ch e, m. Sch p. W Dvn CC
(Tavistock).

WEST QUANTOXHEAD Som
164 ST 1141 3m ESE of Watchet. CP, 366.
Williton RD. P Taunton. Ch e.
Bridgwater CC. St Audries, large Vctrn Tdr
mansion (now a sch), gives its name to the
bay.

WEST RAINTON Co Durham
85 NZ 3246 4m NE of Durham. CP, 2,205.
Drhm RD. P Houghton-le-Spring. Ch e, s, v.
Drhm CC. See also Leamside.

WEST RASEN Lincs (L)
104 TF 0689 3m W of Mkt Rasen. CP, 167.
Caistor RD. P Mkt Rsn. Ch e.
Gainsborough CC. Packhorse br. Thatched
post office.

WEST RAYNHAM Norfolk
125 TF 8725 4m SW of Fakenham. Loc,
Rnhm CP. Walsingham RD. P Fknhm. Ch m.
Sch pe. NW Nflk CC (N Nflk). To E, Rnhm
Hall, 17c, seat of Townshend family.

WEST ROUNTON Yorks (N)
91 NZ 4103 7m NNE of Northallerton.
CP, 145. Nthlltn RD. Ch e, m.
Richmond CC.

WEST ROW Suffolk (W)
135 TL 6775 8m NNE of Newmarket. Loc,
Mildenhall CP. P Bury St Edmunds. Ch b.
Bury St Eds CC.

WEST RUDHAM Norfolk
125 TF 8227 7m WSW of Fakenham.
CP, 257. Docking RD. Ch e. NW Nflk CC
(King's Lynn).

WEST RUNTON Norfolk
126 TG 1842 1m E of Sheringham. Loc,
Rntn CP. Erpingham RD. P Cromer.
Ch e, m. N Nflk CC.

WESTRY Cambs
135 TL 3998 2m NW of March. Loc, Mch UD.

WEST SCRAFTON Yorks (N)
90 SE 0783 4m SW of Middleham. CP, 51. Leyburn RD. Ch m. Richmond CC.

WEST SLEEKBURN Nthmb
78 NZ 2885 5m E of Morpeth. Loc, Bedlingtonshire UD. Blyth BC.

WEST SOMERTON Norfolk
126 TG 4619 8m NNW of Yarmouth. Loc, Smtn CP. Blofield and Flegg RD. P Gt Ymth. Ch e. Sch p. Ymth CC.

WEST STAFFORD Dorset
178 SY 7289 2m E of Dorchester. CP, 157. Dchstr RD. P Dchstr. Ch e. W Dst CC.

WEST STOCKWITH Notts
104 SK 7994 3m NNW of Gainsborough. CP, 362. E Retford RD. P Doncaster, Yorkshire. Ch e, m3. Bassetlaw CC. Trentside vllge looking across to E Stckwth and Lincs.

WEST STOKE Sussex (W)
181 SU 8308 3m NW of Chichester. Loc, Funtington CP. Ch e.

WEST STOUGHTON Som
165 ST 4149 4m SW of Cheddar. Loc, Wedmore CP.

WEST STOUR Dorset
166 ST 7822 5m W of Shaftesbury. CP, 142. Shftsbry RD. Ch e. N Dst CC.

WEST STOURMOUTH Kent
173 TR 2562 6m NW of Sandwich. Loc, Stmth CP. Eastry RD. Ch e. Dover and Deal CC (Dvr).

WEST STOW Suffolk (W)
136 TF 8170 5m NNW of Bury St Edmunds. CP, 159. Thingoe RD. Ch e. Bury St Eds CC.

WEST STOWELL Wilts
167 SU 1362 2m NW of Pewsey. Loc, Alton CP. Psy RD. Devizes CC.

WEST TANFIELD Yorks (N)
91 SE 2678 5m NNW of Ripon. CP, 489. Bedale RD. P Rpn. Ch e, m. Sch pe. Thirsk and Malton CC. See also Binsoe, Nosterfield,

Thornborough. On N bank of R Ure. Marmion gatehouse all that survives of 15c cstle.

WEST TAPHOUSE Cornwall
186 SX 1563 4m NE of Lostwithiel. Loc, Broadoak CP.

WEST THIRSTON Nthmb
71 NU 1800 8m S of Alnwick. Loc, Thstn CP. Morpeth RD. Ch v. Mpth CC.

WEST THORNEY Sussex (W)
181 SU 7602 4m SE of Havant. CP, 1,124. Chichester RD. Ch e. Chchstr CC. Next to airfield on Thny Island, jutting out into Chchstr Harbour. Ch has 11c bell, oldest in Sussex.

WEST THURROCK Essex
161, 171 TQ 5877 4m W of Tilbury. Loc, Thrrck UD. P Grays. Thrrck BC (CC). Large modern power stn. Factories. Quarries.

WEST TILBURY Essex
161, 171 TQ 6677 2m NE of Tilbury. Loc, Thurrock UD. P Grays. Thrrck BC (CC).

WEST TISTED Hants
168, 169, 181 SU 6529 7m NW of Petersfield. CP, 199. Alton RD. P Alresford. Ch e. Ptrsfld CC.

WEST TOFTS Norfolk
136 TL 8392 5m NE of Brandon. Loc, Lynford CP. Swaffham RD. Ch e, r. SW Nflk CC. In Battle Sch area. RC ch in isolated position 1¼m W.

WEST TORRINGTON Lincs (L)
104 TF 1382 5m SSE of Mkt Rasen. CP, 104. Horncastle RD. P LINCOLN. Ch e. Hncstle CC.

WEST TOWN Som
155, 165 ST 4868 7m WSW of Bristol. Loc, Backwell CP.

WEST TYTHERLEY Hants
167 SU 2729 7m NW of Romsey. CP, 636. Rmsy and Stockbridge RD. P Salisbury, Wilts. Ch e, m. Sch pe. Winchester CC.

WEST TYTHERTON Wilts
157 ST 9474 2m E of Chippenham. Loc, Pewsham CP. Ch e.

WEST WALTON Norfolk
124 TF 4713 2m NNE of Wisbech.
CP, 1,196. Marshland RD. P Wsbch,
Cambs. Ch e, m. Sch p, s. NW Nflk CC
(King's Lynn). See also W Wltn Highway.
13c ch: detached twr; 13c wall-paintings.

WEST WALTON HIGHWAY Norfolk
124 TF 4913 3m NE of Wisbech. Loc,
W Wltn CP. Ch m.

WESTWARD Cumb
82 NY 2744 2m SSE of Wigton. CP, 799.
Wgtn RD. Ch e. Penrith and the Border CC.
See also Red Dial, Rosley, W Curthwaite.

WESTWARD HO! Devon
163 SS 4329 2m NW of Bideford. Loc,
Northam UD. P Bdfd. Named after novel by
Charles Kingsley. To N, long stretch of sand;
Nthm Burrows.

WESTWELL Kent
172, 184 TQ 9947 3m SE of Charing.
CP, 942. W Ashford RD. P Ashfd. Ch e.
Ashfd CC. See also Ram Lane.

WESTWELL Oxon
144/157 SP 2209 8m W of Witney. CP, 86.
Wtny RD. Ch e. Mid-Oxon CC (Banbury).
Old Cotswold mnr hse; gdns*.

WESTWELL LEACON Kent
172, 184 TQ 9647 1m SSE of Charing. Loc,
Chrng CP.

WEST WELLOW Hants
180 SU 2919 4m WSW of Romsey. Loc,
Wllw CP. Rmsy and Stockbridge RD.
P Rmsy. Ch e, m3, v. Sch pe.
Eastleigh CC (Winchester).

WESTWICK Cambs
135 TL 4265 5m NNW of Cambridge.
CP, 37. Chesterton RD. Cambs CC.

WESTWICK Norfolk
126 TG 2726 2m SSW of N Walsham.
CP, 128. Smallburgh RD. Ch e. N Nflk CC.

WEST WICKHAM Cambs
148 TL 6149 4m NW of Haverhill. CP, 333.
S Cambs RD. P CAMBRIDGE. Ch e, s.
Sch pe. Cambs CC.

WEST WICKHAM London
171 TQ 3965 2m S of Bromley. Loc,

Brmly LB. P Kent. Ravensbourne BC
(Beckenham).

WEST WINCH Norfolk
124 TF 6316 3m S of King's Lynn.
CP, 1,136. Freebridge Lynn RD. P K's Lnn.
Ch e, m. Sch p. NW Nflk CC (K's Lnn). See
also Setchey.

WEST WITTERING Sussex (W)
181 SZ 7898 6m SW of Chichester.
CP, 1,719. Chchstr RD. P Chchstr.
Ch e, m, r. Sch pe. Chchstr CC. See also
Acre St. Blt-up area at W end of Selsey
peninsula.

WEST WITTON Yorks (N)
90 SE 0688 4m WSW of Leyburn. CP, 329.
Lbn RD. P Lbn. Ch e, m. Sch p.
Richmond CC. See also Swinithwaite.

WESTWOOD Devon
176 SY 0198 7m NE of Exeter. Loc, Broad
Clyst CP. Ch e. NT vllge.

WESTWOOD Wilts
166 ST 8159 3m WNW of Trowbridge.
CP, 771. Bradford and Melksham RD.
Ch e, m. Sch p. Westbury CC. Ch: Perp twr;
15c E window. Wstwd Mnr (NT)*, 15c–17c
hse with gt hall; topiary work in gdn.

WEST WOODBURN Nthmb
77 NY 8986 4m ENE of Bellingham. Loc,
Corsenside CP. Bllnghm RD. P Hexham.
Ch m, v. Hexham CC.

WEST WOODHAY Berks
168 SU 3963 5m SE of Hungerford.
CP, 127. Hngrfd RD. Ch e. Newbury CC.

WEST WOODLANDS Som
166 ST 7744 2m S of Frome. Loc,
Selwood CP. Frme RD. Ch m. Wells CC.

WESTWOODSIDE Lincs (L)
103/104 SK 7599 7m NNW of
Gainsborough. Loc, Haxey CP. P Doncaster,
Yorkshire. Ch m. Sch pe.

WEST WORLDHAM Hants
169 SU 7538 2m ESE of Alton. Loc,
Wldhm CP. Altn RD. Ch e. Petersfield CC.

WEST WORLINGTON Devon
163, 175 SS 7713 9m SSE of S Molton.
Loc, E Wlngtn CP. Ch e.

WEST WRATTING Cambs
148 TL 6052 6m NW of Haverhill. CP, 404.
S Cambs RD. P CAMBRIDGE. Ch e. Sch pe.
Cambs CC.

WEST WYLAM Nthmb
77, 78 NZ 1063 just E of Prudhoe. Loc,
Prdhoe UD. P(W Wlm Colliery), Prdhoe.

WEST YOULSTONE Cornwall
174 SS 2615 7m NNE of Bude. Loc,
Morwenstow CP.

WETHERAL Cumb
76 NY 4654 4m E of Carlisle. CP, 3,852.
Border RD. P Clsle. Ch e, m. Sch j. Penrith
and the Bdr CC. See also Cotehill,
Cumwhinton, Gt Corby, Scotby, Warwick,
Wrwck Br. Priory gatehouse, 15c, S of ch.
Down by river, three man-made caves. To S,
W. Woods, NT.

WETHERBY Yorks (W)
97 SE 4048 8m SE of Harrogate. CP, 4,179.
Wthrby RD. P. Ch e, m, r. Sch p, pe, s.
Barkston Ash CC. Mkt tn. Racecourse.

WETHERDEN Suffolk (E)
136 TM 0062 4m NW of Stowmarket.
CP, 431. Gipping RD. P Stmkt. Ch e, b.
Sch pe. Eye CC. Ch has double
hammerbeam angel roof.

WETHERINGSETT Suffolk (E)
136 TM 1266 4m SSW of Eye.
CP(Wthrngstt-cum-Brockford), 592.
Hartismere RD. P Stowmarket. Ch e.
Sch pe. Eye CC. See also Brckfd St,
Wetherup St. Thatched cottages. 14c ch.
TV mast.

WETHERSFIELD Essex
148, 149 TL 7131 6m NW of Braintree.
CP, 2,774. Brntree RD. P Brntree. Ch e, c, v.
Sch pe. Brntree CC (Maldon). See also
Beazley End, Blackmore End. 1m N,
Wthrsfld RAF/US air base.

WETHERUP STREET Suffolk (E)
136 TM 1464 6m NE of Stowmarket. Loc,
Wetheringsett-cum-Brockford CP. P(Wthrp),
Stmkt.

WETLEY ROCKS Staffs
110 SJ 9649 5m SSW of Leek. Loc,
Cheadle RD. P Stoke-on-Trent. Ch e, m.
Sch pe. Lk CC.

WETTENHALL Ches
110 SJ 6261 4m SW of Winsford. CP, 137.
Nantwich RD. Ch e, m. Nntwch CC.

WETTON Staffs
111 SK 1055 7m NW of Ashbourne.
CP, 200. Leek RD. P Ashbne, Derbyshire.
Ch e, m. Sch pe. Lk CC. In limestone hills of
Peak Distr National Pk; caves in valley of
R Manifold to W.

WETWANG Yorks (E)
98 SE 9359 6m WNW of Driffield. CP, 401.
Drffld RD. P Drffld. Ch e, m. Sch pe.
Howden CC.

WETWOOD Staffs
110, 119 SJ 7733 6m E of Mkt Drayton.
Loc, Eccleshall CP. P STAFFORD. ½m NW
along B5026, Broughton Ch, 17c Gothic:
font, glass, box pews. Hall, across rd, Elizn,
half-timbered.

WEXCOMBE Wilts
167 SU 2759 7m SSW of Hungerford. Loc,
Grafton CP. Marlborough and
Ramsbury RD. Ch m. Devizes CC.

WEYBOURNE Norfolk
125 TG 1143 3m W of Sheringham.
CP, 403. Erpingham RD. P Holt. Ch e, m.
N Nflk CC. Anti-aircraft gunnery range.

WEYBREAD Suffolk (E)
137 TM 2480 8m SW of Bungay. CP, 389.
Hartismere RD. P Diss, Norfolk. Ch e.
Eye CC.

WEYBRIDGE Surrey
170 TQ 0864 2m SW of Walton-on-Thames.
UD(Wltn and Wbrdge), 51,004. P. Chertsey
and Wltn BC (Esher CC). Rsndtl distr.

WEYHILL Hants
168 SU 3146 3m WNW of Andover. Loc,
Penton Grafton CP. P Andvr. Ch e. Sch pe.
Formerly famous for its fair, described by
Hardy in *The Mayor of Casterbridge.*

WEYMOUTH Dorset
178 SY 6779 26m WSW of Bournemouth.
MB(Wmth and Melcombe Regis), 42,332.
P(Wmth). S Dst CC. See also Broadwey,
Preston, Upwey, Wyke Regis. Port for
Channel Islands. Developed as resort in 18c,
when patronized by George III. Ggn centre
with 19c and 20c accretions.

WHADDON Bucks
146 SP 8034 4m W of Bletchley. CP, 347.
Winslow RD. P Bltchly. Ch e, c. Sch pe.
Buckingham CC. Centre of W. Chase,
formerly a forest.

WHADDON Cambs
147 TL 3446 3m N of Royston. CP, 413.
S Cambs RD. P Rstn, Herts. Ch e, m.
Cambs CC.

WHADDON Glos
143 SO 8313 3m S of Gloucester.
CP(Brookthorpe-w-Whddn), 302. Glcstr RD.
Ch e. Stroud CC.

WHADDON Wilts
167 SU 1926 4m SE of Salisbury. Loc,
Alderbury CP. Ch e.

WHALEY Derbys
112 SK 5171 7m NNW of Mansfield. Loc,
Bolsover UD.

WHALEY BRIDGE Derbys
111 SK 0181 6m NNW of Buxton.
UD, 5,232. P Stockport, Cheshire. High
Peak CC. See also Fernilee, Furness Vale,
Taxal. Textile tn. The Gate Inn has curious
sign (cf. Weaverham, Ches.)

WHALEY THORNS Derbys
112 SK 5371 6m N of Mansfield. Loc,
Scarcliffe CP. P Langwith, Mnsfld, Notts.
Ch e, m. Sch p, s.

WHALLEY Lancs
95 SD 7336 4m SSW of Clitheroe.
CP, 3,905. Clthroe RD. P Blackburn.
Ch e, m, r. Sch pe, s. Clthroe CC. Rems of
13c abbey.

WHALTON Nthmb
78 NZ 1381 5m SW of Morpeth. CP, 453.
Cstle Ward RD. P Mpth. Ch e. Hexham CC.
See also Ogle. Stone hses and greens. Four
hses converted into mnr hse by Lutyens,
1908. (Gdns*.) Ch 12c and later. Custom of
Burning the Bale on July 4th.

WHAPLODE Lincs (H)
123 TF 3224 2m W of Holbeach. CP, 2,452.
E Elloe RD. P Spalding. Ch e, m4. Sch p, pc.
Holland w Boston CC. See also Saracen's
Head.

WHAPLODE DROVE Lincs (H)
123 TF 3113 7m SE of Spalding. Loc,
Whplde CP. P Spldng. Ch e, m2.

WHARFE Yorks (W)
90 SD 7869 4m NNW of Settle. Loc,
Austwick CP.

WHARLES Lancs
94 SD 4435 7m NW of Preston. CP(Treales,
Roseacre and Whls), 348. Fylde RD.
S Flde CC.

WHARNCLIFFE SIDE Yorks (W)
102 SK 2994 6m NW of Sheffield. Loc,
Bradfield CP. P SHFFLD. Ch m. Sch p.

WHARRAM LE STREET Yorks (E)
92 SE 8666 6m SE of Malton. Loc,
Whrrm CP. Norton RD. P(Whrrm), Mltn.
Ch e. Howden CC.

WHARRAM PERCY Yorks (E)
92, 98 SE 8564 7m SE of Malton. Loc,
Whrrm CP. Norton RD. Ch e. Howden CC.
Partly Saxon ch belongs to lost vllge.

WHARTON Ches
110 SJ 6666 just E of Winsford. Loc,
Wnsfd UD. P Wnsfd.

WHASHTON Yorks (N)
85 NZ 1506 4m NNW of Richmond. CP, 92.
Rchmnd RD. Ch m. Rchmnd CC.

WHATCOMBE Dorset
178 ST 8301 4m SW of Blandford. Loc,
Winterborne Whitechurch CP.

WHATCOTE Warwicks
145 SP 2944 4m NE of Shipston on Stour.
CP, 84. Shpstn on Str RD. Ch e, m.
Stratford-on-Avon CC (Strtfd).

WHATFIELD Suffolk (W)
149 TM 0246 2m N of Hadleigh. CP, 283.
Cosford RD. P Ipswich. Ch e, s, v. Sch pe.
Sudbury and Woodbridge CC.

WHATLEY Som
166 ST 7347 3m W of Frome. CP, 158.
Frme RD. P Frme. Ch e. Wells CC. See also
Chantry.

WHATLINGTON Sussex (E)
184 TQ 7618 2m NNE of Battle. CP, 333.
Bttle RD. P Bttle. Ch e. Rye CC.

WHATSTANDWELL Derbys
111 SK 3354 4m N of Belper. Loc,
Crich CP. P Matlock. Ch m.

WHATTON Notts
112, 122 SK 7439 11m E of Nottingham.

CP, 318. Bingham RD. P NTTNGHM.
Ch e, m. Rushcliffe CC (Carlton).

WHEATACRE Norfolk
137 TM 4693 3m NE of Beccles. CP, 113.
Loddon RD. Ch e. Sch p. S Nflk CC.

WHEATCROFT Derbys
111 SK 3557 4m ESE of Matlock. Loc,
Crich CP. Ch m.

WHEATFIELD Oxon
159 SU 6899 4m SSW of Thame. CP, 33.
Bullingdon RD. Ch e. Henley CC.
'Georgianised' mdvl ch in pk of Whtfld Hse,
burnt down 1814.

WHEATHAMPSTEAD Herts
147, 160 TL 1713 3m E of Harpenden.
CP, 4,175. St Albans RD. P St Albns.
Ch e, c, m, r. Sch pe, s. St Albns CC. See
also Marshall's Hth.

WHEATHILL Shrops
129, 130 SO 6282 8m NE of Ludlow.
CP, 217. Ldlw RD. Ch e. Ldlw CC. See also
Loughton, Silvington.

WHEATHILL Som
165, 166 ST 5830 7m WSW of Bruton. Loc,
Lovington CP. Ch e.

WHEATLEY Hants
169 SU 7840 4m E of Alton. Loc,
Binsted CP.

WHEATLEY Oxon
158 SP 5905 5m E of Oxford. CP, 2,208.
Bullingdon RD. P OXFD. Ch e, c. Sch pe, s.
Mid-Oxon CC (Henley). Conical lock-up in
corner of recreation grnd.

WHEATLEY HILL Co Durham
85 NZ 3739 4m WSW of Peterlee. Loc,
Wingate CP. P DRHM. Ch e, m, r. Sch p, s.

WHEATLEY LANE Lancs
95 SD 8338 1m W of Nelson. Loc,
Barrowford UD, Burnley RD. Nelson and
Colne BC, Clitheroe CC.

WHEATON ASTON Staffs
119 SJ 8512 7m ENE of Shifnal. Loc,
Lapley CP. P STAFFORD. Ch e, c, m.
Sch pe.

WHEDDON CROSS Som
164 SS 9238 5m SW of Minehead. Loc,
Cutcombe CP. P Mnhd. Ch m.

WHEELER'S GREEN Berks
169 SU 7672 3m E of Reading. Loc,
Woodley and Sandford CP.

WHEELERSTREET Surrey
169 SU 9440 3m SW of Godalming. Loc,
Witley CP.

WHEELOCK Ches
100 SJ 7559 4m NE of Crewe. Loc,
Sandbach UD. P Sndbch.

WHEELTON Lancs
94, 95 SD 6021 2m NNE of Chorley.
CP, 937. Chly RD. P Chly. Ch m. Sch p.
Chly CC. See also Hr Whltn.

WHELDRAKE Yorks (E)
97, 98 SE 6844 7m SE of York. CP, 451.
Derwent RD. P YK. Ch e, m. Sch pe.
Howden CC.

WHELFORD Glos
157 SU 1698 9m E of Cirencester. Loc,
Kempsford CP. Ch e.

WHELPLEYHILL Bucks
159, 160 SP 9904 2m S of Berkhamsted.
Loc, Ashley Grn CP. P Chesham. Sch p.

WHENBY Yorks (N)
92 SE 6369 12m NNE of York. CP, 64.
Easingwold RD. Ch e. Thirsk and Malton CC.

WHEPSTEAD Suffolk (W)
136 TL 8358 4m SSW of Bury St Edmunds.
CP, 357. Thingoe RD. P Bury St Eds.
Ch e, b. Sch p. Bury St Eds CC.

WHERSTEAD Suffolk (E)
150 TM 1540 3m S of Ipswich. CP, 379.
Samford RD. Ch e. Sudbury and
Woodbridge CC. Whstd Pk, late 18c, now
HQ of Eastern Electricity Board.

WHERWELL Hants
168 SU 3840 3m SSE of Andover. CP, 480.
Andvr RD. P Andvr. Ch e, m. Sch p.
Winchester CC (Basingstoke). See also
Fullerton.

WHESTON Derbys
111 SK 1376 5m ENE of Buxton. CP, 37.
Bakewell RD. W Derbys CC. To W of Hall,
complete mdvl vllge cross; height incl steps
over 11 ft.

WHETSTED Kent
171 TQ 6546 4m E of Tonbridge. Loc,
Capel CP.

WHETSTONE Leics
132, 133 SP 5597 5m SSW of Leicester.
CP, 1,460. Blaby RD. P LCSTR. Ch e, b, c.
Sch pe. Blby CC (Harborough).

WHICHAM Cumb
88 SD 1382 3m WNW of Millom. CP, 373.
Mllm RD. Ch e. Sch pe. Whitehaven CC. See
also Silecroft.

WHICHFORD Warwicks
145 SP 3134 5m N of Chipping Norton.
CP, 232. Shipston on Stour RD.
P Shpstn on Str. Ch e. Sch p.
Stratford-on-Avon CC (Strtfd).

WHICKHAM Co Durham
78 NZ 2061 3m W of Gateshead.
UD, 28,704. P NEWCASTLE UPON TYNE.
Blaydon BC(CC). See also Byermoor,
Marley Hill, Street Gate, Sunniside. To SW
in Snipes Dene Wood on Gibside estate,
monmt known as the 'Column of British
Liberty'.

WHIDDON DOWN Devon
175 SX 6992 7m ESE of Okehampton. Loc,
Okhmptn RD. P Okhmptn. Ch m.
W Dvn CC (Torrington).

WHILTON Northants
132, 133 SP 6364 4m ENE of Daventry.
CP, 171. Dvntry RD. P Dvntry. Ch e.
Dvntry CC (S Nthnts).

WHIMPLE Devon
176 SY 0497 8m ENE of Exeter. CP, 885.
St Thomas RD. P Extr. Ch e, c. Sch p.
Tiverton CC. Cider factory amid orchards.

WHIMPWELL GREEN Norfolk
126 TG 3829 6m E of N Walsham. Loc,
Happisburgh CP.

WHINBURGH Norfolk
125 TG 0009 3m SSE of E Dereham.
CP, 268. Mitford and Launditch RD.
P Drhm. Ch e, m. SW Nflk CC. See also
Westfield.

WHIPPINGHAM IOW
180 SZ 5193 1m SSE of E Cowes. Loc,
Cowes UD. P: E Cowes. Vctrn royal estate

vllge. Ch blt by Prince Albert and regularly
used by Queen Victoria.

WHIPSNADE Beds
147 TL 0017 2m S of Dunstable. CP, 574.
Luton RD. P Dnstble. Ch e. S Beds CC.
To S, on edge of Chilterns, W. Zoological
Pk*, branch of London Zoo; wild animals
given degree of freedom. Open daily.

WHIPTON Devon
176 SX 9493 E distr of Exeter. Loc,
Extr CB. P Extr.

WHISBY Lincs (K)
113 SK 9067 5m WSW of Lincoln.
CP(Doddington and Whsby), 352.
N Kesteven RD. Grantham CC.

WHISSENDINE Rutland
122 SK 8314 4m NNW of Oakham.
CP, 612. Oakhm RD. P Oakhm. Ch e, m.
Rtlnd and Stamford CC. Imposing 13c–15c
ch.

WHISSONSETT Norfolk
125 TF 9123 4m S of Fakenham. CP, 440.
Mitford and Launditch RD. P Dereham.
Ch e, m. Sch p. SW Nflk CC.

WHISTLEY GREEN Berks
159 SU 7974 5m E of Reading. Loc; St.
Nicholas, Hurst CP. Wokingham RD.
Wknghm CC.

WHISTON Lancs
100 SJ 4791 3m SW of St Helens.
CP, 10,535. Whstn RD. Ch e, m, v.
Sch p2, s, sb, sg, sr. Widnes CC.

WHISTON Northants
133 SP 8460 5m SSW of Wellingborough.
Loc, Cogenhoe CP. Ch e.

WHISTON Staffs
111 SK 0447 3m NE of Cheadle. Loc,
Kingsley CP. P Stoke-on-Trent. Ch e, m.
Sch pe.

WHISTON Staffs
119 SJ 8914 6m SSW of Stafford. Loc,
Penkridge CP.

WHISTON Yorks (W)
103 SK 4590 2m SE of Rotherham.
CP, 3,629. Rthrhm RD. P Rthrhm. Ch e, m.
Sch p. Rother Valley CC. See also Morthen.

WHITACRE HEATH Warwicks
131 SP 2192 3m NNE of Coleshill. Loc,
Nether Whtcre CP. P BIRMINGHAM.

WHITBOURNE Herefs
130 SO 7156 4m ENE of Bromyard.
CP, 472. Brmyd RD. P WORCESTER. Ch e.
Sch pe. Leominster CC.

WHITBURN Co Durham
78 NZ 4061 3m N of Sunderland. Loc,
Boldon UD. P Sndrlnd. Has a green shaded
by two rows of trees.

WHITBURN COLLIERY Co Durham
78 NZ 4063 4m SE of S Shields. Loc,
Boldon UD.

WHITBY Ches
100, 109 SJ 3975 1m SW of Ellesmere Port.
Loc, Ellesmre Pt MB. P Ellesmre Pt, Wirral.

WHITBY Yorks (N)
86 NZ 8911 17m NNW of Scarborough.
UD, 12,717. P. Cleveland and Whtby CC
(Scbrgh and Whtby). See also Briggswath,
Ruswarp. Fishing tn and resort. Orig St
Hilda's Abbey destroyed by Danes 867.
Present ruins (A.M.) date from 13c. Home
of Caedmon, early Saxon poet. Captain
Cook first sailed hence as a boy; his hse is
preserved. Pannett Pk museum portrays
history of tn.

WHITCHURCH Bucks
146 SP 8020 4m N of Aylesbury. CP, 780.
Aylesbury RD. P Aylesbury. Ch e, m. Sch p.
Aylesbury CC.

WHITCHURCH Devon
175, 187 SX 4972 1m SSE of Tavistock.
CP, 463. Tvstck RD. P Tvstck. Ch e, m.
Sch p. W Dvn CC (Tvstck). See also
Merrivale.

WHITCHURCH Hants
168 SU 4648 6m ENE of Andover.
CP, 2,699. Kingsclere and Whtchch RD. P.
Ch e, b, m, r, s, v. Sch pe, s. Basingstoke CC.
In ch: Anglo-Saxon gravestone.

WHITCHURCH Herefs
142 SO 5417 4m NE of Monmouth.
CP, 804. Ross and Whtchch RD.
P Ross-on-Wye. Ch e, r, v. Sch pe.
Hereford CC. See also Gt Doward.

WHITCHURCH Oxon
158, 159 SU 6377 just N of Pangbourne.
CP, 734. Henley RD. P Pngbne, Reading,
Berks. Ch e. Sch p. Hnly CC.

WHITCHURCH Shrops
118 SJ 5441 14m SW of Crewe.
CP(Whtchch Urban), 7,165. N Shrops RD.
P. Ch e, c, m3, r. Sch ie, je, s2. Oswestry CC.
Mkt and indstrl tn with some handsome
bldngs incl 18c red sandstone ch.

WHITCHURCH Som
155, 156 ST 6167 4m SSE of Bristol.
CP, 1,118. Bathavon RD. P BRSTL. Ch e, c.
Sch p. N Som CC.

WHITCHURCH Warwicks
144 SP 2248 4m SSE of Stratford. CP, 160.
Strtfd-on-Avon RD. Ch e. Strtfd-on-Avn CC
(Strtfd). See also Wimpstone.

WHITCHURCH CANONICORUM Dorset
177 SY 3995 4m ENE of Lyme Regis.
Alternative spelling for Whitechurch
Canonicorum, qv.

WHITCHURCH HILL Oxon
158, 159 SU 6478 2m N of Pangbourne.
Loc, Goring Hth CP. P Reading, Berks.

WHITCOMBE Dorset
178 SY 7188 2m SE of Dorchester. CP, 50.
Dchstr RD. Ch e. W Dst CC.

WHITCOTT KEYSETT Shrops
128 SO 2782 2m NW of Clun. Loc, Cln CP.
Ch m.

WHITE CHAPEL Lancs
94 SD 5641 8m N of Preston. Loc,
Goosnargh CP.

WHITECHAPEL London
160 TQ 3481 3m ENE of Charing Cross.
Loc, Twr Hmlts LB. Stepney and Poplar BC
(Stpny). In Lndn's East End. Rsdntl and
indstrl. Whtchpl Art Gallery. Petticoat Lane
st mkt.

WHITECHURCH CANONICORUM Dorset
177 SY 3995 4m ENE of Lyme Regis.
CP, 635. Bridport RD. Ch e. Sch pe.
W Dst CC. See also Fishpond Bottom,
Morcombelake, Ryall. Cruciform ch with
Perp twr. Tomb of St Wite contains relics.

WHITE COLNE Essex
149 TL 8729 4m E of Halstead. CP, 272.
Hlstd RD. P Colchester. Ch e. Saffron
Walden CC. Colneford Hse has fine
pargetting, dated 1685.

WHITE COPPICE Lancs
95, 101 SD 6119 2m ENE of Chorley. Loc,
Chly RD. Ch v. Chly CC.

WHITECROFT Glos
155, 156 SO 6206 2m NNW of Lydney.
Loc, W Dean CP. W Dn RD. P Ldny. Ch m.
W Glos CC.

WHITECROSS Cornwall
185 SW 9672 1m W of Wadebridge. Loc,
St Breock CP. P Wdbrdge. Ch m.

WHITEFIELD Lancs
101 SD 8006 3m S of Bury. UD, 21,841.
P MANCHESTER. Middleton and
Prestwich BC (CC).

WHITEGATE Ches
110 SJ 6369 3m NW of Winsford. Loc,
Wnsfd UD. P Northwich.

WHITEHAVEN Cumb
82 NX 9718 34m NNW of
Barrow-in-Furness. MB, 26,720. P.
Whthvn CC. See also Hensingham,
Mirehouse, Sandwith. Port; coal mines,
some extending under sea. Tn laid out in
straight lines.

WHITEHILL Hants
169, 181 SU 7934 6m SE of Alton.
CP, 7,381. Altn RD. P Bordon. Ch c.
Petersfield CC. See also Bdn, Lindford,
Longmoor Camp.

WHITE LACKINGTON Dorset
178 SY 7198 5m N of Dorchester. Loc,
Piddletrenthide CP.

WHITELACKINGTON Som
177 ST 3715 1m ENE of Ilminster. CP, 124.
Chard RD. Ch e. Yeovil CC.

WHITE LADIES ASTON Worcs
143, 144 SO 9252 5m ESE of Worcester.
CP, 244. Pershore RD. Ch e. S Worcs CC.

WHITELEY VILLAGE Surrey
170 TQ 0962 2m SE of Weybridge. Loc,
Walton and Wbrdge UD. P Wltn-on-Thames.

Orig blt 1907 by William Whiteley as
almshouses for 350 old people, largest group
of almshses in England.

WHITEMANS GREEN Sussex (E)
182 TQ 3025 3m NW of Haywards Hth.
Loc, Cuckfield UD. P Cckfld, Hwds Hth.

WHITEMOOR Cornwall
185 SW 9757 4m NW of St. Austell. Loc,
St Astll RD. P Nanpéan, St Astll. Ch m.
Sch p. Truro CC.

WHITE NOTLEY Essex
149, 162 TL 7818 4m SE of Braintree.
CP, 500. Brntree RD. P Witham. Ch e.
Sch pe. Brntree CC (Maldon).

WHITEPARISH Wilts
167 SU 2423 7m ESE of Salisbury. CP, 859.
Slsbry and Wilton RD. P Slsbry. Ch e, m2.
Sch pe. Slsbry CC. See also Newton. New
Hse, three-pointed star shape, blt 1619 for
Sir Thomas Gorges of triangular Longford
Cstle (see Alderbury).

WHITE PIT Lincs (L)
105 TF 3777 5m W of Alford. Loc,
Louth RD, Spilsby RD. Ch m. Lth CC,
Horncastle CC.

WHITE RODING Essex
148, 161 TL 5613 6m SW of Dunmow.
CP(White Roothing), 340. Dnmw RD.
P Dnmw. Ch e, c. Saffron Walden CC. One
of eight Rodings, pronounced 'roothing'.
Mdvl ch has Roman bricks in window
arches.

WHITESHILL Glos
156 SO 8407 1m NNW of Stroud.
CP, 1,182. Strd RD. P Strd. Ch e, c. Sch p.
Strd CC.

WHITESMITH Sussex (E)
183 TQ 5213 5m NW of Hailsham. Loc,
Hlshm RD. P Lewes. Lws CC (Eastbourne).

WHITESTAUNTON Som
177 ST 2810 3m WNW of Chard. CP, 164.
Chd RD. Ch e. Yeovil CC.

WHITESTONE Devon
176 SX 8693 3m W of Exeter. CP, 750.
St Thomas RD. P Extr. Ch e, m.
Tiverton CC. See also Oldridge. Ch above
vllge, at over 800ft; prominent landmark
and well known viewpoint.

WHITE WALTHAM Berks
159 SU 8577 3m SW of Maidenhead.
CP, 2,550. Cookham RD. P Mdnhd.
Ch e, m. Sch pe. Windsor and Mdnhd CC
(Wndsr). See also Paley St, Woodlands Pk.

WHITEWAY Glos
143, 144 SO 9110 8m SE of Gloucester.
Loc, Miserden CP.

WHITEWELL Yorks (W)
94, 95 SD 6546 6m NW of Clitheroe. Loc,
Bowland Forest Low CP. Blnd RD. Ch e.
Skipton CC.

WHITFIELD Glos
155, 156 ST 6791 7m E of Severn Rd Br.
Loc, Thornbury RD. S Glos CC.

WHITFIELD Kent
173 TR 2945 3m NNW of Dover. CP, 1,837.
Dvr RD. P Dvr. Ch e, c. Sch p. Dvr and
Deal CC (Dvr).

WHITFIELD Northants
145, 146 SP 6039 2m NE of Brackley.
CP, 156. Brckly RD. P Brckly. Ch e.
Daventry CC (S Nthnts).

WHITFIELD Nthmb
77 NY 7758 6m SW of Haydon Br.
CP(Plenmeller and Whtfld), 304.
Haltwhistle RD. P Hexham. Ch e2. Sch pe.
Hxhm CC. Scatter of bldngs above W Allen
river near its confluence with E Allen.
Heavily wooded area.

WHITFORD Devon
177 SY 2595 3m SW of Axminster. Loc,
Shute CP. P Axmnstr. Ch m.

WHITGIFT Yorks (W)
98 SE 8122 4m E of Goole. CP, 191.
Gle RD. P Gle. Ch e, m. Gle CC.

WHITGREAVE Staffs
119 SJ 8928 4m NNW of Stafford. CP, 156.
Stffd RD. P STFFD. Ch e. Stffd and
Stone CC.

WHITINGTON Norfolk
135 TL 7199 7m ESE of Downham Mkt.
Loc, Northwold CP. Ch e.

WHITLEY Berks
169 SU 7270 S distr of Reading. Loc,
Rdng CB. Rdng S CC (Rdng BC).

WHITLEY Wilts
156, 157 ST 8866 5m SSW of Chippenham.
Loc, Melksham without CP. Bradford and
Mlkshm RD. Ch e, m. Westbury CC.

WHITLEY Yorks (W)
97 SE 5621 7m E of Pontefract. CP, 394.
Osgoldcross RD. P Goole. Ch m. Sch p.
Gle CC.

WHITLEY BAY Nthmb
78 NZ 3572 2m N of Tynemouth.
MB, 37,775. P. Tnmth BC. See also Hartley,
Monkseaton, Murton, Seaton Sluice. Resort;
rsdntl. Good sands.

WHITLEY CHAPEL Nthmb
77 NY 9257 4m S of Hexham. Loc,
Hexhamshire CP. Hxhm RD. Sch pe.
Hxhm CC.

WHITLEY ROW Kent
171 TQ 5052 2m SW of Sevenoaks. Loc,
Chevening CP.

WHITLOCK'S END Warwicks
131 SP 1076 4m WSW of Solihull. Loc,
Hockley Hth CP.

WHITMINSTER Glos
156 SO 7708 5m WNW of Stroud. CP, 392.
Gloucester RD. P GLCSTR. Ch e, m.
Sch pe. Strd CC.

WHITMORE Staffs
110, 119 SJ 8140 4m SW of
Newcastle-under-Lyme. CP, 645.
Ncstle-undr-Lme RD. Ch e. Sch pe.
N-u-L BC. See also Acton, Butterton.

WHITNAGE Devon
164 ST 0215 5m ENE of Tiverton. Loc,
Uplowman CP. Ch m.

WHITNASH Warwicks
132 SP 3263 1m S of Leamington.
CP, 4,486. Warwick RD. P Lmngtn Spa.
Ch e, m. Sch i, j, pe, pr. Wrwck and
Lmngtn CC.

WHITNEY Herefs
141 SO 2647 4m NE of Hay-on-Wye.
CP, 137. Kington RD. P HEREFORD. Ch e.
Leominster CC. See also Millhalf.

WHITRIGG Cumb
75 NY 2257 just N of Kirkbride. Loc,
Bowness CP. Wigton RD. Penrith and the
Border CC.

WHITSBURY Hants
179 SU 1219 3m NNW of Fordingbridge.
CP, 215. Ringwood and Fdngbrdge RD.
P Fdngbrdge. Ch e. New Forest CC. To N,
Iron Age camp; rems of pottery and circular
hse excavated.

WHITSTABLE Kent
173 TR 1166 6m NNW of Canterbury.
UD, 25,404. P. Cntrbry CC. See also
Seasalter, Swalecliffe, Yorkletts. Resort and
rsdntl tn, famous for oysters. Small port,
with fishing and yacht-building.

WHITSTONE Cornwall
174 SX 2698 6m SSE of Bude. CP, 350.
Stratton RD. P Holsworthy, Devon.
Ch e, m. Sch p. N Cnwll CC.

WHITTINGHAM Nthmb
71 NU 0711 7m W of Alnwick. CP, 394.
Rothbury RD. P Alnwck. Ch e, r. Sch pe.
Berwick-upon-Tweed CC. See also
Thrunton. On R Aln near S end of Cheviot
Hills. Partly Saxon ch.

WHITTINGSLOW Shrops
129 SO 4389 3m SSW of Ch Stretton. Loc,
Wistanstow CP.

WHITTINGTON Derbys
111 SK 3875 3m N of Chesterfield. Loc,
Chstrfld MB. P(Whttngtn Moor), Chstrfld.
Revolution Hse, now a museum, was once
an inn, where the Revolution of 1688 was
plotted.

WHITTINGTON Glos
144 SP 0120 4m E of Cheltenham. CP, 157.
Northleach RD. Ch e. Cirencester and
Tewkesbury CC. See also Syreford.
Whttngtn Ct, 16c and later mnr hse in
Cotswold stone; in grnds, rems of Roman
villa.

WHITTINGTON Lancs
89 SD 6076 2m SSW of Kirkby Lonsdale.
CP, 300. Lunesdale RD. P Carnforth. Ch e.
Sch pe. Lancaster CC. See also Newton.

WHITTINGTON Shrops
118 SJ 3231 2m ENE of Oswestry.
CP, 4,524. Oswstry RD. P Oswstry. Ch e, c.
Sch pe. Oswstry CC. See also Babbinswood,
Hindford. Rems of 13c cstle.

WHITTINGTON Staffs
120 SK 1608 3m E of Lichfield. CP, 1,772.
Lchfld RD. P Lchfld. Ch e, r. Sch p. Lchfld
and Tamworth CC. 1m SSW, Whttngtn
Barracks; regimental museum (open by
appointment only).

WHITTINGTON Staffs
130 SO 8582 3m W of Stourbridge. Loc,
Kinver CP.

WHITTINGTON Worcs
143 SO 8752 2m SE of Worcester. CP, 390.
Pershore RD. P WCSTR. Ch e. Sch pe.
S Worcs CC.

WHITTINGTON, GREAT Nthmb
77 NZ 0070 4m NNE of Corbridge. See
Gt Whttngtn.

WHITTLEBURY Northants
146 SP 6944 3m S of Towcester. CP, 366.
Tcstr RD. P Tcstr. Ch e, m. Sch pe.
Daventry CC (S Nthnts).

WHITTLE-LE-WOODS Lancs
94 SD 5821 6m SSE of Preston. CP, 2,900.
Chorley RD. P Chly. Ch e, r. Sch pe, pr.
Chly CC.

WHITTLESEY Cambs
134 TL 2697 5m E of Peterborough.
UD, 10,451. P PTRBRGH. Isle of Ely CC.
See also Coates, Eastrea, Eldernell,
Pondersbridge. Butter cross of 17c in mkt
place.

WHITTLESFORD Cambs
148 TL 4748 7m S of Cambridge.
CP, 1,012. S Cambs RD. P CMBRDGE.
Ch e, c. Sch p. Cambs CC. Large and
rambling. Old timber guildhall. Partly
Norman flint ch. See also Duxford.

WHITTON Co Durham
85 NZ 3822 5m NW of Teesside (Stockton).
CP, 931. Stcktn RD. Easington CC
(Sedgefield).

WHITTON Lincs (L)
98 SE 9024 9m N of Scunthorpe. CP, 180.
Glanford Brigg RD. P Scnthpe. Ch e, m.
Brgg and Scnthpe CC (Brgg). Views across
Humber

WHITTON Nthmb
71 NU 0501 just S of Rothbury. Loc,
Tosson CP. Rthbry RD.
Berwick-upon-Tweed CC. 14c fortified hse.
18c folly, 50ft high.

WHITTON Shrops
129 SO 5772 4m ESE of Ludlow. CP, 84.
Ldlw RD. Ch e. Ldlw CC. Whttn Ct*, 15c
and later mnr hse blt round courtyard.

WHITTON Suffolk (E)
150 TM 1447 NW distr of Ipswich. Loc,
Ipswch CB; CP, 45, Gipping RD. P Ipswch.
Ipswch BC, Eye CC.

WHITTONDITCH Wilts
158 SU 2872 4m NW of Hungerford. Loc,
Ramsbury CP.

WHITTONSTALL Nthmb
77, 78 NZ 0757 5m NW of Consett. Loc,
Shotley Low Quarter CP. Hexham RD.
P Cnstt, Co Durham. Ch e. Sch p. Hxhm CC.

WHITWELL Derbys
103 SK 5276 4m WSW of Worksop.
CP, 4,847. Clowne RD. P Wksp, Notts.
Ch e, m, v. Sch p. Bolsover CC. See also
Hodthorpe.

WHITWELL Herts
147 TL 1821 4m SW of Stevenage. Loc, St
Paul's Walden CP. P Hitchin. Ch b.

WHITWELL IOW
180 SZ 5277 3m W of Ventnor. Loc,
Niton CP. P Vntnr. Ch e, m.

WHITWELL Rutland
122 SK 9208 4m E of Oakham. CP, 51.
Oakhm RD. P Oakhm. Ch e. Rtlnd and
Stamford CC.

WHITWELL-ON-THE-HILL Yorks (N)
92 SE 7265 5m SW of Malton. CP, 147.
Mltn RD. Ch e. Thirsk and Mltn CC.

WHITWICK Leics
121 SK 4316 1m NNE of Coalville. Loc,
Clvlle UD. P Clvlle, LEICESTER. 1½m NE,
Mt St Bernard Abbey, first RC abbey blt in
England since Reformation (1835, mostly
by Pugin).

WHITWOOD Yorks (W)
97 SE 4024 2m WSW of Castleford. Loc,
Cstlfd MB. P Cstlfd.

WHITWORTH Lancs
95, 101 SD 8818 3m N of Rochdale.
UD, 7,417. P Rchdle. Heywood and
Prestwich BC (CC). See also Healey,
Shawforth.

WHIXALL Shrops
118 SJ 5134 3m N of Wem. CP, 900.
N Shrops RD. P Whitchurch. Ch e, c, m2.
Sch pe. Oswestry CC.

WHIXLEY Yorks (W)
97 SE 4458 6m E of Knaresborough.
CP, 764. Nidderdale RD. P YORK. Ch e, m.
Sch pe. Harrogate CC.

WHORLTON Co Durham
84 NZ 1014 4m ESE of Barnard Cstle.
CP, 197. Bnd Cstle RD. P Bnd Cstle. Ch e.
Bishop Auckland CC.

WHORLTON Yorks (N)
91 NZ 4802 9m NE of Northallerton.
CP, 429. Stokesley RD. Ch e (at Swainby).
Sch pe. Richmond CC. See also Swainby.

WHYLE Herefs
129 SO 5560 4m ENE of Leominster. Loc,
Pudlestone CP.

WHYTELEAFE Surrey
170 TQ 3358 4m S of Croydon. Loc,
Caterham and Warlingham UD. P.

WIBDON Glos
155, 156 ST 5697 3m NE of Chepstow.
Loc, Tidenham CP.

WIBTOFT Warwicks
132 SP 4787 5m SSE of Hinckley. CP, 52.
Rugby RD. Ch e. Rgby CC.

WICHENFORD Worcs
130 SO 7860 5m NW of Worcester. CP, 435.
Martley RD. P WCSTR. Ch e. Sch pe.
Kidderminster CC.

WICHLING Kent
172 TQ 9256 5m S of Sittingbourne.
CP, 91. Hollingbourn RD. Maidstone CC.

WICK Glos
156 ST 7072 6m NNW of Bath. CP (Wck and
Abson), 1,524. Sodbury RD. P BRISTOL.
Ch e, c. Sch pe. S Glos CC.

WICK Sussex (W)
181, 182 TQ 0203 1m N of Littlehampton.
Loc, Lttlhmptn UD. P Lttlhmptn.

WICK Wilts
167 SU 1621 6m SSE of Salisbury. Loc,
Downton CP.

WICK Worcs
143, 144 SO 9645 1m E of Pershore.
CP, 381. Pshre RD. P Pshre. Ch e.
S Worcs CC.

WICKEN Cambs
135 TL 5670 6m SSE of Ely. CP, 655.
Newmarket RD. P Ely. Ch e, m. Sch p.
Cambs CC. See also Upware. Wckn Fen
(NT) is nature reserve.

WICKEN Northants
146 SP 7439 3m W of Stony Stratford.
C P , 2 7 8 . T o w c e s t e r R D .
P Wolverton, Bucks. Ch e. Daventry CC
(S Nthnts).

WICKEN BONHUNT Essex
148 TL 4933 4m SW of Saffron Walden.
CP, 156. Sffrn Wldn RD. Ch e. Sffrn
Wldn CC.

WICKENBY Lincs (L)
104 TF 0881 5m SSW of Mkt Rasen.
CP, 150. Welton RD. P LINCOLN. Ch e, m.
Gainsborough CC.

WICKERSLEY Yorks (W)
103 SK 4791 3m E of Rotherham.
CP, 5,029. Rthrhm RD. P Rthrhm.
Ch e, m, r. Sch i, p, pe, s. Rother Valley CC.

WICKFORD Essex
161, 162 TQ 7493 4m NNE of Basildon.
Loc, Bsldn UD. P. Scheduled for conversion
into new tn.

WICKHAM Berks
158 SU 3971 6m WNW of Newbury. Loc,
Welford CP. P Nby. Ch e. Sch pe.

WICKHAM Hants
180 SU 5711 3m N of Fareham. CP, 3,586.
Droxford RD. P Frhm. Ch e, m. Sch pe.
Petersfield CC. Picturesque vllge blt round
large square; bthplce of William of
Wykeham, 1324.

WICKHAM BISHOPS Essex
149, 162 TL 8412 2m SE of Witham.
CP, 911. Maldon RD. P Wthm. Ch e. Sch pe.
Mldn CC.

WICKHAMBREUX Kent
173 TR 2258 5m E of Canterbury.
CP(Wickhambreaux), 379. Bridge-Blean RD.
P Cntrbry. Ch e, m. Sch pe. Cntbry CC. See
also Grove, Stodmarsh.

WICKHAMBROOK Suffolk (W)
149 TL 7454 6m N of Clare. CP, 769.
Clare RD. P Newmarket. Ch e, c, m. Sch p.
Bury St Edmunds CC. See also Clopton Grn,
Thorns.

WICKHAMFORD Worcs
144 SP 0642 2m SE of Evesham. CP, 522.
Eveshm RD. P Eveshm. Ch e. S Worcs CC.
Mkt gdn distr. Ch: Tdr and Jcbn furnishings;
17c monmts incl gravestone of a Washington
showing family arms of stars and stripes (cf
Garsdon, Sulgrave).

WICKHAM MARKET Suffolk (E)
150 TM 3055 5m NE of Woodbridge.
CP, 1,283. Deben RD. P Wdbrdge. Ch e, v2.
Sch p. Eye CC. Small tn on A12 main rd.

WICKHAMPTON Norfolk
126 TG 4205 6m W of Yarmouth. Loc,
Freethorpe CP. Ch e, m.

WICKHAM ST PAUL Essex
149 TL 8336 4m SW of Sudbury. CP, 140.
Halstead RD. P Hlstd. Ch e, m. Sch pe.
Saffron Walden CC.

WICKHAM SKEITH Suffolk (E)
136 TM 0969 4m SW of Eye. CP, 258.
Hartismere RD. P Eye. Ch e, m. Eye CC. See
also Wckhm St.

WICKHAM STREET Suffolk (E)
136 TM 0969 4m SW of Eye. Loc, Wckhm
Skeith CP.

WICKHAM STREET Suffolk (W)
149 TL 7554 6m N of Clare. Loc, Clare RD.
Bury St Edmunds CC.

WICK HILL Berks
169 SU 7964 3m SSW of Wokingham. Loc,
Finchampstead CP. Sch s.

WICKLEWOOD Norfolk
125 TG 0702 3m WNW of Wymondham.
CP, 590. Forehoe and Henstead RD.
P Wndhm. Ch e, m. Sch p. S Nflk CC
(Central Nflk). See also Crownthorpe.

WICKMERE Norfolk
126 TG 1733 4m NNW of Aylsham.
C P , 2 1 0 . E r p i n g h a m R D .
P NORWICH, NOR 43Y. Ch e, m.
N Nflk CC. 1m SW, Wolterton Hall*, brick
and stone hse blt 1724 by Ripley for
Horatio Walpole.

WICK RISSINGTON Glos
144 SP 1921 3m S of Stow-on-the-Wold.
CP, 159. N Cotswold RD. Ch e. Cirencester
and Tewkesbury CC.

WICK ST LAWRENCE Som
155, 165 ST 3665 4m NE of Weston.
CP, 182. Axbridge RD. Ch e, m.
Wstn-super-Mare CC.

WICKWAR Glos
156 ST 7288 10m E of Severn Rd Br.
CP, 888. Sodbury RD.
P Wotton-under-Edge. Ch e, v. Sch p.
S Glos CC.

WIDDINGTON Essex
148 TL 5331 4m S of Saffron Walden.
CP, 329. Sffrn Wldn RD. P Sffrn Wldn.
Ch e. Sffrn Wldn CC.

WIDDRINGTON Nthmb
71 NZ 2595 5m S of Amble. CP, 274.
Morpeth RD. P Mpth. Ch e, m, r, v.
Mpth CC.

WIDECOMBE IN THE MOOR Devon
175, 187, 188 SX 7176 5m NNW of
Ashburton. CP, 557. Newton Abbot RD.
P Ntn Abbt. Ch e. Sch p. Totnes CC. See
also Dunstone, Leusdon, Ponsworthy,
Poundsgate. Dartmoor vllge invaded in
summer as result of popular song. Ch has
120ft twr.

WIDEGATES Cornwall
186 SX 2857 3m NE of Looe. Loc,
Morval CP. P Looe. Ch m. Sch pe.

WIDEMOUTH Cornwall
174 SS 2002 3m S of Bude. Loc,
Poundstock CP. P Bde. Bungalow resort.

WIDE OPEN Nthmb
78 NZ 2472 5m N of Newcastle. Loc,
Longbenton UD. P NCSTLE UPON TYNE.

WIDFORD Essex
161 TL 6905 1m SW of Chelmsford. Loc,
Chlmsfd MB.

WIDFORD Herts
148 TL 4215 4m ENE of Ware. CP, 402.
Ware RD. P Ware. Ch e. Sch p. E Herts CC.

WIDFORD Oxon
144 SP 2712 1m E of Burford.
CP(Swinbrook and Wdfd), 175. Witney RD.
Ch e. Mid-Oxon CC (Banbury).

WIDMER END Bucks
159 SU 8896 3m NNE of High Wycombe.
Loc, Hughenden CP. Wcmbe RD.
Wcmbe CC.

WIDMERPOOL Notts
121, 122 SK 6328 9m SSE of Nottingham.
CP, 160. Bingham RD. Ch e. Rushcliffe CC
(Carlton).

WIDNES Lancs
100, 109 SJ 5185 6m WSW of Warrington.
MB, 56,709. P. Wdns CC. See also Ditton,
Farnworth, Hough Grn. Chemical wks. Rly
and rd brs over R Mersey and Manchester
Ship Canal; rd br is a steel suspension br
with span of 1,082ft.

WIDWORTHY Devon
177 SY 2199 3m ESE of Honiton. CP, 202.
Hntn RD. Ch e. Hntn CC. See also
Wilmington.

WIELD Hants
168 SU 6238 6m W of Alton. CP, 238.
Altn RD. P Alresford. Ch e, m.
Petersfield CC. See also Lr Wld. Small Nmn
ch with early 19c wooden belfry.

WIGAN Lancs
100 SD 5805 17m WNW of Manchester.
CB, 81,258. P. Wgn BC. Coal-mining distr,
but much indstrl diversification, eg
food-canning (Kitt Grn), paper-making
machinery mnfre.

WIGANTHORPE Yorks (N)
92 SE 6672 8m W of Malton. CP(Terrington
w Wgnthpe), 350. Mltn RD. Thirsk and
Mltn CC.

WIGBOROUGH, GREAT Essex
149, 162 TL 9614 5m E of Tiptree. See Gt
Wgbrgh.

WIGGATON Devon
176 SY 1093 4m NNW of Sidmouth. Loc,
Ottery St Mary UD.

WIGGENHALL ST GERMANS Norfolk
124 TF 5914 4m SSW of King's Lynn.
CP, 785. Downham RD. Ch e, m. Sch p.
SW Nflk CC.

WIGGENHALL ST MARY MAGDALEN Norfolk
124 TF 5911 5m N of Downham Mkt. CP, 732. Dnhm RD. Ch e, m. Sch p. SW Nflk CC.

WIGGENHALL ST MARY THE VIRGIN Norfolk
124 TF 5813 5m SSW of King's Lynn. CP, 252. Downham RD. Ch e, m. SW Nflk CC. See also Saddle Bow. Perp ch has fine carved bench-ends.

WIGGINTON Herts
146, 159 SP 9310 1m SE of Tring. CP, 1,184. Berkhamsted RD. P Trng. Ch e, b. Sch pe. Hemel Hempstead CC. To S, a stretch of Grim's Dyke (see Northchurch).

WIGGINTON Oxon
145 SP 3833 6m SW of Banbury. CP, 159. Bnbry RD. P Bnbry. Ch e, m. Bnbry CC.

WIGGINTON Staffs
120 SK 2006 2m N of Tamworth. CP, 903. Lichfield RD. P Tmwth. Ch e. Sch pe. Lchfld and Tmwth CC. See also Comberford, Hopwas.

WIGGINTON Yorks (N)
97 SE 5958 4m N of York. CP, 384. Flaxton RD. Ch e, m. Sch p. Thirsk and Malton CC.

WIGGLESWORTH Yorks (W)
95 SD 8156 4m S of Settle. CP, 177. Sttle RD. P Skipton. Ch m. Skptn CC.

WIGGONBY Cumb
75 NY 2953 4m NE of Wigton. Loc, Aikton CP. Sch pe.

WIGGONHOLT Sussex (W)
182 TQ 0616 1m SE of Pulborough. Loc, Parham CP. Chanctonbury RD. Ch e. Shoreham CC (Arundel and Shrhm).

WIGHILL Yorks (W)
97 SE 4746 2m NNW of Tadcaster. CP, 220. Wetherby RD. P Tdcstr. Ch e, m. Sch pe. Barkston Ash CC.

WIGHTON Norfolk
125 TF 9439 3m SSE of Wells. CP, 318. Walsingham RD. P Wlls-next-the-Sea. Ch e, m. Sch pe. NW Nflk CC (N Nflk).

WIGMORE Herefs
129 SO 4169 7m SW of Ludlow. CP, 308. Leominster and Wigmore RD. P Lmnstr. Ch e, m. Sch p, s. Lmnstr CC. See also Ongar St. Seat of great mdvl family of Mortimers. Scant rems of their cstle.

WIGMORE Kent
172 TQ 8064 2m SE of Gillingham. Loc, Gllnghm MB. P Gllnghm.

WIGSLEY Notts
113 SK 8670 7m W of Lincoln. CP, 59. Newark RD. Nwk CC.

WIGSTON MAGNA Leics
132, 133 SP 6099 4m SSE of Leicester. UD(Wgstn), 30,230. P(Wgstn), LCSTR. Harborough CC. See also S Wgstn. Part of Lcstr blt-up area.

WIGSTON PARVA Leics
132 SP 4689 4m SE of Hinckley. CP, 36. Blaby RD. Ch e. Blby CC (Harborough). 1m SE on main rd at crossing of Fosse Way and Watling St, monmt of 1712 marks site of Roman settlement of Venonae.

WIGTOFT Lincs (H)
114, 123 TF 2636 6m SW of Boston. CP, 505. Bstn RD. P Bstn. Ch e. Sch pe. Holland w Bstn CC.

WIGTON Cumb
82 NY 2548 10m WSW of Carlisle. CP, 4,235. Wgtn RD. P. Ch e, f, m, r, v2. Sch i, ir, j, jr, s2. Penrith and the Border CC. Mkt tn.

WIGTWIZZLE Yorks (W)
102 SK 2495 8m NW of Sheffield. Loc, Bradfield CP.

WIKE Yorks (W)
96 SE 3342 6m NNE of Leeds. Loc, Harewood CP.

WILBARSTON Northants
133 SP 8188 5m W of Corby. CP, 461. Kettering RD. P Mkt Harborough, Leics. Ch e, c. Sch pe. Kttrng CC.

WILBERFOSS Yorks (E)
97, 98 SE 7350 5m WNW of Pocklington. CP, 619. Pcklngtn RD. P YORK. Ch e, m. Sch pe. Howden CC. See also Newton upon Derwent. Ch has brasses.

WILBRAHAM, GREAT Cambs
135 TL 5457 6m E of Cambridge. See Gt Wlbrhm.

WILBURTON Cambs
135 TL 4874 5m SW of Ely. CP, 771. Ely RD. P Ely. Ch e, b. Sch pe. Isle of Ely CC.

WILBY Norfolk
136 TM 0389 4m SSW of Attleborough. Loc, Quidenham CP. Ch e, m. Sch pe. Elizn brick hall now farmhouse.

WILBY Northants
133 SP 8666 2m SW of Wellingborough. CP, 613. Wllngbrgh RD. P Wllngbrgh. Ch e, m. Sch pe. Wllngbrgh CC.

WILBY Suffolk (E)
137 TM 2472 6m NNW of Framlingham. CP, 255. Hartismere RD. P Diss, Norfolk. Ch e. Sch pe. Eye CC.

WILCOT Wilts
167 SU 1461 2m NW of Pewsey. CP, 538. Psy RD. P Psy. Ch e. Devizes CC. See also Oare.

WILCOTT Shrops
118 SJ 3718 8m WNW of Shrewsbury. Loc, Gt Ness CP. Ch c.

WILDBOARCLOUGH Ches
110 SJ 9868 5m SE of Macclesfield. CP, 142. Mcclsfld RD. P Mcclsfld. Ch e. Sch pe. Mcclsfld CC. Elevated position in Peak Distr National Pk. Moorland scenery.

WILDEN Beds
134 TL 0955 5m NE of Bedford. CP, 338. Bdfd RD. P BDFD. Ch e, b. Sch pe. Mid-Beds CC.

WILDEN Worcs
130 SO 8272 1m NE of Stourport. Loc, Stpt-on-Severn UD. P Stpt-on-Svn. Iron wks. Ch has Burne-Jones windows commemorating Baldwin family. To NE, Summerfield government research stn.

WILDHERN Hants
168 SU 3550 4m N of Andover. Loc, Tangley CP. Ch m.

WILDMOOR Worcs
130, 131 SO 9675 3m N of Bromsgrove. Loc, Belbroughton CP.

WILDSWORTH Lincs (L)
104 SK 8097 5m N of Gainsborough. CP, 71. Gnsbrgh RD. Ch e, m. Gnsbrgh CC.

WILKESLEY Ches
110, 118, 119 SJ 6241 5m NW of Mkt Drayton. CP(Dodcott cum Wlksly), 451. Nantwich RD. Sch pe. Nntwch CC.

WILLAND Devon
164, 176 ST 0310 5m ESE of Tiverton. CP, 963. Tvtn RD. P Cullompton. Ch e, m. Sch p. Tvtn CC.

WILLASTON Ches
100, 109 SJ 3377 7m S of Birkenhead. Loc, Neston UD. P Wirral.

WILLASTON Ches
110, SJ 6852 2m E of Nantwich. CP, 1,818. Nntwch RD. P Nntwch. Ch e, m. Sch p. Nntwch CC.

WILLEN Bucks
146 SP 8741 2m S of Newport Pagnell. CP(Woolstone-cum-Wlln), 151. Npt Pgnll RD. Ch e. Buckingham CC.

WILLENHALL Staffs
130, 131 SO 9698 3m E of Wolverhampton. Loc, Walsall CB. P. Wlsll N BC(Wednesbury). Mnfg distr; iron and brass wks.

WILLERBY Yorks (E)
93 TA 0079 6m SSW of Scarborough. CP, 407. Norton RD. Ch e. Sch p. Howden CC. See also Staxton.

WILLERBY Yorks (E)
99 TA 0230 5m WNW of Hull. Loc, Haltemprice UD. P Hll. Hltmprce CC.

WILLERSEY Glos
144 SP 1039 1m NNE of Broadway. CP, 618. N Cotswold RD. P Brdwy, Worcs. Ch e, m. Sch pe. Cirencester and Tewkesbury CC. Hses blt on both sides of long wide grn. Ch has six bells, cast, from orig three, to celebrate treaty of Utrecht, 1713.

WILLERSLEY Herefs
142 SO 3147 6m NE of Hay-on-Wye. CP, 37. Kington RD. Ch e. Leominster CC.

WILLESBOROUGH Kent
172, 173, 174 TR 0241 1m SE of Ashford.
Loc, Ashfd UD. P Ashfd.

WILLESDEN London
160 TQ 2284 5m NW of Charing Cross. Loc,
Brent LB. Brnt E BC (Wllsdn E, Wllsdn W).

WILLEY Shrops
129, 130 SO 6799 3m E of Much Wenlock.
Loc, Barrow CP. Ch e.

WILLEY Warwicks
132 SP 4984 3m W of Lutterworth. CP, 88.
Rugby RD. P Rgby. Ch e. Rgby CC.

WILLEY GREEN Surrey
169 SU 9351 4m WNW of Guildford. Loc,
Normandy CP.

WILLIAMSCOT Oxon
145 SP 4845 3m NNE of Banbury. Loc,
Bnbry RD. Bnbry CC.

WILLIAN Herts
147 TL 2230 1m S of Letchworth. Loc,
Ltchwth UD. P Ltchwth.

WILLINGALE Essex
161 TL 5907 4m NE of Ongar. CP, 534.
Epping and Ongr RD. P Ongr. Ch e2. Sch pe.
Brentwood and Ongr CC (Chigwell). See
also Shellow Bowells.

WILLINGDON Sussex (E)
183 TQ 5802 3m NNW of Eastbourne.
CP, 3,857. Hailsham RD. P Eastbne. Ch e, v.
Sch p, s. Eastbne CC.

WILLINGHAM Cambs
135 TL 4070 8m NNW of Cambridge.
CP, 1,766. Chesterton RD. P CMBRDGE.
Ch e, b, m, s, v. Sch p. Cambs CC. Ch has
double-hammerbeam angel roof. Large
pump on grn. 1m E, Belsar's Hill, named
after Nmn who pursued Hereward the Wake
across Fens.

WILLINGHAM Lincs (L)
104 SK 8784 5m SE of Gainsborough.
CP, 408. Gnsbrgh RD. P Gnsbrgh. Ch e, m.
Sch p. Gnsbrgh CC.

WILLINGTON Beds
147 TL 1149 4m E of Bedford. CP, 510.
Bdfd RD. P BDFD. Ch e, m. Sch p.
Mid-Beds CC. 16c stone dovecote*, blt by

Sir John Gostwick, Wolsey's Master of the
Horse; NT, with 16c stables opposite*.

WILLINGTON Co Durham
85 NZ 1935 4m N of Bishop Auckland.
UD(Crook and Wllngtn), 21,485. P Crk.
NW Drhm CC. Colliery tn.

WILLINGTON Derbys
120, 121 SK 2928 5m NE of
Burton-on-Trent. CP, 1,318. Repton RD.
P DERBY. Ch e, b, m. Sch p. Belper CC.

WILLINGTON Nthmb
78 NZ 3267 2m W of Tynemouth. Loc,
Wallsend MB.

WILLINGTON Warwicks
144 SP 2639 1m SSE of Shipston on Stour.
Loc, Barcheston CP.

WILLINGTON CORNER Ches
109 SJ 5366 8m E of Chester. Loc,
Northwich RD, Tarvin RD.
P(Wllngtn), Tarporley. Ch m. Nthwch CC.

WILLISHAM Suffolk (E)
149 TM 0750 5m SSE of Stowmarket.
CP, 142. Gipping RD. Ch e. Eye CC. See
also Wllshm Tye.

WILLISHAM TYE Suffolk (E)
149 TM 0651 5m SSE of Stowmarket. Loc,
Wllshm CP.

WILLITOFT Yorks (E)
97, 98 SE 7435 7m N of Goole. Loc,
Bubwith CP. Ch m.

WILLITON Som
164 ST 0741 1m S of Watchet. CP, 2,304.
Wlltn RD. P Taunton. Ch e, m. Sch pe, s.
Bridgwater CC.

WILLOUGHBY Lincs (L)
114 TF 4771 3m SSE of Alford.
CP(Wllghby w Sloothby), 541. Spilsby RD.
P Alfd. Ch e, m. Sch pe. Horncastle CC.

WILLOUGHBY Warwicks
132 SP 5167 7m S of Rugby. CP, 541.
Rgby RD. P Rgby. Ch e, m. Sch pe.
Rgby CC.

WILLOUGHBY ON THE WOLDS Notts
121, 122 SK 6325 7m ENE of
Loughborough. CP, 305. Basford RD.
P Lghbrgh, Leics. Ch e, m. Sch p.
Rushcliffe CC. Wllghby monmts in ch.

WILLOUGHBY WATERLESS Leics
132, 133 SP 5792 8m S of Leicester.
CP, 191. Lutterworth RD. P LCSTR.
Ch e, m. Blaby CC (Harborough). Many
18c–19c hses, good examples of the period.

WILLOUGHTON Lincs (L)
104 SK 9393 7m ENE of Gainsborough.
CP, 456. Gnsbrgh RD. P Grnsbrgh. Ch e, m.
Sch p. Gnsbrgh CC. In ch, 6ft long vamping
horn used to call people to ch and to lead
hymns. Vllge full of roses.

WILMCOTE Warwicks
131 SP 1658 3m NW of Stratford. Loc,
Aston Cantlow CP. P Strtfd-upon-Avon.
Ch e, c. Sch pe. Strtfd-on-Avn CC (Strtfd).
Mary Arden's Hse*, half-timbered Tdr hse
prob bthplce of Shakespeare's mother.

WILMINGTON Devon
177 SY 2199 3m E of Honiton. Loc,
Widworthy CP. P Hntn.

WILMINGTON Kent
161, 171 TQ 5372 1m S of Dartford. CP,
6,418. Dtfd RD. P Dtfd. Ch e, v. Sch p2.
Dtfd CC.

WILMINGTON Sussex (E)
183 TQ 5404 5m NW of Eastbourne.
CP, 216. Hailsham RD. P Polegate. Ch e.
Lewes CC (Eastbne). Enormous old yew
tree in churchyard. Rems of 12c priory now
agricultural museum. To S, Long Man of
Wlmngtn, figure cut in chalk of Downs —
origin unknown.

WILMSLOW Ches
101 SJ 8481 6m SSW of Stockport.
UD, 28,982. P. Cheadle BC (Knutsford CC).
See also Dean Row, Handforth, Morley Grn,
Styal. Dormitory area for Manchester distr.
Industries incl engineering, pharmaceuticals.

WILNECOTE Staffs
120 SK 2201 2m SE of Tamworth. Loc,
Tmwth MB. P Tmwth. Lichfield and
Tmwth CC (Meriden).

WILNE, GREAT Derbys
112, 121 SK 4430 7m ESE of Derby. See
Gt Wlne.

WILPSHIRE Lancs
94, 95 SD 6832 3m N of Blackburn.
CP, 1,933. Blckbn RD. P Blckbn. Ch m.
Darwen CC.

WILSDEN Yorks (W)
96 SE 0936 4m SE of Keighley. Loc,
Bingley UD. P Bradford.

WILSFORD Lincs (K)
113, 123 TF 0043 4m WSW of Sleaford.
CP, 430. E Kesteven RD. P Grantham.
Ch e, m. Sch pe. Grnthm CC.

WILSFORD Wilts
167 SU 1057 4m WSW of Pewsey. CP, 102.
Psy RD. P Psy. Ch e. Devizes CC.

WILSFORD Wilts
167 SU 1339 2m SW of Amesbury.
CP(Wlsfd cum Lake), 162. Amesbury RD.
Ch e. Salisbury CC.

WILSHAMSTEAD Beds
147 TL 0643 4m S of Bedford. CP, 1,095.
Bdfd/RD. P BDFD. Ch e, m, v. Sch p.
Mid-Beds CC.

WILSHAW Yorks (W)
102 SE 1109 5m SSW of Huddersfield. Loc,
Meltham UD.

WILSILL Yorks (W)
91 SE 1864 2m ESE of Pateley Br. Loc,
High and Low Bishopside CP. Ripon and
Ptly Br RD. Ch m. Rpn CC.

WILSON Leics
121 SK 4024 6m NNE of Ashby de la
Zouch. Loc, Breedon on the Hill CP.

WILSTEAD Beds
147 TL 0643 4m S of Bedford. Alternative
name for Wilshamstead, qv.

WILSTHORPE Lincs (K)
123 TF 0913 5m NE of Stamford. CP
(Braceborough and Wlsthpe), 169.
S Kesteven RD. Ch e. Rutland and
Stmfd CC.

WILSTONE Herts
146, 159 SP 9014 2m NW of Tring. Loc,
Trng Rural CP. Berkhamsted RD. P Trng.
Ch e, b. Sch p. Hemel Hempstead CC.

WILTON Wilts
167 SU 0931 3m WNW of Salisbury.
MB, 3,815. P Slsbry. Slsbry CC. Carpet
industry dates from 17c. Royal Wltn
Factory*. Ch Vctrn Italianate. Wltn Hse*,
17c and later. In grnds, 18c Palladian br and
riding sch.

WILTON Wilts
167 SU 2661 6m SW of Hungerford. Loc,
Grafton CP. Marlborough and
Ramsbury RD. P Mlbrgh. Ch m. Devizes CC.

WILTON Yorks (N)
92 SE 8682 4m ESE of Pickering. CP, 117.
Pckrng RD. Ch e, m. Scarborough CC
(Scbrgh and Whitby).

WIMBISH Essex
148 TL 5936 3m E of Saffron Walden.
CP, 1,083. Sffrn Wldn RD. P Sffrn Wldn.
Ch e, s. Sch p. Sffrn Wldn CC. See also
Howlett End. 12c–14c ch has 14c brasses.
1m NW, Tiptofts Farm, moated 14c mnr
hse.

WIMBISH GREEN Essex
148 TL 6035 3m N of Thaxted. Loc,
Wmbsh CP.

WIMBLEDON London
160, 170 TQ 2470 7m SW of Charing Cross.
Loc, Merton LB. Wmbldn BC. Rsdntl.
Wmbldn Cmmn is large open space. All
England Lawn Tennis Club Cts, between
cmmn and Wmbldn Pk.

WIMBLINGTON Cambs
135 TL 4192 3m S of March. CP, 1,365.
N Witchford RD. P Mch. Ch e, m2. Sch p.
Isle of Ely CC.

WIMBORNE MINSTER Dorset
179 SZ 0199 7m NW of Bournemouth.
UD, 5,000. P(Wmbne). N Dst CC. Mkt tn,
usually called simply Wimborne. Nmn to
Dec two-towered minster at tn centre.

WIMBORNE ST GILES Dorset
179 SU 0312 8m N of Wimborne. CP, 438.
Wmbne and Cranborne RD. P Wmbne. Ch e.
Sch pe. N Dst CC. See also Monkton Up
Wmbne. Ch: 18c classical. Almshouses. St
Giles Hse*, 17c–18c; shell grotto in grnds.

WIMBOTSHAM Norfolk
124 TF 6105 1m NE of Downham Mkt.
CP, 665. Dnhm RD. P King's Lynn. Ch e, m.
Sch p. SW Nflk CC.

WIMPSTONE Warwicks
144 SP 2148 4m S of Stratford. Loc,
Whitchurch CP.

WINCANTON Som
166 ST 7128 12m NE of Yeovil. CP, 2,525.
Wncntn RD. P. Ch e, b, f, m, r, v. Sch p, s.
Wells CC. Small mkt tn, mainly Ggn, rebuilt
after fire in 1747.

WINCEBY Lincs (L)
114 TF 3268 4m ESE of Horncastle.
CP, 31. Hncstle RD. Hncstle CC.

WINCHAM Ches
101 SJ 6775 1m NE of Northwich. CP, 751.
Nthwch RD. P Nthwch. Ch m. Nthwch CC.

WINCHCOMBE Glos
144 SP 0228 6m NE of Cheltenham.
CP, 3,047. Chltnhm RD. P Chltnhm.
Ch e, bv, r. Sch ie, j, s. Cirencester and
Tewkesbury CC. See also Greet, Gretton.
Attractive small Cotswold tn. Perp ch. 1m
SE, Sudeley Cstle*, mdvl bldng much
rebuilt and restored.

WINCHELSEA Sussex (E)
184 TQ 9017 2m SW of Rye. Loc,
Icklesham CP. P. Ch e, m. Sch pe. Tn laid
out by Edward I. Often attacked by the
French, and the sea. Ch has fine Dec work.

WINCHELSEA BEACH Sussex (E)
184 TQ 9116 3m S of Rye. Loc,
Icklesham CP. P Wnchlsea.

WINCHESTER Hants
168 SU 4829 12m NNE of Southampton.
MB, 31,041. P. Wnchstr CC. County tn of
Hants; ancient capital of Wessex and
England. Cathedral. Boys' public sch,
founded 1382. St Cross pensioners' hsptl*,
founded 1136. Army barracks, museum.

WINCHFIELD Hants
169 SU 7654 7m NW of Farnham. CP, 415.
Hartley Wintney RD. Ch e. Bsngstke CC
(Aldershot). Nmn ch.

WINCHMORE HILL Bucks
159 SU 9394 2m SW of Amersham. Loc,
Penn CP. Ch m.

WINCHMORE HILL London
160 TQ 3294 1m S of Enfield. Loc,
Enfld LB. Southgate BC.

WINCLE Ches
110 SJ 9566 5m SSE of Macclesfield.

CP, 183. Mcclsfld RD. P Mcclsfld. Ch e. Sch pe. Mcclsfd CC. See also Allgreave, Danebridge.

WINDERMERE Westm
89 SD 4198 7m NW of Kendal. UD, 8,063. P. Westm CC. See also Bowness-on-Wndrmere. Largely Vctrn tn, Lake District holiday centre.

WINDERTON Warwicks
145 SP 3240 4m E of Shipston on Stour. Loc, Brailes CP. Shpston on Str RD. Stratford-on-Avn CC (Strtfd). 1m N, Compton Wynyates*, Tdr hse surrounded by low hills.

WINDLESHAM Surrey
169 SU 9364 5m ENE of Camberley. CP, 7,819. Bagshot RD. P. Ch e, m. Sch p. NW Srry CC (Chertsey). See also Bgsht, Lightwater, Updown Hill.

WINDLEY Derbys
111 SK 3045 3m WSW of Belper. CP, 145. Blpr RD. P DERBY. Ch e. Blpr CC.

WINDMILL HILL Som
177 ST 3116 4m WNW of Ilminster. Loc, Ashill CP. Ch c.

WINDMILL HILL Sussex (E)
183 TQ 6412 4m ENE of Hailsham. Loc, Hlshm RD. P Hlshm. Rye CC.

WINDRUSH Glos
144 SP 1913 4m W of Burford. CP, 151. Northleach RD. P OXFORD. Ch e, m. Cirencester and Tewkesbury CC. Cotswold vllge blt round grn. Largely Nmn ch has famous S doorway.

WINDSOR Berks
159, 160, 170 SU 9676 2m SSW of Slough. MB(New Wndsr), 30,065. P. Wndsr and Maidenhead CC (Wndsr). The cstle, blt by William I but much altered, is the chief royal residence. Precincts open daily. St George's Chpl; Perp, fan-vaulting. Home Pk private; Gt Pk open.

WINEHAM Sussex (W/E)
182 TQ 2320 3m NNE of Henfield. Loc, Chanctonbury RD, Cuckfield RD. P Hnfld. Shoreham CC, Mid-Sx CC. (Arundel and Shrhm CC, Lewes CC.)

WINESTEAD Yorks (E)
99 TA 2924 3m SW of Withernsea. Loc, Patrington CP. P Hull. Ch e. Bthplce of Andrew Marvell, poet. Ch: monmts, brasses (incl palimpsest brass).

WINFARTHING Norfolk
136 TM 1085 4m N of Diss. CP, 350. Depwade RD. P Dss. Ch e, m2. Sch pe. S Nflk CC.

WINFORD Som
155, 156, 165 ST 5465 6m SW of Bristol. CP, 1,309. Long Ashton RD. P BRSTL. Ch e. Sch pe. N Som CC. See also Felton, Ridgehill, Upr Tn.

WINFORTON Herefs
142 SO 2947 5m NE of Hay-on-Wye. CP, 151. Kington RD. P HEREFORD. Ch e. Leominster CC.

WINFRITH NEWBURGH Dorset
178 SY 8084 7m WSW of Wareham. CP, 626. Wrhm and Purbeck RD. P(Wnfrth), Dorchester. Ch e, m. Sch pe. S Dst CC. See also E Knighton. To N, Wnfrth Hth and the Atomic Energy Establishment.

WING Bucks
146 SP 8822 2m SW of Linslade. CP, 1,719. Wng RD. P Leighton Buzzard, Beds. Ch e, c, m2. Sch p, s. Buckingham CC. Wing airfield lies to W. To E is Ascott (NT)*, 19c hse with collection of furniture, pictures, Oriental porcelain; hse and grnds open.

WING Rutland
122 SK 8903 3m NE of Uppingham. CP, 242. Uppnghm RD. P Oakham. Ch e, m. Rtlnd and Stamford CC.

WINGATE Co Durham
85 NZ 4037 3m SW of Peterlee. CP, 11,442. Easington RD. P. Ch e, m, r, s, v. Sch i, j, pr, s2. Easngton CC. See also Deaf Hill, Wheatley Hill.

WINGATES Lancs
101 SD 6507 4m ENE of Wigan. Loc, Westhoughton UD. P Wsthghtn, Bolton.

WINGATES Nthmb
71 NZ 0995 5m SE of Rothbury. Loc, Nunnykirk CP.

WINGERWORTH Derbys
111 SK 3867 2m S of Chesterfield.
CP, 3,418. Chstrfld RD. P Chstrfld. Ch e, m.
Sch p2. NE Derbys CC.

WINGFIELD Beds
147 TL 0026 3m NNW of Dunstable. Loc,
Chalgrave CP.

WINGFIELD Suffolk (E)
137 TM 2276 6m ENE of Eye. CP, 377.
Hartismere RD. P Diss, Norfolk. Ch e.
Sch pe. Eye CC. 14c moated cstle (private)
stands at corner of vast grn. Ch has effigies
of Wngflds and de la Poles.

WINGFIELD Wilts
166 ST 8256 2m W of Trowbridge. CP, 323.
Bradford and Melksham RD. P Trwbrdge.
Ch e. Sch pe. Westbury CC. 1m N, gateposts
of Midway Mnr commemorate General
Shrapnel who invented shrapnel in 1785.

WINGHAM Kent
173 TR 2457 6m E of Canterbury.
CP, 1,428. Eastry RD. P Cntrbry. Ch e, v.
Sch p. Dover and Deal CC (Dvr). Old mkt tn
with wide tree-lined main street; much
traffic.

WINGRAVE Bucks
146 SP 8718 5m NE of Aylesbury.
CP(Wngrve w Rowsham), 832. Wing RD.
P Aylesbury. Ch e, bv, m. Sch pe.
Buckingham CC.

WINKBURN Notts
112 SK 7158 6m WNW of Newark. CP, 107.
Southwell RD. Ch e. Nwk CC. Ch is in hall
grnds.

WINKFIELD Berks
169 SU 9072 3m NE of Bracknell.
CP, 7,134. Easthampstead RD. P Windsor.
Ch e. Sch i, je, pe. Wokingham CC. See also
Burleigh, Cranbourne, Woodside.

WINKFIELD ROW Berks
169 SU 8971 2m NE of Bracknell. Loc,
Wnkfld CP. P Brcknll. Ch m.

WINKFIELD STREET Berks
169 SU 9072 3m NE of Bracknell. Loc,
Wnkfld CP.

WINKHILL Staffs
111 SK 0651 6m SE of Leek. Loc,
Waterhouses CP. Ch m.

WINKLEIGH Devon
175 SS 6308 8m NNE of Okehampton.
CP, 934. Torrington RD. P. Ch e, m3. Sch p.
W Dvn CC (Trrngtn). See also Ashley,
Hollocombe.

WINKSLEY Yorks (W)
91 SE 2571 4m W of Ripon. CP, 90. Rpn
and Pateley Br RD. Ch e. Rpn CC.

WINLATON Co Durham
78 NZ 1762 5m W of Gateshead. Loc,
Blaydon UD. P Bldn-on-Tyne.

WINLATON MILL Co Durham
78 NZ 1860 5m WSW of Gateshead. Loc,
Blaydon UD. P Bldn-on-Tyne.

WINMARLEIGH Lancs
94 SD 4748 8m S of Lancaster. CP, 332.
Garstang RD. P Preston. Ch e. Sch pe.
N Fylde CC.

WINNERSH Berks
169 SU 7870 2m NW of Wokingham.
CP, 2,525. Wkngham RD. P Wknghm. Ch m.
Sch p, s. Reading S CC (Wknghm). See also
Sindlesham.

WINSCALES Cumb
82 NY 0226 2m SE of Workington.
CP, 213. Cockermouth RD. Wkngtn CC.

WINSCOMBE Som
165 ST 4257 4m NW of Cheddar.
CP, 2,553. Axbridge RD. P. Ch e, b, f, v.
Sch p. Weston-super-Mare CC. See also
Sandford. Ch has 100ft twr and William
Morris glass.

WINSFORD Ches
110 SJ 6566 5m S of Northwich.
UD, 24,791. P. Nantwich CC. See also
Church Hill, Foxwist Grn, Meadowbank,
Salterswall, Wharton, Whitegate.
Salt-producing tn with modern shopping
centre and indstrl estate.

WINSFORD Som
164 SS 9034 5m N of Dulverton. CP, 362.
Dlvtn RD. P Minehead. Ch e, m. Sch pe.
Taunton CC. Thatched cottages; packhorse
br. To W, Wnsfd Hill (NT), 1404ft; good
viewpoint. Many Bronze Age barrows.

WINSHAM Som
177 ST 3706 4m ESE of Chard. CP, 673.
Chd RD. P Chd. Ch e, c. Sch p. Yeovil CC.

WINSKILL Cumb
83 NY 5834 5m NE of Penrith. Loc,
Hunsonby CP. P Pnrth.

WINSLADE Hants
168, 169 SU 6548 3m SSE of Basingstoke.
CP, 116. Bsngstke RD. Ch e. Bsngstke CC.

WINSLEY Wilts
166 ST 7960 4m NW of Trowbridge.
CP, 1,282. Bradford and Melksham RD.
P Brdfd-on-Avn. Ch e, m. Sch pe.
Westbury CC. See also Turleigh.

WINSLOW Bucks
146 SP 7627 6m SE of Buckingham.
CP, 2,072. Wnslw RD. P Bletchley.
Ch e, b, c, r. Sch pe, s. Buckingham CC.
Wnslw Hall, c.1700, attributed to Wren.

WINSON Glos
157 SP 0908 6m NE of Cirencester. CP, 63.
Northleach RD. P Crncstr. Ch e. Crncstr
and Tewkesbury CC.

WINSTER Derbys
111 SK 2460 4m W of Matlock. CP, 669.
Bakewell RD. P Mtlck. Ch e, m2, v. Sch pe.
W Derbys CC. Old lead-mining tn, famous
for mumming dance. Mkt Hse (NT), c 1700,
in main st.

WINSTER Westm
89 SD 4193 3m S of Windermere. Loc,
Crook CP. P Wndrmre. Ch e.

WINSTON Co Durham
85 NZ 1416 6m E of Barnard Cstle.
CP, 423. Bnd Cstle RD. P Darlington.
Ch e, m. Bishop Auckland CC. See also Lit
Newsham. 18c single-arch br over R Tees.

WINSTON Suffolk (E)
137 TM 1861 6m W of Framlingham.
CP, 145. Gipping RD. Ch e. Eye CC.

WINSTONE Glos
157 SO 9609 6m NW of Cirencester.
CP, 190. Crncstr RD. P Crncstr. Ch e, b.
Crncstr and Tewkesbury CC.

WINSWELL Devon
163, 175 SS 4913 4m S of Torrington. Loc,
Peters Marland CP. P Trrngtn.

WINTERBORNE CAME Dorset
178 SY 7088 2m SE of Dorchester. CP, 67.
Dchstr RD. Ch e. W Dst CC. Winter borne
(or bourne) denotes stream which flows
only in winter. Cme Hse, Palladian hse of
mid-18c. William Barnes, 19c Dorset poet,
rector here for 25 years. His rectory, in
cottage orné style, has thatched roof.

WINTERBORNE CLENSTON Dorset
178 ST 8303 4m SW of Blandford. CP, 86.
Blndfd RD. Ch e. N Dst CC.

WINTERBORNE HERRINGSTON Dorset
178 SY 6888 2m S of Dorchester. CP, 34.
Dchstr RD. W Dst CC.

WINTERBORNE HOUGHTON Dorset
178 ST 8204 4m WSW of Blandford.
CP, 126. Blndfd RD. P Blndfd Forum. Ch e.
N Dst CC.

WINTERBORNE KINGSTON Dorset
178 SY 8697 6m SSW of Blandford.
CP, 361. Blndfd RD. P Blndfd Forum.
Ch e, c, m. Sch p. N Dst CC.

WINTERBORNE MONKTON Dorset
178 SY 6787 2m SSW of Dorchester.
CP, 128. Dchstr RD. Ch e. W Dst CC. To
NW, Maiden Cstle (A.M.), huge oval
prehistoric earthworks.

WINTERBORNE STICKLAND Dorset
178 ST 8304 3m WSW of Blandford.
CP, 474. Blndfd RD. P Blndfd Forum.
Ch e, m. Sch pe. N Dst CC.

WINTERBORNE TOMSON Dorset
178, 179 SY 8897 6m S of Blandford. Loc,
Anderson CP. Ch e. 12c ch with Ggn box
pews.

WINTERBORNE WHITECHURCH Dorset
178 ST 8300 5m SW of Blandford. CP, 503.
Blndfd RD. P Blndfd Forum. Ch e, m, v.
Sch pe. N Dst CC. See also Whatcombe.

WINTERBORNE ZELSTON Dorset
178, 179 SY 8997 6m S of Blandford.
CP, 96. Blndfd RD. Ch e. N Dst CC.

WINTERBOURNE Berks
158 SU 4572 3m N of Newbury. CP, 162.
Nbry RD. Ch e. Nbry CC.

WINTERBOURNE Glos
155, 156 ST 6480 6m NE of Bristol.
CP, 6,097. Sodbury RD. P BRSTL.
Ch e, m3, v. Sch i, j, pe, s. S Glos CC. See
also Hambrook. Ch has brass of c 1370,
oldest in Glos.

WINTERBOURNE ABBAS Dorset
178 SY 6190 5m W of Dorchester. CP, 145.
Dchstr RD. P Dchstr. Ch e. Sch pe.
W Dst CC.

WINTERBOURNE BASSETT Wilts
157 SU 1074 7m SW of Swindon. CP, 156.
Marlborough and Ramsbury RD. P Swndn.
Ch e, m. Devizes CC. To E on Hackpen Hill,
White Horse cut in hillside 1838.

WINTERBOURNE DAUNTSEY Wilts
167 SU 1734 4m NE of Salisbury. Loc,
Wntrbne CP. Amesbury RD. Ch m.
Slsbry CC.

WINTERBOURNE EARLS Wilts
167 SU 1734 3m NE of Salisbury. Loc,
Wntrbne CP. Amesbury RD. Ch e, m.
Sch pe. Slsbry CC.

WINTERBOURNE GUNNER Wilts
167 SU 1835 4m NE of Salisbury. Loc,
Wntrbne CP. Amesbury RD. P Slsbry.
Ch e. Slsbry CC. Army camp to S.

WINTERBOURNE MONKTON Wilts
157 SU 1072 6m WNW of Marlborough.
CP, 166. Mlbrgh and Ramsbury RD.
P Swindon. Ch e. Sch pe. Devizes CC.

WINTERBOURNE STEEPLETON Dorset
178 SY 6289 4m W of Dorchester. CP, 171.
Dchstr RD. Ch e. W Dst CC.

WINTERBOURNE STOKE Wilts
167 SU 0741 5m W of Amesbury. CP, 202.
Amesbury RD. P Salisbury. Ch e. Slsbry CC.

WINTERBURN Yorks (W)
95 SD 9358 6m NW of Skipton. CP(Flasby
w Wntrbn), 110. Skptn RD. Ch v. Skptn CC.

WINTERINGHAM Lincs (L)
98 SE 9322 8m NNE of Scunthorpe.
CP, 863. Glanford Brigg RD. P Scnthpe.
Ch e, m. Sch p. Brgg and Scnthpe CC (Brgg).

WINTERLEY Ches
110 SJ 7457 3m ENE of Crewe. Loc,
Haslington CP. P Sandbach. Ch m.

WINTERSETT Yorks (W)
96, 102, 103 SE 3815 5m SE of Wakefield.
CP, 32. Wkfld RD. Wkfld BC.

WINTERSLOW Wilts
167 SU 2332 6m ENE of Salisbury.
CP, 1,070. Slsbry and Wilton RD. P Slsbry.
Ch e, m. Sch pe. Slsbry CC. See also Cmmn,
Lopcombe Corner, Middle Wntrslw.
Training stables. 1½m N beside A30 rd,
Pheasant Inn, or Wntrslw Hut, where in
1816 a lion killed leading horse of Exeter
mail coach.

WINTERTON Lincs (L)
104 SE 9218 5m NNE of Scunthorpe.
CP, 2,688. Glanford Brigg RD. P Scnthpe.
Ch e, m, s. Sch pe, s. Brgg and Scnthpe CC
(Brgg). Roman villa excavated.

WINTERTON-ON-SEA Norfolk
126 TG 4919 8m NNW of Yarmouth.
CP, 824. Blofield and Flegg RD. P Gt Ymth.
Ch e, m. Sch p. Ymth CC. Nature reserve on
the extensive sand dunes.

WINTHORPE Lincs (L)
114 TF 5665 1m N of Skegness. Loc,
Skgnss UD.

WINTHORPE Notts
113 SK 8156 2m NNE of Newark. CP, 365.
Nwk RD. P Nwk. Ch e, m. Sch p. Nwk CC.

WINTON Westm
84 NY 7810 1m NNE of Kirkby Stephen.
CP, 189. N Westm RD. Ch b. Sch pe.
Westm CC.

WINTRINGHAM Yorks (E)
92, 93 SE 8873 6m E of Malton. CP, 208.
Norton RD. P Mltn. Ch e. Howden CC. See
also Newton.

WINWICK Hunts
134 TL 1080 6m SE of Oundle. CP, 114.
Huntingdon RD. P HNTNGDN. Ch e.
Hunts CC.

WINWICK Lancs
101 SJ 6092 3m N of Warrington.
CP, 3,838. Wrrngtn RD. P Wrrngtn. Ch e, m.
Sch pe. Newton CC. See also Houghton Grn.

WINWICK Northants
132, 133 SP 6273 8m E of Rugby. CP, 92.
Daventry RD. Ch e. Dvntry CC (S Nthnts).

Wirksworth

WIRKSWORTH Derbys
111 SK 2854 4m S of Matlock. UD, 5,151.
P DERBY. See also Bolehill, Middleton.
Small mkt and indstrl tn; several bldngs of
interest. Large ch.

WIRSWALL Ches
118 SJ 5444 2m N of Whitchurch. CP, 154.
Nantwich RD. Nntwch CC.

WISBECH Cambs
124 TF 4609 12m WSW of King's Lynn.
MB, 17,002. P. Isle of Ely CC. See also New
Walsoken. Centre of fruit and bulb growing
area; fruit canning. Tn has Dutch
appearance. Many Ggn hses line river.
Peckover Hse (NT)*, 18c.

WISBECH ST MARY Cambs
124 TF 4208 3m WSW of Wisbech.
CP, 2,603. Wsbch RD. P Wsbch. Ch e, m3.
Isle of Ely CC. See also Tholomas Drove,
Thorney Toll.

WISBOROUGH GREEN Sussex (W)
182 TQ 0525 2m W of Billingshurst.
CP, 1,007. Petworth RD. P Bllngshst.
Ch e, v. Sch p. Chichester CC (Horsham).
See also Newpound Cmmn. Vllge with
enormous grn beside A272 rd.

WISETON Notts
103 SK 7189 6m N of Retford. CP, 103.
E Rtfd RD. P Doncaster, Yorkshire.
Bassetlaw CC.

WISHAW Warwicks
131 SP 1794 4m ESE of Sutton Coldfield.
CP, 207. Meriden RD. P Sttn Cldfld. Ch e.
Mrdn CC.

WISHFORD, GREAT Wilts
167 SU 0835 5m NW of Salisbury. See Gt
Wshfd.

WISLEY Surrey
170 TQ 0659 4m E of Woking. CP, 219.
Guildford RD. Ch e. Dorking CC. To S,
gdns* of Royal Horticultural Society.

WISPINGTON Lincs (L)
114 TF 2071 4m WNW of Horncastle.
CP, 72. Hncstle RD. Ch e. Hncstle CC.

WISSETT Suffolk (E)
137 TM 3679 2m NW of Halesworth.
CP, 268. Wainford RD. P Hlswth. Ch e, c.
Lowestoft CC.

WISSINGTON Suffolk (W)
149 TL 9533 6m NNW of Colchester.
CP(Nayland-w-Wssngtn), 960. Melford RD.
Ch e. Sudbury and Woodbridge CC. Small
Nmn ch.

WISTANSTOW Shrops
129 SO 4385 2m N of Craven Arms.
CP, 662. Ludlow RD. P Crvn Arms. Ch e, m.
Sch pe. Ldlw CC. See also Bushmoor,
Cheney Longville, Cwn Head, Marshbrook,
Strefford, Whittingslow, Woolston.

WISTANSWICK Shrops
118, 119 SJ 6628 3m S of Mkt Drayton.
Loc, Stoke upon Tern CP. P Mkt Drtn. Ch v.

WISTASTON Ches
110 SJ 6853 2m ENE of Nantwich.
CP, 4,519. Nntwch RD. Ch e, m. Sch p2.
Nntwch CC.

WISTON Sussex (W)
182 TQ 1512 2m NW of Steyning. CP, 289.
Chanctonbury RD. P Stnng. Ch e.
Shoreham CC (Arundel and Shrhm). See
also Buncton. Under the S Downs and
Chanctonbury Ring (see Buncton;
Washington). Wstn Hse is Elizn and later.

WISTOW Hunts
134 TL 2781 3m S of Ramsey. CP, 348.
St Ives RD. P HUNTINGDON. Ch e.
Hunts CC.

WISTOW Yorks (W)
97 SE 5935 3m NW of Selby. CP, 628.
Slby RD. Ch e, m. Sch pe. Barkston Ash CC.

WISWELL Lancs
95 SD 7437 3m S of Clitheroe. CP, 778.
Clthroe RD. Clthroe CC. See also Barrow.

WITCHAM Cambs
135 TL 4680 5m W of Ely. CP, 277.
Ely RD. P Ely. Ch e, m. Sch pe. Isle of
Ely CC.

WITCHAMPTON Dorset
179 ST 9806 4m NNW of Wimborne.
CP, 438. Wmbne and Cranborne RD.
P Wmbne. Ch e, m. Sch pe. N Dst CC.

WITCHFORD Cambs
135 TL 5078 2m WSW of Ely. CP, 653.
Ely RD. P Ely. Ch e, b. Sch pe, s. Isle of
Ely CC.

WITCOMBE, GREAT Glos
143, 144 SO 9114 5m SSW of Cheltenham.
See Gt Wtcmbe.

WITHAM Essex
149, 162 TL 8214 9m NE of Chelmsford.
UD, 17,306. P. Braintree CC (Maldon). See
also Chippinghill, Rivenhall End, Silver End.
**Ancient tn now industrialised. Large modern
radio equipment factory (Marconi). Rems of
10c cstle and mdvl ch.**

WITHAM FRIARY Som
166 ST 7441 5m SSW of Frome. CP, 340.
Frme RD. P Frme. Ch e. Wells CC. Ch is sole
rems of first Carthusian monastery in
England, founded 1178 as penance for
murder of Becket.

WITHAM ON THE HILL Lincs (K)
123 TF 0516 4m SW of Bourne. CP, 190.
S Kesteven RD. P Bne. Ch e. Sch pe.
Rutland and Stamford CC.

WITHCALL Lincs (L)
105 TF 2883 4m SW of Louth. CP, 116.
Lth RD. Ch e, m. Lth CC.

WITHERENDEN HILL Sussex (E)
183 TQ 6426 5m NE of Heathfield. Loc,
Burwash CP.

WITHERIDGE Devon
164, 176 SS 8014 10m W of Tiverton.
CP, 699. S Mltn RD. P Tvtn. Ch e, m, v.
Sch pe. N Dvn CC.

WITHERLEY Leics
132 SP 3297 1m E of Atherstone. CP, 703.
Mkt Bosworth RD. P Athrstne,
Warwickshire. Ch e. Sch pe. Bswth CC. See
also Fenny Drayton, Ratcliffe Culey.

WITHERN Lincs (L)
105 TF 4382 4m NNW of Alford. CP(Wthn
w Stain), 296. Louth RD. P Alfd. Ch e, m.
Sch pe. Lth CC.

WITHERNSEA Yorks (E)
99 TA 3427 15m E of Hull. UD, 5,976. P.
Bridlington CC. Resort. Lighthouse.

WITHERNWICK Yorks (E)
99 TA 1940 4m S of Hornsea. CP, 312.
Holderness RD. P Hull. Ch e, m. Sch p.
Bridlington CC.

WITHERSDALE STREET Suffolk (E)
137 TM 2681 7m SW of Bungay. Loc,
Mendham CP. P(Wthrsdle), Harleston,
Norfolk. Ch e, m.

WITHERSFIELD Suffolk (W)
148 TL 6547 2m NW of Haverhill. CP, 345.
Clare RD. P Hvrhll. Ch e, m. Bury
St Edmunds CC. Large grn on slope. Ch has
big iron doorhandle with two salamanders
carved on it.

WITHERSLACK Westm
89 SD 4384 4m NNE of Grange-over-Sands.
CP, 444. S Westm RD. P Grnge-over-Snds,
Lancs. Ch e. Sch pe. Westm CC. See also
Tn End.

WITHIEL Cornwall
185 SW 9965 4m S of Wadebridge. CP, 291.
Wdbrdge and Padstow RD. P Bodmin.
Ch e, m. Bodmin CC. See also Retire.

WITHIEL FLOREY Som
164 SS 9833 6m NE of Dulverton. Loc,
Brompton Regis CP. Ch e.

WITHINGTON Ches
110 SJ 8169 5m NW of Congleton. CP, 590.
Macclesfield RD. Ch e, m. Sch pe.
Mcclsfld CC.

WITHINGTON Glos
144 SP 0315 5m W of Northleach. CP, 458.
Nthlch RD. P Cheltenham. Ch e, b. Sch pe.
Cirencester and Tewkesbury CC.

WITHINGTON Herefs
142 SO 5643 4m NE of Hereford. CP, 403.
Hrfd RD. Ch e, b, m. Sch p. Leominster CC.
The White Stone, wayside cross dated 1770,
used as direction mark.

WITHINGTON Shrops
118 SJ 5713 5m E of Shrewsbury. CP, 180.
Atcham RD. P Shrsbry. Ch e. Shrsbry CC.

WITHINGTON GREEN Ches
110 SJ 8071 7m W of Macclesfield. Loc,
Wthngtn CP. To W is Jodrell Bank radio
telescope; part open.

WITHLEIGH Devon
164, 176 SS 9012 3m W of Tiverton. Loc,
Tvtn MB. P Tvtn.

Withnell

WITHNELL Lancs
94, 95 SD 6322 5m SW of Blackburn.
UD, 3,217. P Chly. Chly CC. See also Abbey
Vllge, Brinscall, Wthnll Fold.

WITHNELL FOLD Lancs
94, 95 SD 6123 5m SW of Blackburn. Loc,
Wthnll UD.

WITHYBROOK Warwicks
132 SP 4384 7m NE of Coventry. CP, 264.
Rugby RD. P Cvntry. Ch e. Rgby CC.

WITHYCOMBE Som
164 ST 0141 4m WSW of Watchet. CP, 345.
Williton RD. P Minehead. Ch e, m.
Bridgwater CC. See also Rodhuish.

WITHYDITCH Som
166 ST 7059 3m NNE of Radstock. Loc,
Dunkerton CP. Ch b.

WITHYHAM Sussex (E)
171, 183 TQ 4935 6m WSW of Tunbridge
Wells. CP, 3,066. Uckfield RD. P Hartfield.
Ch e. Sch p. E Grinstead CC. See also Ball's
Grn, Blackham, Friar's Gate. Ch: Sackville
chpl and monmt, 17c.

WITHY MILLS Som
166 ST 6657 2m NW of Radstock. Loc,
Paulton CP. Ch m.

WITHYPOOL Som
164 SS 8435 6m NW of Dulverton.
CP(Withypoole), 252. Dlvtn RD.
P Minehead. Ch e, m. Sch p. Taunton CC.
See also Hawkridge. Many Bronze Age
barrows, stone circles etc on surrounding
moors.

WITLEY Surrey
169 SU 9439 3m SW of Godalming.
CP, 6,105. Hambledon RD. P Gdlmng.
Ch e, r, v. Sch pe, s. Farnham CC. See also
Brook, Milford, Sandhills, Wheelerstreet,
Wormley. Ch: Saxon and Nmn work; glass;
wall-painting.

WITNESHAM Suffolk (E)
150 TM 1850 4m NNE of Ipswich. CP, 556.
Deben RD. P Ipswch. Ch e, b. Sch p.
Eye CC.

WITNEY Oxon
145 SP 3510 10m WNW of Oxford.
UD, 12,535. P. Mid-Oxon CC (Banbury).

Has made blankets since Middle Ages. Glove
mnfg. Stone hses. Wide main st with central
bldngs. 17c grammar sch.

WITNEY, GREAT Worcs
130 SO 7566 5m SW of Stourport. See Gt
Wtny.

WITTERING Hunts
123 TF 0502 4m SSE of Stamford.
CP, 2,278. Barnack RD.
P PETERBOROUGH. Ch e, m. Sch i, j.
Ptrbrgh BC (CC). RAF airfield. Mainly
Saxon ch.

WITTERSHAM Kent
184 TQ 8927 5m N of Rye. CP, 885.
Tenterden RD. P Tntdn. Ch e, m. Sch pe.
Ashford CC. On ridge above Rother marshes
called Isle of Oxney, of which it is 'capital'.
1m E, Stocks windmill.

WITTON Norfolk
126 TG 3109 5m E of Norwich. Loc,
Postwick CP. P NRWCH, NOR 87Z. Ch e.

WITTON Norfolk
126 TG 3330 3m E of N Walsham. CP, 326.
Smallburgh RD. P(Wttn Br), N Wlshm.
Ch e, m. N Nflk CC. See also Ridlington.

WITTON GILBERT Co Durham
85 NZ 2345 3m NW of Durham. CP, 2,137.
Drhm RD. P DRHM. Ch e, s. Sch p.
Drhm CC.

WITTON LE WEAR Co Durham
85 NZ 1431 3m SSW of Crook. Loc, Crk
and Willington UD. P Bishop Auckland.
Wttn Cstle*, 15c and later; pictures,
furniture. Wooded grnds with lake.

WITTON PARK Co Durham
85 NZ 1730 2m WNW of Bishop Auckland.
Loc, Bshp Aucklnd UD. P Bshp Aucklnd.

WIVELISCOMBE Som
164 ST 0827 6m NW of Wellington.
CP, 1,141. Wllngton RD. P Taunton.
Ch e, m, v. Sch p, s. Tntn CC.

WIVELSFIELD Sussex (E)
182 TQ 3420 2m S of Haywards Hth.
CP, 988. Chailey RD. Ch e, b, v. Sch p.
Lewes CC.

WIVELSFIELD GREEN Sussex (E)
183 TQ 3520 3m SSE of Haywards Hth.
Loc, Wvlsfld CP. P Hwds Hth.

WIVENHOE Essex
149, 162 TM 0321 4m SE of Colchester.
UD, 5,310. P Clchstr. Harwich CC.
Shipyards. Ferry to Fingringhoe. Ch has
early Tdr brasses. Wvnhoe Pk, grnds
landscaped by Richard Wood, is site of
University of Essex.

WIVENHOE CROSS Essex
149, 162 TM 0423 3m ESE of Colchester.
Loc, Wvnhoe UD.

WIVETON Norfolk
125 TG 0443 3m NW of Holt. CP, 141.
Walsingham RD. Ch e. NW Nflk CC
(N Nflk).

WIX Essex
150 TM 1628 4m ESE of Manningtree.
CP, 665. Tendring RD. P Mnnngtree.
Ch e, m. Sch p. Harwich CC. Rems of 12c
abbey incorporated in ch and nearby
farmhouse.

WIXFORD Warwicks
144 SP 0954 7m W of Stratford. CP, 141.
Alcester RD. Ch e. Strtfd-on-Avon CC
(Strtfd). Ch: roof with numerous carved
bosses; 15c brass. Half-timbered hses.

WIXOE Suffolk (W)
148, 149 TL 7142 3m SE of Haverhill.
CP, 80. Clare RD. Ch e. Bury
St Edmunds CC.

WOBURN Beds
146 SP 9433 4m E of Bletchley. CP, 846.
Ampthill RD. P Bltchly, Bucks. Ch e. Sch p.
Mid-Beds CC. 1m E, Wbn Abbey*, 18c seat
of Duke of Bedford, in large pk. Hse and
grnds open, latter daily.

WOBURN SANDS Bucks
146 SP 9235 4m ENE of Bletchley.
CP, 1,481. Newport Pagnell RD. P Bltchly.
Ch e, m. Buckingham CC.

WOKING Surrey
169, 170 TQ 0058 6m N of Guildford.
UD, 75,771. P. Wkng CC. See also Byfleet,
Horsell, Knaphill, Mayford, Pyrford, W Bflt.
Rsndtl; light industry. Mosque of 1889.

WOKINGHAM Berks
169 SU 8168 7m ESE of Reading.
MB, 21,058. P. Wknghm CC.

WOLD Northants
133 SP 7873 6m WSW of Kettering.
Alternative name for Old, qv.

WOLDINGHAM Surrey
171 TQ 3755 7m SSE of Croydon. Loc,
Caterham and Warlingham UD. P Ctrhm.

WOLD NEWTON Lincs (L)
105 TF 2496 8m SSW of Grimsby. CP, 86.
Grmsby RD. P LINCOLN. Ch e. Louth CC.

WOLD NEWTON Yorks (E)
93 TA 0473 6m SW of Filey. CP, 247.
Bridlington RD. P Driffield. Ch e, m. Sch p.
Brdlngtn CC. See also Fordon. Ch largely
Nmn. Meteorite fell here 1795 — monmt
marks spot.

WOLFERLOW Herefs
129, 130 SO 6661 5m N of Bromyard.
CP, 73. Brmyd RD. Ch e. Leominster CC.
See also High Lane.

WOLFERTON Norfolk
124 TF 6528 6m NNE of King's Lynn. Loc,
Sandringham CP. P K's Lnn. Ch e.

WOLFORD, GREAT Warwicks
144 SP 2434 3m ENE of Moreton-in-Marsh.
See Gt Wlfd.

WOLLASTON Northants
133 SP 9062 3m S of Wellingborough.
CP, 2,014. Wllngbrgh RD. P Wllngbrgh.
Ch e, b, c, m, s. Sch p, s. Wllngbrgh CC.

WOLLASTON Shrops
118 SJ 3212 7m ENE of Welshpool. CP, 215.
Atcham RD. Ch e. Sch pe. Shrewsbury CC.
Breiden Hills to W dominate landscape. Ch
contains brass commemorating 'Old Parr',
who reputedly lived from 1483 to 1635.

WOLLERTON Shrops
118, 119 SJ 6230 4m SW of Mkt Drayton.
Loc, Hodnet CP. P Mkt Drtn. Ch c.

WOLSINGHAM Co Durham
84 NZ 0737 3m WSW of Tow Law.
CP, 3,005. Weardale RD. P Bishop
Auckland. Ch e, b, m3, r. Sch p, pr, s.
NW Drhm CC. See also Thornley.

Wolston

WOLSTON Warwicks
132 SP 4175 5m ESE of Coventry. CP, 1,436. Rugby RD. P Cvntry. Ch e, b. Sch pe, s. Rgby CC. Stream flows beside main st; footbridges to hses. Faint rems of 13c Brandon Cstle across R Avon (see Brndn).

WOLVERHAMPTON Staffs
130, 131 SO 9198 12m NW of Birmingham. CB, 268,847. P. BCs: Wlvrhmptn NE, SE, SW. (BCs: Bilston, Wednesbury, Wlvrhmptn NE, SW; CCs: Brierley Hill, Cannock.) See also Blstn, Tettenhall, Wednesfield. Indstrl tn; iron and brass, aircraft components, locks, etc.

WOLVERLEY Staffs
118 SJ 4731 3m WNW of Wem. Loc, Wm Rural CP. N Shrops RD. Oswestry CC.

WOLVERLEY Worcs
130 SO 8279 2m N of Kidderminster. CP, 4,630. Kddrmnstr RD. P Kddrmnstr. Ch e. Sch pe. Kddrmnstr CC. See also Blakeshall, Caunsall, Cookley, Kingsford. Beside R Stour and Staffs and Worcs Canal.

WOLVERTON Bucks
146 SP 8141 6m NW of Bletchley. UD, 13,819. P. Buckingham CC. See also Calverton, Stony Stratford, Upr Weald.

WOLVERTON Hants
168 SU 5558 7m NW of Basingstoke. Loc, Baughurst CP. P Bsngstke. Ch e. Early Ggn ch.

WOLVERTON Warwicks
131 SP 2062 5m N of Stratford. CP, 175. Strtfd-on-Avon RD. Ch e. Sch p. Strtfd-on-Avn CC (Strtfd).

WOLVEY Warwicks
132 SP 4287 4m S of Hinckley. CP, 1,226. Rugby RD. P Hnckly, Leics. Ch e, b, r. Sch pe. Rgby CC. See also Bramcote.

WOLVISTON Co Durham
85 NZ 4525 4m N of Teesside (Stockton). CP. Stcktn RD. P BILLINGHAM, Tssde. Ch e, m. Sch p. Easington CC (Sedgefield).

WOMBLETON Yorks (N)
92 SE 6684 4m E of Helmsley. CP, 263. Kbmsde RD. P YORK. Ch m. Sch pe. Thirsk and Malton CC.

WOMBOURN Staffs
130 SO 8793 4m SW of Wolverhampton. CP. Seisdon RD. P Wlvrhmptn. Ch e, c, m. Sch i, j, p, pe, s. SW Staffs (Brierley Hill).

WOMBWELL Yorks (W)
102, 103 SE 3903 4m SE of Barnsley. UD, 17,933. P Bnsly. Dearne Valley CC. See also Hemingfield, Jump. Colliery tn.

WOMENSWOLD Kent
173 TR 2250 7m SE of Canterbury. CP, 363. Bridge-Blean RD. P Cntrbry. Ch e. Sch pe. Cntrbry CC. See also Woolage Grn.

WOMERSLEY Yorks (W)
103 SE 5319 5m ESE of Pontefract. CP, 372. Osgoldcross RD. P Doncaster. Ch e. Sch pe. Goole CC.

WONERSH Surrey
169, 170 TQ 0145 3m SSE of Guildford. CP, 3,585. Hambledon RD. P Gldfd. Ch e, c, v. Gldfd CC. See also Blackheath, Shamley Grn. Some old cottages in vllge. 1m NNE, Gt Tangley Mnr, 16c moated hse.

WONSTON Hants
168 SU 4739 6m N of Winchester. CP, 1,385. Wnchstr RD. Ch e. Sch p. Wnchstr CC. See also S Wnstn, Stoke Charity, Sutton Scotney.

WOOBURN Bucks
159 SU 9087 3m SW of Beaconsfield. CP, 7,962. Wycombe RD. Ch e. Sch pe. Bcnsfld CC (Wcmbe). See also Bourne End, Cores End.

WOOBURN GREEN Bucks
159 SU 9188 2m WSW of Beaconsfield. Loc, Wbn CP. P High Wycombe. Ch m. Sch p.

WOODACOTT Devon
174 SS 3807 4m NE of Holsworthy. Loc, Thornbury CP. Ch m.

WOODALL Yorks (W)
103 SK 4880 6m W of Worksop. CP(Harthill w Wdll), 1,458. Kiveton Pk RD. Rother Valley CC.

WOODBASTWICK Norfolk
126 TG 3315 2m SE of Wroxham. CP, 569. Blofield and Flegg RD. P NORWICH, NOR 54Z. Ch e. Sch pe. Yarmouth CC. See also Panxworth, Ranworth.

WOODBECK Notts
104 SK 7778 5m ESE of Retford. Loc,
Rampton CP. P Rtfd. Rmptn Criminal
Mental Hsptl.

WOODBOROUGH Notts
112 SK 6347 6m NE of Nottingham.
CP, 747. Basford RD. P NTTNGHM.
Ch b, m. Sch pe. Carlton CC. Stocking
knitters' cottages in vllge.

WOODBOROUGH Wilts
167 SU 1159 3m W of Pewsey. CP, 286.
Psy RD. P Psy. Ch m. Sch pe. Devizes CC.

WOODBRIDGE Suffolk (E)
150 TM 2749 7m ENE of Ipswich.
UD, 7,272. P. Sudbury and Wdbrdge CC.
Small mkt tn at head of Deben estuary. Old
tide mill. Perp ch with seven-sacrament font.
Partly 16c Shire Hall.

WOODBURY Devon
176 SY 0187 4m N of Exmouth. CP, 2,736.
St Thomas RD. P Exeter. Ch b, v. Sch pe.
Honiton CC. See also Ebford, Exton, Wdbry
Salterton.

WOODBURY SALTERTON Devon
176 SY 0189 5m N of Exmouth. Loc,
Woodbury CP. P Exeter. Sch pe.

WOODCHESTER Glos
156 SO 8402 2m SSW of Stroud. CP, 815.
Strd RD. P Strd. Ch e, b, r2. Sch pe, pr.
Strd CC. Rems of Roman villa S of ruined
ch. 2m WSW, uncompleted 19c mansion in
Wdchstr Pk, wooded valley with five lakes.

WOODCHURCH Kent
184 TQ 9434 4m E of Tenterden.
CP, 1,314. Tntdn RD. P Ashford. Ch e, v.
Sch pe. Ashfd CC. See also Redbrook St.
Fine EE ch. To N, well preserved
smock-mill.

WOODCOTE Oxon
158, 159 SU 6482 4m N of Pangbourne.
CP, 1,115. Henley RD. P Reading, Berks.
Ch e, m. Sch p, s. Hnly CC.

WOODCOTE Shrops
119 SJ 7615 3m SSE of Newport. CP, 243.
Wellington RD. Ch e. Sch pe. The
Wrekin CC.

WOODCOTT Hants
168 SU 4354 5m NNW of Whitchurch.
CP(Litchfield and Wdctt), 231. Kingsclere
and Whtchch RD. Ch e. Basingstke CC.

WOODCUTTS Dorset
179 ST 9717 8m ESE of Shaftesbury. Loc,
Sixpenny Handley CP. P Salisbury, Wilts.
Ch m.

WOOD DALLING Norfolk
125 TG 0827 7m S of Holt. CP, 273.
St Faith's and Aylsham RD.
P NORWICH, NOR 12Y. Ch e, m, s. N Nflk
CC (Central Nflk).

WOODDITTON Cambs
135 TL 6559 3m SSE of Newmarket.
CP, 1,134. Nmkt RD. P Nmkt, Suffolk.
Ch e, c, m. Sch pe. Cambs CC. See also Dttn
Grn, Saxon St. Large but elegant concrete
water twr.

WOODEATON Oxon
145 SP 5311 4m NNE of Oxford. CP, 136.
Bullingdon RD. Ch e. Mid-Oxon CC
(Henley).

WOOD END Herts
147 TL 3225 6m E of Stevenage. Loc,
Ardeley CP.

WOODEND Northants
145, 146 SP 6149 5m W of Towcester.
CP, 184. Tcstr RD. P Tcstr. Ch b.
Daventry CC (S Nthnts).

WOODEND Sussex (W)
181 SU 8108 4m NW of Chichester. Loc,
Funtington CP.

WOOD END Warwicks
131 SP 1071 5m NE of Redditch. Loc,
Tanworth CP. Sch p.

WOOD END Warwicks
131 SP 2498 4m SSE of Tamworth. Loc,
Kingsbury CP. P Atherstone.

WOOD ENDERBY Lincs (L)
114 TF 2763 4m SSE of Horncastle.
CP, 101. Hncstle RD. Ch e. Hncstle CC.

WOODFALLS Wilts
167 SU 1920 7m SSE of Salisbury. Loc,
Redlynch CP. P Slsbry Ch m.

WOODFORD Ches
101 SJ 8982 3m ENE of Wilmslow. Loc,
Hazel Grove and Bramhall UD. P Brmhll,
Stockport.

Woodford

WOODFORD Cornwall
174 SS 2113 5m N of Bude. Loc,
Morwenstow CP. Ch m.

WOODFORD Glos
156 ST 6995 9m NE of Severn Rd Br. Loc,
Alkington CP. Thornbury RD. Ch e, b.
Sch pe. S Glos CC.

WOODFORD London
161 TQ 4191 2m WSW of Chigwell. Loc,
Redbridge LB. Wanstead and Wdfd BC.

WOODFORD Northants
134 SP 9676 2m WSW of Thrapston.
CP, 1,361. Oundle and Thrpstn RD.
P Kettering. Ch e, b, m. Sch pe.
Wellingborough CC (Peterborough).

WOODFORD GREEN London
161 TQ 4092 1m NW of Wdfd. Loc,
Redbridge LB. P Essex. Wanstead and
Wdfd BC. Statue of Sir Winston Churchill,
former MP for Wdfd.

WOODFORD HALSE Northants
145 SP 5452 6m SSW of Daventry. Loc,
Wdfd cum Membris CP. Dvntry RD.
P Rugby, Warwickshire. Ch e, v. Sch pe, s.
Dvntry CC (S Nthnts). Paradise for
explorers of closed rly lines.

WOODGATE Norfolk
125 TG 0216 3m NE of E Dereham. Loc,
Swanton Morley CP.

WOODGATE Sussex (W)
181 SU 9304 5m E of Chichester. Loc,
Aldingbourne CP.

WOODGATE Worcs
130, 131 SO 9666 3m S of Bromsgrove.
Loc, Stoke Prior CP.

WOODGREEN Hants
179 SU 1717 3m NNE of Fordingbridge.
CP, 432. Ringwood and Fdngbrdge RD.
P Fdngbrdge. Ch m. New Forest CC.

WOOD GREEN London
160 TQ 3090 6m N of Charing Cross. Loc,
Haringey LB. Wd Grn BC.

WOODHALL Yorks (N)
90 SD 9790 2m NW of Aysgarth. Loc,
Askrigg CP.

WOODHALL SPA Lincs (L)
113 TF 1963 7m SW of Horncastle.
UD, 2,232. P. Hncstle CC. 19c spa tn with
fine golf course. 1½m NE, obelisk with bust
of Wellington records that surrounding wd
grows from acorns planted immediately
after Battle of Waterloo.

WOODHAM Surrey
170 TQ 0462 3m NE of Woking. Loc,
Chertsey UD. P Weybridge.

WOODHAM FERRERS Essex
162 TQ 7999 6m SSW of Maldon.
CP, 2,215. Chelmsford RD. P Chlmsfd.
Ch e, c, v. Sch pe. Chlmsfd CC. See also
Bicknacre, S Wdhm Frrs.

WOODHAM MORTIMER Essex
162 TL 8104 3m SW of Maldon. CP, 434.
Mldn RD. P Mldn. Ch e. Mldn CC.

WOODHAM WALTER Essex
162 TL 8006 3m W of Maldon. CP, 499.
Mldn RD. P Mldn. Ch e, v. Sch pe. Mldn CC.
Ch blt in Elizabeth I's reign, very rare.

WOODHILL Shrops
130 SO 7384 5m S of Bridgnorth. Loc,
Highley CP.

WOODHORN Nthmb
78 NZ 2988 7m ENE of Morpeth. Loc,
Ashington UD. Mining vllge. Ch 12c–14c,
restored 19c; monmts.

WOODHOUSE Leics
121 SK 5415 3m S of Loughborough.
CP, 2,493. Barrow upon Soar RD.
P Lghbrgh. Ch e. Melton CC. See also Wdhse
Eaves.

WOODHOUSE EAVES Leics
121 SK 5314 3m S of Loughborough. Loc,
Wdhse CP. P Lghbrgh. Ch e, b, m. Sch pe.

WOODHOUSES Lancs
101 SD 9100 3m SSW of Oldham. Loc,
Failsworth UD. P Flswth, MANCHESTER.

WOODHURST Hunts
134 TL 3176 3m N of St Ives. CP, 275.
St Ives RD. P HUNTINGDON. Ch e, b.
Hunts CC.

WOODINGDEAN Sussex (E)
183 TQ 3505 3m ENE of Brighton. Loc,
Brghtn CB. P Brghtn. Brghtn, Kemptown BC.

WOODLAND Co Durham
84 NZ 0726 6m NNE of Barnard Cstle. CP, 270. Bnd Cstle RD. P Bishop Auckland. Ch m. Sch p. Bshp Aucklnd CC.

WOODLAND Devon
187, 188 SX 7968 2m ESE of Ashburton. CP, 101. Newton Abbot RD. Ch e. Totnes CC.

WOODLANDS Dorset
179 SU 0509 6m NNE of Wimborne. CP, 336. Wmbne and Cranborne RD. P Wmbne. Ch m. Sch pe. N Dst CC.

WOODLANDS Hants
180 SU 3211 3m NE of Lyndhurst. Loc, Netley Marsh CP. P SOUTHAMPTON.

WOODLANDS Yorks (W)
103 SE 5307 4m NW of Doncaster. Loc, Adwick le Street UD. P Dncstr.

WOODLANDS PARK Berks
159 SU 8578 2m SW of Maidenhead. Loc, White Waltham CP. P Mdnhd. Sch p.

WOODLANDS ST MARY Berks
158 SU 3374 4m N of Hungerford. Loc, Lambourn CP. Ch e.

WOODLEIGH Devon
187, 188 SX 7348 3m N of Kingsbridge. CP, 163. Kngsbrdge RD. P Kngsbrdge. Ch e. Totnes CC.

WOODLESFORD Yorks (W)
96, 102 SE 3629 5m SE of Leeds. Loc, Rothwell UD. P LDS.

WOODLEY Berks
159 SU 7673 3m E of Reading. CP(Wdly and Sandford), 12,461. Wokingham RD. P Rdng. Ch e, c, m. Sch p4, pe, pr, s. Rdng S CC (Wknghm). See also Lit Hungerford, Wheeler's Grn.

WOODMANCOTE Glos
143, 144 SO 9727 4m NNE of Cheltenham. CP, 1,146. Chltnhm RD. P Chltnhm. Ch v. Cirencester and Tewkesbury CC.

WOODMANCOTE Glos
157 SP 0008 4m N of Cirencester. Loc, Crncstr RD. P Crncstr. Crncstr and Tewkesbury CC.

WOODMANCOTE Hants
168 SU 5642 7m SW of Basingstoke. CP(Woodmancott), 31. Bsngstke RD. P Winchester. Ch e. Bsngstke CC.

WOODMANCOTE Sussex (W)
181 SU 7707 6m WNW of Chichester. Loc, Westbourne CP. Ch e.

WOODMANSEY Yorks (E)
99 TA 0537 2m SE of Beverley. CP, 1,648. Bvrly RD. P Bvrly. Sch pe. Haltemprice CC. See also Thearne.

WOODMANSTERNE Surrey
170 TQ 2759 1m E of Banstead. Loc, Bnstd UD. P Bnstd.

WOODNESBOROUGH Kent
173 TR 3056 2m WSW of Sandwich. CP, 948. Eastry RD. P Sndwch. Ch e. Dover and Deal CC (Dvr).

WOODNEWTON Northants
134 TL 0394 4m N of Oundle. CP, 247. Oundle and Thrapston RD. P PETERBOROUGH. Ch e, m. Sch pe. Wellingborough CC (Ptrbrgh).

WOOD NORTON Norfolk
125 TG 0127 6m ESE of Fakenham. CP, 181. Walsingham RD. P Dereham. Ch e, m. NW Nflk CC (N Nflk).

WOODPLUMPTON Lancs
94 SD 5034 4m NW of Preston. CP, 1,694, Prstn RD. P Prstn. Ch e, r. Sch pe, pr. S Fylde CC. See also Catforth, Cuddy Hill.

WOODRISING Norfolk
125 TF 9803 5m ENE of Watton. Loc, Cranworth CP. P NORWICH, NOR 22X. Ch e.

WOODSEAVES Shrops
110, 119 SJ 6831 2m SSE of Mkt Drayton. Loc, Sutton upon Tern CP. Mkt Drtn RD. Ch m. Oswestry CC.

WOODSEAVES Staffs
119 SJ 7925 5m NE of Newport. Loc, High Offley CP. P STAFFORD. Ch m.

WOODSEND Wilts
157 SU 2275 5m NNE of Marlborough. Loc, Aldbourne CP.

WOODSETTS Yorks (W)
103 SK 5583 4m NNW of Worksop.
CP, 589. Kiveton Pk RD. P Wksp, Notts.
Ch e, m. Sch p. Rother Valley CC.

WOODSFORD Dorset
178 SY 7690 5m E of Dorchester. CP, 181.
Dchstr RD. Ch e. W Dst CC. Wdsfd Cstle,
14c fortified hse, now a farm.

WOODSIDE Berks
169 SU 9371 4m SSW of Windsor. Loc,
Winkfield CP.

WOODSTOCK Oxon
145 SP 4416 8m NNW of Oxford.
MB, 1,940. P OXFD. Banbury CC. Glove
mnfg. Old tn — many 18c bldngs, but some
older. Oxfd City and County Museum. On
W side, Blenheim Palace*, blt for Duke of
Marlborough by Vanbrugh early 18c. Vast
hse and pk with lake.

WOOD STREET Surrey
169, 170 SU 9551 3m WNW of Guildford.
Loc, Worplesdon CP. P Gldfd.

WOODTHORPE Derbys
112 SK 4574 5m ENE of Chesterfield. Loc,
Staveley UD. P Chstrfld.

WOODTHORPE Leics
121 SK 5417 2m S of Loughborough. Loc,
Lghbrgh MB.

WOODTHORPE Lincs (L)
105 TF 4380 5m SW of Mablethorpe.
CP(Strubby w Wdthpe), 222. Louth RD.
Lth CC.

WOODTON Norfolk
137 TM 2993 4m NW of Bungay. CP, 392.
Loddon RD. P Bngy, Suffolk. Ch e, m.
Sch p. S Nflk CC.

WOODVILLE Derbys
120, 121 SK 3119 3m NW of Ashby de la
Zouch. CP, 2,203. Repton RD.
P Burton-on-Trent, Staffs. Ch e, m2, v.
Sch i, je. Belper CC.

WOOD WALTON Hunts
134 TL 2180 5m WSW of Ramsey. CP, 271.
Huntingdon RD. P HNTNGDN. Ch e.
Hunts CC.

WOODYATES Dorset
179 SU 0219 10m SW of Salisbury. Loc,
Pentridge CP. Ch m.

WOOFFERTON Shrops
129 SO 5268 4m S of Ludlow. Loc,
Richard's Cstle (Salop) CP.

WOOKEY Som
165 ST 5145 2m W of Wells. CP, 1,042.
Wlls RD. P Wlls. Ch e, m. Sch p. Wlls CC.
See also Henton.

WOOKEY HOLE Som
165, 166 ST 5347 2m NNW of Wells. Loc,
St Cuthbert Out CP. Wlls RD. P Wlls. Ch m.
Sch p. Wlls CC. Vllge largely grown up
round famous cave (floodlit, much visited).
R Axe flows out here from under ground.
To N, Ebbor Gorge (NT), with further caves
(not accessible), where many prehistoric
rems found.

WOOL Dorset
178 SY 8486 5m W of Wareham. CP, 3,709.
Wrhm and Purbeck RD. P Wrhm. Ch e, m, r.
Sch pe, pr. S Dst CC. See also E Burton.
R Frome spanned by Elizn br with
transportation tablet, cf. Durweston. Hard
by, Woolbridge Mnr, Elizn. To E, slight rems
of Bindon Abbey, 12c.

WOOLACOMBE Devon
163 SS 4543 4m WSW of Ilfracombe. Loc,
Mortehoe CP. P. Ch e, m. Sch p. Resort at N
end of long stretch of sands backed by
dunes. View of Lundy.

WOOLAGE GREEN Kent
173 TQ 2349 7m NW of Dover. Loc,
Womenswold CP.

WOOLASTON Glos
155, 156 ST 5899 5m NE of Chepstow.
CP, 786. Lydney RD. Ch e, m2. Sch p.
W Glos CC. See also Netherend.

WOOLAVINGTON Som
165 ST 3441 4m NE of Bridgwater.
CP, 1,049. Brdgwtr RD. P Brdgwtr. Ch e, m.
Sch p. Brdgwtr CC.

WOOLBEDING Sussex (W)
181 SU 8722 1m NW of Midhurst. CP, 207.
Mdhst RD. Ch e. Chichester CC (Horsham).
Wlbdng Hse (NT), 17c hse; gdn has 130ft
tulip tree.

WOOLDALE Yorks (W)
102 SE 1508 5m S of Huddersfield. Loc,
Holmfirth UD. P Hlmfth, Hddsfld.

WOOLER Nthmb
71 NT 9928 16m S of Berwick-upon-Tweed.
CP, 1,976. Glendale RD. P. Ch e, m, r, v.
Sch p, s. Brwck-upn-Twd CC. Small mkt tn
at NE end of Cheviot Hills, on tributary of
R Till.

WOOLFARDISWORTHY Devon
174 SS 3321 8m WSW of Bideford. CP, 505.
Bdfd RD. P(Woolsery), Bdfd. Ch e, m.
Sch p. N Dvn CC (Torrington). See also
Alminstone Cross, Ashmansworthy, Buck's
Cross.

WOOLFARDISWORTHY Devon
176 SS 8208 5m N of Crediton. CP, 163.
Crdtn RD. Ch e. Tiverton CC (Torrington).

WOOLHAMPTON Berks
158 SU 5766 6m E of Newbury. CP, 593.
Nbry RD. P Reading. Ch e, r2. Sch pe.
Nbry CC. 1m N, Douai Abbey and Sch,
former modern.

WOOLHOPE Herefs
142, 143 SO 6135 6m W of Ledbury.
CP, 437. Ldbry RD. P HEREFORD. Ch e.
Leominster CC.

WOOLLAND Dorset
178 ST 7706 7m W of Blandford. CP, 85.
Sturminster RD. P Blndfd Forum. Ch e.
N Dst CC.

WOOLLARD Som
166 ST 6364 6m SSE of Bristol. Loc,
Bathavon RD, Clutton RD. Ch b.
N Som CC.

WOOLLEY Cornwall
174 SS 2516 7m NNE of Bude. Loc,
Morwenstow CP. Ch m.

WOOLLEY Hunts
134 TL 1574 6m WNW of Huntingdon.
CP(Barham and Wlly), 78. Hntngdn RD.
Ch e. Hunts CC.

WOOLLEY Som
156 ST 7468 2m N of Bath. Loc,
Charlcombe CP. Ch e.

WOOLLEY Yorks (W)
102 SE 3213 4m NNW of Barnsley.
CP, 1,184. Wakefield RD. P Wkfld. Ch e.
Sch p, pe. Wkfld BC.

WOOLMER GREEN Herts
147 TL 2518 4m NNE of Welwyn Gdn City.
Loc, Wlwn CP. P Knebworth. Ch e. Sch pe.

WOOLPIT Suffolk (W)
136 TL 9762 5m WNW of Stowmarket.
CP, 963. Thedwastre RD. P Bury St Eds.
Ch e, m, v. Sch p. Bury St Eds CC. Ch has
double hammerbeam angel roof.

WOOLSTASTON Shrops
129 SO 4598 3m N of Ch Stretton. CP, 75.
Atcham RD. Ch e. Shrewsbury CC.

WOOLSTHORPE Lincs (K)
113, 122 SK 8334 5m W of Grantham.
CP, 581. W Kesteven RD. P Grnthm.
Ch e, m. Sch p. Rutland and Stamford CC.
Canal with wharf and lock. Views of Belvoir
Cstle.

WOOLSTHORPE Lincs (K)
122 SK 9224 7m S of Grantham. Loc,
Colsterworth CP. Wlsthpe Mnr (NT)*,
bthplce of Sir Isaac Newton, 1642.

WOOLSTON Lancs
101 SJ 6489 3m ENE of Warrington.
CP, 3,434. Wrrngtn RD. P Wrrngtn. Ch r.
Sch p, pr, s. Newton CC. See also
Martinscroft.

WOOLSTON Shrops
118 SJ 3224 4m SSE of Oswestry. Loc,
W Felton CP. Holy well sacred to
St Winifred at half-timbered cottage.

WOOLSTON Shrops
129 SO 4287 3m N of Craven Arms. Loc,
Wistanstow CP.

WOOLSTONE Berks
158 SU 2987 7m W of Wantage. CP, 81.
Faringdon RD. Ch e. Abingdon CC. Near
Uffington, qv.

WOOLSTONE, GREAT Bucks
146 SP 8738 3m N of Bletchley. See Gt
Wlstne.

WOOLTON HILL Hants
168 SU 4261 4m SW of Newbury. Loc,
E Woodhay CP. P Nbry, Berks. Ch e. Sch pe.

WOOLVERSTONE Suffolk (E)
150 TM 1838 4m SSE of Ipswich. CP, 280.
Samford RD. P Ipswich. Ch e. Sch pe.
Sudbury and Woodbridge CC.

WOOLVERTON Som
166 ST 7954 4m NNE of Frome. Loc,
Tellisford CP. Ch e.

WOOLWICH London
161, 171 TQ 4378 7m E of Lndn Br. Loc,
Greenwich LB. Wlwch E BC, Wlwch W BC.
Thames-side distr S of river; ferry to
N Wlwch and docks on N bank. Rotunda*
contains artillery museum. Thamesmead
housing development to E.

WOONTON Herefs
142 SO 3552 5m SE of Kington. Loc,
Almeley CP. P HEREFORD.

WOOPERTON Nthmb
71 NU 0420 6m SSE of Wooler. Loc,
Roddam CP. P Alnwick. 1m SE is Percy's
Cross, shaft of 15c cross marking spot where
the Lancastrian leader Sir Ralph Percy was
slain in Wars of the Roses battle of 1464.

WOORE Shrops
110, 119 SJ 7342 6m NE of Mkt Drayton.
CP, 853. Mkt Drtn RD. P Crewe, Cheshire.
Ch e, m. Sch p. Oswestry CC. See also
Bearstone, Pipe Gate.

WOOTTON Beds
147 TL 0045 4m SW of Bedford. CP, 1,826.
Bdfd RD. P BDFD. Ch e, b, m. Sch p.
Mid-Beds CC. See also Keeley Grn.

WOOTTON Berks
158 SP 4701 4m SW of Oxford. CP, 2,429.
Abingdon RD. P Boars Hill, OXFD.
Ch e, m, r. Sch pe. Abngdn CC. See also
Bs Hll, Sandleigh.

WOOTTON Hants
179 SZ 2497 5m WNW of Lymington. Loc,
Lmngtn MB. P New Milton.

WOOTTON Kent
173 TR 2246 7m N of Folkestone. CP
(Denton w Wttn), 311. Dover RD. P Canterbury. Ch e, v. Dvr and Deal CC (Dvr).

WOOTTON Lincs (L)
104 TA 0816 5m SE Barton-upon-Humber.
CP, 433. Glanford Brigg RD. P Ulceby.
Ch e, m. Sch pe. Brgg and Scunthorpe CC
(Brgg).

WOOTTON Northants
133 SP 7656 3m S of Northampton.

CP, 1,649. Nthmptn RD. P NTHMPTN.
Ch e, m. Sch p. Daventry CC (S Nthnts).

WOOTTON Oxon
145 SP 4319 2m N of Woodstock. CP, 677.
Chipping Norton RD. P Wdstck, OXFORD.
Ch e, m. Sch pe. Banbury CC.

WOOTTON Staffs
111 SK 1045 5m WSW of Ashbourne.
CP, 117. Uttoxeter RD. Burton CC.

WOOTTON BASSETT Wilts
157 SU 0682 6m W of Swindon. CP, 4,390.
Cricklade and Wttn Bsstt RD. P Swndn.
Ch e, m2, r, v. Sch j, p, pe, s.
Chippenham CC. Hillside tn. Bldngs of
many periods. Restored timbered tn hall of
1700.

WOOTTON BRIDGE IOW
180 SZ 5391 3m NE of Newport. Loc,
Npt MB. P Ryde.

WOOTTON COMMON IOW
180 SZ 5391 2m NE of Newport. Loc,
Npt MB.

WOOTTON COURTENAY Som
164 SS 9343 3m SW of Minehead. CP, 265.
Williton RD. P Mnhd. Ch e. Bridgwater CC.

WOOTTON FITZPAINE Dorset
177 SY 3795 3m NE of Lyme Regis.
CP, 304. Bridport RD. P Brdpt. Ch e.
Sch pe. W Dst CC. See also Monkton Wyld.

WOOTTON RIVERS Wilts
167 SU 1963 3m NE of Pewsey. CP, 239.
Psy RD. P Marlborough. Ch e, m. Sch pe.
Devizes CC.

WOOTTON ST LAWRENCE Hants
168 SU 5953 3m WNW of Basingstoke.
CP, 1,945. Bsngstke RD. P Bsngstke.
Ch e, m2. Bsngstke CC. See also Ramsdell.

WOOTTON WAWEN Warwicks
131 SP 1563 6m NNW of Stratford.
CP, 1,489. Strtfd-on-Avon RD. P Solihull.
Ch e, r. Sch pe. Strtfd-on-Avn CC (Strtfd).
Ch: Saxon twr; monmts; chained books.
Wttn Hall, 17c. Caravans.

WORCESTER Worcs
130/143 SO 8455 24m SSW of Birmingham.
CB, 73,445. P(WCSTR). Wcstr BC. County

and cathedral city on R Severn. Industries incl glove-making, porcelain (Royal Pcln Wks Museum). 14c–15c commandery*, 18c guildhall*; Greyfriars (NT)*, half-timbered hse of 1480 onwards.

WORCESTER PARK Surrey
170 TQ 2165 3m SE of Kingston. Loc, Epsom and Ewell MB. P.

WORFIELD Shrops
130 SO 7595 3m ENE of Bridgnorth. CP, 3,572. Brdgnth RD. P Brdgnth. Ch e. Sch pe. Ludlow CC. See also Ackleton, Hilton, Roughton. Wfld Gdns* of exotic plants.

WORKINGTON Cumb
82 NX 9928 31m SW of Carlisle. MB, 28,414. P. Wkngtn CC. See also Harrington, High Hrrngtn, Siddick, Stainburn. Coal and iron tn. Reclamation work N and S to provide seaside amenities.

WORKSOP Notts
103 SK 5879 15m S of Doncaster. MB, 36,034. P. Bassetlaw CC. See also Hardwick. 'Gateway to the Dukeries.' To SE, Clumber Pk: see Carburton.

WORLABY Lincs (L)
104 TA 0113 4m NNE of Brigg. CP, 295. Glanford Brgg RD. P Brgg. Ch e, m. Sch p. Brgg and Scunthorpe CC (Brgg). 17c almshouses.

WORLD'S END Berks
158 SU 4876 6m N of Newbury. Loc, Beedon CP.

WORLD'S END Bucks
159 SP 8509 4m SE of Aylesbury. Loc, Wendover CP.

WORLE Som
165 ST 3562 3m ENE of Weston. Loc, Wstn-super-Mare MB. P Wstn-spr-Mre.

WORLESTON Ches
110 SJ 6556 3m N of Nantwich. CP, 336. Nntwch RD. P Nntwch. Ch e. Sch pe. Nntwch CC.

WORLINGHAM Suffolk (E)
137 TM 4489 2m E of Beccles. CP, 684. Wainford RD. P Bccls. Ch e. Sch pe. Lowestoft CC.

WORLINGTON Suffolk (W)
135 TL 6973 7m NNE of Newmarket. CP, 337. Mildenhall RD. P Bury St Edmunds. Ch e. Bury St Eds CC.

WORLINGWORTH Suffolk (E)
137 TM 2368 5m NW of Framlingham. CP, 460. Hartismere RD. P Woodbridge. Ch e. Sch pe. Eye CC. See also Fingal St.

WORMALD GREEN Yorks (W)
91 SE 3064 4m S of Ripon. Loc, Markington w Wallerthwaite CP. Rpn and Pateley Br RD. Rpn CC.

WORMBRIDGE Herefs
142 SO 4230 8m SW of Hereford. CP, 52. Dore and Bredwardine RD. P HRFD. Ch e. Sch pe. Hrfd CC.

WORMEGAY Norfolk
124 TF 6611 6m SSE of King's Lynn. CP, 337. Downham RD. P K's Lnn. Ch e. Sch pe. SW Nflk CC.

WORMELOW TUMP Herefs
142 SO 4930 6m S of Hereford. Loc, Hrfd RD. P(Wmlw), HRFD. Hrfd CC.

WORMHILL Derbys
111 SK 1274 4m E of Buxton. CP, 1,240. Chapel en le Frith RD. P Bxtn. Ch e, m2. Sch p. High Peak CC. See also Pk Dale.

WORMINGFORD Essex
149 TL 9331 6m NW of Colchester. CP, 345. Lexden and Winstree RD. P Clchstr. Ch e, m. Sch pe. Clchstr CC.

WORMINGHALL Bucks
158, 159 SP 6408 4m WNW of Thame. CP, 314. Aylesbury RD. P Aylesbury. Ch e. Aylesbury CC.

WORMINGTON Glos
144 SP 0436 4m W of Broadway. Loc, Dumbleton CP. Ch e.

WORMLEIGHTON Warwicks
145 SP 4453 8m N of Banbury. CP, 132. Southam RD. P Leamington Spa. Ch e. Stratford-on-Avon CC (Strtfd). Part of 16c mnr hse, and the 17c gatehouse, remain.

WORMLEY Herts
161 TL 3605 2m N of Cheshunt. Loc, Hoddesdon UD. P Broxbourne. Ch: unusual Nmn font.

WORMLEY Surrey
169 SU 9438 4m SSW of Godalming. Loc,
Witley CP. P Gdlmng.

WORMSHILL Kent
172 TQ 8857 4m SSW of Sittingbourne.
CP, 214. Hollingbourn RD. P Sttngbne.
Ch e. Maidstone CC.

WORMSLEY Herefs
142 SO 4247 7m NW of Hereford. CP, 39.
Weobley RD. Ch e. Leominster CC.

WORPLESDON Surrey
169, 170 SU 9753 3m NNW of Guildford.
CP, 6,399. P Gldfd. Ch e, v. Sch p3. Gldfd CC.
See also Pitch Place, Wd St.

WORRALL Yorks (W)
102 SK 3092 4m NW of Sheffield. Loc,
Bradfield CP. P SHFFLD. Ch c.

WORSBROUGH Yorks (W)
102, 103 SE 3503 2m SSE of Barnsley.
UD, 15,433. P(Wsbrgh Br and Wsbrgh Dale),
Bnsly. Bnsly BC. See also Birdwell, Blacker
Hill. Colliery tn.

WORSLEY Lancs
101 SD 7400 6m WNW of Manchester.
U D, 4 9 , 5 7 3. P M N C H S T R.
Farnworth BC (CC). See also Boothstown,
Lit Hulton, Walkden. Bridgewater Canal
begun here by Brindley in 1759.

WORSTEAD Norfolk
126 TG 3026 3m SSE of N Walsham.
CP, 754. Smallburgh RD. P: N Wlshm.
Ch e, b, m. Sch pe. N Nflk CC. Worsted
cloth made here by Flemish weavers in 12c.

WORSTHORNE Lancs
95 SD 8732 3m E of Burnley.
CP(Wsthne-w-Hurstwood), 1,640. Bnly RD.
P Bnly. Ch e, m. Sch p. Clitheroe CC.

WORSTON Lancs
95 SD 7642 2m ENE of Clitheroe. CP, 90.
Clthroe RD. Clthroe CC.

WORTH Kent
173 TR 3356 1m S of Sandwich. CP, 718.
Eastry RD. P Deal. Ch e, v. Sch p. Dover
and Deal CC (Dvr).

WORTH Sussex (E)
170, 182 TQ 3036 2m E of Crawley.
CP, 5,368. Cuckfield RD. Ch e, r.

Mid-Sx CC (E Grinstead). See also
Copthorne, Crly Down, Turner's Hill.
Restored Saxon ch. To SE, Wth Priory, RC
sch for boys.

WORTHAM Suffolk (E)
136 TM 0877 3m SW of Diss. CP, 545.
Hartismere RD. P Dss, Norfolk. Ch e, m2.
Sch p. Eye CC. Hses dotted round huge
cmmn with football pitch in one corner. Ch
1m N. Beyond ch, another cmmn, hses,
Tumble Down Dick Inn beside R Waveney.

WORTHEN Shrops
118 SJ 3204 7m ESE of Welshpool.
CP, 1,760. Clun and Bishop's Cstle RD.
P Shrewsbury. Ch e, m. Sch pe. Ludlow CC.
See also Aston Pigott, Astn Rogers, Betton,
Bog, Brockton, Hope, Leigh, Meadowtown,
P e n n e r l e y, R o w l e y, Snailbeach,
Stiperstones.

WORTHING Norfolk
125 TF 9919 4m N of E Dereham. Loc,
Hoe CP. Ch e.

WORTHING Sussex (W)
182 TQ 1402 10m W of Brighton.
MB, 88,210. P. Wthng BC. See also
Goring-by-Sea. Seaside resort and rsdntl tn.

WORTHINGTON Leics
121 SK 4020 4m NE of Ashby de la Zouch.
CP, 1,429. Ashby de la Zch RD. P Ashby de
la Zch. Ch e, m2, v. Sch p.
Loughborough CC. See also Newbold.

WORTH MATRAVERS Dorset
179 SY 9777 4m WSW of Swanage.
CP, 580. Wareham and Purbeck RD.
P Swnge. Ch m. S Dst CC. See also Harman's
Cross.

WORTLEY Yorks (W)
102 SK 3099 5m SSW of Barnsley. CP, 588.
Wtly RD. P SHEFFIELD. Ch e. Sch pe.
Penistone CC.

WORTON Wilts
167 ST 9757 3m SW of Devizes. CP, 394.
Dvzs RD. P Dvzs. Ch e, m. Sch p. Dvzs CC.

WORTWELL Norfolk
137 TM 2784 5m SW of Bungay. CP, 348.
Depwade RD. P Harleston. Ch c. S Nflk CC.

WOTHERSOME Yorks (W)
96 SE 3942 4m S of Wetherby. CP, 25.
Wthrby RD. Barkston Ash CC.

WOTHERTON Shrops
118 SJ 2800 6m SE of Welshpool. Loc, Chirbury CP.

WOTHORPE Hunts
123 TF 0205 1m SSW of Stamford. CP, 161. Barnack RD. Peterborough BC (CC). Early 17c mansion, ruined since 18c, stands close to Stmfd bypass (A1).

WOTTER Devon
187 SX 5561 6m NW of Ivybridge. Loc, Shaugh Prior CP. P Plymouth. Ch m.

WOTTON Surrey
170 TQ 1247 3m WSW of Dorking. CP, 660. Dkng and Horley RD. Ch e. Sch pe. Dkng CC. See also Ranmore Cmmn. Wttn Hse, bthplce of John Evelyn, diarist, 1620.

WOTTON-UNDER-EDGE Glos
156 ST 7593 8m W of Tetbury. CP, 3,515. Dursley RD. P. Ch e, b, c, m2, r, v2. Sch pe3, s2. Stroud CC. Small Cotswold tn with several bldngs of interest, incl 17c almshouses.

WOTTON UNDERWOOD Bucks
146, 159 SP 6816 6m N of Thame. CP, 138. Aylesbury RD. Ch e. Aylesbury CC. Home of Grenville family. W. Hse, 18c, restored 19c, in large pk.

WOUGHTON ON THE GREEN Bucks
146 SP 8737 3m N of Bletchley. CP, 160. Newport Pagnell RD. Ch e. Buckingham CC.

WOULDHAM Kent
171, 172 TQ 7164 4m SSW of Rochester. CP, 846. Malling RD. P Rchstr. Ch e, m, s, v. Sch pe. Tonbridge and Mllng CC (Sevenoaks). Chalk pits, marshes, indstrl rems.

WRABNESS Essex
150 TM 1831 5m W of Harwich. CP, 379. Tendring RD. P Manningtree. Ch e, m. Sch pe. Hrwch CC.

WRAGBY Lincs (L)
104 TF 1378 7m S of Mkt Rasen. CP, 796. Horncastle RD. P LINCOLN. Ch e. Sch p. Hncstle CC. Plastics factory and beehive wks.

WRAMPLINGHAM Norfolk
125 TG 1106 3m N of Wymondham.

CP, 157. Forehoe and Henstead RD. Ch e. S Nflk CC (Central Nflk).

WRANGATON Devon
187, 188 SX 6757 3m ENE of Ivybridge. Loc, Ugborough CP. P: S Brent.

WRANGLE Lincs (H)
114 TF 4251 8m NE of Boston. CP, 1,311. Bstn RD. P Bstn. Ch e, m2. Sch p. Holland w Bstn CC.

WRANGLE COMMON Lincs (H)
114 TF 4253 9m NE of Boston. Loc, Wrngle CP. P Wrngle, Bstn.

WRANGWAY Som
164 ST 1217 2m SW of Wellington. Loc, Wllngtn Without CP. Wllngtn RD. Ch v. Taunton CC.

WRANTAGE Som
177 ST 3022 5m ESE of Taunton. Loc, N Curry CP. P Tntn. Ch m.

WRATTING, GREAT Suffolk (W)
148 TL 6848 2m NE of Haverhill. See Gt Wrttng.

WRAWBY Lincs (L)
104 TA 0108 1m NE of Brigg. CP, 827. Glanford Brgg RD. P Brgg. Ch e, m2. Sch pe. Brgg and Scunthorpe CC (Brgg). To E, 18c post-mill*.

WRAXALL Som
155, 156 ST 4971 6m W of Bristol. CP, 1,402. Long Ashton RD. P BRSTL. Ch e. Sch pe. N Som CC. See also Failand, Lr Flnd.

WRAXALL Som
166 ST 6036 3m NW of Cstle Cary. Loc, Ditcheat CP.

WRAY Lancs
89 SD 6067 7m S of Kirkby Lonsdale. CP(Wray-w-Botton), 432. Lunesdale RD. P LANCASTER. Ch e, m. Sch pe. Lncstr CC. Picturesque vllge st.

WRAYSBURY Bucks
159, 160, 170 TQ 0074 2m NW of Staines. CP, 3,372. Eton RD. P Stns, Middx. Ch e, b, r. Sch p. Beaconsfield CC (S Bucks). See also Hythe End. Reservoirs N and S. 1m S in R Thames is island of Runnymede, where Magna Carta was signed, 1215.

WRAYTON Lancs
89 SD 6172 4m S of Kirkby Lonsdale.
CP(Melling-w-Wrtn), 180. Lunesdale RD.
Lancaster CC.

WREA GREEN Lancs
94 SD 3931 6m ESE of Blackpool. Loc,
Ribby-w-Wrea CP. P Preston. Ch e.

WREAY Cumb
83 NY 4349 5m SSE of Carlisle. Loc,
St Cuthbert Without CP. Border RD. Ch e.
Sch pe. Penrith and the Bdr CC. Unusual
mid-19c ch designed as Roman basilica.

WRELTON Yorks (N)
86, 92 SE 7686 2m NW of Pickering.
CP, 192. Pckrng RD. P Pckrng. Ch m2.
Scarborough CC (Thirsk and Malton).

WRENBURY Ches
109 SJ 5947 5m SW of Nantwich.
CP(Wrnbry cum Frith), 815. Nntwch RD.
P Nntwch. Ch e. Sch p. Nntwch CC. Ch has
box pews, and elaborate monmt to Sir
Stapleton Cotton, illustrious Peninsula War
general.

WRENINGHAM Norfolk
137 TM 1698 4m SE of Wymondham.
CP, 376. Forehoe and Henstead RD.
P NORWICH, NOR 90W. Ch e, m. Sch pe.
S Nflk CC (Central Nflk).

WRENTHAM Suffolk (E)
137 TM 4982 4m N of Southwold. CP, 792.
Lothingland RD. P Beccles. Ch e, c, m2.
Sch p. Lowestoft CC.

WRENTHORPE Yorks (W)
96, 102 SE 3122 1m NW of Wakefield. Loc,
Stanley UD. P Wkfld.

WRENTNALL Shrops
118 SJ 4203 7m SW of Shrewsbury. Loc,
Ch Pulverbatch CP. Ch m.

WRESSLE Yorks (E)
97, 98 SE 7031 5m NNW of Goole.
CP, 261. Howden RD. Ch e. Hdn CC. See
also Brind, Newsholme. Wrssle Cstle, 14c,
only fortified rems in E Riding.

WRESTLINGWORTH Beds
147 TL 2547 5m ENE of Biggleswade.
CP, 393. Bgglswde RD. P Sandy. Ch e, c.
Sch pe. Mid-Beds CC.

WRETTON Norfolk
135 TL 6999 5m ESE of Downham Mkt.
CP, 273. Dnhm RD. P King's Lynn. Ch e.
SW Nflk CC.

WRIBBENHALL Worcs
130 SO 7975 just E of Bewdley. Loc,
Bdly MB. P Bdly.

WRIGHTINGTON BAR Lancs
100 SD 5313 4m SW of Chorley. Loc,
Wrghtngtn CP. Wigan RD. Ch e, r, v. Sch pr.
Westhoughton CC.

WRINEHILL Staffs
110 SJ 7547 6m W of Newcastle-under-
Lyme. Loc, Betley CP. P Crewe, Cheshire.
Ch m.

WRINGTON Som
165 ST 4762 2m ESE of Congresbury.
CP, 1,811. Axbridge RD. P BRISTOL.
Ch e, c, m2, s. Sch pe. Weston-super-
Mare CC. See also Lulsgate Bottom, Redhill.
Ch twr, 113ft.

WRITHLINGTON Som
166 ST 7054 1m E of Radstock. Loc,
Norton-Radstock UD. P Rdstck, Bath.
N Som CC.

WRITTLE Essex
161 TL 6706 2m W of Chelmsford.
CP, 3,392. Chlmsfd RD. P Chlmsfd. Ch e, v.
Sch i, j, p. Braintree CC (Chlmsfd). See also
Gt Oxney Grn. Ch has good brasses; monmt
of 1629 to Sir Edward Pinchon.

WROCKWARDINE Shrops
118, 119 SJ 6212 2m W of Wellington.
CP, 1,380. Wllngtn RD. P Telford. Ch e.
Sch pe. The Wrekin CC. See also Admaston,
Walcot.

WROOT Lincs (L)
103 SE 7103 9m E of Doncaster. CP, 391.
Isle of Axholme RD. P Dncstr, Yorkshire.
Ch e, m. Sch pe. Gainsborough CC.

WROTHAM Kent
171 TQ 6159 6m ENE of Sevenoaks.
CP, 1,487. Malling RD. P Svnks. Ch e.
Sch pe, s. Tonbridge and Mllng CC (Svnks).
Pronounced 'rootm'. Old vllge blt round
square. Ch has processional way under twr.

WROTHAM HEATH Kent
171 TQ 6358 7m E of Sevenoaks. Loc,
Platt CP. P Svnks. Famous viewpoint.
TV mast.

WROTTESLEY Staffs
119 SJ 8501 4m WNW of Wolverhampton.
CP. Seisdon RD. SW Staffs CC (Brierley
Hill). See also Perton, Wergs.

WROUGHTON Wilts
157 SU 1480 3m S of Swindon. CP, 5,108.
Highworth RD. P Swndn. Ch e, m, r.
Sch i, j, s. Devizes CC. See also Elcombe,
N Wrghtn.

WROXALL IOW
180 SZ 5579 2m NNW of Ventnor. Loc,
Vntnr UD. P Vntnr.

WROXALL Warwicks
131 SP 2271 5m NW of Warwick. CP, 144.
Wrwck RD. Ch e. Sch pe. Wrwck and
Leamington CC.

WROXETER Shrops
118 SJ 5608 5m ESE of Shrewsbury.
CP, 657. Atcham RD. P Shrsbry. Ch e.
Shrsbry CC. See also Donnington, Rushton.
Rems of Roman stn of *Viroconium*. Ch
exemplifies styles of all periods Nmn to
Vctrn.

WROXHAM Norfolk
126 TG 2917 7m NE of Norwich.
CP, 1,101. St Faith's and Aylsham RD.
P Nrwch. Ch e. Sch p. N Nflk CC (Central
Nflk). Broadland yachting centre.

WROXTON Oxon
145 SP 4141 3m WNW of Banbury.
CP, 598. Bnbry RD. P Bnbry. Ch e, m, r.
Sch pe. Bnbry CC. See also Balscott. Stone
and thatched cottages. Wrxtn Abbey, hse of
early 17c.

WYASTON Derbys
120 SK 1842 3m S of Ashbourne.
CP(Edlaston and Wstn), 191. Ashbne RD.
P Ashbne. Ch m. W Derbys CC.

WYBERTON Lincs (H)
114, 123 TF 3240 2m S of Boston.
CP, 2,889. Bstn RD. Ch e. Sch p. Holland
w Bstn CC.

WYBOSTON Beds
134 TL 1656 3m SSW of St Neots. Loc,
Roxton CP. P BEDFORD. Ch m.

WYBUNBURY Ches
110 SJ 6949 3m ESE of Nantwich. CP, 747.
Nntwch RD. P Nntwch. Ch e, m. Sch pe2.
Nntwch CC. Ch twr generally considered
magnificent.

WYCHBOLD Worcs
130, 131 SO 9265 2m NE of Droitwich.
Loc, Dodderhill CP. Drtwch RD. P Drtwch.
Ch e. Worcester BC.

WYCH CROSS Sussex (E)
183 TQ 4131 4m SSE of E Grinstead. Loc,
Uckfield RD. E Grnstd CC.

WYCHE Worcs
143 SO 7743 1m S of Malvern. Loc,
Mlvn UD.

WYCHNOR Staffs
120 SK 1716 6m NE of Lichfield. CP, 118.
Tutbury RD. Ch e. Burton CC. A38 rd
carried by two brs over Trent and Mersey
Canal to E.

WYCK Hants
169 SU 7539 2m E of Alton. Loc,
Binsted CP.

WYCK RISSINGTON Glos
144 SP 1921 3m S of Stow-on-the-Wold.
Alternative spelling for Wick Rissington qv.

WYCLIFFE Yorks (N)
84 NZ 1114 4m ESE of Barnard Cstle.
CP(Wclffe w Thorpe), 151. Startforth RD.
Ch e, r. Richmond CC.

WYDDIAL Herts
148 TL 3731 6m SSE of Royston. CP, 91.
Braughing RD. Ch e. E Herts CC.

WYE Kent
172, 173, 184 TR 0546 4m NE of Ashford.
CP. E Ashfd RD. P Ashfd. Ch e. Sch pe.
Ashfd CC. Old mkt tn. Wye College,
agricultural sch of London University. 1m
N, Olantigh Twrs, Ggn mansion, with gdns*
where music festival held annually. 1m E,
crown cut in chalk of downs commemorates
Edward VII's coronation.

WYFORDBY Leics
122 SK 7918 3m E of Melton Mowbray.
Loc, Freeby CP. Ch e.

WYKE Surrey
169 SU 9251 4m E of Aldershot. Loc,
Normandy CP. Ch e. Sch p.

WYKE CHAMPFLOWER Som
166 ST 6634 1m W of Bruton. Loc,
Brtn CP. Ch e.

WYKEHAM Yorks (N)
92 SE 8175 3m NE of Malton. Loc, Mltn UD.
Mltn UD.

WYKEHAM Yorks (N)
93 SE 9683 6m SW of Scarborough.
CP, 356. Scbrgh RD. Scbrgh. Ch e. Sch pe.
Scbrgh CC (Scbrgh and Whitby). See also
Langdale End, Ruston.

WYKE MARSH Dorset
166 ST 7926 just W of Gillingham. Loc,
Gillingham CP. P(Wke), Gllnghm.

WYKE REGIS Dorset
178 SY 6677 2m SW of Weymouth. Loc,
Wmth and Melcombe Regis MB. P Wmth.

WYKEY Shrops
118 SJ 3924 7m ESE of Oswestry. Loc,
Ruyton-XI-Towns CP.

WYLAM Nthmb
77, 78 NZ 1164 1m NE of Prudhoe.
CP, 1,495. Hexham RD. P. Ch e, m3, v.
Sch p. Hxhm CC. Bthplce of George
Stephenson, 1781.

WYLYE Wilts
167 SU 0037 10m NW of Salisbury.
CP, 365. Slsbry and Witton RD.
P Warminster. Ch e, c. Sch pe. Slsbry CC.
See also Deptford, Fisherton de la Mere.
Flint and stone chequerwork cottages.

WYMESWOLD Leics
121, 122 SK 6023 5m ENE of
Loughborough. CP, 817. Barrow upon
Soar RD. P Lghbrgh. Ch e, m. Sch pe.
Melton CC.

WYMINGTON Beds
134 SP 9564 1m S of Rushden. CP, 772.
Bedford RD. P Rshdn, Northants. Ch e, v.
Sch pe. Bdfd CC. Ch: 15c 'doom', Jcbn
plpt, notable brasses.

WYMONDHAM Leics
122 SK 8518 6m E of Melton Mowbray.
CP, 694. Mltn and Belvoir RD. P Mltn Mbry.
Ch e, m, v. Sch pe. Mltn CC. See also
Edmondthorpe.

WYMONDHAM Norfolk
136 TG 1101 9m WSW of Norwich.
UD, 8,510. P. S Nflk CC. See also Spooner
Row. Fine 12c and later abbey, now parish
ch. Several Ggn hses; also old weavers'
cottages from time when tn was textile
centre.

WYMONDLEY, GREAT Herts
147 TL 2128 2m E of Hitchin. See Gt
Wmndly.

WYNFORD EAGLE Dorset
177, 178 SY 5895 8m ENE of Bridport.
CP, 73. Dchstr RD. Ch e. W Dst CC. 17c
mnr hse of Ham stone has eagle over central
gable.

WYRE PIDDLE Worcs
143, 144 SO 9647 1m NE of Pershore.
CP, 285. Pshre RD. P Pshre. Ch e, m.
S Worcs CC.

WYRLEY, GREAT Staffs
119 SJ 9907 2m SSE of Cannock. See Gt
Wly.

WYSALL Notts
121, 122 SK 6027 6m NE of
Loughborough. CP, 197. Basford RD.
P NOTTINGHAM. Ch e, m. Sch pe.
Rushcliffe CC.

WYTHALL Worcs
131 SP 0774 5m NNE of Redditch. CP.
Bromsgrove RD. P BIRMINGHAM.
Ch e, b, v2. Sch j, p. Brmsgrve and
Rddtch CC (Brmsgrve). See also Major's
Grn.

WYTHAM Berks
158 SP 4708 3m NW of Oxford. CP, 197.
Abingdon RD. P OXFD. Ch e. Abngdn CC.
Wthm Abbey, Tdr.

WYTHEFORD, GREAT Shrops
118 SJ 5719 6m NE of Shrewsbury. Loc,
Shawbury CP.

WYTON Hunts
134 TL 2772 3m E of Huntingdon.
CP(Houghton and Wtn), 2,908. St Ives RD.
Ch e. Sch i, p. Hunts CC.

WYTON Yorks (E)
99 TA 1733 6m ENE of Hull. Loc,
Bilton CP. Ch m.

WYVERSTONE Suffolk (E)
136 TM 0467 6m N of Stowmarket.
CP, 286. Hartismere RD. P Stmkt. Ch e, m.
Eye CC.

WYVERSTONE STREET Suffolk (E)
136 TM 0367 6m N of Stowmarket. Loc,
Wvrstne CP.

WYVILLE Lincs (K)
122 SK 8829 4m SSW of Grantham.
CP (Wvlle cum Hungerton), 82.
W Kesteven RD. Ch e. Rutland and
Stamford CC.

Y

YADDLETHORPE Lincs (L)
104 SE 8807 2m S of Scunthorpe. Loc,
Bottesford CP. Ch m2.

YAFFORD IOW
180 SZ 4481 6m SW of Newport. Loc,
Shorwell CP.

YAFFORTH Yorks (N)
91 SE 3494 2m W of Northallerton.
CP, 122. Nthlltn RD. Ch e, m.
Richmond CC.

YALDING Kent
171 TQ 6950 5m SW of Maidstone.
CP, 2,457. Mdstne RD. P Mdstne. Ch e, b.
Sch pe. Mdstne CC. See also Benover,
Collier St, Laddingford. In hop-growing
country beside Medway. Much boating at
Y. Lees.

YANWATH Westm
83 NY 5027 2m S of Penrith. CP(Ynwth and
Eamont Br), 237. N Westm RD. Sch p.
Westm CC. Y. Hall incorporates 14c pele
twr. To NE, two prehistoric henge monmts:
Mayburgh and King Arthur's Round Table
(both A.M.).

YANWORTH Glos
144 SP 0713 2m WSW of Northleach.
CP, 138. Nthlch RD. P Cheltenham. Ch e.
Cirencester and Tewkesbury CC.

YAPHAM Yorks (E)
97, 98 SE 7852 2m NNW of Pocklington.
CP, 163. Pcklngtn RD. Ch e, m. Sch pe.
Howden CC. See also Meltonby.

YAPTON Sussex (W)
181, 182 SU 9703 4m NE of Bognor.
CP, 2,023. Chichester RD. P Arundel.
Ch e, c. Sch pe. Arndl CC (Chchstr). See
also Flansham.

YARBURGH Lincs (L)
105 TF 3593 4m NNE of Louth. CP, 149.
Lth RD. P Lth. Ch e, m. Lth CC.

YARCOMBE Devon
177 ST 2408 5m W of Chard. CP, 451.
Honiton RD. P Hntn. Ch e, b2. Hntn CC.
See also Marsh.

YARDLEY GOBION Northants
146 SP 7644 3m NNW of Stony Stratford.
CP, 585. Towcester RD. P Tcstr. Ch e, v.
Sch pe. Daventry CC (S Nthnts).

YARDLEY HASTINGS Northants
133 SP 8656 7m ESE of Northampton.
CP, 759. Nthmptn RD. P NTHMPTN.
Ch e, c. Sch p. Daventry CC (S Nthnts).

YARKHILL Herefs
142, 143 SO 6042 6m ENE of Hereford.
CP, 330. Ledbury RD. Ch e. Sch pe.
Leominster CC. See also Newtown.

YARLET Staffs
119 SJ 9128 3m S of Stone. Loc,
Marston CP.

YARLINGTON Som
166 ST 6529 4m W of Wincanton. CP, 171.
Wncntn RD. P Wncntn. Ch e. Wells CC.

YARM Yorks (N)
85 NZ 4112 4m SSW of Teesside
(Stockton). CP, 1,910. Stokesley RD. P.
Ch e, m, r. Sch j, p, s. Richmond CC.

YARMOUTH IOW
180 SZ 3589 9m W of Newport, 4m SSE of
Lymington (by sea). CP, 984. Isle of
Wight RD and CC. P. Ch e, m. Sch pe. See
also Thorley St. Y. Cstle (A.M.), blt by
Henry VIII for coastal defence. Car ferry to
Lmngtn.

YARMOUTH, GREAT Norfolk
126 TG 5207 18m E of Norwich. See Gt
Ymth.

YARNFIELD Staffs
110, 119 SJ 8632 3m WSW of Stone. Loc,
Swynnerton CP. P Stne. Sch j.

YARNSCOMBE Devon
163 SS 5623 5m ENE of Torrington.
CP, 203. Trrngtn RD. P Barnstaple.
Ch e, m, v. W Dvn CC (Trrngtn).

YARNTON Oxon
145 SP 4712 4m NNW of Oxford.
CP, 1,371. Ploughley RD. P OXFD. Ch e.
Sch p. Mid-Oxon CC (Banbury). Jcbn mnr
hse, restored 1897, blt by Sir Thomas
Spencer. Spncr monmts in ch.

YARPOLE Herefs
129 SO 4764 4m NNW of Leominster.
CP, 394. Lmnstr and Wigmore RD.
P Lmnstr. Ch e, m. Lmnstr CC. See also
Bircher. Ch has detached 13c—14c twr.

YARSOP Herefs
142 SO 4047 8m NW of Hereford. Loc,
Yazor CP.

YARWELL Northants
134 TL 0697 6m NNE of Oundle. CP, 224.
Oundle and Thrapston RD.
P PETERBOROUGH. Ch e.
Wellingborough CC (Ptrbrgh).

YATE Glos
156 ST 7182 10m NE of Bristol. CP, 3,898.
Sodbury RD. P BRSTL. Ch e, b, m, v.
Sch i, p4, pe, s. S Glos CC. Ch: Perp twr;
brass of 1590. New shopping centre.

YATELEY Hants
169 SU 8160 3m W of Camberley.
CP, 4,461. Hartley Wintney RD. P Cmbrly,
Surrey. Ch e, b, r. Sch i, j, pe, s.
Aldershot CC. See also Frogmore.

YATESBURY Wilts
157 SU 0671 4m E of Calne. Loc,
Cherhill CP. P Clne. Ch e.

YATTENDON Berks
158 SU 5574 7m NE of Newbury. CP, 265.
Bradfield RD. P Nbry. Ch e, m2. Sch pe.
Nbry CC.

YATTON Herefs
129 SO 4366 6m NW of Leominster. Loc,
Aymestrey CP.

YATTON Som
155, 165 ST 4365 1m NNW of
Congresbury. CP, 3,063. Long Ashton RD.
P BRISTOL. Ch e, f, m, v2. Sch ie, je.
Weston-super-Mare CC. See also Claverham,
N End.

YATTON KEYNELL Wilts
156 ST 8676 4m NW of Chippenham.
CP, 426. Calne and Chppnhm RD.
P Chppnhm. Ch e, bv. Sch pe. Chppnhm CC.

YAVERLAND IOW
180 SZ 6185 1m NE of Sandown. Loc,
Sndn-Shanklin CP. Ch e.

YAXHAM Norfolk
125 TG 0010 2m SSE of E Dereham.
CP, 364. Mitford and Launditch RD.
P Drhm. Ch e, c. Sch pe. SW Nflk CC. See
also Clint Grn.

YAXLEY Hunts
134 TL 1892 4m S of Peterborough.
CP, 2,690. Norman Cross RD. P PTRBRGH.
Ch e, b, c, m2. Sch pe. Hunts CC.
Brickworks district. Ch has fine twr and
spire.

YAXLEY Suffolk (E)
136 TM 1274 2m W of Eye. CP, 255.
Hartismere RD. P Eye. Ch e. Eye CC.

YAZOR Herefs
142 SO 4046 8m NW of Hereford. CP, 166.
Weobley RD. Ch e. Leominster CC. See also
Moorhampton, Yarsop.

YEADON Yorks (W)
96 SE 2041 6m NNE of Bradford. Loc,
Airborough UD. P LEEDS. Pudsey BC.
Leeds/Brdfd airpt.

YEALAND CONYERS Lancs
89 SD 5074 2m N of Carnforth. CP, 210.
Lancaster RD. Ch e, f, r. Sch pe. Morecambe
and Lonsdale CC. The Quaker Meeting Hse
is of 1692. To W, Leighton Hall*,
neo-Gothic mansion.

YEALAND REDMAYNE Lancs
89 SD 5075 3m N of Carnforth. CP, 278.
Lancaster RD. P(Ylnd), Cnfth. Sch pe.
Morecambe and Lonsdale CC.

YEALMPTON Devon
187 SX 5751 4m SW of Ivybridge.
CP, 1,060. Plympton St Mary RD.
P Plymouth. Ch e, m. Sch p. W Dvn CC
(Tavistock). See also Dunstone.

YEARSLEY Yorks (N)
92 SE 5874 5m NE of Easingwold. CP, 104.
Easngwld RD. Ch e, m. Thirsk and
Malton CC.

YEATON Shrops
118 SJ 4319 6m NW of Shrewsbury. Loc,
Baschurch CP.

YEAVELEY Derbys
120 SK 1840 4m S of Ashbourne. CP, 174.
Ashbne RD. P Ashbne. Ch e, v. Sch pe.
W Derbys CC.

YEAVERING Nthmb
64, 71 NT 9330 5m WNW of Wooler. Loc,
Kirknewton CP. 1m SSW, Y. Bell, 1,182ft,
hill with fine views; large prehistoric fort at
summit.

YEDINGHAM Yorks (E)
92, 93 SE 8979 6m ESE of Pickering.
CP, 95. Norton RD. P Malton. Ch e, m.
Howden CC.

YELDHAM, GREAT Essex
149 TL 7638 4m S of Clare. See Gt Yldhm.

YELFORD Oxon
158 SP 3604 3m S of Witney.
CP(Hardwick-w-Ylfd), 85. Wtny RD. Ch e.
Mid-Oxon CC (Banbury).

YELLAND Devon
163 SS 4932 4m W of Barnstaple. Loc,
Fremington CP. P Bnstple.

YELLING Hunts
134 TL 2662 5m ENE of St Neots. CP, 231.
St Nts RD. P HUNTINGDON. Ch e, b.
Sch p. Hunts CC.

YELVERTOFT Northants
132, 133 SP 5975 6m E of Rugby. CP, 451.
Daventry RD. P Rgby, Warwickshire.
Ch e, r, v. Sch p. Dvntry CC (S Nthnts).

YELVERTON Devon
187 SX 5267 5m SE of Tavistock. Loc,
Buckland Monachorum CP. P. Ch e, m, r.

YELVERTON Norfolk
126 TG 2902 6m SE of Norwich. CP, 104.
Loddon RD. Ch e. S Nflk CC.

YENSTON Som
166 ST 7121 5m S of Wincanton. Loc,
Henstridge CP. Ch m.

YEOFORD Devon
175 SX 7898 3m WSW of Crediton. Loc,
Crdtn Hmlts CP. Crdtn RD. P Crdtn. Ch v.
Sch p. Tiverton CC (Torrington).

YEOLMBRIDGE Cornwall
174, 186 SX 3187 2m NNW of Launceston.
Loc, Werrington CP. P Lncstn. Widened 14c
br spans R Ottery.

YEOVIL Som
177, 178 ST 5516 21m ESE of Taunton.
MB, 25,492. P. Yvl CC. See also Preston
Plucknett. Mnfg tn producing light aircraft
and helicopters, leather, gloves, agricultural
goods. Mdvl ch known as 'Lantern of the
West' in well laid out tn centre.

YEOVIL MARSH Som
177, 178 ST 5418 2m N of Yeovil. Loc, Yvl
Without CP. Yvl RD. Ch e. Yvl CC.

YEOVILTON Som
166, 177 ST 5423 2m E of Ilchester.
CP, 1,319. Yeovil RD. Ch e. Yvl CC. See
also Bridgehampton, Podimore. Fleet Air
Arm museum.

YETMINSTER Dorset
177, 178 ST 5910 4m SE of Yeovil.
CP, 576. Sherborne RD. P Shbne. Ch e, m.
Sch p. W Dst CC.

YETTINGTON Devon
176 SY 0585 5m NE of Exmouth. Loc,
Bicton CC.

YIELDEN Beds
134 TL 0166 3m E of Rushden.
CP(Melchbourne and Yldn), 342.
Bedford RD. P BDFD. Ch e, m. Bdfd CC.
Cstle mounds. Ch has plpt from which
Bunyan preached on Christmas Day 1659.

YIEWSLEY London
160 TQ 0680 2m S of Uxbridge. Loc, Hillingdon LB. P: W Drayton, Middx. Uxbrdge BC (CC).

YOCKLETON Shrops
118 SJ 3910 6m WSW of Shrewsbury. Loc, Westbury CP. P Shrsbry. Ch e. Sch pe.

YOKEFLEET Yorks (E)
98 SE 8224 5m E of Goole. Loc, Blacktoft CP.

YORK Yorks
97 SE 6052 22m NE of Leeds. CB, 104,513. P(YK). Yk BC. Ancient city, the Roman *Eboracum,* with mdvl walls largely intact; many mdvl bldngs (incl huge minster, cstle, guildhall), many now museums. Seat of archbishop. Important rly centre. University (see Heslington), chocolate factories, barracks, racecourse.

YORKLETTS Kent
172, 173 TR 0963 3m SW of Whitstable. Loc, Whtstble UD. P Whtstble.

YORKLEY Glos
155, 156 SO 6307 2m N of Lydney. Loc, W Dean CP. W Dn RD. P Ldny. Ch b, m. Sch p2. W Glos CC.

YORTON Shrops
118 SJ 5023 3m S of Wem. Loc, Broughton CP. N Shrops RD. Oswestry CC.

YOULGREAVE Derbys
111 SK 2164 3m S of Bakewell. CP, 1,442. Bkwll RD. P Bkwll. Ch e, m2, v. Sch ie, je. W Derbys CC. Ch: large and impressive; font, c 1200, with side stoup. 3m W, Arbor Low (A.M.), circle of 40 stones on the moors.

YOULTHORPE Yorks (E)
97, 98 SE 7655 5m NNW of Pocklington. Loc, Bishop Wilton CP.

YOULTON Yorks (N)
91, 97 SE 4963 6m ESE of Boroughbridge. CP, 38. Easingwold RD. Thirsk and Malton CC.

YOUNG'S END Essex
148, 149, 162 TL 7319 3m SSW of Braintree. Loc, Brntree RD, Chelmsford RD. Brntree CC. (Maldon CC, Chlmsfd CC.)

YOXALL Staffs
120 SK 1419 6m NNE of Lichfield. CP, 1,029. Tutbury RD. P Burton-on-Trent. Ch e, m2, r. Sch pe. Btn CC. See also Hadley End, Morrey, Newchurch.

YOXFORD Suffolk (E)
137 TM 3968 4m N of Saxmundham. CP, 800. Blyth RD. P Sxmndhm. Ch e, m2. Sch p. Eye CC. Picturesque vllge partly on A12 rd. Old Tdr hse, Wisbech's, on rd to Peasenhall, past ch.

Z

ZEAL MONACHORUM Devon
175 SS 7104 8m WNW of Crediton. CP, 286. Crdtn RD. P Crdtn. Ch e, c. Tiverton CC (Torrington).

ZEALS Wilts
166 ST 7831 5m ENE of Wincanton. CP, 436. Mere and Tisbury RD. P Warminster. Ch e, m. Sch pe. Westbury CC.

ZELAH Cornwall
185, 190 SW 8151 5m N of Truro. Loc, St Allen CP. P Truro. Ch m.

ZENNOR Cornwall
189 SW 4538 4m WSW of St Ives. CP, 246. W Penwith RD. Ch e, m. St Ives CC. See also Porthmeor. Mermaid on carved bench-end in ch. Spectacular coast scenery to N. To SE, Z. Quoit, cromlech with 18ft capstone.

INDEX OF BUILDINGS
MENTIONED UNDER PLACES OF A DIFFERENT NAME
Buildings marked with an asterisk are regularly open to the public.
(Museums, although open to the public, are not so marked.)

Building	Mentioned under
* Abbey Hse	Minster, Kent (TR 3064)
Abbot Hall	Kendal
* Abbot's Fish Hse	Meare
Acorn Bank	Temple Sowerby
Acrise Place	Elham
* A La Ronde	Exmouth
Albright Hussey	Albrighton, Shrops (SJ 4918)
* Allington Cstle	Maidstone
Alscot Pk	Preston on Stour
* Althorp Pk	Harlestone
Ammerdown Pk	Kilmersdon
* Angel Corner	Bury St Edmunds
* Anglesey Abbey	Lode
* Anne Hathaway's Cottage	Shottery
* Appuldurcombe Hse	Godshill, IOW
* Arbury	Astley, Warwicks
* Ark, The	Tadcaster
* Ascott	Wing, Bucks
* Ashdown Hse	Ashbury, Berks
Ashdown Hse	Forest Row
Ashridge	Lit Gaddesden
Ashurst Beacon	Dalton, Lancs
Aske Hall	Gilling W
* Astley Hall	Chorley, Lancs
* Attingham	Atcham
* Audley End	Saffron Walden
* Barden Twr	Burnsall
* Bardon Mnr	Washford
* Bateman's	Burwash
* Bayham Abbey	Bells Yew Grn
Bedales	Sheet
* Bede Hse	Lyddington
Bedgebury Pk	Goudhurst
* Beeleigh Abbey	Maldon
* Belchamp Hall	Belchamp Walter
* Belloc's Mill	Shipley, Sussex
* Berrington Hall	Eye, Herefs
Bickham Hse	Roborough, Devon (SX 5062)
* Bladon Gallery	Hurstbourne Tarrant
Blagdon Hall	Stannington, Nthmb
Blake Hall	Bobbingworth
* Bleak Hse	Broadstairs
* Blenheim Palace	Woodstock
* Blithfield Hall	Admaston, Staffs

Building	Mentioned under
* Blue Br Hse	Halstead
Blundell's Sch	Tiverton, Devon
Bollitree Cstle	Weston under Penyard
* Bonner's Cottages	E Dereham
* Boscoble Hse	Tong
* Boughton Monchelsea Place	Boughton Grn
Boughton Pk	Weekley
Bowood Pk	Calne
* Bradley Mnr	Highweek
* Braithwaite Hall	Middleham
* Brantwood	Coniston, Lancs
Brattles Grange	Brenchley
Brewer Street Farm	Bletchingley
* Brickwall	Northiam
Broadlands	Romsey
Broke Hall	Levington
* Broomfield Hse	Southgate, London
Broomholme Priory	Bacton, Norfolk
* Brougham Cstle	Eamont Br
* Browsholme Hall	Bashall Eaves
Bruce Cstle Museum	Tottenham
Burderop Pk	Chiseldon
* Burghley Hse	Stamford, Lincs (K)
* Burton Ct	Eardisland
Butthouse	King's Pyon
* Byland Abbey	Wass
* Cadhay	Fairmile
Caerhays Cstle	St Michael Caerhays
Camoys Ct Farm	Chislehampton
* Capesthorne Hall	Siddington, Ches
Captain Cook Monmt	Easby, Yorks (N) (NZ 5708)
Captain Cook Museum	Gt Ayton
* Carr Hse	Bretherton
Castle Drogo	Drewsteignton
* Castle Hse	Dedham
* Castle Howard	Coneysthorpe
* Cedar Hse	Cobham, Surrey
Chadacre Pk	Shimpling
* Charl(e)ston	Westdean, Sussex (E)
Charterhouse	Farncombe
* Chartwell	Crockham Hill
Chateau Impney	Droitwich
* Chatsworth Hse	Edensor
Chavenage Hse	Beverstone
Chequers	Ellesborough
* Chillington Hall	Brewood
Chipchase Cstle	Wark, Nthmb (NY 8677)
Christ's Hsptl	Itchingfield
* Churche's Mansion	Nantwich
* Claremont	Esher
* Cleeve Abbey	Washford

Building	Mentioned under
* Cliffe Cstle	Keighley
* Clifton Pk	Rotherham
* Clouds Hill	Briantspuddle
Colneford Hse	White Colne
Columbine Hall	Stowupland
Column of British Liberty	Whickham
* Combe Bank	Sundridge
Compton Verney Pk	Combrook
* Compton Wynyates	Winderton
Conygar Twr	Dunster
* Cooke's Hse	W Burton, Sussex (W)
* Coombe Abbey	Brinklow
Cornbury Pk	Charlbury
* Cotehele Hse	Calstock
* Cothay	Greenham, Som
* Courts, The	Holt, Wilts
* Cowdray	Midhurst
Cragside	Rothbury
Cranbury Pk	Otterbourne
Crichel Hse	Moor Crichel
Crittenden Hse	Matfield
Crossways Farm	Abinger Hammer
* Cusworth Hall	Doncaster
* Danny	Hurstpierpoint
* Ditchley Pk	Over Kiddington
* Dorford Hall	Acton, Ches (SJ 6353)
Dorney Wd	Burnham, Bucks
* Dorton Hse	Brill
Douai Abbey	Woolhampton
* Dove Cottage	Grasmere
Downside Abbey	Stratton on the Fosse
Drayton Hse	Lowick, Northants
Duncombe Pk	Helmsley
* Dunstanburgh Cstle	Craster
* Eastbury Mnr Hse	Barking, London
Easton Neston Hse	Towcester
* Egglestone Abbey	Barnard Cstle
	Greta Br
Emmetts	Brasted
* Encombe	Kingston
Fardel	Cornwood
Farringford	Freshwater
* Fenton Hse	Hampstead
Ferne Hse	Berwick St John
Field Place	Broadbridge Hth
Finchcocks	Goudhurst
Flatford Mill	E Bergholt
Flemings Hall	Bedingfield
Flounders' Folly	Culmington
Foley Hse	High Garrett
* Forde Abbey	Thorncombe, Dorset (ST 3703)

Building	Mentioned under
* Forty Hall	Enfield
* Fountains Abbey	Studley Roger
Foxcote	Ilmington
* Foxdenton Hse	Chadderton
* Friars, The	Aylesford
Gadshill	Higham, Kent
* Gainsborough's Hse	Sudbury, Suffolk (W)
Garnons	Mansell Gamage
* Gawthorpe Hall	Padiham
* Gibside Chpl	Rowland's Ghyll
Glassenbury Pk	Cranbrook
Glendurgan Hse	Mawnan Smith
* Godington Pk	Ashford, Kent
* Goodwood Hse	Strettington
* Gorhambury	St Albans
* Grange, The	Rottingdean
Gray's Inn	Holborn
* Great Dixter	Northiam
* Greathead Mnr	Dormans Land
* Great Maytham	Rolvenden
Great Tangley Mnr	Blackheath, Surrey
	Wonersh
Gresham's Sch	Holt, Norfolk
* Greys Ct	Rotherfield Greys
Grimshaw Hall	Knowle, Warwicks
Gryffon Hse	Coddenham
Gulbenkian Museum	Durham
* Gun Hill Place	Dedham
* Haddon Hall	Rowsley
Haileybury College	Hertford Hth
* Hall i' th' Wd	Bolton, Lancs
Hall Place	Leigh, Kent
* Hardwick Hall	Ault Hucknall
* Haremere Hall	Etchingham
* Harvard Hse ·	Stratford-upon-Avon
* Hatchlands	E Clandon
Haumond Abbey	Uffington, Shrops
* Hayes Barton	E Budleigh
* Heaton Hall	Prestwich
* Hellens	Much Markle
* Heriots	Stanmore, London
Hewell Grange	Tardebrigge
* Hill Top	Near Sawrey
* Hogarth Hse	Chiswick
Holbech Hse	Himley
Hole Pk	Rolvenden
* Holker Hall	Cark
* Holy Cross Priory	Blackboys
Hood Monmt	Butleigh
Horne's Place	Appledore Hth
Horselunges	Hellingly

Building	Mentioned under
* Lullingstone Silk Farm	Ayot St Lawrence
Lumley Cstle	Chester-le-Street
* Lyme Hall	Disley
* Lytes Cary	Kingsdon
Magdalen College Sch	Brackley
* Maison Dieu	Ospringe
Mannington Hall	Itteringham
* Marble Hill Hse	Twickenham
* Markenfield Hall	Markington
* Mary Arden's Hse	Wilmcote
* Mary Mitford's Cottage	Threemile Cross
Max Gate	Dorchester, Dorset
Medford Hse	Mickleton, Glos
Mere Hall	Hanbury, Worcs
* Michelham Priory	Upr Dicker
Midway Mnr	Wingfield, Wilts
* Milton's Cottage	Chalfont St Giles
Misarden Pk	Miserden
* Moigne Ct	Owermoigne
Mole Hall	Debden
* Monk Bretton Priory	Barnsley, Yorks (W)
Moot, The	Downton, Wilts
Moreton Hall	Weston Rhyn
* Moseley Old Hall	Featherstone, Staffs
* Mount Edgcumbe	Cremyll
* Mount Grace Priory	Osmotherley
Mount St Bernard Abbey	Whitwick
Moyles Ct	Ellingham, Hants
Moyns Pk	Birdbrook
* Moyse's Hall	Bury St Edmunds
Mulgrave Cstle	Lythe
Murtholme	Gt Harwood
Narford Hall	Narborough
* Naworth Cstle	Brampton, Cumb
Newburgh Priory	Coxwold
* Newby Hall	Skelton, Yorks (W)
New Hse	Whiteparish
* Newtimber Place	Pyecombe
* New Wardour Cstle	Tisbury
Norris Cstle	E Cowes
Norton Place	Bishop Norton
* Nostell Priory	Foulby
Notley Abbey	Long Crendon
* Oakwell Hall	Birstall Smithies
* Odiham Cstle Keep	N Warnborough
Olantigh Twrs	Wye
Old Blundell's Sch	Tiverton, Devon
Old Mnr	Littlehampton
* Old Place, The	Boveney
* Old Soar	Plaxtol
* Old Wardour Cstle	Tisbury

Building	Mentioned under
Orchardleigh	Lullington, Som
Orwell Pk	Nacton
* Osborne Hse	E Cowes
* Osterley Pk	Heston
* Otterden Pk	Charing
* Owletts	Cobham, Kent
Owl Hse	Lamberhurst
* Packwood Hse	Hockley Hth
Palace Hse	Beaulieu
Pannett Pk Museum	Whitby
* Parham Hse	Rackham
* Paycocke's	Coggeshall
* Peckover Hse	Wisbech
* Pelham Mausoleum	Gt Limber
* Pendennis Cstle	Falmouth
Pendon Museum	Long Wittenham
* Penfound	Poundstock
* Penjerrick Gdns	Budock Water
* Pepys Hse	Brampton, Hunts
* Percival Hall	Appletreewick
Peterson's Twr	Sway
* Peveril Cstle	Castleton, Derbys
* Phillipps Hse	Dinton, Wilts
Pigeon Hse	Angmering
Pitt-Rivers Museum	Farnham, Dorset
Place Farm	Kirtling
Place Farm	Tisbury
* Polesden Lacy	Gt Bookham
* Porch Hse	Potterne
Portledge	Alwington
* Prestwold	Hoton
Prior Pk	Combe Down
* Puttendon Mnr	Lingfield
Pynsent Monmt	Curry Rivel
* Pyte Hse	Newtown, Wilts
Quarr Abbey	Binstead
Quarters Hse	Alresford, Essex
* Quebec Hse	Westerham
* Queen Elizabeth's Hunting Lodge	Chingford
Quenby Hall	Hungarton
* Quex Pk	Birchington
* Raby Cstle	Staindrop
* Ragley Hall	Arrow
* Redheath	Croxley Grn
* Restormel Cstle	Lostwithiel
Revolution Hse	Whittington, Derbys
* Richborough Cstle	Ash, Kent (TR 2858)
	Sandwich
* Roche Abbey	Maltby, Yorks (W)
Rokeby Hall	Greta Br
Roos Hall	Beccles

Building	Mentioned under
* Rose Cstle	Raughton Head
* Rudding Pk	Harrogate
Ruskin Museum	Coniston, Lancs
* Rycote Chpl	Gt Haseley
Rydale Folk Museum	Hutton-le-Hole
Rymans	Apuldram
St Audries	W Quantoxhead
* St Cross Hsptl	Winchester
St David's Ruin	Harden
* St Giles Hse	Wimborne St Giles
St John's College	Hurstpierpoint
* St John's Jerusalem	Sutton-at-Hone
St Leonard's Hsptl	Tickhill
* St Leonard's Twr	W Malling
* St Mary's	Bramber
Salford Hall	Abbot's Salford
* Salisbury Hall	Shenley
* Salmestone Grange	Margate
* Saltram	Plympton
* Sandham Memorial Chpl	Burghclere
* Scotney Cstle	Lamberhurst
Serby Hall	Scrooby
* Sewerby Hall	Bridlington
Sezincote	Bourton-on-the-Hill
* Shallowford	Norton Br
Shardeloes Pk	Amersham
Sharpham Hse	Ashrpington
Sheffield Pk	Fletching
Shrubland	Coddenham
* Shugborough	Gt Haywood
Sir John Soane's Museum	Holborn
Sir Tatton Sykes Monmt	Garton-on-the-Wolds
* Sizergh Cstle	Sedgwick
* Smedmore	Kimmeridge
* Smithills Hall	Bolton, Lancs
* Spade Hse	Sandgate
* Sqerrys Ct	Westerham
* Steeton Hall Gatehouse	S Milford
* Stoneacre	Otham
Stone Gappe	Glusburn
Stonemason's Museum	Gt Bedwyn
Stonyhurst College	Hurst Grn, Lancs
Storr's Twr	Hilton
* Stourhead	Stourton, Wilts
Stowe	Chackmore
Studley Royal	Studley Roger
* Sudeley Cstle	Winchcombe
Sundorne Cstle	Uffington, Shrops
* Swakeleys	Ickenham
* Swarthmoor Hall	Ulverston
Swinsty Hall	Fewston

Buildings	Mentioned under
Woolbridge Mnr	Wool
Wool Hse	Loose
Woollas Hall	Eckington, Worcs
Wordsworth Museum	Grasmere
Wrest Pk	Silsoe
* Yardhurst	Gt Chart

ACKNOWLEDGEMENTS

The following works of reference have been consulted:-

Index of Place Names (Census 1961)	HMSO
Census 1971 Preliminary Report	HMSO
Postal Addresses	Issued by the Post Office
Official List Part III, 1965 Annual Addenda 1966—9	HMSO
Boundary Commission for England, Second Periodical Report	HMSO
Crockford's Clerical Directory	OUP

Of the many works consulted for the descriptive matter, in addition to my own notes, I specially acknowledge the debt I owe to Sir Nikolaus Pevsner's *Buildings of England* series, and to various *Shell County Guides* and *Travellers Guides*. For general background I have found Professor W.G. Hoskins' *The Making of the English Landscape* particularly helpful.

I am happy to acknowledge the assistance I have received from officials of the Ministry of Education & Science and the Department of the Environment, and from county education officers.

Finally, I gratefully acknowledge the invaluable help given by my wife in the compilation of this gazetteer.